# Data Intensive Storage Services for Cloud Environments

Dimosthenis Kyriazis
*National Technical University of Athens, Greece*

Athanasios Voulodimos
*National Technical University of Athens, Greece*

Spyridon V. Gogouvitis
*National Technical University of Athens, Greece*

Theodora Varvarigou
*National Technical University of Athens, Greece*

BUSINESS SCIENCE Reference

An Imprint of IGI Global

| | |
|---|---|
| Managing Director: | Lindsay Johnston |
| Editorial Director: | Joel Gamon |
| Production Manager: | Jennifer Yoder |
| Publishing Systems Analyst:: | Adrienne Freeland |
| Assistant Acquisitions Editor: | Kayla Wolfe |
| Typesetter: | Christina Barkanic |
| Cover Design: | Jason Mull |

Published in the United States of America by
Business Science Reference (an imprint of IGI Global)
701 E. Chocolate Avenue
Hershey PA 17033
Tel: 717-533-8845
Fax: 717-533-8661
E-mail: cust@igi-global.com
Web site: http://www.igi-global.com

Library of Congress Cataloging-in-Publication Data

Data intensive storage services for cloud environments / Dimosthenis P. Kyriazis, Athanasios S. Voulodimos, Spyridon V. Gogouvitis, and Theodora A. Varvarigou, editors.
    pages cm
 Includes bibliographical references and index.
 Summary: "This book provides an overview of the current and potential approaches towards data storage services and its relationship to cloud environments, bringing together research on storage technologies in cloud environments and various disciplines useful for both professionals and researchers"--Provided by publisher.
 ISBN 978-1-4666-3934-8 (hardcover : alk. paper) -- ISBN 978-1-4666-3935-5 (ebook : alk. paper) -- ISBN 978-1-4666-3936-2 (print & perpetual access : alk. paper) 1. Cloud computing. 2. Data warehousing. 3. Web services. I. Kyriazis, Dimosthenis P., 1973-
 QA76.585.D38 2013
 004.67'82--dc23

                         2013009979


British Cataloguing in Publication Data
A Cataloguing in Publication record for this book is available from the British Library.

All work contributed to this book is new, previously-unpublished material. The views expressed in this book are those of the authors, but not necessarily of the publisher.

# Table of Contents

# Detailed Table of Contents

**Chapter 1**
Commercial and Distributed Storage Systems ............................................................................ 1
*Spyridon V. Gogouvitis, National Technical University of Athens, Greece*
*Athanasios Voulodimos, National Technical University of Athens, Greece*
*Dimosthenis Kyriazis, National Technical University of Athens, Greece*

Distributed storage systems are becoming the method of data storage for the new generation of applications, as it appears a promising solution to handle the immense volume of data produced in today's rich and ubiquitous digital environment. In this chapter, the authors first present the requirements end users pose on Cloud Storage solutions. Then they compare some of the most prominent commercial distributed storage systems against these requirements. Lastly, the authors present the innovations the VISION Cloud project brings in the field of Storage Clouds.

**Chapter 2**
Key Distributed Components for a Large-Scale Object Storage ......................................................... 9
*Miriam Allalouf, Jerusalem College of Engineering, Israel*
*Ghislain Chevalier, Orange Labs, France*
*Danny Harnik, IBM Haifa Research Labs, Israel*
*Sivan Tal, Infinidat Ltd., Israel*

This chapter discusses distributed mechanisms that serve as building blocks in the construction of the VISION Cloud object service. Two are fundamental building blocks in the creation of a large-scale clustered object storage. These are distributed file systems and distributed data management systems. In addition, the authors study two complimentary topics that aim to improve the qualities of the underlying infrastructure. These are resource allocation mechanisms and improvements to data mobility via data reduction.

**Chapter 3**

*Michael C. Jaeger, Siemens AG, Corporate Technology, Germany*

*Uwe Hohenstein, Siemens AG, Corporate Technology, Germany*

Content-centric storage represents an approach for handling large amounts of data. It is one of the innovations pursued by the VISION Cloud project. The goal of the VISION Cloud project is the development of an industry grade storage system using cloud technology. The envisaged use of the VISION Cloud involves the storage and management of millions of data items, potentially several hundreds of terabytes in size. On the one hand, the technical foundations must be capable of efficiently storing such an amount of data. On the other hand, the VISION Cloud must provide adequate means of an API for allowing the efficient navigation, search, and access for the right data item in this storage. For the latter purpose, VISION Cloud provides a data access layer, which is called "Content Centric Interface." Applications can use this data access layer for accessing the VISION Cloud storage from a content-centric point of view, abstracted from actual storage representation. The content centric interface is different from existing cloud storage interfaces and is similar, from an architectural point of view, to object relational mapping frameworks for traditional applications with relational database systems.

**Chapter 4**

*Javier Martínez Elicegui, Telefónica I+D, Spain*

*Lei Xu, Umeå University, Sweden*

*Emilio García Escobar, Telefónica I+D, Spain*

The advent of the Cloud has leveraged a number of challenges, both for customers and service providers. Companies willing to embrace the new paradigm must face some entrance barriers, such as security, privacy and trust concerns, vendor locking risk, legal issues, etc. While service providers may work to minimize these barriers, they must be especially careful when defining what may constitute the most crucial aspect for the success of their offerings: the business model. Different incarnations of the cloud (IaaS, PaaS, and SaaS) add to the possibility of offering public or private solutions, or even federated models. On top of this is the billing strategy: the ubiquitous pay-per-use approach (either in its most common post-paid incarnation, or in a novel pre-paid version) is only the starting point for a wide range of innovative solutions, including bundling or QoS considerations, which European project VISION Cloud is tackling as part of its research efforts. This chapter aims to provide a comprehensive discussion on the most relevant business factors that the Cloud confronts.

**Chapter 5**

*Sebastian Dippl, Siemens AG Corporate Technology, Germany*

*Michael C. Jaeger, Siemens AG Corporate Technology, Germany*

*Achim Luhn, Siemens AG Corporate Technology, Germany*

*Alexandra Shulman-Peleg, IBM Haifa Research Lab, Israel*

*Gil Vernik, IBM Haifa Research Lab, Israel*

While it is common to use storage in a cloud-based manner, the question of true interoperability is rarely fully addressed. This question becomes even more relevant since the steadily growing amount of data that needs to be stored will supersede the capacity of a single system in terms of resources, availability, and network throughput quite soon. The logical conclusion is that a network of systems needs to be created that is able to cope with the requirements of big data applications and data deluge scenarios. This chapter shows how federation and interoperability will fit into a cloud storage scenario. The authors take a look at the challenges that federation imposes on autonomous, heterogeneous, and distributed cloud systems, and present approaches that help deal with the special requirements introduced by the VISION Cloud use cases from healthcare, media, telecommunications, and enterprise domains. Finally, the authors give an overview on how VISION Cloud addresses these requirements in its research scenarios and architecture.

*Nikoletta Mavrogeorgi, National Technical University of Athens, Greece*

*Spyridon V. Gogouvitis, National Technical University of Athens, Greece*

*Athanasios Voulodimos, National Technical University of Athens, Greece*

*Vasilios Alexandrou, National Technical University of Athens, Greece*

The need for online storage and backup of data constantly increases. Many domains, such as media, enterprises, healthcare, and telecommunications need to store large amounts of data and access them rapidly any time and from any geographic location. Storage Cloud environments satisfy these requirements and can therefore provide an adequate solution for these needs. Customers of Cloud environments do not need to own any hardware for storing their data or handle management tasks, such as backups, replication levels, etc. In order for customers to be willing to move their data to Cloud solutions, proper Service Level Agreements (SLAs) should be offered and guaranteed. SLA is a contract between the customer and the service provider, where the terms and conditions of the offered service are agreed upon. In this chapter, the authors present existing SLA schemas and SLA management mechanisms and compare various features that Cloud providers support with existing SLAs. Finally, they address the problem of managing SLAs in cloud computing environments exploiting the content term that concerns the stored objects, in order to provide more efficient capabilities to the customer.

*Ciro Formisano, Engineering Ingegneria Informatica SPA, Italy*

*Lucia Bonelli, Engineering Ingegneria Informatica SPA, Italy*

*Kanchanna Ramasamy Balraj, Engineering Ingegneria Informatica SPA, Italy*

*Alexandra Shulman-Peleg, IBM Haifa Research Lab, Israel*

Cloud storage systems provide highly scalable and continuously available storage services to millions of geographically distributed clients. In order for users to trust their data to these systems, they need to be confident that their data is secure. Thus, cloud services should implement an access control mechanism preventing unauthorized access and manipulation of their data. This chapter presents the existing access control mechanisms and describes their advantages and limitations in the Cloud set-up. The authors address the main access control aspects that include managing the identities and defining access policies. Furthermore, they describe more complex scenarios of identity federation and integration of separate identity silos which is required in various scenarios, like collaboration, merge on acquisition, or migration. For each topic, the authors present the existing solutions and describe the motivation for the architecture developed by the VISION Cloud project.

## Chapter 8

*Lucia Bonelli, Engineering Ingegneria Informatica, Italy*

*Luisa Giudicianni, Engineering Ingegneria Informatica, Italy*

*Angelo Immediata, Engineering Ingegneria Informatica, Italy*

*Antonio Luzzi, Engineering Ingegneria Informatica, Italy*

Despite the huge economic, handling, and computational benefits of the cloud technology, the multitenant and geographically distributed nature of clouds hides a large crowd of security and regulatory issues to be addressed. The main reason for these problems is the unavoidable loss of physical control that costumers are forced to accept when opting for the cloud model. This aspect, united with the lack of knowledge (i.e. transparency) of the vendor's infrastructure implementation, represents a nasty question when costumers are asked to respond to audit findings, produce support for forensic investigations, and, more generically, to ensure compliance with information security standards and regulations. Yet, support for security standards compliance is a need for cloud providers to overcome customers hesitancy and meet their expectations. In this context, tracking, auditing, and reporting practices, while transcending the compliance regimes, represent the primary vehicle of assurance for security managers and auditors on the achievement of security and regulatory compliance objectives. The aim of this chapter is to provide a roundup of crucial requirements resulting from common security certification standards and regulation. Then, the chapter reports an overview of approaches and methodologies for addressing compliance coming from the most relevant initiatives on cloud security and a survey of what storage cloud vendors declare to do in terms of compliance. Finally, the SIEM-based approach as a supporting technology for the achievement of security compliance objectives is described and, the architecture of the security compliance component of the VISION Cloud architecture is presented.

## Chapter 9

*Mirko Lorenz, Deutsche Welle, Germany*

*Linda Rath-Wiggins, Deutsche Welle, Germany*

*Wilfried Runde, Deutsche Welle, Germany*

*Alberto Messina, RAI, Italy*

*Paola Sunna, RAI, Italy*

*Giorgio Dimino, RAI, Italy*

*Maurizio Montagnuolo, RAI, Italy*

*Roberto Borgotallo, RAI, Italy*

Why do media organizations look out for cloud storage? In short, the media industry as a whole is facing various challenges. Due to digital convergence there is more material, less time, and multiple channels to fill, while budgets get smaller. TV, video on demand, and mobile content have become big drivers in pushing a search for innovative storage solutions. In addition to that, the opportunity to work with raw data, which can be used for deeper analysis, mapping, visualization, and personalized services is another aspect of why there is a need for novel storage solutions, preferably in the cloud. The media industry could lower production costs and increase speed to market of time critical reporting. This book chapter provides an overview of how far VISION Cloud can provide novel concepts for these demands.

The operators Telefónica, Orange, and Telenor represent the telecommunication industry in the VISION Cloud project. Together, they provide a telco-oriented use case, which provides feedback and requirements to the work on the reference architecture being developed. The use cases are developed based on the challenges and opportunities that are identified that relate to storage and mobility technologies. The use cases validate the reference architecture of VISION Cloud based on prototype tests and experimentations that enable the use case to be evaluated in scenarios. Telecommunication industry challenges are being addressed by the advancements made in the VISION Cloud project iterations, which takes the inputs from the telco use case and other use cases into consideration. This chapter is a study in the telecommunication industry challenges and possibilities with respect to the cloud storage technology advancements made in VISION Cloud.

Today almost all big enterprises act globally, which results in a growing need for a new kind of data analytics. Imagine a company where data from distribution and sales needs to be combined with increasing online sales on multiple platforms and marketing across new social media channels. Here, new real-time analytics using Cloud Computing concepts can open new perspectives. SAP has had a strong presence in the Business Intelligence (BI) market. The company pioneered concepts to collect, combine, and analyze company wide information. As a result, SAP customers enjoy BI capabilities that are strongly integrated with their SAP operational systems (e.g., ERP, CRM). In recent years, companies have leveraged Cloud Computing as a means for lowering the Total Cost of Ownership (TCO) of various types of business applications that are provided On-Demand. SAP already offers products such as SAP Business ByDesign, which is offered as a Software-as-a-Service (SaaS) On-Demand product. Feature-rich Cloud storage solution such as VISION Cloud enables SAP to integrate new innovations to its On-Demand software portfolio. This chapter describes how VISION Cloud enriches SAP's Instant Business Intelligence analytical On-Demand service.

This chapter elaborates on the impact and benefits Cloud Computing may have on Earth Observation. Earth Observation satellites generate in fact Tera- to Peta-bytes of data, and Cloud Computing provides many capabilities that allow an efficient storage and exploitation of such data. Several scenarios related to Earth Observation activities are analyzed in order to identify the possible benefits from the adoption of Cloud Computing. As concrete proofs-of-concept, several activities related to Cloud Computing in the context of Earth Observation are exposed and discussed. Technical details are provided for a particular framework used by Earth Observation applications that has made the transition from using Grid services towards using Cloud services. A special attention is given to the avoidance of the vendor-lock-in problem.

## Chapter 13

*João Barreto, Technical University Lisbon, Portugal*
*Pierangelo Di Sanzo, Sapienza Università di Roma, Italy*
*Roberto Palmieri, Sapienza Università di Roma, Italy*
*Paolo Romano, Technical University Lisbon, Portugal*

By shifting data and computation away from local servers towards very large scale, world-wide spread data centers, Cloud Computing promises very compelling benefits for both cloud consumers and cloud service providers: freeing corporations from large IT capital investments via usage-based pricing schemes, drastically lowering barriers to entry and capital costs; leveraging the economies of scale for both services providers and users of the cloud; facilitating deployment of services; attaining unprecedented scalability levels. However, the promise of infinite scalability catalyzing much of the recent hype about Cloud Computing is still menaced by one major pitfall: the lack of programming paradigms and abstractions capable of bringing the power of parallel programming into the hands of ordinary programmers. This chapter describes Cloud-TM, a self-optimizing middleware platform aimed at simplifying the development and administration of applications deployed on large scale Cloud Computing infrastructures.

## Chapter 14

*Shantanu Pal, University of Calcutta, India*

Cloud computing has leaped ahead as one of the biggest technological advances of the present time. In cloud, users can upload or retrieve their desired data from anywhere in the world at anytime, making this the most important and primary function in cloud computing technology. While this technology reduces the geographical barriers and improves the scalability in the way we compute, keeping data in a Cloud Data Center (CDC) faces numerous challenges from unauthorized users and hackers within the system. Creating proper Service Level Agreements (SLA) and providing high-end storage security is the biggest barrier being developed for better Quality of Service (QoS) and implementation of a safer cloud computing environment for the Cloud Service Users (CSU) as well as for the Cloud Service Providers (CSP). Therefore, cloud applications need to have increased QoS and effective security measures and policies set in place to provide better services and to decline unauthorized access. The purpose of this chapter is to examine the cloud computing technology behind innovative business approaches and establishing SLA in cloud computing applications. This chapter provides a clear understanding of different cloud computing security challenges, risks, attacks, and solutions that exist in the present heterogeneous cloud computing environment. Storage security, different cloud infrastructures, the many advantages, and limitations are also discussed.

## Chapter 15

*Jalil Boukhobza, University of Western Brittany, France*

Data and storage systems are one of the most important issues to tackle when dealing with cloud computing. Performance, in terms of data transfer and energy cost, predictability, and scalability are the main challenges researchers are faced with, and new techniques for storing, managing, and accessing huge amounts of data are required to make cloud computing technology feasible. With the emergence of flash memories in mass storage systems and the advantages it can provide in terms of speed and power efficiency as compared to traditional disks, one must rethink the storage system architectures accordingly. Indeed, the integration of flash memories is considered a key to leverage the performance of data-centric computing. The purpose of this chapter is to introduce flash memory storage systems by focusing on their specific architectures and algorithms, and finally their integration into servers and data centers.

**Chapter 16**

*Jan Stender, Zuse Institute Berlin, Germany*

*Michael Berlin, Zuse Institute Berlin, Germany*

*Alexander Reinefeld, Zuse Institute Berlin, Germany*

Cloud computing poses new challenges to data storage. While cloud providers use shared distributed hardware, which is inherently unreliable and insecure, cloud users expect their data to be safely and securely stored, available at any time, and accessible in the same way as their locally stored data. In this chapter, the authors present XtreemFS, a file system for the cloud. XtreemFS reconciles the need of cloud providers for cheap scale-out storage solutions with that of cloud users for a reliable, secure, and easy data access. The main contributions of the chapter are: a description of the internal architecture of XtreemFS, which presents an approach to build large-scale distributed POSIX-compliant file systems on top of cheap, off-the-shelf hardware; a description of the XtreemFS security infrastructure, which guarantees an isolation of individual users despite shared and insecure storage and network resources; a comprehensive overview of replication mechanisms in XtreemFS, which guarantee consistency, availability, and durability of data in the face of component failures; an overview of the snapshot infrastructure of XtreemFS, which allows to capture and freeze momentary states of the file system in a scalable and fault-tolerant fashion. The authors also compare XtreemFS with existing solutions and argue for its practicability and potential in the cloud storage market.

# Foreword

By now, the concept of storing data on the Cloud needs no introduction. We keep our email and our photographs on the Cloud, pass documents between our mobile devices on the Cloud, and even do our tax returns on the Cloud. Yet, Cloud Computing, and in particular, storage services for Cloud environments, is still an emerging field. The rise in popularity of storage Clouds holds the promise of gaining value from data in ways that are only now starting to be investigated. The ability of storage Clouds to swallow vast amounts of heterogeneous data is outpacing our ability to efficiently search and manage this data.

*Data Intensive Storage Services for Cloud Environments* is a visionary book. Realizing that the value of a storage Cloud comes from the ability to easily locate and manipulate vast amounts data while providing a secure and scalable infrastructure, this book surveys the state of the art in a wide number of technologies required to create a cutting-edge storage Cloud.

The choice of chapters in this book was guided largely by the experience gained through the creation of VISION Cloud, an innovative storage Cloud created under the auspices of the European Union's FP7 funding. Gathering together leading researchers from academia and industry across Europe, VISION Cloud has created a prototype of a next generation storage Cloud, which deals with such concepts as efficiency in big data environments, federation of data to avoid vendor lock in, security, multi-tenancy, and scalability. VISION Cloud's development was guided by actual use cases from industry, which in turn helped those industrial partners realize new business opportunities afforded by adoption of VISION Cloud technologies.

This book will take the reader from a survey of storage Clouds commercially available today, to a survey of the existing technologies required to create the infrastructure for a storage Cloud, such as distributed file systems and distributed management systems. Design decisions made in VISION Cloud are explained and will be instructive to others. The technologies considered to allow efficient searching of data stores are analyzed in light of VISION Cloud's goal of implementing a rich API for accessing content.

This book examines those management aspects required to make a storage Cloud commercially viable, such as providing for accounting and billing of services used, and the creation and management of Service Level Agreements – contracts between Cloud customers and service providers that create obligations on Cloud infrastructure. Security measures are studied, both for creating Cloud access mechanisms and for tracking compliance in the Cloud. Presented use cases from different industrial sectors illustrate new and improved workflows that storage Clouds can enable.

*Data Intensive Storage Services for Cloud Environments* will be useful to a technical audience ranging from students wanting to learn about Cloud Computing to engineers and researchers interested in developing Cloud technologies. The technology chapters can be read separately and in any order, and the chapters describing the use cases help to present a unifying picture of convergence of all of these technologies into a coherent solution. It is expected that many of the topics presented here can be researched future for potential Master and PhD topics.

*Eliot Salant*
*IBM Haifa Labs, Israel*

**Eliot Salant** *has held a number of managerial and technical leadership positions over the last twenty years at the IBM Haifa Labs. Additionally, he has served as Project Coordinator for several large European Union sponsored Cloud computing projects, including RESERVOIR and VISION Cloud. Eliot holds a B.Eng. degree in Mechanical Engineering from McGill University, an M.S. degree in Biomedical Engineering from The Technion – Israel Institute of Technology, and an M.S. degree in Computer Science from Union College.*

# Preface

The explosion of personal and organisational digital data is presently recognised as one of the most significant characteristics of the last few years. Market reports indicate that since 2007 generated data is growing faster than the ability of humanity to store it. In parallel with the explosion of digital data, our society has become critically dependent on services to extract valuable information from data and driven by decision making by individuals, businesses, and government, across all aspects of life.

In the emerging era of the Future Internet, the explosion of raw data and the dependence on data services is expected to be further amplified due to two important trends, namely the strong proliferation of data-intensive services and the digital convergence of Telco, Media, and ICT.

In this context, emerging Cloud-based infrastructures for storage have been widely accepted as the next-generation solution to address the data proliferation and the reliance on data. Such infrastructures promise essentially infinite scalability and capacity, with continuous and ubiquitous availability at substantially lower costs than traditional storage solutions. Nevertheless, today's cloud environments need to overcome specific limitations with regard to data intensive services.

Creating an innovative storage cloud calls for progressing beyond the state-of-the-art in several technologies. The book at hand surveys the existing technologies pertaining to infrastructure as well as management aspects of a storage cloud, thus aiming at becoming a reference point for the research community.

The target audience for the book ranges from PhD or Masters' students to researchers and teachers. From the domain or community point of view, researchers in data-intensive services and cloud storage can discover through this book the particularities, strengths, weaknesses, and future trends of different research areas, and potentially draft a "research agenda" for future projects according to these.

The book initially (Chapter 1) presents a survey of storage clouds commercially available today, compared and contrasted against the most important requirements that end users pose on Cloud storage solutions. Chapter 2 discusses two fundamental building blocks in the creation of large-scale clustered object storage, namely distributed file systems and distributed data management systems. Furthermore, resource allocation mechanisms and data reduction are explored as a means of improving the underlying infrastructure. The innovative concept of content centric storage is analyzed in Chapter 3. The content centric interface is different from existing cloud storage interfaces, being similar from an architectural point of view to object relational mapping frameworks for traditional applications with relational database systems. Chapter 4 addresses a crucial aspect behind any commercial Cloud offering: the business model. Special emphasis is placed on billing strategy: the ubiquitous pay-per-use approach (either in its most common post-paid implementation, or in a novel pre-paid version) is only the starting point for a wide range of innovative solutions, including bundling or QoS considerations. Chapter 5 shows how federation and interoperability can fit into a cloud storage scenario, describing the challenges that federation imposes on autonomous, heterogeneous, and distributed Cloud systems and presenting approaches that help deal with the special requirements introduced by healthcare, media, telecommunications, and enterprise use cases. The significant topic of SLA management in storage cloud is addressed in Chapter 6. The authors present existing SLA schemas and SLA management mechanisms, and also propose new solutions based on VISION Cloud's content centric concept presented in a previous chapter. Chapter 7 presents existing access control mechanisms and describes their advantages and limitations in the Cloud set-up. The authors address the main access control aspects that include managing the identities and defining access policies. Moreover, they describe more complex scenarios of identity federation and integration of separate identity silos which is required in various scenarios like collaboration, merge on acquisition, or migration. Chapter 8, on the other hand, investigates another security-related aspect, that of compliance in the Cloud. Tracking, auditing, and reporting practices, while transcending the compliance regimes, represent the primary vehicle of assurance for security manager and auditors on the achievement of security and regulatory compliance objectives. The chapter provides a roundup of crucial requirements resulting from common security certification standards and regulation. It also reports an overview of approaches and methodologies for addressing compliance and details the SIEM-based approach as a supporting technology for the achievement of security compliance objectives. The following three chapters deal with Cloud-related use cases from three different domains. Chapter 9 provides an overview in how far a novel storage Cloud such as VISION Cloud can provide innovative concepts in the media industry, thus helping lower production costs and increase speed to market of time critical reporting. Subsequently, a study of telecommunication industry challenges and possibilities with respect to Cloud storage technology advancements is given in Chapter 10. The authors of Chapter 11 explore the added value that a cutting-edge storage Cloud can offer to companies that leverage on Cloud Computing as a means for lowering the Total Cost of Ownership (TCO) of various types of business applications that are provided on-demand. Turning to a more scientific domain, Chapter 12 elaborates on the impact and benefits Cloud Computing may have on Earth Observation. Earth Observation satellites generate in fact Tera to Peta bytes of data and Cloud Computing provides many capabilities that allow an efficient storage and exploitation of such data. Several scenarios related to Earth Observation activities are analyzed in order to identify the possible benefits from the adoption of Cloud Computing. In the next chapter, the authors pinpoint a major pitfall in Cloud environments: the lack of programming paradigms and abstractions capable of bringing the power of parallel programming into the hands of ordinary programmers. In this context, Chapter 13 describes Cloud-TM, a self-optimizing middleware platform aimed at simplifying the development and administration of applications deployed on large-scale Cloud Computing infrastructures. Moving on to Chapter 14, the authors examine the Cloud Computing technology behind innovative business approaches and establishing SLA in Cloud Computing applications. This chapter also provides a clear understanding of different Cloud Computing security challenges, risks, attacks, and solutions that exist in the present heterogeneous Cloud Computing environment. Storage security, different Cloud infrastructures, the many advantages, and limitations are also discussed. The purpose of Chapter 15, on the other hand, is to introduce flash memory storage systems by focusing on their specific architectures and algorithms, and finally their integration into servers and data centers. Finally, in Chapter 16 the authors present XtreemFS, a file system for the Cloud. XtreemFS reconciles the need of Cloud providers for cheap scale-out storage solutions with that of Cloud users for a reliable, secure, and easy data access. Special emphasis is put on the internal architecture, the security infrastructure, the replication mechanisms, and the snapshot infrastructure of XtreemFS, which allows capturing and freezing momentary states of the file system in a scalable and fault-tolerant fashion.

Covering a vast range of topics pertaining to data-intensive storage services in Cloud environments, we believe that this publication provides a substantial point of reference for the research community in its endeavor to find innovative ways to efficiently search and manage the great amounts of heterogeneous data produced across all aspects of life today.

*Dimosthenis Kyriazis*
*National Technical University of Athens, Greece*

*Athanasios Voulodimos*
*National Technical University of Athens, Greece*

*Spyridon V. Gogouvitis*
*National Technical University of Athens, Greece*

*Theodora A. Varvarigou*
*National Technical University of Athens, Greece*

# Acknowledgment

First and foremost, we would like to thank all the chapter authors who have contributed their research results to this book. Without their efforts this book would not exist. We also owe a debt of gratitude to the reviewers who have provided valuable comments on the book chapters. We would also like to acknowledge the members of the Editorial Advisory Board for their assistance and constructive comments. Last but not least, special thanks are given to Mr. Joel Gamon of IGI Global for his assistance in the book preparation.

*Dimosthenis Kyriazis*
*National Technical University of Athens, Greece*

*Athanasios Voulodimos*
*National Technical University of Athens, Greece*

*Spyridon V. Gogouvitis*
*National Technical University of Athens, Greece*

*Theodora A. Varvarigou*
*National Technical University of Athens, Greece*

# Chapter 1
# Commercial and Distributed Storage Systems

**Spyridon V. Gogouvitis**
*National Technical University of Athens, Greece*

**Athanasios Voulodimos**
*National Technical University of Athens, Greece*

**Dimosthenis Kyriazis**
*National Technical University of Athens, Greece*

## ABSTRACT

*Distributed storage systems are becoming the method of data storage for the new generation of applications, as it appears a promising solution to handle the immense volume of data produced in today's rich and ubiquitous digital environment. In this chapter, the authors first present the requirements end users pose on Cloud Storage solutions. Then they compare some of the most prominent commercial distributed storage systems against these requirements. Lastly, the authors present the innovations the VISION Cloud project brings in the field of Storage Clouds.*

## INTRODUCTION

Distributed storage systems are becoming the method of data storage for the new generation of applications - Web applications by companies like Google, Amazon and Yahoo!. There are several reasons that explain the increasing trend towards distributed processing. On one hand, programs should be scalable and should take advantage of multiple systems as well as multi-core CPU architectures. On the other hand, Web servers have to be globally distributed for low latency and

failover. Object systems differ from file systems in the data model and access semantics they provide. Distributed object stores support wide distribution of data and access to data with high availability, even in presence of frequent node failures. They support data storage cloud services in which data is read and written by a wide variety of client applications running anywhere and typically using HTTP interfaces to access the storage service and their data. Several main differences in the characteristics of distributed object stores compared to file systems are:

DOI: 10.4018/978-1-4666-3934-8.ch001

- **Flat namespace:** Each object is addressed individually and independently of other objects, eliminating the hierarchical directory structure of file systems. With a flat namespace, each operation affects a single object, which helps keep consistency in widely distributed systems. Object metadata support provides some data management capabilities that compensate for the absence of directories. Some object stores provide the notion of containers, or buckets, that act as collections of objects and divide the namespace into multiple ones, also serving as a means of managing data and isolation between different data sets and multiple clients.

- **Fixed content:** Objects are typically written as a whole, rather than updated at the byte range level. This also helps keeping data consistency in the presence of multiple geographically distributed writers, while keeping the object stored highly available for read and write.

- **Relaxed consistency models:** Storage clouds consisting of distributed object stores deploy an eventual consistency model, meaning that when no node and network failures occur, eventually all nodes will have the same view of the data.

- Modern distributed object stores are typically built for world-wide spread with nodes distributed over a WAN. Data redundancy is typically supported through replication rather than RAID. Replicating data across distant locations also improves the availability and latency in access to the data. Each object storage cloud service has its own HTTP based API, and each API evolves over time by adding more features support through the API. The flexible APIs are developer-friendly and allow for rapid enhancements of the service. On the other hand, lack of standardization in this area results in lack of interoperability and the data lock-in problem. Providing storage as a cloud service introduces a new ICT delivery model for storage. Businesses and individuals can consume flexible, variable and unlimited amount of storage without acquiring hardware, managing and maintaining it, paying per use for storage consumed "on demand".

In this chapter, we first present the requirements end-users pose on cloud storage services. Then we provide a high-level overview of the most prominent commercial offerings in cloud storage and compare them against the requirements set out. Lastly, we briefly present how the innovations of VISION Cloud compare to the presented commercial solutions

## REQUIREMENTS

Within the context of the VISION Cloud project a number of requirements for a storage service have been identified. These can be basically broken down to the following categories:

- Basic access to the storage and interface requirements. The service should support the Create, Read, Update and Delete (CRUD) operations on the data objects and metadata through a standard interface such as CDMI.

- Requirements having to do with the efficient tagging of data with metadata, as well as the efficient search and retrieval of objects based on these metadata.

- Computational requirements. The storage service should allow for computations to be defined and executed on the stored objects and their metadata.

- Security and Compliance requirements. The issue of security is of major importance in storage clouds. This is not limited to providing encryption mechanisms, but also the means to control access to the stored data through elaborate Access Control Lists (ACLs), Digital Rights Management issues, supporting Single-Sign-On features and others.

- Federation requirements. The storage system should be able to be seamlessly interconnected with other storage systems. This avoids vendor lock-in problems as the user is able to easily migrate to other providers. Moreover, it is desired that a user will be able to have a unified view of the data he/she owns in different providers.
- SLA Requirements. User requirements are typically defines in terms of Service Level Agreements which define specific Key Performance Indicators of the provided service as well as costs and penalties in case these are not met.
- Accounting and Billing requirements. Every commercial storage cloud needs to have proper mechanisms to accurately bill its customers. The more agile these mechanisms are the more use cases can be covered.

## APPROACHES AND IMPLEMENTATIONS

### Amazon S3

Amazon Simple Storage Service (S3) (Amazon Simple Storage Service (Amazon S3), n.d.) is one of the most prominent commercial cloud storage services. Amazon S3 is reported to store more than a trillion objects as of June 2012 [1].

The organization of data in S3 follows a two-level approach. At the top level are buckets that are identified by a user-assigned global key. Buckets can contain an unlimited amount of data objects, where each object can be up to 5 terabytes in size. Each object also has a set of system defined metadata as well as user defined metadata in the form of name-value pairs. Objects are stored in multiple devices in multiple locations to provide high durability levels. S3 provides read-after-write consistency for PUTS of new objects and eventual consistency for overwrite PUTS and DELETES.

Users are able to interact with the service through a REST or a SOAP interface. Moreover, S3 provides the ability to download any publicly available data through the use of the BitTorrent protocol. S3 also provides various services to users such as versioning capabilities. A user is able to define that a bucket should have versioning enabled in which case all objects are preserved in cases of PUT, POST, COPY or DELETE operations on them. A user is able to retrieve any version by supplying the version number. Also the service provides a Multipart Upload API that can be used to upload objects of sizes from 5 MB up to 5TB. Multi-Object Delete is another feature of the service that can be used to delete multiple objects in one request, thus speeding up the process. The user is also able to define expiration rules per bucket. Every object defined in the rule will be deleted once the expiration period has elapsed. S3 also provides a reduced redundancy storage (RRS) option at reduced pricing but with a lower promised durability level of 99.99% over a given year.

Amazon's pricing model follows a tiered approach based on the overall storage purchased by each user. Moreover, there are additional charges for data transfer out of the S3 Cloud as well as per PUT, COPY, POST, LIST and GET Requests. S3 comes with a 99.9% monthly uptime guarantee giving 10% Service Credits back in case the Monthly Uptime Percentage is equal to or greater than 99% and less than 99.9% and 25% back in case the Monthly Uptime is less than 99% (*Amazon S3 service level agreement*, 2009). Amazon also promises 99.999999999% durability over a given year, something not included in the SLA.

S3 provides four different access control mechanisms: Identity and Access Management (IAM) policies, Access Control Lists (ACLs), bucket policies, and query string authentication. Moreover, Amazon promises that objects stored in a Region never leave the Region unless the user explicitly transfers them out. Data can be encrypted through Server Side Encryption in which case Amazon handles the management of all security keys or through client libraries before uploading the data to S3. Amazon S3 also supports data access auditing through access log records for all requests made against it.

It is also worth mentioning that Amazon has started to provide an archiving service named Glacier[2]. Glacier is "optimized for data that is infrequently accessed and for which retrieval times of several hours are suitable" according to Amazon. S3 plans to incorporate an option to seamlessly move data between S3 and Glacier using lifecycle policies.

## Google Cloud Storage

Google also provides a storage service through Google Cloud Storage (Google Cloud Storage, n.d.). It follows the same organization as Amazon S3 through the use of buckets and objects. Objects in Google Cloud Storage are immutable, meaning that no append or truncate operations are allowed. The consistency model followed is strong read-after-write consistency for upload and delete operations on objects and eventual consistency for list operations on objects and buckets. Users can interact with the service through a REST interface.

Google Cloud Storage, much like S3, follows a tiered pricing model, charging for the overall storage consumed, network used for data exiting the cloud as well as the number of requests handled. Google Cloud Storage comes with a 99.9% monthly uptime guarantee giving 10% Service Credits back in case the Monthly Uptime Percentage is equal to or greater than 99% and less than 99.9% and 25% back in case the Monthly Uptime is between 95.0% and 99.9% and 50% back if it less than 95.0%.

Google Cloud Storage uses OAuth 2.0 for authorization and authentication as well as ACLs for controlling access to buckets and objects.

## Windows Azure Storage

Microsoft provides a storage service through the Windows Azure Platform (Windows Azure Storage Services API Reference, 2010). Data are stored in the form of Blobs (Binary Large Objects) and each blob needs to reside within a container. Blobs come in two types, namely block blobs, which are more common, are optimized for streaming, and have a maximum size of 200GB and page blobs, which are usually used as virtual hard drives, since they are optimized for random read/write operations and provide the ability to write to a range of bytes in a blob. Page blobs have a maximum size of 1TB. Blobs and containers can have custom metadata in the form of name-value pairs. Each data object is replicated three times in the same sub-region (locally redundant option) and the user is also able to choose to have the data replicated to another sub-region to provide disaster recovery functionalities (geographically redundant option). Each account in Windows Azure Storage can hold up to 100 TB of data.

The Windows Azure also provides a Tables service, which provides basic CRUD operations for non-relational tabular data, a SQL Database service which provides a scalable relational database, a Windows Azure Drives service which provides a mechanism for applications to mount a single volume NTFS VHD as a Page blob and a Queue service for storing messages.

The Windows Azure SDK offers a REST API and a managed API for working with the storage services. The storage services may be accessed from within a service running in Windows Azure or directly over the Internet from any application that can send and receive data over HTTP/HTTPS.

Windows Azure Storage follows a tiered pricing scheme based on the storage consumed and whether local or geographical redundancy was chosen. Transactions are billed flatly ($0.01 per 100000 transactions). Windows Azure Storage comes with a monthly uptime guarantee of 99.9% giving 10% Service Credits back in case the Monthly Uptime Percentage less than 99.9% and 25% back in case the Monthly Uptime is less than 99%. It is also worth noting that the SLA defines specific metrics for when a transaction is considered to have failed. For example, a PutBlob or GetBlob (includes blocks and pages) operation must complete within the product of 2 seconds multiplied by the number of MBs transferred in processing the request, a CopyBlob operation must complete processing within 90 seconds, a PutBlockList or a GetBlockList operation must complete processing within 60 seconds, etc.

## Rackspace Cloud Files

Cloud Files (Rackspace Cloud Files, n.d.) is the Rackspace's cloud storage offering powered by open-source OpenStack[3]. Rackspace provides a REST API for accessing the storage service as well as language specific bindings. The data model of Cloud Files follows a two level scheme, with objects being the basic storage entities which are located inside containers. There is no hierarchy of containers, i.e. containers cannot be nested. Objects cannot be larger than 5GB, but there is the option to upload larger objects in 5GB segments than can be later downloaded as a single concatenated object. This is achieved through a manifest object that when retrieved returns the concatenated objects. Custom metadata can be defined for objects and containers, but should not exceed 90 individual key/value pairs and the total byte length should not exceed 4KB. Since Rackspace Cloud Files is based on Opestack Swift it follows an eventual consistency model. Redundancy is achieved by replicating every data object three times in different storage nodes. Cloud Files also allows for an expiration date to be set when creating an object, which leads to the object

being deleted when the target time limit is met. It also provides a versioning option by which when new data is written to an object the non-current version is moved to a different container. One of the most prominent features of Cloud Files is the ability to integrate with Akamai's Content Delivery Network (CDN). This is achieved by defining a container to be CDN-enabled. Each CDN-enabled container also has a streaming URL that can be used to stream content.

Cloud Files has a fixed cost per Gigabyte, irrespective of the storage consumed and does not charge for the requests handled, while still charging for outgoing bandwidth. The price for outgoing bandwidth is the same whether Akamai's CDN is used or not.

Cloud Files provides a 99.9% availability SLA while reductions are depicted in Table 1.

Rackspace gives the following definition for unavailability: *Unavailability means: (1) The Rackspace Cloud network is down, or (2) the Cloud Files service returns a server error response to a valid user request during two or more consecutive 90 second intervals, or (3) the Content Delivery Network fails to deliver an average download time for a 1-byte reference document of 0.3 seconds or less, as measured by The Rackspace Cloud's third party measuring service.*

Security in Cloud Files is enforced through an authentication token that is received during login and used in all subsequent requests to the service.

*Table 1. Cloud files SLA*

| Total Cloud Files Available Time | | Credit Amount |
|---|---|---|
| 100% - 99.9% | | 0% |
| 99.89% | - 99.5% | 10% |
| 99.49% | - 99.0% | 25% |
| 98.99% | - 98.0% | 40% |
| 97.99% | - 97.5% | 55% |
| 97.49% | - 97.0% | 70% |
| 96.99% | - 96.5% | 85% |
| Less than 96.5% | | 100% |

There is no option to encrypt data on the server side, but each customer is responsible for encrypting the data prior to uploading it to the service.

## EMC Atmos

EMC Atmos (Atmos Online Programmer's Guide, 2010) is different to the solutions presented thus far in that it is not a commercial storage service, but a storage platform that can be used to build private or public clouds. EMC Atmos has two different deployment models. The standard EMC Atmos where specific hardware along with appropriate software is used and Atmos Virtual Edition, where the software stack can be installed on third-party storage systems.

The platform provides REST and SOAP Web-based APIs, as well as CIFS/NFS traditional file access. It has two data models, an object interface and a namespace interface that is similar to a file system with folders. Objects in Atmos have metadata associated with them, which are both system as well as user defined. Moreover, each object has an ACL specifying which users and groups are allowed access to the data object.

EMC Atmos has a rich account model, supporting a three-level hierarchy of tenants, subtenants and users. Each tenant can be assigned its own interface nodes and dedicated resources while subtenants as logically separated by each having its own namespace.

The notion of policies also exists in EMC Atmos, through which various management operations can be set, such as number of replicas, compression, deduplication, retention and deletion periods. Replication policies can be set through the metadata of each object. Atmos provides the options of having a mixture of synchronous and asynchronous replicas, while also allowing for geo-constraints to be defined.

EMC provides security through ACLs per data object, while there are no capabilities for server side encryption.

## COMPARISON

Table 2 compares the five services under investigation against the high-level requirements set forth.

## VISION CLOUD APPROACH

Comparing VISION Cloud to the presented commercial offerings leads to the following conclusions:

### Rich Metadata

While the notion of coupling data with metadata is not new, VISION Cloud allows for much richer metadata than what is currently offered by commercial solutions. Metadata in VISION Cloud can be used for active indexing and other content management support operations inside the storage infrastructure. This option is only available in EMC Atmos, in a more basic form.

### Content-Centric Access

VISION Cloud also goes a step beyond in the use of metadata by providing the ability to set relations between objects. Therefore, content networks can be created dynamically and automatically by discovery and construction processes that are integrated into the infrastructure, driven by user-provided specifications for the specific domains of interest.

### Computational Storage

VISION Cloud also promotes the idea of bringing computations close to the storage, through the notion of storlets. While most commercial offerings provide computational resources apart from storage resources, these are considered as separate services and there is no guarantee of their co-location. Storlets, on the other hand, provide

*Table 2. Comparison of commercial offerings to VISION cloud requirements (grouped)*

| | Amazon S3 | Google Cloud Storage | Windows Azure Storage | Rackspace Cloud Files | EMC Atmos |
|---|---|---|---|---|---|
| Interface | REST, SOAP, Bit-Torrent | REST | REST, Managed API | REST | REST, SOAP, CIFS. NFS, Atmos file-system |
| Query Capabilities on Metadata | NO | NO | NO | NO | YES (only by meta-data key) |
| Computations | Through EC2 instances | Through Google Compute Engine | Through Azure Compute Service | Through Cloud Servers | NO |
| Federation | NO | NO | NO | NO | YES (with Atmos public providers) |
| Security | IAM policies, ACLs, bucket policies and query string authentication | OAuth 2.0, ACLs | ACLs, Shared Access Signatures | Authentication Key | Authentication Key, ACLs |
| Server-side encryption | YES | NO | NO | NO | NO |
| SLA metrics | Availability metric | Availability metric | Availability, clearly defined max. processing times for operations | Availability | N/A |

a programming framework able to run computations close to the data. Moreover, storlets can be activated by events such as uploading of a new object, adding metadata to it etc.

## Federation

By leveraging and extending the CDMI standard, as well as implementing the appropriate mechanisms, VISION Cloud is able to provide federation capabilities, allowing for companies to bridge private cloud installations to public cloud storages hosted at different providers.

## Security

VISION Cloud supports the authentication both with the internal user services as well as with external identity providers through SAML SSO. Moreover, it combines ACL-based and ABAC models for granting authorization on the object or container levels, allowing for versatile authorization schemes. While VISION Cloud does

not currently provide a server-side encryption mechanism, this can be relatively easily achieved by using storlets.

## Rich SLAs and Billing Mechanisms

Current commercial offerings provide rudimentary SLAs that are focused on service provisioning, storage resources, capacity, and service availability. In VISION Cloud SLAs are more dynamic in nature and able to accommodate more of the customers' needs. This coupled with advanced billing mechanisms that can accommodate not only post-paid but also pre-paid scenarios allows VISION Cloud to support new business models.

## CONCLUSION

Providing storage as a service is an important aspect of the emerging Cloud ecosystem. Commercial offerings are nowadays well established, but still issues such as ease of management, data mobility and federation, coupling storage with computing power and guaranteeing QoS need to be researched to address the increasing volumes of data that are being produced and need to be processed and stored. In this chapter we investigated how commercial cloud offerings differ and what the VISION Cloud project proposes as a means to advance in this field.

## REFERENCES

Amazon Simple Storage Service (Amazon S3). *(n.d.)*. Retrieved from http://aws.amazon.com/s3/

*Atmos Online Programmer's Guide*. (2010). Retrieved from https://community.emc.com/docs/DOC-3481

*Google Cloud Storage*. (n.d.). Retrieved from http://www.google.com/enterprise/cloud/ storage/

*Rackspace Cloud Files*. (n.d.). Retrieved from http://www.rackspace.com/cloud/cloud_hosting_products/files/

*Windows Azure Storage Services API Reference*. (2010). Retrieved from http://msdn.microsoft.com/en-us/library/dd179355.aspx

## KEY TERMS AND DEFINITIONS

**Cloud Computing:** Cloud computing is a model of offering compute, network and storage, possibly virtualized, resources over a network.

**Distributed Computing:** Distributed Computing refers to any computing system that individual nodes are distributed and cooperate through a network to solve a problem.

**Federation:** The ability to use more than one Cloud provider and have their services interoperate.

**Service Level Agreement (SLA):** A SLA is the negotiated contract between a customer and a provider of a service. The SLA defines the quality of the service, its cost, the responsibilities of the provider and the customer and other binding terms.

**Virtualization:** The creation and provision of resources which are virtual, rather than actual, enabling them to be used as a service.

## ENDNOTES

1   http://aws.typepad.com/aws/2012/06/amazon-s3-the-first-trillion-objects.html
2   http://aws.amazon.com/glacier/
3   www.openstack.org/

# Chapter 2
# Key Distributed Components for a Large-Scale Object Storage

**Miriam Allalouf**
*Jerusalem College of Engineering, Israel*

**Ghislain Chevalier**
*Orange Labs, France*

**Danny Harnik**
*IBM Haifa Research Labs, Israel*

**Sivan Tal**
*Infinidat Ltd., Israel*

## ABSTRACT

*This chapter discusses distributed mechanisms that serve as building blocks in the construction of the VISION Cloud object service. Two are fundamental building blocks in the creation of a large-scale clustered object storage. These are distributed file systems and distributed data management systems. In addition, the authors study two complimentary topics that aim to improve the qualities of the underlying infrastructure. These are resource allocation mechanisms and improvements to data mobility via data reduction.*

## INTRODUCTION

Building a large-scale object storage requires the ability to distribute storage across multiple disks, nodes, racks and eventually data centers. Our design identified two main tools that can form the foundation of such a large object storage. The first is a distributed file system that should form the storage backbone for the actual data of the objects. The second is a distributed data management mechanism that will serve as a central management tool for metadata (both system metadata and user metadata). The properties and performance of these components will have major influence on the ability of the storage cloud to serve requests both in terms of speed and in terms of scale. As such, they must fulfil the following crucial requirements (as referenced in the requirements section): Scalability (in terms of number of objects, total capacity, containers, etc, the ability to support performance at a high scale (scale out performance), Elasticity, Availability and eventual consistency. In addition, we survey in this chapter two additional topics regarding

DOI: 10.4018/978-1-4666-3934-8.ch002

highly distributed mechanisms. Unlike the above mentioned distributed file system and data base, that are fundamental building blocks for the object service, the next two topics study means and methodologies of gaining added value to the VISION Cloud over existing designs. The first topic is a resource allocation mechanism across a global cloud, with an emphasis on placement of object containers. The goal here is to make smarter allocations of resources such as disk, bandwidth and CPU both on a cloud wide basis and locally in a cluster. The ultimate goal is to improve performance and reduce overall cost in the cloud. The second is methodologies of reducing traffic and improving data mobility in the cloud with a positive side effect of reducing the required storage capacity. Since the amount of data being transferred across a WAN in the cloud is huge (this can be for replication, for user applications or for recovery), the time and resources spent on this transfer make bandwidth a scarce resource and moving data harder to handle. The aim of this work package is to reduce this burden and the underlying technique is by using data reduction methodologies, and most notably deduplication (finding repeating data across the cloud, and thus not transferring data that is already at the target location).

## DISTRIBUTED FILE SYSTEMS

### Overview

File systems evolved over time. Starting with local file systems over time additional file systems appeared focusing on specialized requirements such as data sharing, remote file access, distributed file access, parallel files access, HPC, archiving, etc. A Distributed file System (DFS) is a network file system whose clients, servers, and storage devices are dispersed among the machines of a distributed system or intranet. Using a networking protocol between nodes, a DFS allows a single file system to span across all nodes in the DFS cluster, effectively creating a unified Global Namespace for all files:

- Unifying files on different computers into a single namespace.
- Files are distributed across multiple servers appearing to users as being stored at a unique place on the network.
- Users no longer need to know and specify the actual physical location of files in order to access them.

Distributed file systems may include facilities for transparent replication and fault tolerance. When a limited number of nodes in a file system go offline, the system continues to work without any data loss or unavailability. Distributed File Systems (DFS) maintain control of file and data layout across the nodes and employ metadata and locking mechanisms that are fully distributed and cohesively maintained across the cluster, enabling the creation of a very large global pool of storage. A DFS can seamlessly scale to petabytes of storage. A fully distributed file system can handle metadata operations, file locking, and cache management tasks by distributing operations across all the nodes in the cluster.

### Approaches, Implementations, and Comparisons

#### GPFS

GPFS (General Parallel File System) (Schmuck & Haskin, 2002) is IBM's clustered file system. The following description is taken from (IBM General Parallel File System, n.d.).

IBM's high-performance shared-disk clustered file system GPFS (General Parallel File System) powers many of the world's largest scientific and commercial applications requiring high-speed access to large volumes of data such as:

- Digital media
- Engineering design
- Business intelligence
- Financial analytics
- Seismic data processing
- Geographic information systems
- Scalable file serving

GPFS provides online storage management, scalable access, and integrated information life-cycle management tools capable of managing petabytes of data and billions of files. Virtualising your file storage space and allowing multiple systems and applications to share common pools of storage provides you the flexibility to transparently administer the infrastructure without disrupting applications, improving cost and energy efficiency, while reducing management overhead. IBM's Scale Out NAS (SONAS) product exports the clustered file system through industry standard protocols like CIFS, NFS, FTP and HTTP. Released in 2010, SONAS is a second generation file services architecture first used within IBM to store employees' files since 2001. All of the file system nodes export all files of all file systems simultaneously (they are called interface nodes in SONAS terminology). This is a different approach from some other clustered NAS solutions which pin individual files to a single node or pair of nodes thus limiting the single file performance. Each file system can be multiple Petabytes in size. SONAS combines proprietary IBM technology (storage & server hardware and GPFS) with open source components like Linux, Samba (free software re-implementation of SMB/CIFS networking protocol) and CTDB (cluster implementation of the TDB database used by Samba and other projects to store temporary data).

## OneFS

OneFS is Isilon System's clustered file system support, as described in Isilon's Web site (Isilon OneFS Operating System, n.d.): OneFS is Isilon's sixth-generation operating system that provides the intelligence behind all Isilon scale-out storage systems. It combines the three layers of traditional storage architectures-file system, volume manager and RAID-into one unified software layer, creating a single intelligent file system that spans all nodes within a cluster. Isilon's OneFS enables:

- Independent or linear scalability of performance and capacity to over 85 Gigabytes per second of throughput and more than 15.5 petabytes of capacity in a single file system.
- A single point of management for large and rapidly growing repositories of data.
- Mission-critical reliability and high availability with state-of-the-art data protection.

Unlike simple NAS namespace aggregation products, Isilon's OneFS operating system is truly distributed and stripes data across all nodes in a cluster to create a single, shared pool of storage. OneFS offers mission-critical reliability and industry-leading drive rebuild times. OneFS also delivers cluster-aware Symmetric Multiprocessing (SMP) capabilities that enable the system to move tasks between processors for extremely efficient workload balancing. In conjunction with OneFS' ability to stripe data across all nodes in a cluster, Isilon achieves the high aggregate bandwidth and transactional performance required to power next generation enterprise data centers. Each node in an Isilon clustered storage system is a peer, so any node can handle a request. Using InfiniBand for intracluster communication and synchronization, OneFS provides each node with knowledge of the entire file system layout and where each file and part thereof is located. OneFS controls the placement of files directly on individual disks and dramatically improves the performance of the disk sub-system by optimally distributing files across the cluster. By laying data on disks in a file-by-file manner, OneFS is able to control the redundancy level of the storage system at the volume, directory, and even file levels.

## GlusterFS

GlusterFS (GlusterFS, n.d.) is a general purpose distributed file system for scalable storage. A summary of its main concept is presented below and taken from (GlusterFS wiki, n.d.): GlusterFS aggregates so called "storage bricks" over Infiniband or TCP/IP interconnect into one large parallel network file system. Its design supports a stack-able user space design without compromising performance and has been used for a variety of applications ranging from Cloud Computing, Biomedical Sciences to Archival Storage. GlusterFS has a client and server component. Servers are typically deployed as storage bricks, with each server running a glusterfsd daemon to export a local file system as a volume. The glusterfs client process, which connects to servers with a custom protocol over TCP/IP, InfiniBand or SDP, composes remote volumes into larger ones. Applications doing large amounts of file I/O can also use the libglusterfs client library to connect to the servers directly and run translators in-process, without going through the file system and incurring extra overheads.

The main features supported by GlusterFS are the following, as is implemented by so called "translators":

- File-based mirroring and replication
- File-based striping
- File-based load balancing
- Volume failover
- Scheduling and disk caching
- Storage quotas

The GlusterFS server exports an existing file system as-is, leaving it up to client-side translators to structure the store. The clients themselves are stateless, do not communicate with each other, and are expected to have translator configurations consistent with each other. This can cause coherency problems, but allows GlusterFS to scale up to several petabytes on commodity hardware by avoiding bottlenecks that normally affect more tightly-coupled distributed file systems.

## Lustre

Lustre (Lustre, n.d.) is a massively parallel distributed file system, generally used for large scale cluster computing. The name Lustre is derived from Linux and cluster. Available under the GNU GPL, the project aims to provide a file system for clusters of tens of thousands of nodes with petabytes of storage capacity, without compromising speed, security, or availability. Lustre is designed, developed, and maintained by Oracle Corporation, by way of its 2010 acquisition of Sun Microsystems, with input from many other individuals and companies. Lustre file systems are used in computer clusters ranging from small workgroup clusters to large-scale, multi-site clusters. Fifteen of the top 30 supercomputers in the world use Lustre file systems, including the world's fastest supercomputer (as of October 2010). The Lustre architecture is comprised of a single Metadata Target (MDT) per filesystem and multiple Object Storage Servers (OSSes) that store file data on one or more Object Storage Targets (OSTs). In addition, there are client components for accessing the data. Lustre exposes to the clients a standard POSIX interface with a unified namespace for all of the files and data in the filesystem, and allows concurrent reads and writes. In typical installations, the MDT and OST functions are located on separate nodes communicating over a network. Lustre supports several network types, including native Infiniband verbs, TCP/IP on Ethernet and a variety of other networks. The storage attached to the servers is typically accessed using the ext4 file system. In Lustre clients do not directly modify the objects on the OST filesystems, but, instead, delegate this task to OSSes. This is in contrast to some shared block-based filesystems that allow direct access to the underlying storage by all of the clients in the filesystem.

## GoogleFS

Google File System (GFS) (Ghemawat, Gobioff, & Leung, 2003) is a file system designed by Google to support its applications. As such, it is not designed for the general purpose use of a file system interface, but rather for the internal use of Google's search engine data collecting mechanisms. The most frequent operation in this environment is an append operation of chunks of data onto large existing files. Only rarely are files modified, so operations that edit exiting content can have very bad response times without hurting the main cause. The basic architecture of a GFS cluster is composed of many Chunkservers along with one single Master node that serves for metadata queries. Actual chunks are communicated directly between Clients and Chunkservers, while the Master's sole purpose is to manage and answer periodic queries regarding chunk distributions across the nodes. Other design points are the preference of providing high throughput rather than low latency and the use of cheap commodity hardware. The later calls for intensive replication of data to avoid data loss, and indeed each chunk is replicated across at least three Chunkservers. As opposed to many filesystems, GFS is not implemented in the kernel of an operating system, but is instead provided as a userspace library.

## HDFS

The Hadoop Distributed File System (HDFS) (HDFS, Apache Hadoop Project, n.d.) is a distributed, scalable, and portable filesystem written in Java for the Hadoop framework. Much like GFS (which HDFS originally attempted to mimic) HDFS stores large files across multiple machines, and is designed to handle very large files. It has a primary Namenode for metadata handling and numerous data nodes. HDFS achieves reliability by replicating data across multiple hosts, where data is typically stored on three nodes: two on the same rack, and one on a different rack. Data nodes can talk to each other to rebalance data, to move copies around, and to keep the replication level of data. HDFS is not fully POSIX compliant because the requirements for a POSIX filesystem differ from the target goals for a Hadoop application, namely, increased performance for data throughput (on the other hand, high availability is not one of HDFS's stated target goals). File access is supported through the native Java API or the Thrift API (for generating a client in other languages). Being built to be used by Hadoop jobs, HDFS cannot be directly mounted by an existing operating system. Getting data into and out of the HDFS file system, an action that often needs to be performed before and after executing a job, can be inconvenient. A Filesystem in Userspace (FUSE) virtual file system has been developed to address this problem, at least for Linux and some other Unix systems.

## PVFS

The Parallel Virtual File System (PVFS) (Blumer & Ligon, 1994) is an open source parallel file system. A parallel file system is a type of distributed file system that distributes file data across multiple servers and provides for concurrent access by multiple tasks of a parallel application. PVFS was designed for use in large scale cluster computing. PVFS focuses on high performance access to large data sets. It consists of a server process and a client library, both of which are written entirely of user-level code. A Linux kernel module and a pvfs-client process allow the file system to be mounted and used with standard utilities. The client library provides for high performance access via the Message Passing Interface (MPI). PVFS is being jointly developed between the Parallel Architecture Research Laboratory at Clem-son University and the Mathematics and Computer Science Division at Argonne National Laboratory, and the Ohio Supercomputer Centre and has been funded by NASA Goddard Space Flight Centre, DOE Argonne National Laboratory, NSF PACI, and HECURA programs, and other government and private agencies. In a cluster using PVFS nodes are designated as one or more of: client, data server, and metadata server. Data servers hold file data, metadata servers hold metadata including stat-info, attributes, and datafile-handles as well as directory entries. Clients run applications that utilize the file system by sending requests to the servers over the network. The above information was collected from (Parallel Virtual File System wiki, n.d.).

## XtreemFS

XtreemFS (XtreemFS, n.d.) is introduced as a distributed and replicated file system for the Cloud. In its framework, distributed Clients and servers can be distributed world-wide. XtreemFS supports installations across many data centers and is able to handle the failures that occur in wide-area installations. Clients can mount XtreemFS volumes from anywhere with an Internet connection. XtreemFS has been under development since early 2007 and a first public release was made in August 2008. XtreemFS is part of the XtreemOS project which is funded by the European Commission's IST programme. Some of the main features are:

- **Replication:** All XtreemFS services can be replicated with hot stand-byes which automatically take over when the primary server fails.
- POSIX compatibility.
- **Elasticity:** An XtreemFS installation can add or remove storage serves and scale to thousands of storage and metadata servers.
- **Security:** Supports SSL and X.509 certificates to allow running XtreemFS over the Internet without a VPN.
- **Extensibility:** Has a plug-in architecture through which one can modify the behavior of XtreemFS, e.g., to better integrate with a security infrastructure.

- Striping of files over several storage servers (similar to RAID-0) for increased I/O bandwidth and capacity.

## Microsoft DFS

Microsoft DFS (What is DFS?, n.d.) is a set of services allowing administrators to group shared folders located on different servers by transparently connecting them to one or more DFS namespaces. A DFS namespace is a virtual view of shared folders in an organization. Using the DFS tools, an administrator selects which shared folders to present in the namespace, designs the hierarchy in which those folders appear, and determines the names that the shared folders show in the namespace. When a user views the namespace, the folders appear to reside on a single, high-capacity hard disk. Users can navigate the namespace without needing to know the server names or shared folders hosting the data. Some of the benefits that DFS also provides include:

- **Simplified data migration:** Users do not need to readjust to the fact that data has changed its location.
- **Increased availability of file server data:** In the event of a server failure, DFS refers client computers to the next available server.
- **Load sharing:** DFS provides a degree of load sharing by mapping a given logical name to shared folders on multiple file servers.
- **Security:** The existing NTFS file system and shared folder permissions are used on each target in DFS.

## CONCLUSION

The VISION Cloud project intends to provide scalable, metadata-rich object services with a new data model that is not compatible with file system POSIX API. The approach that will be taken in this project is to leverage state of the art distributed file systems rather than expand their capabilities. In particular:

1. Distributed file systems may be used within a data center, while other advanced data distribution mechanisms will be deployed across sites. The challenge then becomes how to synchronize between the data that is replicated on two or more different file systems, taking into account latencies and possible separation in the network topology. This is a major shift from an architecture that is based on a single file system that handles the entire pool of files in a centralized manner (using locking, centralized meta data server, etc).
2. Diverging from the POSIX semantics requires a definition of a new type of semantics.
3. A cloud storage infrastructure capable of providing services, with accounting and billing for users, required richer meta data and monitoring at the system level than currently supplied by file systems.

This includes information on capacity used by entities (rather than directories), access statistics to files, bandwidth and more. The challenge is then to (1) extend the reporting and accounting within a given distributed file system (2) aggregate this information across many file systems. IBM's GPFS SNC (shared nothing cluster) produce was selected for use in VISION Cloud. It fulfills the general requirements of VISION Cloud, namely Scalability, scale out performance, elasticity, and availability. The selection of this technology was heavily influenced by GPFS's strong commercial track record, as well as IBM HRL's ability to provide a high level of support if required, and license-free installations for the VISION Cloud test bed. Other potential solutions were either proprietary (e.g., OneFS, GFS, MS-DFS) or open source solutions that do not carry the maturity and insurance of stability as a product such as GPFS (XtreemFS, PVFS, HDFS, GlusterFS, Lustre).

The unique accessibility to this product provided by IBM HRL made it the leading candidate for the VISION Cloud.

## DISTRIBUTED DATA MANAGEMENT SYSTEMS

### Overview

Modern distributed database systems have become a central tool for massive data storage (in the order of petabytes) that store large amount of metadata information. Distributed database systems use an architecture that distributes storage and processing across multiple servers to address performance, scalability requirements, caching, flexible graph handling and easy query manipulation. All these requirements cannot be met by traditional relational databases mainly because requests inside the same transaction have to be run by a single node of the database. With the rise of scale and Internet applications, more and more companies made the choice to skip relational databases in favor of simpler and more scalable "NoSQL" databases (DeWitt & Gray, 1990; Distributed Databases Survey, n.d.; NoSQL Databases, n.d.). These types of databases allow simple requests like single row transaction, but do not allow complex SQL request such as join operations. Notable production implementations include Google's BigTable (Chang et al., 2006), Amazon's Dynamo (DeCandia et al., 2007a), and Cassandra (The Apache Cassandra Project, n.d.; Lakshman & Malik, 2009).

### Approaches, Implementations, and Comparisons

In the following, we try to give a short summary of the main characteristics of NoSQL databases and highlight some implementations most relevant to our requirements.

## NoSQL Databases Characteristics

The excellent survey by Randy Guck (Distributed Databases Survey, n.d.; NoSQL Databases, n.d.) describe NoSQL databases as ones that follow most or all of the following characteristics:

- **No pre-defined Schema for "Tables":** Traditional databases typically require a predefined scheme that each entry (row) in the table should follow. In modern NoSQL databases such a requirement is not mandatory and entries can vary from row to row.
- **Partitioning (Ganesan, Bawa, & Garcia-Molina, 2004; Ford et al., 2010):** Storage rows are partitioned into small storage entities (usually managed by a single server), and replicated.
- **Shared nothing architecture:** According to the above mentioned partition, each node handles the entries at its responsibility locally, rather than using some shared storage with a global view.
- **Elasticity (Stonebraker et al., 2007):** Storage and server capacity can be increased by adding more servers without downtime.
- **Asynchronous replication and BASE instead of ACID:** Reliability is handled by replication of elements across different nodes in the system. In order to avoid latency in write operations, this replication is done in asynchronous fashion (Belaramani et al., 2006; Belaramani, Dahlin, Nayate, & Zheng, 2008), allowing the write to complete after the first replica is in place, and assuring *eventual consistency* (Das, Agrawal, & El Abbadi, 2010; Vogels, 2009; Burrows, 2006) rather than atomicity. This is a choice to adopt the BASE (Basically Available, Soft state, Eventual consistency) principle over ACID (Atomicity, Consistency, Isolation, Durability) (Pritchett, 2008): NoSQL da-

tabases emphasize performance and availability. According to the well-known CAP (Consistency, Availability, Partition tolerance) theorem (Gilbert & Lynch, 2002) one cannot have all three properties together and due to the emphasis on performance and availability in cloud applications the consistency is typically relaxed.

In VISION Cloud, the distributed database is designated for an efficient management of metadata of objects in the cloud. Scale is perhaps the most dominant factor in this cloud, and thus we focus our attention to solutions that seems appropriate. The most relevant categories of distributed databases types for the VISION project are the *key/value stores* and *"Big Table" databases*. Other categories can be examined in (*Distributed Databases Survey*, n.d.; *NoSQL Databases*, n.d.). We highlight some of the properties of these categories and some existing solutions for them (note that some solutions fall into both categories).

## NoSQL Database Implementations

The simplest implementations of DBs are key/value stores by which each entry can be accessed solely by its key. More sophisticated NoSQL DBs have additional mechanisms for indexing data entries. This is typically carried out by handling multiple tables for the same data and enabling synchronization between them. The exact data model can vary from one example to the other and typically relies on the target application of the product. In the following section, we list some prominent implementations of such DB:

- **Google's BigTable (Chang et al., 2006):** This DB has been the initial model for many of the other implementations to come. Initially designed for the use of the search engine operations, it is now also a data storage solution known as datastore in Google's Cloud Computing framework

- the Google App Engine (GAE). It is a distributed schema-less DB that supports multiple updates within a single transaction and has an indexing system that serves the mechanism to returns entities in different desired orders (typically predefined). GAE datastores can be accessed with Python or Java.

- **Cassandra (Apache) (The Apache Cassandra Project, n.d.):** An open source project that originated from Facebook. This project is surveyed in greater depth in the following section as it was chosen to be a central clustered DB for the VISION Cloud.

- **HBase (Apache HBase Reference Guide, n.d.):** An Apache open source project that gives an analogue of Google's Bigtable built upon Hadoop's HDFS.

- **Hypertable (Hypertable inc., n.d.):** Another open source, "Web scale" database modeled after Google's BigTable. It is available under the GNU GPLv2. Hypertable can be deployed on top of the Hadoop HDFS or CloudStore KFS file systems. It supports an SQL-like language for creating tables called HQL.

- **Azure Tables (Windows Azure – Data Management, n.d.):** Microsoft's Azure cloud computing platform, first came into production use in 2010. The underlying Azure fabric provides distributed computing services such as communication, service management, replication, and failover and also several storage options, including: file system, storage objects, "big table" like storage structures and limited version of SQL.

- **SimpleDB (Amazon SimpleDB, n.d.):** Amazon's simpleDB is a non-relational data store that serves Amazon's Web services. It carries the flexibility of a pay per use service, and has the benefit that the data model can be modified on the fly with automatic indexing.

- **Voldemort (Voldemort Distributed Database, n.d.):** Originating from LinkedIn, it is now an open source project.

- **PNUTS (Platform for Nimble Universal Table Storage) (Cooper et al., 2008):** Internally called Sherpa, is a Yahoo! project for big table-like distributed storage. It is currently a research project. Its goals are high availability, autosharding, multi-data center replication, and failover, similar to BigTable, Cassandra, and others.

## Cassandra

In this section, we give a more in depth account of the solution that was chosen for the VISION Cloud. The information in this section is collected from the Cassandra documentation (*The Apache Cassandra Project*, n.d.). Cassandra is a distributed second generation database that has an instance running on each interface node, providing access to a cluster-wide database from each node. Cassandra is a highly scalable, eventually consistent, distributed column-oriented database. Cassandra brings together the distributed systems technologies from Amazon's Dynamo (DeCandia et al., 2007b) and the data model from Google's BigTable (Chang et al., 2006). Like Dynamo, Cassandra is eventually consistent and provides different levels of consistency at different cost of availability and performance. Like BigTable, Cassandra provides a ColumnFamily-based data model richer than typical key/value systems. Cassandra was open sourced by Facebook in 2008, and designed by one of Dynamo's original authors (Avinash Lakshman), who also designed the Voldemort database for LinkedIn. It is used by many large companies such as Rackspace, Digg, Facebook, Twitter, and Cisco. The largest production server has over 150 TB of data. Following is a list of key features in Cassandra:

- **Decentralized:** All nodes are equal; there is no single point of failure.
- **Fault tolerant:** Data is automatically replicated to multiple nodes for fault-tolerance. Replication across multiple data centers is supported. Failed nodes can be replaced with no downtime.
- **Eventually consistent:** Data uses an eventually consistent model with optimizations such as Hinted Handoff and Read Repair to minimize inconsistency windows.
- **Elasticity:** New machines can be added dynamically with no downtime, and read/write operations scale linearly as new servers are added.
- **Rich data model:** More complex records are supported than simple key/value stores.
- **Content-abstraction support:** Version 0.7 support dynamic creation of column family and keyspace, identified by 'variable' identified that hides application and content semantics.
- Cassandra reports impressive performance numbers compared to MySQL.

Cassandra is written in Java. It uses the Apache Thrift service framework to provide access in many languages. Based on its roots, it emphasizes the Linux platform though it is being used on Windows as well. In mid-March, 2010, Cassandra was moved from an incubator project to a top-level project.

## CONCLUSION

Due to VISION Cloud's requirement to be scalable across the cloud - i.e. across multiple clusters, relational databases were ruled out in favor of a No-SQL based database. Of the big table solutions mentioned above, the field was thinned down to open source project that seem the most stable in terms of user reports and apparent interests of applications and community activity. The main leading prospects were HBase and Cassandra that both show a high level of activity and involvement from industrial communities and fulfill the basic requirements of scalability, performance, elasticity, availability and eventual consistency. After much consideration, Cassandra was chosen. The main properties that influenced this decision were its relatively simple installation requirements, OpenSource availability, and its automatic scalability - when adding more servers it will reconfigure itself redistributing load among the servers.

## RESOURCE ALLOCATION AND ENERGY MANAGEMENT

### Overview

There are a multitude of parameters and considerations involved in the decision of where and when to place data objects and compute tasks (VM execution in general and storlets in the case of VISION Cloud) in a global cloud. A major challenge is to take into account all the considerations and tradeoffs, and allocate resources in the cloud in a manner that will benefit both the user and the various cloud providers. Among the main considerations are:

- **Performance:** The global position of both the data centres and the users of the cloud dictate a central role in the placement considerations. It is most sensible that data will reside as close as possible to its end user, thus reducing network latencies to minimum. However, this becomes tricky in many cases. For example, (1) users move around; (2) data centres become overloaded; (3) some data should be accessible from many locations simultaneously (sometimes very far apart); and (4) data objects often manipulated by computationally intense storlets may be better placed in data centres with powerful compute nodes than in ones close to the user. Load balancing plays a central role in achieving good performance: it is advisable that the use of many resources of the cloud (e.g., storage capacity, network, spindles, and compute power) is evenly distributed. This is also true within a single data centre, where resources should be utilised accordingly.

- **Reliability and continuous availability:** One of the central goals for cloud storage is reliability and availability. To achieve this data is replicated across multiple (at least two) geographical zones. An automated allocation procedure should distribute replicas of data in numbers and locations that coincide with the requirements for that data, taking into account the importance of the data, its expected usage frequency, and the reliability of the different data centres.

- **Total cost of ownership (TCO):** Also a central goal for the cloud. An overall resource allocation mechanism should attempt to place data in locations that are cheaper, yet still provide good performance. It is clear that there are often tradeoffs between the overall cost on one hand and performance, reliability, and availability one the other.

- **Energy management:** A significant part of the cost of the cloud is its energy utilisation. The electricity consumed by IT today is estimated to be ≈ 2% of the world power usage. Coupled with the high cost of energy and growing environmental considerations, reducing power consumption has become a central goal when managing data centres. This is ever more crucial in cloud environments due to their large scale and the critical importance of low operational costs. Placement of storlets (VISION Cloud's notion of a storage-oriented computation) and scheduling of data movement activities can play a central role towards reducing power consumption.

## Approaches, Implementations, and Comparisons

Data and compute allocation and placement problems are well studied both from theoretical aspects and as practical means of spreading data in a large distributed environment. Most of the work though considers only a subset of the complexities involved in actual automated placement, and in fact, many operating data centers, data placement, and allocation are done manually. We scan a number of directions studied and point to recent publications that represent the topic out of the vast amount of literature. Other references can be found within these representatives. There has been a line of theoretical works on load balancing objects (could be storage, compute or network packets) into variable size containers (data centers, disks, storage controllers, etc.). Some simple and more challenging approaches are studied, along with mathematical analysis of their success. Most of the works do not consider a multitude of parameters. Some recent works study allocation in the presence of replication (Mense & Scheideler, 2008). Peer2Peer environments are large clusters of small compute and storage nodes and it is challenging to allocate space for objects in a balanced fashion while allowing for quick lookup of an object. A long line of works consider efficient and manageable techniques for large networks with growing diversity of the nodes and more requirements such as location constraints and local optimizations (Weil, Brandt, Miller, & Maltzahn, 2006; MacCormick et al., 2009). There have also been studies of incorporating placement with error correction and redundancy mechanisms in large clustered storage environments (Brinkmann & Effert, 2008). In this respect, some basic balancing mechanisms have been instated into just about every distributed file system or distributed DB (as mentioned in Sections 1 and 2). A large body of work addresses allocation within SAN storage systems, in which compute consideration are taken into account. The placement of storage and computation are coordinated to some extent, and migration options are discussed. These studies take weight in the considerations of the traffic required between the computation taking place and the actual data (Cardosa, Korupolu, & Singh, 2009; Gulati, Kumar, Ahmad, & Kumar, 2010; Gulati, Ahmad, & Waldspurger, 2009). These studies are limited to a single data center scenario, but techniques may be highly relevant to a multi-DC cloud. (Agarwal et al., 2010) looks at a global dispersal of information in the cloud, and studies placement issues that are related to the geographical location of the cloud users and attempts to put data in the geographical vicinity of its main users. Regarding power consumption, there are a number of ongoing efforts to model and integrate global energy saving techniques at the data center and cloud levels.

## Green Grid

The Green Grid (Green Grid, n.d.) is a standardization body that set out to define metrics for power efficiency of data centers. FIT4Green (Fit4Green, n.d.) is an EU funded project aims at contributing to ICT energy reducing efforts by creating an energy-aware layer of plug-ins for data centre automation frameworks, to improve energy efficiency of existing IT solution deployment strategies so as to minimize overall power consumption, by moving computation and services around a federation of IT data centres sites.

## GAMES

GAMES (Green Data Centers, n.d.) is an EU funded project aiming at developing a set of methodologies, software tools and services, and innovative metrics for the Energy Efficiency Design and Management of the Data Centres of the next generation (namely IT Service Centres). There are also numerous academic efforts that aim at power saving methodologies. Examples follow (and see other references within): (Kaushik, Cher-

kasova, Campbell, & Nahrstedt, 2010) describes using power efficient data tiers, (Harnik, Naor, & Segall, 2009) looks for opportunities of powering down resources and (Le, Bianchini, Martonosi, & Nguyen, n.d.) aims at clever utilization of data centers with lower electricity prices.

## CONCLUSION

As mentioned, existing works do not capture the full complexity of allocation of storage and compute resources in a global multi-DC cloud environment. While many of the techniques used today are relevant to this setting as well, it is likely a combination of these techniques and new innovations that would capture the new challenges introduced by a geographically dispersed cloud. Using the large scale of the cloud and its geographical distribution allows us to benefit from aggressive thin provisioning and to lower the overall cost of the cloud, and balance this desire with the need to support a high quality of service and adhere to SLAs for the clouds customers. Work on energy management is deferred to the second and third years of the VISION Cloud project. In general the cloud should utilise its global distribution across geographies and time zones to minimise both power costs and the total use of electricity. For example, one can power down resources in certain locations and during the periods at which they are unlikely to be necessary. Distributing the data in a manner that would maximise such opportunities is a priority. Among our objectives are: (1) To predict the overall usage patterns and identify long-term and short-term future events. (2) To leverage global scheduling of operations (storage and compute) to optimise the total power usage. This will be achieved by placement of system components and events in response to spatial and temporal characteristic of the usage patterns. By leveraging and integrating the energy and modelling we plan to study and develop algorithms for system-wide placement and migration of servers and storage with a special focus on to energy utilisation. Energy management is highly related to the previous two allocation tasks, and is given its separate task due to its importance and due to the natural tradeoffs that arise between saving power and improving performance.

## DATA MOBILITY

### Overview

A key aspect that is missing today from large storage systems and cloud storage systems in particular is comprehensive and true data mobility. Data mobility is critical in achieving improved quality of service, improving reliability (by achieving faster replication and recovery times), and reducing costs (both in terms of network related hardware – one of the more costly resources of a data center, and in terms of energy consumption). In addition, improved data mobility can aid in to avoid data lock in (discussed separately under the chapter on federation). VISION Cloud will address the fundamental technological barriers for data mobility today. The main areas of research for data mobility will be techniques for data deduplication and data reduction.

### Approaches, Implementations, and Comparisons

#### Data Deduplication

A key technique that VISION Cloud intends to exploit for achieving improved data mobility is data deduplication. Network deduplication, WAN deduplication, source based deduplication or client side deduplication are all terms used to describe methodologies that first test if data already appears in its target destination, and then forgoes unnecessary data transfers if they already exist at the target. The prominent technique for performing deduplication is by fingerprinting data using a hash function with a short output. The data is

first broken into a basic deduplication chunk. This can be done in one of several granularities:

- **Full file:** The basic duplication unit is a whole file/object. This is most suitable for immutable data, e.g. images or compressed data (where a sub file granularity is typically not useful).
- **Fixed blocks:** Typically at size of 2KB, 4KB or 8KB. This can match a lower level page size being used and is easy to work with. It can benefit from duplications at the sub file granularity, as long as they are aligned with the block size.
- **Variable sized blocks:** A methodology for chunking data at variable size, with a predefined average size (say 4KB) that allows for deduplication at block granularity even if data is not aligned with a fixed block size.

Once the data is broken into its deduplication granularity, each chunk is given a fingerprint using a hash function, typically using a cryptographic hash (such as SHA1 or SHA256). Each new chunk is then compared to all previous existing chunks (via a fingerprint search) and duplicate chunks can then be stored in compact manner. Moreover, by comparing chunk fingerprints, data chunks that exist at the target destination do not have to be sent from the host at all. The main technical challenges are therefore: 1) Maintaining existing fingerprints and identifying existence of repeating fingerprints efficiently. 2) Storing data in a succinct non-duplicated manner that can be accessed efficiently. Each existing deduplication strategy tackles the above issues. There are a multitude of products and implementations, mostly from the realm of backup applications that perform network deduplication. A partial list is below:

- IBM TSM and TSM Fastback (Tivoli Storage Manager, n.d.), EMC Avamar (EMC Avamar, n.d.), Symantec Netbackup (Symantec Netbackup, n.d.) (and many more) - These are backup and CDP appliances, typically with a central backup and deduplication across a number of source locations. To save data transfer bandwidth, deduplication is done at the source side. These applications typically work at the block level.

- Mozy (Mozy, n.d.), Dropbox (Dropbox, n.d.), Memopal (Memopal – Online Backup, n.d.) (and many more) - These are cloud based backup services. They serve a large number of users and perform cross user, client side data deduplication. This is typically done at a full file level and cover huge amounts of data (Mozy proclaims they handle 50 petabytes of data).

There are a number of academic papers that discuss tackling the problem of deduplication in large scales of data. Among these are works from Data Domain (EMC) (Zhu, Li, & Patterson, 2008), (Dong et al., 2011), Diligent (IBM) (Aronovich et al., 2009), and HP/UCSC (Bhagwat, Eshghi, Long, & Lillibridge, 2009; Lillibridge et al., 2009).

## CONCLUSION

Much of the data in a cloud has replicas or near replicas in different locations. If this duplication can be identified, one can greatly reduce the amount of data that needs to be moved. The sheer scale and the multi-location nature of the VISION Cloud poses design challenges that do not appear in smaller scale environments. Existing solutions typically have a single target (or in some cases a cluster) and numerous clients. In our cloud setting, we deal with several distributed sources and numerous distributed targets. The challenge is to architect a solution that can identify duplications at an extremely high scale and with very high performance. Moreover, not all data is suitable for deduplication, and if it is, the same strategy may

not be good for all applications. Thus, identifying the suitable technique automatically is a challenge that can greatly improve performance for a large and diverse cloud. Finally, there are some crucial security issues that arise when doing deduplication across many clients, especially need when deduplicating from the client side. These issues have so far gone unattended and we plan to advance the state of the art in this respect.

## REFERENCES

Agarwal, S., Dunagan, J., Jain, N., Saroiu, S., Wolman, A., & Bhogan, H. (2010). Volley: Automated data placement for geo-distributed cloud services. In *Proceedings of the 7th Usenix Conference on Networked Systems Design and Implementation* (p. 2). Berkeley, CA: USENIX Association. Retrieved from http://portal.acm.org/citation.cfm ?id=1855711.1855713

*Amazon simpledb.* (n.d.). Retrieved from http://aws.amazon.com/ simpledb/

*Apache Hbase Reference Guide.* (n.d.). Retrieved from http://hbase.apache.org/book.html

Aronovich, L., Asher, R., Bachmat, E., Bitner, H., Hirsch, M., & Klein, S. T. (2009). The design of a similarity based deduplication system. In *Proceedings of Systor 2009: The Israeli Experimental Systems Conference* (pp. 6:1–6:14). New York, NY: ACM. Retrieved from http://doi.acm.org/10.1145/1534530.1534539

Belaramani, N., Dahlin, M., Gao, L., Nayate, A., Venkataramani, A., Yalagandula, P., & Zheng, J. (2006). PRACTI replication. In *Proceedings of the USENIX Symposium on Networked Systems Design and Implementation (NSDI).* USENIX.

Belaramani, N., Dahlin, M., Nayate, A., & Zheng, J. (2008). *PADRE: A policy architecture for building data replication systems.*

Bhagwat, D., Eshghi, K., Long, D. D. E., & Lillibridge, M. (2009). Extreme binning: Scalable, parallel deduplication for chunk-based file backup. In *Proceedings of Mascots* (pp. 1–9). Mascots. doi:10.1109/MASCOT.2009.5366623.

Blumer, A., & Ligon, W. B. (1994). *The parallel virtual file system.* Paper presented at the 1994 PVM Users Group Meeting. New York, NY.

Brinkmann, A., & Effert, S. (2008). Redundant data placement strategies for cluster storage environments. In *Proceedings of the 12th International Conference on Principles of Distributed Systems* (pp. 551–554). Berlin: Springer-Verlag. Retrieved fromhttp://dx.doi.org/10.1007/978-3-540-92221-6 38

Burrows, M. (2006). The chubby lock service for loosely-coupled distributed systems. In *Proceedings of the 7th Symposium on Operating Systems Design and Implementation* (pp. 335–350). Berkeley, CA: USENIX Association. Retrieved from http://portal.acm.org/citation.cfm?id=1298455.1298487

Cardosa, M., Korupolu, M. R., & Singh, A. (2009). Shares and utilities based power consolidation in virtualized server environments. In *Proceedings of the 11th IFIP/IEEE International Conference on Symposium on Integrated Network Management* (pp. 327–334). Piscataway, NJ: IEEE Press. Retrieved from http://portal.acm.org/citation.cfm?id=1688933.1688986

Chang, F., Dean, J., Ghemawat, S., Hsieh, W. C., Wallach, D. A., Burrows, M., et al. (2006). Bigtable: A distributed storage system for structured data. In *Proceedings of the 7th USENIX Symposium on Operating Systems Design and Implementation* (vol. 7, p. 15). Berkeley, CA: USENIX Association. Retrieved from http://portal.acm.org/citation.cfm?id=1267308.1267323

Cooper, B. F., Ramakrishnan, R., Srivastava, U., Silberstein, A., Bohannon, P., Jacobsen, H.-A., et al. (2008). Pnuts: Yahoo!'s hosted data serving platform. *Proceedings of VLDB Endowment, 1*(2), 1277–1288. Retrieved fromhttp://dx.doi.org/10.1145/1454159.1454167

Das, S., Agrawal, D., & El Abbadi, A. (2010). G-store: A scalable data store for transactional multi key access in the cloud. In *Proceedings of the 1st ACM Symposium on Cloud Computing* (pp. 163–174). New York, NY: ACM. Retrieved from http://doi.acm.org/10.1145/1807128.1807157

DeCandia, G., Hastorun, D., Jampani, M., Kakulapati, G., Lakshman, A., Pilchin, A., et al. (2007). Dynamo: Amazon's highly available key-value store. *SIGOPS Operating Systems Review, 41*, 205–220. Retrieved from http://doi.acm.org/10.1145/1323293.1294281

DeWitt, D. J., & Gray, J. (1990). Parallel database systems: the future of database processing or a passing fad? *SIGMOD Record, 19*, 104–112. Retrieved from http://doi.acm.org/10.1145/122058.122071 doi:10.1145/122058.122071.

*Distributed Databases Survey.* (n.d.). Retrieved from http://wiki.toadforcloud.com/index.php/Surveydistributeddatabases#Overview

Dong, W., Douglis, F., Li, K., Patterson, H., Reddy, S., & Shilane, P. (2011). Tradeoffs in scalable data routing for deduplication clusters. In *Proceedings of the 9th USENIX Conference on File and Storage Technologies* (p. 2). Berkeley, CA: USENIX Association. Retrieved from http://portal.acm.org/citation.cfm?id=1960475.1960477

*Dropbox.* (n.d.). Retrieved from https://www.dropbox.com/

*Emc Avamar.* (n.d.). Retrieved from http://www.emc.com/collateral/software/data-sheet/h2568-emc-avamar-ds.pdf

*Fit4green*. (n.d.). Retrieved from http://www.fit4green.eu/

Ford, D., Labelle, F., Popovici, F. I., Stokely, M., Truong, V.-A., Barroso, L., et al. (2010). Availability in globally distributed storage systems. In *Proceedings of the 9th USENIX Conference on Operating Systems Design and Implementation* (pp. 1–7). Berkeley, CA: USENIX Association. Retrieved from http://portal.acm.org/citation.cfm?id=1924943.1924948

Ganesan, P., Bawa, M., & Garcia-Molina, H. (2004). Online balancing of range-partitioned data with applications to peer-to-peer systems. In *Proceedings of the Thirtieth International Conference on Very Large Data Bases* (vol. 30, pp. 444–455). VLDB Endowment. Retrieved from http://portal.acm.org/citation.cfm?id=1316689.1316729

Ghemawat, S., Gobioff, H., & Leung, S.-T. (2003). The google file system. *SIGOPS Operating Systems Review, 37*, 29–43. Retrieved from http://doi.acm.org/10.1145/1165389.945450

Gilbert, S., & Lynch, N. (2002). Brewer's conjecture and the feasibility of consistent, available, partition-tolerant web services. *SIGACT News, 33*, 51–59. Retrieved from http://doi.acm.org/10.1145/564585.564601

*GlusterFS*. (n.d.). Retrieved from http://www.gluster.org/

*Glusterfs Wiki*. (n.d.). Retrieved from http://en.wikipedia.org/wiki/ GlusterFS

*Green Data Centers*. (n.d.). Retrieved from http://www.green-datacenters.eu/

*Green Grid*. (n.d.). Retrieved from http://www.thegreengrid.org/

Gulati, A., Ahmad, I., & Waldspurger, C. A. (2009). Parda: Proportional allocation of resources for distributed storage access. In *Proceedings of the 7th Conference on File and Storage Technologies* (pp. 85–98). Berkeley, CA: USENIX Association. Retrieved from http://portal.acm.org/citation.cfm?id=1525908.1525915

Gulati, A., Kumar, C., Ahmad, I., & Kumar, K. (2010). Basil: Automated io load balancing across storage devices. In *Proceedings of the 8th USENIX Conference on File and Storage Technologies* (p. 13). Berkeley, CA: USENIX Association. Retrieved from http://portal.acm.org/citation.cfm?id=1855511.1855524

Harnik, D., Naor, D., & Segall, I. (2009). Low power mode in cloud storage systems. In *Proceedings of the 2009 IEEE International Symposium on Parallel & Distributed Processing* (pp. 1–8). Washington, DC: IEEE Computer Society. Retrieved from http://portal.acm.org/citation.cfm?id=1586640.1587438

*Hdfs, Apache Hadoop Project*. (n.d.). Retrieved from http://hadoop.apache.org/hdfs/

*Hypertable Inc*. (n.d.). Retrieved from http://hypertable.com/

*IBM General Parallel File System*. (n.d.). Retrieved from http://www-03.ibm.com/systems/software/gpfs/

*Isilon Onefs Operating System*. (n.d.). Retrieved from http://www.ndm.net/isilonstore/isilon/isilon-onefs-operating-system

Kaushik, R. T., Cherkasova, L., Campbell, R., & Nahrstedt, K. (2010). Lightning: Self-adaptive, energy-conserving, multi-zoned, commodity green cloud storage system. In *Proceedings of the 19th ACM International Symposium on High Performance Distributed Computing* (pp. 332–335). New York, NY: ACM. Retrieved from http://doi.acm.org/10.1145/1851476.1851523

Lakshman, A., & Malik, P. (2009). Cassandra: Structured storage system on a p2p network. In *Proceedings of the 28th ACM Symposium on Principles of Distributed Computing* (p. 5). New York, NY: ACM. Retrieved from http://0-doi.acm.org.millennium.lib.cyut.edu. tw/10.1145/1582716.1582722

Le, K., Bianchini, R., Martonosi, M., & Nguyen, T. D. (n.d.). *Cost-and energy-aware load distribution across data centers.*

Lillibridge, M., Eshghi, K., Bhagwat, D., Deolalikar, V., Trezise, G., & Camble, P. (2009). Sparse indexing: Large scale, inline deduplication using sampling and locality. In *Proceedings of the 7th Conference on File and Storage Technologies* (pp. 111–123). Berkeley, CA: USENIX Association. Retrieved from http://portal.acm.org/citation. cfm?id=1525908.1525917

*Lustre.* (n.d.). Retrieved from http://www.lustre. org

MacCormick, J., Murphy, N., Ramasubramanian, V., Wieder, U., Yang, J., & Zhou, L. (2009). Kinesis: A new approach to replica placement in distributed storage systems. *Transitional Storage, 4,* 11:1–11:28. Retrieved from http://doi.acm. org/10.1145/1480439.1480440

*Memopal – Online Backup.* (n.d.). Retrieved from http://memopal.com/ en/

Mense, M., & Scheideler, C. (2008). Spread: An adaptive scheme for redundant and fair storage in dynamic heterogeneous storage systems. In *Proceedings of the Nineteenth Annual ACM-SIAM Symposium on Discrete Algorithms* (pp. 1135–1144). Philadelphia, PA: Society for Industrial and Applied Mathematics. Retrieved from http://portal.acm.org/citation.cfm?id=1347082.1347206

*Mozy.* (n.d.). Retrieved from http://mozy.com

*Nosql Databases.* (n.d.). Retrieved from http:// en.wikipedia.org/wiki/NoSQL

*Parallel Virtual File System (PVFS) Wiki.* (n.d.). Retrieved from http://en.wikipedia.org/wiki/ ParallelVirtualFileSystem

Pritchett, D. (2008). Base: An acid alternative. *Queue, 6(3),* 48–55. doi:10.1145/1394127.1394128.

Schmuck, F., & Haskin, R. (2002). GPFS: A shared-disk file system for large computing clusters. In *Proceedings of the 1st USENIX Conference on File and Storage Technologies.* Berkeley, CA: USENIX Association. Retrieved from http://portal.acm.org/citation.cfm?id=1083323.1083349

Stonebraker, M., Madden, S., Abadi, D. J., Harizopoulos, S., Hachem, N., & Helland, P. (2007). The end of an architectural era: It's time for a complete rewrite. In *Proceedings of the 33rd International Conference on Very Large Data Bases* (pp. 1150–1160). VLDB Endowment. Retrieved from http://portal.acm.org/citation. cfm?id=1325851.1325981

*Symantec Netbackup.* (n.d.). Retrieved from http:// www.symantec.com/ netbackup

*The Apache Cassandra Project.* (n.d.). Retrieved from http://cassandra.apache.org/

*Tivoli Storage Manager.* (n.d.). Retrieved from http://www-01.ibm.com/software/tivoli/products/ storage-mgr/

Vogels, W. (2009). Eventually consistent. *Communications of the ACM,* 40–44. doi:10.1145/1435417.1435432.

*Voldemort Distributed Database.* (n.d.). Retrieved from http://project -voldemort.com/voldemort/

Weil, S. A., Brandt, S. A., Miller, E. L., & Maltzahn, C. (2006). Crush: Controlled, scalable, decentralized placement of replicated data. In *Proceedings of the 2006 ACM/IEEE Conference on Supercomputing.* New York, NY: ACM. Retrieved from http://doi.acm.org/10.1145/1188455.1188582

*What is DFS?* (n.d.). Retrieved from http://technet. microsoft.com/en-us/library/cc779627.aspx

*Windows Azure – Data Management.* (n.d.). Retrieved from http://www.windowsazure.com/ en-us/home/features/data -management/

*XtreemFS.* (n.d.). Retrieved from http://www. xtreemfs.org/

Zhu, B., Li, K., & Patterson, H. (2008). Avoiding the disk bottleneck in the data domain deduplication file system. In *Proceedings of the 6th USENIX Conference on File and Storage Technologies* (pp. 18:1–18:14). Berkeley, CA: USENIX Association. Retrieved from http://portal.acm.org/citation. cfm?id=1364813.1364831

# Chapter 3
# Content Centric Storage and Current Storage Systems

**Michael C. Jaeger**
*Siemens AG, Corporate Technology, Germany*

**Uwe Hohenstein**
*Siemens AG, Corporate Technology, Germany*

## ABSTRACT

*Content-centric storage represents an approach for handling large amounts of data. It is one of the innovations pursued by the VISION Cloud project. The goal of the VISION Cloud project is the development of an industry grade storage system using cloud technology. The envisaged use of the VISION Cloud involves the storage and management of millions of data items, potentially several hundreds of terabytes in size. On the one hand, the technical foundations must be capable of efficiently storing such an amount of data. On the other hand, the VISION Cloud must provide adequate means of an API for allowing the efficient navigation, search, and access for the right data item in this storage. For the latter purpose, VISION Cloud provides a data access layer, which is called "Content Centric Interface." Applications can use this data access layer for accessing the VISION Cloud storage from a content-centric point of view, abstracted from actual storage representation. The content centric interface is different from existing cloud storage interfaces and is similar, from an architectural point of view, to object relational mapping frameworks for traditional applications with relational database systems.*

## INTRODUCTION

Content centric storage represents a novel research topic. When investigating major search engines at the start of the VISION Cloud project, we have found a few hits referring to content centric storage, mostly referring to research efforts such as the CIMPLE project (cf. Delaet and Joosen, 2009).

The term content centric storage forms an analogy to the term content centric networking or content centric routing. In the area of networking and routing, the idea of content "centricness" comes from the need to perform routing efficiently, even with a rising amount of data. Content centric networking / routing refers to the idea that the content is not (directly) routed from the logical location of a source to the logical location of a recipient, but an additional layer of content publishers and

DOI: 10.4018/978-1-4666-3934-8.ch003

content sinks is placed above and routing efforts are performed more efficiently on this layer.

Among other authors, Ted Nelson's work was one of the first that have discussed this idea (cf. Nelson 1988). The goal is to implement a more efficient handling of content. Modeling the problem of getting content from A to B from a content-perspective enables a couple of useful mechanisms that improve the efficiency of the system, among them are (cf. Koponen 2007):

- The system can cache content that is subject to delivery to multiple consumers. The system can react more efficiently to congestion, as the awareness of the content will allow for a more suitable rerouting/exception handling than with network-based routing.
- Security functions can be implemented on a content level at distribution, which appears more suitable than at a central or isolated location.
- The system can be seen as a store for content rather than relying on the actual network or storage structure that holds the information.

A storage service appears similar to a network service, as the semantics of the operations of a storage service and a message-oriented middleware have strong similarities (cf. Gray1995). A message-oriented middleware can be seen as storage service to when considering that both a network service and a storage service have similar data sink and data source semantics. Also, a message-oriented middleware must offer similar characteristics as database servers do, when referring to the ACID paradigm (atomicity, consistency, isolation and durability) in the database world.

Consequently, we see content centric storage as an approach to provide a storage service at the content level that shall enable similar advantages as with content centric networking or routing. In

the VISION Cloud project, the front most goals are simplified and efficient storage access. The basic idea for the content centric access in VISION Cloud is to provide a persistence service at the content-level, hiding specialties of the implementation, such as the storage location, server addresses, etc.

## BACKGROUND: REQUIREMENTS FROM VISION CLOUD PROJECT

Besides the research background for content centric storage, the VISION Cloud project has also engineered requirements for the content centric access to the data. In general, the requirements emerge from the intended application use cases of the project, which intends to deliver applications in four domains: healthcare, media production, business intelligence applications, and telecommunications services. We identify the following main areas for requirements:

- The so named "Big Data" capability, the goal of which is to actually enable the management of big data.
- The capability of working with metadata, also enabling richer data models from the application domain.
- Efficient search access and retrieval.
- Execution of tasks on the storage to save bandwidth and round-trip latency. This involves analysis or metadata handling in order to provide statistical data or other functionalities on metadata.

When we look at the application use cases in the VISION Cloud project, we have had a couple of very concrete requirements that have outlined what content centric storage actually means. In the following, we summarize the demands from the application use cases for such an access layer.

## Media Use Case: A Large Archive for Media Production

The efficient access to an archive is very important in the media domain. The producer has a limited amount of time for searching media from the archives is considered time consuming. The media use case involves the storage of movies, video tracks, ultra HD material that is difficult to query for specific characteristics. Therefore, the use case requires two capabilities from such content centric access layer:

1. Metadata is necessary for the identification of content. Moreover, metadata already exists in different forms or as part of different domain specific file formats. Therefore, the metadata capabilities must support the metadata data models already established in the media domain. This metadata is very important for searching across the content.
2. The data items, scenes, videos, audio tracks, different sequels etc have important relations between each other that should be supported by the storage. A producer searching in the archive of media assets requires information about which audio tracks belong to which video tracks, which material belongs together because it represents a sequel of shots, etc. Therefore the content centric access layer should support relations between the items in the storage.

## Telecommunications Use Case: Large Scale Storage

The requirements from the telecommunications service application use case are similar to the requirements of the media use case—to some extent—although, the application is certainly different. For the telecommunications case, the idea is also the creation of an archive. But this archive is for the sharing of user-generated content, which is generated by the cameras of smart phones, tablet computers, and which is shared over the telecommunications network.

Therefore, we can expect a high level of dynamics among the items in the store: media will be created and added constantly and also media will be removed again. Also the use case involves a high level of distribution since the content is generated among the subscribers of a national cell phone network—even allowing subscribers being out of this own network and connecting via roaming. The direction for the requirements is, however, similar to the telecommunications case:

1. **Capture and management of metadata:** It is assumed that the user-generated content will also involve important metadata, such as the name and location of the generating persons, but also metadata resulting from the file's content, such as media duration, the encoding format, etc.
2. **Support for metrics:** The support for metrics is twofold: on the one hand, this can represent user ratings, just as seen on most Web applications. On the other hand, this can also represent a kind of proximity metrics that allows bringing content together by keywords or other user metadata.

The use case seems to share some similarity with existing video portals such as YouTube. However, this application is different because it is about the integration of such functionality into the service landscape of a telecommunications infrastructure. The integration of YouTube is not feasible for that. But, YouTube represents a relevant benchmark about what is possible with technology today. Nevertheless, the requirements for the content access layer are primarily the above mentioned metadata issues.

## Healthcare Use Case: Medical Imaging Data

The idea of the healthcare use case is the use of VISION Cloud as an archive for medical data, more precisely the storage of medical imaging data. For this use case, an established file format is considered, the DICOM file format (cf. DICOM). This file format does not only contain a set of metadata values, but also involves a data model that reflects the handling of medical imaging data in the healthcare domain. For example, different images are part of a series. And this relation between the series should also be reflected in the storage. Therefore, the resulting requirements or the required capabilities are as follows:

1. Support for the metadata as existing in the healthcare domain: The idea here is to have a first test on what is required for the automated extraction of DICOM file metadata for VISION Cloud.
2. Support of the data model relations: As outlined, in the healthcare domain, different images stand in relation to each other, and such relations should be reflected.

It must be noted that support for the metadata data model and support for the relations implies also the ability to search for items by using the stored relations in the store. Therefore, the relations should not only be stored in the way that this information is retrieved when retrieving the data item. But a useful implementation of this functionality is to quickly identify objects belonging together. This applies also to the other two mentioned domains.

## STATE OF THE ART: FUNCTIONALITY AND APPROACHES

The content centric interface is a novel approach of blending a cloud-technology-based data object store with a rich API for accessing content. However, parts of the approach, for example, the data objects store has been already developed by projects, software vendors or open source communities outside the cloud computing domain. As a consequence, it is indispensable for the design and development to precisely identify the innovation hub of the content centric part of the VISION Cloud interface compared to existing approaches. The following overview explains main differences (and similarities) to other approaches found among traditional technology such as relational database servers.

Our approach is to summarize the main sections of the requirements and the capabilities of the content centric access layer as intended for the VISION Cloud project and discuss these requirements or capabilities with existing technology or existing approaches.

- Storage of large amount of documents, which is the primary purpose of the VISION Cloud. This is about the so named "Big Data" capability.
- Flexibility for managing (unstructured) metadata, which represents the additional functionality that the VISION Cloud puts in addition to the basic data object services of VISION Cloud.
- Content centric access in terms of an API that provides a content-oriented view on the data objects for retrieval, finding and access.

In addition to the requirements, the capability for computational executions directly on the storage is also relevant. It does not represent a requirement in the area of content centric capabilities itself. However, since the storlet capability is a corner stone in the VISION Cloud project, this capability is also subject of the examination. This capability can support the creation of indices, analysis data or statistics about the data objects which support the content centric access.

## Relational Database Management Systems (RDBMS): On Premises

RDBMS are very common in enterprise applications. Since their invention and developments already decades ago they have matured to capable and widely adopted software. Examples are Oracle, Microsoft SQLServer, DB2, MySQL/MariaDB, or PostgreSQL. RDBMSes use tables to store data with a fixed predefined structure using some predefined basic data types such as INT, FLOAT and VARCHAR (i.e., strings of variable length). Typically, the length of values is limited, e.g., the VARCHAR data type in Oracle cannot exceed 4000 bytes, which makes them unusable for storing documents.

But most RDBMSs offer the possibility to store BLOBs (binary large objects) and CLOBs (character large objects) as some uninterpreted chunk of data which cannot directly be used in SQL queries, i.e., it is not possible to query for rows that have some specific BLOB/CLOB content. Anyway, the BLOB/CLOB of a certain row is accessible after having qualified the rows by a query. Moreover, most products offer some full-text search capabilities by special functions that allow full-text retrieval and XML query functionality (XPath, XQuery) for XML processing on BLOB/CLOB columns. BLOB/CLOBs still have a fixed upper size, e.g., 4 GB for Oracle. BLOBs and CLOBs can be used as column types and are certainly appropriate to manage documents unless the limit is insufficient. All the associated metadata can be managed in ordinary tables in the following manner:

```
MyDocuments (docId INT, someMeta-
data VARCHAR, creationDate DATE, ...,
theDocument BLOB)
```

Such a table is suitable if the metadata has a fixed structure that fits into columns such as someMetadata of any predefined data type. That is, having a fixed metadata structure, a table for keeping the metadata and having a special BLOB/CLOB column for the document offers powerful query capabilities given by SQL combined with very efficient query functionality. Metadata can be even split across several tables if their structures are more complex. If the metadata is required to have a more flexible nature that does not allow for a fixed schema, key/value pairs can be used for keeping unstructured metadata:

```
MyDocumentsWithKeyValues(docId INT,
theDocument BLOB)
KeyValues(docId INT, key VARCHAR,
value VARCHAR
```

The KeyValues table stores the metadata for the document that is referred to by column docId. That is, KeyValues is able to maintain for each document (docId resp.) several key/value records. The structure of such a relational key/value store can be even more complex. However, there are performance issues, since key/value pairs cannot benefit from indexing, which makes searches for specific key/values rather slow.

As an alternative, in case of XML-based metadata, the metadata can be stored in some kind of XMLType column (if supported by the RDBMS, for example, by SQL Server as a XML data type) instead of having several metadata columns of basic data type. This provides a much higher flexibility for storing metadata, but also has some query efficiency since XPath/XQuery functionality is usually available for querying the values. This means a query can ask for XMLType contents such as having a certain XML element, XML attribute or values. An XMLType can possess an associated XML Schema, a flexible definition of structure, which will be checked during storage. To sum up, this approach combines flexibility (given by XML) with powerful query capabilities (given by XML query extensions) and enough efficiency.

In any case, the interface for querying is SQL with corresponding extensions for XML handling, BLOB handling etc. Concerning the computational storage concept of VISION Cloud, RDBMSs provide powerful trigger mechanisms with some ECA (Event, Condition, Action) rules: Before or after inserting, updating (specific columns) or deleting records, whenever a certain condition is satisfied, some actions can take place. The action itself can mostly be implemented in Java, C++, or proprietary stored procedure languages. It is important to note that any ECA rule is triggered by a database operation. The user cannot trigger an ECA rule directly. Even events such as login, CREATE TABLE operations etc. can be intercepted.

Usually, an RDBMS uses disks, disk arrays or NAS/SAN storage for keeping the table data with the corresponding redundancy of RAID systems etc. Most commercial RDBMSs provide additional means for redundant storage and data replication. However, this usually requires additional replication or fault tolerance options such as database cluster solutions.

Concerning data distribution, table partitioning is the established concept for creating and managing very large databases. A table can be subdivided into several partitions using a predefined partition schema. According to this schema, data is inserted into the corresponding partition. Queries are still referring to the table, however, only those partitions that can contribute to query processing are considered. Usually, partitions are stored in different storage devices. Even if several partitions are involved in query processing, a query can be run in parallel with relevant partitions. Relational databases have proven capabilities for high performance needs.

## Relational Database Management Systems in the Cloud

In the beginning of Cloud Computing, the large providers have offered simple data stores. However, customers have complained about the limited or difficult migration path for their existing applications to such simplified storage solutions. In order to allow for a migration path for existing application, Amazon and Microsoft have started offerings that are based on classical RDBMSs. Examples are Amazon Relational Database Service (RDS) and Microsoft SQL Azure.

There is nothing really specific to mention for SQL-like RDBMSs in the cloud. These are more or less standard RDBMS such as MySQL 5.0 or Oracle database server software in case of Amazon RDS or SQL-Server in case of Microsoft SQL Azure with a couple of restrictions. Anyway, the principles for managing metadata are quite the same.

One important difference is the automatic built-in replication that is (SQL Azure) or will be (Amazon RDS) part of the cloud solutions: Data is replicated to multiple database servers (for example 3) in the same availability zone. The capability for a massive parallel use of the database server is limited by the offered computing instance. Furthermore, for supporting a large number of concurrent requests, a special architecture of Cloud relational database servers is required if the demand cannot be served by the largest offered database instance. Another important characteristic is the provisioning model: the customer orders a database server instance that runs on a specific computing instance and is not concerned with administration or maintenance of the infrastructure.

## Object-Oriented Database Management Systems on Premises

Object-Oriented Database Management Systems (ODBMSs) pursue a different approach than RDBMSs: They are able to store objects in an object-oriented programming language fashion, such as objects are handled in Java, C++, or Smalltalk. From a programming point of view, the handling is similar to object/relational persistence (O/R) frameworks (see the next section), products like Hibernate, JDO, JPA), i.e., an object is stored and objects are retrieved. The major difference to O/R frameworks is that no RDBMSs is used as the persistence medium, objects are more or less directly written to disk. That is, all the parts that belong to an object are physically close to that object. From a modeling point of view, all the object-oriented primitives such as arrays, pointers, collections etc. can be used besides primitive data types. The structure is fixed and defined by a class. There are also BLOB/CLOB-like data types that are appropriate for storing documents.

This means that in contrast to RDBMSs, metadata can be structured in an object-oriented manner, i.e., relating the document to some kind of object-oriented metadata objects describing the contents. Even if the modeling power of defining metadata is higher since being object-oriented, the same problems concerning the flexibility arise. It is also important to note that the query capabilities of ODBMSs are less powerful than SQL for RDBMSs just as their performance is.

Another characteristic of ODBMSs is the fact that classes can possess methods to implement behavioral aspects. Methods can certainly be used to define storlet behavior, however, there is no real triggering mechanism in the sense of RDBMSs. That is, methods must be invoked explicitly.

In the following, we summarize some specific concepts for two major ODBMS candidates, Objectivity/DB and Versant Object Store based on the given information by the vendors (cf. Versant Developer Center 2012c and Objectivity.com 2012b).

## Example: Objectivity/DB

For the setup of a high performance installation or offering, Objectivity/DB allows for a federated database setup and multiple databases. This appears similar to the RDBMSs partitioning concept, but lacks of transparency since there is no equivalent 'virtual class' concept that brings together the objects from several databases. Furthermore, Objectivity's storage hierarchy has the concept of a container for organizing objects (Objectivity.com 2012b, page 14). A container is basically supposed to be used as some kind of cluster, i.e., objects in the same container are also put together physically. Anyway, containers can also be used to logically group objects, i.e., the metadata of documents.

To cope with high availability demands, there is also a so named Fault Tolerant Option (FTO) (Objectivity.com 2012a). It allows dividing a federated database into independent pieces, so-called autonomous partitions. Each autonomous partition is maintained as a self-completed entity in the case a network or system failure occurs in another partition. Each partition has all the system resources necessary to run the application on top of it. In addition, it is possible to replicate data between several partitions with the Data Replication Option (DRO, Objectivity.com 2012a). With the DRO, each image of a database contains all the data in the covered database. Each image is created and managed by an autonomic partition. If a system's boot partition contains an image of the database, the database server will use that image; otherwise the database accesses an image from a different partition. If one image of a database fails due to a network or machine error, work may continue with a different available image.

There is some support for stored procedures in the way that the user can call a C or C++ procedure directly (Objectivity.com 2012b). This feature lets the developer / user define C++ and C procedures right ahead. Additionally, Objectivity/DB supports triggers, which are C++ procedures that are called whenever the database server performs a database modification. A developer can implement and register own triggers. It must be noted that the concept of storlets is richer than stored procedures as they offer a full high-level language programming environment capability that is required for video encoding, for example.

## Example: Versant Object Store

The object-oriented database Versant supports some interesting features with respect to VISION Cloud in terms of distribution and scalability. According to Versant, objects can be migrated while applications still have transparent access to them. Object migration is possible, because objects have ids that stay with the object for their lifetime, which means that the physical locations of objects are abstracted from the application. This feature supports a federated environment or supports parallel deployment of multiple servers to balance the expected load.

Another feature is so called schema evolution (Versant Developer Center 2012a, page 20). This is a functionality allowing variable metadata structures, which directly refers to the variable nature of the key/attribute value metadata of VISION Cloud. Schema evolution in Versant is when an existing persisted object classes, i.e., the database schema, are changed. Versant stores the class definition of each class. When this definition is changed, existing instances of the changed class should be updated: Therefore, when the application accesses an object, Versant automatically adjusts the structure to the latest class definition. This lazy conversion behavior can be considered as a feature that distributes the cost of conversion operation at the server over the run time.

Furthermore, there is a dedicated support for Microsoft Cluster Server software on Windows. This feature allows defining one node in the cluster as a main or central database server and failing over automatically to another node if the system crashes. Database sessions, which are active at failure time, will be lost and their transactions

will be rolled back, but new database connections will stay and will be served by the second node. Then, a fault tolerant version is possible by adding an optional software module for the plain server. It provides some kind of automated fail-over and error recovery (Versant Developer Center 2012b, section 15.2). The functionality is almost hidden to the application. Two database servers, a primary server and a secondary replica server, are synchronized at each transaction.

The software transparently switches the application over to the second replica server if a hardware or software failure at the first server occurs. Once the original primary server turns available again, the software automatically re-synchronizes the pair and returns to a fully fault tolerant mode.

Versant does not support any form of stored procedures at all. By their approach, such logic belongs to the client side, which is the application software that actually uses Versant.

## BLOB Storage Services in the Cloud

Major cloud platform providers have their products for the storage of large data objects: Amazon S3 or Microsoft Azure BLOB Service, or as an available implementation as a part of the Eucalyptus framework, the Walrus project. These services provide some primary support for the management of BLOBs and containers.

The basic concepts of BLOB storage are containers, which must possess a unique name and contain the real BLOB data. Users can create several containers, up to a certain limit. A BLOB also possesses a unique name within its container and contains the real data, e.g., a document. A BLOB can be understood as a file having additional metadata. Some metadata is predefined such as HTTP-Metadata (ETag, Last-Modified, Content-Length, Content-Type, Content-Encoding, Content-Language etc.), however, users can also attach user-defined metadata. Since the BLOB name may contain a separator '/', BLOBs can be organized in a form of directory hierarchies. The size of BLOBs is usually limited, e.g., to 5 GBs in S3 or 1 TB in Microsoft Azure.

Typical operations for BLOB storage are CRUD operations on Containers and BLOBs and the setting of properties or metadata attached to a BLOB. Addressing containers and BLOBs is done by means of special Uniform Resource Identifications (URIs). The URI *http://photos.s3.amazonaws.com/2009/ Barbados/beach.jpg* addresses an object *2009/ Barbados/beach.jpg* in a container named photos. The element s3.amazonaws.com is a predefined host name to be used. The path elements 2009 and Barbados can be understood as subdirectories of the container. However, there is no further subdirectory support such as determining all subdirectories for 2009.

The URI *http://myaccount.BLOB.core.windows.net/?comp=list\&maxresults=10\&include=metadata* is an example for the Microsoft Azure BLOB service. Here, the part BLOB.core.windows.net is predefined; "myaccount" is a registered user account. Using this URI all containers including their metadata (include=) are listed (comp=list), whereby the result is limited to maximal 10 records (maxresults=10).

Access is given by two protocols, SOAP and REST (Representational State Transfer (RFC 2616)) over HTTP(S). REST is an HTTP-based protocol, which uses HTTP operations such as POST, GET, DELETE, and PUT for performing corresponding CRUD data manipulations. Since handling HTTP operations in a programming language is cumbersome, specific APIs for various programming languages (e.g., JetS3t for Amazon S3) are provided, thus releasing programmers from the complicated HTTP programming APIs.

Additional functionalities are sometimes available to cover performance or capability issues. For instance, the Microsoft Azure BLOB Storage distinguishes between block and page BLOBs, one for optimized sequential access while another resembles a random accesses scheme respectively. The BLOB services typically maintain multiple copies of a BLOB, in general 3 redundant copies

with eventual consistency. As already mentioned, BLOBs can have system-defined and user-defined metadata attached to them. A GET operation also retrieves the associated metadata. But here is no mean to search for BLOBs with certain metadata. This limits the usage of metadata.

Furthermore, the concept of storlets is missing from the existing BLOB storage solutions. Both Amazon S3 or Microsoft Azure offer notification functionality once an operation takes place, however, the programming and runtime environment that VISION Cloud provides for storlets must be provided on its own.

## Hadoop Distributed File System (HDFS) On Premises

A special, local deployable (e.g. on premise deployment) solution is the Hadoop Distributed File System (HDFS Apache Hadoop Project 2012a). It was originally built as infrastructure for the Apache Nutch project that was originally a search engine project. And it is now a subproject of the Apache Hadoop framework. HDFS is a distributed file system designed to run on normal, not special grade hardware, just as one of the basic ideas of Cloud Computing. HDFS design goals are fault-tolerance, deployability on low-cost hardware and the ability to serve so named "big data," meaning the handling of large data sets. The capabilities are based on parallelization approaches. As a consequence, a HDFS system can be comprised of hundreds or thousands of server computers (HDFS Apache Hadoop Project 2012a). Internally, the use of parallelization in HDFS divides individual files into chunks that are stored on different computers. This addresses the goal of HDFS to support large files in the area of Terabytes in size. HDFS has a master-slave or a primary-secondary architecture; inside the cluster there is a single master server named NameNode. A NameNode server covers the management of operations for a file system name space and controls or manages the access to files by clients.

A HDFS system provides the traditional hierarchical file system view. One can create directories and store files inside these directories. The hierarchy is similar to most other existing file systems; of course, one can create and remove files, move a file from one directory to another, or rename a file. A Java API is available for applications to use (HDFS Apache Hadoop Project 2012b). In addition, an HTTP browser can be used to browse the files of an HDFS instance. Furthermore, HDFS provides a command line interface named FS shell that lets a user interact with the data in HDFS. The syntax of this command set is similar to other shells (e.g. bash, csh).

A metadata handling is one of a couple of points that VISION Cloud addresses and that are currently missing in HDFS. There is only a small amount of system-defined metadata such as file name and number of replicas, which can be specified by applications.

Nevertheless, HDFS functionality covers a data placement mechanism, which is very important for performance. This is a feature which makes HDFS special compared to other distributed file systems: For managing three replicas, one replica is put on one node in the local rack, another on a node in another remote rack, and a third on a different node but same remote rack. This policy presumes the statistical observation that the chance of a rack failure is far less than that of a node failure (cf. "rack-aware replica placement'", HDFS Apache Hadoop Project 2012a).

## Apache HBase on Premises

As an alternative for looking at the HDFS, there is another Hadoop project, which is HBase (HBase Apache Hadoop Project 2012). HBase is the name of the Hadoop database software project. The major design goal for HBase is the hosting of very large tables and similar to HDFS, running on clusters of commodity hardware opposed to server grade installation of machines with redundant power supplies etc (HBase Apache Hadoop

Project 2012, section 8.1). Technically, speaking of NoSQL technology, HBase is a distributed data storage which supports versioning. It uses the idea of Google's BigTable approach, which takes advantage of some Google File System one layer below, the HBase runs on top of HDFS. Therefore, this relation between the two components allows for distribution of the system, since the file storage can be distributed across several nodes.

An HBase table is a sorted map, which is indexed by a row key, a key for a column, and a time stamp. The system uses the time stamp for a versioning capability. As a consequence, the primary entry point is the row key (and the time stamp if necessary). As with the table stores of cloud offerings, and unlike relational database servers, a table does not require a predefined schema (HBase Apache Hadoop Project 2012, section 5). One key/value pair in a table represents a row. The row consists of a key, a time stamp, and a value that consists of columns. Rows are sorted by the row key in byte-order. A column is assigned to a particular column family. A column family represents a map of key/value pair. In this setup, the key is the name of the column family and the value represents a list of key/values specifying columns in that one family; each table has a fixed set of associated column families, however, contrary to that the actual count of columns is flexible.

The following is a sample table (in JSON syntax):

```
{ 'key1': // row
  { 'A': { 'a1': 'val11' }, { 'a2':
'val21' } }, // column family A
  { 'B': { 'b1': 'val31' } } column
family B
},
{ 'key2': // row
  { 'A': { 'a1': 'val12' }, { 'a2':
'val22' } }, // column family A
  { 'B': { 'b1': 'val32' } } // col-
umn family B
},
```

```
{ 'key3': // row
  { 'A': { 'a4': 'val34' } } } // col-
umn family A
```

The first two rows (key1 and key2) have the columns A:a1, A:a2 (both assigned to family A), and B:b1 (assigned to family B). The third row has a definition for just one column A:a3. It must be notes that a column family belonging of a table is specified when the table is created. This is static information. Anyway, the columns are not static, i.e., a row can fill (or not) any defined column family and any column in a family. Moreover, a row can define new columns in a column family. The key/value pairs are kept in an alphabetical order, which means that similar keys are close to each other. This supports measures for performance issues that are present when choosing a key-based approach for storage.

All data is versioned by using a time stamp (as long integer, "seconds since the epoch") or another passed integer (HBase Apache Hadoop Project 2012, section 5.8). The time stamp can be used for querying as well. If no time stamp is provided in a query, the most recent version is returned by the system, otherwise the version newer or equal to the assigned time stamp is provided (depending if equal is present).

There is no built-in way to query for a list of all columns in all rows. However, it is possible to query for a list of all column families. Although at a conceptual level tables may be viewed as a lightly filled set of rows, the storage groups them together on a per column-family basis. New columns can be added to any column family having no preceding statements required, just the new column declaration. As a storage unit, column families are grouped together on the file system (HBase Apache Hadoop Project 2012, section 5.5). Moreover, each column family may have its own rules regarding how many versions of a given value to keep (MAX_VERSIONS) and other settings such as compressions (BLOCK, RECORD), BLOOM_FILTER, IN_MEMORY etc.

The basic operations on HBase are GET (retrieving data for a given key), SCAN (scanning from a start row to a stop row), PUT, and DELETE. These operations take into account versioning, e.g., it is possible to delete a version at a specific time stamp or all versions older than a certain time stamp.

## Table Storage Services in the Cloud

Another approach is the use of Table storage technology that is offered by large cloud providers as a service and available as software project as well. Examples for the services are Amazon SimpleDB, Microsoft Azure Table Service. An example for a software project is the BigTable implementation "MyNoSQL." These offer a flexible table structure without any predefined table schema. However, these BigTables are unable to store the documents directly due to very strict data size limitations, usually 2 KB. Hence, the only usage for metadata storage in addition to a separate document store, without any further support for linking both together and querying. That is merely the VISION Cloud approach, keeping documents and metadata apart from each other.

## EMC Atmos

The product Atmos from the company EMC is a cloud storage platform to manage content. As the previously discussed software, it is also targeted for storing large amounts of data. The vendor characterizes Atmos as not being a clustered file system or a network attached storage product, but rather a cloud-optimized storage offering. The design emphasis has been put a) on data distribution and b) access on a global scale (EMC Corporation Website 2012).

The Atmos technology is focused on distribution approaches. Their approach incorporates the use of scriptable policies for automated data placement across integrated or involved internal and external data stores. The policy control enables management of data handling at the object level, which is a requirement that is often presented as a part of the compliance issues. A scriptable policy engine allows the developer to define policies such as where content should be placed and replicated based upon requirements such as popularity, traffic, or business characteristics. Atmos possesses a couple of important characteristics when compared to the idea of a content centric storage:

- Handling of objects and metadata.
- Ability to optimize queries or object retrieval.
- Offering high availability when needed.
- Complimentary, metadata-driven policy-based management to manage data placement, protection, and efficiency of massive amounts of content as well as other data services.

Contrary to the other different approaches, Atmos runs in a virtualized environment with own storage solutions or within EMC sold hardware. As the vendor states, it runs on standard hardware components involving consumer market technology such as Gigabit Ethernet and S-ATA drives. Cloud storage services are available from a growing number of worldwide active service providers in Internet-busy countries. The integrated handling of metadata allows a developer for using an API to create and manipulate objects and metadata. There are two main categories of metadata (EMC Corporation Community Network 2012, page 16 ff.):

- System metadata is generated automatically and cannot be modified or deleted by users. Examples are last access and modification time, the size of an object, a name for a policy, or the type.
- User-defined metadata enables users to tag objects. User-defined metadata can be either non-listable or listable. If a metadata element is listable, it refers for the ability for applications to issue queries or basically to search. Apparently there is no search

for values. It must be noted that the Atmos API supports attribute-value pairs, which are restricted to 1 KB in size. The user-defined metadata can be used for defining triggers for policies that allow for optimizations for performance or data protection or compliance. The latter feature can provide the basics for the computational storage of VISION Cloud. (EMC Corporation Community Network 2012)

The EMC Atmos solution provides Web services access to data and management, also in a single tenant or multi tenant setup. SOAP and REST both support an object view and an interface view similar to a file system. The basic principle is object based: Every object to be stored has a object identifier, the main access method for later retrieval. This is the so-called object interface. As an alternative, a file-system like interface exists for getting objects in a hierarchical path style. The REST-based API uses the HTTP operations for performing CRUD operations.

Corresponding URL endpoints /rest/namespace and /rest/objects let one choose between filesystem and object interface, e.g.,\GET /rest/namespace/photos/mypicture.jpg or GET /rest/objects/photos/499ad542a1a8bc200499ad5a6b05580499c3168560a4. Both, object identifiers and path names can be used to reference objects. Storing a document, naming it photos/mypicture.jpg with the file-system-like interface can look like the following (example taken from EMC Programmer's guide (EMC Corporation Community Network 2012, page 45):

```
POST /rest/namespace/photos/mypic-
ture.jpg HTTP/1.1
x-emc-listable-meta: part4/part7/
part8=quick
x-emc-meta: part1=buy
accept: */*
x-emc-useracl: john=FULL_
CONTROL,mary=READ
```

```
date: Wed, 18 Feb 2009 16:08:12 GMT
content-type: application/octet-
stream
x-emc-date: Wed, 18 Feb 2009 16:08:12
GMT
x-emc-groupacl: other=NONE
host: 168.159.116.96
content-length: 211
x-emc-uid: 33115732f3b7455d9d2344ddd2
35f4b9/user1
x-emc-signature: GTOC-
1GqFELjMMH9XIKvYRaHdyrk=
```

In this example, additional metadata is also passed by x-emc-listable-meta (listable) and x-emc-meta (non-listable). Atmos can support different tenants and its sub-tenants. Creating a new object, access can be limited by ACL for specific users and/or groups of users. Currently, only the group "other" is supported. Possible access rights for user groups and single users are for reading, writing, and full control while these setting can be applied to objects and directories. For directories, the access settings are applied to all new objects in it. There is a simple example from the EMC Atmos Programmer's Guide for setting an access control setting for an object:

```
POST /rest/objects/499ad542a1a8bc2004
99ad5a6b05580499c3168560a4?acl
HTTP/1.1
x-emc-useracl: fred=FULL_CONTROL
x-emc-groupacl: other=NONE
```

*Policies as Storlet Alternative:* Atmos has also a policy engine (EMC Corporation White Papers 2012, page 20 ff.). Policies can be created to act on objects to apply different functionality and to implement or to control different service levels to different types of users and their data. An administrator defines the general storage policies. They are invoked through the creation operation on the storage elements, such as the putting of user-defined metadata. Storage policies cover or define the durability demands or availability set-tings of the data. Moreover, they cover attributes which are assigned to a single data object or to a group of them: versioning, number of replicas, de-duplication setting, and placement of data on particular hardware, what is important for compliance issues such as "ready for confiscation". It offers also a setting called "retention period", which specifies a time duration in which the data cannot be modified by the users. And it offers an expiration setting, which defines when a data object is automatically deleted by the system. As an example, by updating an object's user metadata value (like setting `importance=high'), a referring policy can start the creation of additional copies in the system.

*Distribution and Performance:* As already mentioned, a basic functionality of the policy management takes care that content is available and accessible by replication. EMC Atmos creates replicas synchronously or asynchronously. This means that Atmos offers some level of resiliency regarding the data, data objects are divided into multiple parts and are distributed among the computers of the Atmos cloud. Also, there is functionality for content availability checking, to match frequency of use, geographic location etc. From a client point of view, an object within Atmos can be retrieved from any node that has been defined as a storage node.

## STATE OF THE ART: APPROACHES AND ARCHITECTURE

So far storage solutions, particularly database systems, have been discussed that usually are embedded in a layered architecture. In order to complete the discussion of different approaches, an assessment is necessary to identify the level of abstractions present in current persistence system architecture. The main question is here. How is it done today? Which technology do applications use when creating large scale / enterprise solutions? When looking at the current state-of-the-art at the architectural level (in particular, for example at the

JEE or at the .NET platform), Figure 1 identifies the following major tiers in the architecture for storage based application: the basics of persistence along with the equivalents in current application server technology, namely the JEE and the .NET platform.

At the lowest level, there is the physical storage which presumably is common for most storage systems. One level above, there is the operating system that implements the abstract access to the physical storage device. A data management layer is located one level above. This could be a database server as well as a file system; such items use the storage device abstraction from the operating system. As common practice, most database servers as well as other storage technologies, use language environment adapters allowing access to the database server or the file system from different run time environments. In the area of database servers and the Java environment, such an adapter is the JDBC driver. On top of the adapter is another layer that performs the conversion of data entities from the application to the data management. Most common technology in this stack is Object-Relational (O/R) mapping software. Other data entity adapters are also possible, for example, software that converts data entities to XML data for storing them into a file system.

It is certainly possible that an application uses the data entity adapter directly. However, in some applications it is also common practice to provide an additional layer on top of the data entity adapter, which controls the access to this layer. Examples are templates for transaction processing or exception handling combined with a retry mechanism.

Referring to these layers, it can be discussed where content centric storage is located when looking at application server storage: In the layered storage architecture, a content centric view is possible above the language runtime environment adapter. Indeed, from the application perspective most O/R mapping software offers a content view on the data entities and related operations like storing or retrieving them, while all technology that is related to the management of the storage or the technical implementation of a storage is hidden by the O/R mapping software if necessary. Accordingly, there are state-or-the-art technologies that provide corresponding interfaces. Table 1 lists examples of state-of-the-art conceptual technol-

*Figure 1. Abstraction tiers in state-of-the-art storage architectures*

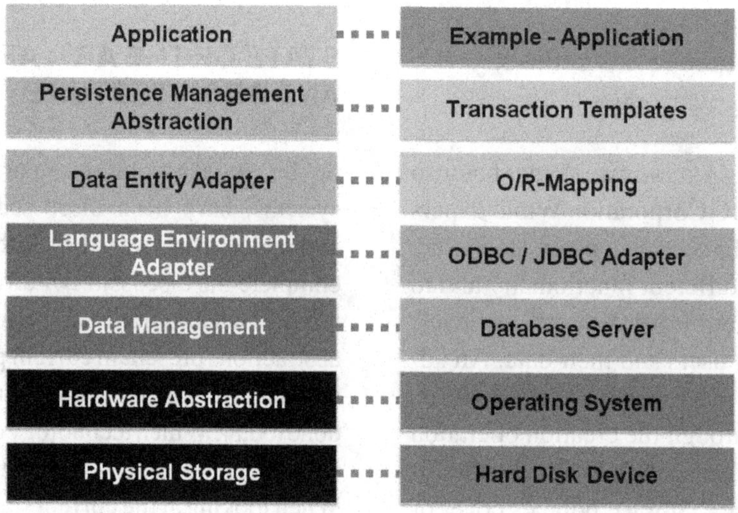

ogy options from the Java world at the level of data entity adapters and their basic characteristics.

Three main approaches for software at data entity level exist in the Java world: the O/R mapping software, which is today represented by the JPA (Java Persistence API) standard, the conceptually more open JDO (Java Data Objects) standards, and proprietary solutions. Hibernate was a long time the de facto standard O/R mapping framework in the Java world until the JPA standard was proposed in its version 1.0. From then, the Hibernate project lost some of its popularity, presumably because Oracle/Sun declared EclipseLink as a reference implementation of the JPA standard. It must be noted that Hibernate's concepts have apparently influenced the JPA standard, also beyond version 1.0, e.g., the Criteria interface for composing queries was adopted by JPA 2.0. In addition to the mentioned items, Table 2 lists implementations and projects that for the current state-or-the-art software at the data entity adapter level along with the main characteristics.

While Table 2 presents the state-of-the-art storage approaches in the Java world, further technologies about storage are certainly available in the Cloud Computing area. Generally, current Cloud Computing storage offerings are manifold and offer many services that have their equivalents in the on premises world. Figure 2 picks up the layered architecture of storage systems and maps two popular storage offerings, the Amazon SimpleDB and the Microsoft Azure Table Service, to these layers.

This figure outlines that the relevant spot, the data entity adapter level, is not directly referring to the SimpleDB or the Microsoft Azure Table service offerings. Rather higher abstraction layers come into place one level above for a content centric interface. For SimpleDB, the project of SimpleJPA offers some first steps of a content-based interface similar to JPA. In the Microsoft world, the storage client library provides the equivalent for the table service. Accordingly, with the SimpleJPA or the storage client library, all the envisaged advantages are implemented or can be implemented: Caching of content, the distribution of content on the underlying storage, the dynamic change of underlying storage locations, etc. However, some important goals of the VISION Cloud project are not covered, such as scalability, the domain specific optimizations, and the interoperability aspects, as the abovementioned technologies work only within their technology platform.

*Table 1. List of approaches for data entity adapters in the Java world*

| Java Persistence API (JPA) | Java Data Objects (JDO) | Proprietary Entity Mapping |
|---|---|---|
| • With EJB 3.0 standard (includes JPA 1.0 wide adoption in Java community (JEE 6: JPA 2.0) <br>• Standard as JSR 220 (1.0) or JSR 317 (2.0) <br>• Seamless integration into JEE application frameworks, for example, EclipseLink in Glassfish <br>• Runs in application server context as well as with stand alone applications <br>• Requires JDBC and Java 1.5 | • Standards such as JSR 12 and JSR 243 <br>• First real standard on Data Entity Level, gained wide popularity, was losing its popularity against Hibernate <br>• True independent data entity mapping software, works with file systems, object oriented databases, relational databases, XML-marshalling <br>• JDO 1.0 was not comprehensive enough, resulting in different almost incompatible JDO solutions <br>• JDO 2.0 has more coverage against JPA 1.0 (UUID, pessimistic transactions) <br>• Newest JDO implementations also implement JPA | • Proprietary technology like iBATIS have coverage for particular fields of functionality <br>• Relatively low market or community relevance <br>• Usage poses risk of vendor lock in. <br>• Proprietary (pre-JPA) interface of Hibernate |

*Table 2. Examples of Java data entity mapping software*

| JBoss Hibernate | Eclipse EclipseLink | Apache OpenJPA | DataNucleus |
|---|---|---|---|
| • Largest popularity<br>• Mature implementation<br>• LGPL License<br>• Comprehensive parameters and functions for tuning performance<br>• Support for many relational database servers<br>• Part of JBoss AS distribution | • Based on Toplink from Oracle<br>• Founded as open source project in 2007<br>• Mature implementation<br>• Apache License<br>• Reference Implementation of JPA 2.0<br>• Comprehensive support of Oracle server<br>• Part of Glassfish distribution | • OpenJPA is open source derivate of BEA's Kodo software<br>• Apache License<br>• Mostly mature product, although, release 1.X has shown problems with stability and run time behavior | • Apache License<br>• Implements JDO and JPA<br>• Google App Engine uses DataNucleaus as data entity adapter for the BigTable as well as with other storage<br>• No similar adoption as with Hibernate or other JPA implementing software |

Figure 3 shows the correspondences of this architecture with the traditional storage architecture model of the VISION Cloud project.

In the VISION Cloud setup, storage clusters that provide a file system equivalent service will provide the hardware abstraction and the physical storage. Then, a data operation layer will offer the data entity adapter, the language environment adapter and the data management tier. The content centric interface will enhance the data entity adapter tier and provide the persistence management abstraction in order to provide special functions. The novel parts in the VISION Cloud content centric access are:

• The data entity adapter will be implemented in the data operation layer as well as in the content centric interface or the data access layer of VISION Cloud. The data operation layer of the VISION Cloud will translate basic data entities of the application into the equivalent concepts of the underlying storage. However, the intention is to provide this at a basic level in order to ensure optimal scalability and support a distributed infrastructure.

• The adoption of storage technologies that support distributed concurrent updates of the metadata with according actions run on the storage entities. In addition, the content centric storage approach will implement the platform for domain specific additions to content handling of particular domains.

*Figure 2. Comparison of Amazon SimpleDB and Microsoft Azure table service*

*Figure 3. Layered architecture of the VISION content centric storage*

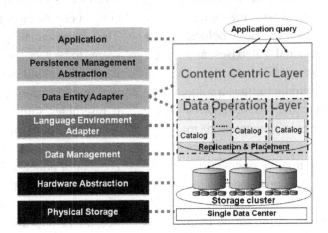

In summary, the content centric storage approach of VISION Cloud envisages two major functional blocks above the operating system level that operate on two levels of abstraction: One upper block, the content centric interface, implements the front end with rich data adapter features for an optimal support of domain specifics and sophisticated queries the content. Another building block implements basic data entity mapping and distributed data management features for optimal scalability and storage distribution.

## RELEVANCE TO VISION CLOUD AND CONCLUSIONS

For VISION Cloud, the short assessment of the state-of-the-art shows that some of the content centric ideas are already present with similar concepts from traditional technology. However, they do not quite cover all of the goals of VISION Cloud with regard to the novel approach of the content centric access or the extent of the interface: scalability on the interface level, interoperability, optimization for domains, computational storage and the query abilities of metadata. The content centric access proposes also relations between data objects, managed as data object metadata which has not been found at any of these systems.

Table 1 summarizes the difference of the given approaches to the VISION Cloud content centric access idea. From this summary in the table, we can conclude for the different other approaches:

- Classic relational databases support complex data models, provide query interfaces and a robust and well-proven infrastructure. However, they are not very suitable for the storage of large files, because in most software products the size of a binary large object is limited to few Gigabytes in most database servers.

- A relational database as a cloud service has the same characteristic as the classic relational database. Moreover, the service providers limit relational databases in terms of the total database size, which require additional mechanisms to overcome this limitation, for example use of multiple database servers in a federation.

- Object oriented databases provide a data model which might suit better the idea for storing data objects, because the metadata of a data objects becomes an intrinsic characteristic for objects in a object-oriented database. However, largest concern is still the limitation on the maximal object size.

- Basically, Hadoop and HBase overcome the limitation on maximal sizes mentioned for the different technologies before. However, while relational databases and object-oriented database have developed into mature and rich product suites, a solution based on Hadoop and HBase requires much of proprietary implementation to achieve richer features. Therefore it offers no advantages referring the innovations for VISION Cloud, most prominently, the content centric storage.

- The Cloud table store and the Cloud blob store technologies represent a similar combination as the HBase and Hadoop combination. And as the analysis has shown, also a large amount of additional proprietary implementation is required to cover the VISION cloud innovations, including the content centric storage.

- The commercial product EMC Atmos seems to be very similar at the first sight, as it provides cloud storage for large files for use in industrial applications. Moreover, it resembles some ideas as envisaged for VISION Cloud, for example the computational capabilities of the storage with the concept of policies. However, although the metadata capabilities are more advanced than those of a standard cloud BLOB storage, the EMC Atmos capabilities are not as advances as the content centric approach in VISION Cloud.

Overall, the summary points out that while related technologies discussed in this work may one or more innovations also pursued by the VISION

*Table 3. Comparison of VISION cloud content centric storage and discussed approaches*

| Product / Category | Large Files | Distribution and Performance | Unstructured Key-Values | Content Centric Access | Computational Storage / Storlets; |
|---|---|---|---|---|---|
| RDBMS On-Premises | Yes - but not in range of Tera bytes | Most offer cluster deployment | Table schema obligatory | Based on query capabilities | Different stored procedure approaches; |
| RDBMS Cloud | Yes - but not in range of Tera bytes | Implicit in cloud offering | Table schema obligatory | Based on query capabilities | Different stored procedure approaches; |
| ODBMS Objectivity | Yes - but not in range of Tera bytes | Distributed deployment as option | Yes -Relations typical for object orientation | Basic Metadata CRUD | Some kind of runtime for C/C++ available; |
| ODBMS Versant | Yes - but not in range of Tera bytes | Distributed deployment as option | Yes -Relations typical for object orientation | Basic Metadata CRUD | Not supported; |
| Hadoop and HBase | Yes -Inherent design characteristic | Yes - Inherent design characteristic | No relations etc. | Basic Metadata CRUD | Must be added by proprietary implementation; |
| Cloud BLOB service | Yes -Inherent design characteristic | Basic support | no queries and must use Table Service | Nothing - just data object URL | Must be added by proprietary implementation; |
| Cloud Table service | Limits to field size in table value. For example Azure limit is 64Kb for string data. Use BLOB Service | Inherent design characteristic | Yes | No relations or similar just basic Metadata CRUD | Must be added by proprietary implementation; |
| EMC Atmos | Yes -Inherent design characteristic | Possible | No relations | no statistics | Related concept of policies; |

Cloud project, none of them fits the orientation of VISION Cloud. Moreover, none of them follows the idea of VISION Cloud. Also, none of the proposed solutions follows the idea of providing a content centric interface, which provides a different view on the storage for the management with a large amount of files as envisaged in the VISION Cloud use cases (see Table 3).

# REFERENCES

Delaet & Joosen. (2009). Managing your content with cimple-a content-centric storage interface. In *Proceedings of Local Computer Networks, 2009*. IEEE.

EMC Corporation Community Network. (2012). *Atmos programmer's guide 1.4.1*. Retrieved April 2012, from https://community.emc.com/docs/DOC-10508

EMC Corporation Website. (2012). *Atmos - cloud storage, big data - EMC*. Retrieved April 2012, from https://http://www.emc.com/storage/atmos/atmos.htm

EMC Corporation White Papers. (2012). *Emc atmos cloud optimized storage for web services*. Retrieved April 2012, from http://www.emc.com/collateral/software/white-papers/h7067-atmos-cloud-optimized-storage-wp.pdf

Gray, J. (1995). Queues are databases. In *Proceedings 7th High Performance Transaction Processing Workshop*. Asilomar, CA: Prentice Hall.

HBase Apache Hadoop Project. (2012a). *Apache HBase reference guide*. Retrieved April, 2012, from http://hbase.apache.org/book.html

HDFS Apache Hadoop Project. (2012b). *Hdfs architecture guide*. Retrieved April 2012, from http://hadoop.apache.org/common/docs/r1.0.2/hdfs_design.html

HDFS Apache Hadoop Project. (2012c). *Hadoop 1.0.2 java api*. Retrieved April 2012, from http://hadoop.apache.org/ common/docs/current/api/

Koponen, C., & Chun, E. K. Shenker, & Stoica. (2007). A data-oriented (and beyond) network architecture. In *Proceedings of the 2007 Conference on Applications, Technologies, Architectures, and Protocols for Computer Communications, SIGCOMM '07*, (pp. 181–192). New York, NY: ACM Press.

Nelson, T. (1988). *Literary machines*. New York: Mindful Press.

Objectivity.com. (2012a). *Data replication in objectivity/db*. Retrieved April 2012, from http://www.objectivity.com/pdf/documents/DataReplication.pdf

Objectivity.com. (2012b). *The objectivity/db technical overview*. Retrieved April 2012, from http://http://www.objectivity.com/pages/downloads/whitepaper/pdf/oodb_techOverview.pdf

Versant Developer Center. (2012a). *How to evaluate an object database*. Retrieved April 2012, from http://developer.versant.com/developer/resources/objectdatabase/whitepapers/WP_Evaluate2002.pdf

Versant Developer Center. (2012b). *Versant object database fundamentals manual*. Retrieved April 2012, from http://developer.versant.com/developer/resources/objectdatabase/documentation/VODFundamentals.pdf

Versant Developer Center. (2012c). *Versant object database*. Retrieved April 2012, from http://developer.versant.com/developer/resources/objectdatabase/overview

# ADDITIONAL READING

Amber, S. W. (n.d.). *Mapping objects to relational databases: O/R mapping in detail*. Retrieved from http://www.agiledata.org/ mappingObjects.html

Armbrust, M. Fox, Griffith, Joseph, Katz, Konwinski, ... Zaharia. (2009). *Above the clouds: A Berkeley view of cloud computing*. Retrieved from http://www.eecs.berkeley.edu/Pubs/TechRpts/2009/EECS-2009-28.html

Cianutti, J. (2012). *5 lessons we've learned using AWS*. Retrieved from http://techblog.netflix.com/2010/12/5-lessons-weve-learned-using-aws.html

Fielding, R. T. (2000). *REST: Architectural styles and the design of network-based software architectures*. (Doctoral dissertation). University of California, Irvine, CA.

Gilbert, S., & Lynch, N. (2002). *Brewer's conjecture and the feasibility of consistent available partition-tolerant web services*. ACM SIGACT News. doi:10.1145/564585.564601.

ISO/IEC. (1996). *ITU.TS recommendation X.902 —ISO/IEC 10746-1: Open distributed processing reference model - Part 1: Overview*. Geneva: ISO.

Quinlan & Dorward. (2002). Venti: A new approach to archival storage. In *Proceedings of the FAST 2002 Conference on File and Storage Technologies, 2002*. FAST.

Rabinovici-Cohen, Factor, Naor, Ramati, Reshef, Ronen, ... Giaretta. (2008). Preservation data stores: New storage paradigm for preservation environments. *IBM Journal of Research and Development, 52*(4-5), 389–400.

# KEY TERMS AND DEFINITIONS

**Content Centric Storage:** A data storage that offers a content oriented view or performs content oriented management of stored items in order to improve efficiency and effectiveness for storage, retrieval and management tasks.

**NoSQL Database:** NoSQL ("Not only SQL") is a new database technology that dispenses from well-established relational concepts such as ACID consistency and SQL query capabilities, while on the other side putting emphasis on high availability and horizontal scaling. According to http://en.wikipedia.org/wiki/NoSQL, the NoSQL movement also covers ODBMSs and XML databases.

**Object-Oriented Database Management System (ODBMS):** A data storage that organizes data by means of objects, as defined by an object oriented programming language, such as Java, C++, and C#, and their relationships. In contrast to object-relational frameworks, those objects are also stored as objects at the physical level.

**Relational Database Management System (RDBMS):** A data storage that organizes data by means of flat tables and offers a corresponding powerful query language SQL.

**VISION Cloud:** For the authors, VISION Cloud is a project that develops a cloud storage system for an efficient and federated storage of all types of content-centric data. In contrast to public cloud offerings, for example Amazon S3 or Microsoft Blob Service specific hardware appliances, VISION Cloud stresses supporting metadata flexibly and as an integral part of the storage.

# Chapter 4
# Business Models and Billing Challenges

**Javier Martínez Elicegui**
*Telefónica I+D, Spain*

**Lei Xu**
*Umeå University, Sweden*

**Emilio García Escobar**
*Telefónica I+D, Spain*

## ABSTRACT

*The advent of the Cloud has leveraged a number of challenges, both for customers and service providers. Companies willing to embrace the new paradigm must face some entrance barriers, such as security, privacy and trust concerns, vendor locking risk, legal issues, etc. While service providers may work to minimize these barriers, they must be especially careful when defining what may constitute the most crucial aspect for the success of their offerings: the business model. Different incarnations of the cloud (IaaS, PaaS, and SaaS) add to the possibility of offering public or private solutions, or even federated models. On top of this is the billing strategy: the ubiquitous pay-per-use approach (either in its most common post-paid incarnation, or in a novel pre-paid version) is only the starting point for a wide range of innovative solutions, including bundling or QoS considerations, which European project VISION Cloud is tackling as part of its research efforts. This chapter aims to provide a comprehensive discussion on the most relevant business factors that the Cloud confronts.*

## INTRODUCTION

"The Cloud" is a new paradigm that is increasingly consolidating itself inside IT industry and that will change computing inside companies they way we know it. The same way that in past times bread was kneaded and raised at each home, and nowadays this has become quite odd, in a few years time it will be strange for a company or public institution not to have its own IT platform in the Internet. The reasons behind this change are the clear advantages that the Cloud offers: flexibility to obtain resources on demand, easy management, access from any geographical location, cost shifting from CAPEX to OPEX (allowing finer control of expenditure and avoiding costly acquisition of assets), and cost reduction due to economies of scale and strong competition among cloud providers.

DOI: 10.4018/978-1-4666-3934-8.ch004

As of now, there are still great differences between the speed at which this paradigm change is taking place in one place or another. In some cases there are not yet enough companies demanding these kind of services to form a critical mass, or the services offered are scarce. Even in those places where there are strong cloud providers, the problem is often related to medium-to-large company CEOs that are reluctant to change. People in charge of IT in those companies are aware of the advantages of having a Cloud infrastructure, but they are hesitant to make the move, and prefer to be cautious and wait to have feedback from related companies in their sector before making a decision. On the other hand, small companies (except maybe those in technological sectors) do not show either a rapid transition to embrace cloud services, even if they could offer a competitive advantage, key to their survival. There are still high barriers, such as concerns over availability and business continuity (there are some recent examples of failures), concerns over security of the stored data, vendor locking, risks and costs for moving current IT platforms to Cloud, amortization of recent IT investments… that handicap a quicker adoption rate.

This context leads to different business models that this chapter will analyse in detail. A business model represents the set of characteristics to classify the different paths to make money by offering cloud services. These characteristics include the type of services offered, target market segment, billing models, alliances between providers to create different value chains…

The actual situation in cloud services development is creating a clear supremacy of a few companies that drive the development of this industry, by pushing their own rules. In contrast, some movements such as the "Open Cloud Manifesto"[1] have appeared, to bet on some principles that enable the development of an open industry where much more players can participate, supporting rules in the interest of the end-user. It is expected that these principles and objectives make progressively their way into customer needs, which will force cloud providers to include them in their business models.

## BACKGROUND

The Use Cases developed inside VISION Cloud (Enterprise, Telco, Media and Healthcare) have leveraged a number of requirements for the billing (and accounting) mechanisms to be deployed there. The general requirement is, of course, to have a distributed billing mechanism in place that is able to charge all tenants for their actual consumption, in a pay-per-use basis (*ENRQ15: Automatic billing mechanisms*). To this extent, it is required that comprehensive list of metrics is identified, so that it covers the most common concepts related to the usage of a storage cloud (*TCRQ45: Billing concepts*): storage used, inbound/outbound traffic… considering also the particularities of VISION Cloud, such as *Storlets*. Accounting and billing mechanisms have to be agile enough to enable mechanisms for the tenants to control consumption prior to the generation of the bill (*TCRQ44: Balance Query, TCRQ46: Billing alerts*)

It is assumed that there are SLA agreements between VISION Cloud and its tenants, to control the quality of the service offered. In case of infringement of the SLA terms, the billing subsystem must keep track of this fact, and compensate the user for it (*TCRQ36: User storage space SLA enforcement*, ENRQ02, *TCRQ58: SLA durability, TCRQ61: SLA latency*, ENRQ46, TCRQ62, MDRQ40, HCRQ0408: *Bandwidth requirements*).

Finally, Use Cases demand that is performed following at least two different models: post-paid, where users is charged at the end of regular cycles, for the consumed resources (*TCRQ47: Post-paid billing*); and pre-paid, where users have available a variable amount of credit that enable them to operate for a cost, until their credit is exhausted (*TCRQ48: Pre-paid billing*).

## ENTRANCE BARRIERS

Even if Internet usage is widespread nowadays, most businesses have not yet embraced IT services from Cloud providers. Companies typically continue hosting their own datacenters, with complex system layouts (CRM, BSS, OSS, Billing, Human Resource Management, …).

Differences in penetration of the Cloud paradigm in companies can be clearly seen from a geographical point of view. USA holds a significant lead over the rest of the world, which some studies (Bradshaw, 2012) rate at three-to-five years ahead of Europe. This fact has pushed European administration to identify structural barriers in Cloud adoption, and to stimulate economically its development. There is the non-negligible risk that this technological gap could widen, threatening the competitiveness of the global European industry.

Similarly to other technologies, four different acceptance groups for Cloud computing can be identified: innovators, early adopters, majority adopters, and laggards. Most business fit in the latest two groups; the reasons behind their delay in embracing these services are described below:

- **Security and Privacy:** Many organizations are uncomfortable with the idea of storing their data and applications on systems they do not control.
- **Trust:** Concerns over availability and business continuity of Cloud Providers (there are some recent examples of failures).
- **Vendor Locking:** The lack of common standards pose a significant risk in the election of a particular Cloud, at the prospect of not being able to easily switch providers at a later stage.
- **Cost:** When moving to the Cloud model, it is not an easy task to estimate the costs, where they are usually aggregated (communications, storage, computation, pay-per-use applications, additional SLAs…)
- **Heterogeneity of Legislation:** There are currently quite different regulations on security, privacy, trust and digital rights aspects, even among countries in the EU. Moreover: what happens with intellectual property rights and data protection when you access Europe data from China?
- **Transition:** Moving IT systems from the traditional datacenter to Cloud solutions means facing substantial problems and technical risks, and the need to justify recent IT investments. Cloud industry tries to minimize these barriers by offering soft transitions based on hybrid cloud models.
- **Internet Connection:** Evolving towards a Cloud model means increasing the bandwidth of the communication links, and many businesses do not have yet a fast and reliable Internet connectivity.

## CLASSIFICATION OF BUSINESS MODELS

The following paragraphs will analyse some of the characteristics that, on their own, or in combination with others, can help on the task of classifying the existing business models around the Cloud paradigm. Attending to those characteristics, the following classifications can be made:

- Service Models
- Deployment Models
- Federation Models
- Other Business Models

### Service Models

Service-based business models show a definition of how services shall be used by the customer, while not revealing the details of how they work or their implementation. A large pool of physical resources is shared among all customers, maximizing efficiency. This scheme generates important economics of scale benefits that Cloud Providers could translate in cheaper services.

Another important aspect is the service on-demand characteristic. Customers could ask for IT resources and change their needs anytime. Customers perceive IT services as the usual water or electricity service, where everyone could think there are infinite resources available at any moment.

Virtualization technologies have played an important role in offering these kinds of services. By using these technologies, clients do not need to care about the security or performance of those resources assigned to him from the shared pool. Furthermore, actual operation of the IT resources from one client does not impact the rest of clients. Each one is guaranteed a slice, subject to a Service Level Agreement; if that slice is idle at a given time, it can be temporarily reallocated for other purposes.

There is a common agreement to classify the Cloud Service Models in the following three categories (see Figure 1):

- **Infrastructure as a Service (IaaS):** The cloud provider owns a large amount of physical resources: storage, computation and communications. Customers can request virtual resources for a period of time, without knowledge about the mapping to the underlying physical infrastructure.

*Figure 1. Cloud computing services and deployment models*

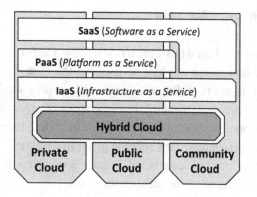

Popular examples include Amazon Web Services S3 and EC2.

- **Platform as a Service (PaaS):** This offers a higher level of abstraction on top of the functionalities offered by an IaaS. Instead of a virtual infrastructure of physical resources, PaaS offers a platform or software stack (development tools, database services, application server, Web Access, billing, metering, mash-ups…) over which clients develop and run their applications. Some examples are Google App Engine and Microsoft Azure.

- **Software as a Service (SaaS):** The latest category focuses on services for business, instead of developers. Providers offer a set of Web-based applications, eliminating the need for companies to purchase, operate and support them locally. Typical examples are CRM SalesForce, and Google Apps such as Gmail or Docs.

A significant barrier working against the adoption of these services is vendor lock-in. Unfortunately for customers, there is not yet a standard which allows a smooth handover from one cloud services provider to a different one. This is partly due to being in an expansive phase where new services appear regularly, or their characteristics change rapidly. It can be expected that this evolution comes to a rest in the next few years, leading to the creation of standards that will be crucial in the success of the commercialization of the Cloud.

## Deployment Models

Other important aspect of cloud industry is the way of deploying cloud-computing services. This decomposition is also shown in the lower part of Figure 1.

- **Public Cloud:** This comprises cloud services that are used by the general public. Public clouds require significant investment, so they are usually owned by large corporations such as Microsoft, Google or Amazon.

- **Private Cloud:** A cloud that is used exclusively by one organisation. The cloud may be operated by the organisation itself (usually in their own premises) or by a third party (either internally or externally). VMware and RedHat are popular examples.

- **Community Cloud:** A cloud that is shared by several organisations and is usually setup for their specific requirements. The Open Cirrus cloud test bed could be regarded as a community cloud that aims to support research in cloud computing.

- **Hybrid Cloud:** A cloud that is setup using a mixture of the aforementioned three deployment models. The more common case for a hybrid cloud is that composed of private (in-house) and public (external) clouds. In this configuration applications and data can be moved from private to public cloud when more resources are required. VMware and RedHat offer solutions for hybrid clouds.

While Public and Private Cloud solutions have been sold for a while, Hybrid Cloud solutions are becoming increasingly popular. This is an option that is particularly interesting for those customers seeking to mitigate transition risks when embracing public cloud solutions, while allowing for the amortization of their investments in equipment in their datacenters.

There is a delicate aspect in hybrid when it comes to ensuring a seamless experience: secure and adequate communications. From a security point of view, the customer of a hybrid cloud expects to see the public cloud part as an extension of its private cloud, integrated in its corporate LAN, and compliant with its existing policies. From a communications point of view, private and public clouds often need to share resources, such as a database or a Web server. This turns into critical some features like having good latency

and link speeds. These technological challenges present themselves as opportunities to companies that have a great experience in these topics, such as Citrix, Intel or telco operators in general.

## Federation Models

The concept of "Federated Cloud Computing" is emerging. The most common model nowadays, in which a Cloud provider offers its infrastructure only to its customers, needs to change progressively as the Cloud business is consolidating and becoming ubiquitous. Following the example of the banking business, which evolved from the model where a local office lent money only to its customers to a global interbanking market where clients can order payments worldwide, the Cloud market will need to evolve towards federated and collaborative models.

Some of the federated models that can be identified are the following ones:

- **Cloud Wholesale Market:** The cloud provider obtains computational and/or storage resources from other cloud providers, offering them transparently to its customers. An example of this approach are virtual cloud providers, which purchases resource blocks in the wholesale market, and resells them to retail clients, under an assortment of pricing and service level policies.

- **Confederation of Services:** Under this model, the client has contracts with different cloud providers that are interlinked and/or have collaboration agreements. For example, a multinational company may have deals with local services providers in each country where it operates. Whenever an employee of that company moves from one country to another one, virtual machines are automatically relocated in order to guarantee better latency. This model also enables load balancing, shared application licences, an integrated security model...

- **Aggregation of Cloud Services:** This model is offered to the client as an integrated service where different cloud providers collaborate and share benefits. An example is the Cloud Federation Business Model for CDN Services (Content Delivery Networks), where a CDN provider offers a technological solution for distributing high-quality video streaming to millions of customers spread in different continents. To this extent, some cloud providers collaborate by offering storage (cache) services in each country; others offer computational solutions for video transcoding; some others offer their low-cost communication solutions that take advantage of off-peak hours in some of their network segments...

- **Academic or Research Collaborations:** Open Cirrus is a global Cloud computing testbed that federates 10 distributed datacenters across North America, Europe and Asia. In Open Cirrus, each joining site contains physical resources and different services (Hadoop, MPI, Virtual Machine, cluster storage, etc.) that are shared among the community.

## Other Business Models

A close examination of current publications about cloud models leads to the identification of the following references:

- **Cloud: Seven Clear Business Models (Chou, 2009):** This interesting work describes the evolution of software commercialization by the most relevant software companies, under the influence of the explosion of Internet. The book identifies seven possible models: Traditional, Open Source, Outsourcing, Hybrid, Hybrid+, Software as a Service, and Internet.

- **Cloud Cube Model (CCM) proposed by Jericho's Forum[2]:** The CCM is used to enable secure collaboration in cloud formations to business needs. An interesting classification of business models into eight types using CCM is found in (Chang, 2010): (1) Service Provider and Service Orientation; (2) Support and Services Contracts; (3) In-House Private Clouds; (4) All-In-One Enterprise Cloud; (5) One-Stop Resources and Services; (6) Government Funding; (7) Venture Capitals; and (8) Entertainment and Social Networking.

- **Linear Value Chain and Ecosystem Models proposed (Luhn & Jaekel, 2009):** The author exposes how the traditional Value Chains for IT services is changing as a result of cloud computing concepts. The result is a new cloud computing ecosystem of IT service providers where new stages in the value chain, such as service brokering and aggregation, trust and reputation assessments are incorporated.

- **Green Cloud (Castro-Leon, 2012):** In a cloud environment it would be possible to improve "green" credentials by utilising more efficient processors and memory. This author exposes a new business model where new regulation and carbon emissions taxes are incorporated on the market and where the carbon footprint of applications is calculated on the cloud. In this scenario, "going green" is relevant not only to reduce additional costs of energy consumption, but also to reduce the carbon footprint and provide to customer a green service with less tax.

## BILLING CHALLENGES

It is crucial for commercial systems, such as Clouds, to generate revenues for their providers. The following paragraphs will introduce the manner to charge customers for usage and yield profits for the investors, including the approach for billing Cloud services, the payment model widely deployed in Clouds, how the model can adapt to competitive markets, and future work of the VISION Cloud on accounting and billing.

## The "Pay-per-Use" Approach

Among the multiple approaches for billing cloud services provided to the end-user, the most commonly used one, due to its simplicity, is the one based on "Pay-per-use" (also referred as "Pay-as-you-go" and "Utility computing"). In this model, the customer pays for the amount of processing power, disk space, network traffic… that you actually consume from each virtualized resource from the IaaS or PaaS. Occasionally these services are offered for free until a threshold is reached; this helps lowering the entry barrier.

Pay-per-use model is progressively becoming adopted also in SaaS. Until now, the traditional model for selling applications implies that the customer pays for one or several software licences, and may be charged with additional annual fees for updates. The customer holds the responsibility of owning the hardware and installing and managing the application, as well as associated exploitation duties, such as performing backups, supervising logs, launching batch processes….

Following the cloud paradigm, the same companies selling software copies see now an opportunity of extending their services at a moderate cost, by building over-the-top solutions using existing IaaS / PaaS platform. They can deploy their applications into the cloud, and offer them to customers as SaaS, who will be happy to adopt them being spared of their administration and exploitation.

This way of organizing Cloud business enables the creation of a rich ecosystem where each and all parties can draw significant benefits. IaaS and PaaS providers, which have made great investments in IT physical resources, now find a way to share those expenses among their clients, while holding appreciable margins thanks to economies of scale. The broad market for application providers, now offering SaaS services in a pay-per-use model, which can request more IaaS and PaaS resources as their customer base increases. Finally, end-users, which now externalize their IT workloads (turning CAPEX into OPEX), and can focus in the activities that are essential for their businesses.

An interesting challenge for small companies in the SaaS field is commercializing, billing and charging geographically sparse clients. One solution to this problem is proposed by large IaaS / PaaS providers, which include in their portals, together with their services, a marketplace where third parties can introduce their SaaS services. The large provider takes then the responsibility of reselling the service, and performing accounting and billing to the end-user on behalf of these third parties.

## Pre-Paid and Post-Paid

Billing can be realized as post-paid or pre-paid. Post-paid customers receive bills and pay for usage periodically. This payment model assumes that customers are trusted and willing to pay. It requires the subscription and identification of its customers. Post-paid model is in wide use whilst pre-paid one is gaining in popularity since it offers effective economic management for both customers and providers. Pre-paid customers deposit an amount of credit into their accounts prior to any consumption. The accounts will be supervised and credit will be reserved during resource usage. Once the balance of a customer reaches a certain bottom limit, the customer will be invited to transfer more credit to the account. Compared with post-paid model, pre-paid model is more available for the customers with low consumption profiles and preferring to hide their identifications, since this model requires no fixed subscription fee or customer identification.

In post-paid model, the consumption cost of both event-based and session-based resources are calculated in the same way: usage records are collected and correlated, and then transformed into a common format that is suitable for further operations; afterwards, the processed data are mapped into monetary units periodically. Contrarily, in pre-paid model, the consumption of event-based and session-based resources can be charged in different manners: the usage of event-based resources may cause an immediate debit or be charged with unit reservations whilst session-based ones are normally charged with unit reservations. The reservation-based charging is performed as follows, which is graphically depicted in Figure 2.

1.    The Cloud forwards the resource request to the accounting and billing system. The accounting and billing system calculates an amount of credit that needs to be reserved before the consumption.
2.    The accounting and billing system checks the target customer's account and then reserves the amount of credit if the customer's balance covers this amount of credit. Otherwise, the consumption request will be denied.
3.    During resource consumption, the granted credit units are monitored within the Cloud and upon their exhaustion, the credit reservation is repeated.
4.    When the resource session is terminated, the amount credit consumed is determined and then debit from the customer' account. Meanwhile, the unused reserved credit units are released.

## Evolution to Highly Competitive Markets

Instead of calculating cost of resource usage based on a single and static parameter, both post-paid and pre-paid model can charge consumptions based on multiple influencing parameters flexibly. This enables providers to offer more attractive price plans, and enforces a more efficient use of resources by charging for the use and availability of these resources. The charging influencing parameters in Clouds can include the following ones:

- **Duration:** Duration of resource consumption is an obvious parameter to charge for in systems in which QoS terms are fixed. Even in the case of some storage clouds where resource usage is expressed in other ways, such as read/write bytes, duration is still considered a valid parameter, since a typical customer may not be aware of the technologies to offer resources and therefore she will be confused if the same amount of data kept in the cloud for the same duration varies in cost.
- **Volume:** It is one of the important charging parameters in storage clouds since it represents the resource consumption in a straightforward manner. It is a way to offer incentives for customers, and enforce a more efficient use of resources. However, it has the limitation that usage data based on

*Figure 2. Pre-paid model: typical sequence*

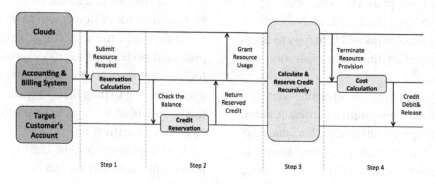

volume can be hard to understand for the customers without technical background.

- **Quality of Service (QoS):** To stay in competitive and keep customers, providers need to offer compensation for SLA violations. Meanwhile, to make efficient use of Cloud resources, there should be an incentive for customers to choose among a variety of available QoS terms. Therefore, QoS is crucial in the definition of attractive and flexible price plans. Charging for resource usage based on each parameter constituting a QoS set can lead to large and complex tariff tables that are hard to be interpreted. A better solution is to define QoS in multiple classes, and charge consumptions based on the classes (Ghys et al., 2003).

- **Time Interval:** Resources are typically consumed at different time intervals. It is common knowledge that much more traffic is generated during perk days or hours. Resource providers can counter this by defining tariff rates based on time of day, day of week or absolute time intervals that are intended to persuade customers to shift their non-urgent consumptions to a cheaper time period (Ghys et al., 2003) and balance the load on the their systems.

- **Commercial Relationships between Multiple Providers:** A customer may consume a bundle of resources that are offered by different providers, and the providers may want their commercial relationships to be reflected in the way their resources are charged for. For example, provider A may give a 10% discount if one or more of its resources are used in conjunction with one or more resources provided by provider B. This common business practice is known as price bundling of service offering (Simon & Wuebker, 1999). Taking into account such commercial relationships makes cost calculation closer to the business model.

In Clouds, the consumption cost of resources can be based on the multiple parameters discussed above. However, statically specifying all possible tariffs on these parameters would lead to big tariff tables that are difficult to maintain whilst they depends on the prior-knowledge of the context in which resources are consumed. An attractive approach to tackle this issue is to deploy a component to apply the charging rules of the single parameters based on the runtime environment (Xu & Jennings, 2009). This will reduce the cost of charging scheme configuration and facilitate the offering of resources.

## FUTURE RESEARCH DIRECTIONS

The VISION Cloud deploys the "Pay-per-use" approach, and supports both post-paid and pre-paid model. This Cloud system consists of multiple clusters, a customer may consume resources of different clusters. In the case, deploying a centralized system to track and charge resource consumption may limit the capacity of providers to offer their resources, since such a single component can be a bottleneck when a huge number of resources are consumed simultaneously. We have to investigate the manner to release the potential bottleneck, meanwhile the manner to tackle the billing challenges faced by the storage Cloud, and adapt to competitive market.

### VISION Cloud Approach

VISION Cloud will deploy a distributed accounting solution to offer accounting records to billing (covering requirement *ENRQ15: Automatic billing mechanisms*). It is fully distributed that can improve the scalability and performance of the accounting system (complying with requirement *TCRQ61: High performance*). Usage data are synchronised between different clusters in the post-paid model (covering requirement *TCRQ47: Post-paid billing*) based on a distribution approach. To support pre-paid model (*TCRQ48: Pre-paid billing*), distributed accounting components that constitute the accounting system of VISION Cloud will map tariff of long-running resources into a time-based function, and supervise the consumption of these resources based on that calculated time interval; the credit of a given customer is distributed between different accounting components. Practically, it may be hard to synchronize credit balance in real-time in clouds. To avoid termination of resource offering in VISION Cloud, a small overdraw can be allowed in the accounting solution that may result in a miniscule loss of revenue but can reduce the burden of the accounting system.

From the management point of view, flexible charging mechanisms applied in both payment models that reflect business models and polices can enhance the linkage between the technical and economical perspective of a cloud infrastructure. This will be achieved in VISION Cloud by charging consumptions based on a lot of charging parameters like volume or duration, compensations of service level agreement violations (coping with requirements *TCRQ36: User storage space SLA enforcement*; ENRQ02, *TCRQ58: SLA durability*; *TCRQ61: SLA latency*; and *ENRQ46, TCRQ62, MDRQ40, HCRQ0408: Bandwidth requirements*) variable prices depending on special prices obtained from contracting service bundles (e.g. bundles of Storlets) (Simon & Wuebker, 1999) (covering requirement *TCRQ45: Billing concepts*), etc.

## Justification of the Approach

Deploying a distributed accounting and credit management solution will release the potential bottleneck of service provision—the centralized accounting system. In the case, an accounting component is deployed on each cluster constituting a Cloud that collects usage data generated on the cluster. In post-paid model, an accounting data consumer may connect to an arbitrary accounting component to retrieve records that are collected by other accounting components. Therefore, the

accounting components have to synchronize their data. However, it is hard to keep every record from other accounting components up-to-date since the synchronization can be expensive and the communication may be delayed. In the case, a challenge arises for the post-paid model since the consumption data on a given customer within a specific period of time obtained by a data consumer from different accounting components should be identical. The usage data distribution and synchronization approach is intended to tackle this challenge.

Except for the usage data synchronization, a distributed pre-paid solution deployed in VISION Cloud has to tackle the real-time credit supervision. In pre-paid model, for session based resources, a customer's account has to be checked periodically whilst consumption cost needs to be calculated in real-time. Each of the real-time credit supervision is expensive that represents a considerable cost driver of the total offering cost. However, the reduction of the number of real-time supervision will increase the possibility of revenue loss due to credit overuse.

In VISION Cloud, multiple customers may consume a large number of pre-paid resources simultaneously. In the case, its accounting system has to perform real-time checking on every resource consumed by each customer individually and periodically. As the number of customers and the number resources used by each of these customers increase, the cost of resource provision and the workload of the accounting system increase dramatically. Furthermore, there are some resources that are used close to a set of data objects in a storage Cloud, such as the resources consumed by the media-rich data transformation service used to support telco/media applications. These resources are consumed on behalf of customers, and they are potentially long-lived. To keep supervising the usage of each of the resources at short intervals can impose high overhead for accounting systems.

The solution given in VISION Cloud could tackle the challenges faced by pre-paid model that deploys an accounting component on each cluster constituting clouds, and these accounting components synchronize credit of customers when it is necessary. To further tackle the scalability issue of each of the distributed accounting components and reduce the cost of resource provision, tariff of resources can be mapped into time-based functions. This enables every accounting component supervises resource consumption based on a calculated time interval for a bundle of resources instead of single resource individually.

## CONCLUSION

"The Cloud" is a new paradigm that will change computing inside companies the way we know it. Reasons behind these change include all the clear advantages that the Cloud offers: flexibility to obtain resources on demand, easy management, access from any geographical location, cost shifting from CAPEX to OPEX, and cost reduction. However, there are still great differences between the speeds at which this paradigm change is taking place in different places of the world. USA holds a significant technological and commercial lead over the rest of contenders, while Europe struggles to keep the pace by stimulating Cloud development and eliminating existing structural barriers: security and privacy, trust, vendor locking, cost, legislation.

As relevant as the underlying technology may appear to be, one of the most crucial aspects in the success of the Cloud is the business model applied to it, involving billing, provisioning, or new ways to offer the service (consider, for example, Google's advertising model). Among the different business models found today are those based on the type of service, type of deployment, or federation/collaboration agreements. Furthermore, new models keep on appearing: while being less mature than "traditional" ones, they consider some novel aspects: green credentials, reputation assessment, or social networks support.

Billing therefore constitutes a differentiating factor in business models. VISION Cloud project is making significant effort tackling the elevated number of challenges that a provider may face. One of these difficulties is managing adequately and in real-time the billing for pre-paid cloud services contracts. Even if it is a relatively simple task to define it, it can be quite complex to achieve it in a scalable and cost effective way over a distributed or federated Cloud infrastructure. Other challenge is offering flexible price plans that can be tailored to the needs of each market segment, where billing is performed by combining complex business rules over a list of parameters that define the use of cloud resources: duration, volume, resource type, special prices on bundles or packages of services or during rush hours, temporal offers, compensations for Service Level Agreement (SLA) infringements.

The consolidation of the Cloud industry will bring a wide commercial offer that will need the support of new business models and varied contracting and billing schemes produced by the innovative efforts on-going nowadays.

## REFERENCES

Bradshaw, D. (2012). *Cloud in Europe: Uptake, benefits, barriers, and market estimates.* Academic Press.

Castro-Leon, E. et al. (2012). *Global IT manageability policies across service boundaries in a cloud environment.* Intel Technology Journal. doi:10.1109/SRII.2012.48.

Chang, V., Wills, G., & De Roure, D. (2010). A review of cloud business models and sustainability. [IEEE.]. *Proceedings of IEEE CLOUD, 2010*, 43–50.

Chou, T. (2009). *Seven clear business models.* New York: Active Book Press.

Ghys, F., Mampaey, M., Smouts, M., & Vaarani-emi, A. (2003). *3G multimedia network services, accounting, and user profiles*. Boston: Artech House.

Jeffery, K. et al. (2010). *The future of cloud computing: Opportunities for European cloud computing beyond 2010*. Academic Press.

Lawson, J. (2009). *The cloud: OSS model 3.0*. Paper presented at the O'Reilly Conference. San Jose, CA. Retrieved from http://en.oreilly.com/oscon2009/public/schedule/detail/10369

Luhn, A., & Jaekel, M. (2009). *Cloud computing – Business models, value creation dynamics and advantages for customers*. Retrieved from https://www.it-solutions.siemens.com/b2b/it/en/global/Documents/Publications/CloudComputing_Whitepaper_PDF_e.pdf

Schubert, L., & Jeffery, K. (2012). *Advances in cloud – Research in future cloud computing*. Academic Press.

Simon, H., & Wuebker, G. (1999). Bundling – A powerful method to better exploit profit potential. In Fuerderer, R., Herrmann, A., & Wuebker, G. (Eds.), *Optimal Bundling: Marketing Strategies for Improving Economic Performance* (pp. 7–28). Berlin: Springer Verlag. doi:10.1007/978-3-662-09119-7_2.

Xu, L., & Jennings, B. (2009). A framework for automated creation and deployment of consolidated charging schemes for service compositions. In *Proceedings of the 7th European Conference on Web Services* (pp. 49-57). IEEE.

## ADDITIONAL READING

Chang, M., & Yang, W. (2002). Performance of mobile prepaid and priority call services. *IEEE Communications Letters*, 6(2), 61–63. doi:10.1109/4234.984693.

Chang, V., David, B., Wills, G., & De Roure, D. (2010). *A categorisation of cloud business models*. Paper presented at the 10th International Symposium on Cluster, Cloud and Grid Computing. Melbourne, Australia.

Courcoubetis, C., & Weber, R. (2003). *Pricing communication networks: Economics, technology, and modelling*. Chichester, UK: John Wiley & Sons, Ltd. doi:10.1002/0470867175.

3. GPP. (2005a). *3rd generation partnership project, technical specification group services and systems aspects, telecommunication management, charging management, charging principles (release 5)*. 3G TS 32.200 version 5.9.0 (2005-09).

3. GPP. (2005b). 3rd generation partnership project, technical specification group services and systems aspects, telecommunication management, charging management, charging data description for the circuit switched (CS) domain (release 5). 3G TS 32.205 version 5.9.0 (2005-03).

3. GPP. (2005c). 3rd generation partnership project, technical specification group services and systems aspects, telecommunication management, charging management, charging data description for the packet switched (PS) domain (release 5). 3GTS 32.215 version 5.9.0 (2005-06).

3. GPP. (2005d). 3rd Generation Partnership Project, Technical Specification Group, Telecommunication management, Charging management, Charging data description for application services (release 5). 3G TS 32.235 version 5.5.0 (2005-09).

3. GPP. (2006a). 3rd generation partnership project, technical specification group services and system aspects, telecommunication management, charging management, charging architecture and principles (release 6). 3G TS 32.240 version 6.4.0 (2006-09).

3. GPP. (2006b). 3rd generation partnership project, technical specification group service and system aspects, telecommunication management, charging management, online charging system (OCS), applications and interfaces (release 6). 3G TS 32.296 version 6.3.0 (2006-09).

3. GPP. (2006c). 3rd generation partnership project, technical specification group service and system aspects, telecommunication management, charging management, charging data record (CDR) file format and transfer (release 6). 3G TS 32.297 version 6.2.0 (2006-09).

3. GPP. (2007). 3rd generation partnership project, technical specification group service and system aspects, telecommunication management, charging management, diameter charging applications (release 6). 3G TS 32.299 version 6.12.0 (2007-09).

Ilango, S., & Khajeh-Hosseini, A. (2010). *Research agenda in cloud technologies CoRR abs/1001.3259*. Academic Press.

Jaekel, M., & Luhn, A. (2009). *Cloud computing – Business models, value creation dynamics and advantages for customers*. Academic Press.

Koutsopoulou, M., Kaloxylos, A., & Alonistioti, A. (2004). Charging, accounting and billing management schemes in mobile telecommunication networks and the Internet. *IEEE Communications Surveys and Tutorials*, *6*(1), 50–58. doi:10.1109/COMST.2004.5342234.

Lin, P., Lin, Y., Yen, C., & Jeng, J. (2006). Credit allocation for UMTS prepaid service. *IEEE Transactions on Vehicular Technology*, *55*(1), 306–317. doi:10.1109/TVT.2005.858190.

Lin, Y., & Sou, S. (2009). *Charging for mobile all-IP telecommunications*. Chichester, UK: John Wiley & Sons, Ltd..

*Open Cloud Manifesto*. (n.d.). Retrieved from http://www.opencloudmanifesto.org/opencloud-manifesto1.htm

Plummer, D. C., Bittman, T. J., Austin, T., Cearley, D. W., & Smith, D. M. (2008). *Cloud computing: Defining and describing an emerging phenomenon*. Academic Press.

Rayport, J. F., & Heyward, A. (2009). *Envisioning the cloud: The next computing paradigm*. Marketspace.

Ruehl, T. S. (2010). *The efficacy of cloud computing in vertical industries as measured by profitability*. (Thesis). University of Wisconsin, Platteville, WI.

Xu, L., & Elmroth, E. (2011). A time interval-based credit reservation approach for prepaid composite services in cloud environments. In *Proceedings of the 9th European Conference on Web Services* (pp. 158–165). IEEE.

Xu, L., Lakew, E. B., Hernandez-Rodriguez, F., & Elmroth, E. (2012). A scalable accounting solution for prepaid services in cloud systems. In *Proceedings of the 9th International Conference on Service Computing*. IEEE.

Zimory Gmb, H. (2009). *Zimory enterprise cloud – Whitepaper*. Retrieved from http://www.zimory.com/fileadmin/images/content_images/pdf/WP_Enterprise_Engl_020409.pdf

## ENDNOTES

1    http://www.opencloudmanifesto.org
2    https://collaboration.opengroup.org/jericho/

# Chapter 5
# Towards Federation and Interoperability of Cloud Storage Systems

**Sebastian Dippl**
*Siemens AG Corporate Technology, Germany*

**Michael C. Jaeger**
*Siemens AG Corporate Technology, Germany*

**Achim Luhn**
*Siemens AG Corporate Technology, Germany*

**Alexandra Shulman-Peleg**
*IBM Haifa Research Lab, Israel*

**Gil Vernik**
*IBM Haifa Research Lab, Israel*

## ABSTRACT

*While it is common to use storage in a cloud-based manner, the question of true interoperability is rarely fully addressed. This question becomes even more relevant since the steadily growing amount of data that needs to be stored will supersede the capacity of a single system in terms of resources, availability, and network throughput quite soon. The logical conclusion is that a network of systems needs to be created that is able to cope with the requirements of big data applications and data deluge scenarios. This chapter shows how federation and interoperability will fit into a cloud storage scenario. The authors take a look at the challenges that federation imposes on autonomous, heterogeneous, and distributed cloud systems, and present approaches that help deal with the special requirements introduced by the VISION Cloud use cases from healthcare, media, telecommunications, and enterprise domains. Finally, the authors give an overview on how VISION Cloud addresses these requirements in its research scenarios and architecture.*

DOI: 10.4018/978-1-4666-3934-8.ch005

## INTRODUCTION

There is always a point in time, when one system is not enough anymore. History showed that applications always managed to require more resources than a single instance of a system can provide at a time. There are several reasons why one would go beyond a single cloud storage system besides the simple need of more storage space. In real life, there are enterprise borders and there is data that is not allowed to leave the enterprise for legal or compliance issues. There are geographical constraints and it is sometimes simply not efficient enough to access data at the other side of the globe, just because a company's cloud storage is located there. Furthermore, sometimes other storage offers may simply be cheaper. We notice that there is more than enough motivation to take a closer look on federation and interoperability of cloud storage systems.

The term federation describes the interworking of two or more otherwise autonomous and possibly heterogeneous systems. Creating a federation of existing cloud systems supports the user with a unified and combined view of storage and data services across several providers and systems. A storage federation allows users to seamlessly migrate, backup, synchronize, and monitor data and resources across connected cloud storage systems and supports various use cases such as collaboration, storage outsourcing, hybrid storage management and geographical data distribution to different providers or company branches. Federating resources to multiple cloud providers to scale beyond the storage limits of a single provider, guarantees reliability in case of failures and thus leads to higher data security. How does that relate to the term interoperability of cloud systems? Even though this turns out to be a religious discussion, we define interoperability as the technical base on which we can build up a federated system. As an example, we use the interoperability characteristics of HTTP, REST, and CDMI to create a combined, federated view of user's resources.

Federation is an important consideration for cloud storage providers and for companies consuming storage services. Storage providers have an interest in keeping their costs low which leads to an economical best practice of operating clusters at full capacity whenever possible to be cost efficient. If peak loads are to be expected, the provider needs to make the same decision as a potential cloud user: How much CAPEX (own infrastructure) should be turned to OPEX (variable cost of renting infrastructure)? Given the technical possibility of a cloud federation, a cloud provider can dimension his cluster for average load scenarios and use federated resources on a "Pay per Use" basis if needed. The same is true for supplying customers with compute resources in countries where no dedicated infrastructure is available, to grant a certain service level. Users of cloud storage solutions will also benefit from federation: using more than one cloud allows to mitigate the risk of storage failures and prevents data lock-in.

Recently, it also became obvious that there is an emerging need for hybrid clouds, that use federation and interoperability technologies to combine access to public and private clouds in parallel (*Managing Private and Hybrid Clouds for Data Storage*, 2010). Hybrid clouds essentially federate access to multiple pools of resources in order to meet business, performance and compliance requirements. For example, an enterprise may choose to store sensitive data in the private storage cloud, while utilizing the low cost and the elasticity of the public storage cloud for other less sensitive data. In addition, hybrid clouds are useful for creating storage tiers, with lower cost tiers being exported to public clouds, while storing only the higher level data that needs to meet the low latency requirements in private clouds. Similarly, replicating the data to external public clouds, may lower the overall cost of data backup and archiving. Finally, hybrid storage clouds are useful when elastic demand for storage exceeds the available internal resources (*Managing Private and Hybrid Clouds for Data Storage*, 2010).

Another not to be underestimated driver for federation, especially for new cloud service providers on the market, is the possibility to allow customers an easy migration or on-boarding between different storage clouds, while keeping data accessible for the users.

Interoperable federated and hybrid cloud systems introduce a set of new challenges that do not appear in unfederated setups, such as:

- Heterogeneity of data access semantics and data models.
- The process of distributing data and queries to the right storage cloud.
- Management and configuration of the federation.
- Mechanisms for access control, authentication and authorization.
- Billing, accounting, monitoring and auditing in federated clouds.

Even if federation in cloud environments is a research topic today, some of the basic concepts and architectures of federations have been already researched intensively within the area of federated database management systems as the article "Federated Database Systems for Managing Distributed, Heterogeneous, and Autonomous Databases" (Sheth & Larson, 1990), published in 1990, shows. Sheth and Larson define within this work a federated database system as a "collection of cooperating but autonomous component database systems" including a "software that provides controlled and coordinated manipulation of the component database systems," which is called a federated database management system. This definition places the federated database layer outside and on top of the component database systems that make up the federation. The article also introduces a possible characterization of systems of multiple databases along the dimensions of distribution, heterogeneity and autonomy, differentiates between tight (administrators create and maintain federation, global schema) and loosely (users

create and maintain federation) coupled systems and describes a reference architecture for federated database systems. A general focus is put on the transformation and integration of the database schemas of the federated component database systems and the respective querying language.

This chapter is organized as follows. First, we present the background section which describes the federation requirements and sample scenarios recognized by the VISION Cloud project. Then, we present the existing cloud federation and interoperability approaches. Finally, the section on future research directions presents the VISION Cloud approach, justifying its design decisions and describing its advantages.

## BACKGROUND

The VISION Cloud project consortium defined four use cases from different enterprise domains (healthcare, enterprise, media, telecommunications) as drivers for the architectural requirements. The industrial partners within VISION Cloud became the owners of these use cases. The requirements on interoperability and federation where derived from a survey that was done among those use case owners. The results of this survey lead to the main research pillars of the interoperability and federation working group.

The survey results identified several important requirements for the federation layer.

- Support for data backup at different providers.
- Creation of higher availability through redundancy.
- Interoperable interfaces in cloud storage systems.
- Avoidance of vendor lock in and being able to change providers on demand.
- Support for storage brokerage on a public storage marketplace.

- Unified view on all resources of a federated storage infrastructure.
- Secure access to data.

Less important in the view of the partners is the ability to share information via public cloud systems or the business to business integration via federation built into a storage system. Also the rapid elasticity feature of a cloud storage federation was not rated very high, which could be explained by the VISION Cloud focus on large data objects that cannot easily be redistributed because of the available network throughput.

For the deployment and access types, all the use case owners shared the opinion that access to federated storage with the companies identities and existing public key infrastructure is essential. Furthermore federation and interoperability should not only deal with operations between VISION Clouds but also with interactions to third party providers on different technology stacks like the Amazon cloud or the Microsoft Azure platform. It also became evident, that in a federated scenario read and write access will be required on all of the cloud systems taking part in a federation. Placement control via metadata attached to objects is seen as a viable way to establish this control. Most of the partners would prefer to set up a VISION Cloud system on their own premises and would use a publicly provided VISION Cloud only as an extension if it comes with a significant cost reduction or special feature set. Gathering the information of resources usage for billing and monitoring is seen as a prerequisite for all federation relevant scenarios.

Below are two sample federation scenarios recognized by the enterprise and content/media use cases of the VISION Cloud project.

## Enterprise Data Mobility and Federation

One of the main motivations for moving to the cloud is lowering the Total Cost of Ownership (TCO). In order to achieve this, a service provider may decide to move data to a cheaper storage provider or federate content from the storage of several providers. This requires introducing federation at the infrastructure level using the same APIs for accessing and managing the different clouds. Throughout the life time of the deployed Business Intelligence On-Demand (BIOD) offering, this will enable, for example, choosing the cheapest provider for accumulating new objects, while not effecting in any way the consumption of these stored data objects. Other alternative is to have objects with different SLAs (Service Level Agreements) and use different providers to guarantee these SLAs at best price. For example, this could be useful for video streaming applications, which may have different SLAs in different countries allowing giving good service at peak hours.

## Federated Access to Content Networks

In this scenario, customers will have the ability to use several services to store their content, while sharing the data from all the sources in a seamless way with friends or relatives. For example this can be as part of social networks applications or content delivery services. Another example is the integration between legacy or institutional content and personal/professional content, which is important in such fields as journalism. The underlying federation should be transparent to the user who should not be aware of the exact data location, but should have a unified view of his content.

## CLOUD FEDERATION AND INTEROPERABILITY APPROACHES

There are several possibilities to establish a basic interworking of systems. We describe the most common approaches that can be used for cloud storage systems.

## Multi Cloud APIs

The simplest way to achieve federation between otherwise autonomous cloud storage systems is to access all of the involved systems from a single client. The common way to achieve efficient application development in such a scenario, is to define a storage interface that is implemented by different adapters. The combination of such interfaces and adapter implementations is known as a multi cloud API. A very popular multi cloud API that abstracts from the different underlying storage providers is JClouds (*Jclouds*). JClouds is an open source Java based library, which gives the user the freedom to use different blob storage and compute providers without changing their application code. JClouds includes adapters for many existing clouds like Amazon, VMWare, Azure, and Rackspace (*Jclouds,*). Almost as popular, but not available to the Java world is the Apache incarnation of multi cloud APIs called libcloud (*Apache LibCloud*). Apache libcloud is currently Python only, but allows the user not only to access storage and compute but also gives access to DNS infrastructure and load balancers. Another Apache project, which is now adopted by Red Hat distributions, is called Deltacloud (*Apache DeltaCloud*). It aims to implement multiple provider APIs on a language agnostic basis by providing a REST interface to applications. Apart from that, DeltaCloud also provides native support for C and Ruby programming languages. The commercial SMEStorage service (*SMEStorage*) on the other hand introduces a service based approach for users to access remote storage, may it be Amazon blobs, box.net accounts, FTP servers or even Google docs storage. The SME Storage API is more ajar to a file system API than the blob-like storage interfaces of the other multi cloud APIs. The RightScale Multi Cloud Platform (*RightScale Multi Cloud Platform*) provides a commercial version of a multi cloud storage API and comes with a set of graphical management tools. One of the big disadvantages of all the multi cloud APIs is the limited support for different functional aspects of special cloud provider. This becomes evident if we compare the rich metadata model and query possibilities of VISION Cloud to the simple metadata fields of current blob cloud storage implementations. While it is true, that most cloud providers like Amazon and Microsoft provide scalable table store implementations, which could be used for rich metadata, these table abstractions are usually not provided on the level of the multi cloud APIs.

## Resource Federation

Resource Federation describes a model of interworking where the federation logic is contained in one of the cloud systems that make up the federation. In this topology each cloud has its own users and accessible objects, and clouds use each other via agreed interfaces. One example of this type of federation was presented by the Reservoir project, which followed the principles of the electrical power plants (Rochwerger et al., 2011). Just as power utilities deal with shortage of capacity by buying additional capacity from neighboring plants, cloud computing infrastructure providers create a federated cloud where capacity beyond the limits of a particular provider are met by delegating some of the requests to another provider. The Reservoir project has defined a model and an open architecture for federation and the interoperability of autonomous clouds to form a global fabric of resources that can be provided on demand with guaranteed service levels (Rochwerger et al., 2009). Additional work on extending the monitoring architectures used in Grid computing by technology neutral interfaces and architectural additions for handling placement, migration, and monitoring of VMs in federated cloud environments (Elmroth & Larsson, 2009) has also been done. However, these works addressed only the federation of the compute resources (VMs) and did not deal with the federation of the storage resources.

## Layered Federation

Layered federation in contrast to resource federation is managed from a component that is not part of the autonomous cloud systems that participate in the federation. From an architectural point of view, in layered federation the federation management component (Cloud broker) is situated in a layer above the systems that are part of the federation. The Federated systems itself in some cases don't even have to know that they are part of a federation. Although layered federation has already been exploited in the Grid context (Elmroth & Tordsson, 2005), cloud based solutions are still in their infancy. Recently, Tordsson et al (Tordssona, Monterob, Moreno-Vozmedianob, & Llorente), presented an architecture for cloud brokering and multi-cloud VM management. They described a placement optimization model for compute-intense applications deployed in multicloud environments. Their model incorporates price and performance, as well as constraints in terms of hardware configuration and load balancing. They demonstrate that multi-cloud placement can improve performance, fault tolerance and can lower the costs. Similar to Reservoir, they focused on VM management and did not deal with storage resources. Extending the considered resources to also take into account network and storage resources, InterCloud (Buyya, Ranjan, & Calheiros, 2010) presented the high level components of a service-oriented architectural framework consisting of client's brokering and coordinator services that support application scheduling, resource allocation and migration of workloads. The architecture couples the administratively and topologically distributed storage and computes capabilities of Clouds as parts of a single resource leasing abstraction. The system eases the cross-domain capability integration for flexible, on demand, energy-efficient, and reliable access to the infrastructure based on the emerging virtualization technologies. Another example of such a layered federation system is RACS, which is a proxy-type system that transparently spreads the storage load over many providers (Abu-libdeh, Princehouse, & Weatherspoon). User data is striped across multiple clouds by applying a RAID-like techniques at the cloud storage level.

## Standardized Interfaces

A desirable way to exchange information and data in federated systems is to use standardized interfaces. The Cloud Data Management Interface (CDMI) (Silk, 2010) is a SNIA standard that specifies a RESTful protocol for using and administrating cloud storage systems. Within these efforts also federation topics are addressed and relevant terminology has been defined. Standardizing federations is planned for the CDMI 1.1 standard.

According to CDMI a federation is a process by which two systems can establish a trusted relationship to exchange content via CDMI. In a federation, there are typically two main actors:

- **Federation Initiator:** The CDMI system that initiates operations within a federation relationship.
- **Federation Target:** The CDMI system that processes operations within a federation relationship.

Based upon these actors there are basically two ways to access data in federated CDMI systems:

- **Proxy Access:** The initiating cloud is using the target cloud to outsource data. A user only accesses data on the target cloud via the initiator cloud in a proxy type pattern. The user might or might not know if his data is federated to another storage system. This type of access enables scaling the storage capacity and allows for a better distribution of data.
- **Peering Access:** Data is accessed concurrently from initiator and target cloud. This type of federation is used in scenarios,

where data is synchronized between enterprise branches or distributed to providers in different geographical locations.

As an additional dimension, a proxy or peering federation can be unidirectional or bidirectional, depending on the directions in which data is replicated or synchronized. These combinations have been presented as federation use cases by the CDMI consortium. Federation to Non-CDMI systems is done by providing a CDMI compatible wrapper or proxy implementation for the Non-CDMI system that maps the CDMI requests to requests on the native system.

## Commercial Cloud Integration Solutions

Most commercial systems that deal with cloud interoperability and federation are only addressing the notion of identity federation and access control in distributed systems (e.g. Microsoft Active Directory Federation Services or IBM Tivoli federated Identity Manager). However, there are several available IT integration solutions that we detail below.

*IBM CastIron:* WebSphere Cast Iron Cloud Integration (*IBM Cast Iron*) enables companies to rapidly interconnect their hybrid world of public clouds, private clouds, and on-premise applications. It maps different data structures located on different storage and database systems and creates integration solutions that can be executed either on an on-premise integration appliance or the multitenant WebSphere Cast Iron Live cloud service.

*DELL Boomi (Dell Boomi, 2011):* Dell Boomi AtomSphere simplifies the introduction of cloud and SaaS applications into an existing IT environment. It allows exchanging and mapping of data structures in different formats, such as XML and EDI. Boomi combines support for Webservices, filesystems and database systems with connectors for SaaS solutions like SalesForce, Netsuite,

RightNow, JIRA, Autotask as well as on premise stacks from SAP, Peoplesoft and Oracle.

*CloudSwitch (CloudSwitch, 2011):* CloudSwitch enables enterprises to easily migrate to the cloud without re-architecting the application or changing management tools and policies.

All of these solutions are more integration than federation solutions. They integrate two or more systems to a third new system instead of creating a loosely coupled aggregation where each system remains autarkic. Common for all of them is the approach of a configuration approach over a programmatic way to establish interoperability.

## FUTURE RESEARCH DIRECTIONS

When inspecting the existing products available on the market, it became apparent that federation is not a new topic in computer science, but federation in cloud based, virtualized infrastructures is still in its infancy. Especially a standardized interworking as suggested by CDMI is not yet established. Furthermore federating VISION Clouds rich metadata model, access control and computational storage services is an open field for research. Together with the requirements of the VISION Cloud use cases this led to the definition of the following research scenarios in the scope of VISION Cloud project.

- **On-Boarding:** An enterprise wants to move all his data from an old storage provider to a new storage provider while having access to data and a unified view on data while the data is in transit. The challenges addressed in this scenario are the management of the possibly parallel federation tasks, the distribution of the federation relevant information to the background processes that actually transfer the data to the new provider and the propagation and delegation of user access rights and identities to enable the transfer.

- **Resource Federation:** Two or more cloud systems store different shards of a tenant's data. Requests and queries need to be routed to the right place in an efficient way. This scenario enables one cloud to transparently purchase storage services from one or more federated clouds. However, the federation between the clouds is transparent to the user. The system managing the federation is responsible for providing a unified view of all the resources.

- **Identity Federation:** This scenario is dealing with the integration of storage federation and identity federation efforts. It solves the problem of a company wanting to use own identities across federated storage systems.

- **Cross-Providers Protocols and Services:** The approach here is to exploit open standards such as CDMI and to create proposals for new standards or extensions to existing standards.

- **Automated Negotiation Over SLAs and Pricing:** This subject is an active area of research in VISION Cloud and its research results can be proposed as the foundation for general mechanisms that will be employed by other clouds to achieve competitive service.

- **Transformation of Data Models and Semantics:** Federations with storage systems having different data and metadata schemas requires a layer that transforms these representations into VISION Cloud understandable format. Also ways of mapping the rich metadata schemes of VISION Cloud to popular storage services are treated within this scenario.

## VISION CLOUD APPROACH

We use a simple usage scenario to introduce the federation architecture of VISION Cloud. The scenario contains only two cloud systems that make up a federation. In this scenario, users access data only via the initiator cloud. The initiating cloud system has the possibility to outsource storage to an external target cloud. Data objects within VISION Cloud are stored in containers. Creating a federation in VISION Cloud basically connects a local container in the initiator cloud to a federated container in the target cloud. A federator component manages placement of objects and access to objects stored in the federation. The complete scenario is shown in Figure 1.

If a user needs to access an object in the federated storage space, he issues a standard CDMI HTTP GET Object request to the initiator VISION

*Figure 1. Simple federation usage scenario*

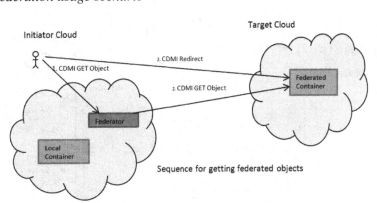

Cloud system. The VISION Cloud internal request dispatching will forward the requests to the federator component, if the container holding the object is in an federated state. The federator now can implement logic that determines where the data is placed. Depending on the use cases, different strategies are possible here.

- **Request from all:** If the federator component gets a request, it queries all federated containers for the object and delivers the object from the first response back to the user.
- **Procedural approach:** If the federator component gets a request, it starts querying the most local container before querying the federated containers.
- **Distributed placement index:** The federators of the federated cloud systems are interoperable and keep and update an index of which objects are stored in which cloud. If a get request is coming in, the index is queried for the cloud system, where the request needs to be forwarded to.

On top of these strategies, the federator component also has the possibility of redirecting the request completely to the target cloud instead of proxying the whole request which might be useful if big datasets have to be transferred.

Internally the federator component is split up to several components with different responsibilities. A federation administration component, a direct federation and a background federation component as well as an adapter layer for accessing different storage clouds (see Figure 2).

There are two main flows of information in the federation architecture. As described in usage scenario above, there is an application running on top of VISION Cloud, which stores and retrieves objects. These requests arrive at the direct federation component and are redirected to their real targets, usually via storage adapters. The background federator component's responsibility is to transfer data objects in the absence of a user initiating the federation, as it happens in the backup or onboarding scenarios. The background job needs to access local and federated storage on behalf of the user that created the federation or with a context that has read and write access to the needed resources in order to ensure the security of the system. This is done through a delegation of access rights, which can be managed either

*Figure 2. Components in VISION cloud federation architecture*

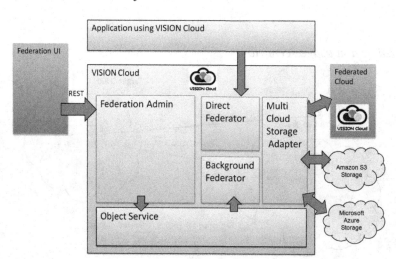

by the Identity Provider (IdP) of the cloud or by an external IdP kept at customer premises.

Another flow of information is the management flow, which is initiated by the administrator of a federation. In this setup, an administrator (of tenant or cloud) can use a graphical user interface of the federation administration component (or the REST API directly) to create, update and delete federations between containers on different cloud systems. In the most simplistic use case (Federated cloud is VISION Cloud, HTTP Basic Authentication, Credentials are provided), a federation is defined by the attributes illustrated in Figure 3. In the scenarios with background data transfer, such as backup or on-boarding, the federator reads the federation attributes and schedules data transfers with respect to attributes like current network or system load.

## Justification of the Approach

As already said, the main driver behind the technical architecture of the federation components are the requirements from the use case partners. The architecture fulfils all of the use case owners input that was discussed in the background chapter. We addressed the issue of interoperability and prevention of data lock-in by providing storage adapters and interfaces, which are based on the

CDMI standard. We have the possibility to use the framework in different scenarios to share, distribute and migrate data back and forth between cloud storage systems and we can provide a unified view on a tenants or users storage. The concepts behind VISION Cloud Federation allow companies to bridge private cloud installations to public cloud storages hosted at a different provider, while keeping control over the data. All of this is integrated into the whole VISION Cloud project where federation interacts with the Service Level Agreement (SLA), account management, billing and not to forget all security features (e.g., identity federation and access control) that are outcomes from other work packages. By using and extending CDMI for federated storage management, we push the work on standardization forward and deliver valuable input for the next generation of the CDMI Standard.

## CONCLUSION

We showed that research in federation and interoperability is essential for next generation storage clouds. Storage providers need federation technologies to transparently increase their amount of resources while consumers benefit from data lock in avoidance. Several different approaches

*Figure 3. Federation info JSON hash contents*

```
"federationinfo" : {
    //information about target cloud
    "eu.visioncloud_federation_target_cloud_URL" : "http://target.visioncloud.eu",
    "eu.visioncloud_federation_target_cloud_root_URI" : "/vision-cloud/object-service/",
    "eu.visioncloud_federation_target_cloud_type":"CDMI".
    "eu.visioncloud_federation_target_container_name":"oldContainer",
    "eu.visioncloud_federation_target_tenant":"MyCompany",
    //Credentials to access target cloud
    "eu.visioncloud_federation_target_cloud_auth_type": "HTTP Basic",
    "eu.visioncloud_federation_target_user":"onboarding_context_at_target_cloud",
    "eu.visioncloud_federation_target_password":"very_secret",
    //Unix Timestamp
    "eu.visioncloud_federation_generated_at":"131069017",
    //enable disable onboarding process
    "eu.visioncloud_federation_is_onboarding_enabled":"Enable|Disable"
}
```

to federation are possible starting with standardized cloud storage interfaces up to multi layered cloud architectures that manage data flow and data access in federated scenarios. Federation certainly is not a new topic and we can base our research scenarios on work that has been done in relational database management systems and grid computing environments. But the amount of data which we are dealing with today and the usage of more and more complex metadata structures lead to new requirements that are unsolved in distributed and federated systems. The defined federation scenarios for research within VISION Cloud are backed by industrial applications and will provide deep insights and architectural visions for future storage solutions. Since these scenarios are embedded in the VISION Cloud architecture as a whole also the integration of the outcomes into a working platform is secured.

# REFERENCES

Abu-libdeh, H., Princehouse, L., & Weatherspoon, H. (n.d.). *Racs: A case for cloud storage diversity.* Academic Press.

*Apache DeltaCloud.* (n.d.). Retrieved from http://deltacloud.apache.org/

*ApacheLibCloud.* (n.d.). Retrieved from http://libcloud.apache.org/

Buyya, R., Ranjan, R., & Calheiros, R. N. (2010). *Intercloud: Utility-oriented federation of cloud computing environments for scaling of application services.* CoRR, abs/1003.3920.

Cloudswitch. (2011, May). *CloudSwitch enterprise.* Retrieved from http://www.cloudswitch.com/page/enterprise-cloud -computing-product-overview Dell boomi

*Dell Press Releases.* (n.d.). Retrieved from http://content.dell.com/us/en/corp/d/press-releases/2011-10-25-dell-boomi-fall11-v5

Elmroth, E., & Larsson, L. (2009). Interfaces for placement, migration, and monitoring of virtual machines in federated clouds. In *Proceedings of the 2009 Eighth International Conference on Grid and Cooperative Computing* (pp. 253–260). Washington, DC: IEEE Computer Society. Retrieved from http://dx.doi.org/10.1109/GCC.2009.36

Elmroth, E., & Tordsson, J. (2005). An interoperable, standards-based grid resource broker and job submission service. In *Proceedings of the First International Conference on E-Science and Grid Computing* (pp. 212–220). Washington, DC: IEEE Computer Society. Retrieved from http://13portal.acm.org/citation.cfm?id=1107836.1107876

*IBM Cast Iron.* (n.d.). Retrieved from http://www-01.ibm.com/software/integration/cast-iron-cloud-integration/#

*Jclouds.* (n.d.). Retrieved from http://code.google.com/p/jclouds/

*RightScale Multi Cloud Platform.* (n.d.). Retrieved from http://www.rightscale.com/products/multicloud-platform.php

Rochwerger, B., Breitgand, D., Epstein, A., Hadas, D., Loy, I., Nagin, K., et al. (2011). Reservoir - When one cloud is not enough. *Computer, 44*, 44–51. Retrieved from http://dx.doi.org/10.1109/MC.2011.64 doi: http://dx.doi.org/10.1109/MC.2011.64

Rochwerger, B., Breitgand, D., Levy, E., Galis, A., Nagin, K., Llorente, I. M., et al. (2009). The reservoir model and architecture for open federated cloud computing. *IBM Journal of Reservoir Development, 53*, 535–545. Retrieved from http://portal.acm.org/citation.cfm?id=1850659.1850663

Sheth, A. P., & Larson, J. A. (1990). Federated database systems for managing distributed, heterogeneous, and autonomous databases. *ACM Computing Surveys, 22*, 183–236. doi:10.1145/96602.96604.

Silk, D. (2010). *CDMI and cloud federation.* Paper presented at the SNIA Storage Developer Conference. New York, NY.

*SMEStorage.* (n.d.). Retrieved from http://www.smestorage.com/

SNIA. (2010). *Managing private and hybrid clouds for data storage.* Retrieved from www.snia.org/forums/csi/Private-HybridCloudWhitePaper.pdf

Tordssona, J., Monterob, R. S., Moreno-Vozmedianob, R., & Llorente, I. M. (n.d.). *Optimized placement of a computational cluster across multiple clouds.* Academic Press.

## KEY TERMS AND DEFINITIONS

**CAPEX:** The expenditures creating future benefits.

**Federation:** Interworking of two or more otherwise autonomous and possibly heterogeneous systems.

**On-Boarding:** A process of moving customer data from one cloud storage provider to another.

**OPEX:** An ongoing cost for operating a system.

**TCO:** Total Cost of Ownership.

# Chapter 6
# SLA Management in Storage Clouds

**Nikoletta Mavrogeorgi**
*National Technical University of Athens, Greece*

**Spyridon V. Gogouvitis**
*National Technical University of Athens, Greece*

**Athanasios Voulodimos**
*National Technical University of Athens, Greece*

**Vasilios Alexandrou**
*National Technical University of Athens, Greece*

## ABSTRACT

*The need for online storage and backup of data constantly increases. Many domains, such as media, enterprises, healthcare, and telecommunications need to store large amounts of data and access them rapidly any time and from any geographic location. Storage Cloud environments satisfy these requirements and can therefore provide an adequate solution for these needs. Customers of Cloud environments do not need to own any hardware for storing their data or handle management tasks, such as backups, replication levels, etc. In order for customers to be willing to move their data to Cloud solutions, proper Service Level Agreements (SLAs) should be offered and guaranteed. SLA is a contract between the customer and the service provider, where the terms and conditions of the offered service are agreed upon. In this chapter, the authors present existing SLA schemas and SLA management mechanisms and compare various features that Cloud providers support with existing SLAs. Finally, they address the problem of managing SLAs in cloud computing environments exploiting the content term that concerns the stored objects, in order to provide more efficient capabilities to the customer.*

## OVERVIEW

The evolution of Internet provides a platform for using IT services. Many transactions are executed by Web services, such as data storage, online purchasing etc. Companies, media, and other fields need to store large amount of data, to retrieve data and/or to exchange data online from any geographic location anytime. The need of a formal contract for describing what functionalities are provided and under which terms (e.g. cost, conditions, obligations, etc.) is essential.

DOI: 10.4018/978-1-4666-3934-8.ch006

The document that captures that information is commonly referred as Service Level Agreement.

A Service Level Agreement (SLA) is an agreement between the provider and the consumer of the service that specifies the function performed by the service, the obligations on both the provider and the consumer, the agreed-upon constraints of performance (QoS) for the service, and how deviations are handled (exceptions and compensation). In this sense, an SLA is a contract between the participants in the service, which are typically the provider and the consumer, but can also include mediators or other actors that are stakeholders in the service lifecycle.

An SLA is made in some business context, which may include decisions made by each party leading up to the agreement, the presence of an endorser for the agreement and simply some prior conditions that make the terms of the agreement acceptable by both sides. An SLA is typically established before deploying a service and covers the whole lifecycle including execution and monitoring through decommissioning. However, it is also possible to form an SLA with an existing service, e.g. through a federation process orchestrated by an existing consumer that produces new interactions with other consumers. SLAs therefore have a huge influence on all aspects of the service, from as early as design time, to the infrastructure the service is deployed and executed on and the monitoring components that will be required for the provider to successfully offer a service. While many aspects of context following the creation of an SLA can be shared or agreed (e.g. roots of trust, expected QoS, etc.), some should not (e.g. no commercial service provider is likely to reveal their resource plan to a consumer).

Currently, cloud providers tend to use existing monitoring tools from other environments, such as Grid. The disadvantage is that these tools do not cover all the needs of the cloud environments. Most of them are restricted to locality and homogeneity of monitored objects, are not scalable, and do not support mapping of low-level resource metrics (e.g. uptime and downtime) to high-level applica-

tion SLA parameters (e.g. availability). What is more, current cloud storage providers offer SLAs (Amazon S3; Windows Azure; Nirvanix) that only guarantee service availability and they give service credit or refunds for lack of the agreed availability.

In the following sections, we will present some state-of-the-art scientific proposals for SLA schemas and mechanisms. Additionally, the features that are supported by the most known Cloud providers are analyzed. Finally, the proposed SLA Management in Cloud environments developed in VISION Cloud is presented.

# BACKGROUND

In this chapter, we consider SLA for storage cloud services which store and manage the data for customers by a third party.

The SLA is the service level agreement between the user and the service provider, where the level of a service is formally defined. Some of the elements that are defined in the SLAs are the parties involved, the contract date, the terms of agreement and the data cost. The properties that are used in the terms of agreement can be divided in functional and non-functional. The latter can contain quantitative (e.g. availability, durability, latency) and qualitative properties (e.g. adherence to safety properties and absence of deadlocks and livelocks). The quantitative properties are constrained through thresholds, commonly named as Service level objectives (SLOs).

A lot of research and protocols have been done as far as Service Level Agreements (SLA) and the SLA Management are concerned.

SLA schemas are XML schemas that represent the content of an SLA. Some existing approaches for SLA schemas and the corresponding languages to define service description terms are: WS-Agreement (Andrieux, et al., 2005), SLAng (Lamanna, et al.., 2003), WSLA (Keller & Ludwig, 2003), WSOL (Tosic, et al., 2003), and SWAPS (Oldham, et al., 2006).

However, weaknesses exist. SWAPS is quite complex and the implementation is not publicly available. WSLA and SLAng have not been developed further since 2009. Moreover, with SLAng one cannot define management information such as financial terms and WSLA has not formal definition of metrics semantics. WSOL lacks SLA related functionalities, such as the capture of the relationship between service provider and infrastructure provider.

The WS Agreement (Web Services Agreement) is a Web Services protocol for establishing agreement between two parties using an extensible XML language for specifying the nature of the agreement, and agreement templates to facilitate discovery of compatible agreement parties. It allows arbitrary term languages to be plugged-in for creating domain-specific service description terms.

Many European infrastructure projects address the question of SLA management, such as IRMOS, RESERVOIR, SLA@SOI, SOA4ALL and SLA4D-Grid. Most of them create SLAs based on WS-Agreement or a protocol close to WS-Agreements.

Some of the negotiation protocols are: discrete offer, invitation to treat and offer, multi-round negotiation, and auction-based negotiation. The multi-round negotiation protocol offers the flexibility in terms of negotiation to achieve SLAs between Service Provider and Infrastructure Provider. Moreover, this protocol is available as WS-Agreement Negotiation extension together with WS-Agreement.

There are two common challenges in this area (1) the requirements translation from high-level metrics to low-level requirements and vice versa and (2) the proactive violation detection. Many proposals have addressed these issues, but very little is applicable for cloud environments. For instance, GRIA SLAs (Boniface, et al., 2007) suggest a solution for avoiding violations but concerns only Grid environments.

Grid computing has been using SLAs for many years and much work has been done. However, in Cloud computing, which is an evolution of Grid computing, the work on SLAs is immature. Cloud providers offer some specific predefined SLAs with no many choices allowed to the customer. Most of them guarantee only for the availability as SLO. Therefore, more research should be done in order to provide SLAs that cover customers' needs in Cloud environments.

## Requirements

SLAs contain requirements that are agreed upon between the tenant and the provider. In this section, we present some basic requirements. We also examined thoroughly the requirements that the uses cases of VISION Cloud desire.

One important requirement is the throughput, which is a common requirement of all use cases, but at different granularity. Some requirements concern throughput aggregated in the level of tenant, whereas other concern the throughput per request.

Additionally, many non-functional requirements are desired, for instance the durability (and the availability. Also, constraints regarding the duration of the requests, i.e. the latency and the response time are desired. Latency is the time spent by a packet to travel from the cloud storage to the customer, whereas response time is measured from the instant when the user requests an object, to the time the system responds (e.g. starts transmitting the object). It is understood that Cloud providers cannot take responsibility over the Internet network latency, as this depends on customer's connectivity, but it should take care of the internal latency of the cloud.

Another aspect that comes out from the analysis of use cases requirements are security and privacy. Authorization, authentication, and guarantee of proper use are supported in VISION Cloud.

Geographic constraints are an additional requirement. A user determines in which regions he desires to store his data and which regions he forbids (black list).VISION Cloud ensures that objects of that user are stored in a datacenter located in a specific region obeying the above constraints.

All the requirements should be checked and be during the SLA lifecycle. VISION Cloud should be able to enforce SLAs or compensate to the tenant in case of violation. For SLA enforcement, the system should automatically monitor metrics of the stored objects and if the QoS falls below the level specified in the SLA, the necessary corrective actions should be performed.

Clouds also provide CRUD operations. An important capability in VISION Cloud is storlets. Storlets are executables which provide capabilities for supporting and improving the services that are offered to the tenants, such as data compression, file transformation in various formats etc. During the SLA negotiation, the SLA templates contain section for available storlets selection.

Finally, all these requirements are associated with billing rules. VISION Cloud charges the tenant for the services provided and, in case of violation, penalties are paid by the provider.

In Figure 1, essential requirements are displayed. The last column displays the related CDMI metadata field if it exists. CDMI (Cloud Data Management Interface (SNIA, 1997)) is a standard for managing cloud storage using RESTful HTTP requests.

## SLA Schema Approaches

In this section, we present some of the main specifications that are designed to describe the syntax of SLAs.

### WS-Agreement

The Web Services Agreement Specification (WS-Agreement) (Andrieux, et al., 2005) of the Open Grid Forum (OGF) describes a protocol for establishing an agreement on the usage of

Services between the provider and the consumer of a service. It defines a language and a protocol to represent the services of providers, create agreements based on offers and monitor agreement compliance during runtime. An agreement defines a dynamically established and dynamically managed relationship between two parties. The objective of such relationship is the provision and delivery of a service by one of the parties. In the agreement each party agrees on the respective roles, rights and obligations. Thus, in an agreement a provider offers a service according to the conditions described within it, while a consumer enters the agreement with the intention to obtain guarantees on the availability of one or more services offered by the provider. Agreements can also be negotiated by entities acting on behalf of the provider and/or the consumer. An agreement is created by the filling of an agreement template by the user. The schema for the agreement and the template is an extensible XML language.

The structure of a WS-Agreement consists of the following elements (Figure 2):

- **Name:** Contains the name of the agreement. It is an optional field.
- **Context:** Defines the meta-data for the agreement, such as the involved participants, the contract date, the template reference used and the termination time of the agreement.
- **Terms of Agreement:** Define the content of the agreement and a detailed description of the provided service(s). It consists of the service terms and the guarantee terms:
  - **Service Terms:** Contain data regarding the description of the service. It consists of the following terms:
    - **Service Description Terms:** Contain a functional description of the provided service.
    - **Service References:** Provide a way to refer to existing services within an agreement.

*Figure 1. Requirements table*

| requirement | description | unit | CDMI metadata field |
|---|---|---|---|
| availability | availability is the proportion of time a system is in a functioning condition. to be continuously available, every request received by a non-failing node in the system must result in a response. | % | |
| durability | the probability that the object will remain intact and accessible after a period of one year | % | |
| throughput | maximum data rate on retrieve, in bytes per second. The desired bandwidth to the primary copy of data, as measured from the edge of the cloud and factoring out any bandwidth capability between the client and the cloud | Mbps | cdmi_throughput |
| latency | maximum time to first byte, in milliseconds. The desired latency (in milliseconds) to the first byte of data in a primary copy, as measured from the edge of the cloud and factoring out any propagation latency between the client and the cloud | ms | cdmi_latency |
| response time | the time a system or functional unit takes to react to a given input. In other words, the maximum response time a service is permitted when handling user requests | ms | |
| access time (on reading /writing) | | ms | |
| redundancy | #copies. Contains the desired number of complete copies of the data object to be maintained. This number determines the minimum number of primary copies of the data that the cloud shall maintain. Additional primary copies may be made to satisfy demand for the value. | # replicas | cdmi_data_redundancy |
| data dispersion | distance (km) between the copies replicas. Contains the desired distance (km) between the infrastructures supporting the multiple copies of data. This metadata is used to separate the (cdmi_infrastructure_redundancy number of) infrastructures by a minimum geographic distance to prevent data loss due to site disasters. | km | cdmi_data_dispersion |
| geographic constraints | regions where the object is permitted or not permitted to be stored.data is physically stored in a given region | | cdmi_geographic_placement |
| jitter | variations in node to node i.e., variance of latency between network packages of a video stream) | ms | |
| reliability | consist of availability guarantees over a period of time. The ability of a system or component to perform its required functions under stated conditions for a specified period of time. (reliability parameters: MTBF,FITS (=failures in a billion hours),MTTR,availability, downtime) | % | |
| mean time between failures (MTBF) | is the predicted elapsed time between inherent failures of a system during operation | ms | |
| mean time to recovery/repair (MTTR) | the average time that a device will take to recover from any failure | ms | |
| RPO (recovery point objective) | the largest acceptable duration in time between an update and when the update may be recovered, specified in seconds. This is used to indicate the desired backup frequency from the primary copy(s) of the data to the secondary copy(s). It is the maximum acceptable duration between a write to the primary copy and the backup to the secondary copy during which a failure of the primary copy(s) shall result in data loss. | sec | cdmi_RPO |
| RTO (recovery time objective) | Contains the largest acceptable duration in time to restore data, specified in seconds. This metadata is used to indicate the desired maximum acceptable duration to restore the primary copy(s) of the data from a secondary backup copy(s). | sec | cdmi_RTO |
| data loss | an error condition in which information is destroyed by failures or neglect in storage, transmission, or processing | % | |
| retention (id) | Contains a user-specified retention identifier. it is used to tag a given object as being managed by a specific retention policy | | cdmi_retention_id |
| retention (period) | Contains an ISO 8601:2004 time interval during which the object is under retention | | cdmi_retention_period |
| retention (autodelete) | It is used to indicate if the object is to be automatically deleted when retention expires. | | cdmi_retention_autodelete |
| throttling | measure to regulate network traffic and minimize bandwidth congestion. It wowrks by limiting (throttling) the rate at which a bandwidth intensive device (a server) accepts data. If this limit is not in place, the device can overload its processing capacity. | | |
| privacy | data will be not unduly accessed by actors internal or external to VISION Cloud | | |
| encryption | the server shall encrypt the object using the encryption algorithm and key length specified | | cdmi_encryption |

*Figure 2. WS-agreement: SLA elements (Andrieux, et al., 2005)*

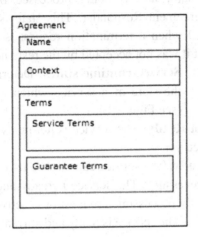

- **Service Properties:** Contain measurable properties related to the provided service(s). These properties are used at the guarantee terms definition.
  ○ **Guarantee Terms:** Include the service guarantees, that is, the Service Level Objectives (SLOs) that should be followed in this agreement and under which conditions these guarantees should be valid. It also contains information regarding the violations and the penalties that the provider is obliged to pay It consists of the following elements:
    - **Service Scope:** Determines which services concern this guarantee term.
    - **Qualifying Condition:** determines the preconditions that must be fulfilled before a guarantee applies.
    - **Service Level Objective (SLO):** Defines the targets for Key Performance Indicators (KPIs) which are measurable properties associated to the provided service(s) and described

in the service properties of the element service terms. These targets must be met in order to provide a service with a particular service level or with a particular Quality of Service (QoS). During the SLA lifecycle, the actual QoS properties are computed by the monitoring system. The SLOs contain the logical expression of the agreed QoS properties with the actual ones in order to determine the fulfillment of a guarantee. The WS-Agreement Specification allows the usage of any domain specific or standard condition expression language to define SLOs.

- **Business Value List:** Specifies the strength and the importance of the guarantee, customer preferences and the penalty that the provider is obliged to pay in case that an assurance is not met.

The agreement template contains the aforementioned elements having also optionally the agreement creation constraints. This element contains constraints on possible values of terms for creating an agreement. It is permitted to set the valid ranges or distinct values that the terms may take.

An agreement creation process usually consists of the following steps:

- The initiator retrieves the available agreement templates that advertise the types of offers the responder is willing to accept.
- The initiator chooses a template from the responder that better fits to him.
- The initiator then makes an offer, which is either accepted or rejected by the responder.

The WS-Agreement, in order to check if the agreement is met, has defined states in three sections. The accepted states transitions are displayed in the corresponding states graphs.

- **Agreement states**: Concern the states of the whole agreement which are the following (see Figure 3):
- **Pending:** An Agreement offer has been made but it has been neither accepted nor rejected.
- **Observed:** An Agreement offer has been made and accepted.
- **Rejected:** An Agreement offer has been made and rejected.
- **Complete:** An Agreement offer has been received and accepted.
- **Terminated:** An Agreement offer has been terminated by the Agreement Initiator and the obligation no longer exists.
- **Pending and Terminating:** An Agreement offer has been made and it has not been accepted or rejected. Furthermore a Terminate operation has been issued by the Agreement Initiator and is being processed. This state is realized when a termination request is made but it was not accepted by the responder.
- **Observed and Terminating:** An Agreement offer has been made and accepted. Furthermore, a Terminate opera-

tion has been issued from the Agreement Initiator and is being processed by the Agreement Responder. This state is realized when a termination request is made but it was not accepted by the responder.

- ○ **Service runtime states:** Determines the state of a service which can be (see Figure 4):
- **Not Ready:** The service is not ready to be used yet.
- **Ready:** The service can now be used
- **Processing:** The service is ready and currently processing a request or is active.
- **Idle:** The service is ready and currently not being used.
- **Completed:** The service is completed and cannot be used anymore.
- ○ **Guarantee states:** Describes the fulfillment of a guarantee and the states are (see Figure 5):

- **Fulfilled:** The guarantee is fulfilled.
- **Violated:** The guarantee is violated.
- **NotDetermined:** No activity regarding this guarantee has happened yet or is currently happening that allows evaluating whether the guarantee is met.

*Figure 3. WS-agreement: agreement states (Andrieux, et al., 2005)*

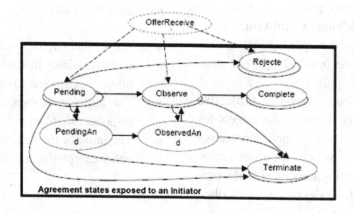

*Figure 4. WS-agreement: service states (Andrieux, et al., 2005)*

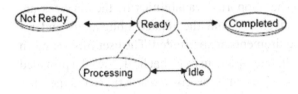

*Figure 5. WS-agreement: guarantee states (Andrieux, et al., 2005)*

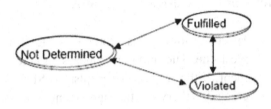

## Web Service Level Agreement (WSLA)

WSLA (Keller & Ludwig, 2003) is a framework developed by IBM which addresses SLA management issues for Web Services and it is mainly focused on the SLAs definition and the monitoring (Seidel, et al., 2007; Dan, et al., 2002; WSLA documents). This framework monitors the QoS parameters of a Web Service, checks the SLOs and reports violations to the concerned parties. WSLA provides a language, based on XML schema, which permits to specify SLAs, their parameters and the way they are measured. The runtime architecture consists of several SLA monitoring services. These monitoring services are automatically configured to enforce an SLA upon receipt and they may be outsourced to third supporting parties, fact that ensures a maximum of objectivity. The SLA management life cycle of WSLA consists of five distinct stages:

1. **Negotiation/Establishment:** In this stage an agreement between the provider and the consumer of a service is arranged and signed. An SLA document is generated.

2. **SLA Deployment:** The SLA document of the previous stage is validated and distributed to the involved components and parties.

3. **Measurement and Reporting:** In this stage, the SLA parameters are computed by retrieving resource metrics from the managed resources and the measured SLA parameters are compared against the guarantees defined in the SLA.

4. **Corrective Management Actions:** If an SLO has been violated, corrective actions are carried out. These actions range from opening a trouble ticket to automatically communicate with the management system to solve potential performance problems. Before any actions involving the managed system are taken, the Business Entity of the service provider is consulted to verify if the proposed actions are allowable.

5. **SLA Termination:** The parties of an SLA can negotiate the termination the same way the establishment is done. Alternatively, an expiration date can be specified in the SLA.

## SLAng (SLA Notification Generation)

The SLAng (Lamanna, et al., 2003) provides a language, which addresses the specification of contractual relationships between customers and application service providers. The supported SLAs define the responsibilities of each party with respect to non-functional properties. The SLAng language permits to describe the QoS properties based on which the SLAs are created. This language may be used as input for automated reasoning systems or QoS-aware adaptive middleware.

SLAng introduces a reference model for inter-organizational service provision at storage, network, middleware, and application level for distributed component architecture. Figure 6 depicts the reference model.

This traditional layered architecture points out that service provisioning could occur at any level of the architecture and different parties could provide or consume services. SLAng defines six different types of SLAs: four vertical and three horizontal. These concern all the possible agreements that can exist between the different kinds of parties of this architecture and are depicted in Figure 7. The horizontal ones concern interaction between same type of providers, whereas the vertical ones concern interactions between subordinated pairs.

This cross-layered architecture considers all the cases of interactions between the actors taking a share in an e-business model.

The primary shortcoming of these approaches is that they do not provide dynamic negotiation, and various types of cloud consumers need a different structure of implementation of SLAs to integrate their own business rules with the guarantees that are presented in the targeted SLA (Alhamad, Dillon & Chang, April 2010).

## SLA Negotiation

The SLA negotiation is the mechanism where the customer negotiates the quality of the provided service and which concludes to an SLA creation in case that both involved parties agree. The SLA negotiation is realized using agreement templates. The supported capabilities of the services are advertised and the related obligations and requirements are presented. The user fills the given SLA template in case that he desires the provided services with the given restrictions and the SLA is created. Otherwise, he negotiates with different requirements until both parties agree. The remainder of the section presents the existing protocols for the negotiation of SLA.

- **Discrete offer:** This protocol is the simplest one. The initiator proposes an agreement. If the responder accepts, the SLA is created, otherwise the agreement is cancelled. For convenience, the responder may provide templates to the initiator by which the initiator can create his proposals.
- **Invitation to treat and offer:** This is another one-phase negotiation protocol. This protocol permits to request pricing for imminent SLAs. This pricing is not bounding.
- **Multi-round negotiation:** In the multi-round negotiation protocol, the user creates

*Figure 6. Service provision reference model (Lamanna, et al., 2003)*

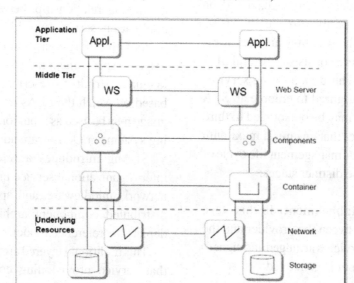

*Figure 7. SLAng: SLA types*

| category | SLA type | pairs | | |
|---|---|---|---|---|
| vertical | application | web services | components | |
| | hosting | service provider | host | |
| | persistence | host | storage service provider | |
| | communication | container | network service provider | |
| horizontal | service | component and web service providers | | |
| | container | containers providers | | |
| | networking | network providers | | |

quote for an SLA template and asks from the provider to accept this quote or to suggest a new one. In any case, these quotes are not binding. If both parties agree then an SLA can be created. The user can request quotes from different providers in order to compare and choose the best fitted for him. This protocol is not supported from WS-Agreement, but it is examined at the WS-Agreement Negotiation

- **Auction-based**: This protocol permits the pricing negotiation when the other parameters are fixed. There are variants of this protocol:
  - **English Auction:** In this protocol, the initial price is low and it is raised. The last binding wins.
  - **Dutch Auction:** In this protocol, the initial price is high and it is lowered until the customer to accept this price. This is the opposite of the English Auction
  - **Vickrey Auction:** In this protocol, the initial price is low and it is raised. The last pricing wins. The winner pays the second highest quote. This protocol forces the bidders to give true value quotes.

## WS-Agreement Negotiation

WS-Agreement Negotiation, which sits on top of WS-Agreement, describes the re/negotiation of agreements. The WS-Agreement Specification allows the usage of any domain specific or standard condition expression language to define SLOs. The specification of domain-specific term languages is explicitly left open (Andrieux, et al., 2005; Seidel, et al., 2007).

WS-Agreement supports a one-phase negotiation where the negotiating capabilities are very limited. For this reason the WS-Agreement Negotiation was designed which supports advanced features regarding the negotiation. The negotiation is dynamic and,, renegotiation and negotiation in multiple round are supported. For instance, WS-Agreement Negotiation supports the negotiation of a service provisioning time in co-allocation scenarios, the renegotiation of existing agreements in order to cope with peaks in a service usage, and the negotiation of related service parameters such as the resources number and the pricing of a provided service.

During the negotiation, the negotiation participants exchange negotiation offers for determining their negotiation goals and requirements. A negotiation offer is a non-binding proposal for a potential agreement that one negotiation participant makes to another. The offer describes the desired service and its quality in terms of guarantees. During renegotiation, most of the times, the new offer that is created is based on a previous one and it is called Negotiation counter offer.

The WS-Agreement Negotiation is conjunct with WS-Agreement. The agreement offer created by the WS-Agreement Negotiation can be used as input in the agreement creation at the WS-Agreement.

The schema of an SLA offer is similar with the SLA template schema of the WS-Agreement, It contains a context, service terms and guarantee terms as the WS-Agreement, but it has additionally the negotiation constraints. The negotiation constraints provide a method for the negotiation process and are used to express the desired requirements of the parties by defining structure and value spaces for negotiation counter offers. The negotiation context apart from the data that were described at the WS-Agreement contains metadata regarding the negotiation, such as if the negotiation concerns a new agreement or renegotiation of existing agreement, the negotiation round, the expiration time, the id of the offer etc..

The WS-Agreement Negotiation model consists of three layers: the negotiation layer, the agreement layer and the service layer.

- **Negotiation layer:** This layer sits on top of the agreement layer and provides a protocol and a language to negotiate agreement offers and to create agreements based on negotiated offers. In this layer is realized the exchange of the negotiation offers.
- **Agreement layer:** This layer provides the basic functionality to create and monitor agreements.
- **Service layer:** At this layer the agreed services are provided. These services are governed by the agreement layer.

A negotiation offer has states that are related to its life cycle. The negotiation offer state contain data that can be used by the negotiating participants to exchange information related to the offer life cycle, and advance the negotiation process in an efficient way. Figure 8 depicts the possible states of a negotiated offer and their valid transitions.

- **Advisory State:** This state concerns negotiation offers with no further obligations associated and which need further negotiation.
- **Solicited State:** This state indicates that a negotiation party wants to start a negotiation process. The requirement is that the counter offers are either in the acceptable state or the rejected one.
- **Acceptable State:** This state indicates that a negotiation party accepts a negotiation offer as is and no further negotiation is required. As the negotiated offers are non-binding, there is no guarantee that an agreement will be created.
- **Rejected State:** This state indicates that a negotiation offer is rejected. In this case, the rejected offer is sent back to the inquiring party associated optionally with the reason of the rejection.

*Figure 8. States of negotiation offers (Seidel, et al., 2007)*

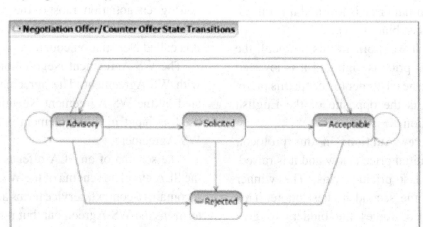

## WSAG4J Framework

The WS-Agreement for Java (WSAG4J) (Waldrich) framework is the most advanced implementation of the WS-Agreement. It provides operations regarding the SLAs in distributed systems. There are implemented domain independent operations that permit an automatic SLA Management, such as template publishing, SLA offer validation, SLA creation, monitoring the agreements runtime states and agreement guarantee evaluation and accounting.

The WSAG4J framework contains the agreement factory, which is responsible for the agreement creation and is depicted in Figure 9.

The main tasks of the agreement factory are the template processing, the offer validation, the service instantiation and the agreement creation. The interface provides services for getting the supported SLA templates and for creating agreements based on incoming offers.

Regarding the agreement creation, a client gets the lists of the supported templates and makes an agreement offer using the desired template. The template, as it follows the WS-Agreement standard, contains a template name, a context and the agreement terms, but also includes information on agreement creation constraints to describe a range of agreements it might accept.

Finally, the WSAG4J uses digital signatures to enforce message integrity (WS-Security) and provides the listing of existing agreements via WS-Service Groups.

## SLAs for Cloud Computing

In this section we describe researches that have been done in Cloud Environments regarding the SLAs.

In (Alhamad, Dillon & Chang, 2010) the authors describe different SLA parameters for four types of services that can be offered in Cloud Computing environments, i.e. infrastructure as a service, platform as a service, software as a service, and storage as a service. For example, the parameters for data storage service metrics

*Figure 9. WSAG4J agreement factory (Waldrich, n.d.)*

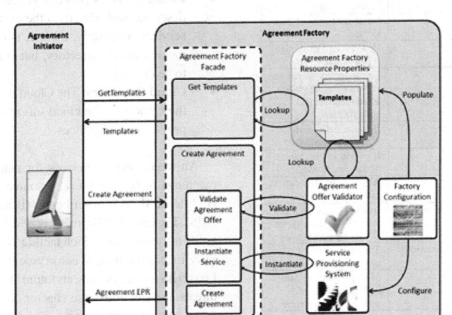

(Figure 10) are basic requirements for negotiation with storage providers.

The same authors go one step further to propose an architecture and a protocol for an SLA-based trust model for Cloud Computing (Alhamad, Dillon, & Chang, 2010). The constituent components of the proposed architecture are depicted in Figure 11 and are described in the following:

- **SLA Agent:** An SLA agent is an intermediary agent between consumers and cloud providers and it is used for the execution of the following operations:
  - Grouping cloud consumers according to different classes based on business needs.
  - Designing SLA metrics based on the consumers' needs.
  - Negotiating with cloud providers.

*Figure 10. SLA metrics for storage as a service*

| Parameter | Description |
|---|---|
| Geographic location | Availability zones in which data are stored |
| Scalability | Ability to increase or decrease storage space |
| Storage space | Number of units of data storage |
| Storage billing | How the cost of storage is calculated |
| Security | Cryptography for storage and transferring of data, authentication, and authorization |
| Privacy | How the data will be stored and transferred |
| Backup | How and where images of data are stored |
| Recovery | Ability to recover data in disasters or failures |
| System throughput | Amount of data that can be retrieved from system in specific unit of time |
| Transferring bandwidth | The capacity of communication channels |
| Data life cycle management | Managing data in data centres, and use of network infrastructure |

- Selecting cloud providers based on non-functional requirements.
- Monitoring business activities for consumers.
- Monitoring SLA parameters.
- **Cloud Consumer Model:** This model is responsible for the request of the external services execution. There are pricing models by which the user bill is evaluated in case of completed services execution. This model contains the following elements:
  - **Trust management model:** This model is responsible for the management of the trust relationships between the cloud providers and the users. For this management, it requires 1) the local experiences with cloud providers and users, 2) the opinions of external cloud services and 3 the reports of the SLA agent.
  - **Business activities management:** This model is responsible for the business activities and determines the responsibilities for the profits and the violations.
- **Cloud Services Directory:** This directory describes and advertises the existing cloud services. Currently, there is not an implemented public directory, but it is planned to be created.
- **Cloud Providers:** The Cloud providers are the owners of the cloud infrastructure and provide cloud services.

An interesting framework for managing the mappings of the Low-level resource metrics to High-level SLAs is described in (Brandic, et al., 2010). The LoM2HiS framework is embedded into FoSII infrastructure, which facilitates autonomic SLA management and enforcement. Thus, the LoM2HiS framework detects future SLA violation threats and can notify the enactor component to act so as to avert the threats.

*Figure 11. SLA-based trust model for cloud computing (Alhamad, Dillon, & Chang, 2010)*

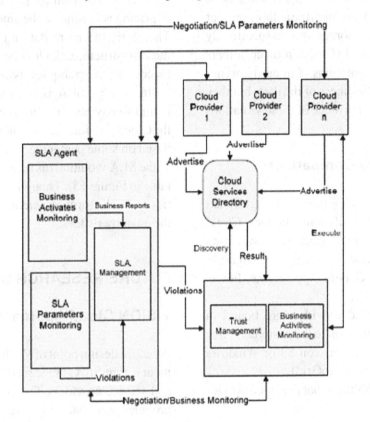

The LAYSI framework (Brandic, et al., 2010) provides a new approach for sla violation detection. It supports two kinds of monitors sensors, the host monitor, and the runtime monitor sensor. The former monitors data and the latter senses future SLA violation threat based on resource usage experiences and predefined threat thresholds.

Another novel approach for mapping low-level resource metrics to SLA parameters necessary for the identification of failure sources is presented in (Emeakaroha, et al., 2010). The authors devise a layered cloud architecture for the bottom-up propagation of failures to the layer, which can react to sensed SLA violation threats. They also present a communication model for the propagation of SLA violation threats to the appropriate layer of the cloud infrastructure, which includes negotiators, brokers, and automatic service deployer.

In DesVi (Vincent, et al., 2011), another architecture is proposed for preventing SLA violations. The proactive violation detection takes into consideration resource usage experiences and historical data. The detection is realized based on a knowledge database and Case-Based Reasoning (CBR) (Maurer, et al., 2010). CBR is the process of solving problems based on past experience. The main steps of this process are:

- Retrieving the most similar cases.
- Reusing the information and knowledge in the similar cases to solve the problem.
- Revising the proposed solution.
- Update knowledge database.

The needed requirements translation is realized using the aforementioned LoM2HiS framework.

Finally, the lack of security support is addressed in (Popa, et al., 2011), in which the authors present CloudProof, a secure storage system specifically designed for the cloud. In CloudProof, customers can not only detect violations of integrity, write-serializability, and freshness of the data, but they can also prove the occurrence of these violations to a third party.

## Cloud Providers Comparison

In the tables depicted in Figures 12-14 significant commercial offerings of some famous Cloud providers (e.g. Amazon S3, Rackspace, Windows Azure, etc.) are compared (Amazon S3; Windows Azure; Rackspace; Google App Engine; Force.com; GoGrid; Harris).

Most of the Cloud providers are bound in availability as commitment to the customer. They start from 99.9% (e.g. Amazon S3 or Windows Azure) up to 100% (e.g. GoGrid).

Some of the capabilities that the cloud providers support are:

- **Data centers selection:** A customer can choose the geographic locations for storing the data from a list of datacenters supported by the providers.
- Support (free or not and some provide and maximum response time).
- Free charge for the initial usage (for some amount of data and/or for some period), trial editions, etc.

Regarding the pricing of using cloud storage, this is calculated in multiple ways (see Figure 14). Most of providers charge the customer according to the amount of the stored data, the number of the requests (PUT, GET, DELETE, etc.) that they execute and the data transferred (based on the region that they transfer the data and on the amount of the transferred data). Some providers charge the customer according to the amount of data that they use (e.g. Rackspace), whereas oth-

ers such as Amazon S3 provide different levels of pricing according to the amount of data stored. Therefore, the more data a customer stores on the infrastructure, the less he has to pay per GB (according to pricing levels).

In case an SLA is not met, the provider is bound to pay penalties to the customer. Most of the Cloud providers reduce the customer's charges based on some percentages according to the type of the SLA violation (as it can be concluded from table in Figure 15). Though, the provider's penalties are in the form of a credit and will not exceed the customer's fees.

## FUTURE RESEARCH DIRECTIONS

## VISION Cloud Approach

A central design point of VISION Cloud management is that SLAs are signed between customers and service providers. Our proposed framework provides automated SLA Management using an SLA schema enriched with content terms.

The SLA schema is the schema that represents an SLA. It defines what data can be contained in an SLA (e.g. cost, contract dates, user requirements, fines, etc) and in which format. The SLA has a unique identifier. The language that is used for the SLA schema is XSD (XML Schema Document). Based on this schema, the SLA Management handles its responsibilities.

An SLA's lifecycle can be divided into two main steps, namely SLA negotiation, where the QoS requirements of the customer as well as associated cost and penalties are defined and SLA enforcement, where the platform is responsible for adhering to the requirements set.

The main operations of the SLA Management component in VISION Cloud are:

- SLA negotiation.
- SLA templates creation.

*Figure 12. Cloud providers comparison (1)*

| | maximum limits | SLA availability | support pricing policy |
|---|---|---|---|
| **Amazon AWS** | • Amazon S3 - Store object up to 5 TB<br>• Amazon EC2 - Elastic Block storage volume sizes: 1GB-1TB<br>• (20 TB/account limit while in beta) | • Amazon S3: available with Monthly Uptime ≤ 99.9% per monthly billing cycle<br>• Amazon EC2: available with Annual Uptime ≤ 99.95% per Service Year | Premium Support - Silver and Gold support available and are charged accordingly |
| **Rackspace** | Infinite scalability | • 100% Network Uptime Guarantee<br>• 1-Hour Hardware Replacement<br>• 2-Hour Commencement of Onsite Data Restores | 24x7x365 Live Support & Expertise [Pricing details not mentioned in the website] |
| **Google App Engine** | • Automatic scaling is built in with App Engine<br><br>• No matter how many users you have or how much data your application stores, App Engine can scale to meet your needs | 99.95% available (monthly) | Free Support is available 24x7x365 from on-site cloud hosting experts |
| **Windows Azure** | Azure has a 64MB limit on individual blobs and also allows you to split a blob into blocks of 4MB each | 99.9% uptime | Support is charged per incident basis. (or utilize support incidents from existing programs e.g. MSDN, MPN). |
| **Force.com** | In the unlimited edition,<br>• Number of sites - 25 [Features available more for additional fee]<br>• 2,000 Database objects total<br>• storage:120MB/user<br>• API calls/day: 5,000/user, 5 million total<br>• Page views/month: 1,000,000 [Features with rolling 24-hour time period]<br>• Sites bandwidth/day - 40GB<br>• Sites page generation time/day [Rolling 24-hour time period] - 60 server hours | 99.9+ % uptime | Basic Support, Premier Support, Premier Support with Administration. Developer Support is only available for a fee, on a per-case basis |
| **GoGrid** | • Horizontal server scaling: rapidly deploy new servers to meet sudden spikes in demand. Delete the servers when demand drops, paying only for the resources used.<br>• Vertical server scaling: scale RAM by deploying a GSI to a new server with a higher RAM allotment and then deleting the old server.<br>• Server parking: bundle and park a server for $0.15 – $3.00/month. | 100% Uptime:<br>• network outage: none<br>• packet loss < 0.1%<br>• latency < 5ms<br>• jitter < 0.5ms<br>• maximum jitter: 10 msec in 15-minutes | • FREE 24/7 Phone Support<br>• Free 24/7 Premium Support |

- Configuration of the other components when a new SLA is created.
  ○ Creating policies that should be checked during the SLA lifecycle.
  ○ Sending the parameters to be monitored to the Monitoring component.
  ○ Informing Accounting and Billing of the new SLA and its related cost.
  ○ etc.
- Proactive SLA violation detection and handling.

VISION Cloud supports dynamic SLAs, as the SLA templates are generated according to the current supplies. VISION Cloud templates permit the user to choose from a variety of requirements his desired SLOs and they are not restricted to the availability as the most of the current Cloud providers. Apart from the measured requirements such as throughput, latency, durability etc, there are supported geographic constraints where the user can determine in which regions he prefers to store his data and in which ones he doesn't allow

*Figure 13. Cloud providers comparison (2)*

| | support response time | data centers | new user trial credentials |
|---|---|---|---|
| **Amazon AWS** | Severity level vs response time<br>• Urgent: 1 hour<br>• High : 4 business hours<br>• Normal:1 business day<br>• Low: 2 business days | 8 regions: US East (Northern Virginia), US West (Oregon), US West (Northern California), EU (Ireland), Asia Pacific (Singapore), Asia Pacific (Tokyo), South America (Sao Paulo), and AWS GovCloud. | free:<br>Amazon S3<br>• 5 GB of Amazon S3 storage<br>• 20,000 Get Requests<br>• 2,000 Put Requests<br>• 15GB of data transfer out each month for one year<br><br>Amazon EC2<br>• 750 hours of EC2 running Linux/Unix Micro instance usage<br>• 750 hours of EC2 running Microsoft Windows Server Micro instance usage<br>• 750 hours of Elastic Load Balancing plus 15 GB data processing<br>• 30 GB of Amazon Elastic Block Storage (EBS) plus 2 million IOs and 1 GB snapshot storage<br>• 15 GB of bandwidth out aggregated across all AWS services<br>• 1 GB of Regional Data Transfer |
| **Rackspace** | 24 x 7 x 365 online live chat and toll free phone support backed by Fanatical Support | USA(TX,IL,VA)., UK, Hong Kong | - |
| **Google App Engine** | - | | An efficient application on a free account can use up to 500MB of storage and up to 5 million page views a month |
| **Windows Azure** | - | zone 1:North Europe, Western Europe, East US, North Central U,S South Central US, West US, zone 2: East Asia, Southeast Asia | • During Community Technology Preview: services without charge (subject to certain limits).<br>• For commercial use: priced through consumption and offers.<br>• 90 days free trial |
| **Force.com** | Support type vs response time<br>• Basic Support: 2 business days<br>• Premier Support: 2 hours<br>• Premier Support with Administration: 2 hours | | Force.com free edition |
| **GoGrid** | Emergency cases:30min<br>• Server down<br>• Packet loss<br>• Routing issue<br>All other cases: 120min | San Francisco, Virginia, Amsterdam | • Included free with every account.<br>• f5 Hardware Load Balancing<br>• 10GB of Cloud Storage per month<br>• Unlimited inbound Data Transfer<br>• 24/7 Premium Support |

to store them. Also, during the SLA negotiation the user can choose if he desires to permit federation in the future and if so he can choose specific Cloud providers.

During the SLA lifecycle, the SLA Management framework checks if the SLA requirements are met. It computes policies for checking the SLOs and detecting proactively SLA violations based on analysis of the monitored data and forecasts. In case that an imminent violation is detected, corrective actions are taken and reconfiguration is realized. If an SLA violation occurs, then the Cloud provider is obliged to pay penalty to the user according to the signed SLAs.

## Justification of the Approach

As it can be deduced by examining the state of the art in SLA schemas concerning Web service provision in general, as well as cloud storage in

*Figure 14. Cloud providers comparison: pricing*

**pricing**

**Amazon**

| Storage Pricing | Standard Storage | Reduced Redundancy Storage | Request Pricing | | Data Transfer Pricing | |
|---|---|---|---|---|---|---|
| First 1 TB/month | $0.125/GB | $0.093/GB | request type | pricing | Data Transfer IN | |
| Next 49 TB/month | $0.110/GB | $0.083/GB | PUT, COPY, POST, LIST | $0.01/ 1,000 requests | All data transfer in | $0.000/GB |
| Next 450 TB/month | $0.095/GB | $0.073/GB | | | Data Transfer OUT | |
| Next 500 TB/month | $0.090/GB | $0.063/GB | GET and all other | $0.01/10,000 requests | First 1 GB/month | $0.000/GB |
| Next 4000 TB/month | $0.080/GB | $0.053/GB | | | Up to 10 | $0.120/GB |
| Over 5000 TB/month | $0.055/GB | $0.037/GB | DELETE | 0 | Next 40 TB/month | $0.090/GB |
| | | | | | Next 100 TB/month | $0.070/GB |
| | | | | | Next 350 TB/month | $0.050/GB |
| | | | | | Next 524 TB/month | Contact |

**Windows Azure**

| Storage Pricing | Geographically Redundant | Locally Redundant | Storage Transactions | Price | Data Transfer Pricing | | |
|---|---|---|---|---|---|---|---|
| First 1 TB/month | $0.125/GB | $0.093/GB | 100,000 | $0.01/100,000 | inbound data trasfe free | | |
| Next 49 TB/month | $0.11/GB | $0.083/GB | | | Transfer Outbound | Zone 1 | Zone 2 |
| Next 450 TB/month | $0.095/GB | $0.073/GB | | | First 10 TB/month | $0.12/GB | $0.19/GB |
| Next 500 TB/month | $0.09/GB | $0.063/GB | | | Next 40 TB/month | $0.09/GB | $0.15/GB |
| Next 4,000 TB/month | $0.08/GB | $0.053/GB | | | Next 100 TB/month | $0.07/GB | $0.13/GB |
| Next 4,000 TB/month | $0.055/GB | $0.037/GB | | | Next 350 TB/month | $0.05/GB | $0.12/GB |
| Over 9,000 TB/month | Contact | Contact | | | > 500 TB/month | Contact | Contact |

**Rackspace**

| Pricing | |
|---|---|
| Unlimited Files and Media Storage | 7p/GB |
| Outgoing Bandwidth | 12p/GB |
| Incoming Bandwidth | Free |
| PUT, POST, LIST Requests | Free |
| HEAD, GET, DELETE Requests | Free |

**Google App Engine**

| Hosting | Free quota/app/day | Pricing if you exceed your free quota |
|---|---|---|
| On-demand Frontend Instances | 28 instance hours | $0.08 / hour |
| Reserved Frontend Instances | | $0.05 / hour |
| High Replication Datastore | 1G | $0.24/G/month |
| Outgoing Bandwidth | 1G | $0.12 / G |
| Incoming Bandwidth | 1G | Free |
| Datastore API | 50k read/write/small | $0.10/100k write |
| | | $0.07/100k read |
| | | $0.01/100k small |

particular, current SLA schemas tend to be focused on service provision, storage resources, capacity, and service availability. These are indeed some of the core elements involved and VISION Cloud will define and specify models for storage resource and service characteristics, models for attributing the usage and utilization of storage resources and services to applications, metadata to express storage service requirements for applications running over the VISION storage cloud, and SLA definitions. However, the novelty introduced by VISION Cloud is allowing these models, requirements and

*Figure 15. Penalties in case of SLA violation*

| Amazon AWS | | Rackspace | | Google App Engine | | Windows Azure | | GoGrid |
|---|---|---|---|---|---|---|---|---|
| Amazon S3 | | available time | credit amount | availability (monthly) | credited % of future bill | uptime | credit | violation => 10% SC |
| availability (monthly) | service credit | 100% - 99.9% | 0% | 99–99.95% | 10% | compute connectivity < 99.95% uptime | 10% | "10 % Service Credit (SC)" is a credit equivalent to 100 times Customer's fees for the impacted Service feature for the duration of the Failure |
| | | 99.89% - 99.5% | 10% | 95-99% | 25% | | | |
| | | 99.49% - 99.0% | 25% | < 95% | 50% | role instance uptime or storage < 99.9% uptime | 10% | |
| | | 98.99% - 98.0% | 40% | | | | | |
| 99-99.9% | 10% | 97.99% - 97.5% | 55% | not exceed 50% of the amount | | availability< 99% | 25% | |
| < 99% | 25% | 97.49% - 97.0% | 70% | | | availability: 99-99.9% | 10% | |
| | | 96.99% - 96.5% | 85% | | | | | |
| Amazon EC2 | | < 96.5% | 100% | Customer Must Request Financial Credit within 30 days | | | | |
| availability (annualy) | service credit | 5% of the fees (up to 100%) for each : • 30' network downtime • 30' infrastructure downtime • additional hour of downtime • additional hour of downtime | | | | | | |
| <99.5% | 10% | | | | | | | |

SLA schemas to be expressed not only on storage resources and services, but also on the content descriptions for the underlying storage objects, in support of content centric storage. Therefore, the SLA frameworks that currently only deal with typical terms included in the SLAs such as cost, availability, performance etc., will be extended to address content-related information. In order to implement an advanced SLA framework that takes into consideration the stored content and realizes the Content-Centric Access to Storage innovation of VISION Cloud, it is essential to advance current SLA specifications. Thus, we will research on expressive SLA specification that will be rich-enough to contain content-related terms (e.g. different content types in an SLA may be linked with different pricing models and performance estimation for data transfer). The content tagging will be explored in order to include the necessary information in the proposed SLA schemas and linked with SLA terms. These are of major importance and closely coupled with the SLA Enforcement Framework of VISION Cloud since new SLA and Term Containers will be implemented by taking into consideration the content-related SLA terms during the SLA life-cycle. To this direction, we will analyze and design SLA and Terms schemas as well as implement them along with the corresponding containers.

Furthermore, emphasis will be given to proactive SLA violation detection. Work will be carried out on specifying what monitoring data and analysis (e.g. trends, patterns) of them should require the SLA Management framework. The SLA Management framework needs the mapping of high-level application parameters with the low-level hardware metrics in order to create policies for detecting proactively SLA violations.

Models and patterns will be studied to automate the definition and determine the parameters that need to be monitored and analyzed based on the SLA terms on a dynamic way. Research on monitoring and SLA schemas and management will thus have to interact, so as to work towards the realization of a proactive SLA violation prevention mechanism, which will be an important aspect of the framework.

One of the goals of VISION Cloud is to substantially extend the limited data migration capabilities available in contemporary infrastructures so as to migrate and federate data across geographically distributed administrative domains, thus ensuring comprehensive and transparent data interoperability and overcoming the problem of data lock-in. Taking this into account, research on SLA schemata and management frameworks will also focus on the innovative aspects of the infrastructure for Cloud federation and interoperability, which cannot be fulfilled by the state of the art SLA schemata.

Finally, examination of complicated requirements should be done and renegotiation should also be added in the proposed framework in order to provide a complete automated SLA Management.

# REFERENCES

Alhamad, M., Dillon, T., & Chang, E. (2010a). Conceptual SLA framework for cloud computing. In *Proceedings of Digital Ecosystems and Technologies (DEST)*. IEEE. doi:10.1109/DEST.2010.5610586.

Alhamad, M., Dillon, T., & Chang, E. (2010b). SLA-based trust model for cloud computing. In Proceedings of Network-Based Information Systems (NBiS). NBiS. doi: doi:10.1109/NBiS.2010.67.

Amazon S3. (2009). *Amazon simple storage service*. Retrieved from http://aws.amazon.com/s3/

Amazon S3 SLA. (2009). *Amazon S3 service level agreement*. Retrieved from http://aws.amazon.com/s3-sla/

Andrieux, A., Czajkowski, K., Dan, A., Keahey, K., Ludwig, H., & Nakata, T. ... Xu, M. (2005). *Web services agreement specification (WSAgreement)*. Retrieved from http://www.ggf.org/Public_Comment_Docs/Documents/Oct-2005/WS-AgreementSpecificationDraft050920.pdf

Boniface, M., Phillips, S. C., Sanchez-Macian, A., & Surridge, M. (2007). Dynamic service provisioning using GRIA SLAs. In *Proceedings of the 5th International Workshops on Service-Oriented Computing, ICSOC'07*. ICSOC.

Brandic, I., Emeakaroha, V. C., Maurer, M., Dustdar, S., Acs, S., Kertesz, A., & Kecskemeti, G. (2010). LAYSI: A layered approach for SLA-violation propagation in self-manageable cloud infrastructures. In *Proceedings of Computer Software and Applications Conference Workshops (COMPSACW)*. IEEE.

Dan, A., Franck, R., Keller, A., King, R., & Ludwig, H. (2002). *Web service level agreement (WSLA) language specification*. Academic Press.

Emeakaroha, V. C., Brandic, I., Maurer, M., & Dustdar, S. (2010). Low level metrics to high level SLAs - LoM2HiS framework: Bridging the gap between monitored metrics and SLA parameters in cloud environments. In Proceedings of High Performance Computing and Simulation (HPCS). HPCS.

Emeakaroha, V. C., Netto, M. A. S., Calheiros, R. N., Brandic, I., Buyya, R., & De Rose, C. A. F. (2011). Towards autonomic detection of SLA violations in cloud infrastructures. *Future Generation Computer Systems*. doi: doi:10.1016/j.future.2011.08.018.

*Force.com*. (n.d.). Retrieved from http://www.force.com/

*GoGrid.* (n.d.). Retrieved from http://www.gogrid.com/

*Google App. Engine.* (n.d.). Retrieved from https://developers.google.com/appengine/

Hui, L. (2009). Challenges in SLA translation. *SLASOI, FP7216556, 1-6. Sla translation 27 30 Violation 28 29.*

Keller, A., & Ludwig, H. (2003). The WSLA framework: Specifying and monitoring service level agreements for web services. *Journal of Network and Systems Management*, 11.

Kolodner, E. K., Tal, S., Kyriazis, D., Naor, D., Allalouf, M., & Bonello, L. ... Wolfsthal, Y. (2011). A cloud environment for data-intensive storage services. In Proceedings of Cloud Computing Technology and Science (CloudCom). IEEE.

Kolodner, H., Naor, D., Tal, S., Koutsoutos, S., Mavrogeorgi, N., & Gogouvitis, S. ... Salant, E. (2011). Data-intensive storage services on clouds: Limitations, challenges and enablers. In *Proceedings of eChallenges e-2011 Conference.* eChallenges.

Lamanna, D. D., Skene, J., & Emmerich, W. (2003). SLAng: A language for defining service level agreements. In *Proceedings of the Ninth IEEE Workshop on Future Trends of Distributed Computing Systems (FTDCS'03).* IEEE.

Maurer, M., Brandic, I., Emeakaroha, V. C., & Dustdar, S. (2010). Towards knowledge management in self-adaptable clouds. In *Proceedings of the 4th International Workshop of Software Engineering for Adaptive Service-Oriented Systems, SEASS'10.* SEASS.

Microsoft Corporation. (2009). *Windows Azure pricing and service agreement.* Retrieved from http://www.microsoft.com/windowsazure/pricing/

*Nirvanix Service Level Agreement.* (n.d.). Retrieved from http://www.nirvanix.com/sla.aspx

Oldham, N., Verma, K., Sheth, A., & Hakimpour, F. (2006). Semantic WS-agreement partner selection. In *Proceedings of the 15th International Conference on World Wide Web (WWW '06).* ACM.

Popa, R. A., Lorch, J., Molnar, D., Wang, H. J., & Zhuang, L. (2011). Enabling security in cloud storage SLAS with cloudproof. In *Proceedings of the 2011 USENIX Conference on USENIX Annual Technical* Conference *(USENIXATC'11).* USENIX Association.

*Rackspace.* (n.d.). Retrieved from http://www.rackspace.com/

Seidel, J., Wäldrich, O., Ziegler, W., & Yahyapour, R. (2007). Using SLA for resource management and scheduling-a survey. *Network, 8,* 335–347. Retrieved from http://www.coregrid.net/mambo/images/stories/TechnicalReports/tr-0096.pdf.

*SNIA.* (1997). Retrieved from http://www.snia.org/cdmi

Torry Harris. (n.d.). *Cloud computing services - A comparison.* Retrieved from http://www.thbs.com/pdfs/Comparison of Cloud computing services.pdf

Tosic, V., Pagurek, B., & Patel, K. (2003). WSOL - A language for the formal specification of classes of service for web services. In Zhang, L.-J. (Ed.), *ICWS* (pp. 375–381). CSREA Press.

*VISION Cloud.* (2010). Retrieved from http://www.visioncloud.eu/

Voulodimos, A., Gogouvitis, S., Mavrogeorgi, N., Talyansky, R., Kyriazis, D., & Koutsoutos, S. ... Varvarigou, T. (2011). A unified management model for data intensive storage clouds. In *Proceedings of the IEEE First International Symposium on Network Cloud Computing and Applications.* Toulouse, France: IEEE.

Wäldrich, O. (n.d.). *WS-agreement for JAVA (WSAG4J).* Retrieved 2012, from http://packcs-e0.scai.fraunhofer.de/wsag4j/

*Windows Azure*. (n.d.). Retrieved from http://www.windowsazure.com/en-us/

*WSLA Documents*. (n.d.). Retrieved from http://researchWeb.watson.ibm.com/wsla/documents.html

*WSLA*. (n.d.). Retrieved from http://www.research.ibm.com/wsla/

## KEY TERMS AND DEFINITIONS

**Content Centric Storage:** Storage that provides services based on object's content.

**Proactive SLA Violation Detection:** Mechanism for detecting and handling proactively imminent violations.

**Service Level Agreement (SLA):** A formal contract describing what functionalities are provided and under which terms.

**Service Level Objectives (SLO):** The quantitative properties that are constrained through thresholds.

**SLA Management:** The management of operations regarding an SLA (e.g. SLA negotiation, SLA enforcement, proactive SLA violation detection).

**SLA Requirements:** The requirements that are defined in the SLA and which can be functional or non-functional.

**SLA Schema:** The XML schema that represents an SLA and based on which the SLA Management runs.

# Chapter 7
# Cloud Access Control Mechanisms

**Ciro Formisano**
*Engineering Ingegneria Informatica SPA, Italy*

**Lucia Bonelli**
*Engineering Ingegneria Informatica SPA, Italy*

**Kanchanna Ramasamy Balraj**
*Engineering Ingegneria Informatica SPA, Italy*

**Alexandra Shulman-Peleg**
*IBM Haifa Research Lab, Israel*

## ABSTRACT

*Cloud storage systems provide highly scalable and continuously available storage services to millions of geographically distributed clients. In order for users to trust their data to these systems, they need to be confident that their data is secure. Thus, cloud services should implement an access control mechanism preventing unauthorized access and manipulation of their data. This chapter presents the existing access control mechanisms and describes their advantages and limitations in the Cloud set-up. The authors address the main access control aspects that include managing the identities and defining access policies. Furthermore, they describe more complex scenarios of identity federation and integration of separate identity silos which is required in various scenarios, like collaboration, merge on acquisition, or migration. For each topic, the authors present the existing solutions and describe the motivation for the architecture developed by the VISION Cloud project.*

## INTRODUCTION

The cloud architecture, and storage cloud in particular, opens up new security related issues and intensifies other known vulnerabilities and threats. For example, most cloud storage services are offered by external providers on infrastructures also used for storing other customer's data. Thus, many customers are rightfully worried about moving their data to a storage cloud and data security risks are a key barrier to the wide adoption of cloud storage (Wilson, 2009; Mitchel, 2009; Messmer, 2009). Storage cloud providers must, therefore, implement a secure access control system in order to reduce the risk of unauthorized access to a reasonably low level.

DOI: 10.4018/978-1-4666-3934-8.ch007

Security has its costs and the structure of very large scale storage systems incurs a trade-off between performance, availability and security (Leung, Miller, & Jones, 2007). Balancing this trade-off is particularly challenging in the cloud environment due to the scalability and high availability requirements. Moreover, even though the consistency of the data itself can be reduced to improve availability (Trusted Computer System Evaluation Criteria, 1985), the access control configurations and their enforcement should be always consistent across all access points. Furthermore, since data in the storage cloud resides on a shared infrastructure, it may be repeatedly migrated, hosted and managed by parties which may be untrusted and can be exposed to unauthorized access. The early cloud storage offerings mostly neglected security or provided minimal security guarantees. However, recently security is gaining more and more attention. This issue becomes central both to the existing vendors, that improve their offerings, as well as new companies and services that aim to add an additional level of security or access control over the existing solutions.

In addition to the scale and availability requirements, today's new Web applications introduce new characteristics to data access. For example, data is not necessarily accessed directly by its owner but rather through various applications, in flexible sharing scenarios and with various billing methods. These applications put forth new functional requirements that include, for example, the requirement for the federated identity and Single Sign On (SSO) as well as the ability of a client to delegate a subset of his access rights, supporting the related notion of Discretionary Access Control (DAC) (Messmer, 2009). Another requirement is a support for hierarchical management of rights, assigning administrators' privileges to domains and allowing them to delegate partial access to other principals under their control.

An access control system is considered to be safe if no permission can be leaked to an unauthorized or uninvited principal. Thus, it is essential to ensure that the access control architecture cannot lead to leakage of permissions to an unauthorized principal. When considering the highly distributed architecture of cloud storage systems, this is an extremely challenging task. Each architectural component can introduce new threats. Furthermore, there is a requirement to support multi-tenancy while isolating the configuration parameters and the data of the different tenancy. This is a very ambitious goal, especially since even a well-known functionality, such as deduplication, in a cloud setting can lead to privacy violations (Harnik, Pinkas, & Shulman-Peleg, 2010). Unfortunately, when addressing the required rich functionality together with the next generation cloud scale, most of the existing solutions require high performance overhead or lead to new security threats and bottlenecks.

This chapter is structured as follows. First, we present the background section, which describes the requirements of the cloud access control mechanisms as recognized by the VISION Cloud project. The section titled "Access Control Models and Components" describes the access control fundamentals, presenting the existing access control models. It compares the various schemes describing the challenges that occur in the Cloud Storage set up. The section titled "Access Policy Modelling and Management" focuses on existing solutions in the field of policy based management and the section on "Federated Identity" addresses the important issue of identity federation, which gives clients a unified access control system. Finally, the section on "Future Research Directions" presents the VISION Cloud approach, justifying its design decisions and describing its advantages.

## BACKGROUND

The challenge of access control is to control the access and allow only users with the proper privilege to carry out operations. There are two basic access control components: (1) Authentication, which determines and verifies the identity of a user in the system; and (2) Authorization, which determines the access rights of a user to a specific resource. VISION Cloud project recognized several requirements that should be satisfied by these components in the cloud set-up.

## Authentication

- **Internal Identity Management Service:** For the public cloud scenario there should be an option to perform authentication with the Cloud provider, who will manage the use identities.
- **Integration with External Identity Providers (IdPs):** Enterprise customers might require one of the two solutions: (1) Working with the Identity Provider (IdP) of the Cloud as above. (2) Integrating an IdP kept at customer premises. The Cloud service will use the authentication mechanism of this server, which is managed outside the Cloud.
- **Federated Identity and Single-Sign On (SSO):** It should be possible to allow users to work with a single set of credentials that will allow access to applications residing at different security domains. Furthermore, there is a need to provide a generic way to integrate separate identity silos managing the trust relationships, access control polices and identity mapping mechanics.

## Authorization

- **Internal Authorization Service:** For the public cloud scenario the Cloud should provide an option for internal authorization for data access and management request.
- **Supporting ACL-based Access Control:** For compatibility with existing systems, the Cloud should support the ACL-based access control model and allow the configuration of ACLs through a RESTful

API (e.g., as required by the Cloud Data Management Interface [CDMI] [SNIA, n.d.]).

- **Role and Attribute-based Access Control Models:** It should be possible to manage the access rights based on the user roles. There should be a mechanisms for the specification of rich access policies, which can be based on the user roles or attributes of the resources (e.g., type of objects).

## ACCESS CONTROL MODELS AND COMPONENTS

Access control refers to managing identities, defining access policies, and controlling access to resources in a secure manner.

## Overview

Authentication is one of the biggest issues concerning information security in the Cloud and it ensures that a person who tries to connect to the system is who he or she claims to be. The traditional Unix authentication is performed through validating a username and a password that are provided during the login process. To allow an easier replacement of the authentication scheme, some systems implement BSD auth or NSS (GNU, 2001), which are an advance but still require library modifications to add a new mechanism. PAM (Pluggable Authentication Modules) introduced by Sun in Solaris solves this problem and allows adding new authentication mechanisms without the need for recompilation or modification of the existing programs. PAM is currently used by most major Unix systems, like Linux, Solaris, Mac OS X or FreeBSD and its modules supports a number of authentication schemes such as Kerberos, NIS, NIS+ and LDAP. These modules provide a technical solution for integrating external identity management servers. However, when addressing the expected scale of the storage clouds, these solutions are expected to create bottlenecks at the data access path.

The main types of authorization schemes are:

1.  **Access Control Lists (ACLs):** Which are stored with the resource, define the users authorized to access the resource along with their access rights. These systems allow easily answering the question "who are the users that have access to this resource?", but it is difficult to determine all privileges of a user over all resources. In enterprise environments it is difficult to centrally administrate ACLs, especially with a large number of users and groups (e.g., switching from one enterprise policy to another is very difficult). Finally, ACLs are platform-dependent and different systems have their own syntax of ACL.

2.  **Capabilities:** Unforgeable tokens that identify one or more resources and the access rights granted to their holder. Capability-based protocols consist of two main stages: (1) The client requests a credential from the security manager, which authenticates and authorizes the clients and grants the credentials; (2) The client accesses the data on the storage servers, presenting the credential to the storage server that enforces access

control. Selecting the best access control model has been an issue of debate for many decades and theoretically best models are not always widely adopted (Miltchev, Smith, Prevelakis, Keromytis, & Ioannidis, 2008; Close, 2009). Table 1 presents some of the advantages and the disadvantages of each approach. In capability based systems it is easy to know "which resources can a user access?" But we cannot determine all the users who can access a specific resource.

3.  **Role-based and access control models:** Which enables to carry out a broad range of authorized operations through the establishment and definition of roles, role hierarchies, relationships, and constraints. System administrators can control access at a level of principles which is suitable to the way that enterprises control their business.

## Cloud Access Control Solutions

Although distributed file systems were used for file sharing within organizations for many years, most systems, such as NFS, AFS, and CIFS were not designed for file sharing across organizational borders. When users in distinct administrative domains try to share files, they either need to ask their system administrators to create new accounts

*Table 1. Overview of authentication mechanisms*

|  | **ACLs - list the users authorized to access the resource along with their access rights.** | **Capabilities – unforgeable tokens that identifies the resources and access rights** | **Role-based access control** |
|---|---|---|---|
| Advantages | 1. Used in most production systems. | 1. Supports the property of least privilege. 2. Do not require explicit authentication on the data path. 3. Allows efficient delegation. | 1. Supports control at the level of principles, which gives the enterprises an appropriate level of control. |
| Disadvantages | 1. Authorization depends on prior authentication. 2. Insecure for interactions with more than two principals (Confused deputy problem). | 1. Capabilities must be carefully protected from theft (e.g., by transmission over secure and authenticated channels). 2. May be more difficult for later auditing. | 1. Not suitable for managing a cloud-scale number of objects. 2. Role management across different administrative domain is difficult. |

for their partners or share their account passwords. This leads to either cumbersome exchange of information or compromising the security (Trusted computer system evaluation criteria,, 1985). Obviously these solutions are not suitable for storage clouds. While some experimental systems, like Fileteller (Ioannidis, Ioannidis, Keromytis, & Prevelakis, 2003), DisCFS (Miltchev et al., 2003) and WebDAVA (Levine, Prevelakis, Ioannidis, Ioannidis,&Keromytis, 2003) allow more efficient file sharing services, they are based on Public Key Infrastructure (PKI), which was shown to have multiple limitations for adoption in cloud-scale systems (Niu et al., 2009).

One of the most popular authentication schemes was pioneered by the Amazon S3. It is based on user identifiers (unique within S3) and secret keys shared between the users and the system. The requester includes his identifier in the request and signs key parts of the request message with a keyed hash (HMAC) using his secret key. By embedding the authentication information in the HTTP request, an authorized user can create an authenticated request and pass it to another user to get one-time access to a specific object. Furthermore, since the authentication information can be passed in a query string as part of the URL of the HTTP request, this method can be used by Web applications interacting with Web browsers to provide seamless access delegation. This scheme is also adopted by EMC Atmos, Microsoft Windows Azure Storage and many more. Azure also supports a limited capability-based access. This is done by handing a user Shared Access Signature, which encodes a capability to perform specified operations on a specified object (container or blob) for a specified period of time. As in S3, the Signature is encapsulated in a URL and is signed with the owner's secret key (Windows Azure Storage Services API Reference, 2010).

## Comparison

Most of the cloud offerings use internal identity management services and do not support easy integration of customer managed IdPs. Recently, Amazon Web Services (AWS) made an important step forward by introducing an Identity and Access Management (IAM) service (AWS Identity and Access Management [IAM]). It enables customers to create and manage their users in AWS's identity management system. It also enables granting access to AWS resources for users managed outside of AWS. These users, termed "federated users" can be managed, for example, in the corporate directory. Although this service is an important milestone in cloud storage access control, it is still very basic. For example, it does not support role based access control for S3 as well as standard identity federation protocols like SAML SSO. Furthermore, although most cloud offerings support ACLs, many of them use proprietary syntax. This prevents compatibility, complicating federation and data migration.

## ACCESS POLICY MODELING AND MANAGEMENT

A key aspect of security is access control model. Access control models define a set of abstractions capable of expressing access policy statements for a wide variety of information resources. Access control techniques are categorized as either discretionary or non-discretionary. The three most widely recognized models are the following:

- **Discretionary Access Control (DAC):** Where access policies are determined by the owner of an object.
- **Mandatory Access Control (MAC):** Which consists in the enforcing of access control rules defined by a central authority.

- **Role Based Access Control (RBAC):** Which uses the roles assigned to users as a criteria to allow or deny access to system resources.

Policy based management is one of the most widely used approaches followed in network and distributed computing. Access Policy management specifies how to deal with situations that are likely to occur via priorities and access control rules for system resources. The system will have a Policy Decision Point (PDP) for interpreting the policies and a Policy Enforcement Point (PEP) for applying the policies.

## Access Policy Models and Products

Besides the already mentioned ones, a number of models have been developed to address various aspects of policy management. IBAC (Identity Based Access Control) provides access control based on the identity of the requester. Such a model requires policy definitions for each identity: it is easy to understand that this model is not scalable. A possible solution takes into the account that actually policies are not defined basing on the single user but on user categories. A category of users associated with a fixed set of access policies is defined as role: the access control model based on roles is called Role Based Access Control (RBAC). In this model the main way to control user access is to assign a particular role to a particular user. Challenges with RBAC became apparent when it was extended across domains like in the Cloud. Reaching an agreement between the parties regarding the rights that should be associated with each role proved to be difficult. Adding, deleting, or modifying the duties of a role involved updating too many policy stores. Further, RBAC had limited support for context, such as day vs. night or war vs. peace, when it was important in the access decision. Attribute Based Access Control (ABAC), sometimes referred to as Policy Based

Access Control (PBAC) or Claims Based Access Control (CBAC), was proposed as a solution to these new issues. The access decision would be based on attributes that the user can prove to have, such as clearance level or citizenship. This approach makes it easy to include context in the access decision. This model has the issue of reaching agreement on the meaning of attributes when spanning organizations because of the need to reconcile complex and extensive lexicons. ZBAC (Karp, n.d.) (authoriZation Based Access Control) is an approach where users are authorized based on global agreements between the domains involved. This model provides an approach for authorization which does not require SSO/Federated Identity, where the user is authenticated in local domain and the local domain delegates the rights to user, based on the rights provided to the local domain by the service domain (by making a global agreement). The request for resource is authorized based on the delegated rights issued by local domain. This approach requires all participating domains to agree on a global agreement with each other.

However the lack of standards defined to reach a global agreement between the domains for this model and the need for understanding the semantics of access rights delegated, and mapping internally is a disadvantage to adopt the model. Any policy model has to be associated with an appropriate policy management framework which manages the policies and renders access decisions. Policies can be applied to sets of resources to configure them uniformly and adapt their behaviour to suit changing requirements. Policies provide abstractions that can be used for the configuration and management of resources without having to change their implementation. The level of abstraction can be broad, from high-level management goals to low-level actions. A policy specification is a description containing a policy model consisting of the technical aspects and relevant concepts and a language to describe the desired behaviour of the concepts.

A complete policy management framework must support:

- Policy specification.
- Policy analysis, verification, and validation.
- Policy enforcement.

More precisely it must include:

- A policy specification language that allows the expression of policies.
- Built-in support and authoring tool for policy creation (policy editors and policy definition environments, like syntax checkers), verification, consistency analysis (and redundancy) and conflict detection and resolution (in case of multiple policies, to ensure the correctness and quality of the policies specified). For conflict resolution and detection there are rule and policy combination algorithms.
- A policy deployment model for the distribution of policies.
- A policy analysis mechanism for making the correct policy enforcement decisions (this is usually a distinct component called decision engine).
- A policy enforcement mechanism that facilitates execution of policy actions.

For consumer users, all the policies are specified locally at the cloud service. However, the use of cloud services by members of corporations and other organizations introduces the possibility that access control policies may be specified in one place, such as the organization, and transmitted to another place, such as the cloud service provider. If every cloud service provider and every customer invent their own format for representing policy information, an unsustainable situation results. The industry standard eXtensible Access Control Markup Language (XACML) represents access control policies in a standard way.

Argus (Argus Authorisation Framework, n.d.) is Policy management framework developed for EGEE project. It is based on XACML language and provides consistent authorization decisions for distributed services.

Enterprises, including the healthcare enterprise, need a mechanism to exchange security and privacy policies, evaluate consent directives and determine authorizations in an interoperable manner. The Cross-Enterprise Security and Privacy Authorization (XSPA) profile of XACML (Cross-Enterprise Security and Privacy Authorization—XSPA—Profile of XACMLv2.0 for Healthcare Version 1.0, n.d.) describes several mechanisms to authenticate, administer, and enforce authorization policies controlling access to protected information residing within or across enterprise boundaries. The policies being administered and enforced relate to security, privacy, and consent directives. This profile specifies the use of XACML 2.0 to promote interoperability within the healthcare community by providing common semantics and vocabularies for interoperable policy request/response, policy lifecycle, and policy enforcement.

WS-Policy is a lesser-known alternative, for those using the WS-Federation standard for Web services.

## Comparison

Below is a comparison of XACML policies and JSON (Javascript standard object notation) policies, which are selected by Amazon for definition of policies on S3 buckets (see Table 2).

## FEDERATED IDENTITY

In cloud-computing environment, federation of identity plays a key role in enabling allied enterprises to authenticate, provide single or reduced sign-on and exchange identity attributes among Administrative Domains.

*Table 2. Comparison of XACML policies and JSON policies*

| Features | JSON Policies | XACML Policies |
|---|---|---|
| Specifications available? | No - Amazon policy language reference http://docs. amazonWebservices.com/AmazonS3/latest/dev/AccessPolicyLanguage.html | Yes |
| Open source implementations | Not known | Available at http://www.oasis -open.org/ committees/ tc home.php?wg abbrev= xacml#other |
| Schemas | Custom schema, data types, policy combining mechanisms for the policy need to be defined | Schemas are available as xsds, data types. Policy evaluation functions can be specified. |
| General characteristics | Simple | Powerful and very expressive |
| Policy distribution and indexing | Requires customization - one option is to index the JSON policies using Cassandra. | XACML policies are distributed and policy indexing approaches are well defined. |
| XPath based access control | Any such access control need to be designed and implemented | XPAth based access control is available. |
| Protocols | Custom request/response protocols need to be defined | XACML defined policy request/ response protocol |
| Adoption | Not widely adopted | Widely adopted in many implementations |
| Granularity | The model of S3 is at the granularity of buckets and not objects | Fine grained |
| Size | The model of S3 limits the size to be less than 20K | Flexible (can be limited on demand) |
| Policy security between access control components | Not supported | Many different techniques may be used to provide authentication, such as collocated code, a private network, a VPN or digital signatures. Authentication may also be performed as part of the communication protocol used to exchange the XACML contexts. In this case, authentication may be performed either at the message level or at the session level. |
| REST architecture support | Policy manipulations functions should be mapped to HTTP methods. Policies should be carried in the payload of the request/response. | Policy manipulations functions should be mapped to HTTP methods. Policies should be carried in the payload of the request/ response. |
| Access control over policies | ACEs are needed to control the users rights to policy definitions | ACEs are needed to control the users rights to policy definitions |

Making cloud components securely interoperable across Administrative Domains requires interoperability as well as stable, well-established standards: there should be a unified access control mechanism with authentication and authorization interoperability. Furthermore, every Administrative Domain, in the most of cases representing a Cloud, should support trust with the other Domains composing the Federation.

## Models, Technologies, and Products

Identity Management plays a critical role in cloud infrastructure security and in access management. There are two main approaches to manage identity in the Cloud:

- **Identity Proxy/Mediator:** Accounts and credentials are centrally managed through an Identity Proxy that intercepts the access requests and performs a map with external accounts/identities. The main problems of this approach are the scalability, accountability, and global compliance issues that make it much more suitable to environments composed by a single administrative domain, such as enterprises, which need Single Sign On for the various services exposed.

- **Identity Federation:** This approach is based on the interaction between an Identity Provider (**IdP**) which manages the Identities of the users in a certain domain (e.g. the Cloud Provider could be the Identity Provider of its cloud) and a Service Provider (**SP**), protecting the service of a federated domain. Under this approach, security and privacy constraints can be implemented at the Identity Provider site and it is possible to create circle of trusts for auditing and compliance checking. However, as a result the IdP becomes a bottleneck/central point of control which limits the scalability across multiple Cloud Providers. Moreover, governance and compliance issues are managed at IdPs side and not by the infrastructure.

Organizations considering federated identity management in the cloud should understand the various challenges and possible solutions to address those challenges with respect to identity lifecycle management, authentication methods, token formats, and non-repudiation. Non-repudiation is a major potential benefit of federation, as it provides a mechanism to trust or verify that the identity assertions came from the trusted IdP rather than an impostor.

The Security Assertion Markup Language SAML, an OASIS standard, is a structured way to transport authentication and attributes information across security domains. The use of SAML allows a user from one site (for example, a user within her own company's portal) to seamlessly access content at another site (for example, information outsourced to a third party) without being challenged for another authentication. The ability to perform such exchanges in a secure and standard manner has allowed orchestrating more sophisticated business processes spanning administrative boundaries. For example, OpSource, an infrastructure services provider focusing on cloud integration, uses TriCipher's SAML-based MyOneLogin. TriCipher, through MyOneLogIn and other applications, provides business users anywhere access, VPN and multifactor authentication, and user management for 200 in-the-cloud business applications providers, including Google, Salesforce.com, ADP, Concur and others.

Several protocols have been built on SAML, in order to meet different context and use cases of Identity Federation: for example the requirements to federate two sites are different than those to federate two SOAP Services. A consistent combination some of these protocols is called SAML Profile: there is a group of five profiles related to Single Sign On, and another group providing SSO-related services. In particular, the SSO profiles are:

- **Web Browser SSO:** Provides federation and SSO among sites accessed by Web Browser.
- **Enhanced Client or Proxy:** Provides federation and SSO for services accessed by enhanced clients or proxies.
- **Identity Provider Discovery:** Helps to discover an Identity Provider. Single Logout: provides the logout from the whole federation
- **Name Identifier Management:** Provides a management mechanism for Name Identifiers, which are used to identify the person that the IdP has issued an assertion about.

The other SAML profiles are:

- **Artifact Resolution:** To resolve a SAML Assertion from an ID.
- **Assertion Query/Request:** To query the IdP for a SAML Assertion.
- **Name Identifier Mapping:** To link different accounts in the. federation
- **SAML Attribute:** To manage the attributes.

Shibboleth (Shibboleth, n.d.) implements SAML Web Browser SSO and Enhanced Client or Proxy profiles: it also provides some protocols for artifact resolution and attribute management. Shibboleth is the most complete and widely used SAML implementation: the identity management is performed by a configurable Identity Provider (IdP), from which it is possible to get the attributes of the identity; the services are protected by a Service Provider (SP) which, with the help of the so-called Where Are You From Service, finds the home domain of the request and redirects it to authenticate. Shibboleth is widely adopted; in particular several research and university federations are based on Shibboleth, such as 12 GRTNF (Greece), IDEM GARR (Italy), Gakunin (Japan), SWITCHaai (Switzerland), SWAMID (Sweden).

Another popular model used for federating different administrative domains is OpenID (OpenID, n.d.), which is an open standard of decentralized authentication adopted by important sites, such as Google or Facebook. OpenID bases the authentication process on a trusted OpenID Provider and several Relying Parties. The protocol flow is the following:

- The User who wants to access the Relying Party, presents her OpenID.
- The Relying Party parses the OpenID and gets the url of the OpenID. Provider: if the Provider is trusted, the request is redirected there to authenticate.
- The Authentication Process is performed by the provider.
- The authenticated request is redirected to the Relying Party.

There are several public OpenID Provider, e.g. Myid.net, Myopenid, Claimid; some Internet Service Provider also acts as OpenID provider, such as Google, Yahoo, Flickr, Orange.

OpenID provides a federation model similar to SAML Web SSO profile with a more limited set of options. For example, in addition to the possibility to choose a suitable profile, SAML can indicate the strength of authentication used by the external authentication service. With the wide variety of single sign-on authentication implementations, it is important not to enable inadequate authentication mechanisms for access to sensitive services. "Strong authentication" typically refers to multifactor authentication or authentication protected by cryptographic means. Strong authentication methods such as Kerberos, and token or smart-card systems are common within enterprise networks, and the enterprises are increasingly leveraging this technology for use in the IaaS cloud, especially for privileged access management or shell access using Secure Shell (SSH).

However, the increasing number of such business transactions has exposed a new challenge. All of the transactions are dependent on the notion that the user identity already exists at the secondary site. Put differently, the use case assumes that the user has already been provisioned with the access to the appropriate systems on both sides of the 'fence'. Without this assumption being met, the value of cross-domain transactions, such as those enabled using SAML, cannot be fully realized. The current workaround for this problem is to facilitate the provisioning of user identities to secondary sites using manual or out-of-band mechanisms. At best, this is a cost-inefficient model due to the proliferation of manual processes that need to be implemented and executed. More importantly, this model prevents many of the dynamic processes that require late-binding or just-in-time provisioning to take place between multiple business domains. Protocols are emerging to provide an elegant and effective solution to this challenge. These include SCIM (Simple Cloud Identity Management), SPML (Service provisioning markup language), as well as SAML Attribute query which is being advocated by Google and OASIS respectively. SPML exists since a decade now and has evolved over time. While SCIM is new and is being advocated by Google, Salesforce claims to overcome the shortcomings of SPML.

Regarding user authorization, OAuth (open protocol for secure API authorization) (OAUTH 2.0, n.d.), has become adopted among developers and cloud providers since it allows for more granularity of data controls across cloud applications. OAuth was formalized in December of 2007, and Google and MySpace have been the first to adopt it as an API development standard. Yahoo and others have since followed, but many large cloud service providers still don't support OAuth. Still, OAuth is likely to be one of the technologies that will replace the proprietary version of delegated authorization, allowing secure transactions between different service providers. Amazon supports Query string authentication for giving HTTP or browser access to resources that would normally require authentication. This is useful for enabling direct third-party browser access to Amazon S3 data, without proxying the request.

There are two key specifications related to federated identity schemes: the Identity Assurance Framework (IAF) and Identity Governance Framework (IGF). These frameworks follow the development of the widely adopted Security Assertion Markup Language (SAML). The SAML 2.0 is the de-facto standard for federated relationships, addressing privacy and trust considerations. IAF provides policy criteria to allow organizations to link identity systems based on a uniform definition of the security and privacy risks at each of four levels of assurance. Level 1 requires essentially no assurance that a person is who he claims to be. Level 2 requires a moderate level of ID proofing. Level 3 is a more stringent level, probably requiring multifactor authentication, and Level 4 is the most stringent, requiring strong multifactor authentication. IGF is a technical specification for defining privacy issues based on the Extensible Markup Language. It is an auditable, open standards' based framework to help meet regulatory requirements for using, managing and protecting personally identifiable information.

Below is a comparison of the different token formats for exchanging authentication and authorization data between security domains to achieve federated identity. The following three tokens types are discussed – JWT (JSON Web token) tokens, SAML SimpleSign (SAML SimpleSign, n.d.), SAML tokens. With cloud storage providers providing RESTful interfaces, the token formats provide a comparison that can be analyzed based on the federated identity and RESTful token exchange requirements. Due to its advantages and wide adoption, SAML is one of the best solutions for exchanging assertions with existing service providers, aiding interoperability (see Table 3).

## FUTURE RESEARCH DIRECTIONS

Analysis of the existing solutions, combined with the requirements specified by the VISION Cloud project, led to the following observations regarding the components that should be implemented by the next generation Cloud Storage platform:

- **ACL-based access control:** To allow compatibility and federation with existing systems there is a need to support ACLs with standard syntax and RESTful API.
- **ABAC support:** To allow enterprise-level control with rich access rules and policies there is a need to support attribute-based access control based on a standard policy language.

*Table 3. Comparison of token formats*

| Features | JWT Tokens | SAML SimpleSign | SAML Tokens |
|---|---|---|---|
| Service provisioning markup language used in user/resource provisioning bw Idp and SPs(is recommended by CSA) | Not available | SAML 2.0 Profile for SPML | SAML 2.0 Profile for SPML |
| Token security | JSON Web signature HMAC SHA-256, RSA SHA-256, and ECDSA P256 SHA-256 | SAML assertions are signed as simple 'BLOBs' | XMLSig and XMLEnc specifications for XML signature and encryption available |
| Token length | Lightweight | Lightweight | Heavy |
| Token validation time | Less as it involves just hashing | Less | High as it requires XML validation and canonicalization |
| SSO | Can be achieved | Can be achieved | Can be achieved |
| Federation | Can be achieved | Can be achieved | Can be achieved |
| General characteristics | Simple, lean and less standardized token | Less standardized token, not widely adopted - http://www.oasisopen.org/committees/download.php/28046/ sstcsamlbindingsimplesigncs-01.pdf | Standardized, rich, expressive, verbose |
| Delegation | Lacks delegation capabilities | Lacks delegation capabilities | Lacks delegation capabilities |
| Token format | JSON object | XML based | XML based |
| Strength of security | Medium | Medium | High |
| Adoption | Google & Microsoft | Shibboleth | Emerging as a widely supported federation standard - Microsoft, Shibboleth, Oracle Ping Identity and so on |

- **Federated identity and SSO:** Required to use the same user credentials for authentication with a wide range of services. Furthermore, it is required to provide trust and identity federation across organizational boundaries.

## VISION CLOUD APPROACH

Based on the above observations, the access control modules of the VISION Cloud combine the following components.

## Authentication

Each tenant can select one of the following two authentication options:

1. Authentication with an internal identity manager provided by the VISION Cloud as part of its User Services.
2. Authentication with his existing identity management server, which is located at the customer premises. In this case, the authentication is based on SAML SSO.

## Authorization

VISION Cloud combines the following two authorization options:

1. **ACL-based access control**: Where the system associate ACLs (Access Control Lists) with every resource, such as object or container. Their configuration is done with a RESTful API as specified by CDMI (SNIA, n.d.), where the syntax is NFSv4 compatible and allows migration from existing systems.
2. **ABAC support**: Which uses attributes as building blocks in a structured language used to define access control rules and to describe access requests. Attributes are sets of labels or properties which can be used to describe all the entities that must be considered for authorization purposes. Each attribute consists of a key-value pair such as "Role=Assistant Manager."

VISION Cloud combines the ACL-based and ABAC models allowing to grants permissions based on roles and attributes, while protecting the access to each and every object/container by ACLs which are distributed as part of the object's/container's meta data.

## Justification of the Approach

Below we explain the motivation for the choices and decisions made by the VISION Cloud project.

## Selection of the Policy Language

Policy languages are mostly proprietary and the adoption of standards based policies could provide transparency and facilitate interoperability. In VISION, XACML has been selected for the following reasons:

- XACML has a standard structure allowing creation of complex policies.

- There are some Open Source implementation of XACML based policy managers.
- A complete message exchanging protocol has been defined.
- It is currently widely adopted.

The policy management of VISION is based on an ABAC policy model that has particular advantages when it is deployed in a Federated environment. Access is determined by the agreement on attributes between two entities (business, organizations, governments, etc.). The enterprise could simply leverage the attributes exchanged and map them to the authorization information to determine what type of access to allow. This provides the benefit of enterprises not needing to create additional accounts for users who are already known to a partner organization. In addition, constraints would be passed along with authorization decisions based on context/environment attributes (e.g., time of day, day of a week etc.) that are defined in the policies, thus allowing context based access decisions.

Since XACML based policies are not very human-friendly, it is vital to provide an interface for authoring policies and viewing policies in a simpler way. In order to simplify CRUD operations on XACML policies a JSON syntax has been defined and applied as interface for Vision Cloud Policy Management System, allowing simple definition of multi-attributes policies. XACML is agnostic about the semantic of those attributes, which can be, for example, roles, groups or time of the day. The chosen solution based on a XACML core with JSON interface will exploit the advantages of both the models.

## Identity Federation with SAML SSO

VISION's use cases go far beyond simple Web browser SSO: they concern federation among different domains exposing resources not accessible by Web browser sessions, but by REST calls. SAML is flexible enough to cover a wide set of use cases: the different SAML profiles can answer to different requirements and different deployment models. A SAML token, containing authentication information and user attribute, can be efficiently referenced by a key inserted in an HTTP header: the *Artifact Resolution Protocol* has been defined for this purpose. The high level of flexibility is the most important reason by which SAML has been chosen as Identity Federation technology for VISION: it is independent from the authentication factor used and, since it is a standard, it could enable federation with non-VISION infrastructures if the feature will be required in the future.

## CONCLUSION

Selecting the best access control model has been an issue of debate for many decades. Each approach has its advantages and disadvantages. When applying these schemes to the Cloud set-up with a huge amount of users and objects the advantages and the disadvantages of each scheme become even more dominant. Thus, the VISION Cloud project combines several schemes benefiting from the advantages of several models, while minimizing the disadvantages by limiting their scope. We envision that such combinations will become more and more popular when the cloud storage solutions become more mature.

## REFERENCES

*Argus Authorization Service*. (n.d.). Retrieved from https://twiki.cern.ch/twiki/bin/view/EGEE/AuthorizationFramework

*AWS Identity and Access Management (IAM)*. (n.d.). Retrieved from http://aws.amazon.com/iam/

Close, T. (2009). *ACLS don't*. Retrieved from http://www.hpl.hp.com/techreports/2009/HPL-2009-20.pdf

*Cross-Enterprise Security and Privacy Authorization - XSPA- Profile of XACMLv2.0 for Healthcare Version 1.0*. (n.d.). Retrieved from http://www.oasis-open.org/committees/document.php?document id=34164&wg abbrev=xacml

GNU. (2001). *The GNU C library reference manual*. Retrieved from http://www.gnu.org/software/libc/manual/htmlnode/Name-Service-Switch.html

Harnik, D., Pinkas, B., & Shulman-Peleg, A. (2010). Side channels in cloud services: Deduplication in cloud storage. *IEEE Security and Privacy, 8*, 40–47. Retrieved from http://doi.ieeecomputersociety.org/10.1109/MSP.2010.18

Ioannidis, J., Ioannidis, S., Keromytis, A. D., & Prevelakis, V. (2003). Fileteller: Paying and getting paid for file storage. In *Proceedings of the 6th International Conference on Financial Cryptography* (pp. 282–299). Berlin: Springer-Verlag. Retrieved from http://portal.acm.org/citation.cfm?id=1765278.1765298

*JSON Web Token*. (n.d.). Retrieved from http://self-issued.info/docs/draft-jones-json-Web-token.html

Karp, A. H. (n.d.). *From ABAC to ZBAC: The evolution of access control models*. Retrieved from http://www.hpl.hp.com/techreports/2009/HPL-2009-30.pdf

Kernel. (2005). *Linux-pam*. Retrieved from http://www.kernel.org/pub/linux/libs/pam

Leung, A. W., Miller, E. L., & Jones, S. (2007). Scalable security for petascale parallel file systems. In *Proceedings of the 2007 ACM/IEEE Conference on Supercomputing* (pp. 16:1–16:12). New York, NY: ACM. Retrieved from http://doi.acm.org/10.1145/1362622.1362644

Levine, A., Prevelakis, V., Ioannidis, J., Ioannidis, S., & Keromytis, A. D. (2003). Webdava: An administrator-free approach to web file-sharing. In *Proceedings of the Twelfth International Workshop on Enabling Technologies: Infrastructure for Collaborative Enterprises*. Washington, DC: IEEE Computer Society. Retrieved from http://portal.acm.org/citation.cfm?id=938984.939757

Messmer, E. (2009). *Are security issues delaying adoption of cloud computing*. Retrieved from http://www.networkworld.com/news/2009/042709-burning-securitycloud-computing.html

Miltchev, S., Prevelakis, V., Ioannidis, S., Ioannidis, J., Keromytis, A. D., & Smith, J. M. (2003). Secure and flexible global file sharing. In *Proceedings of the USENIX 2003 Annual Technical Conference (Freenix Track)* (pp. 165–178). USENIX.

Miltchev, S., Smith, J. M., Prevelakis, V., Keromytis, A., & Ioannidis, S. (2008). Decentralized access control in distributed file systems. *ACM Computer Survey, 40*, 10:1–10:30. Retrieved from http://doi.acm.org/10.1145/1380584.1380588

Mitchel, R. L. (2009). *Cloud storage triggers security worries*. Retrieved from http://www.computerworld.com/s/article/340438

Niu, Z., Jiang, H., Zhou, K., Yang, T., & Yan, W. (2009). Identification and authentication in large-scale storage systems. In *Proceedings of the 2009 IEEE International Conference on Networking, Architecture, and Storage* (pp. 421–427). Washington, DC: IEEE Computer Society. Retrieved from http://dx.doi.org/10.1109/NAS.2009.72

*OAUTH 2.0*. (n.d.). Retrieved from http://oauth.net/2/

*OpenID*. (n.d.). Retrieved from www.openid.net

*SAML SimpleSign*. (n.d.). Retrieved from http://www.oasis-open.org/committees/download.php/28046/sstc-saml-binding-simplesign-cs-01.pdf

*Shibboleth*. (n.d.). Retrieved from http://www.shibboleth.net/

*Simple Cloud Identity Management*. (n.d.). Retrieved from https://sites.google.com/site/clouddir/draft1

SNIA. (n.d.). *Cloud data management interface (CDMI)*. Retrieved from http://snia.org/cdmi

*Trusted Computer System Evaluation Criteria*. (1985). Retrieved from http://csrc.nist.gov/publications/history/dod85.pdf

Wilson, T. (2009). *Security is chief obstacle to cloud computing adoption, study says*. Retrieved from http://www.darkreading.com/securityservices/security/perimeter/showArticle.jhtml?articleID=221901195

*Windows Azure Storage Services API Reference*. (2010). Retrieved from http://msdn.microsoft.com/en-us/library/dd179355.aspx

## KEY TERMS AND DEFINITIONS

**Access Control Lists (ACLs):** Define the users authorized to access the resource along with their access rights.

**Capabilities:** Are unforgeable tokens that identify one or more resources and the access rights granted to their holder.

**eXtensible Access Control Markup Language (XACML):** The industry standard which provides a standard way to represent access control policies.

**Identity Provider (IdP):** An identity management service.

**Role Based Access Control (RBAC):** A model which uses the roles assigned to users as a criteria to allow or deny access to system resources.

# Chapter 8
# Compliance in the Cloud

**Lucia Bonelli**
*Engineering Ingegneria Informatica, Italy*

**Luisa Giudicianni**
*Engineering Ingegneria Informatica, Italy*

**Angelo Immediata**
*Engineering Ingegneria Informatica, Italy*

**Antonio Luzzi**
*Engineering Ingegneria Informatica, Italy*

## ABSTRACT

*Despite the huge economic, handling, and computational benefits of the cloud technology, the multitenant and geographically distributed nature of clouds hides a large crowd of security and regulatory issues to be addressed. The main reason for these problems is the unavoidable loss of physical control that costumers are forced to accept when opting for the cloud model. This aspect, united with the lack of knowledge (i.e. transparency) of the vendor's infrastructure implementation, represents a nasty question when costumers are asked to respond to audit findings, produce support for forensic investigations, and, more generically, to ensure compliance with information security standards and regulations. Yet, support for security standards compliance is a need for cloud providers to overcome customers hesitancy and meet their expectations. In this context, tracking, auditing, and reporting practices, while transcending the compliance regimes, represent the primary vehicle of assurance for security managers and auditors on the achievement of security and regulatory compliance objectives. The aim of this chapter is to provide a roundup of crucial requirements resulting from common security certification standards and regulation. Then, the chapter reports an overview of approaches and methodologies for addressing compliance coming from the most relevant initiatives on cloud security and a survey of what storage cloud vendors declare to do in terms of compliance. Finally, the SIEM-based approach as a supporting technology for the achievement of security compliance objectives is described and, the architecture of the security compliance component of the VISION Cloud architecture is presented.*

DOI: 10.4018/978-1-4666-3934-8.ch008

# INTRODUCTION

Although the distributed computing models and virtualization technologies have introduced substantial benefits, the facts that both physical and software resources can be geographically distributed and shared by different users and the customer has not control over the physical security of the infrastructure that host their business services, have heightened the common security and regulatory issues of traditional IT infrastructure.

As a result, it is fundamental for a cloud provider to guarantee and demonstrate that the security level of its infrastructure is at least the same of the customer's one.

According to this, most important initiatives on security compliance, including CSA (Cloud Security Alliance) and ENISA – European Network and Information Security Agency, emphasizes the importance to certify the cloud offering to the common security standards such as ISO27001 and PCI-DSS and audit framework such as SAS-70 II, in order to cushion cloud computing security issues.

Providing evidence of adherence to these standards is binding for cloud providers that are supposed to host critical applications or sensitive data. For example: getting PCI DSS certification is mandatory in the context of for credit card management system, while HIPAA prescribes a rigorous security checklist in order to preserve the integrity and confidentiality of personal health records.

Among the key requirements derived from these standards, the aspect of auditing and its impact to the cloud computing is sticking out more and more. It implies the need for cloud provider to put in place logging management and reporting mechanisms in order to gather information about the behavior of the hardware, software and network infrastructure used to run specific tenant applications, and process them to elaborate security and compliance reports that are needed for audit purposes. In synthesis, logging

and reporting practices are essential for auditor and management to control on the compliance objectives achievement.

In this chapter, the privacy compliance and the storage infrastructure compliance regulations and standards and their applicability to storage clouds, as well as the derived key requirements, are firstly discussed. Then an overview of the most accredited works on security compliance best practices, recommendations and guidelines in the cloud is provided, along with a survey of how the most common cloud providers approach the problem of compliance.

Finally, the chapter presents the architecture of the VISION Cloud compliance component is presented. It is a SIEM (System Information and Event Management) based, scalable and flexible system that can be deployed in a variety of distributed and virtualized infrastructure and which provides the following capabilities: collection in a secure way of audit records from different sources (and in different format) of the distributed infrastructure, normalization records in a standard an common format independent from the source, application of security polices over the normalized messages and (in case of events that may require corrective actions or other types of responses) generation of alert, summary of data in reports in conformity with ISO 27001.

## THE PROBLEM OF BEING COMPLIANT

Security responsibilities of both the provider and the consumer differ between cloud service models. Security controls, at a glance, can be divided into three macro-areas which directly derive from the corresponding cloud service models defined above. The first ones are Infrastructure-Level (IL) security controls. Controls performed at this level can refer up to the physical, environmental and virtualization layers. The second ones are

Platform-Level (PL) security controls. Controls performed at this level can refer up to the operating system and running environment layer. The last ones are Software-Level (SL) security controls. Controls performed at this level can refer up to the application layer.

As an example, Amazon EC2 IaaS offering can provide only IL security controls while PL and SL are fully missed. The reason for that is the lack of knowledge about the applications that will run upon the virtualized infrastructure and, more important, the type of managed data and data processing to be performed. Indeed, responsibilities tied to the remaining security issues entirely relay on the consumer. However, the kind of data transferred to the provider and the processing defined upon this data still raise accountability concerns the consumers need to face with. It is worth to be noticed that cloud users still remain responsible for the security and privacy assurance of transmitted data, especially in the case of personal and sensitive information. In Ashimmy's article[1] this concept is efficaciously paraphrased: "No matter where your assets are, no matter the cloud you rely on, if your company has a compliance requirement, you are accountable to be compliant... you can outsource responsibility for compliance in the cloud, but you remain accountable and suffer the consequences of non-compliance."

Especially in public and distributed storage cloud, customer data can be stored on any of multiple servers that form the cloud infrastructure, potentially around the world, and can be moved or copied to another server at any time. This can result in a crucial issue for customers that are requested to provide audit trail of where data has been stored for regulatory or legal purposes. Then, just because the responsibility of compliance cannot be "outsourced" along with the outsourced services and data, the customer should be enabled to get information from the cloud provider on where and by whom/what its data is accessed, stored, transferred and eventually tempered with.

## THE REFERENCE LEGAL FRAMEWORK

Data stored in the cloud are subject to international information privacy and security laws (e.g. the EU Data Protection Directives), which are often in conflict each other. The assignment of compliance responsibilities to cloud providers and costumers must be clearly investigated. From a practical point of view, this separation should depend on the effective means available to the parties involved in order to install security policies and controls and verify their operation and effectiveness. Nevertheless, law and regulatory provisions often fall upon the cloud users who, as a consequence of the transferring of control to the provider, simultaneously lose capability in performing many essential controls. The size of this loss depends on the adopted cloud service model as already mentioned.

It's therefore necessary to identify regulatory requirements applicable to a given cloud service model. For the most part they derive from geographical considerations (about the physical location of the provider's servers, about the provider's jurisdiction and the data owner's jurisdiction) and from the categories of data to be processed (e.g. sensitive, financial or health data).

Below follows a short description of the EU Directives that are widely adopted as a reference legal framework and that we've considered for the VISION Cloud infrastructure.

### EU Directive 95/46/EC

The EU Directive was adopted by the European Commission on October 24, 1995, and took effect on October 25, 1998 . Its stated purpose was two fold: to harmonize divergent data protection regimes in the Member States in order to remove obstacles to the free flow of information and, to "protect fundamental rights and freedoms, notably the right to privacy" by establishing minimum safeguards for the use of personal data.

## EU Directive 2002/58/EC

Directive 2002/58/EC concerns the processing of personal data and the protection of privacy in the electronic communications sector. The provisions characteristic of this directive, give and complement of Directive 95/46/EC. The Directive aims to harmonize the provisions of the Member States concerning the obligations on providers of electronic communications services accessible to the pub- lic or a public disclosure related to retention of certain data in order to ensure their availability for the detection, investigation and prosecution of serious crime.

## EU Directive 2006/24/EC

The Directive 2006/25/EC concerns the retention of data generated or processed in the provision of publicly available electronic communications services or of public communications networks. The Directive aims to harmonize the provisions of the Member States concerning the obligations for providers of electronic communications services available to the public or a public communication. These obligations are about retention of certain data or processes in order to ensure their availability for the purposes of investigation, detection and prosecution of serious crime, as defined by each Member State in its national legislation. It applies to traffic data and location data of persons and legal entities, and the related data necessary to identify the subscriber or registered user. Do not apply to the content of electronic communications.

## EU Data Protection Reform and Cloud Computing

In the last period the European Commission is working on a overall EU-wide Cloud Computing Strategy, initially scheduled for mid-2012, to propose a single set of rules for EU in order to develop a European Cloud Market[2] "The strategy will set out how different actions can serve the goal to get clarity on issues like standards, privacy, data portability, legal liability and applicable jurisdiction." The target of this initiative is to create a European Cloud Partnership between public authorities and industry with the idea to agree on common requirements for public Cloud procurements.

The European Commission has presented a proposal designed to improve privacy online and to reform the EU data protection policy. Their main objectives are to discuss the issues related to the technology from policy, business, technology and user perspectives, to highlight the need for a EU Cloud policy and regulatory framework and to look into the necessity of standardisation to guarantee interoperability between Cloud providers in order to create a competitive European market for Cloud services. Their intent is to "make Europe not just Cloud-Friendly but Cloud Active."

They have proposed a Regulation to replace a Directive: that means a single set of rules for Europe instead many different ones and than the same rules should apply to the data. Alongside that, under the new rules you will get a one-stop-shop of enforcement. So that, even if an operator is active in several EU countries, it will only have to deal with one data protection authority. Companies that are active in the EU, offer services to EU citizens and handle personal data outside the union are subject to the proposed rules. The main principles developed and proposed are:

- **Right to be Forgotten:** Organization that are responsible of the collection of sensitive data, are obliged to delete such information upon owner request. Furthermore, these organization must be obtain the explicit consensus of the owner to collect certain data.
- **Data Portability:** Individuals should be enabled to access to their own data, request a copy of their stored data and move it to another service provider in a common portable format. Individuals must be informed on how organization handle their data.

- **Data Breach:** Organization must notify regulators of a data breach and notify affected individuals. Organization should produce data protection assessment.
- **Data Protection Authorities (DPAs):** Organisations should refer only to a single national data protection authority.

## REFERENCE SECURITY AND AUDIT CERTIFICATION STANDARDS

The absence or inadequacy of automation in the audit practices and methodology of a cloud infrastructure increases the risks of non-compliance. This inhibits enterprises from outsourcing their more valuable business processes onto the Cloud and prevents the full realization of the economic potential of Cloud Computing. In order to stimulate enterprise confidence in cloud services, the central objective is certifying cloud offerings for their adherence to regulatory requirements. Certifications provide means to address the complexity associated with achieving and maintaining compliance in the cloud. Standards and compliance certifications include SAS-70 Type I and Type II Attestation, ISO 27001 Certification, PCI DSS Compliance, HIPAA Business Associate, U.S. Commerce Department Safe Harbor Certification, and others. Below a short description of some certifications of particular interest which also affect the European vendors follows.

- **SAS 70 type I and type II Attestation:** Statement on Auditing Standards N. 70 is a widely recognized auditing standard developed by the American Institute of Certified Public Accountants (AICPA). Service organizations or service providers must demonstrate that they have adequate controls in place when they host or process data belonging to their customers. SAS70 certifies that a service organisation has had an in-depth audit of its controls (including control objectives and control activities). SSAE 16 effectively replaces SAS 70 as the standard for reporting on service organizations since June 15, 2011.

- **ISO/IEC 27001:2005:** This is an information security standard. It specifies the requirements for establishing, implementing, operating, monitoring, reviewing, maintaining and improving a documented Information Security Management System (ISMS) within the context of the organization's overall business risks. It is designed to ensure the selection of adequate and proportionate security controls that protect information assets and give confidence to interested parties. Currently ISO/IEC 27001 is being revised. Updating of the standard has been delayed partly by the JTCG (Joint technical Coordination Group) decision to harmonized all its management systems standards. Consequently, the revised standard is unlikely to be published much before the end of 2013.

- **ISO 31000:2009:** It was published as a standard on the 13th of November 2009, and provides a standard on the implementation of risk management. It provides generic guidelines for the design, implementation and maintenance of risk management processes throughout an organization. The purpose of ISO 31000:2009 is to be applicable and adaptable for "any public, private or community enterprise, association, group or individual". As a family of risk management standards ISO 31000 provides a generic best practice structure and guidance to all operations concerned with risk management. ISO/IEC 2700k are being revised to harmonize all its management systems standards and the part concerning risk management will take into account ISO 31000.

- **SSAE 16:** Statement on Standards for Attestation Engagements (SSAE) No. 16, is an attestation standard issued by the Auditing Standards Board (ASB) of the American Institute of Certified Public Accountants (AICPA). Specifically, SSAE 16 is an attestation standard geared towards addressing engagements conducted by auditors on service organizations for purposes of reporting on the design of controls and their operating effectiveness. SSAE 16 engagements on service organizations will result in the issuance of either a SSAE 16 Type 1 or Type 2 Report. A Type 1 report is technically known as a "Report on Management's Description of a Service Organization's System and the Suitability of the Design of Controls". Regarding a Type 2 Report, it is technically known as a "Report on Manage- ment's Description of a Service Organization's System and the Suitability of the Design and Operating Effectiveness of Controls".

- **ISAE 3402:** International Standards for Assurance Engagements (ISAE) No. 3402 and Service Organization Con- trol (SOC) reporting. This is a standard put forth by the International Auditing and Assurance Standards Board (IAASB), a standard-setting board within the International Federation of Accountants (IFAC). It is a global standard for assurance reporting on services organizations. It is interesting to note that in ISAE 3402 there are two crucial components: the service organization must produce a description of its system and the service organization must provide a written statement of assertion. SAAE 16 and ISAE 3402 are essentially similar standards; they are the convergence of auditing standards for reporting on controls at service organizations.
- **PCI DSS:** The Payment Card Industry Data Security Standard (PCI DSS) is a worldwide information security standard that applies to organisations that hold, process

or exchange cardholder information. Cardholder data includes primary account number, expiration date, name as it appears on the card, CVV, CVV2 and magnetic stripe. This standard helps preventing credit card fraud through increased con- trols around data and its exposure to compromise. The PCI DSS includes requirements for security management, policies, procedures, network architecture, software design. PCI DSS compliance in- clude Self Assessment Questionnaires - PCI DSS SAQ - that is a validation tool. A SAQ includes a series of yes-or-no questions about security posture and practices and it depends on the business scenario. PCI Security Standards Council published new guidelines regarding the PCI DSS Virtualization section in June 2011 to provide guidance on the use of virtualization in accordance with the PCI DSS. They explain how PCI DSS applies to virtual environments including: evaluating the risks of a virtualized environment, implementing additional physical access controls for host systems and securing access, isolating the security processes that could put the card data at risk and identifying which virtualized elements should be considered "in scope" for the purposes of PCI compliance.

- **COBIT:** The Control Objectives for Information and related Technology (COBIT) is a model (framework) for the Management of Information and Communication Technology (ICT) created in 1992 by the Amer- ican Information Systems Auditor (Information Systems Audit and Control Association - ISACA), and the IT Governance Institute (ITGI). COBIT provides managers, auditors and users of IT systems a grid of reference: structure of the IT processes a series of theoretical and practical tools related to the processes with the aim of assessing whether it is in place effective governance of the IT function (IT governance) or to provide guidance to restore it. COBIT has achieved the status of internationally recognized standard; the European Union has set COBIT as one of three standards that can be used to ensure the security of information systems.

- **NIST SP800-53:** The SP 800-53 standard, titled 'Recommended Security Controls for Federal Information Systems and Organizations', was co-developed by the Computer Security Division of NIST, DoD and the U.S. Intelligence Community, as well as the Industrial Control System community. It benefited by extensive public review and comments. It represents the best practices and guidance available today, not only for the government but for private enterprises as well. The purpose of SP800-53 is to achieve information system security and effective risk management, in part, by providing a common information security language for all information systems and by providing consistent and repeatable guidelines for selecting and specifying standard security controls. On February 2012 NIST (NIST, 2012) presented the Special Publication SP 800-53, Revision 4 Draft to update the content of the security controls catalogue and the guidance for selecting and specifying security controls for federal information systems and organizations. Many of the changes rise from particular security issues and questions including, for example, application security, cloud computing, insider and advanced persistent threats, firmware integrity. The controls and enhancements are distributed throughout the control catalogue in several families and provide specific security features that are required to support new computing technologies and approaches.

- **HIPAA:** The Health Insurance Portability and Accountability Act (HIPAA) is a set of standards created by Congress that aim to safeguard protected health information (PHI) by regulating healthcare providers. HIPAA has been around since 1996 but has never been taken seriously before the new act called HITECH (The Health Information Technology for Economic and Clinical Health Act) was enacted that became effective on February 2010. HIPAA mandates standardized formats for all patient health, administrative and financial data.

## KEY REQUIREMENTS

This section reports the most relevant security compliance requirements for storage cloud deriving from the legal and security reference frameworks previously described. In order to derive this list also the work done by ENISA, has been taken into account. ENISA is a public agency dealing with cyber security issues of the European Union, a centre of expertise and information exchange among Member States. Among other works, it carried out some studies (ENISA, 2009) to identify the potential security issues and limitation of the introduction of the Cloud technologies.

- **Data Center Security:** The customer should be aware of the physical location of cloud provider's data centre(s). Futhermore, appropriate measures should be taken in order to prevent data centre from unauthorized access.

- **Geolocalization and Georeplication:** The provider should guarantee that user data are maintained in a specific jurisdiction and/or to avoid certain jurisdictions. As well known, data stored on the cloud is, in many cases, subject to transferring or copying from one server to another, either in different data centre locations. Changing location of data, even on a temporary basis, could imply customers to become subject to the laws of the specific jurisdiction where the data has been transferred.

- **Security of data in transit:** When data is moved from a server to another in the cloud, it is problematic to identify and determine the policies around the sensitive data. The related security policies should accompany the data during their migration in order to meet the initial constraints of security and privacy, such as confidentiality and integrity. Furthermore data in transit should be protected, e.g., by using protocol such as FTP over SSL, HTTPS, etc, especially when data is transferred across the Internet. Providers should implement security policies in order to prevent lost or fall into the wrong hands during the transit.

- **Data Protection: access control policies, confidentiality, integrity:** Cloud provider should implement appropriate technical and organizational security measures on the processing of private data, and also provide the customer with auditable proofs of the accomplishment of those measures. Adequate security policies on data handling/ management and access control should be determinate, in order to prevent impermissible copying or removal of customer data (e.g. by unauthorized employees of the organization, even infrastructure administrator, by external user,...). Access control is needed to guarantee the confidentiality of data and it includes both authentication and authorization. Usually, protection of data stored in the cloud involves the use of encryption and, as a consequence, it is important to know which encryption algorithm is used and which encryption key management mechanisms are in place in the cloud. Data protection should also be guaranteed for ancillary data, for example

accounts or transaction data, which need to have the same treatment as any other sensitive data.

- **Information classification:** This means assigning a degree of severity to data, which determines the adequate protection measures that must be taken in order to prevent the risk of loss or disclosure. The A2.7.1 ISO27001 requirement literally says "Data, and objects containing data, shall be assigned a classification based on data type, jurisdiction of origin, jurisdiction domiciled, context, legal constraints, contractual constraints, value, sensitivity, criticality to the organization and third party obligation for retention and prevention of unauthorized disclosure or misuse". Classifying information is a basic requirement for data protection and access control, in fact security controls such as those on data retention, deletion and sanitisation can be performed only if data is stored along with the classification information. Also the type encryption should depend on the degree of severity.

- **Segmentation and data segregation:** Currently, most cloud service providers offer their services on a shared server basis (multitenancy). Within the same physical machine can coexist more than virtual machines belonging to different organizations. Also storage can be offered on a virtualization basis, as in VISION Cloud, where virtual storage containers that potentially reside in the same physical storage which can be owned by different organizations. In this case, it is important to have a segmentation of the system with the separation of the roles to be associated with individual entities in order to prevent an entity might accidentally get data of which her is not the owner. From this point of view, customer should be informed on the procedures/ security policies that are in place in the cloud in order to ensure that another customer does not have access its data, even if data of both customers are hosted on the same server, and that violation attempts are detected.

- **Data retention:** This requirement refers to how long the private data that is transferred to the cloud is kept in and which retention policy governs the data. Private data should not be retained for longer than needed to perform the task for which it was collected, or as required by laws or regulations. Data should be destroyed in a secure way at the end of the retention period (see next point). Another point is about ownership of data, that is whether data is actually owned by the organization or by the cloud provider and who enforces the retention policy in the cloud.

- **Data deletion and sanitisation (on data remanence):** Data remanence is the physical data that can remain on a storage device after that data is deleted and it is caused by the fact that standard deletion methods are rarely as effective as they are supposed to be. Data remanence may cause inadvertent disclosure of sensitive information. The cloud storage provider should guarantee and provide evidence that, after the retention period, a proper sanitisation procedure has been carried out to the storage device which hosted the customer data during the service contract period.

- **Backup and replication:** Backup and discovery practices should be applied in the storage cloud. Having multiple instances of data replicated by geography is a key capability for distributed data centre replication. The provider should conduct regular backup and recovery tests and, whenever an event of lost or compromised data occurs, the data should be backed up and easily restored from the backup.

- **Vulnerability disclosure:** The storage provider is required to disclose any new vulnerability that may impact the confidentiality of customer data, or the availability and integrity of their services.

- **Logging, auditability, accountability:** As previously mentioned, this is likely the most important aspect (along with access control) related to security compliance as well as a focus area in all security certification standards. Most of rules defined in the standards like ISO 27001 and SAS 70 II are on logging management and audit aspects and can be summarized as follows:
  ○ Trace all significant events.
  ○ Specify which are the threat events.
  ○ Specify the corrective actions in case of event happening.
  ○ Log event and related corrective actions.
  ○ Make available both the events and corrective actions related logs for Audit purposes.
  ○ Securely store all logs and provide evidence on how long they are maintained.

Cloud provider should be able to produce a secure audit trail that can be inspected in case of problem, according to the following principles of accountability:

- **Non-repudiability:** Each operation should be incontrovertibly linked to the entity (e.g. user, service, infrastructure node) that executes it.

- **Secure record:** All operations should be recorded in a secure way.

- **Auditing:** The recorded operations should be inspected by other domains or by a trusted third party and exclusively upon secure access on the audit recorded information.

## APPROACHES AND IMPLEMENTATIONS

Addressing compliance means defining a compliance program based on a risk analysis, on the identification of the needed security controls, and on the regular assessment of those controls.

These controls should tailor the number of regulatory, industry, and internal organization obligations to the governed infrastructure, in accordance to the most accredited best-practice framework and guidelines.

And, actually, most of all current works on the compliance in the cloud just reflect the effort to apply the common IT Security management practices and the necessity to adapt existing and/or define new common standards and specifications for the cloud paradigm and the virtualization technologies it relies on. For example, virtualization introduced the need to consider new type of security policies such as for controlling the creation, use, and modification of virtual machines and for configuring new infrastructure elements, including the hypervisor, virtual networks and storage, that can dynamically change the boundaries of the governed perimeter. Furthermore, this exacerbates the need to perform continuous enforcement and assessment of compliance program.

However, the process of evolving traditional compliance and security practices for the cloud model is quite hard and it has not resulted yet in universally recognized practices and methodologies.

Cloud Security Alliance – CSA, ENISA and NIST are the most active organizations promoting the use of best practices aiming at offering security assurance within Cloud Computing. Several approaches and methodologies are proposed to support security, compliance, and data management in the Cloud context. It is just a recent news the collaboration between CSA and the ISO team in order to extend the ISO27k certification standards also to the cloud model.

This section provides an outline on the most accredited works aim at identifying recommendation and best practices and provides a survey on how the most common cloud providers approach the problem of compliance.

### CSA

The Cloud Security Alliance[3] is a non-profit organization with the intent to support the use of best practices in order to provide security assurance within Cloud Computing. Among their proposed initiatives, it worth mentioning the following:

- **CSA Security Guidance (for Critical Areas of Focus in Cloud Computing):** Foundational best practices for securing cloud computing. Recently the version 3 published included 14 domains of analysis each of which reported either recommendations and requirements.

Each domain (Cloud Architecture, Governance and Enterprise Risk Management, Legal: Constraints and Electronic Discovery, Compliance and Audit, Information Management and Data Security, Portability and Interoperability, Traditional Security, Business Continuity and Disaster Recovery, Data Center Operations, Incident Response, Notification and Remediation, Application Security, Encryption and Key Management, Identity and Access Management, Virtualisation, and Security as a Service) represent a perspective or focus of the potential risks around the adoption of Cloud services for the Enterprise Data or Processes/Applications.

- **Cloud Controls Matrix:** Security controls framework for cloud provider and cloud consumers.
- **Consensus Assessments Initiative:** Research tools and processes to perform consistent measurements of cloud providers.

- **GRC Stack:** An integrated suite of 4 CSA initiatives: Cloud Audit, Cloud Controls Matrix, CAI Questionnaire, the Cloud Trust Protocol.
- **Security as a Service:** Research for gaining greater understanding for how to deliver security solutions via cloud models.

In particular, the Cloud Security Alliance Cloud Controls Matrix (CCM)[4] is designed to provide fundamental security principles to guide cloud vendors and to assist cloud customers in assessing the security risk of a cloud provider.

The CCM represents an attempt for a synthetic set of controls each compared with the Certifications or standards. It includes more than 100 controls are listed and mapped into Industry standards (e.g. ISO 27001/27002, ISACA COBIT, PCI, NIST, Jericho Forum and NERC CIP). These controls when actually implemented allow to report relevant information needed by standard reporting certifications such as the SAS 70.

CCM is a part of the CSA GRC (Governance, Risk Management and Compliance) Stack, which provides a controls framework that gives a detailed understanding of security concepts and principles that are aligned to the Cloud Security Alliance's 13 domains (which include Identity Assurance, Audit and Secure Access).

CSA STAR is open to all cloud providers and allows them to submit self-assessment reports that document compliance to CSA published best practices. The registry will allow cloud customers to review the security practices of providers, accelerating their due diligence and leading to higher quality procurement experiences. CSA STAR is intended to promote industry transparency and to encourage providers to provide fundamental security capabilities.

Cloud providers can submit two different types of reports to indicate their compliance with CSA best practices: Consensus Assessments Initiative Questionnaire (CAIQ) or the Cloud Controls Matrix (CCM).

- **Security as a Service (Secaas) and System Information and Event System (SIEM):** CSA suggests the use of SIEM tools to correlate cloud application access log data and policy data for compliance purposes. An innovative aspect introduced in the "Security Guidance for Critical area of focus in cloud computing v3.0" is the concept of the Security as a Service (Secaas). It is described as "one of the milestone of the maturity of cloud as a platform for business operations". Their point is that predominantly cloud security discussions have focused on how to migrate to the Cloud and how to ensure Confidentiality, integrity, availability and location are maintained when using the Cloud. Secaas (Security as a Service) looks from the other side to secure systems and data as well as hybrid and traditional enterprise network via cloud- based services.

As highlighted by CSA the most interesting security service categories are: Identity and Access Management (IAM), Data Loss Prevention, Web Security, Email Security, Security Assessments, Encryption, Business Continuity and Disaster Recovery, Network Security, Security Information and Event Management (SIEM).

Among the most significant areas of Cloud Security as a Service, the attention of the authors of this chapter was focused predominantly on Security Information and Event Management (SIEM) as a technology supporting certification and audit on the infrastructure and the achievement of the security objectives. The CSA SIEM definition is:

"SIEM systems aggregate log and event data from virtual and real networks, applications, and systems. This information is then correlated and analyzed to provide real time reporting and alerting on information or events that may require intervention or other types of responses. The logs are typically collected and archived in a manner that prevents tampering to enable their use as evidence in any investigations or historical reporting. The SIEM Security as a Service offering is a Detective technical control but can be configured to be a protective and reactive technical control".

## CAMM: COMMON ASSURANCE MATURITY MODEL

CAMM (Common Assurance Maturity Model) is a standards-based information security metrics that has been created by a consortium of end user organizations, service providers, associations. It is also mentioned in the CSA Consensus Assessments Initiative Questionnaire. CAMM will provision a top down view of the providers capabilities in the areas of Security, Governance, and Compliance.

CAMM Maturity Model of Security Controls has the goal of providing a framework in support of necessary transparency attesting the Information Assurance Maturity of a Third Party Providers such as Cloud providers. Their intent is the publication of results in an open and transparent manner without the mandatory need for third party audit functions. CAMM model focuses on Information Assurance in comparison to other supplier's levels of compliance, and security profiles.

The methodology they use is: to apply existing standards such as ISO 27001, ISO 27002, CobIT, PCI-DSS, to develop a series of control questions specific to the organisation; to make responses to such questions public and available; to include a score that details the providers Common Assurance Maturity score.

## RC3: REGULATORY COMPLIANT CLOUD COMPUTING

In order to manage the issue of securing sensitive data and ensuring compliance to security regulations the Regulatory Compliant Cloud Computing (RC3) is a model of computing where business transactions involve in regulated areas and public clouds. The basic idea is storing and managing sensitive data within regulated areas inside a secure perimeter, while all non-sensitive data can be computed, stored and managed in public clouds. Therefore, sensitive data is encrypted, tokenized and managed in the regulated area within the secure perimeter of an enterprise (or a delegated out-sourcing company), while all non-sensitive data resides in the public cloud.

RC3 applications require data classified into three categories:

- **C1 - Sensitive and regulated data:** Data whose disclosure to the public would result in potential lawsuits, and loss of goodwill to the breached entity. Examples are: credit card numbers, social security numbers, bank account numbers, etc. This kind of data will be processed and stored in regulated areas, within a secure network perimeter. These areas will prove they are compliant with applicable data-security regulations. Sensitive data that has been encrypted and replaced with tokens may be stored in public clouds.

- **C2 - Sensitive but non-regulated data:** Data which is not regulated, but whose disclosure to the public would be detrimental to a company and/or result in some loss of goodwill to the breached entity. Examples are: an employee's salary, sales figures for specific product-lines, name, gender and age of a customer, etc. These kind of data will be processed in secure, but not necessarily regulated, areas. Data-tokens may be stored in public clouds.

- **C3 - Non-sensitive data:** All other data. Examples are: product descriptions, images, etc. These kind of data may be processed and stored in public clouds.

## COMPARISON

Taking as reference the certification standards recommended by the CSA, below is a general survey of some cloud providers and which standards they declare to be compliant to. It worth noticing that, while these information are disclaimed by the providers themselves, there is no public knowledge about any specific procedure, best practice and automatism they adopt to address compliance.

In the last two years the most notable Public Cloud providers (e.g. AWS, RackSpace, Microsoft) recognised the need for acquiring security certifications. However the level of auditability is almost null and the compliance to regulation is still to be proved.

SoftLayer offers CloudLayer[5] for scale computing resource on-demand and allowing: Public Cloud: A multi-tenant environment that is designed for workloads that require rapid provisioning. Private Cloud: An environment dedicated to a single customer that leverages virtualization tools to deliver a secure computing platform. Bare Metal Cloud: Designed for workloads with high I/O and that do not require a virtualization layer. CloudLayer doesn't support any standard except for SAS 70 Type II certification.

Gogrid[6] specializes in IaaS and allows building scalable cloud infrastructure in multiple data centers using dedicated and cloud servers, elastic F5 hardware load balancing, and cloud storage with total control through automation and self-service. GoGrid is a service of ServePath, LLC, San Francisco who received the same SAS 70 Type II Report that includes GoGrid. GogGrid, in partnership with Sentrigo[7], offers "Integraded Databse Security Suite" that allow GoGrid users to quickly and easily satisfy regulatory requirements (SOX, PCI-DSS, SAS70, HIPAA).

Logicworks offers the IaaS service Infini-Cloud. Logicworks[8] has been certified PCI DSS level 1 http://www.logicworks.net/tech-specs/compliance.

Rackspace has received the final report for SAS 70 Type II reports that now covers Cloud Files, Cloud Servers and all of our global datacenters has been assessed and found compliant with the requirements of ISO 27001:2005[9]. This Certificate is valid for the activities specified below: "The management of information security in the design, implementation and support of Hosted Systems at our LON 3 data centre facility".

Atlantic.Net[10] is a market-leading Hosting Solutions Provider renowned for providing exceptional Infrastructure as a service, simplifying complex technologies and building a brand that people trust since it was established in 1994. Atlantic.Net operates SAS 70 Type II audited and certified hosting solutions platform to assist businesses around the globe with their advanced IT needs. Atlantic.Net is SSAE 16 (SOC 1) TYPE II (Formerly SAS 70) compliant[11].

Amazon specializes in IaaS. It offers through Amazon Web Services (AWS): Amazon Elastic Compute Cloud (EC2), Amazon SimpleDB, Amazon CloudFront, Amazon SQS. Amazon Web Services has in the past successfully completed multiple SAS70 Type II audits, and as of September 30, 2011 publishes a Service Organization Controls 1 (SOC 1) report, published under both the SSAE 16 and the ISAE 3402 professional standards. In addition, AWS has achieved ISO 27001 certification, has been successfully validated as a Level 1 service provider under the Payment Card Industry (PCI) Data Security Standard (DSS), and has completed the control implementation and independent security testing required to operate at the FISMA-Moderate level[12]. AWS platform permits the deployment of solutions that meet industry-specific certification requirements. For instance, customers have built healthcare applications compliant with HIPPA. AWS participates in the safe harbour programs[13].

Google specializes in PaaS and SaaS. As SaaS it offers Google Apps: a Web-based communication, collaboration and security apps which include, Gmail, Google Calendar, Google Talk, Google

Docs and Google Sites. As PaaS it offers Google App Engine: a platform for developing and hosting Web applications in Google-managed data centers. Currently, the supported programming languages are Python and Java. The controls, processes, and policies that protect data in our systems have successfully completed a SSAE 16 Type II audit. Google Apps is the first cloud based messaging and collaboration suite to achieve FISMA (Federal Information Security Management Act) certification, indicating that the General Services Administration has reviewed and certified their security processes and documentation[14].

Microsoft Cloud offers Azure, a Windows-as-a-service platform consisting of the operating system and developer services that can be used to build and enhance Web-hosted applications. The Microsoft cloud has obtained ISO/IEC 27001:2005 certification and SAS 70 Type 1 and II attestations[15]. MS Azure AWS participates in the safe harbour programs[16]. Windows Azure has published its security controls in response to the standards set by the Cloud Security Alliance (CSA) Security, Trust & Assurance Registry[17] (STAR).

Salesforce is leader in SaaS. Offers Salesforce CRM (Sales Cloud 2, Service Cloud 2) & Force.com Platform (Custom Cloud 2, Development Platform). The complete list of Saleforce certifications are available on its site[18]. Salesforce is now Payment Card Industry, Data Security Standard (PCI DSS) certified at Compliance Level 1 as well as ISO27001, TRUSTe Certified Privacy, SysTrust, and SAS70 Type II certified.[19]

Joyent is the only cloud computing company that has developed a complete software stack, runs a major public cloud on that stack, and offers its cloud data center software to any company that wants to build a cloud. Joyent did not declare in its Website[20] whether it has received or not certifications like SAS 70 or PCI DSS. Joyent just declared to respect individual privacy because participates to the safe harbour programs[21].

NetSuite specializes in SaaS. It offers SuitCloud Platform, which is a comprehensive offering of on- demand products, development tools and services designed to help customers and software developers take advantage of the significant benefits of cloud computing. Also a leading provider of Web-based Business Software Suite for CRM, ERP tools and Accounting. NetSuite Provides an SSAE 16 (SOC1)/ISAE 3402.Type II Report[22]. The other certifications of NetSuite concern data services and not cloud services[23].

CA 3Tera offers AppLogic[24], it is a turnkey cloud computing platform for composing, running and scaling distributed applications. It uses advanced virtualization technologies to be completely compatible with existing operating systems, middleware and Web applications. CA 3Tera hasn't disclaimed any information about its certification program.

VMware, in joint venture with Salesforce.com, offers VMforce, which is the first enterprise cloud for Java.

Looking at the Figure 1, the following considerations result:

- Almost all cloud providers are certified SAS70.
- Only Amazon is a HIPAA compliance. While, some of them provide the tools or libraries to get certified HIPAA.

## FUTURE RESEARCH DIRECTIONS

### VISION Cloud Approach

### Introduction

The "Approaches" section introduced the concept of SIEM and the recommendation from CSA to adopt this technology as a best practice supporting the security posture of organization and achievement of security and certification objectives.

For this reason, in the Management Interface Layer of VISION Cloud a Compliance Component, made up of auditing and reporting mechanisms and based on SIEM approach, has been included. It is basically a set of functionalities

*Figure 1. Cloud provider survey*

| Cloud Provider | SAS70 II | EU Privacy | ISO:27001 | PCI DSS | HIPAA |
|---|---|---|---|---|---|
| SoftLayer CloudLayer | YES | | | | |
| GoGrid | YES | | | | |
| infiniCloud logicwork | YES | | | V.1.2 | |
| Rackspace | YES | | YES | | |
| atlantic.net | YES | | | | |
| Amazon AWS | YES | Safe Harbor framework | YES | Level 1 | YES |
| Google Apps for Business | YES | Safe Harbor framework | | | |
| Microsoft Cloud | YES | Safe Harbor framework | YES | | |
| Salesforce | YES | Safe Harbor framework | YES | | |
| Joyent | | Safe Harbor framework | | | |
| NetSuite | YES | Safe Harbor framework | | | |
| CA 3tera | | | | | |
| VMWare VMforce | YES | | YES | | |
| Verizon CaaS | YES | | | | |

enabling centralization, storing and processing of the security events that occur within the storage infrastructure and that have to be collected and processed for security and audit purposes. In accordance to the SIEM model, the proposed solution provides the following main capabilities:

- Secure and reliable retention of audit events for reliability and accountability, even in case of the source of event/log fails or the logs on it are accidentally or intentionally cancelled.
- Correlation of events in order to identify violation of security policies in the distributed data centre of the storage infrastructure, which it would be impossible to do if each data center processed events separately.
- Alerting and notification to the interested parties (e.g. security manager of the storage infrastructure).
- Controlling on the status of the corrective actions.
- Reporting at different levels (for basic audit inspection, statistical) and for different purposes (for final users, for internal purposes, for auditing).

The audit events, generated by all the components of VISION Cloud through a dedicated library, are propagated in the Cloud infrastructure through the compliance system and also stored in a secure dedicated server, in accordance to log retention requirement deriving from the most common regulatory and certification standards.

In order to support interoperability and to streamline correlation, the event are formatted in the XDAS[25] standard and essentially log a list of activities that are performed within the infrastructure of VISION Cloud. The information contained in every XDAS event can be related to the source and destination host of a request, to the identity of the user/entity that invoked the operation, and the type of operation.

XDAS events are propagated through a the JMS[26] or TCP/IP sockets protocols, to a dedicated module which store them in a secured database.

In the following, more details on the proposed architecture and its strengths are reported.

## Architecture

The compliance module consists of two main components, as illustrated in the Figure 2 and one API library:

- **Compliance Agent Node:** A software component installed in each server of VISION Cloud (either physical or virtual machine).
- **Compliance Agent Server:** A software component installed on a dedicated (or pool of) server and unique within each perimeter of VISION Cloud, where perim-

*Figure 2. Cloud computing services and deployment models*

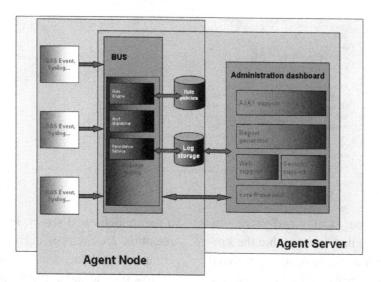

eter is defined as a set of IP and security rules of the Cloud infrastructure that are governed by the same security policies and that can be required to get ISO27001, PCI-DSS or other standards certified.

- **XDASLog4j:** A library for generating audit events in XDAS format and for propagating them to Agent Node.

The Agent Node is responsible for collecting XDAS events exposed through a JMS Topic, which is a distribution mechanism for publishing messages that are delivered to multiple subscribers. In addition, when an Agent Node is started, it searches for other agents (by auto-discovery) and joins them in the cluster by creating a Clustered Bus. Each event published in the Agent Node is propagated to the Agent Server. In fact, events are routed through Agent Nodes, which act as a Clustered Message Broker.

The Bus has a dual task: on the one hand it routes all the XDAS events in a topic so that all subscribers can apply all the security policies; on the other hand, it adds a level of decoupling between the XDAS producer and the Agent Node consumer, using the pattern of Publisher and Subscriber.

All VISION Cloud components are enabled to produce and propagate XDAS events in the Bus through a dedicated library. Among other things, this library supports a failover protocol: if an Agent Node is not reachable, it tires to publish XDAS events to the other Agent Nodes until this operation is successful. Figure 3 shows this aspect.

The Agent server collects all the events/alerts produced by the various Agent Nodes and provides a dashboard for management and report generation, management of alerts to display static metrics and production of events.

According to regulation and audit guidelines, the Agent Server must be placed in a secure network and only the Security Manager of the infrastructure can access it for security reason, thus preventing malicious activities on audit logs. It can be considered as a safe collector of audit / alert events that are inspected during the process of audit certification like ISO 27001.

In the proposed architecture, the Agent Node always guarantees that events are propagated to the Agent server. Moreover, if for some reason the Agent Server is unreachable, events are stored in the clustered bus until the Server is reachable again. This is depicted in Figure 4.

*Figure 3. High availability: case agent node died*

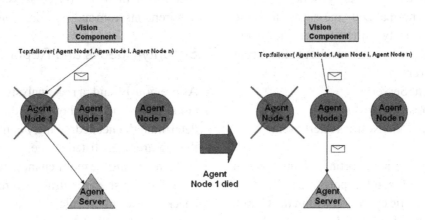

The aforementioned features (failover, auto-discovery, and the Compliance Clustered Bus) provide high reliability guarantees: no event message should are lost in any condition, even in case one of the Agent Nodes is unreachable. The only exception is when none of the Agent Nodes is accessible by the XDAS propagation library, but this is a borderline case very unlikely to happen.

A final aspect to highlight is the modularity of the proposed architecture, where each component can be added and removed at runtime without affecting the reliability and performance.

For a better understanding of the compliance module from the functional point of view, Figure 5.

Business Process Model and Notation (BPMN) illustrates the process of collection, aggregation and correlation of events produced by the aforementioned library:

- **Pool VISION:** A VISION Component generates an XDAS event.
- Pool Agent Node:
  - Collects the audit messages from different nodes of VISION.
  - Normalizes message in XDAS format.
  - Propagates the messages to Agent Server.

*Figure 4. High availability: case agent server died*

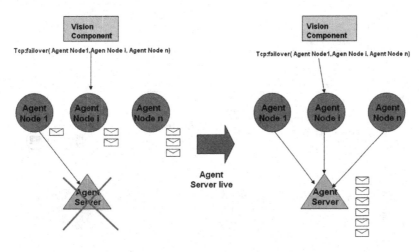

○ Applies the security police over every normalized message; in case of security policy failure the Agent Node propagates an alert to the Agent Server.
- Pool Agent Server:
  ○ Stores Audit events
  ○ Stores and Notifies Alert events

Finally, there is a Reporting Module which provides a set of audit reports, classified by standards or specific operation within the Cloud, thus enabling a potential audit and compliance assessment of the infrastructure.

The administration console of the Agent Server allows security administrator to analyze the events occurred in the system, to support activity of risk inspection and decision management by alerting and notification and to visualize statistical reports on significant events.

The functionalities offered by the Administration Console are protected by Authentication and Authorization mechanism, where the latter is RBAC-based. Users are managers or administrators in charge of analysis and management of audit logs and alerts. All activities related to the management of audit messages, including the login and logout to the application that allows inspection on them, are traced as well according to requirements from audit standards and regulations.

## Security Checks and Reports

As previously said, a risk analysis on the storage cloud infrastructure should be done in order to determine the needed security controls targeting the requirements listed above.

Considering the multitenancy caracteristic of the reference storage infrastructure, the security checks in the engine rule of the compliance component can be also defined on a per–tenant basis, thus addressing different compliance constraints that any tenant may have.

The security policies are applied on every XDAS event trough a CEP - Complex Event Processing. The CEP is a technology for analyzing data about certain event that happen within the governed perimeter, and deriving a conclusion from them. If one security policy fails, then the Agent Node propagates an alert to the Agent Server. The processing of audit events leverages on Esper[27], which is an ESP-Event Stream Processing, that is processing a stream of events in real time, so it can apply correlation and decision. Targeted for real-time processing, Esper is capable of triggering custom actions written as

*Figure 5. Compliance architecture: BPMN process*

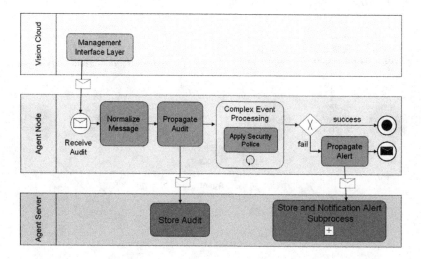

Plain Old Java Objects (POJO) when event conditions occur among event streams. It is designed for high-volume event correlation where it would be impossible to store millions of events using classical database architecture. Thanks to Esper, it is possible to analyze every stream of audit message and perform the correlation needed to apply security policies.

An example of correlation is when a user fails three time the authentication in three minutes. The rule policy written in EPL- Event Processing Language would be the following:

```
select * from XdasV1Model(hdr_event_
number='XDAS_AE_CREATE_SESSION' and
(hdr_outcome='XDAS_OUT_INVALID_IDEN-
TITY' OR hdr_outcome ='XDAS_OUT_IN-
VALID_CREDENTIALS' OR hdr_outcome
='XDAS_OUT_FAILURE')).win:length(180)
group by int_domain_specific_id having count(*)
>=3
```

The Agent node formats the event in Java Pojo Bean and then passes the output to Esper, which in turn applies the security policy above and, in case of failure, propagates the alert to the Agent Server.

Figures 6 and 7 are two examples of security controls for the VISION Cloud architecture enabled in the compliance component and the requirements they address (among those introduced in the requirements section).

There are many types of reports to be produced depending on the specific requirements that an organization has and the scope of audit and assessment. Nevertheless, there are some categories of reports particularly significant which are highlighted below.

Access control events are among the most important to track for compliance purpose. For example PCI DSS requires "track and monitor all access to network resources and cardholder data", ISO 27002 Access control state "regulates access to network and operating systems,

user access management generally and user responsibilities";HIPAA requirements (164.308) clearly state that user accesses to the system be recorded and monitored for possible abuse.

The types of access control reports useful for compliance that are enabled in the Security Compliance component of VISION Cloud include the followings:

- Logon and Logoff access reports related to the accesses to infrastructure resources and to the operating systems, to user access management and user responsibilities.
- Logon Failure reports related to all unsuccessful login attempts. the user name, date and time are included in this report.
- Audit Logs Access reports, which allow to regularly inspect audit logs.
- Object Access reports related to the accesses to objects, on the type of access (e.g. read, write, delete) and whether or not access was successful, and who performed the action.
- System Events reports related to who performed actions on local system such as system start-up and shutdown and changes to the system time or audit log.

The following reports provide information on account management events and are produced in association with main account management operations. The principal involved in the event may be a user or a service within the system. Events considered include:

- Create/deletion/disablement/enablement of account.
- Query account attributes: the requesting of the attributes associated with a principal within a domain.
- Modify account attributes: the modification of the attributes associated with a principal within a domain.

## Justification of the Approach

The background section discussed the aspects of auditability and accountability, and how logging and reporting practices constitute important assets of compliance management in order to guarantee and provide evidence that security, stability and conformity objectives are met.

The implementation approach for addressing security compliance requirements in VISION cloud is based on the shaping of the SIEM (system Information and Event Management) model to the cloud storage infrastructure, introducing as much automation as possible in the processing of auditable security events and in the compliance reporting.

Considering regulations, standards and models, the proposed solution is a system potentially capable of receiving relevant (security) information generated by different kinds of resources of the governed perimeter and to format them in auditable events using a common standard format.

Though these resources can potentially vary among systems, firewalls, routers, and any software component of the storage cloud infrastructure, the compliance perimeter considered in VISION Cloud is the one composed of all instances of the components that form VISION Cloud software stack within the distributed storage cloud infrastructure.

The capabilities provided by the compliance system include real-time reporting and alerting on those collected events that may require intervention (such as violation of a security policy) and enable the administrator to govern the security of perimeter(s), that is the set of data centers, clusters and related security policies, of the storage cloud infrastructure, even in a multi-tenant basis.

Currently, not all the SIEM products are able to manage virtualized environments as the ones in a cloud infrastructure. Furthermore, most of them that offer tools to control the security of virtual machines do not provide the same level of details especially for communications between VMs on the same host or virtual network as in physical infrastructures. Finally, very vendor, and actually in many cases different products by one vendor, uses a different proprietary event data format. Even in cases where standards such as Syslog are used, these standards are not enough powerful and well suited for the final audit purpose.

The proposed architecture presents the following key values:

- The usage of a unique and standard format for audit events facilitates the correlation, analysis and check of security policy constraints. It makes the module of compliance independent from the source which produces the events, thus enabling interoperability. Also, XDAS specification defines a wide list, also customizable, of the possible events which can be mapped into most of the control area of the CSA CCM (introduced in the approaches section).

- It leverages totally on open source technologies.

- Its clustered architecture provides high scalability thanks to its auto-discovery capability. The fact that each atomic agent can be installed automatically on each physical or virtual device (even at hypervisor level) makes the designed architecture fully modular. Furthermore, it enables a system administrator to decide where to install the agents and the rules for compliance to be applied on each component of the storage cloud architecture.

- The messaging bus technology used to propagate XDAS records allows decoupling the source producing events (the components of the VISION Cloud stack) from the compliance component, which analyzes them, in an asynchronous flow, thus guaranteeing high throughput. Furthermore, the messaging bus could be used also by other components whenever

*Figure 6. Security policy*

| Requirement | Information Classification - VISION Cloud architecture must support classification of Data Objects and Containers based on data type, jurisdiction of origin, jurisdiction domiciled, context, legal constraints, contractual constraints, value, sensitivity, criticality to the organization and third party obligation for retention and prevention of unauthorized disclosure or misuse |
|---|---|
| Type | Preventive |
| Description | This control aims to assure that only Data Objects having classification metadata (e.g. jurisdiction of origin, jurisdiction domiciled, legal constraints, sensitivity) are returned to the caller of the getObject operation. |
| Event | This control MUST be triggered whenever the Object Service receives a getObject service request. |
| Condition | None. |
| Action | The Object Service MUST:<br>• Invoke the getObjectMD operation provided by the Object Service.<br>• If the value returned by the getObjectMD operation misses classification metadata (e.g. jurisdiction of origin, jurisdiction domiciled, legal constraints, sensitivity) block the processing of the request and return a metadata-failure to the caller.<br>• Allow processing of the getObject request. |
| Generated Events | GETMD_STARTED (before step 1)<br>GETMD_COMPLETED(action= BLOCK) (is conditions of step 2 is true)<br>GETMD_COMPLETED(action=ALLOW) (step 3) |

an asynchronous distribution of messages is needed.

• The compliance rules which determine the controls to be performed on the audit events are only defined in the engine rule of the compliance architecture. This allows adding dynamically new compliance controls with a minimum impact to the other components of the storage cloud infrastructure.

• It is ideally suited for today's compliance-oriented requirements, since it provides a consolidated view of the security status of the critical assets of the infrastructure, and on-demand reports via the secure Web-based console.

• According to CSA recommendation, the capabilities provided by the proposed SIEM-based architecture constitute a mean a support to security manager of the infrastructure and auditor, allowing to perform compliance checks against a set of controls areas of reference standards and regulations that are considered of particular in-

terest for the VISION Cloud context and can be considered as a SaaS (Software as a service) solution.

In particular, the security checks concern the following control areas: data integrity, accesses to resources, access to sensitive data, geolocalization, data deletion. In conformity with ISO27001 requirements, particular attention is placed in access controls to resources and in the management of sensitive data, for which mechanisms of notification about suspicious conditions (e.g.: geo-localization constraint violation, reserved data violation etc.) are provided.

## CONCLUSION

In this chapter, we have presented an overview on the most critical requirements for cloud storage coming from regulations and common IT certification standards and best practices and how

*Figure 7. Security policy*

| Requirement | Logging/Audit - VISION Architecture MUST provide mechanisms to retain audit logs recording privileged user access activities, authorized and unauthorized access attempts, system exceptions, and information security events, complying with applicable policies and regulations. VISION Architecture MUST support at least daily review of Audit logs. VISION Architecture MUST restrict logical user access to audit logs to authorized personnel. |
|---|---|
| Type | Preventive |
| Description | The objective of this control is to assure that each operation on a Data Object is logged within the audit log. |
| Event | This control MUST be triggered whenever the Object Service receives an operation request for a Data Object. |
| Condition | None. |
| Action | The Object Service MUST:<br>• Allow processing of service request. |
| Generated Events | OBJECTACTION_STARTED (before step 1)<br>OBJECTACTION_COMPLETED(action=COMPENSATED) (after step 1) |

these should be reflected in the cloud provider security program.

A number of regulations that contain provisions relating to the storage, protection, or transfer of data require that the relevant data and/or operations be auditable. This is of particular importance considering the fact that the customer is the final responsible of and it remains accountable for all data and services it outsource to the cloud.

Moving to cloud entails addressing not only technical risks related to the lost of governance, but also legal risks related to the lack of due diligence as required by national laws. On this, certifications of the datacenter are not enough. There are psychological barriers that need to be overcome.

Governance, transparency, data protection, and auditability constitute the key factors to build trust in the cloud. At this purpose, having an efficient and well documented security program and of a robust security event and management system are essential best practices. In fact, they constitute a mean for cloud provider to control and maintain the security objectives and to be open towards customer. Consequently, this helps overcoming customer's hesitancy when considering migrating from traditional IT infrastructure to the cloud computing model.

# REFERENCES

ENISA. (2009). *Cloud computing - Benefits, risks and recommendations for information security.* ENISA.

NIST. (2012). *Security and privacy controls for federal information systems and organizations.* Retrieved from http://securecloudreview.com/2011/10/cloud-security-transfers-some-responsibility-but-not-accountability/

# ADDITIONAL READING

Krutz, R. L., & Dean Vines, R. (2010). *Cloud security - A comprehensive guide to secure cloud computing.* Academic Press.

NIST. (2011). *Guidelines on security and privacy in public cloud computing.* NIST.

Symantec, VMWare. (2011). *Securing the cloud for the enterprise.* Symantec.

## KEY TERMS AND DEFINITIONS

**Cloud Computing:** Based on NIST definition[28], the Cloud model consists in enabling the seamless access to shared IT resources on-demand and on a pay-as-you-go basis. This model stands over the recent developments in virtualization and network technologies. Such technologies enabled the delivery of rapidly available, easily configurable and highly reliable resources. The sharing of physical resources implied reduced financial and management costs.

**Security Assessment:** In IT systems, it is a (systematic) measurement of the effectiveness of the safeguards and countermeasures that are in place to meet the identified security requirements and control objectives. It optionally proposes recommendation to correct inadequacies and enhance the existing conditions. An assessment usually provides a gap analysis (or a score) about the current status vs the desiderata.

**Security Certification Audit:** It focuses on compliance and conformance of the system to a given Security Standard and it is regularly performed in order to obtain and maintain the Certification. It consists on (systematically) gathering evidence of conformance or nonconformance and can result in a success or a failure.

**Security Compliance:** In IT systems, it concerns the state of conformance of the system with respect to security requirements prescribed by Security Certification standards (e.g. ISO27001) and/or legal (e.g. European Directives on Data Protection) and regulatory frameworks, and providing evidence (assurance) of it.

## ENDNOTES

1    http://securecloudreview.com/2011/10/cloud-security-transfers-some-responsibility-but-not-accountability/

2    http://europa.eu/rapid/pressReleasesAction.do?reference=SPEECH/12/40

3    CSA, www.cloudsecurityalliance.org

4    https://cloudsecurityalliance.org/research/projects/cloud-controls-matrix-ccm/

5    http://www.softlayer.com/cloudlayer

6    http://www.gogrid.com/

7    http://www.sentrigo.com/

8    http://www.logicworks.net/tech-specs/compliance

9    http://client.certificationeurope.com/print/5053

10   http://www.atlantic.net/

11   http://www.atlantic.net/Cloud-Computing/cloudcomputing.html

12   http://aws.amazon.com/security/

13   http://aws.amazon.com/agreement/.

14   http://www.google.com/apps/intl/en/business/infrastructure_security.html

15   http://download.microsoft.com/download/5/C/4/5C4CAE76-9DAD-4977-81F3-64D06D763A74/SecuringtheMSCit-it.pdf

16   http://www.microsoft.com/windowsazure/Whitepapers/securityoverview/

17   https://cloudsecurityalliance.org/research/initiatives/star-registry/

18   http://trust.salesforce.com/trust/

19   http://blogs.salesforce.com/product/2012/01/announcing-pci-certification.html

20   http://www.joyentcloud.com/

21   http://www.joyentcloud.com/about/policies/safe-harbor/.

22   (http://www.netsuite.com/portal/platform/infrastructure/ssae16-soc1-cer shtml)

23   http://www.netsuite.com/portal/pdf/ds-netsuite-datacenter-factsheet.pdf

24   (http://www.ca.com/us/cloud-platform.aspx),

25   https://collaboration.opengroup.org/projects/security/xdas/?gpid=534

26   http://www.jcp.org/en/jsr/detail?id=914

27   http://esper.codehaus.org/

28   http://csrc.nist.gov/publications/nistpubs/800-145/SP800-145.pdf

# Chapter 9
# Media Convergence and Cloud Technologies:
## Smart Storage, Better Workflows

**Mirko Lorenz**
*Deutsche Welle, Germany*

**Paola Sunna**
*RAI, Italy*

**Linda Rath-Wiggins**
*Deutsche Welle, Germany*

**Giorgio Dimino**
*RAI, Italy*

**Wilfried Runde**
*Deutsche Welle, Germany*

**Maurizio Montagnuolo**
*RAI, Italy*

**Alberto Messina**
*RAI, Italy*

**Roberto Borgotallo**
*RAI, Italy*

## ABSTRACT

*Why do media organizations look out for cloud storage? In short, the media industry as a whole is facing various challenges. Due to digital convergence there is more material, less time, and multiple channels to fill, while budgets get smaller. TV, video on demand, and mobile content have become big drivers in pushing a search for innovative storage solutions. In addition to that, the opportunity to work with raw data, which can be used for deeper analysis, mapping, visualization, and personalized services is another aspect of why there is a need for novel storage solutions, preferably in the cloud. The media industry could lower production costs and increase speed to market of time critical reporting. This book chapter provides an overview of how far VISION Cloud can provide novel concepts for these demands.*

## INTRODUCTION

Media companies from all domains are in the midst of a complex convergence process, including the now irreversible transition from analogue to digital content. At the same time, current business models are becoming increasingly obsolete in the face of recent structural changes in the media market. Furthermore, new competitors are on the rise (e.g. search engines as new journalistic curators, social networks providing news streams, etc.) and user generated content becomes more important. On the technical side, IP traffic is going up, a higher variety of end-user devices calls for an increase

DOI: 10.4018/978-1-4666-3934-8.ch009

in various technical formats (e.g. video codecs) and changing user demands (interactivity and participation). An addition to that, the emergence of new platforms (e.g. social networks) is presenting an added challenge to existing media companies. In order to stay relevant, media companies need to understand the most important changes, figure out both business and technology models to adapt to multi-channel production. These changes combined call for a restructuring from the ground up. Cloud storage solutions could create a new foundation in this space.

## BACKGROUND

Leading European broadcasters have to manage growing content archives. For instance, estimates of the available amount of content in RAI archives count more than 500.000 hours of previously published programs, ranging in a fifty-year span of broadcasting activity. A rough count exemplifies that a complete digitization of such repository would need 15 petabytes of online storage. This is obviously something currently unmanageable with ad-hoc solutions based on incremental ("evolutionary") engineering of existing storage technologies: there is a need for a revolutionary step. A similar situation can be observed elsewhere. Deutsche Welle, as an international broadcaster, has to multiply content not only across all channels (Internet, TV, radio) but also in 30 different languages. Content in general has an important role in new productions as well as in new media channels, where the "long tail effect" (Anderson, 2006) is considered a key driver for the restoration and digitization of archived assets. Furthermore, HD video production creates an entirely different set-up in terms of storage needs for raw material, handling of workflows, broadcasting, and distribution of such content across all channels.

A second, equally relevant trend in the media space is the rise of data journalism. From a technological perspective, the trend can be understood as a move from what is today known as "business intelligence" and data warehousing for commercial companies, to an extended use of data as a basis for analysis and reporting – potentially to be called "public intelligence" in the future. Media companies anticipate that by being able to work with large amounts of data sets, the journalists are provided with new options to find relevant content, provide context and deep analysis. This sub-form of journalism is not news, it is a variation of what has been described as "Computer-Assisted Reporting" (CAR) and data visualization. However, since 2010, there is an increasing interest in what is now called "data-driven journalism". This concept extends the range and scope of CAR, because data is not only used in the story development internally. Instead, small and large data sets becoming available in different countries of the world are offered as open data (Manocha, 2011). The open data movement is in some ways related to creative commons licensing of software on platforms such as Twitter, Flickr, Facebook, and YouTube. As a pre-requisite, large data repositories are mandatory for daily access to content (video, data, and more).

The current media market is even more critical if we consider the efficiency of current media production workflows, measured as the ratio between the length of a published content and the cumulative length of rough acquired material for its production (video, audio, pictures, data, etc.).

To sum up: Online video combined with big data, multi-channel strategies and the pressure to find efficient media production workflows are drivers pushing a search for innovative storage solutions, preferably supported by cloud computing. Finding new architectures could contribute to the media market as a whole. What can be expected is a fast development spiral towards much higher storage sizes and specifically "active archives" which could support faster digital workflows in content acquisition, content production, and digital distribution.

## TRANSITION TO MEDIA CLOUDS

The focus of development is on cloud storage, which could support production processes, providing new options to editors on a deadline. One basic assumption is that the storage needs will quickly exceed what media companies can host as single companies, thus driving migration to cloud computing concepts. The ability to aggregate content and to collaborate with others on-demand underlines the importance of migrating towards the cloud as a foundational technical enabler for production and distribution of content. Broadcasters and media producers could benefit greatly from a cloud-based system where each step of the production workflow is benefitting from features made possible by a cloud. For the past years barriers between dedicated technologies like VTRs and SDI networks and IT components are fading to nought. Therefore, the transition from traditional tape-based production paradigms to entirely file-based workflows is by now a reality to be efficiently managed, and no more a futuristic vision. In this scenario, the availability of off-the-shelf distributed services for creation, manipulation, production and publication of content is considered "the" reference architecture of the future. Cloud computing, in its "Software-as-a-Service" embodiment, and distributed storage technologies represent a viable solution for implementing such an architecture in a sustainable and future-proof way.

What media companies will need from a cloud-computing platform are four basic elements:

- Cost flexibility, reducing costs in the whole media gathering, production and distribution process.
- Media-orientated storage/delivery platforms, that are flexible enough to switch between data formats.
- Reliable ways to collect, merge and use metadata helping to find relevant items of content.
- Adaptable workflows, channeling data through the process of ingestion/production/presentation and delivery to the public.

## OUTLINE OF THE MEDIA USE CASE

At the heart of every media company lies the ability to provide compelling content to a target audience. Especially in regards to public broadcasters, such as Germany's Deutsche Welle and Italian's RAI, the newsworthiness of a story constitutes the essence of its relevance. Key factors for the newsworthiness of a story include, among others (Rogers, 2012): timeliness, proximity, exceptional quality, prominence, and conflict. These factors call for a digital platform, where every phase of the production could be enhanced, e.g. by merging steps or by automating what is so far done manually.

Therefore, the scenario of VISION Cloud's media use case is an online feature and can serve as a modern day scenario with which broadcasters are typically confronted with today. The online feature (e.g. a special Website or an integrated special site on an existing Website) can be enriched with multimedia items such as online video content (professionally produced by journalists as well as user generated content), interactive maps, (near-)realtime participatory data from social networks and data-based information (e.g. statistics from other public sources). The target audiences for this feature are people who are interested in either Italy's capital in general or who are actually traveling to Rome and now trying to find insight information online. Consequently, the journalists and editors need to find appealing ways in order to get attention, come up with informative angles and several ways to use the content over time via TV, computers, tablets and mobile phones. Therefore, they can prepare the feature by, for instance, interviewing people from Rome in HD video in order to get an insight perspective from the people living there, or aggregating already existing video material from an archive or from social video platforms, such as YouTube. Furthermore, the journalists can include pictures in the feature, either taken with a camera or curated from online photo platforms, such as Flickr. Also, journalists can record an HD video of a motorcycle trip through the streets of Rome so that the audience will see the city from a new angle. In addition to that, the journalists can prepare audio snippets of live music events in Rome, create an interactive map of the most interesting spots in town, and link to informative external sites. Also, the feature can include compelling data-driven stories based on research done at national archives or public ministries (e.g. average salary of taxi drivers over the last 20 years or traffic penalties by Rome's tourists from last week). The objective of the "A trip to Rome" feature is to present Rome in a new, interactive, and appealing multimedia way that can be published at one point and then updated whenever there are any changes necessary.

This relatively simple example of a multimedia production already poses many challenges in today's versatile media market and raises issues that have to be addressed by going along the production cycle.

The production cycle can be summarized in seven consecutive stages: (1) collaboration as a team of editors/journalists who are responsible for producing the feature "A trip to Rome," (2) ingesting the previously produced material (can be any kind of material: audio, video, pictures, text, data, links, etc.) into back-end systems, such as the content management systems (CMS) in order to work with it in a multimodal way, (3) filtering the information as a means to find the most relevant items first and be able to convert formats in order to create a solid base for subsequent phases, (4) the production phase which results in curation and editing the content (video, data, etc.), (5) publishing the feature for end-users to use on a Website, (6) distributing the features for end-users to find and (7) measuring the popularity of content for further use.

All these different phases of the production cycle encompass requirements that are prevalent for an effective production of a feature. When going along the phases, requirements can be concluded as follows:

### Phase (1): Team

- Allowing to collaborate as a team and work on the same project for a particular time frame according to a rights management system that pre-defines sharing and editing rights. This should be supported by a digital platform that could be accessed online from everywhere, to enable collaboration.

### Phase (2): Ingestion

- Manual upload of content which was gathered/shot by journalists/editors.
- Options to manipulate or transform content to the maximum quality.
- Automatic upload of content, e.g. through social network APIs which was selected by journalists/editors.
- Enrichment of material ingested by handling metadata (automatically or manually).

### Phase (3): Filter

- Easy access to any source of content, regardless of where the ingested content is located (e.g. different servers).
- Ability to annotate the data in order to complete and enrich stored files.

### Phase (4): Production

- Curating and managing editorial as well as technical formats by defining an editorial concept and going along with it.
- Provision of versioning of formats.

### Phase (5): Publish

- Formats must be considered that allow end-users to consume the content, regardless of which platform they are using (mobile device, smart TV, Webpages, etc.).

### Phase (6): Distribution

- Fast spread of content - flexible access to content for end-users.
- Searchability and findability of content via metadata.

### Phase (7): Popularity

- Content must be measured in order to understand the usage of data.
- Metadata collection over time.
- Enriching both finished material as well as raw material, single data sets or snippets of video for re-use, enriching the cloud storage media archive over time for the organization as a whole.

As noted above, media's specific needs for storage will increase tremendously and will drive migration to cloud computing concepts. Therefore, a media cloud needs to be introduced where access and use of the stored material is "wrapped" into features that actually help journalists in the process of production. Preferably, it will be an "active media archive," where content is provided not only after, but at the start and during production of any given content. This in turn creates a perspective to combine cloud storage with a middleware layer that connects to next generation content management systems.

## CLOUD ISSUES IN THE MEDIA USE CASE

A successful cloud-strategy for media companies is based on specific objectives that need to be set beforehand. These specific strategic and business objective are based on the production cycle of the media use case and include:

### Phase (1): Team

- Set up of a (temporary, project-oriented) data storage on a case by case basis (depending on the project the team is working on), with different storage quality levels (in operational and development media processes it is often required to have high flexibility in storage availability and disposal that need to be achieved by a storage cloud).
- Cloud infrastructure that allows users to define quality levels for storage in terms of performance and capacity (e.g. depending on the amount of data or video).
- Full control over development and deployment of new features and options to merge tasks when performing operations on content (data, video, etc.) in the cloud (e.g. by administrators of a specific media project).
- Distributed production by different journalists with different responsibilities and various degrees of seniority, and sensitivity of projects' content to privacy laws.
- Manage data content, gain cost flexibility from the cloud (there is a need to flexibility in storage cost due to the utilization of a storage cloud. In addition to that, variable costs gain percentage of total cost with regards to possible overheads).

### Phase (2): Ingestion

- Many different data formats need to be considered in the ingestion phase due to heterogeneous data formats (e.g. data formats changing over time based on new cameras, new types of data, etc.). This can be achieved by compliance to standards (e.g. regarding automatic media encoding standards: MXF, MPEG family of standards, H264; Publication Standards: HTML, HTML5, XML).

- Security alliance.
- High Data Capability due to large amounts of incoming data.
- Infrastructure scalability.
- Data mobility (e.g. data moving from one cloud to another).
- Security requirements (Data integrity, Data availability, Data non repudiation, Data deduplication).
- Co-existence and integration with external or legacy equipment (Transmitters, Schedulers, Traffic Control, Archives Legacy Databases).

**Phase (3): Filter**

- In order to be able to filter and find the content for the actual production, an automated indexing of media content is necessary (manually annotating ingested content is not affordable anymore). Automated information analysis and extraction platforms are highly complex artefacts that need highly-qualified resources to be designed, engineered and maintained. The most common content analysis and indexing tools at the storage cloud level will lower the total cost of setting up and owning such platforms, and increase interoperability at the same time.
- Rich Data/Metadata: Ability to annotate the data in order to complete and enrich stored files.
- Compliance: metadata standards (e.g. EBU Core (5), MPEG-7 AVDP (6)) have to be

supported as common dictionaries due to their generality and flexibility.

**Phase (4): Production**

- Seamless management of all kinds of data relevant in the multimedia production.
- Leverage some content management/editing functionalities built in the cloud. Modern multi-media production is highly based on non-linear editing functionalities that are typically implemented by dedicated HW/SW stacks, which are only minorly interoperable with each other (silos). Having content management/editing functionalities in the cloud will improve interoperability and flexibility of such systems.
- Ubiquitous management of media content: generation, access, search and retrieval. Nowadays production of content can be highly distributed in responsibilities, location, and final target users. Means of accessing and managing multimedia content are expected to substantively increase in efficiency if a common layer of APIs are developed on top of a distributed storage layer.
- Data filtering and aggregation are becoming more and more a strategic process for modern media production. It is envisaged that several such functionalities are provided natively through the storage layer.
- Visualisation of multimedia data is key for some publications leveraging data analytics like data-driven journalism. It is expected that such capabilities are offered by a storage cloud natively.

**Phase (5): Publish**

- Automatic encoding mechanisms must be considered that allow end-users to consume the content, regardless of which platform they are using (mobile device, smart TV, Webpages, etc.).

### Phase (6): Distribution

- Integrated file-based distribution is needed. Nowadays production facilities work on established (legacy) workflows that may depend on the type of program being produced, the location, and the final delivery platform. Intelligent storage can act as a middleware to integrate production and distribution processes more efficiently.

### Phase (7): Popularity

- Keeping track of usage of the data, and of the relationships among data sources.
- In order to optimise storage capacity and production processes that make intensive use of archive assets it is essential to track the usage of data.

From a technological perspective, recent analyses conducted among key experts in the European Broadcasting Union (EBU, 2002) also led to very similar conclusions regarding cloud requirements, in support of the issues outlined above:

- There is the need for a paradigm shift from monolithic vertical dedicated systems to horizontally- integrated highly-interchangeable, component-based ones.
- Introduction of Content Management Systems is a key enabler for content sharing in distributed file- based production.
- Metadata and content semantic indexing is considered as a key factor for the optimization of production workflows and overall abatement of costs related to content ownership.

- Re-engineering of processes has priority over local substitution of technologies and devices.
- A common set of file formats fulfilling a set of baseline requirements has to be defined and agreed.
- Material eXchange Format (MXF) is considered the "de facto" technological reference.

## CHALLENGES IN THE MEDIA INDUSTRY

Although several technologies based on computer standards and components are already available from the market, there are still some major issues hindering the path towards a completely integrated cloud solution for the media industry. These issues can be summarized as follows:

- Complexity of file formats. Existing standards like MXF are too complex to allow developers conceive a general interoperable solution; therefore, only limited parts of the standard are developed by different vendors. This ends in a serious lack of interoperability among devices, even when the same family of formats (but different "flavors") are declared.
- Proprietary solutions. Existing integrated solutions are based on proprietary developments and factory standards, which are not available to external developers. This has the direct effect of locking-in particular vendors, considerably limiting system integration possibilities.
- No common metadata. Content-related metadata are important enablers in media production work- flows. However, there is not currently an overall accepted solution in terms of dictionaries and structures, so that different systems may result not

interoperable, or interoperability can be reached only through complex and lossy information mapping overloads.

- Limited openness and verticality of systems. Existing products are rarely open products, i.e. they are not typically shipped together with well-documented and pervasive API support. When APIs are present, they are limited to the upper levels of the architecture, thus enabling only application- level integration. Lower levels (like storage) are not accessible and their maintenance and/or upgrade typically require product specialists' intervention.

## BEST PRACTICES IN THE MEDIA INDUSTRY

The following section provides an overview of cloud technologies currently used by specifically pre-selected media companies. This overview does not qualify for a complete representation of all the industry's cloud usage. Instead, remarkable best practice examples were used in this qualitative analysis to understand the future's demands. In addition to that, the overview depicts the challenges and shortcomings of today's solutions and what will be needed to meet the demands.

Three different iterations of data-intensive software have been picked for the qualitative solution. The platforms provide a good starting point for future research and development, specifically with the media use case in mind:

- **Media Workflows:** *Signiant* (Commercial US-Company)
- **Media Collections:** *DocumentCloud* (funded by Knight Foundation)
- **Working with Data:** *Guardian Data Blog and Data Stor*

## Innovation in Media Workflows with Signiant

The company is one of several new entrants, though potentially the most advanced in terms of using technology to solve common bottlenecks. Traditional media workflows have been based on high quality and reliability, which were major drivers for broadcasters in radio and television for a long time, resulting in cost- and labour intensive workflows. While some of the quality that can be achieved with such equipment, todays changing media landscape results in rising pressure on all media organizations to find new ways to efficiently capture, store and provide media data. Without reliable storage and evolving metadata for each file the benefits of going digital can only partially be leveraged, therefore calling for new and better solutions. Signiant implements a novel approach worth looking into. The company has developed a digital, partly automated workflow to move large media files through a production and distribution process that can include delivery of one file to multiple channels (i.e. TV, cable, Internet, mobile) and automated reformatting and right-sizing of the files based on customer needs. Signiant is a US-based company, providing transportation services and automated workflows for digital media companies, that need to handle very large files and streams of content. On a low level, Signiant provides an alternative to transport large media files timely and securely - the company's solutions provide a better and more reliable FTP solution (including better use of available bandwidth). According to CrunchBase (2011), a directory of venture-funded companies maintained by US-Blog TechCrunch, Signiant was founded in 2000 and received a 10M Dollar funding in 2006. Headquarted in Boston, Massachusetts, Signiant employs 70 people. Customers include a number of large media brands. They describe their software as "more than simple file transport - we automate, accelerate, manage, and securely control the movement of high-value digital content within and between organizations and ecosystems. Signiant solutions streamline content supply chain management operations from production through distribution and upload of digital files - enabling customers to build new business models, reduce costs, and integrate with existing investments" (Signiant, 2012). One of the most interesting and well-developed aspects of what Signiant has to offer is the workflow editor that can automate workflows from a source (e.g. FinalCut) to multiple distribution channels. Such a need to map a certain workflow process into very specific channels arises often in the media industry (see media use case above). That way, media companies can adapt the production/storage process to their specific needs, supported by software. Furthermore, the software offers support for API access and can incorporate Amazon Cloud Services for pure storage. Signiant defines four main challenges for digital media and media workflows: (1) secure transport of media via the Internet, (2) time sensitive delivery of content across town or around the globe, (3) distribution of content to multiple stakeholders and (4) processing files and status aggregation of content.

Media management, production workflow, and distribution might be the most obvious uses of cloud computing and smart storage in the near future. Signiant provides a good example of how such services need to be flexible and adaptable. Competitors in such a market would be both companies specialized on storage such as EMC, Extensis as well as Content Management Specialists like Open Text Digital Media. Other new entrants will be start-ups in the cloud market that might try to establish businesses in markets like media.

## Media Collections on DocumentCloud

Regarding data journalism, new perspectives have to be taken into consideration, such as the collaborative use of storage in the cloud, adding crowdsourcing and sharing functionalities

for not only investigations but also for possible use by end-users. DocumentCloud provides just that. DocumentCloud (DocumentCloud, 2012) is a digital platform, founded by journalists and funded by a grant from the Knight News Foundation (Foundation, 2012). One can upload, share and conduct structured searches on documents, and also go through analyses based on extracted entities, such as people, places, and organizations mentioned in the text. As a contributor, one can download a lightweight document viewer to embed documents on your Website. The goal is to provide a system for primary source analysis, anticipating that the size of available data for investigation and the complexity of extracting meaning will rise steeply in coming years. Therefore, DocumentCloud is both a repository of primary source documents and a tool for document-based investigative reporting and supports excessive collaboration on documents by journalists, researchers, and archivists. On the technical side, DocumentCloud has been developed based on Ruby (Rails, Sinatra), which along with Python/Django is one way to use a scaffolding programming language for faster development and easier changes or addition of features. There is an API allowing for calls and integration of the DocumentCloud into other platforms. DocumentCloud uses special software to understand text (Tesseract) and OpenCalais for entity extraction. As of late 2010 a variety of media companies and newsrooms uses the platform for different projects, large and small (DocumentCloud, 2011). On an entry level, DocumentCloud describes itself as "an index of primary source documents and a tool for annotating, organizing and publishing them on the Web" (DocumentCloud, 2012). At the foundation of this platform are several new ways of approaching challenges that were not present in the past.

## Guardian Data Blog and Data Store

The Guardian is a good example how former print-newspapers can use and combine digital production for all channels (Guardian, 2012). Since starting the Guardian Data Blog in early 2010 the newsroom is widely regarded as a forerunner in the field of data journalism. The newspaper detected the trend towards Open Data, meaning that large data sets collected by public bodies and the government are opened up for analysis to the public. The level of openness differs greatly as of now from country to country, but there is a quite strong movement calling for opening in countries across Europe. The US and the UK governments have reacted by setting up huge data outlets allowing newspapers, companies and the public to see and work with collected data. In the case of the Guardian, the newspaper set up a Guardian Data Blog, where reporters publish new stories based on data analysis (Rogers, 2012). A second means was the creation of the Guardian Data Store, where all the data sets used by the Guardian are publically accessible. Often these filtered and controlled sub-sets are much better in quality and easier to handle than the large raw data collections. The Guardian Data Store can therefore be used as a "data market". Notable scoops of the Guardian so far were the published data on the UK budget (Rogers, 2010), the Afghanistan War Logs (Leigh & Davies, 2010) and the UK Expense scandal (Rogers, 2010) which all have led to rising interest in such platforms. The Guardian Data Store uses a collection of mostly free tools, such as Many Eyes (IBM), Timetric (2012) for visualization. Data is coming in from a variety of sources, some from open data platforms, others from surveys run by the editors. Publishing and visualizing data as part of the editorial offering is a new trend, so popularity with readers is very high. The Guardian Data Blog for example has risen into the top sections on the Guardian Website with more than one million views each month.

## Concluding Remarks

The findings from the media use case and the technical components of VISION Cloud can be used to describe future needs beyond the state of the art.

1.  Media cloud computing applications will have to make sure that they are rock-solid in terms of stability and elasticity. Furthermore, they should be designed for scalability, as the demand for media storage is rising quickly. These basic needs are well covered in the VISION Cloud effort. As shown, the current competitors and market offerings focus on moving stored files - media companies expect speed while the IT focuses on stability.

2.  Understanding how the end user will use platforms like VISION Cloud storage is the basis, but based on the qualitative analysis above, an increasing demand for easily usable GUIs are expected that help to (a) configure and monitor the media cloud resources, (b) manage applications, and (c) set up simple, time-saving services to be used in media production workflows. This last aspect is well addressed in VISION Cloud through the storlet concept, meaning that VISION Cloud foresees a high flexibility to create new storlets or APIs to connect other resources when needed.

In conclusion, to develop the approaches of VISION Cloud for the media domain, whether working with videos, data or mixed, unstructured media files, efficient platforms where workflows can be tested to solve specific problems are expected.

## SOLUTIONS AND RECOMMENDATIONS

To address the issues outlined above and to address the requirements posed by the media use case "A trip to Rome", the most relevant objectives are pursued by the VISION Cloud project. The project is developing a reference architecture for a futuristic storage cloud aiming to support data intensive services, and being verified against several industry use cases. Built upon direct attached storage and clustered, commodity servers, VISION Cloud combines a scalable, resilient (active-active replication) architecture with advanced storage functionality to offer features much more attuned to today's world of cloud storage than traditional storage systems implemented on the cloud. This functionality includes:

- Allowing access to stored databases on an object model abstraction, rather than at the level of hierarchical file storage. For example, in VISION Cloud, data is enriched with both user and system metadata, and storage as a data object abstraction, rather than as a series of files.
- Associated data objects can be accessed in a content-centric manner that is independent of the location of the data, but rather based on the content, properties and relationships between data objects.
- The ability to run computation close to the data (computational storage), on the storage cloud, in a secure manner, rather than incur the data transfer costs and latencies incurred by downloading data from a cloud for processing and then even potentially uploading the results.
- Advanced functionality for cloud storage, included Quality of Service and security guarantees.

Furthermore, in order to disrupt obstacles represented by verticality of content storage systems, a distributed content persistence layer which will act as a horizontal middleware for all applications in the media production workflow is needed. This layer (ideally, an open distributed media content persistence layer) should be constituted by a set of standard functionalities accessible through visual and/or programmatic interfaces, ideally implementing a media-aware operating system built on top of the generic VISION Cloud architecture. In addition to that, in order to lower the negative impact of the lack of interoperability at the essence level, abstract data structures representing the content of audiovisual files independently from the actually implemented operational pattern or file format are needed. At the metadata level, a set of structural metadata, which will be directly mapped onto the Data Access Layer of the VISION Cloud architecture, has to be conceived, providing basic semantic indexing services automatically fed during the content ingestion phase. Last but not least, a baseline of media processing services based on the media content persistence layer and on the abstract essence and metadata structures have to be seamlessly integrated to perform typical content processing chains. These will include in essence transcoding, visualization, rendering, and basic edit operations (rough cut).

Four innovations make the VISION Cloud project stand out and address very media-specific needs in cloud computing. (1) The computational storage level ensures innovation during the filter and production phase (see media use case above) by efficiently running computations such as content transcoding or multimedia data mining on the data near the storage as opposed to bringing that content to a local machine, transform, and then store back to the cloud. (2) The content-centric data access enables innovation during the production, publishing, and distribution phase (see media use case above) by allowing rapid access to data and its related metadata. The creation of relationships between data can provide benefits for deeper analysis of data and is a natural way to preserve informative relations that are pre-existing the upload of data in the storage cloud. (3) The advanced functionality for cloud storage during the publishing and distribution phase (see media use case above) ensures quality of service that can be used to guarantee the rapid accessibility to the data, which may be required. In addition to that, security guarantees on the data to be distributed are needed. Furthermore, publication and distribution are phases that may imply crossing business boundaries. This can leverage advanced functionalities as federation among storage clouds. (4) Last but not least, the access based on object model abstraction makes access to data possible based on metadata-based searches which is crucial throughout all stages of both the contemporary use case, and future scenarios.

## FUTURE RESEARCH DIRECTIONS

The previous sections have enlightened how in recent years modern media production has been diverging from its traditional role, tied up with the roots of 20th century broadcasting, and embracing a new environment in which tight integration with the IT world started to become a key enabler for survival in today's complex market of information.

This divergence is still happening in several dimensions: from one(active)-to-many (passive) delivery to full interactivity, from traditional media (audio and/or video) to multimedia, from terrestrial and satellite channels to Internet.

The price to be paid is the revolutionary impact that new technologies have in established media workflows, which had previously been grown in vertical and isolated environments, and thus naturally not made robust by continued market competition, typical of the IT-world. Though a first attempt at bounding this impact in a controlled domain had started in the early 2000s, when file-based digital formats for audiovisual material saw

their birth together with consolidated end-to-end solutions for digital content management, however it came soon to evidence that these attempts were prone to a serious lack of interoperability, in terms of media formats, integration of services and metadata semantics. Thus, the natural evolution was once again a world of silos technologies and systems, barely communicating at the media exchange interface (e.g., through MXF), and retaining mostly proprietary metadata schemas, storage structures and data access protocols.

In this context, the advent of media clouds, i.e. of distributed, scalable and virtualized infrastructures with advanced media production-awareness, like the one VISION Cloud is addressing in the media use case, can be considered as a real technological breakthrough enabling modern media players to play a dominant role in the new scenario. In fact, such frameworks represent transversal general-purpose middlewares for storing and managing media transformations in a safe and efficient way, accessing media assets content-wise, and easily integrating services using standard protocols based on the RESTful conceptualisation of media resources. It is now becoming increasingly foreseeable a future media production scenario dominated by thin applications on top of such frameworks, easily extensible and adaptively configurable to the ever-changing needs of modern media users.

## CONCLUSION

By taking advantage of emerging technologies in the cloud, the media industry stands to gain both by lowering production costs and increasing the speed to market of time critical reporting. Additionally, new emerging forms of journalism based on social media, crowd sourcing and data mining will rely on advanced ICT infrastructures to add value to traditional news gathering, which is now starting to be taken over by online (Anderson, 2006) communities which essentially operate for free.

# REFERENCES

Anderson, C. (2006). *The long tail: Why the future of business is selling less of more.* New York: Hyperion.

Crunchbase. (2011). *Crunchbase.* Retrieved from http://www.crunchbase.com/company/signiant

DocumentCloud. (2011). *DocumentCloud.* Retrieved from http://www.documentcloud.org/featured

DocumentCloud. (2012). *DocumentCloud.* Retrieved from http://blog.documentcloud.org/blog/2011/06/new-home-at-ire/

EBU. (2002). *EBU.* Retrieved from http://www.ebu.ch/CMSimages/en/DSG_final_report_E_tcm6-5090.pdf

Foundation, K. (2012). *Knight foundation.* Retrieved from http://knightfoundation.org/about/

Guardian. (2012, June 30). *Guardian.* Retrieved from www.guardian.co.uk

IBM. (2012). *Many eyes.* Retrieved from http://www-958.ibm.com/software/data/cognos/many-eyes/page/About.html

Leigh, D., & Davies, N. (2010). *Guardian data blog.* Retrieved from http://www.guardian.co.uk/world/2010/jul/25/afghanistan-war-logs-military-leaks

Manocha, I. (2011). *IDG connect.* Retrieved from http://www.idgconnect.com/blog-abstract/263/ian-manocha-uk-on-road-open-data

Rogers, S. (2010). *Guardian data blog.* Retrieved from http://www.guardian.co.uk/news/datablog/2010/nov/19/government-spending-data

Rogers, S. (2012). *Guardian data blog.* Retrieved from http://www.guardian.co.uk/news/datablog/2012/jun/28/open-data-white-paper

Rogers, T. (2012). *About journalism.* Retrieved from http://journalism.about.com/od/reporting/a/newsworthy.htm

Signiant. (2012). *Signiant.* Retrieved from http://www.signiant.com/company/company-profile/

# Chapter 10
# Telecommunication Industry:
## Storage and Mobility

**Fredrik Solsvik**
*Telenor ASA, Norway*

**Michel Dao**
*Orange Labs, France*

## ABSTRACT

*The operators Telefónica, Orange, and Telenor represent the telecommunication industry in the VISION Cloud project. Together, they provide a telco-oriented use case, which provides feedback and requirements to the work on the reference architecture being developed. The use cases are developed based on the challenges and opportunities that are identified that relate to storage and mobility technologies. The use cases validate the reference architecture of VISION Cloud based on prototype tests and experimentations that enable the use case to be evaluated in scenarios. Telecommunication industry challenges are being addressed by the advancements made in the VISION Cloud project iterations, which takes the inputs from the telco use case and other use cases into consideration. This chapter is a study in the telecommunication industry challenges and possibilities with respect to the cloud storage technology advancements made in VISION Cloud.*

## INTRODUCTION

The telecommunication industry experiences competition from Internet players and content providers. Not only does telephony, Internet, and broadcasting technologies converge, but also the combination of media and ICT services converge. As all types of content have been digitalized value-added services are offered to users as services integrate content with resources such as storage, network and computing.

DOI: 10.4018/978-1-4666-3934-8.ch010

Rich content can be over the Internet in big volumes and with high quality, but is constantly pressured for new demands in capacity and overall costs. In response to the convergence the telecom operators' business shift from management of network infrastructure to service and content management.

This chapter looks at the challenges and opportunities in the telecommunication industry and identifies some needs that should be addressed to better position telecom operators in a converged industry with a focus on storage and mobility aspects. The chapter looks at how VISION Cloud can be used in such a setting and presents the telco use casework done and planned.

## CHALLENGES AND OPPORTUNITIES IN THE TELECOMMUNICATION INDUSTRY

Telecommunication operators (telcos) are witnessing declines in revenue due to lower ARPU (Average Revenue per User) in their traditional markets as a result of that the willingness to pay for communications is declining. The loss of income from voice is not offset by the increase in data traffic volume. At the same time IT business and Internet companies are taking traditional telco market shares as a result of the convergence of voice and data communication. The competition from Over-the-Top (OTT) service providers is expected to increase with a higher penetration of mobile broadband. Smart phones give access to services on the handset, services that no longer are controlled by the telco, but made accessible through the device manufacturer. Telcos are left to have some services preloaded on devices they sell to customers at subsidized prices.

OTT players challenge not only the traditional voice revenue, but also content related services are seen as a threat. New positions in the service delivery chain and novel service offerings must be exploited by telcos in order to avoid being reduced to a simple bit provider. (Green, 2012) states the impact on revenues to be considerable, nearly $500 billion in lost revenues over the next eight years. Prices will continue to fall as the markets mature and become saturated. Data traffic will be increasing in the coming year, but revenue from that traffic will not offset the decline in voice income (Telco 2.0, 2012). The Internet age has value chains and payment models that are an ill fit with traditional telecom models.

OTT players that play nice with the telco operations are of interest to protect the revenue streams and can also extend existing offerings. One option is to establish cannibalizing OTT operations that can be controlled and take otherwise lost market shares that competitive OTT would have taken. Equally important, telcos must utilize their strengths and enhance their networks in order to offer something more than the competing OTT providers are capable of.

The combination of smart networks and cloud services will be one area where telcos offer a superior service. Cloud computing has indeed been embraced by many telecom operators lately, whether the cloud services are produced and delivered by the operator itself or through partnerships. The telco network is an important asset in both of these cases and telcos can provide an end-to-end cloud service that pure IT cloud providers are not able to do.

The shift in source of future revenue requires telcos to invest in adapting their infrastructure. This requires a significant engineering effort with people with the right qualifications. Telco background may be seen as not optimal for the new age of mobile applications, and right people are hard to find.

Traditionally new telco services are slow to get out to market, but with the new mobile application platforms such as Google Play and App Store has significantly reduced the Time to Market for services.

Management of data and data traffic is important for a telco and will be increasingly important if the forecast (Cisco, 2012) on the increase in Internet traffic in general and video content traffic in specific is shown to hold. Storage services that can target limitations in network bandwidth and availability, handset capabilities etc. is of interest, but should still be tailored for optimal end user experience to have a competitive advantage over traditional storage services. Such an advantage will be even more important with the adoption of devices that are well suited for the accelerated consumption of multimedia content. Telcos have an advantage here as they can influence the placement of data. On-net placement of data not only reduces interconnect costs but also increases the return of investments of existing infrastructure if server hosting and similar services are also offered. Telcos also have a huge asset in controlling the last mile of access to customers; an opportunity here can be to extend that to a last mile CDN. This can ensure the profitability as the QoS for customers and core network load can be controlled.

The business market can be addressed by telcos where they can act as a Single Point Of Contact (SPOC) for small business. This enables such businesses to focus on the core of their business. One relevant position for a telecom operator is to look at the cloud broker role, combined with offering cloud connectivity (Nesse, 2011; Ried, 2011). A cloud broker is expected to become an important part of the cloud ecosystem. This intermediary role will be bigger as more and more services are offered as cloud services, and brokering those between customers and providers relieves some of the management burdens. Typical added value by a broker can be identity management, consolidated billing, SLA management, etc. If services also can be made interchangeable the telco in a broker role can make migration decisions based on network conditions and customer experience.

## Needs for Telecommunication Mobility and Storage

The demands sets premises for what a cloud storage infrastructure should aim to achieve for a telecom operator. We have identified some areas that should be addressed to cover the challenges and opportunities from the convergence in the telco domain.

### Shared Infrastructure

A shared infrastructure that serves several market segments of a telecom operator is an approach that may help keep TCO (Total Cost of Ownership) low, while still fulfilling the special requirements of market segments such as consumer and SME/

enterprise. Telcos share network and infrastructure with competitors in some markets (3gis, 2012; Telenor, 2011) in order to reuse infrastructure and get more out of the investments. Global players also consolidate part of their operations to leverage group scale, e.g. by sharing data centers, cross border integration and realize synergies. In the markets where infrastructure is shared with other operations the customers experience increased connectivity and the need for additional sites for base towers and antennas are reduced. The operators can have increased return of investments as they limit duplicated infrastructure investments, and reduce maintenance and upgrade costs. Setting up a new operation in a new market is high risk with costly fixed investments, such as Telenor Group has experienced with their operation in India (The Hindu, 2012).

### Flexible Billing

Telecom business use many billing approaches, including plain tariffs, consumption bonuses, free offers, both in postpaid and prepaid modalities to maximize the potential in all types of markets. What works for teenagers in a mature market where we see decline in income from voice-based services is not the correct approach for customers in e.g. India where the ARPU is extremely low and customers have multiple SIM cards. Also the cloud paradigm has brought into light the convenience of paying only for consumed resources, be it computation or storage. Telecom demands a variety of flexible billing mechanisms that offer intelligent pricing of voice and data connectivity, as well as producing detailed accounting records that they can use for their customers together with new options for payment.

### Customer Experience

Many telcos have developed strategies that address the highly competitive market they are in, e.g. (Telenor Group, 2012). Customer centricity, where they want to be preferred by customers to reduce churn and retain high ARPU customers is a common strategy where strengthening the customer relationships and improving the customer experience has significant value creation potential. One approach to this is to bundle service options together, e.g. storage of photos taken on the mobile phone. The touch points between telecom operators and customers are being challenged by device manufacturers, device platforms (e.g. Android and iOS) and mobile marketplace owners (e.g. Apple and Google). They take increasing parts of the value chains of modern telecom. Lean and flawless customer processes imply cost reductions, as the focus is to create value for the customer that makes it harder for them to choose competitors. Increasing the Quality of Experience, where focus can be on responsive services and customer care, through seamless mobility and SLAs, can also enhance this. When telcos can spend less on winning backs customers, they reduce churn, and increase the ARPU.

## Smart Networks

One of the main sources for the increase in mobile traffic growth is smartphones. The forecasts are pointing to the skies. Networks risk being overloaded and out of control costs, which needs to be managed. Smartphones enables a wider range of applications and consumption of richer content. The handsets have become powerful and versatile which opens up for individualized services and over-the-top video services. Making networks smarter enables the operators to tackle the video traffic better. Today that traffic comes from CDNs and the cloud and is delivered to the consumer end user eyeballs. Networks risk being congested, and telcos needs to better control the flow of data in order to avoid that while maintaining network QoS that the customer expects (Videonet, 2010). Telcos internationally are building CDNs to exploit the fact that they own the last mile. Content can then be cached deep in the telco network and improve overall connectivity and media consumption. Data traffic then becomes a source for income rather

than a cost. Some telcos have even opted to connect their CDNs with one another, in a federated CDN (Raybum, 2011). What is hosted On-net and what is hosted Off-net need to be managed in a smart way and prepared to meet the demand for capacity and capability. Techniques that may minimize the load on the core networks are suitable, such as balancing by prices, by geography, by compression, tiered service offers, differentiation, etc. The end goal is an optimal user experience for Internet access customers

## Service Management

There is an increasing need to manage services efficiently, both in-house and those offered externally and offer differentiation possibilities to target different markets and tailor service bundles for the customer. The data transfers, service messaging and complex service compositions all need to be elastic to use minimal resources. This potentially also saves costs as a service can use resources from a shared pool when burst is needed and thus minimize the size of data centers. Together this is offering both a technical and commercial flexibility that improves the total customer experience. However telecom is also challenged with the time to market for new services, where so far Internet companies have proved more flexible and targeted. Not only do the TTM need to be reduced, but core network capabilities should be integrated with third-party services to enable more use of third party services that utilize the telco capabilities. New telco assets could also be enabled via APIs, such as payment and identity management. Efficient service platforms, service monitoring and service management is needed that can cross borders (Telco 2.0 Research, 2012).

## Content from Consumers

More and more consumers adopt smart phones and tablets in markets such as Europe. Such devices are tailored for a more heavy consumption of content. Video content is already demanding more than half of the network capacity, and with more commercial content choices and changes in consumption trends more is expected. Customers access content anywhere at anytime, and expect ubiquitous connectivity. The use of social networks such as Facebook also accelerates media consumption as people communicate more with images and videos in addition to text. Customers upload data and store them in hosted services; such as popular cloud data services such as Dropbox or at big Internet companies such as Apple, Microsoft and Google. Some of the content could instead be hosted by telecom, and that content needs efficient methods of retrieval and searching, which implies an efficiently managed set of metadata. A storage cloud that serves this need should manage data volumes, data placement and data transfer, all while efficiently manage searches and locating the correct data.

## Enterprise Data

Enterprises and SMEs are a target for telecoms addressing the business market. They do not have the same data volume and data composition as end consumers, but may still need a lot of storage capacity. Sensitive data needs to be managed and secured and it is important that the telco can ensure the desired level of data security and integrity (Owen, 2012). Those business that looks into entering the cloud needs to have their concerns addressed and telcos have a history of covering their needs (Symantec, 2011). Done correctly a storage infrastructure can host both in-house data and hosted data from business customers. Data from business market may also have another profile with more metadata associated with it, both structured and unstructured. Identifying patterns and optimize the use of such data may give the data owners a competitive edge in their business.

## Big Data

Data sets that grow so large that they become hard to work with is often called Big Data. The big data domain can be used by telecom business, and with optimal use of an optimal infrastructure it provides a benefit by providing actionable information. The capture of data can come from external companies and services, but also internal sources, such as; service logs and data, Call Detail Records, user and usage data, data from BSS/OSS, data from use of telecom enablers (position, call control, oneAPI, etc), and the emerging M2M market. The data have to be searchable, with efficient query times and data loading times. The data should be shared with minimal load on network and hardware storage cost. Tools for analytics should be available to be optimized and give insight, preferably in real time (Banerjee, 2011).

## Positioning in the Cloud Ecosystem

Some large telcos have entered the cloud ecosystem as cloud providers (e.g. Verizon, AT&T, and KT). Others have chosen to partner with SaaS providers and offer cloud services as part of a bundle (e.g. Deutsche Telecom). In an advanced form, these positions can be seen as brokers of cloud services, as explained in details in (Liu, 2011). A cloud broker in the simplest form should offer some added value such as identity management and settlement/billing. Next, a cloud broker should be able to combine cloud services from different providers as well as having the functionality for choosing the best cloud service providers to fulfill specific customer requirements. The cloud broker should thus also be responsible for negotiating and monitoring the SLAs on behalf of the customer.

For a telco, the cloud broker model additionally provides the opportunity for combining cloud and network services. Cloud services can thus be chosen and delivered based on network availability and performance. We foresee a scheduler with an optimization algorithm responsible for making cloud deployment choices based on cloud provider cost as well as network cost and quality. The scheduler will thus move customer data and applications between different cloud infrastructures when the experienced quality of the cloud or network service declines, in order to deliver the service with the lowest possible cost and highest possible quality.

For the enterprise market, the trend is that enterprises are moving their business critical applications and data to the cloud. A cloud broker can provide a one-stop shop for SMEs and enterprises that look for a complete cloud service portfolio covering all their IT needs. A combined view of cloud and network service is valuable and the network connecting the enterprise and the cloud data center must be available and provide the required latency for the enterprise to be satisfied. Other important challenges with respect to interoperability between different cloud services and federation across different cloud providers must also be solved, as well as the management of SLAs across the different providers.

The consumer market demands another set of important requirements to the telecom cloud service provisioning; ubiquitous access to services and data, from all types of accesses and all types of terminals is fundamental. This convergence is happening and consumers expect the same piece of data to be delivered to any device anywhere and at any time. Services for the consumer market utilize the increased capabilities of handsets, resulting in bandwidth hungry services such as video services being consumed on mobile devices. Although these services and other new types of services are capable of running on handsets such as tablets and smart phones, the capabilities are still limited. Bandwidth is limited to the network available at any given location and how many concurrent users there are, CPU is limited by battery capacity and power consumption, while screen size, memory and storage is limited by the physical size of the device.

Telecom operators need to meet the expectations from consumers, SMEs and enterprises and offer services and infrastructure that is future proof in this respect. The latter poses specific requirements on storage and cloud storage are becoming more and more important. The objective should be to manage the data for different market segments, tenants and users, and through managed data traffic ensure the desired levels of QoS.

## Use of VISION Cloud

The telecommunication operators overall needs for a cloud storage infrastructure have been presented above. The innovations proposed by VISION Cloud are good candidates to fulfill those needs. Even though not all of them will be assessed within the duration of the project, following is an analysis of this potential fulfillment classified by innovation:

- **Raise Abstraction Level of Storage:** Objects with user- and system-defined metadata.
  - **Content from consumers and enterprise data:** To help consumers and enterprise staff to access their data thanks to metadata (Y1, Y2, Y3).
- **Computational Storage:** Technology for specifying/executing computations close to storage.
  - **Smart networks:** To process data in the cloud storage, thus preventing bandwidth consuming data transfer (Y1, Y2, Y3).
  - **Facility management:** To design facilities based on storlets allowing automation of triggering and modularity (Y2, Y3).
- **Content-Centric Storage:** Facilitate access to data by content and its relationships.

◦ **Customer experience:** Help customers to browse and easily retrieve their data (Y1, Y2, Y3).

◦ **Facility management:** Allow different facilities to share a common organization of data within the cloud storage (Y1, Y2, Y3).

- **Advanced Capabilities for Cloud-based Storage:** Support delivery of data-intensive services securely, at the desired QoS, at competitive costs (Y2, Y3).

    ◦ **Customer experience:** Rely on VISION Cloud SLA management to ensure high level of QoS and QoE (Y2, Y3).

    ◦ **Enterprise data:** Rely on VISION Cloud advanced security model and implementation (Y2, Y3).

    ◦ **Flexible billing**: Rely on VISION Cloud billing and accounting capabilities (Y2, Y3).

- **Data Mobility and Federation:** Enable comprehensive data migration and interoperability across remote locations.

    ◦ **Customer experience:** Move mobile customers data close to them to ensure optimal access performance (Y3).

◦ **Shared infrastructure:** Foster optimal use of storage capabilities within a telecommunication operator IS by use of VISION Cloud federation mechanisms (Y3).

◦ **Content from consumers:** Help customers to have a unique view of their data by federating VISION Cloud and external storage capabilities (Y3).

VISION Cloud telecommunication use case is being developed iteratively. The first iteration focused on assessing the core functional features of the infrastructure by implementing a consumer-oriented scenario allowing a telecommunication operator customer to manage multimedia content in the VISION Cloud test infrastructure. It includes the following aspects: storing and retrieving pictures, videos and associated metadata; using storlets to process stored content and metadata; using content-centric capability to organize content.

Figure 1 shows the overall functional architecture of the first iteration of the telecommunication use case where customers can use several services that access VISION Cloud infrastructure through a common "Telco hub." This component is a gateway to the VISION Cloud infrastructure and is shared by services that a telecommunication operator offers to its mass-market customers. Its purpose

*Figure 1. General architecture of a telco operator, giving access to VISION Cloud through a telco hub*

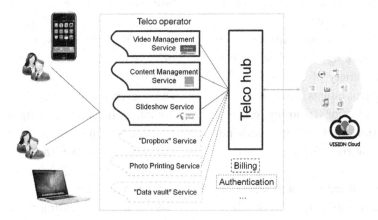

is to enable services to access VISION functional and non functional capabilities in a uniform way. Devices used to access services can be of different types: smartphones, tablets, laptops, etc.

Three service prototypes have been developed: the "Video Management Service" which transcodes uploaded videos to several formats and allows searches on metadata; the "Image Management Service" which allows a customer to store and organize images using VISION Cloud infrastructure; the "Slideshow Service" which produces slideshows of images stored thanks to the Image Management Service. The openness of the architecture allows easily adding new services making use of the Telco hub and sharing data organization and processing capabilities present inside the VISION Cloud infrastructure. In this first iteration the Telco hub only provides functional features and the goal is to add non functional features such as billing or authentication as they become available.

In the "Video Management Service" service, video objects, along with user metadata, are uploaded onto the cloud infrastructure. In general, those video objects could have been obtained by any source, such as the VISION Cloud media use-case, which produces videos in a professional format. The upload subsequently triggers a computational task near the storage (namely "Storlet"), which:

- Uses the provided metadata and technical metadata extracted from the video to identify a set of suitable operations.
- Transcodes the video into different common formats, making it suitable for consumption in a variety of end-user devices (e.g. smartphones, tablets, computers).
- Prepares the video for streaming, enabling easy distribution on low bandwidth networks of varying conditions.

Finally, the user is offered an interface though which he can make complex queries on all the video objects by metadata keys and values. When the desired content is located, the user receives the video object in the format corresponding to the device used.

The "Image Management Service" proposes to upload images to the VISION Cloud infrastructure. Upon uploading, a storlet is triggered that:

- Extracts metadata from the image and stores it as VISON Cloud metadata. EXIF (technical metadata such as camera type, resolution or GPS coordinates) and IPTC (informational metadata such as country, city, location or copyright are extracted.
- Computes clusters of image based of their GPS coordinates and creates "Sets" according to their nearness; sets are a VISION Cloud content-centric capability that allows establishing relations between stored objects; this clustering can be used to classify images according to the site at which they were taken.

The set structure created can be browsed and images can be downloaded along with their metadata.

The "Slideshow Service" reuses the set structure created by the "Image Management Service" to produce a slideshow per set of images, which can be adapted to be displayed on the user's device.

This first iteration allowed assessing the core functional aspects of the VISION Cloud infrastructure: storing and retrieving data and associated metadata using a distant test bed through the Internet. Furthermore, two of the major innovations of VISION Cloud were successfully used: storlets to transcode video extract and populate metadata and, together with the content-centric capability, organize objects. Querying objects using metadata and sharing organization of data within the infrastructure showed that VISION Cloud allowed raising the level of abstraction when accessing data. Nevertheless, the size of the objects stored did not allow assessing the performance of the infrastructure and non functional aspects were not part of this first iteration.

The objectives of the second iteration of the telecommunication use case are the following:

- Explore the use of VISION Cloud for a enterprise oriented scenario as business customer are important for telecommunication operators.
- Assess non functional capabilities such as billing, Service Level Agreements (SLA), performance of the infrastructure.
- Investigate the use of storlets as a way to easily manage in house and third party facilities.

Including and going beyond first iterations capabilities, the "Telco hub" should offer:

- Proxy for functional VISION Cloud operations, storing and retrieving objects and associated metadata using content-centric interface.
- Proxy for non functional VISION Cloud capabilities such as billing, authentication, SLA management.

- Management of facilities implemented as starlets.
- Management of customers and their storage spaces (VISION Cloud containers).

Regarding management of facilities, the "Telco hub" should provide 3rd party facilities providers with means to offer their facilities as storlets. Customers should be able to buy facilities and the "Telco hub" should take care of the ingestion and of the activation of the corresponding storlet into a container of a customer. Billing of the service usage should be managed by the "Telco hub", taking advantage of the billing capability of VISION Cloud covering both storage and processing usage. The "Telco hub" should also act as a bridge between the telco infrastructure and VISION Cloud with respect to customer information management. If the telco has taken a broker role, 3rd party services could be managed in the same way as internal services. The brokered services would use the cloud broker functionalities (see Figure 2).

The demonstration of the new capabilities of the Telco hub will be shown in a "Call Center" service proposed by a telecommunication opera-

*Figure 2. Telco use case second iteration prototype*

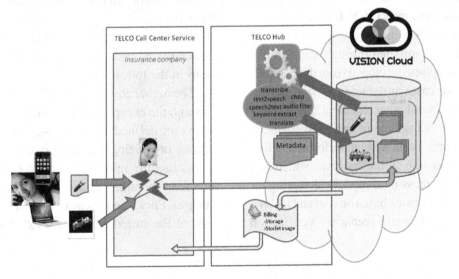

tor to its enterprise customers. This service will offer core facilities such as recording and storing a conversation in the VISION Cloud infrastructure, transcribing a conversation to a text, etc. One of the objectives is to assess the ability of the computational storage innovation of VISION Cloud to enable the customer to easily add new facilities to its call center service.

The call center service will be illustrated by an insurance company using the service to manage conversations recorded when a policy holder calls for a claim. Other data such as pictures of the resulting damage of an accident, scan of an accident report, etc. will also be stored. Metadata will be associated to the objects stored (destination number, originating number, time stamp, … for a conversation, metadata used in first iteration for pictures, etc.). The insurance company might want either to develop new facilities or buy 3rd party ones (such as keywords extraction or translation) and integrate them to its call center service thanks to the facility management offered.

The large amount of metadata stored by an insurance company using the call center service can be queried thanks to the content-centric complex query service in order to identify trends (frequency of accidents in an area and/or timeframe), fraudulent claims, etc.

Last iteration of the telecommunication use case should focus on the use of the federation capabilities offered by VISIOn Cloud.

The revenue potential analysis from storage based services is initiated through a qualitative scenario description developed from the VISION cloud telco use cases introducing service innovations, customers and other technical and business related issues. An update of the telco partners' exploitation ambitions will be performed before moving to next step in the analysis, which is a quantitative business case model calculating alternative business cases based on cost and income figures extracted from the scenarios. Verification

and improvement of these business cases and model input variables will be performed together with the telcos' throughout the VISION Cloud project iterations.

## FUTURE RESEARCH DIRECTIONS

### VISION Cloud Approach

The scenario highlights a number of challenges that need to be addressed in order to enable the utilization of storage clouds for telecommunication service provision. These challenges mainly refer to content-centric access to the stored objects, i.e. access to data objects through information about their content and its relationships rather than details of underlying storage container, and to computational storage, i.e. computational agents—namely storlets—activated by events on data in order to perform computation close to data) The specific challenges, addressed in the framework of the EU-funded VISION Cloud project, set forth to solve issues related to limited network bandwidth, which is considered of major importance both in the consumer and in the enterprise market. In addition, processing of data allows the presentation of the content on different types of devices, thus reducing both the network bandwidth consumption and the requirements to the terminals.

The first prototype developed for the telco use case takes advantage of VISION Cloud innovations in the following way.

The higher abstraction level of storage access, through the encapsulation of storage into objects with user-defined and system-defined attributes, allows organizing the images uploaded to the infrastructure into sets similar to collections provided by online image management systems such as Flickr and Picasa. This organization is part of the stored data, and thus allows it to be shared by different services. In this first validation prototype, the Slideshow Service reuses the organization of data by producing a slideshow on the fly for a set of images.

Computational storage based on the storlets, computational units stored and triggered in the storage infrastructure, was used to build the sets automatically each time an image is uploaded in a customer storage space. In the prototype, metadata is extracted from the images among which GPS coordinates. These coordinates are then used to create the sets according to the geographic closeness of the images. Besides the obvious benefit of having computations processed within the storage infrastructure and avoiding otherwise necessary data transfer, computational storage also fosters modularity. Units of computation can subscribe to events and trigger execution within a customer storage space. This allows computation at will and in compositions, designed by the triggered events, such as changed metadata fields.

The general architecture where customers can use several services that access VISION Cloud infrastructure can be accessed through a common "Telco hub". Devices used to access services can be of different types: smartphones, tablets, laptops, etc. The "Telco hub" should offer:

- Proxy for functional VISION Cloud operations, storing and retrieving objects and associated metadata using content-centric interface.
- Proxy for non-functional VISION Cloud capabilities such as billing, authentication, SLA management.
- Management of services implemented as starlets.
- Management of customers and their storage spaces (VISION Cloud containers).

Regarding management of services, the "Telco hub" should provide 3rd party service providers with means to offer their services as storlets.

Customers should be able to buy services and the "Telco hub" should take care of the ingestion and of the activation of the corresponding storlet into a container of a customer. Billing of the service usage should be managed by the "Telco hub," taking advantage of the billing capability of VISION Cloud covering both storage and processing usage. The "Telco hub" should also act as a bridge between the telco infrastructure and VISION Cloud with respect to customer information management. If the telco has taken a broker role, 3rd party services could be managed in the same way as internal services. The brokered services would use the cloud broker functionalities.

## CONCLUSION

VISION storage innovations like video and image management will provide telco customers more flexible and rich services allowing them to do more with large amounts of data and improve the user experience and reduce cost at the same time. The storage features will enable the customer to access data in a simpler and more efficient way than before since access here is facilitated through content and its relationships, rather than details of the underlying storage containers. This will consequently enable an easier metering, accounting, and billing performance than before. Furthermore VISION cloud aim to offer storage services with QoS and security guarantees, which should be a good selling point especially towards business customers considering deployment of critical business applications and data in the cloud. Coordinating these service innovations in a telco hub demands development of a data oriented service platform. A broker function owned by the telco would be a natural actor to develop and manage such a hub bundling storage-based services with conventional telecom and data services and call centre capabilities.

# REFERENCES

Banerjee, A. (2011). *Addressing big data telcom requirements for real-time analytics.* Retrieved August from http://www.sybase.com/files/White_Papers/Sybase-Big-Data-WP-3-9-11.pdf

Cisco. (2012). *Cisco visual networking index: Global mobile data traffic forecast update, 2011-2016.* Retrieved from http://www.cisco.com/en/US/solutions/collateral/ns341/ns525/ns537/ns705/ns827/white_paper_c11-520862.pdf

3. *GIS.* (2012). Retrieved from http://www.3gis.net/default.asp?lang=eng

Green, J. (2012, July 31). *OTT VoIP to cost telcos $479 billion to 2020.* Retrieved from http://ovum.com/2012/07/31/ott-voip-to-cost-telcos-479-billion-to-2020/

Liu, F. (2011). NIST cloud computing reference architecture. *Special Publication 500-292.*

Nesse, P. E. (2011). Exploiting cloud computing - A proposed methodology of generating new business. In *Proceedings of ICIN 2011.* ICIN.

Owen, T. (2012, April 18). *Data security and the small/medium enterprise (SME).* Retrieved August 2012, from http://www.allenport.com/blog/2012/04/18/data-security-and-the-smallmedium-enterprise-sme-part-2/

Raybum, D. (2011, June 27). *Telcos and carriers forming new federated CDN group called OCX.* Retrieved August 31, 2012, from http://blog.streamingmedia.com/the_business_of_online_vi/2011/06/telco-and-carriers-forming-new-federated-cdn-group-called-ocx-operator-carrier-exchange.html

Ried, S. (2011). *Cloud broker - A new business model paradigm.* Forrester Research Report.

Symantec. (2011). *State of cloud survey.* Retrieved August 2012, from http://www.symantec.com/content/en/us/about/media/pdfs/symc-state-of-cloud-report-global.pdf

Telco 2.0. (2012). *Euro telcos: Fiddling while the platform burns?* Retrieved August 31, 2012, from http://www.telco2research.com/articles/EB_euro-telcos-fiddling-while-platform-burns_Summary

Telco 2.0 Research. (2012). *The value of smart pipes to mobile network operators.* Retrieved August 2012, from http://www.telco2research.com/articles/WP_the-value-of-smart-pipes_Summary

Telenor. (2011, June 14). *Telenor and Telia join forces to create Denmark's best network.* Retrieved August 2012, from http://telenor.com/news-and-media/press-releases/2011/telenor-and-telia-join-forces-to-create-denmarks-best-network/

Telenor Group. (2012). *Strategy.* Retrieved from http://telenor.com/about-us/our-strategy/

The Hindu. (2012, July 24). *Uninor to scale down in four circles.* Retrieved August 2012, from http://www.thehindu.com/business/companies/article3679206.ece

Videonet. (2010, September 23). *Broadband ready to become a serious TV platform.* Retrieved August 31, 2012, from http://www.v-net.tv/Broadband-ready-to-become-a-serious-TV-platform/

## KEY TERMS AND DEFINITIONS

**Call Center:** Centralized function to receive inquiries from consumers and provide service support.

**CDN:** Content Delivery Network is a large distributed system of servers. They serve content to end-users with high performance and offload traffic served directly from content providers.

**Cloud Ecosystem:** The term used to describe the complex system that enable cloud services, e.g. providers, software, infrastructure, partners, integrators, components, etc.

**Cloud Services:** Services enabled and offered by cloud computing technologies, e.g. infrastructure, communication, office productivity service.

**OTT Services:** Services typically offered by global Internet players without own infrastructure or restricted to specific geographic regions.

**Telco Hub:** A global backend offering traditional telco enablers as well as new ones such as VISION Cloud storage, ID, and billing.

**Telecommunication Industry:** Companies that offer telecommunication services.

# Chapter 11
# Data Intensive Enterprise Applications

**Peter Izsak**
*SAP Research Israel, Israel*

**Aidan Shribman**
*SAP Research Israel, Israel*

## ABSTRACT

*Today almost all big enterprises act globally, which results in a growing need for a new kind of data analytics. Imagine a company where data from distribution and sales needs to be combined with increasing online sales on multiple platforms and marketing across new social media channels. Here, new real-time analytics using Cloud Computing concepts can open new perspectives. SAP has had a strong presence in the Business Intelligence (BI) market. The company pioneered concepts to collect, combine, and analyze company wide information. As a result, SAP customers enjoy BI capabilities that are strongly integrated with their SAP operational systems (e.g., ERP, CRM). In recent years, companies have leveraged Cloud Computing as a means for lowering the Total Cost of Ownership (TCO) of various types of business applications that are provided On-Demand. SAP already offers products such as SAP Business ByDesign, which is offered as a Software-as-a-Service (SaaS) On-Demand product. Feature-rich Cloud storage solution such as VISION Cloud enables SAP to integrate new innovations to its On-Demand software portfolio. This chapter describes how VISION Cloud enriches SAP's Instant Business Intelligence analytical On-Demand service.*

## INTRODUCTION

In the enterprise use case SAP aims to develop new concepts for on-demand analytics, which could potentially be faster, more accurate and covering many more data sources using cloud storage. The key idea is to come closer to "Instant Business Analytics" (IBI), where even very big datasets can be capture and analyzed in real-time or near

real-time, thus helping to understand shifts in supply and demand better.

VISION Cloud provides various features, which enables enriching the features of SAP IBI:

- High availability of the data.
- Identity and on-boarding federation.
- Compute engine close to the data – in form of Storlets.
- Multi-tenancy support.
- Accounting and billing information.

DOI: 10.4018/978-1-4666-3934-8.ch011

SAP is at the forefront of enterprise software technology, it offers a wide verity of solutions for managing business processes from large enterprises to small and medium sized businesses. In recent years, the Business Intelligence (BI) software market has gained more attention as the ability to produce meaningful insights from the collected data held by an enterprise became more productive. SAP offers its customers Business Intelligence capabilities that are strongly integrated with their SAP operational systems (e.g., ERP, CRM). Like other vendors in the enterprise software market, SAP offerings include data flows from the operational systems into departmental and organizational data warehouses, where decision support and other on-line analytical processing takes place.

SAP's Instant Business Intelligence is an offering by SAP which provides on-demand analytical and business intelligence capabilities for SAP customers without the need of on-premise installation or integration.

In this chapter, we will explain the integration of VISION Cloud with SAP IBI and show the benefits of using it compared to other solutions offered.

## BACKGROUND

Why is there a need for innovation in the analytics field? Since 2009, we have observed two significant trends that can become a differentiating factor in the market:

- Providing sophisticated analytical capabilities in real time on up-to-date fresh data. The availability of servers with very large main memories, along with the advancements of Main-Memory Database System (MMDBs) (Garcia-Molina & Salem, 1992), put these real time capabilities within reach. SAP has introduced a first

line of products in this area of MMDBs and in particular main-memory BI in 2010.
- Leveraging cloud computing as a means for lowering Total Cost of Ownership (TCO) of various types of business applications that are provided On-Demand. Software-as-a-Service (SaaS)(Software as a Service [SaaS], n.d.) models are gaining significant traction in various segments of the enterprise software market. SAP already provides a complete ERP suite on-demand for small and medium businesses referred to as Business ByDesign.

This leads to several motivations:

- The issue of TCO has become a means for lowering IT costs and improving sustainability of a company's IT infrastructure.
- Companies have recognized the benefits of SaaS models, and have developed intentions for providing new benefits for their customers by adopting the new technology.
- Companies expect high-end solutions to be available in a service oriented model, and with minimal IT implementation and cost.
- The features and capabilities of a SaaS solution can significantly impact the sustainability of a solution built on top of it on the long run.

### Multi-Tenanted Analytics On-Demand

Multi-Tenanted Analytics On-Demand, Large scale analytics in the enterprise domain is enabled with the advances in main memory size and in MMDB technology along with the integration of new cloud based business models which now offer traditional ERP services in an on-demand service model. We are looking at providing analytics services on-demand - Instant Business Intelligence (IBI). Such a scenario is based on:

- Inherent multi-tenancy since it is a SaaS model.
- Data ingress and periodic refresh flow for keeping tenants data up-to-date.
- Analytics of the data in a multi-tenanted setup.
- High-availability of the data.
  Reviewing of State-of-The-Art:
- **SAP BI On Demand 1.0 (SAP BusinessObjects BI OnDemand, n.d.):** So far, SAP has only limited presence in the BI On-Demand market http://www. ondemand.com/businessintelligence - the current offering is a multi-tenant solution allowing for sharing of reports among users the actual data source remains in on-premise thus requiring the existing costly implementation of OLAP cubes on-premise.
- **Oco Business Analytics (Oco Analytic Applications for SAP BusinessObjects OnDemand, n.d.):** Is an offering for SAP CRM and ERP customers who already have an OLAP deployment on-premise. What is placed on-demand is a rich analytics dashboard, thus enabling fancier aggregated analytics reports created for existing customers with OLAP deployed on-premise.

## Analysis of Client Application I/O Workload

We now present an auxiliary research area especially needed for evaluation of storage solutions for complex business applications. This move away from on-site data warehousing/data centers offers new avenues to scale data operations and can potentially lower costs at the same time. We propose the usage of low-overhead I/O profiling tools on the client machine. We can then use the recorded trace information as a means for recreating the I/O load of the given business application per-scenario without the need of running the actual business application software stack on VISION

Cloud test landscape. I/O traces serve for defining the qualitative performance requirements that arise from the enterprise use case.

- Traditional system call monitoring tool such as UNIX STRACE (Strace, n.d.) can attach to a specific process and collect the storage related system call accesses made during a given scenario. The downside of such tools is that they don't work on the full OS system-wide level and they incur high overhead due to running in user-mode.
- Using SystemTap (Eigler, 2006) (a Linux kernel dynamic probe and debug tool) as a basis for I/O profiling would require developing SystemTap specific scripts. Additionally SystemTap is not natively supported in all commercial Linux distributions, thus requires in some cases a Kernel rebuild. Finally SystemTap requires the full kernel-debuginfo which again does not always exist on all Linux distributions.

## ENTERPRISE USE CASE

### Multi-Tenanted Analytics On-Demand

What is missing in existing solutions?

- The existing solutions still require an OLAP (Online Analytical Processing, n.d.) (in addition to OLTP [Online Transaction Processing, n.d.]) service set-up on- premise.
- If the OLAP data store exists on-premise then it can't scale seamlessly as cloud based storage.
- True multi-tenancy with per-user billing and accounting does not exist.
- Various levels of raw data replication including cross-site replication none existent.

In *VISION based IBI*: We go beyond the state of the art by offering the actual analytics engine to run atop the cloud while storing massive data sets securely on the extensible and scalable cloud storage being able to expand as additional tenants are added to the system. The concept of "tenants" is increasingly complex and relevant, because in today's business environment data might come from multiple sources, partners, systems and countries. This creates a need to look at data from multiple angles – on a department level, a country level or along one line of the organization, e.g. logistics. Effectively this approach can open many new options to "know" what is happening and why, thus creating business intelligence at multiple touch-points in the enterprise.

Multi-tenancy is supported inherently by VISION Cloud Account management service. A cloud tenant can define sub-tenants to be provisioned under its own tenant definition in VISION Cloud. SAP sub-tenants are defined under SAP's tenant, which is a dedicated tenant used by SAP in VISION Cloud. This provides the ability for SAP to control the installations of SAP IBI instances along with the management capabilities of account usage and billing aggregated and disaggregated per tenant. Moreover, role based user management allowed SAP's customer to manage its own SAP IBI instance users and roles.

The support of multi-tenancy also provides the ability to manage users in a tenant - sub-tenant structure. SAP IBI users of a certain instance can be defined by an administrative user pre-installed when the instance is initiated, and it is provided the capability of managing the end-users of SAP IBI instance.

## On-Boarding Federation

VISION Cloud supports the action of federating a tenant's data, including container structure, object structure and content between service providers which support VISION Cloud services. Federation adds flexibility and can help to overcome thorny and often costly migration issues when data has to be made available in a new context, an action which usually not available or is highly complex.

SAP customers store their content in a pre-defined and agreed service provider which was decided when the service agreement was signed. Nevertheless, the customer has the ability to switch supported service providers if he desires to. Reasons for switching service providers might me physical location, price, performance or resiliency.

Integration of a tenant instance within a service provider is transparent to the customer (a SAP customer in this case). A tenant has the ability to move to a new service provider. On-boarding federation supports semi non-disruptive relocation of data within supported VISION Cloud providers:

- New agreement is signed between SAP customer user and storage service provider.
- New credentials are pre-configured on new service provider.
- Tenant instance is paused.
- Federation is defined between old and new providers.
- Tenant instance is resumed.

## Storage Compute: Storlets

VISION Cloud offers a novel technology of compute engine which is close to the stored data referred to as Storlets. Storlets are effectively small, specialized programs or routines.

Technically, Storlets are compute objects which are capable of performing small computation task on object in pre-defined event hooks, e.g. when a certain threshold is reached or pre-defined levels of activity are reached. In such an event, storlets are invoked via a metadata label which is added to an object and on different hooks, such as, right after a *PUT* Rest operation, after metadata label delete, etc. Storlets can be defined a synchronous, such as a *GET* Rest operation done on an object, thus must be performed on-the-fly when the request is called. Or asynchronous, which will be invoked asynchronously by the Storlet Runtime Environment (SRE) at the defined invocation hook.

There are several key benefits provided by the SRE:

- A novel runtime environment that has no alternative in common cloud providers in the market.
- Execution of Storlets is done close to the data. Meaning, no network resources are used for data transferring. The Storlet is executed locally within a cluster or a host. This concept of performing computation in the storage cloud opens up a wide field of applications and novel data flows.
- Ability to transfer programmable batch compute operations from the application to the cloud host.

SAP IBI harnesses the state-of-the-art features offered by the SRE by offering several key features:

- Automatic metadata label generation pre-defined by customer instance customization.
- **Data transformation and normalization tenant data:** Perform simple but data intensive processes locally on the VISION Cloud hosts to save networking resources and billing costs, while also offloading computing resources from SAP IBI on-premise and the tenants' systems.
- **Compression and on-the-fly uncompressing:** Archived data is compressed to save storage space and billing cost, while also performing uncompressing of the data if a request for transfer is initiated. Moreover, the compression algorithm is stored along-side with the archived object, enabling technology independent compression solution.
- **On-demand programming environment:** Ability to upload customized storlets programmed by the customer to be executed on the data used by its instance of SAP IBI.

## Analysis of I/O Workload

Trace recording is a common practice for I/O workload analysis, code debugging, performance evaluation of storage solutions and file-systems. However, inserting profiling applications in an execution stack of an application might introduce abnormalities in the behavior of the application; this is unacceptable for it is contradicting the purpose of application trace analysis.

Going beyond State-of-the-Art would require low overhead system-wide I/O profiling per application. A direction we are currently exploring is running a profiler, which traps I/O calls at the VFS level in the Linux kernel. By doing so we enjoy both low-overhead (as there are no needless memory copying between the kernel space to user-mode application) and additionally enjoying low-overhead processing, by running on the VFS level makes the tool ideal for profiling most any file system including local, network, and even FUSE (Filesystem in Userspace, n.d.) based file-systems.

## VISION Cloud in the Enterprise Use Case

SAP offers SAP IBI, an on-demand large-scale analytics engine which uses state-of-the-art MMDB technology. SAP IBI integrates with customer on-premise ERP systems and produces advanced analytical dashboards using SAP's latest MMDB solution.

As means to reduce costs SAP customers turn to on-demand services which provide the same benefits of an on-premise installation without having the costs of hardware and IT maintenance required for operating.

**System architecture:**

- SAP's customer has on-premise installation of ERP systems.
- SAP has an on-premise SAP IBI system for serving on-demand instances of SAP IBI stored locally in SAP's datacenter and in VISION Cloud as objects in containers.

### Pre-loading and updating:

- Each customer pre-loads it SAP IBI instance with ERP data to be analyzed.
- Periodically, new information generated in the on-premise ERP system of a customer is transferred to SAP IBI instance to update the analytical engine with the most recent information.
- The customer pushes new updates into VISION Cloud and updates its instance to load the new information.
- Add pre-configured storlets and customized metadata to be applied on the pushed updates.
- Each update is recognized by SAP IBI engine and loaded into the customers instance and processed in the MMDB.

### Periodical Snapshotting:

- Aggregate periodical updates and current SAP IBI instance data of a customer into a snapshot image to be stored in VISION Cloud – in case of application failure this provides the ability to restore the activity of the instance.
- Keep at least 2 snapshots.

### Per-year archiving:

- Aggregate information collected in a period of 1 year.
- Compress data to save space and save compression algorithm along with data.
- Uncompress on-the-fly when needed.

### Sub-tenant and user management:

- SAP IBI application administrator defines an instance owner as VISION Cloud sub-tenant of the tenant SAP.
- SAP IBI application administrator defines an administrator role to be assigned to a SAP customer instance.

- The customer's administrative user can create administrative roles and end users roles.

### On-boarding federation:

- On-boarding federation is supported in the level of tenants.
- Ability to initiate federation between pre-configured service providers.
- Federation requires a new sub-tenant to be set-up and configured, when federation has initiated successfully old sub-tenant instance is assigned to the new sub-tenant.

### Storlet selection:

- SAP IBI administrator along with the customer agree on a pre-defined set of storlets to be included in the containers:

  ○ Row count of each update.
  ○ Compress data stored in archive.
  ○ Uncompress data when reading.

### Billing:

- Display accounting and billing information of SAP's tenant and sub-tenant

### End-user analytical data:

- End users are the users of SAP IBI analytical engine.
- SAP IBI provides an on-demand analytical dashboard generated by the instance update with the data of the customers ERP system.

## CHALLENGES

SAP's IBI solution stands out from other similar solutions by the ability to deploy instances on-demand by SAP customers on a different data center, to reduce TCO costs as much as possible while also having the latest analytical application for its use.

Application performance and reliability are the key points for providing a successful on-demand application:

- **Low storage use:** Space used equals money spent, the means of using a cloud based storage system should be cheaper than using on-premise NAS (Network-Attached Storage, n.d.) or SAN (Storage Area Network, n.d.) storage solutions.
- **Reliable storage:** Store data in several locations, different providers and verify that the stored data is not corrupt.
- **Fast storage:** As the number of tenant of a cloud storage system grows, the load on the hardware, network devices and physical hosts, grow. Scalability and sustainability should be considered when designing storage cloud.
- **Computation power:** For enabling storlets, a certain computational resources must be devoted for this purpose, overloading the hosts with storlets could reduce the performance of the storage system.

## SOLUTIONS AND RECOMMENDATIONS

There are several solutions for dealing with potential problems that might arise from the challenges noted above. These challenges are the core of the research performed in VISION Cloud. They address typical problems in such flexible and dynamic data storage environments.

One big issue is Data De-Duplication, meaning the management of data objects that are stored multiple times in the same form. Data De-duplication (Data Deduplication, n.d.) systems are a common solution for reducing the amount of space used by storage systems. A de-duplication system is hashes chunks of data and saves only one copy of that

certain chunk, while also saving the information of the user (which in this case – an application).

There are several ways for providing reliable storage in a data center. Either by using a RAID (Redundant Array of Independent Disks, n.d.) solution or storage solutions offered in form of NAS or SAN which provide integrated fault-tolerance.

The SRE should be disaggregated from the storage but not from the data center. Dedicated machines should be devoted only for computation jobs initiated by storlets – this will allow near local I/O performance on objects (since it is located in a fast LAN) and will allow the reduction of computation hurdle on the object storage hosts. Moreover, asynchronous storlets do not require on-the-fly computation thus making the disjoint of storlet cluster machines a positive solution.

## CONCLUSION

SAP envisions a computational data storage concept that could lead to a number of innovations and new options. Advanced storage cloud systems such as VISION Cloud provide the ability of on-demand applications, such as SAP IBI, capabilities that were never possible before or required on-premise installation of supporting applications. Near seamless federation enables service provider change almost without disruption to the user experience. In addition, close to storage computation engine is a feature never seen before from cloud providers, as it opens up almost unlimited potential for SAP IBI's customers to customize their cloud data. To SAP, VISION Cloud provides a means for providing new advanced technology services for SME businesses, which are interested in cloud services for their business.

## REFERENCES

*Data Deduplication.* (n.d.). Retrieved from http://searchstorage.techtarget.com/definition/data-deduplication

Eigler, F. C. (2006). Problem solving with Systemtap. In *Proceedings of the Linux Symposium*. Ottawa, Canada: Linux.

*Filesystem in Userspace*. (n.d.). Retrieved from http://fuse.sourceforge.net/

Garcia-Molina & Salem. (1992). Main memory database systems: An overview. *IEEE Transactions on Knowledge and Data Engineering*, 4(6), 509–516. doi:10.1109/69.180602.

*Network-Attached Storage*. (n.d.). Retrieved from http://en.wikipedia.org/wiki/Network-attached_storage

*Oco Analytic Applications for SAP BusinessObjects OnDemand*. (n.d.). Retrieved from http://ecohub.sap.com/catalog/#!solution:bisolutions

*Online Analytical Processing*. (n.d.). Retrieved from http://en.wikipedia.org/wiki/Online_analytical_processing

*Online Transaction Processing*. (n.d.). Retrieved from http://en.wikipedia.org/wiki/Online_transaction_processing

*Redundant Array of Independent Disks*. (n.d.). Retrieved from http://en.wikipedia.org/wiki/Redundant_array_of_independent_disks

*SAP BusinessObjects BI OnDemand*. (n.d.). Retrieved from http://www.biondemand.com/businessintelligence

*Software as a Service (SaaS)*. (n.d.). Retrieved from http://www.gartner.com/it-glossary/software-as-a-service-saas/

*Storage Area Network*. (n.d.). Retrieved from http://en.wikipedia.org/wiki/Storage_area_network

*Strace*. (n.d.). Retrieved from http://linux.die.net/man/1/strace

# Chapter 12
# Cloud Computing for Earth Observation

**Roberto Cossu**
*European Space Agency (ESRIN), Italy*

**Claudio Di Giulio**
*European Space Agency (ESRIN), Italy*

**Fabrice Brito**
*Terradue, Italy*

**Dana Petcu**
*Institute e-Austria, Austria & West University of Timisoara, Romania*

## ABSTRACT

*This chapter elaborates on the impact and benefits Cloud Computing may have on Earth Observation. Earth Observation satellites generate in fact Tera- to Peta-bytes of data, and Cloud Computing provides many capabilities that allow an efficient storage and exploitation of such data. Several scenarios related to Earth Observation activities are analyzed in order to identify the possible benefits from the adoption of Cloud Computing. As concrete proofs-of-concept, several activities related to Cloud Computing in the context of Earth Observation are exposed and discussed. Technical details are provided for a particular framework used by Earth Observation applications that has made the transition from using Grid services towards using Cloud services. A special attention is given to the avoidance of the vendor-lock-in problem.*

## INTRODUCTION

Nowadys Earth Observation satellites generate Tera to Peta bytes of raw data. When looking at the future, new high-resolution sensors, either multi-, super-, or hyperspectral, will lead to even higher data quantities to be processed. This huge amount of data needs to be stored, preserved, processed to higher levels and be distributed to the user communities.

The IT infrastructures for Earth Observation (EO) need to harness processors, applications and services and cope with peaks of demand of EO data (this demand can be data access and/or processing) that can lead to a reduction of the IT infrastructure QoS. Furthermore, the cost of these computing infrastructures is often very high, such that the required investments may not be motivated.

DOI: 10.4018/978-1-4666-3934-8.ch012

Earth Observation computing infrastructures have particular requirements often not easy to address:

- Provide access to near-real time and historical data.
- Put data and processor together.
- Be able to ensure common functions.
- Allow on-demand processing.
- Be able to host "any" processor.
- Be sizeable, scalable, secure, and reliable.

The growing number of user communities develops applications that need to deal with the processing of large quantities of data. These applications can be global, regional, or local; they have alternative uses for the data at different resolutions; they require access to large historical and distributed archives (these have long term data and knowledge preservation issues) as well as access to near real-time data for processing, value adding and dissemination. In this context, the Cloud computing offer for elastic e-infrastructure use is attractive for the Earth observation communities. In what follows, we describe the steps that were made recently to adapt to the Cloud technologies at European initiatives.

The chapter is structured as follows. Meant as light introduction as well as motivating the actions that were undertaken and are partially reported in this chapter, Section 2 is shortly explaining the benefits of using Cloud technologies by Earth Observation communities. Thereafter, Section 3 is providing several hints about the on-going activities and recent results in the use Cloud Computing in Earth Observation in Europe. Section 4 starts with technical details, while exposing the functionality of a particular framework, namely *ify*, and its recent migration towards using Cloud resources. A special attention is provided to the avoidance of vendor lock-in problem using a platform that is ensuring the application code portability, namely mOSAIC. Same section is pointing towards real applications that are using

the framework. Finally, some conclusions and future work are shortly described.

## EARTH OBSERVATION ACTIVITIES THAT MAY BENEFIT FROM CLOUD COMPUTING

In what follows we analyze several Earth Observation typical activities having in mind the infrastructure needs. Some examples are shortly reported herein after. Others are present in literature as in (Markatchev et al, 2009) where an Interactive Application Service (IAS), a service providing to users on-demand access to applications interactively over the Internet, has been successfully deployed in the GeoChronos portal (http://geochronos.org/), a portal enabling members of the Earth observation science community to share applications and data. Other example is in (Golpayegani et al, 2009) where Cloud Computing solution for Satellite Data Processing on High End Compute Clusters is discussed. In recent literature, (Li et al, 2010) presents the design and implementation of a MODIS (http://earth.esa.int/MODIS/) satellite data re-projection and reduction pipeline in the Windows Azure cloud computing platform and (Wang et al, 2010) design and present a framework for retrieving, indexing, accessing and managing spatial data in the Cloud environment.In the following paragraphs other European Space Agency activities for the Earth Observation and benefits the Cloud Computing may have, are discussed in detail.

### Earth Observation Mission Re-Processing

The Earth Observation mission re-processing targets improvements of the EO data quality. These improvements can be of different nature: radiometric, geo-location and spatial resolution, among others.

These improvements can be achieved with the development of new and enhanced algorithms, tuning of auxiliary parameters, processor re-design, instrument calibration, or threshold and scaling factor corrections.

The volumes of data of an Earth Observation mission to be processed can be impressive. One month of Envisat MERIS Reduced Resolution Level 1 (http://envisat.esa.int/handbooks/meris/CNTR2.htm) corresponds to some 250 GB of data (Fusco et al., 2008). Considering six years the volume reaches almost 20 TB. The processing time of a single product may vary depending on its nature and type of processing. This time can also vary due to the hardware of the computing resource used.

When planning an Earth Observation mission reprocessing a number of variables need to be accessed. The time required to perform the reprocessing is one of these variables, the shorter the better. The sooner the reprocessed products reach the user communities, the sooner scientific results can be obtained. The processing time is directly proportional to the number of processing nodes used.

The trade-off between the processing time and number of processing nodes is then associated to the cost of the computing infrastructure to be procured.

To summarize, the EO mission re-processing scenario has a set of requirements:

- Storage for the input data to be reprocessed.
- Storage for the re-processed products.
- Possible on-line data access for the reprocessed products.
- Computing Infrastructure.

*Impact and benefits Cloud Computing may have on this type of EO activity:* Cloud Computing claims to have virtually infinite storage. The input data can then be pushed into Cloud storage for the duration of the processing. The reprocessed data can be published on Cloud storage with the extra benefit of possibly being used for on-line data access and distribution. All this constitutes a simple cost model which is easy to budget. Cloud Computing offers computing services with scalable capacity. The number of processing nodes can then be raised with no impact on the overall budget. The processing time is automatically diminished, shortening the reprocessed time to user and leaving more resources for quality control.

## Routine Production

Earth Observation routine production includes the generation, archiving and eventually the distribution of higher-level products following data or date driven scheduled services. These products may have different goals and purposes.

The set of 16 Envisat MERIS Level 3 products (http://earth.eo.esa.int/level3/meris-level3/) are considered demonstration products, produced on a daily and monthly basis and made available via a dedicated Web portal. The same input data, MERIS Level 2 Reduced Resolution (http://envisat.esa.int/instruments/meris/data-app/dataprod.html#level2), is processed 14 times per day (the MGVI products are not generated on a daily basis) to generate the daily Level 3, and 16 times per month to generate the monthly Level 3. Another type of product, also using MERIS Level 2 Reduced Resolution, the true-colour global mosaic, is generated for communications purposes.

There are other examples of routine production feeding product subscription services. A common point in these scheduled services is that it is the same data being processed over and over again during specific moments of the production cycle and then no longer used.

*Impact and benefits Cloud Computing may have on this type of EO activity:* Cloud storage could host the monthly amount of input data required for the generation of these products using Cloud computing processing power.

## Earth Observation On-Line Data Access

Earth Observation users want to be able to discover, select, and download data eventually combined with some processing services to do spatial or radiometric sub-setting. Initiatives have been implemented to provide near-real time access to EO data with the rolling archives. Other initiatives provide data via satellite-based data dissemination to allow users in remote areas where the network is too low or even not available to receive near-real time satellite data using simple receiving stations.

When designing these on-line data access systems, an important issue that must be carefully considered is how to respond to peaks of demand. In certain situations, these peaks may lead to a strong reduction of the data distribution QoS.

Furthermore, historical data can cover 20 years of acquisitions leading to volumes of tens of Terabytes per sensor. Providing on-line access to such huge amounts of data can be a quite challenging exercise.

The mistake of mixing on-line data access with data archiving and preservation is often made: archives should not be used to provide on-line data access, and online data access should not be seen as solutions for data archiving and preservation. The result of this common mistake is that historical archives are used for online data access, putting strain on access to the data itself.

Moreover, additional issues must be addressed: not all EO data access policies are the same. While a number of datasets can be addressed by a common data policy, other datasets may be subject to more restricted data policies. On-line data access systems should be able to address different data policies and controlled access.

*Impact and benefits Cloud Computing may have on this type of EO activity:* Cloud Computing for EO on-line data access would clearly split the archiving/preservation from the on-line data access while providing a number of clearly identified benefits:

- **Controlled access:** Access to data can be made private or public and specific rights can be granted to specific users: it implements data policy.
- **High uptime rates:** Protected by Service Level Agreements.
- Controlled and simple cost model.
- **Several data access protocols:** HTTP/HTTPs and BitTorrent (http://www.bittorrent.com/) being the most common among Cloud Computing providers.

## Fast Data Access for Crisis Situations

Earth Observation data has proven to be an excellent source of information for damage assessment for both natural and man-made disasters. There are several initiatives and projects fully dedicated in providing EO-based crisis mapping. A common issue for these services is the fast access to post-crisis data in near-real time and to archived historical data and the computing power for providing higher-level products (e.g. co-registered SAR data, http://envisat.esa.int/handbooks/asar/CNTR5-2.htm) and crisis mapping. On the one hand, and fortunately, the number of crisis event is relatively small, with a small number of activations per month. On the other, the computing resources have to be "on-call", that is, continuously available for processing in case of a crisis event.

Another important issue in the context of fast data access in crisis situations is the fact that the interest for related data is concentrated in a short time span: many users will need to access it in a short period of time. This situation may put strain on the on-line data distribution and eventually lead to its unavailability.

*Impact and benefits Cloud Computing may have on this type of EO activity:* Cloud Computing provides scalable storage capacity, the Earth Observation historical archive and near-real time data could be hosted on such infrastructure. Furthermore, the processing resources needed to provide the higher-level products and maps could also be provided by Cloud Computing thus removing the need for maintaining "on-call" computing resources. Furthermore, Cloud Computing storage provides high transfer rates even when numerous users access the same data at the same time.

## EXAMPLES OF ON-GOING EARTH OBSERVATION ACTIVITIES AT ESA BASED ON CLOUD COMPUTING

After the short introduction in the basic EO activities from the previous section, in what follows we focus on and discuss several examples of some ESA on-going activities where Cloud Computing is used in the context of Earth Observation. One example is shortly reported herein after.

Some initial theoretical conclusions were introduced in the scenarios above:

- EO data can be stored in Cloud Computing storage.
- Cloud Computing stored EO data can be accessed and distributed.
- Cloud Computing stored EO data can be processed over and over.
- Cloud Computing stored EO data separates on-line data access from archiving and preservation of the data.
- Security and reliability are issues addressed by the service provider.

Earth Observation computing infrastructures could be highly enhanced by being extended with Cloud IaaS (Infrastructure as a Service) as it provides virtually "infinite" storage space, large and scalable computing power and allows for running "any" application and claims to be secure and reliable.

The GeoHazard Supersites (http://eo-virtual-archive4.esa.int/) by ESA Virtual Archive it's a first example how Cloud Computing could impact in the Earth Observation activity.

## The Supersites

Geological extreme events such as large earthquakes, volcanic eruptions and landslides unfold as natural disasters when they meet with vulnerability. Precise geophysical measurements prior to, during, and following the events lead to a better scientific understanding of these events.

The Geohazard Supersites partnership pool and coordinate the existing space-based and ground-based observation resources of GEO members to mitigate and to improve the preparedness for geologic disasters. It is a membership-based consortium of universities, research institutions, national agencies responsible for geohazard observations, and space agencies. The aim is to systematically acquire, and provide access to, remote sensing and in-situ geophysical data for selected regional areas exposed to geological threats ("Supersites").

The Geohazard Supersites provide a cyber-infrastructure platform allowing fast, easy and free of charge access to complete satellite and ground-based geophysical data sets derived from different sources and different disciplines. This inter-disciplinary approach of using satellite radar data (SAR interferometry), seismology, and other earth science domains, provides the unique potential in making scientific steps in narrowing down the uncertainty of future disastrous events and providing information to policymakers for urbanization in geohazards endangered areas. These are a representative selection of areas exposed to geological threats (large earthquakes, volcanic eruptions or landslides) for which events are expected in the near future and which are appropriate places to stimulate fundamental research. These areas are monitored by the national agencies in charge of geohazards using in-situ networks (seismic and GPS) and by the participating space agencies with radar SAR satellites. All in-situ and most satellite data are accessible from the Supersites data portal (http://supersites.earthobservations.org/).

Most data are accessible through the Supersite data portal but are physically located elsewhere. The satellite data are located at the Space Agency premise.

The European Space Agency is using a Cloud Computing asset, the Virtual Archive to make the very large data set of 20 years observation robustly and fast available (example: ESA Virtual Archive for Haiti Earthquake, details at http://haiti-earthquake.esa.int/).

ESA Virtual Archive procures ICT capacity to bring large data volumes faster (80 SAR scenes in 300 sec) and shorter distances to the user by putting SAR product copies close to the user, distributed around the world.

The ESA Virtual Archive using the edge caching service by Content Delivery Network (CDN) procured by Cloud providers, allow a very fast SAR product access. The frequently accessed SAR data are temporary storage on servers that are located close to the end user, avoiding bottlenecks.

The Geohazard Supersites allow to stimulate an international effort to study selected sites by establishing open access to relevant datasets according to GEO principles fostering the collaboration between all partners and end-users.

## The mOSAIC, G-POD, and GENESI-DR/DEC Projects

mOSAIC is a multi-national joint effort (supported by the FP7-ICT programme of the European Commission, details at http://www.mosaic-cloud.eu) to build an open-source language-independent and paradigm-free API for developing applications based on Cloud services and elastic components, as well as a proof-of-concept platform that support the selection of the Cloud services to be used in the deployment phase of the applications using complex multi-agent and semantic processing technologies (Di Martino, et al., 2011). It focuses on providing the seamless deployment of data-intensive applications with a primary orientation towards Earth observation community. Recent publications of the project (Panica et al., 2011; Petcu et al., 2011) describe the steps necessary to achieve the independence from the Cloud vendor when migrating an application towards Clouds.

Initiated in 2003-2004 in ESA, transferred in Operations, G-POD project (http://gpod.eo.esa.int/) has been industrialized in 2006 by Terra-due, which maintains, enhances and integrates scientific and operational applications processors.

The EC FP7 project GENESI-DR (http://www.genesi-dr.eu/) and GENESI-DEC (http://www.genesi-dec.eu/), lead by ESA establish open data and services access, allowing European and worldwide Digital Earth Communities to seamlessly access, produce and share data, information, products and knowledge. This creates a multi-dimensional, multi-temporal, and multi-layer information facility of huge value in addressing global challenges such as biodiversity, climate change, pollution, and economic development. GENESI-DEC evolves and enlarges the platform developed by the predecessor GENESI-DR project by federating to and interoperating with existing infrastructures.

The processing service provided by GENESI-DEC enlarges the platform using the Cloud services supported by mOSAIC project as described in (mOSAIC Consortium: D3.1, 2011 and D3.2, 2011).

## THE GENESI-DEC PROJECT AND BENEFIT FROM CLOUD COMPUTING

In this section we are providing details about the GENESI-DEC activities, previously mentioned. The focus is put on the ify framework. Moreover, a special attention is pay to the solutions provided by Cloud Computing and by mOSAIC project.

## The Ify Framework

The ify framework is a Terradue solution providing a "user-segment" putting Earth Observation data and processors together. This framework feeds several operational services at ESA (e.g. ESA Grid Processing on-Demand) and Research and Development projects such as EC-FP7 GENESI-DR/GENESI-DEC.

EC FP7 project GENESI-DR and GENESI-DEC creates a multi-dimensional, multi-temporal, and multi-layer information facility of huge value in addressing global challenges such as biodiversity, climate change, pollution and economic development. GENESI-DEC evolves and enlarges the platform developed by the predecessor GENESI-DR project by federating to and interoperating with existing infrastructures. Both these projects are built on the ify framework for what it concerns data discovery, access, and processing.

The ify framework is a generic Grid-based operational environment and infrastructure for Earth Observation applications where specific data handling applications can be seamlessly plugged into the system. Coupled with high-performance and sizeable computing resources managed by Grid technologies, it provides the necessary flexibility for exploiting an application virtual environment with quick accessibility to data, computing resources and results.

Together with the Web Portal, the ify framework offers a Web services interface that enables on-demand processing that can be used as external virtual resources. The Web portal component delivers a flexible, secure, generic and distributed platform where the user can easily manage all its tasks. From the creation of a new task to the result publication, passing by the data selection and the job monitoring, the user goes through a friendly and intuitive interface accessible from everywhere.

The ify framework (see Figure 1) used in G-POD and GENESI-DEC projects aims at the promotion of:

- Access and use of EO mission data available at ESA and Earth Science data available in federated digital resources, offering on-line access to products with attached computing infrastructure and tools to assist the generation of scientific added value products.

*Figure 1. The framework offers access to earth observation data associated to GRID/cloud driven computing resources to host operational and science applications to generate high-level products*

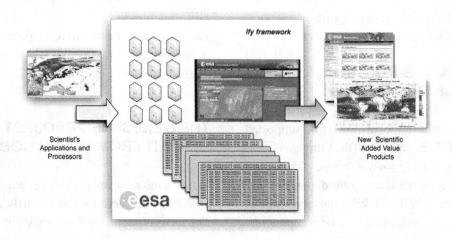

- Development of Earth Science applications requiring significant data and processing resources (data fusion, modelling, data mining).
- Hosting of third party processors and scientific applications.
- Fostering of new partnerships with entities in Earth Science research, algorithm development and validation, and operational deployments of value-added applications.

Seen and exploited as a Service, the ify framework solution used in G-POD manages over 300 computing nodes in the ESA-ESRIN establishment in Italy and at the ESA UK-PAC facility in UK, hosting a large number of EO processors and scientific applications running against several tens of Terabytes of on-line EO data. Furthermore it allows an easy integration of legacy applications.

GENESI-DEC federation allows the user to access not only ESA EO data but several millions of Earth Science products scattered around the world and enabling the users to address complex and challenging applications such as climate change and disaster management.

## Dealing with Third Party Processors and Scientific Applications

In the context of EO domain, several scientific and commercial applications already exist and it is so of fundamental importance to have tools and frameworks allowing an easy integration of such third party SW.

The ify framework hosts third party processors and scientific applications where the third parties are Principal Investigators (PIs) from heterogeneous domains and/or industrial partners developing satellite data processors.

The ify framework offers scientists the possibility to perform bulk processing and/or validation of their own algorithms exploiting the large ESA Earth Observation data available on Virtual Archives together with its available GRID/Cloud

driven computing and dynamic storage resources. Today, several third-party applications and services are currently integrated in G-POD at the European Space Agency and GENESI-DEC. This opportunity creates a partnership opportunity for conducting Earth Science research activities through Grid/Cloud technology. Within this ify framework, we offer processing services coupled with processing power and Earth Observation data to host and run the third-party applications.

Along the last six years, the application integration engineering process described below has been put in place (Figure 2):

1. **Proposal Submission:** In this phase, the third party submits a proposal for the application integration on the ify framework. In turn, the responsible for the project (e.g. G-POD or GENESI-DEC) does an evaluation of the proposal and decides if the project is object of an engineering cycle and becomes a ify service. A positive evaluation triggers the Service Design phase.

2. **Service Design:** During this phase, the PI is invited to submit additional information regarding his/her application by carefully describing:
   a. The data and processing flow.
   b. The modules and applications interfaces.
   c. The Input/Output ify Web Portal interfaces (GUI).
   d. Validation and Verification test scenarios.

The Engineering team, like Terradue, based on the information provided consolidates the project service design by producing the application design document. Its approval by the PI triggers the implementation phase.

3. **Application Integration:** An environment compatibility testing sub-phase is conducted for each project: the Engineering team tests

*Figure 2. Third-party application integration engineering cycle showing the roles of the PI, operations team, the engineering team and the phases of the cycle: proposal submission, application design, implementation, and exploitation*

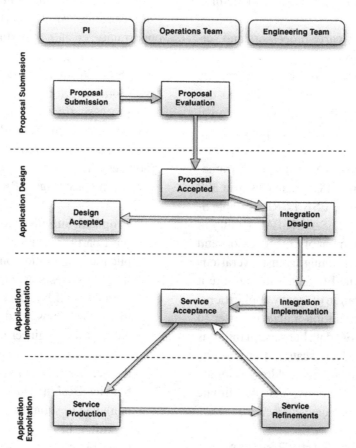

the compatibility with the ify framework computing environment of the application supplied by the project team. This is followed by the implementation sub-phase where the service is implemented against the design document and implementation and validated/verified using the test scenarios. Once validated/verified, the access to the service is granted to the final users for its final acceptance. After the successful application integration acceptance, a team of engineers maintain the application within the general procedures of the maintenance package.

4. **Application Refinements:** When the applications of the selected projects are deployed, a last phase is foreseen where small refinements of the integration can be applied. These changes may include improvements of the GUI, or extend the information returned by the application back to the ify Web Portal, or even, in special cases, workflow changes.

5. **Service Exploitation**: Once in operations, the service enters the exploitation phase and several processing scenarios are possible:

a. On-demand processing where the PI autonomously defines his/her processing tasks and monitors its submission and results retrieval.

b.  Schedule processing where the PI configures the scheduled processing (date/data driven, backward/forward, etc). The generated products can be published on remote defined server using standard communication protocols (e.g. FTP, GridFTP, scp).

## Candidate Legacy Applications

The candidate legacy applications are those third-party applications that will be used to validate and verify that the system is able to use Cloud computing resources to process data.

Two candidate legacy applications have been selected SBAS and GMTSAR. Both are dealing with InSAR (http://www.esa.int/esaMI/ESA_Publications/SEM867MJC0F_0.html), a radar technique used in geodesy and remote sensing.

Synthetic Aperture Radar (SAR, details at https://earth.esa.int/Web/guest/missions/esa-operational-eo-missions/ers/instruments/sar) is a microwave imaging system. It has cloud-penetrating capabilities because it uses microwaves. It has day and night operational capabilities because it is an active system. Finally, its 'interferometric configuration', Interferometric SAR or InSAR, allows accurate measurements of the radiation travel path because it is coherent. Measurements of travel path variations as a function of the satellite position and time of acquisition allow generation of Digital Elevation Models (DEM) and measurement of centimetric surface deformations of the terrain. A satellite SAR can observe the same area from slightly different look angles. This can be done either simultaneously (with two radars mounted on the same platform) or at different times by exploiting repeated orbits of the same satellite. The latter is the case for ESA satellites ERS-1, ERS-2 and Envisat (http://orbits.esa.int/). For these satellites, time intervals between observations of 1, 35, or a multiple of 35 days are available. The distance between the two satellites (or orbits) in the plane perpendicular to the

orbit is called the interferometer baseline and its projection perpendicular to the slant range is the perpendicular baseline. The SAR interferogram is generated by cross-multiplying, pixel-by-pixel, the first SAR image with the complex conjugate of the second. Thus, the interferogram amplitude is the amplitude of the first image multiplied by that of the second one, whereas its phase (the interferometric phase) is the phase difference between the images.

Both candidate applications have great importance in the SuperSites context where they can be used to generate interferograms on areas affected by earthquakes. On the one hand DiNSAR techniques benefit from the Supersite initiatives where long time series of SAR data are available over specific geographic area (prone to geo-hazard). On the other hand Supersite Initiatives benefits from DINSAR taking, thanks to the ability of these techniques to produce accurate ground deformation maps (starting from the raw data available in Supersites Virtual Archive).

*SBAS – Small Baseline Subset Differential SAR Interferometry:* Differential SAR Interferometry (DInSAR) has been demonstrated to be an effective technique to detect and monitor ground displacements with centimetre accuracy. Moreover, the recent development of advanced DInSAR techniques, aimed at the generation of deformation time series, has led to an effective exploitation of the large archives of SAR data acquired by the ERS, ENVISAT and RADARSAT satellites.

Among these advanced approaches, the Small BAseline Subset (SBAS) algorithm developed by CNR IREA relies on the combination of DInSAR data pairs, characterized by a small separation between the acquisition orbits (baseline), in order to produce mean deformation velocity maps and the corresponding time series, maximizing the coherent pixel density of the investigated area. Similarly to other advanced DInSAR techniques, the SBAS approach requires extended data storage and processing capabilities due to the large amount of data exploited for the generation of the final products. Details can be found in (Cossu et al, 2010), while a simulator is also available (http://www.egnos-pro.esa.int/sbassimulator/).

*GMTSAR – an InSAR Processing System Based on Generic Mapping Tools:* GMTSAR (http://topex.ucsd.edu/gmtsar/) is an open source (GNU General Public License) InSAR processing system designed for users familiar with Generic Mapping Tools (GMT, details at http://gmt.soest.hawaii.edu/). The system has three main components:

1.  A preprocessor for each satellite data type (e.g., ERS, Envisat, and ALOS) to convert the native format and orbital information into a generic format.
2.  An InSAR processor to focus and align stacks of images, map topography into phase, and form the complex interferogram.
3.  A postprocessor, mostly based on GMT, to filter the interferogram and construct interferometric products of phase, coherence, phase gradient, and line-of-sight displacement in both radar and geographic coordinates.

GMT is used to display all the products as postscript files and KML-images for Google Earth. A set of C-shell scripts has been developed for standard 2- pass processing as well as image alignment for stacking and time series. GMTSAR differs from other InSAR systems such as ROI_PAC (http://www.roipac.org/), Gamma (http://www.gamma-rs.ch/software/isp-interferometric-sar-processor.html), and DORIS (http://doris.tudelft.nl/) because it relies on sub-meter orbital accuracy to greatly simplify the SAR and InSAR processing algorithms. Moreover large batches of SAR images can be automatically processed with no human intervention. The down side of this approach is that SAR satellites having less accurate orbits (> 10 m, e.g., RADARSAT-1 and JERS-1) cannot be easily processed using GMTSAR. This is not applicable to our case since data on Virtual Archive used here is all ERS-1/2 and Envisat satellites.

*Figure 3. Scope of the GMTSAR legacy application*

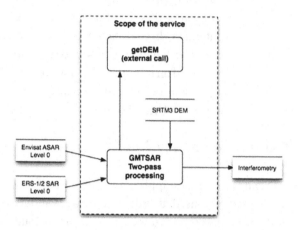

Figure 3 depicts the high-level scope of the GMTSAR processing service and Figure 4 shows the L'Aquila earthquake of April 2009 interferogram.

## Processing EO Data in the Cloud with the Selected Legacy Applications

The candidate legacy applications are those third-party applications that will be used to validate and verify that the system is able to use Cloud computing resources to process data.

Main phases in an EO application are:

*   **Discovering EO data:** The Catalogue Access Service.
*   **Access to EO data:** Virtual Archives.
*   Processing EO data.

1.  **Discovering EO Data: The Catalogue Access Service:** The Catalogue Access Service (CAS) is responsible for all the ingestion, cataloguing, and discovery of all the EO products metadata. It includes a Web service that allows clients querying metadata values and data resources locations on the Catalogues instances. The technologies used to provide such features are based on OpenSearch and expose REST Web service interfaces:

*Figure 4. l'aquila earthquake interferogram using GMTSAR and Envisat SAR data*

a. **OpenSearch:** It allows the description on how to query the catalogue server and query parameters supported by each dataset. The OpenSearch Description Documents (http://www. genesi-dec.eu/info/?id=117) list the available search result responses formats and use extensions that allow search engines to request a specific and contextual query parameter from search clients for each dataset. The CAS uses geospatial, temporal, earth observation products and other suitable extensions to allow the definition of specific queriables. The OpenSearch protocol lists the different access points available for each result type (ATOM, GeoRSS, GeoJSON, Metalink, EOP/ HMA, KML and HTML5) to allow the easy integration in other services and mash-up applications. Using an OpenSearch interface and extensions allows to do queries over topic categories and the predefined metadata attributes defined in the core metadata schema, interferometric search and a free text search to specific metadata fields. Basic comparison and range queries shall be defined over individual attributes and these can be combined with Boolean operators to form arbitrarily complex queries. Together with the use of the OpenSearch Suggestion Extension, it guides the user in the discovery process. This extension offers a convention by which search engines can return a set of search terms for a given search prefix. The suggested items lists together with search filters will guide the user in the exploration of the catalogue contents and avoiding the "no results found" messages.

b. **Metadata:** In the CAS, the metadata elements are aggregated in items covering the identification (including resource location), classification, keywords, geographic location, temporal reference, quality and validity, conformity, usage constrains, responsible organizations, and additional element regarding the metadata creation (according to the preliminary definition and the INSPIRE Directive and INSPIRE metadata implementation rules, details at http://inspire.jrc.ec.europa.eu/). The information model needs to be extensible to accommodate different dataset information models without a compromise in performance. While some of these elements are generic to an entire dataset originating from a given sensor, others are specific to each of the available products. For example, each and every product might have its own identification, spatial-temporal, quality indicators and resource location elements but most probably will share common elements to the dataset.

c. **Native Dataset:** The main and basic unit of the catalogue is the native dataset that groups the products the same product type from a specific EO processing level, sensor and mission. To optimize storing and search capabilities this information model follows a inheritance model as defined in ISO19115 where the product inherits the properties of the associated dataset (respectively dataset and series in ISO19115). For example a dataset may be defined to a specific geographical area or temporal range that aggregates all the associated products. Any discovery performed on the products first validates the corresponding dataset. Conversely, product inherits the metadata fields that are common to an entire dataset. This federated approach already used in other implementations allows a strong optimization of the metadata storage and discovery mechanisms by distributing the server load in several logical or physical data servers.

2. **Access to EO Data: Virtual Archives:** Virtual Archives are online archives that provide an easy access to EO data by coupling high bandwidth, large storage space and software. One of the currently available Cloud based virtual archives is used for storing and providing access to ESA' Synthetic Aperture Radar (SAR) data.

This virtual archive represents ESA contribution to the supersites initiative. This huge amount of SAR data (over than ten thousand products) is accessible to science communities dealing with interferometry, landslide and change detection. In the last 20 years, scientists have ordered ERS-1/2 and Envisat data from ESA. Now, they can ship this data to UNAVCO that deals with the upload to the virtual archive. Coupled with state-of-the-art data discovery mechanisms, it now easier to discover and access the repatriated SAR data. The virtual archive is a Cloud solution provided Storage-as-a-Service for storing the data and is coupled with complementary services:

a. User authentication and authorization.
b. Data discovery implementing simple interfaces such as OpenSearch and results in Atom, RDF and KML format.
c. Data access via common Web protocols such as HTTP(s).

The Supersites have data for the study of natural hazards in geologically active regions, including information from Synthetic Aperture Radar (SAR), GPS crustal deformation measurements, and earthquakes. The data are provided in the spirit of GEO, ESA, NASA and the National Science Foundation (NSF), that easy access to Earth science data will promote their use and advance scientific research, ultimately leading to reduced loss of life from natural hazards.

Supersites is an initiative of the geohazard scientific community. The Supersites provide access to spaceborne and in-situ geophysical data of selected sites prone to earthquake, volcano or other hazards. The initiative began with the "Frascati declaration" at the conclusion of the 3rd International Geohazards workshop of the Group of Earth Observation (GEO) held in November 2007 in Frascati, Italy. The recommendation of the workshop was "to stimulate an international and intergovernmental effort to monitor and study selected reference sites by establishing open access to relevant datasets according to GEO principles to foster the collaboration between all various partners and end-users". This recommendation is formalized as GEO task DI-09-010 (http://www.geo-tasks.org/stc_disaster_review/DI-09-01A.html).

The spaceborne portion of the Supersite initiative was initiated at the Second International Workshop on the Use of Remote Sensing Techniques for monitoring Volcanoes and Seismogenic Areas held in November 2008 in Naples, Italy (USEReST, details at http://www.userest.org/). Many of the workshop participants from research institutions and geological surveys around the world agreed to make SAR and in-situ data available Supersites. ESA agreed to provide the IT infrastructure for access to the SAR data (ESA's Virtual Archive).

3. **Processing EO data: Applying a New Computing Resource Based on Apache Hadoop Map/Reduce and Oozie:** The Apache Hadoop software library (http://hadoop.apache.org/) is a framework that allows for the distributed processing of large data sets across clusters of computers using a simple programming model. It is designed to scale up from single servers to thousands of machines, each offering local computation and storage. Rather than rely on hardware to deliver high-availability, the library itself is designed to detect and handle failures at the application layer, so delivering a highly available service on top of a cluster of computers, each of which may be prone to failures.

The remote execution of job triggered by a command line on the computing resource will be performed using Hadoop streaming. It is a job execution mode that comes with the Hadoop distribution. This mode allows creating and running map/reduce jobs with any executable or script as the mapper and/or the reducer.

The mapper and the reducer are POSIX executable files that read the input from stdin (line by line) and produce the output to stdout. The streaming utility will create a map/reduce job, submit the job to an appropriate cluster, and monitor the progress of the job until it completes.

EO applications are often made of a number of processing modules that are invoked as Directed Acyclic Graph (DAG). In mathematics and computer science, a DAG is a directed graph with no directed cycles. DAGs may be used to model several different kinds of structure. By definition a DAG is a directed graph with no path that starts and ends at the same vertex. This notion is in place in the ify framework processing flows (it is also widely used in ESA EO software toolboxes such as BEAM and NeST). The EO service workflow is described using a DAG where nodes will be the processing steps.

Figure 5 shows an example of a simple DAG with seven processing steps.

Oozie is an open-source workflow/coordination service to manage data processing jobs for Apache Hadoop (http://incubator.apache.org/oozie/). Oozie workflows are actions arranged in a control dependency DAG (Direct Acyclic Graph) as per ify task and therefore they can be mapped directly. Furthermore, Oozie workflow may contain many types of actions nodes and especially Hadoop streaming job. Actions and decisions can be parameterized with job properties, actions output (i.e. Hadoop counters) and HDFS file information (file exists, file size, etc). Running

*Figure 5. Example of a directed acyclic graph applied to processing modules (jobs)*

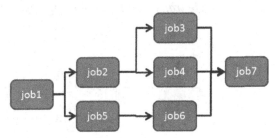

workflow job is done via command line tools or a WebServices API as well as monitoring the system and workflow jobs. Oozie is a transactional system and it has built in automatic and manual retry capabilities.

The DAG shown in Figure 5 is transformed into an Oozie DAG as depicted in Figure 6.

## An Additional Interface to the Ify Framework Computing Resources: OGC's WPS

Today, the ify framework defines one type computing resources based on Grid computing (which can use physical or Cloud based working nodes. We want to add a new computing resource in the ify framework that:

- Uses Hadoop Map/Reduce as underlying computational and storage resources.
- Uses Oozie as DAG orchestrator.
- Use OGC Web Processing Service as interface.

Web Processing Service (WPS, details at http://www.opengeospatial.org/standards/wps) is a specification from the Open Geospatial Consortium that proposes a solution for developing Web-based geoprocessing plugins, and for easily sharing algorithms and geo-processing functionality. It defines a standard for publishing, discovery, and binding to geospatial processes thus providing a standard way for defining a Web services interface for geospatial processing.

A WPS server may offer calculations as simple as subtracting one set of spatially referenced numbers from another, or as complicated as a global climate change model. The data required by the WPS can be delivered across a network, or available at the server. This interface specification provides mechanisms to identify the spatially referenced data required by the calculation, initiate the calculation, and manage the output from the calculation so that the client can access it. This Web Processing Service is targeted at processing both vector and raster data. The WPS specification is designed to allow a service provider to expose a Web accessible process, such as polygon intersection, in a way that allows clients to input data and execute the process with no specialized knowledge of the underlying physical process interface or API. The main advantage of WPS is interoperability of network-enabled data processing. It allows organizations to deliver calculations to users independent of the underlying software. This independence helps to ensure the longevity of code. WPS has many other advantages:

- Supports multiple Web service approaches. It defines equivalent KVP Get, XML Post, and SOAP interfaces, allowing the user to choose the most appropriate interface.
- Exploits the power of distributed computing. WPS is designed to enable distributed processing of geospatial data located anywhere on the Internet.
- Fast, reliable access to "near real-time" calculations. Because WPS makes calculations available as Web services, the most

*Figure 6. Oozie translated DAG showing nested meshes and control nodes (start, fork, join, end)*

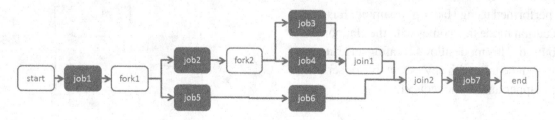

up-to-date data can be accessed directly from the source organization responsible for its maintenance.

- Reusability. Exposing processes through WPS allows organizations to reuse the same process (and code) in multiple applications.
- Flexibility. Exposing processes through WPS allows organizations to change their underlying software without impacting users and client applications.
- Scalability. WPS is scalable, both in terms of the potential for unlimited parallel interfaces, and through the exposure of gridded, cloud, or super-computers through a simple middleware interface.
- Security. Access to WPS processes can be restricted using a variety of standard Web service security mechanisms such as firewalls and HTTPS.

The WPS specification has three mandatory operations:

1. **GetCapabilities:** This operation allows clients to retrieve the list of exposed processes (equivalent to ify framework processing services) metadata. The response is a XML file including metadata describing all processes (services) using identifiers (and not URLs) exposed by the server via the WPS.

2. **DescribeProcess:** This operation allows clients to retrieve the full description of a WPS process using its identifier (returned by the GetCapabilities operation). The description includes information about parameters, input data and formats of the process.

3. **Execute:** This operation allows the WPS clients to submit the execution of a given WPS process. The request includes the service, request, version, identifier, datainputs, response form and language. The response can either be in the form of a RawDataOutput (example: a geotif) or an ExecuteResponse XML document.

## The Ify Framework and the Cloud

While the ify framework infrastructure uses mainly Grid protocols, models and resources for processing and data access, the inner concept of application encapsulation and virtualization can be extended to other models. The growing interest and availability of Cloud computing resources opens a new opportunity to expand this model to a new economic framework. In fact, Cloud Computing provides a dynamically scalable and often virtualized resource as a service over the Internet

The ify framework was used to start exploratory activities in mid-2009 with the G-POD Cloud project lead by Terradue (Figure 7), to include the capability to manage Cloud computing resources where Cloud-based computing nodes are transparently managed by a common middleware, whether Grid nodes, commercial Cloud computing nodes or private Cloud computing nodes. Coupled with the ify framework generic services such as the triggering, submission, status pooling of tasks and jobs, the data discovery and access, routine and on-demand production management and resources monitoring, Cloud IaaS processing and storage service are transparently used to cope with specific processing requirements.

The ify framework Cloud high-level architecture, depicted in Figure 8, has a number of components split into the framework and Cloud IaaS services:

1. **ify framework services:**
   a. Processing triggering and monitoring of routine and on-demand production
   b. Storage data access and monitoring fed by the near-real-time and historical data
   c. Data discovery
   d. EO Catalogue including metadata and file location
   e. EO processors hosting
2. **Cloud IaaS services:**
   a. Processing and storage
   b. Security

*Figure 7. G-POD physical deployment depicting the G-POD core elements with the web portal and the application engine (LGE) using grid technologies to manage both physical resources in ESRIN and UK-PAC and commercial Amazon Cloud computing resources*

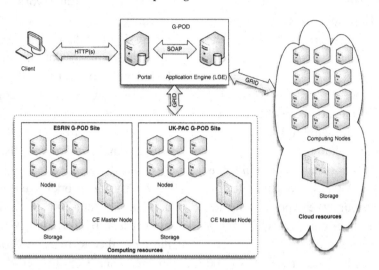

This Cloud approach was validated in two real-life re-processing scenarios with the re-reprocessing of ERS-1/2 SAR Wave Level 0 data to Level 1 and 2 products (https://earth.esa.int/Web/guest/data-access/browse-data-products?p_r_p_564233524_assetIdentifier=sar-wave-mode-wvi-product-7828) and ERS-1/2 Wind Scatterometer Level 0 data to Level 1 products (https://earth.esa.int/Web/guest/data-access/browse-data-products?p_r_p_564233524_ assetIdentifier=wind-scatterometer-fast-delivery-product-1476). For the first scenario, ERS-1/2 SAR Wave, G-POD Cloud has generated six tera-bytes of data using as input over five terabytes and this exclusively using Amazon AWS IaaS Cloud computing resources. This project had a surprising impact since the processing of 80 cycles of SAR Wave data and represented a cost below 10 KEuros. These results have demonstrated the potential of

*Figure 8. Ify framework Cloud high-level architecture with: processing triggering and monitoring of routine and on-demand production; storage data access and monitoring fed by the near-real-time and historical data; data discovery; EO catalogue including metadata and file location; EO processors hosting; and the Cloud IaaS services: processing, storage, and security*

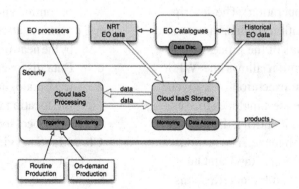

using off-the-shelf purchased processing power to remotely process large amounts of EO data.

In summer 2011, the same approach was applied to test a new version of the MIPAS processor Level 1b to Level 2 (details at http://earth.esa.int/pub/ESA_DOC/ENVISAT/Vol12_Mipas_4C.pdf). MIPAS is an instrument onboard Envisat satellite. The Michelson Interferometer for Passive Atmospheric Sounding (MIPAS) is a Fourier transform spectrometer for the detection of limb emission spectra in the middle and upper atmosphere. It observes a wide spectral interval throughout the mid infrared with high spectral resolution. Operating in a wavelength range from 4.15 microns to 14.6 microns, MIPAS detects and spectrally resolves a large number of emission features of atmospheric minor constituents playing a major role in atmospheric chemistry. Due to its spectral resolution capabilities and low-noise performance, the detected features can be spectroscopically identified and used as input to suitable algorithms for extracting atmospheric concentration profiles of a number of target species.

The processing campaign processed over 30.000 MIPAS L1b products to L2 and consumed over 120.000 CPU/hours in less than four weeks. The Cloud approach reduced the time-to-market i.e. delivery of the Level 2 products to the quality working group for assessing their quality. The processing campaign was faster and cheaper than the traditional approach.

G-POD Cloud project has successfully demonstrated that using Cloud Computing IaaS could be a valid alternative to provide the ify framework with computing and storage resources.

## The Ify Framework and the mOSAIC Solutions

The ify framework has been used to experiment the Cloud in the EO domain with the two reprocessing campaigns run in Amazon AWS. The outcomes of these activities have shown the great potential for running science and industrial applications against the large and growing sets of data made available by the European satellites.

Since the ify framework was born in the Grid computing era and context, it seemed the natural choice to create virtual clusters based on Grid middleware. The solution experimented was then limited to Amazon AWS. For Terradue and in particular for ESA this vendor lock-in situation and on top of that an American provider the future of the usage of Cloud in EO would have to be revisited.

Two aspects of the Cloud have a huge potential in EO:

- Infrastructure-as-a-Service where computing, network and storage are dynamically procured in the Cloud to address the needs of handling EO data: discovery, access and processing. Dissemination of the results of these activities can also occur with IaaS.
- Platform-as-a-Service where an environment for science applications development is provided to the PIs.

The first is addressed in the EO application proposed in this document where mOSAIC brings a huge benefit and evolution in relation to the previous Amazon AWS approach.

The second requires clarifying the concept of the EO platform for applications development. Terradue under contract with ESA has deployed over 50 science processors on a Grid environment. Each of these processors had particularities and often is a patchwork of PhD students including pieces of software written with toolboxes such as Matlab or programming languages such as Fortran or IDL. None of the PIs really use good programming practices. Furthermore, the applications IPR needs to stay in full control of the PI. It is in this context that we see applications hosted as third party applications and not something we can re-engineer in modern programming languages.

An EO platform is then a platform that offers tools for the discovery, access and processing (for testing purposes before going in production) of EO data along side with compilers, toolboxes and project tool suite tools (versioning, issue tracking, etc.).

This document refers also to a technological shift in the way processing resources are managed: a shift of transitions from Grid middleware to Hadoop Map/Reduce that is induced by the need to have more flexibility in the dynamic deployment/disposal of computing resources.

The goal is to use mOSAIC for the procurement of computational resources using the Cloud Agency to create Virtual Clusters to run the WPS server and Hadoop framework. This represents an important and valuable enhancement over the current situation where different Cloud providers must be used to exploit better conditions (prices, SLA, functionalities, etc.) and avoid vendor lock-in or technology lock-in as introduced above. This is fully in line with ESA's mandate where ESA is forced it to foster open and transparent tendering for the procurement of activities and thus the ability to be able

The Earth Observation application in mOSAIC will demonstrate the IaaS capacities in a very computing resources demanding environment. This is driven by the fact that the hosted applications are third-party software (known as legacy software in mOSAIC).

We use mOSAIC's OS, mOS-0.7, to build a set of Virtual Machines that will contain the Hadoop Map/Reduce framework, the Oozie framework (for the orchestration of the processing flows) and the EO applications and toolboxes. Those VMs are then used to deploy the Virtual Clusters on Cloud resources identified by the Cloud Agency.

## EO Software Architecture Overview

In what follows we present the main components of the system, the identified relationships, the different statuses in which the system is operat-

ing, as well as the model of the main information items handled.

The system architecture is divided into four macro components:

1.  **The GENESI-DEC Web Portal**: This is the Web server running the main user interface. This sub-system is an existing product that will be enhanced to support connection to a new processing interface and underlying processing resource procurement;

2.  **The Earth Observation Catalogue**: Known as the Catalogue Access Service (CAS), this component holds the Earth Observation products metadata to allow their discovery (e.g. swath, geospatial coverage, temporal coverage, etc.) and their physical location to allow accessing the products;

3.  **The Earth Observation Virtual-Archive**: This is the data store for holding the physical satellite products. It provides data access mechanisms and implements authentication/authorization services;

4.  **The Processing Engine**: This component provides the front-end to the processing resources and it is this component that has to manage the negotiation, setup and disposal of the computing resources.

Figure 9 depicts the main components and its sub-systems.

The sub-components are the followings:

1.  **GENESI-DEC Web Portal**: The GENESI-DEC Web Portal relies on Terradue's *ify* framework enabling the user front-end for the EO data discovery, access and processing platform.

    a.  Graphical User Interface handling requests via the Web interface. It is a generic module on the ify Web Portal that enables a graphical user interface to the underlying component.

*Figure 9. Earth observation application components and sub-systems*

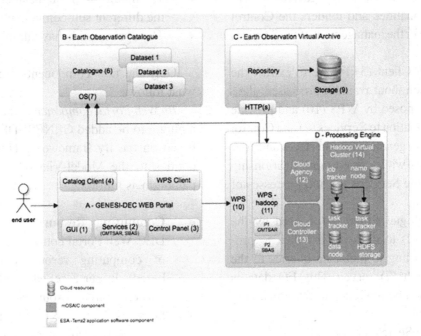

b. Services which process requests from the graphical user interface for managing the creation of processing tasks.

c. Control Panel handles the management of the ify entities (services, users, computing resources, etc.)

d. Catalogue Client handles the requests and responses to and from the Catalogue Access Service.

e. WPS Client handles the requests and responses to and from the WPS servers registered as computing resources in the Control Panel and generated Services

2. Earth Observation Catalogue

a. Catalogue hold the EO product metadata and online resources (URL to products' physical location)

b. OpenSearch (OS) Server exposes the OpenSearch interface to manage the queries and to provide the responses in the format requested (e.g. atom)

3. Earth Observation Virtual Archive

a. Repository exposes access to products store in the Storage

b. Storage holds the EO products

4. Processing Engine

a. WPS Server implements the OGC Web Processing Services and allows implementing processes

b. WPS-hadoop links the WPS server to the Hadoop Virtual Cluster

c. Cloud Agency manages the procurement of Cloud IaaS resources (Virtual Cluster)

d. Cloud Controller holds pre-defined Virtual Machines and generates the Cloud Agency CFP and responses

e. Hadoop Virtual Cluster is used to process the data.

The relationship between components is given below:

1. The Graphical User Interface (1) is the rendered views of the Web Portal components.

It renders the Services (2) pages and exposes its functionalities and renders the Control Panel (3) for the management of the Services (2).

2. The WPS Client (5) is able to extract the information about available processes (algorithms) exposed by WPS (10) and provide that information to Services (2) and Control Panel (3) to generate the interfaces and configurations with a one-to-one relationship between the Services (2) and processes of WPS (10).

3. The Catalogue Client (4) is used by the Services (2) to discover EO data to process according to metadata queries to the OpenSearch (7) server. This EO data is then passed by reference to the processing resources.

4. The OpenSearch (7) server contacts the Catalogue to render the information contained in the query results.

5. Services (2) are instantiated and the related process is triggered in WPS (10)

6. WPS-hadoop (11) which knows the process business logic implemented instantiates a request to the Cloud Agency (12).

7. The Cloud Agency (12) returns a provisioning resource to WPS-hadoop (11) which in turn will trigger the deployment of an Hadoop Virtual Cluster (14) via the Cloud Controller (13).

In what follows we provide more details about two types of components: EO Software components and GENESI-DEC components.

## EO Software Components

The architectural decomposition of the system implementation includes:

- The software components functions and processing.

- The relationship and the interfaces between the different sub-components.
- The dynamical behaviour of the system.

Only the new components are described in what follows:

*Ify Web Portal component:* The WPS client is a plugin to be added GENESI-DEC Web Portal based on the ify framework. This plugin adds entities to the Model-View-Controller (MVC) paradigm as follows:

- **Computing Resources:** The GENESI-DEC Web Portal connects to several types of computing resources (mostly Grid based). In our case, each WPS server is a new computing resource;
- **Services:** Each WPS based computing resource will add as many services to the GENESI-DEC Web Portal as WPS processes listed in the WPS GetCapabilities response and describe in the WPS DescribeProcess responses.

*WPSComputingResource:* This software component is responsible for registering a WPS server as a *ify* computing resource by registering the access point to the WPS server (URL). This new computing resource is an implementation of the *ify* framework Computing Resource abstract class.

The functions are:

- Register the WPS access point URL.
- Allow the submission of processing tasks.
- Allow the monitoring the processing status.
- Allow the retrieval of the processing results.

*WPS and Hadoop components:* These components link the WPS server implementation to the Hadoop framework and allow implementing processes.

*WPS-hadoop:* This component allows connecting the WPS server implementation to the Hadoop framework.

WPSprocess component, defines the handling of the process input/output and business logic.

*Cloud Agency component:* The Cloud Agency is a mOSAIC component. The Cloud Controller component:

- Implement the handling of input parameters
- Implement the business logic:
  - Communicate with the Cloud Agency
  - Communicate with the Cloud Controller
  - Trigger and monitor the business logic
  - Implement the handling of output results

## GENESI-DEC Components

In addition to the components previously described, an EO application will make use of several already existing GENESI-DEC components.

In particular, the GENESI-DEC architecture can be seen as composed of three tiers:

- The Client tier that contains all the software that are part of the communities world such as client programs, client tools, browsers, communities' portals and the common access point the is the GENESI-DEC Web portal.

- The Central Site tier contains all the common services and functionalities that provide needed functionalities for the infrastructure to be used such as security services, Central Site catalogue, the Series and Services registries.
- The Infrastructure tier that encompass all data/service provider software that operate with GENESI-DEC available services including data access services, processing services, specific security implementations, workflow services.

For these services which interact the Table 1 provides a summary of the supported protocols and interface specification for the different kind of services.

## CONCLUSION

The Earth Observation communities have strong reasons to employ Cloud computing services as the current infrastructure services, either for computer, either for storage, are not satisfying their increasing demands. First steps in adopting Cloud technologies in Earth Observation activities have been proved to be successful. In this context, we have pointed in this chapter towards several such usage scenarios. Moreover, we have provided several technical details about the first implementations in Europe of the concepts for real applications.

*Table 1. Protocols and interfaces*

| Service Type | Available Protocols | Supported Interfaces |
|---|---|---|
| Data Search | HTTP/s | OpenSearch |
| Data Access | HTTP/s, | gridFTP (http://www.globus.org/toolkit/docs/latest-stable/gridftp/), OPeNDAP (http://docs.opendap.org/index.php/QuickStart), WMS, WFS (http://www.opengeospatial.org/standards/wfs/), WCS (http://www.opengeospatial.org/standards/wcs/) |
| Processing | HTTP/s | WPS, Web Services |

Note that due to the complexity of the algorithms, software, and even of the data structures and catalogues used in Earth Observation, reimplementation from scratch, as usually encountered in the Web applications for which Cloud computing has been very successful, is not an option. The migration of the existing frameworks and software products relaying on earlier types of distributed systems towards Clouds is the safe way to be followed in these early stage of adoption of Cloud computing paradigm.

However, such migration is not straightforward, as the example provided in this chapter for a special framework has proved. Moreover, due to the current status of Cloud computing affected by the vendor-lock in problem, the migration effort should be multiplied in order to tackle with the differences at the service level between different Cloud providers. Therefore, we have emphases the need of vendor agnosticism in the design phase of the Cloud aware applications or frameworks, and point towards a recent platform that ensures the code portability over infrastructure services provided by different Clouds.

## FUTURE RESEARCH DIRECTIONS

The migration of the existing codes from an existing distributed system towards Cloud services is the most common path encountered until now in Earth Observation. In this process, the Cloud-enabled applications can benefit from the bursting concept promoted with the Cloud computing paradigm. Most of the scenarios are related to batch processing or backups on remote premises.

A less exploited characteristic is the elasticity in terms of Cloud resources, since it requires a re-writing of the applications to include an auto-scaling mechanism. Such mechanism is useful in the case when the solution to the problem to be solved allows an adaptation at the run-time to the number of resources. A study of the existing Earth Observation algorithm is needed to perform

to identify such cases. Moreover, the design of Cloud native Earth Observation applications are expected to emerge and to be implemented using a higher Cloud delivery model, the platform-as-a-service (contrary to the current dominant use of infrastructure-as-a-service delivery model).

The European initiatives presented in this chapter are considered at this moment as early experiments that have proved that Cloud computing can bring benefits for Erath Observation communities. The time has come to move to another level, closer to production. Therefore another European initiative has been recently started by a large consortium of academic and commercial stakeholders involved in early experiments: the Helix Nebula – the Science Cloud. One of the three use cases of Helix Nebula is related to the improvement of SuperSites, transforming it into an Exchange Platform for secure solid Earth data sharing on the Cloud.

## REFERENCES

Cossu, R., Pacini, F., Goncalves, P., & Fusco, L. (2010). Data and computing intensive applications in GENESI-DR. In *Proceedings of EGU General Assembly Conference* (p. 14169). EGU.

Di Martino, B., Petcu, D., Cossu, R., Goncalves, P., Gulyas, L., & Loichate, M. (2011). Building a mosaic of Clouds. *Lecture Notes in Computer Science, 6586*, 529–536. doi:10.1007/978-3-642-21878-1_70.

Fusco, L., Cossu, R., & Retscher, C. (2008). Open grid services for Envisat and earth observation applications. In Plaza, A., & Chang, C. (Eds.), *High Performance Computing in Remote Sensing* (pp. 237–280). London: Chapman & Hall.

Golpayegani, N., & Halem, M. (2009). Cloud computing for satellite data processing on high end compute clusters. In *Proceedings of the IEEE International Conference on Cloud Computing* (pp. 88-92). IEEE.

Li, J., Agarwal, D., Humphrey, M., van Ingen, C., Jackson, K., & Ryu, Y. (2010). eScience in the cloud: A MODIS satellite data reprojection and reduction pipeline in the Windows Azure platform. In *Proceedings of the 2010 IEEE International Symposium on Parallel & Distributed Processing* (pp. 1-10). IEEE.

Markatchev, N., Curry, R., Kiddle, C., Mirtchovski, A., Simmonds, R., & Tan, T. (2009). A cloud-based interactive application service. In *Proceedings of the Fifth IEEE International Conference on e-Science* (pp. 102-109). IEEE. mOSAIC Consortium. (2011a). *D3.1: Cloud usage patterns*. Retrieved from www.mosaic-cloud.eu

mOSAIC Consortium. (2011b). *D3.2 platform use cases*. Retrieved from www.mosaic-cloud.eu

Panica, S., Neagul, M., Craciun, C., & Petcu, D. (2011). Serving legacy distributed applications by a self-configuring cloud processing platform. In *Proceedings of the 6th IEEE International Conference on Intelligent Data Acquisition and Advanced Computing Systems: Technology and Applications* (pp. 139-145). IEEE.

Petcu, D., Panica, S., & Neagul, M. (2011). From grid computing towards sky computing: Case study for earth observation. In *Proceedings of the Cracow Grid Workshop 2010* (pp. 11-20). Cracow.

Wang, Y., Wang, S., & Zhou, D. (2009). Retrieving and indexing spatial data in the cloud computing environment. *Lecture Notes in Computer Science*, *5931*, 322–331. doi:10.1007/978-3-642-10665-1_29

## ADDITIONAL READING

An, J., Chengqi, C., Fuhu, R., & Shuhua, S. (2011). An index model of global subdivision in cloud computing environment. In *Proceedings of the 19th International Conference on Geoinformatics* (pp. 1 – 5). IEEE.

Aysan, A. I., Yigit, H., & Yilmaz, G. (2011). GIS applications in cloud computing platform and recent advances. In *Proceedings of the 5th International Conference on Recent Advances in Space Technologies* (pp. 193 – 196). IEEE.

Berriman, G. B., Juve, G., Deelman, E., Regelson, M., & Plavchan, P. (2010). The application of cloud computing to astronomy: A study of cost and performance. In *Proceedings of the Sixth IEEE International Conference on e-Science* (pp. 1-7). IEEE.

Caspar, C., Colin, O., Laur, H., Tell, B. R., Tandurella, G., & Mathot, E. ... Brito, F. (2007). Generation of ENVISAT ASAR mosaics. In *Proceedings of the International Geoscience and Remote Sensing Symposium* (pp. 1405-1408). IEEE.

Casu, F., Cossu, R., Fusco, L., Guarino, S., Lanari, R., & Manunta, M. ... Sansosti, E. (2009). Satellite ground deformation measurements: An on-demand Grid-InSAR processing system exploiting the SBAS algorithm. In *Proceedings of the International Geoscience and Remote Sensing Symposium* (pp. 949-952). IEEE.

Chen, Z., Chen, N., Yang, C., & Di, L. (2012). Cloud computing enabled web processing service for earth observation data processing. *IEEE Journal of Selected Topics in Applied Earth Observations and Remote Sensing, 5*(6).

Cossu, R., Petitdidier, M., Linford, J., Badoux, V., Fusco, L., & Gotab, B. et al. (2010). A roadmap for a dedicated earth science grid platform. *Earth Science Informatics, 3*(3), 135–148. doi:10.1007/s12145-010-0045-4

Cossu, R., Schoepfer, E., Bally, P., & Fusco, L. (2009). Near real-time SAR-based processing to support flood monitoring. *Journal of Real-Time Image Processing*, *4*(3), 205–218. doi:10.1007/s11554-009-0114-4.

Deqiang, G., Keping, D., Yonghua, Q., Yuzhen, Z., & Linli, L. (2012). Remote sensing algorithm platform in Windows Azure. In *Proceedings of the 20th International Conference on Geoinformatics* (pp. 1 – 6). IEEE.

Dong, C., Yunlong, W., & Qiang, Z. (2010). Massive spatial data processing model based on cloud computing model. In *Proceedings of the Third International Joint Conference on Computational Science and Optimization*, (vol. 2, pp. 347 – 350). IEEE.

Gorgan, D., Bacu, V., Rodila, D., Pop, F., & Petcu, D. (2010). Experiments on ESIP - Environment oriented satellite data processing platform. *Earth Science Informatics*, *3*(4), 297–308. doi:10.1007/s12145-010-0065-0.

Humphrey, M., Hill, Z., Jackson, K., van Ingen, C., & Youngryel, R. (2011). Assessing the value of cloudbursting: A case study of satellite image processing on Windows Azure. In *Proceedings of the IEEE 7th International Conference on E-Science* (pp. 126-133). IEEE.

Jing, D., Yong, X., Ziqiang, C., Hui, X., & Yingjie, L. (2011). Analysis of remote sensing quantitative inversion in cloud computing. In *Proceedings of the IEEE International Geoscience and Remote Sensing Symposium* (pp. 4348 – 4351). IEEE.

Kseneman, M., Geich, D., & Chowdhury, A. (2010). Despeckling synthetic aperture radar images with cloud computing using graphics processing units. In *Proceedings of the 5th International Conference on Pervasive Computing and Applications* (pp. 195 – 200). IEEE.

Lee, C. A., Gasster, S. D., Plaza, A., Chang, C., & Bormin, H. (2012). Recent developments in high performance computing for remote sensing: A review. *IEEE Journal of Selected Topics in Applied Earth Observations and Remote Sensing*, *4*(3), 508–527. doi:10.1109/JSTARS.2011.2162643.

Liu, M., Ai, J., & Ji, T. (2012). Workflow process service research based on cloud computing platform for remote sensing quantitative retrieval. In *Proceedings of the 2nd International Conference on Remote Sensing, Environment and Transportation Engineering* (pp. 1 – 4). IEEE.

Petcu, D. (2009). Challenges of data processing for earth observation in distributed environments. In *Proceedings of the Intelligent Distributed Computing III, Studies in Computational Intelligence SCI 237* (pp. 9-19). SCI.

Petcu, D. (2011). Portability and interoperability between clouds: Challenges and case study. *Lecture Notes in Computer Science*, *6994*, 62–74. doi:10.1007/978-3-642-24755-2_6.

Petcu, D., Macariu, G., Panica, S., & Craciun, C. (2012). Portable cloud applications - From theory to practice. *Future Generation Computer Systems*. doi: doi:10.1016/j.future.2012.01.009.

Petcu, D., Panica, S., Frincu, M., Neagul, M., Zaharie, D., & Macariu, G. et al. (2012). Experiences in building a grid-based platform to serve earth observation training activities. *Computer Standards & Interfaces*, *34*, 493–508. doi:10.1016/j.csi.2011.10.010.

Petcu, D., Panica, S., Neagul, M., Frincu, M., Zaharie, D., Ciorba, R., & Dinis, A. (2010). Earth observation data processing in distributed systems. *Informatica*, *34*, 463–476.

Petcu, D., Zaharie, D., Panica, S., Hussein, A. S., Sayed, A., & El-Shishiny, H. (2011). Fuzzy clustering of large satellite images using high performance computing. *Proceedings of the Society for Photo-Instrumentation Engineers*, *8183*(818302). doi:10.1117/12.898281.

Qi-Shuang, W., Dong, Z., & Zhen-Chun, H. (2012). Research on the performance of virtualization-based remote sensing data processing platform. In *Proceedings of International Conference on Systems and Informatics* (pp. 900 – 904). IEEE.

Suakanto, S., Supangkat, S. H., Suhardi, S. R., Nugroho, T. A., & Nugraha, I. G. B. B. (2012). Environmental and disaster sensing using cloud computing infrastructure. In *Proceedings of the International Conference on Cloud Computing and Social Networking* (pp. 1 – 6). IEEE.

Yang, X., & Deng, Y. (2010). Exploration of cloud computing technologies for geographic information services. In *Proceedings of the 18th International Conference on Geoinformatics* (pp. 1 – 5). IEEE.

## KEY TERMS AND DEFINITIONS

**Application Portability:** Application that can function in different environments.

**Data Intensive Applications:** Applications that are using large volumes of data.

**Distributed Data Management Systems:** A software system that manages a collection of multiple databases.

**Earth Observation:** Gathers information about Earth systems via remote sensing technologies.

**Placement of Virtual Machines:** A process of mapping virtual machines to physical resources.

**Resource Allocation:** A plan for using the available resources.

# Chapter 13
# Cloud–TM:
## An Elastic, Self–Tuning Transactional Store for the Cloud

**João Barreto**
*Technical University Lisbon, Portugal*

**Pierangelo Di Sanzo**
*Sapienza Università di Roma, Italy*

**Roberto Palmieri**
*Sapienza Università di Roma, Italy*

**Paolo Romano**
*Technical University Lisbon, Portugal*

## ABSTRACT

*By shifting data and computation away from local servers towards very large scale, world-wide spread data centers, Cloud Computing promises very compelling benefits for both cloud consumers and cloud service providers: freeing corporations from large IT capital investments via usage-based pricing schemes, drastically lowering barriers to entry and capital costs; leveraging the economies of scale for both services providers and users of the cloud; facilitating deployment of services; attaining unprecedented scalability levels. However, the promise of infinite scalability catalyzing much of the recent hype about Cloud Computing is still menaced by one major pitfall: the lack of programming paradigms and abstractions capable of bringing the power of parallel programming into the hands of ordinary programmers. This chapter describes Cloud-TM, a self-optimizing middleware platform aimed at simplifying the development and administration of applications deployed on large scale Cloud Computing infrastructures.*

## INTRODUCTION

The rapidly expanding market of commercial Cloud Computing infrastructures currently offers solutions of different flavors. Depending on the nature of the resources made available

on demand by the Cloud platform, such flavors include Infrastructure-as-a-Service (IaaS), Platform-as-a-Service (PaaS), and Software-as-a-Service (SaaS). While some of these solutions are reminiscent of the Application Service Provider (ASP) paradigm, in practice, cloud computing platforms work differently than ASPs. Examples include those offered by Amazon Web Services,

DOI: 10.4018/978-1-4666-3934-8.ch013

AT&T's Synaptic Hosting, AppNexus, GoGrid, Rackspace Cloud Hosting, and to an extent, the HP/Yahoo/Intel Cloud Computing Testbed, and the IBM/Google cloud initiative.

Instead of owning, installing, and maintaining the software for their costumers (often in a multi-tenancy architecture), cloud computing vendors typically maintain little more than the hardware, and give customers a set of virtual machines in which to install their own software. However, getting additional computational resources is not as simple as a magic upgrade to a bigger, more powerful machine on the fly (with commensurate increases in CPUs, memory, and local storage); rather, the additional resources are typically obtained by allocating additional server instances to a task. For example, Amazon's Elastic Compute Cloud (EC2) apportions computing resources in small, large, and extra large virtual private server instances, the largest of which contains no more than eight cores. If an application is unable to take advantage of the additional server instances by offloading some of its required work to the new instances which run in parallel with the old instances, then having the additional server instances available will not be much help.

Thus, one of the main challenges that needs to be faced to bring about the potential of cloud computing, and ultimately consolidate its business model, is the development of programming models and tools that simplify the design and implementation of applications for the cloud, so as to bring the power of parallel computing into the hands of ordinary programmers.

Unfortunately, designing and implementing software services that are actually able to match the scalability potentialities of large scale, shared-nothing Cloud infrastructures is far from being a trivial task.

One of the most crucial issues to tackle when developing large scale distributed application is certainly related to how to manage concurrent manipulations to the shared state of the application. The challenge here is to identify mechanisms that able to ensure adequate consistency levels while being:

1. Simple and familiar for the programmers, highly efficient and scalable.
2. Fault-tolerant and highly available.

Decades of literature and field experience in areas such as replicated databases, Web infrastructures, and high performance computing have led to the development of a plethora of different approaches to ensure state consistency in distributed platforms, and taught a fundamental, general lesson. The design space of distributed state consistency mechanisms is so vast that no universal, one-size-fits-all solution exists, as the efficiency of individual state management approaches is strongly affected by both:

1. The characteristics of the incoming workload, such as the ratio of read/write operations, as well as the spatial/temporal locality in the data access patterns.
2. The scale of the system, e.g. number of nodes and local vs. geographical distribution.

The complexity of this problem is hence further exacerbated in Cloud Computing platforms precisely because of the feature that is regarded as one of the key advantages of the cloud: its ability to elastically acquire or release resources, de facto dynamically varying the scale of the platform in real-time to meet the demands of varying workloads.

This chapter describes the architecture of a novel middleware platform for service implementation in Cloud Computing platforms that is being developed in the context of the EU project Cloud-TM.

At the core of the Cloud-TM platform lies the abstraction of a Distributed Software Transactional Memory (DSTM). DSTM is a recently proposed extension of the Transactional Memory (TM) programming paradigm, which was originally introduced to simplify the development of concurrent, though not distributed, programs.

TMs free programmers from the pitfalls of conventional explicit lock-based thread synchronization by relying on the proven, familiar notion of atomic transactions to transparently guarantee the consistency of concurrent memory manipulations by multithreaded applications. By relishing the programmer from the burden of managing locks or other error-prone low-level concurrency control mechanisms, TMs have been shown to enable a significant boost in productivity, shortening development times, and increasing code reliability in complex concurrent applications.

DSTMs enrich the traditional TM model, to breach the boundaries of a single machine and transparently leverage the resources of commodity, shared-nothing clusters, hiding the complexities underlying the implementation of consistent, scalable and fault-tolerant data distribution and replication schemes. DSTMs are a recent research topic, which represents, in some sense, the confluence of the research areas on TM, Distributed Shared Memory (DSM) and database replication. The few currently available DSTMs (Cachopo, 2007; Kotselidis et al., 2008; Bocchino, Adve, & Chamberlain, 2008; Manassiev, Mihailescu, & Amza, 2006; 20; Carvalho, Romano, & Rodrigues, 2010) have shown very promising preliminary results, highlighting how the reliance on the atomic transaction abstraction allows devising highly efficient synchronization schemes that avoid the well-known performance limitations of classical DSM systems while ensuring strong consistency guarantees and scaling up to hundreds of nodes in data center environments.

On the other hand, existing DSTM solutions are all preliminary prototypes that have been experimented only on a restricted number of workloads. Further, existing DSTM platforms lack essential support for cloud computing platforms, such as transparent data caching, automatic data partitioning, fault-tolerance and persistence, delegating to the programmers the responsibility of implementing these low-level, error prone mechanisms.

Building on the abstraction of DSTM, the Cloud-TM project aims at an innovative data platform for cloud environments that addresses the following major challenges:

- Offering a simple and intuitive programming model for the implementation of services in Cloud computing platforms that will allow a major reduction in the costs of the development process by letting service developers focus on delivering differentiating business value instead of managing low-level, error prone mechanisms such as inter-process synchronization, caching, persistence and fault tolerance.
- Maximizing the scalability and efficiency (i.e. the costs/benefits ratio in the Cloud Computing usage-based pricing model) of the user-level services via autonomic mechanisms allowing to transparently alter the state consistency schemes adopted at the middleware level in face of workload fluctuations and on the basis of the amount of resources currently acquired in the cloud.
- Minimizing the monitoring and administration costs by automatizing the provisioning of resources from the Cloud Computing infrastructure, based on user specified target QoS/operational costs criteria.

It has to be noted that, at the time of writing, the Cloud-TM project is still ongoing. Consequently, the development of several of the components of the Cloud-TM platform is still ongoing, and component integration is still at an early stage. The focus of this chapter will therefore be on illustrating the key motivations and challenges that were accounted for during the design phase of the Cloud-TM platform, as well as on illustrating some of the results achieved so far by the researchers involved in the project.

The remainder of the chapter is organized as follows. We start by introducing the background to Cloud-TM, describing its most relevant related work. We then present an overview of the Cloud-TM platform, addressing its main high-level components. Finally, we discuss future research directions and draw conclusions.

## BACKGROUND

### Programming Paradigms for the Cloud

The promise of infinite scalability catalyzed much of the recent hype about Cloud Computing. However, this promise is still menaced by one major pitfall: the lack of programming paradigms and abstractions capable of bringing the power of parallel programming into the hands of ordinary programmers. This is a hot research area and several novel programming paradigms for simplifying large scale computations across shared nothing clusters have been recently proposed.

MapReduce (Jeffrey & Sanjay, 2008) represents probably one of the first, and more popular programming paradigms explicitly targeted to meet the scalability challenges of large-scale cloud infrastructures. MapReduce is a functional programming model which permits automatic parallelization and execution on large scale clusters. By forcing developers to adhere to a restricted, though neatly defined, programming model, the MapReduce's run-time system is able to automatically take care of issues such as input data partitioning, scheduling the program's execution across multiple machines and handling of node failures. MapReduce is being extensively used in large scale Google data centers to analyze in parallel huge data sets in domains such as Web log and graph analysis. Its automatic parallelization and fault-tolerance features have attracted the attention of a growing community of enthusiastic users that have developed a complete open

source porting of the original proprietary system, Hadoop (Hadoop Wiki, 2012). Nevertheless, it is nowadays widely recognized that, depending on the nature of the problem to be addressed, casting a known solution algorithm into the functional MapReduce programming model might be far from being trivial, possibly forcing to fragment the computation into a sequence of MapReduce tasks or inducing unnatural additional steps which can lead to significant performance drawbacks with respect to conventional parallel programming approaches (Ranger, Raghuraman, Penmetsa, Bradski, & Kozyrakis, 2007).

To address this issue a number of MapReduce extensions, e.g. Cascading, DryadLINQ (Yu, 2008), or Pig (Olston, Reed, Srivastava, Kumar, & Tomkins, 2008), have been recently proposed. These solutions greatly simplify the approach to large data analysis problems, not forcing developers to "think" in MapReduce, but rather exposing simpler SQL-like programming interfaces, which are then automatically mapped to an underlying MapReduce implementation.

However, the actual efficiency of MapReduce is currently matter of a controversial debate (Abadi, 2009; DeWitt & Stonebraker, 2009), with several well-known scientists critically highlighting several performance issues of MapReduce and its derivatives, based both on a comparison with the mechanisms supported by modern parallel databases, as well as on benchmarking results showing MapReduce to be about an order of magnitude slower than alternative systems (Hadoop Wiki, 2012).

### Transactional Memory

Along the route of simplify the exploitation of advantages offered by Cloud Computing, data manipulation is of course another major hot topic. In particular, the techniques typically used for managing the concurrency among data and taking care of their availability and reliability need to be revised in order to exploit the Cloud Computing advantages. Moreover, the recent adoption of affordable multicore and manycore chips as the architecture-of-choice for mainstream computing is demanding a radical shift in the way software is developed, moving parallel programming from the niche of scientific and high performance computing to ordinary application domains. Unfortunately, writing scalable parallel programs using traditional lock-based synchronization primitives is a hard, time consuming, and error-prone task, mastered by only a minority of programmers. A first issue with lock-based synchronization is associated with the choice of the lock granularity. Coarse grained locking strategies, e.g. based on a single, mutual exclusion section, are of course very simple to program, but can seriously hamper parallelism. On the other hand, the design of fine grained locking schemes is an extremely challenging engineering task. First because ensuring the correctness of a lock-based program is very difficult, as a single misplaced or missing lock may easily compromise the consistency of data. Second, it is difficult to compose applications that rely on locks without knowing their internals.

Transactional Memories (TMs) respond exactly to the urge for a simpler programming model for concurrent, multi-threaded applications. When using TMs the programmers are simply required to specify which operations on shared data structures are to be executed within the scope of an atomic and isolated transaction. The task of ensuring the consistent execution of the transactions is delegated to the TM, which transparently takes care of regulating the concurrent access to shared data, by automatically aborting unserializable transactions, avoiding deadlocks and priority inversions.

Originally introduced in the seminal paper from Herlihy and Moss (Herlihy, Eliot, & Moss, 1993), as a purely hardware implemented mechanism, the first software realization of the same idea, referred to as Software Transactional Memory (STM), was proposed by Shavit and Touitou (1995). Since these seminal papers, the research on Transactional Memory remained mostly dormant until 2003, when the interest in the area was spurred again by a couple of influential papers (Herlihy, Luchangco, Moir, & Scherer, 2003; Harris & Fraser, 2003) and by the advent of multicore chips. Since then, research on TMs has deserved much attention in computer science and engineering, with hundreds of papers published in prestigious international conferences and journals addressing a wide range of complementary aspects including hardware and Operating Systems (OSs) support (Ramadan et al., 2007), language integration (Harris & Fraser, 2003; Shpeisman, Adl-Tabatabai, Geva, Ni, & Welc, 2009), as well as algorithms and theoretical foundations (Guerraoui, & Kapalka, 2008; Gramoli, Harmanci, & Felber 2008). In the last years several STMs have been released (e.g., (Moir, 1997; Herlihy et al., 2003; Felber, Fetzer, & Riegel, 2008; Cachopo, & Rito-Silva, 2006; Carvalho, Cachopo, Rodrigues, & Rito-Silva, 2008; Ramadan et al., 2007)).

An important conclusion that has been highlighted by the large body of research on STMs, and in particular by some recent, independent results (Guerraoui, Herlihy, & Pochon, 2005; Riegel, Fetzer, & Felber, 2008; Sonmez, Cristal, Harris, Unsal, & Valero, 2009), is that the search for a "one size fits all" solution in the vast multi-dimensional design space of STMs remains inconclusive: up to date, no single "panacea" solution has been identified that is able to maximize the performances of any STM workload.

Even if STMs have garnered a huge research interest over the last years, most of the research efforts in this area have been in the context of non-distributed, cache coherent, shared-memory systems. By contrast, the problem of how to extend the STM abstraction across the boundaries of a single machine and to employ transactions as a first class abstraction for large scale distributed programming has only very recently started to be addressed. However, this topic needs to be considered mandatory if the facilities offered by STMs for managing transactions want to be brought in

Cloud Computing environments in which, typically, much more then few computational nodes are involved. Indeed, only a handful of distributed STM (DSTM) platforms (Couceiro, Romano, Carvalho, & Rodrigues, 2009; Aguilera, Merchant, Shah, Veitch, & Karamanolis, 2007; Manassiev, Mihailescu, & Amza, 2006; Kotselidis et al., 2008; Bocchino et al., 2008) have been proposed.

## Distributed Transactional Memory

Two decades of research have clearly highlighted that distributed shared memories (DSMs) are capable of achieving good performance and scalability only provided that programmers embrace relaxed consistency models (Keleher, Cox, & Zwaenepoel, 1992). Unfortunately, relaxed consistency models are typically challenging for ordinary programmers, because they are forced to understand all the subtleties of complicated consistency properties to avoid endangering correctness, and this contrast with the goal of simplifying the development of concurrent application to the programmers. On the other hand, as highlighted by the experimental evaluation of several of the aforementioned DSTM platforms (Manassiev, Mihailescu, & Amza, 2006; Kotselidis et al., 2008; Bocchino et al., 2008), DSTMs use the transaction abstraction not only as way to simplify parallel programming but also as a natural means to aggregate communication efficiently, avoiding the performance pitfalls proper of DSM systems without sacrificing programming simplicity. In fact, unlike strongly consistent DSMs, which require expensive remote synchronizations at each single memory access, atomic transactions allow for optimistic implementations that permit to batch any consistency action within a single synchronization phase taking place at commit time (Aguilera et al., 2007; Kotselidis et al., 2008; Couceiro et al., 2009). This approach amortizes communication overheads across a (possibly large) number of memory accesses, with clear benefits in terms of performance. Taking a closer look at

existing DSTM platforms, it is relatively easy to draw a line between solutions, such as those in (Kotselidis et al., 2008; Manassiev, Mihailescu, & Amza, 2006; Couceiro et al., 2009), which were designed for being deployed in small scale clusters, and those, such as Cluster-STM (Bocchino et al., 2008) and Sinfonia (Aguilera et al., 2007), which were architected to scale up to several hundreds of nodes.

In the former group of solutions, all of them are based on full replication schemes and, when fault-tolerance is addressed, this is done by using Group Communication Systems that provide support for Virtual Synchrony and Atomic Broadcast (Amir, Danilov, & Stanton, 2000; Miranda, Pinto, & Rodrigues, 2001). These strategies have shown encouraging performance results when employed in clusters of at most 10 nodes, but it is very unlikely that they sustain the scalability challenges of the largest cloud computing environments.

Sinfonia (Aguilera et al., 2007) and Cluster-TM (Bocchino et al., 2008), on the other hand, have shown that DSTM platforms can achieve impressive scale-ups (up to several hundreds of nodes) thanks to the usage of lightweight and highly optimized distributed commit protocols and partial replication schemes.

Unfortunately, none of these solutions have been designed for operating in a Cloud Computing environment, characterized by an elastic, dynamic scaling of the number of nodes in the DSTM platform. This raises a number of important technical issues related both to the efficiency and consistency of the DSTM platform. On the performance side, the efficiency of key mechanisms used to ensure the consistency of the DSTM is strongly affected by the number of replicas and by the cost of inter-replica communication (which may be highly heterogeneous and variable in Cloud platforms, such as the Amazon EC2, made up of large datacenters spread across the globe). For instance, distributed contention management approaches that rely on a centralized coordinator, or fully replicated caching schemes, are known to be a winning solution in small-scale clusters (Kotselidis et al., 2008; Couceiro et al., 2009). However, centralized contention management schemes are also known to suffer of scalability problems, as the coordinating node is naturally prone to become the system's bottleneck. Despite their higher complexity, data partitioning and partial replication are definitely more appealing in large scale data centers than full replication.

## Automated Resource Provisioning

Another highly desirable feature for a DSTM platform operating in a Cloud Computing platform is the ability to automatically determine how many resources should be acquired from the cloud to face the current load pressure. However, existing approaches to the problem of automatic resource provisioning in Cloud Computing, e.g. (Kalyvianaki, Charalambous, & Hand, 2009; Xu, Zhao, Fortes, Carpenter, & Yousif, 2007), cannot be straightforwardly used in the context of a DSTM platform. As just discussed, in fact, the performance of DSTM platforms are deeply affected by a number of factors (e.g. commit/caching schemes, workload characteristics) that are peculiar to the DSTM approach and require novel ad hoc cost/performance forecasting models. Elastically scaling up and down the number of nodes of a DSTM platform also requires facing consistency issues, such as the release of a node holding the freshest copy of a data item, e.g. in multi-master replication schemes (Pacitti, Coulon, Valduriez, & Özsu, 2005), cannot obviously determine data losses.

## Relational Databases and Cloud-Oriented Storage

In traditional, multi-tiered service-oriented applications persistence support is typically pro-

vided by a relational database, which also ensures ACID transactional guarantees. Unfortunately, the reliance on relational databases to synchronize concurrent accesses to application data represents a largely suboptimal solution for what concerns both the ease of programming and the efficiency/scalability of the system. For what concerns programming simplicity, an important issue is related to the mismatch between the object oriented model that is used to code the application logic and the relational model supported by commercial off-the-shelf DBMSs. Since the mapping between the relational model and the object-oriented model is far from being trivial, it is common practice to use platforms (Sun MicroSystems, 2003) or generic frameworks (Hibernate, 2009; iBATIS, 2009) that perform or facilitate the mapping between the relational database and the object-oriented model. Unfortunately, these approaches represent a patch to the problem, rather than a solution to it, and can bias the development of an object-oriented rich domain model (Cachopo, & Rito-Silva, 2006) and be a source of overheads and complexity.

Generally speaking, current support for persistence in cloud computing environments focuses on high availability of resources, on-demand scalability, flexibility of the persistent representation, and on simplifying the distribution of the resources through the cloud. On the other side, they do not focus yet on being programmer-friendly. Instead, they force application design to meet certain API limitations. In some aspects, this is a step back in some of the best object-oriented programming practices. They also impose an impedance mismatch and the programmer must explicitly code the persistency of the non-transient data, implying a cost in development time. Last but not least, existing persistency mechanisms either cannot be composed with transactions, or just support the persistency of data local to a node in the context of a transaction.

## OVERVIEW OF THE CLOUD-TM PLATFORM

### Overview

The high level architecture diagram of the Cloud-TM platform is presented in Figure 1. This diagram will be used as a starting point to derive, in a top-down fashion, more refined versions of the platform's main building blocks, which will be described in detail in the remainder of this document.

The Data Platform is responsible for storing, retrieving and manipulating data across a dynamic set of distributed nodes, elastically acquired from the underlying IaaS Cloud provider(s). It will expose a set of APIs, denoted as "Data Platform Programming APIs" in Figure 1, aimed at increasing the productivity of Cloud programmers from a twofold perspective:

1.  To allow ordinary programmers to store and query data into/from the Data Platform using the familiar and convenient abstractions provided by the object-oriented paradigm, such as inheritance, polymorphism, associations.
2.  To allow ordinary programmers to take full advantage of the processing power of the Cloud-TM platform via a set of abstractions that will hide the complexity associated with parallel/distributed programming, such as load balancing, thread synchronization and scheduling, fault-tolerance.

Lower in the stack we find the backbone of the Data Platform, namely a highly scalable, elastic and dynamically Reconfigurable Distributed Software Transactional Memory (RDSTM).

Cloud-TM uses Red Hat's Infinispan (JBoss/ Red Hat, 2001) as the base component that implements the RDSTM. Infinispan is a recent in-memory transactional data grid designed from the ground up to be extremely scalable. Cloud-TM extends Infinispan with innovative algorithms (in particular for what concerns data replication and distribution aspects), and real-time self-tuning schemes aimed at guaranteeing optimal performance even in highly dynamic Cloud environments.

At its lowest level, the Data Platform supports the possibility to persist its state over a wide range of heterogeneous durable storage systems, ranging from local/distributed file systems to Cloud storages (such as Amazon's S3 or Cassandra).

The Autonomic Manager is the component in charge of automating the elastic scaling of the Data Platform, as well as of orchestrating the self-optimizing strategies that will dynamically reconfigure the data distribution and replication mechanisms to maximize efficiency in scenarios entailing dynamic workloads.

Its topmost layer will expose an API allowing the specification and negotiation of QoS requirements and budget constraints.

The Autonomic Manager leverages on pervasive monitoring mechanisms that do not only track the utilization of heterogeneous system-level resources (such as CPU, memory, network and disk), but also characterize the workload sustained by the various subcomponents of the transactional Data Platform (local concurrency control, data replication and distribution mechanisms, data contention level) and their efficiency.

The stream of raw data gathered by the Workload and Performance Monitor component is then filtered and aggregated by the Workload Analyzer, which distils workload profiling information and alert signals that serve as input for the Adaptation Manger.

Finally, the Adaptation Manager hosts a set of optimizers that rely on techniques of different nature, including analytical or simulation-based models and machine-learning-based mechanisms. These optimizers self-tune the various components of the Data Platform and control the dynamic auto-scaling mechanism. Their ultimate goal is to meet QoS/cost constraints.

*Figure 1. Architectural overview of the Cloud-TM platform*

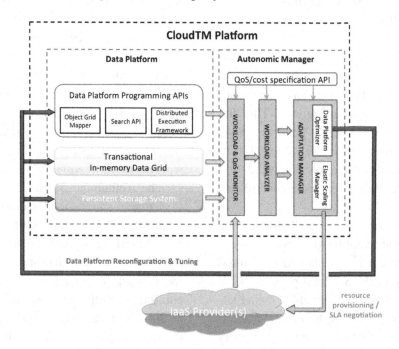

The next subsections describe each main high-level components of Cloud-TM in greater detail.

## Data Platform

This section is devoted to discuss the architectural aspects associated with the development of the key building blocks of the Cloud-TM Data Platform. In particular we will describe the APIs that will be exposed by the Data Platform to the programmers, and the architectural organization of the main building blocks that will expose these APIs.

As depicted in Figure 1, the APIs exposed by the Data Platform can be grouped into three main building blocks:

- **The Object Grid Mapper**: A key feature of the Cloud-TM platform is the support for the development of object-oriented programs based on object domain models; that is, programs that maintain their states as sets of entities, which are represented by

instances of various classes with relationships among them.

As we will discuss more in detail later on the chapter, the Transactional In-Memory Data Grid component of the Cloud-TM architecture is a key-value store and its API is not the most adequate for a programmer that wants to store a large graph of entities interconnected via complex relationships. So, the proposed architecture of the Cloud-TM platform includes a layer on top of the Transactional In-Memory Data Grid that is responsible for providing the higher-level API needed to develop an application that is based on an object-oriented domain model.

- **The Search API**: Any complex data-centric application requires supporting ad-hoc queries to retrieve and manipulate portions of the state that it manages. Given that we want the Data Platform to provide support for development of object-oriented applications, the module in charge of implementing the querying functionality should be able to deal with some intrinsic aspects of the object-oriented model, e.g. supporting notions such as polymorphism and inheritance.

These functionalities will be implemented by the Search API component. This component will expose to the programmer the Java Persistent API - Query Language (JPA-QL) interface, which represents, at the time of writing, the industry standard for encoding queries on an object-oriented database at least for what concerns the Java platform. This same API will be used to support advanced full-text queries, supporting notions such as ranked searching, search by fields, proximity queries, phrase queries etc.

Under the hood, this component will rely on an innovative design strategy that will integrate some of the leading open-source projects in the area of data management and indexing, namely Hibernate OGM and Lucene, with a fully-fledged distributed query engine providing support for complex data manipulation/queries (such as joins or aggregate queries).

- **The Distributed Execution Framework**: This framework will provide a set of APIs aimed at simplifying the development of parallel applications running on top of the Cloud-TM platform. It will essentially consist of two main parts:

  ○ An adaptation of the java.util.concurrency framework, providing a set of building blocks for the development of classic imperative parallel applications deployed on the Cloud-TM platform. These will include abstractions such as task executors and synchronizers (e.g. countdown latches) and transaction-friendly concurrent data collections.

  ○ An adapted version of the popular Google's MapReduce framework. This will allow developers to transparently parallelize their tasks and execute them on a large cluster of machines, consuming data from the underlying in-memory data grids rather than using input files as it was defined by the original proposal.

We address each of these modules in the following subsections.

## Object Grid Mapper

The Object Grid Mapper module is responsible for implementing a mapping from an object-oriented domain model to the Infinispan's key-value model. Thus, a programmer that is developing an application to execute in the Cloud-TM platform will use the API provided by this module not only to develop his application's object-oriented domain model, but also to control the life-cycle of the application's entities.

Given the maturity of the Java Persistence API (JPA) (Oracle, 2012) and its wide acceptance by Java software developers, we decided that the Cloud-TM platform should provide an implementation of the JPA standard as one of its options for mapping an object-oriented domain model. The adoption of JPA will make the Cloud-TM platform standards compliant, easing its adoption by the masses of programmers already familiar with JPA, and providing a smoother migration path for those applications already built on top of JPA. Hibernate OGM, discussed below, is the implementation of JPA for the Cloud-TM platform.

Cloud-TM also offers another API based on the Domain Modeling Language (DML) of the Fénix Framework (Cachopo, 2007). The main reason for having an alternative is because JPA imposes some constraints on the implementation of the mapping from objects to the underlying distributed transactional memory platform that may make it difficult or completely prevent some of the approaches that we would like to explore in the Cloud-TM project.

## Search APIs

The Search APIs provides two main functionalities, namely full-text search queries and support for the JPA query language (JP-QL).

- **Full text queries:** The engine supporting full text queries in the Cloud-TM platform is based on two popular open source frameworks, Hibernate Search and Apache Lucene. These have been extended in order to manipulate/query/index data maintained in the Cloud-TM's Distributed Transactional Memory platform.

*Hibernate Search is an Object/Index Mapper:* It consists of an indexing and an index search component. Both are backed by Apache Lucene, which is a (non-object oriented) full-text indexing and query engine. As a result of this composition, Hibernate Search allows performing full-text queries over object-oriented databases. In the following, it is briefly described how these two components interact, and how they are being integrated in the Cloud-TM platform.

Hibernate Search uses the Lucene index to search an entity and return a list of managed entities. Hence, it saves the programmer the tedious task of taking care of the object to Lucene document mapping. Further, each time an entity is inserted, updated or removed in/from the database, Hibernate Search keeps track of this event (through the Hibernate Core event system) and schedules an update of the Lucene index, in a totally transparent fashion for the programmer. This makes the data in the datastore inlined with the index information and thus makes queries accurate.

To interact with Apache Lucene indexes, Hibernate Search has the notion of DirectoryProviders. A directory provider will manage a given Lucene Directory type. Traditional directory types are file system directories and (non-distributed) n-memory directories.

Integration with the Cloud-TM's data platform is being pursued by developing a Lucene directory capable of efficiently persisting the index information that will be stored in a distributed fashion, in the Cloud-TM's in-memory transactional data grid. This way, the Cloud-TM's data store will contain both the data and the meta-data associated to it.

To maximize efficiency, Hibernate Search batches the write interactions with the Lucene index. There are currently two types of batching. Outside a transaction, the index update operation is executed right after the actual database operation. This is really a no-batching setup. In the case of an ongoing transaction, the index update operation is scheduled for the transaction commit phase and discarded in case of transaction rollback. The batching scope is therefore the transaction. This provides two immediate benefits:

- **Performance:** By amortizing indexing cost across multiple update operations analyzed in a batch, the Lucene indexing can achieve much higher throughput levels.
- **ACIDity:** The work executed has the same scoping as the one executed by the database transaction and is executed if and only if the transaction is committed. This is not ACID in the strict sense of it, but ACID behavior is rarely useful for full text search indexes since they can be rebuilt from the source at any time.
- **JP-QL support:** Support for JP-QL APIs in the Cloud-TM platform is being achieved in two steps:
  - Convert JP-QL queries into Lucene queries, and then execute them via the Hibernate Search APIs.
  - Convert JP-QL queries into Teiid queries where Teiid sources will be the various Lucene indexes exposed via Hibernate Search.

As a first step, we are building a JP-QL parser that converts JP-QL queries into one or more Lucene queries. This approach is limited in what JP-QL queries are supported, as it can only provide for simple selective queries (e.g. where user. age > 30, where order.price > 10 and user.city = 'Paris') and *-to-one joins.

In order to support more complex queries, such as aggregate or join operations, the next step will consist of integrating Teiid within the Cloud-TM platform. Teiid (JBoss/Red Hat, 2012b) is a data virtualization system that allows applications to use data from multiple, heterogeneous data stores. The heart of Teiid is a high-performance query engine that processes relational, XML, XQuery and procedural queries from federated data sources. Teiid's features include support for homogeneous schemas, heterogeneous schemas, transactions, and user defined functions.

Using Teiid, the query execution would:

- Convert the JP-QL query into a Teiid query tree.
- Let Teiid convert the query tree into one or more Hibernate Search / Lucene queries.
- Execute Lucene queries on each dedicated index.
- Aggregate and or do the Cartesian join if necessary.
- Return the results to Hibernate OGM.

## Distributed Execution Framework

The Distributed Execution Framework (DEF) aims at providing a set of abstractions to simplify the development of parallel applications. This will allow ordinary programmers to take full advantage of the processing power available by the set of distributed nodes of the Cloud-TM platform without having to deal with low level issues such as load balancing, thread synchronization and scheduling, fault-tolerance, or asymmetric processing speeds in different nodes.

The DEF will consist of two main parts:

1. An extension of the java.util.concurrency framework, designed to transparently support, on top of the in-memory transactional data grid:
   a. Execution of Java's Callable tasks, which may consume data from the underlying data grid.
   b. Synchronization of tasks/threads via, e.g., queues, semaphores, countdown latches and other classic concurrency tools.
   c. Concurrent, transactional data collections, such as sets, hashmaps, skiplists, arrays.
   d. Processing of data streams, via the definition of pipelines of data stream processing tasks.
2. An adapted version of the popular Google's MapReduce (Jeffrey & Sanjay, 2008) framework. MapReduce is a programming model and a framework for processing and generating large data sets. Users specify a map function that processes a key/value pair to generate a set of intermediate key/value pairs, and a reduce function that merges all intermediate values associated with the same intermediate k. MapReduce framework enables users to transparently parallelize their tasks and execute them on a large cluster of machines. The framework is defined as "adapted" because the input data for map reduce tasks is taken from the underlying in-memory data grid rather than using input files as it was defined by Google's original proposal. Unlike most other distributed frameworks, the Cloud-TM DEF uses data from the transactional data platform's nodes as input for execution tasks. This provides a number of relevant advantages:
   a. The availability of the transactional abstraction for the atomic, thread-safe manipulation of data allows drastically simplifying the development of higher level abstractions such as concurrent

data collections or synchronization primitives.

b. The DEF capitalizes on the fact that input data in the transactional data grid is already load-balanced (using a Consistent Hashing scheme (Karger, 1997)). Since input data is already balanced, the execution of tasks will be automatically balanced as well; users do not have to explicitly assign tasks to specific platform's nodes. However, our framework accommodates users to specify arbitrary subsets of the platform's data as input for distributed execution tasks.

c. The mechanisms used to ensure the fault-tolerance of the data platform, such as redistributing data across the platform's nodes upon failures/leaves of nodes, can be exploited to achieve failover of uncompleted tasks. In fact, when a node F fails, the data platform's failover mechanism will migrate, along with the data that used to belong to F, also any task T that was actively executing on F.

d. Both node failover and task failover policy will be pluggable. Our initial implementation will define interfaces to implement various node failover policies. Currently, we provide only a simple policy that throws an exception if a node fails. In terms of task failure the default initial implementation will simply re-spawn the failed task until it reaches some failure threshold. Future implementations might migrate such a task to another node, etc.

e. As the in-memory transactional data grid will provide extensive support for data replication, more than one node can contain the same entry. Running the same task on the same node would lead to redundant computations, useful possibly for fault-tolerance reasons, but otherwise superfluous. In order to avoid this problem, it is necessary to schedule the processing of disjoint input data in nodes, keeping into account the fact that they possibly maintain replicas of the same data. Thus, the input entries for the task have to be split by the framework behind the scene. Once split, approximately the same number of non-overlapped input entries will be fed to the task on each replica.

Ideally, the split input entries do not need to be merged or re-split. However, there are two cases that need to be considered. The task might run faster on a certain replica while slower on some others, even if the input entries were split evenly depending on how the task was implemented by the user. In such a case, the idle nodes could process the input entries that were not processed yet by the busy nodes (i.e. work stealing) only if the cost of work-stealing does not cancel the gain. Also, during task execution, a replica can go offline for some reason. In such a case, other replicas have to take over the input entries that the offline replica was assigned to. This is basically implemented in the same way with work stealing because we can consider the offline node as "the busiest one". Note that, once the input entries are fed to a node, they can split again to fully utilize all CPU cores. Proper scheduling needs to be done so that only the same number of threads with the number of available cores run at the same time, in order to avoid excessive context switching. Work stealing also needs to be implemented to address the problem mentioned above in a local level.

- **Distributed Execution Model:** The main interfaces for distributed task execution are DistributedCallable and DistributedExecutorService. DistributedCallable is a subtype of the existing Callable from the java.util.concurrent package. DistributedCallable can be executed in a remote JVM and receive input from the transactional in-memory data grid. The task's main algorithm could essentially remain unchanged, only the input source is changed. Existing Callable implementations will most likely get their input in the form of some Java object/ primitive while DistributedCallable gets its input from the underlying transactional data platform in form of key/value pairs. Therefore, programmers who have already implemented the Callable interface to describe their task units would simply extend their implementation to match DistributedCallable and use keys from the data grid as input for the task. Implementation of DistributedCallable can in fact continue to support implementation of an already existing Callable while simultaneously be ready for distributed execution by extending DistributedCallable.

DistributedExecutorService is a simple extension of the familiar ExecutorService interface from the java.util.concurrent package. Existing Callable tasks, instead of being executed in JDK's ExecutorService, are also eligible for execution on the distributed Cloud-TM data platform. The DEF would migrate a task to one or more execution nodes, run the task and return the result(s) to the calling node.

Of course, not all Callable tasks will benefit from parallel distributed execution. Excellent candidates are long running and computationally intensive tasks that can run concurrently and/ or tasks using input data that can be processed concurrently.

The second advantage of the DistributedExecutorService is that it allows a quick and simple implementation of tasks that take input from Infinispan cache nodes, execute certain computa-

tion and return results to the caller. Users would specify which keys to use as input for specified DistributedCallable and submit that callable for execution on the Cloud-TM platform. The DEF's runtime would locate the appropriate keys, migrate DistributedCallable to target execution nodes and finally return a list of results for each executed Callable. Of course, users can omit specifying input keys, in which case Infinispan would execute DistributedCallable on all keys for a specified data store.

- **Map Reduce Execution Model:** The MapReduce model supported by the Cloud-TM platform is an adaptation of Google's original MapReduce. There are four main components in each map reduce task: Mapper, Reducer, Collator and MapReduceTask.

Each implementation of a Mapper interface (see Listing 4) is a component of a MapReduceTask that is invoked once for each input entry $<K,V>$, namely a key/value pair of the underlying in-memory data grid. Given a cache entry $<K,V>$ input pair, every Mapper instance migrated to a node of the data platform, transforms that input pair into intermediate key/value pair emitted into a provided Collator. Intermediate results are further reduced using a Reducer.

Finally, MapReduceTask is a distributed task uniting Mapper, Reducer and Collator into a cohesive large scale computation to be transparently parallelized across the Cloud-TM Data Platform nodes. Users of MapReduceTask need to provide a cache whose data is used as input for this task. The DEF's execution environment will instantiate and migrate instances of provided mappers and reducers seamlessly across Infinispan nodes.

## Reconfigurable Software Transactional Memory

The implementation of the in-memory transactional data grid is based on Infinispan (JBoss/Red Hat, 2001), a recent open source project led by JBoss/Red Hat. In the remainder of this section we will first provide a high level overview of the current architecture of Infinispan, and then focus on how it will be enriched to meet the Cloud-TM's requirements of dynamic reconfiguration.

### Infinispan's Main Operational Modes

Infinispan architecture is extremely flexible and supports a range of operational modes.

*Standalone (non-clustered) mode:* In this mode, Infinispan acts as a Software Transactional Memory. Unlike classical STMs, however, Infinispan does not ensure serializability (or opacity) (Guerraoui & Kapałka, 2008), but, in order to maximize performance, it guarantees more relaxed consistency models. Specifically, it ensures the ISO/ANSI SQL isolation levels Read-committed and Repeatable-read isolation levels (JBoss/Red Hat, 2001), in addition to what is called Write skew anomaly avoidance. In the following, we briefly overview these isolation criteria, and how they are ensured.

- In the read committed isolation level, whenever the application wants to read an entry from Infinispan for the first time, the application is provided directly with the current value in the underlying data container that only contains committed values. When and if the application writes an entry, the modifications are not immediately applied; conversely, the updated data value is stored in a private transaction's workspace. Any later read by the same transaction returns the value that had previously written.

- In the repeatable read isolation level when the application issues for the first time a read request for an entry, it is provided with the value from the committed values container; this value is stored in a private transaction's workspace, and is returned whenever a new read operation is issued on that same data item.

- If the write-skew check is enabled, Infinispan checks if, between a read and a write operation on a data item X issued from a transaction A, there has been some transaction B that has updated (and committed) X. In this case the transaction A is aborted.

Independently from the isolation level, read operations are always lock-free; on the other side, every write operation requires the acquisition of a lock in order to avoid concurrent modifications on the same entry. Infinispan provides the per-entry lock mode, meaning that each <key,value> pair is protected by its own lock, and the striped lock mode, meaning that each lock is shared by a set of <key,value> pairs. This second option reduces memory consumption for lock management, but has the drawback of incurring in false lock contentions. Lock contention is solved through a simple and configurable timeout scheme; further, Infinispan provides a simple and lightweight deadlock detection mechanism to detect cyclic dependencies between pairs of transactions.

*Full replication mode:* In this mode, Infinispan is deployed over a set of interconnected nodes, each one holding a replica of the same key set. This mode is mainly intended for small scale deployments, given that the need to propagate updates to all the nodes in the system hampers the global scalability of this operational mode. The replication mechanism employed by Infinispan is based on the usage of the classical two-phase commit protocol (Gray & Reuter, 1993), which ensures that, in order for a transaction to be committed, it must acquire locks successfully across all the nodes in the platform (thus ensuring replica-wide agreement on the transaction serialization order).

More in detail, upon the issuing of a commit request from a transaction, the prepare phase is initiated: the set of the keys updated by the transaction together with the relevant modification that it wants to perform is broadcast to all nodes. The transaction is then re-run remotely on every node following the aforementioned locking scheme; if a node can successfully acquire all the locks needed, it sends an acknowledgement to the issuer of the prepare phase, otherwise it communicates its impossibility to proceed.

If all nodes send a positive reply, then the node of the original transaction sends a final commit message and all nodes can safely propagate the modifications on the affected keys.

*Partial replication mode:* In this mode every Infinispan replica stores a subset of the data globally managed by the system; every <key, value> pair is replicated (using a Consistent Hashing scheme (Karger, 1997) to distribute keys among nodes, described in the following) over a subset of the total nodes, thus leading to the possibility to meet availability and fault tolerance requirements without the drawbacks that are endemic to the full replicated mode. Upon the commit of a transaction, only the nodes which store keys affected by it are involved in the two-phase commit.

## High Level Architecture

In this section, we will provide some details about the inner structure of Infinispan, describing the main building blocks that are at its core.

At the highest level of abstraction, the main components are the following: the Commands, which are objects that encapsulate the logic of the methods invoked by the user on the Cache; the Visitors, which are intended to "visit" the commands in order to execute them; special Visitors are the Interceptors, which act as a chain and interact with the subsystems which are affected by

a command; the Managers, which are responsible for managing the subsystems.

The main building blocks of the Infinispan architecture are shown in Figure 2, and a brief description for each of them is provided in the following. We start by describing the modules that are common to any operational mode of Infinispan (which we call Core modules). Next we describe, in an incremental fashion, the additional modules that come into play in the full and partial replication modes.

### Core Modules

1.  **DataContainer:** It embeds a ConcurrentHashMap which ultimately stores the <key,value> pairs handled by users. Infinispan gives to the user the possibility to define a lifespan for the entries, after which they are removed from the data container. Moreover it supports several eviction algorithms (FIFO, LRU, LIRS [JBoss/ Red Hat, 2010]) in order to avoid extreme usage of the memory heap. Evicted entries are completely removed, coherently with their lifespan, or stored through the registered CacheLoader, if any. Passivation of entries is also supported.

2.  **CommandFactory:** It is responsible for mapping methods invoked by the application into commands which are visited by the Interceptors.

3.  **EntryFactory:** It is responsible for wrapping DataContainer's entries when accessed. This component interacts with TxInterceptor, which is responsible for implementing the concurrency control algorithms that enforce the isolation level specified by the user.

4.  **LockManager:** It deals with all aspects of acquiring and releasing locks for cache entries. It can support both lazy locking mode, meaning that upon a write the lock is taken only locally, postponing the system-wide lock acquisition until the prepare phase, and

*Figure 2. Architectural overview of Infinispan*

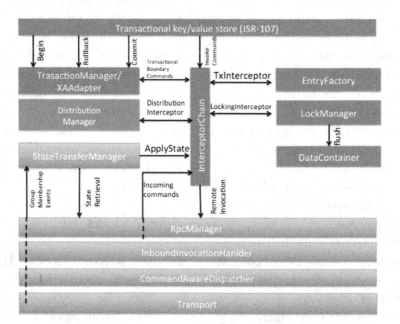

eager locking, in which a lock is taken immediately on all Infinispan's replica when a request is issued. As already mentioned, lock contentions are solved through timeout and in the case of multiple transactions waiting for the same lock fairness is not guaranteed. The Interceptor responsible for interacting with this component is the LockingInterceptor.

5. **Transaction Manager:** It allows to define transactions' boundaries. Infinispan is shipped with a simple DummyTransactionManager, but any JTA compliant transaction manager can be used. Infinispan provides also a XAAdapter class which implements the XAResource interface in order to support distributed transactions among heterogeneous resources.

6. **InterceptorChain:** It is the entry point for any command to be performed. It triggers the visit of the command from all the registered interceptors.

7. **ComponentRegistry:** It acts as a lean dependency injection framework, allowing components and managers to reference and initialize one another.

## Additional Modules Involved in Full Replication Mode

1. **Transport:** It provides a communication link with remote caches and allows remote caches to invoke commands on a local cache instance. This layer ultimately relies on JGroups, to implement lower level's Group Communication Service's abstractions (such as view synchrony, failure detection, reliable broadcast, etc (Chockler, Keidar, & Vitenberg, 2001)).

2. **CommandAwareDispatcher:** It's a JGroups (Bela Ban/Red Hat, 2002) RPC dispatcher which knows how to deal with replicated commands.

3. **InboundInvocationManager:** It is a globally-scoped component which is able to reach named caches and trigger the execution of commands from remote ones by setting up the interceptor chain for them.

4. **RpcManager:** Provides a mechanism for communicating with other caches in the cluster, by formatting and passing requests down to the registered Transport. This

component dialogues directly with the ReplicationInterceptor, which triggers the re-execution of transactions via remote procedures calls.

5.  **StateTransferManager:** It handles generation and application of state on the cache.

## Additional Modules Involved in Partial Replication Mode

*DistributionManager:* It is responsible for both handling the correspondence between any data entry and its owner Infinispan node, as well as the caching policy of entries that are retrieved from remote instances when locally accessed. It communicates with the DistributionInterceptor, which is mutually exclusive with respect to the Replication one.

To determine which instances store which entries, the DistributionManager exploits a Consistent Hashing algorithm (Karger, 1997): both keys and caches are hashed onto a logical circle and each cache contains all keys between itself and the next clockwise one on the circle. This mechanism allows to detect the owner of an entry without additional communication steps and is extremely efficient since upon the leave/join of a node, only a reduced set of entries has to be redistributed, involving in this operation only the nodes which are logically adjacent to the one that has just left/joined the system.

This component is also responsible for managing a level one cache aimed at temporary storing entries which are not a burden, coherently with the consistent hashing, of a specific instance. If a transaction requests an entry that is not local to the node, a remote procedure call is issued, aimed at retrieving and storing it in the level one cache. DistributionManager is responsible for defining eviction policies for those entries.

Moreover, the DistributionManager module is in charge of removing from the DataContainer entries which a node is no longer responsible for

(e.g. upon the join of a new instance) or of moving them to the level one cache.

## Extensions to Support Complex Dynamic Reconfigurations

In order to deal with runtime reconfigurations, Cloud-TM enriches Infinispan's architecture with a Reconfiguration Manager. The Reconfiguration Manager is designed to communicate with the Autonomic Manager via JMX and, when a reconfiguration request is triggered, it orchestrates the switch operations of the various components via the native Infinispan's visitor-based design pattern.

A subsystem that wants its internals to be dynamically tuned must implement a Reconfigurable interface, exposing methods supporting the specification of generic reconfiguration commands, and returning a future (Goetz et al., 2006) associated with the outcome of the requested reconfiguration operation.

By exploiting the future semantics, we allow the invocation to the methods that encapsulate the reconfiguration logics to return asynchronously. This allows reconfigurations of modules that are not subject to specific causality constraints to be executed in parallel, reducing the total reconfiguration latency.

The final commit of the switch from a configuration to another one is issued by the Reconfiguration Manager, which can also act as a system-wide synchronization element to guarantee that, if the configuration switch has a global scope, then all Infinispan replicas have reached agreement on it before declaring the reconfiguration phase concluded. More in detail, upon the request for a reconfiguration, every subsystem involved in the reconfiguration has to perform modifications on its internal state and on its relevant fields on the Infinispan's Configuration object, which stores all state information concerning the configuration of a given instance of Infinispan.

At its core, a ConfigInfo object is a set of String and Objects: the Strings are the names of the methods exposed by the Configuration and are invoked via Reflection; the Objects can represent the parameters for such methods or any other element needed by a subsystem to perform the reconfiguration. The semantics of an Object as well as its specific class are determined at runtime, based both on the method currently invoked via Reflection and the specific logic implemented by the Reconfigure method.

Thanks to the Reconfiguration Manager, the above described architecture also encompasses the possibility to orchestrate complex reconfiguration operations that would be difficult to split into several, component-specific minor reconfigurations. For instance, this design pattern allows to modify the interceptor chain at run-time. The latter can therefore be seen as both the means through which reconfiguration commands are spread in the system, and as a reconfigurable object itself. A practical example for this scenario is the switch from Replicated to Distributed mode, which entails the substitution of the ReplicationInterceptor with the DistributionInterceptor.

## Autonomic Manager

The Autonomic Manager (AM) is the component of the Cloud-TM platform that is in charge of automating the elastic scaling of the Data Platform, as well as of orchestrating the self-optimizing strategies to dynamically reconfigure the data distribution and replication mechanisms. The AM aims at minimizing the infrastructure cost by minimizing the amount of resources required by the applications and optimizing their usage, avoiding at the same time Quality of Service (QoS) violations.

Figure 1 from Section "Overview of the Cloud-TM Platform" depicts the AM architecture. Its topmost layer exposes an API allowing the specification and negotiation of QoS requirements and budget constraints. In order to implement self-optimization strategies, the AM relies on the Workload & Performance Monitor (WPM) component for sensing the execution environment. Figure 3 depicts the WPM. WPM collects information from several heterogeneous components of the platform. Gathered statistics refer to both the utilization of hardware resources and performance metrics at data platform level. The streams of statistical data are used by another component of the AM, the Workload Analyzer (WA). The WA implements workload and resource demand characterization and prediction functionalities by relying on aggregated and filtered data views. The WA also offers the possibility to set alerts to be triggered when specific pre-defined conditions are met (e.g. QoS violations).

Finally, another component, namely the Adaptation Manager (AdM), is in charge of actuating the platform reconfiguration throughout the functionalities provided by the WA and by using both off-line adaptation policies (e.g. based on alerts) and on-line performance forecasts.

## Workload and Performance Monitor

The Workload and Performance Monitor (WPM) provides audit data for both infrastructure resources and platform (or application) level components in an integrated manner. An important feature of WPM is that it does not target any specific platform or application. Instead, it is flexible and adaptable, so to allow integration with differentiated platform/application types. On the technological side, the development of WPM leverages on (a) Lattice, a monitoring framework tailored for cloud infrastructures, which has been developed in the context of the RESERVOIR EU project, and on (b) JMX, a monitoring framework suited for the audit of Java-based components.

The WPM, whose architecture is shown in Figure 3, has been defined according to the need for supporting Statistical Data Gathering (SDG) and Logging (SDL) functionalities.

*Figure 3. WPM architectural organization*

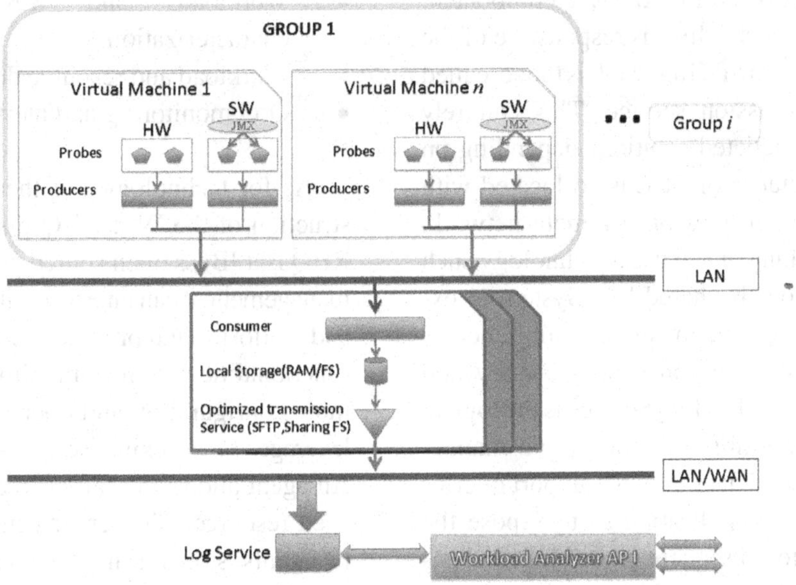

The SDG functionality maps onto an instantiation of a flexible, fault-tolerant and easy to reconfigure system that is able to interconnect all the components of the monitoring infrastructure. In order to be more general and maximize the coverage of the possible configurations of a distributed system, the elements belonging to the monitored infrastructure, such as Virtual Machines (VMs), can be logically grouped, and each group will entail per-machine probes targeting two types of resources: (a) hardware/virtualized and (b) logical ones. Statistics related to the first kind of resources could be directly collected over the Operating System (OS), or via an OS-decoupled library, while statistics related to logical resources (e.g. the data-platform) are collected at the application level. The latter approach does not necessarily require an instrumentation of the monitored application but, relying on the JMX Java framework, WPM is able to directly query any Java applications. Also, it can be exploited to build a Java wrapper for non-Java applications/ components. The data collected by the probes is sent to the producer component via the facilities

natively offered by the interconnection systems. Each producer is coupled with one or many probes and is responsible of managing them. The consumer is a component that receives the data from the producers, via differentiated messaging implementations, which could be selected on the basis of the specific system deployment. A classical network configuration is composed by a LAN-based clustering scheme such that the consumer is in charge of handling one or multiple groups of machines belonging to the same LAN. Anyway, the number of consumers is not meant to be fixed. Conversely, it can be scaled up/down depending on the amount of instantiated probes/producers. Overall, the consumers can be instantiated as centralized or distributed processes. Beyond collecting data from the producers, the consumer is also in charge of performing a local elaboration aimed at producing a suited stream representation to be provided as the input to the Log Service component, which is in charge of supporting the SDL functionality.

An easy way to implement the consumers is to decide to exploit their locally available file systems, to temporarily keep the stream instances to be sent towards the Log Service component. The functional block which is responsible of the interaction between SDG and SDL is the so-called optimized-transmission service. This can rely on top of differentiated solutions depending on whether the instance of SDL is co-located with the consumer or resides on a remote network. Generally speaking, it can use a technology such as SFTP or a locally-shared File System to exchange data. Also, stream compression schemes can be actuated to optimize both latency and storage occupancy. The Log Service is the logical component responsible for storing and managing all the gathered data. It must support queries from any external application so to expose the statistical data to subsequent processing/analysis tasks. The Log Service could be implemented in several manners, in terms of both the underlying data storage technology and the selected deployment (centralized vs. distributed). As for the first aspect, different solutions could be envisaged in order to optimize access operations depending on, e.g. suited tradeoffs between performance and flexibility. This is also related with the data model ultimately supported by the Log Service, which might be a traditional relational model or, alternatively, a <key,value> model. Further, the Log Service could maintain the data onto a stable storage support or within volatile memory, for performance and reliability tradeoffs. The above aspects could depend on the functionalities/architecture of the application that is responsible for analyzing statistical data, which could be designed to be implemented as a geographically distributed process in order to better fit the WPM deployment (hence taking advantage from data partitioning and distributed processing).

## Workload Analyzer

The WA is placed between the WPM and the AdM. The WA bears the following responsibilities:

- Data aggregation and filtering.
- Workload and resource demand characterization.
- Workload and resource demand prediction.
- QoS monitoring and alert notification.

As for technologies at the base of the construction of the WA, RHQ plays a central role. RHQ is a JBoss open source product for systems management. It can interface with several products and platforms and provides various management functionalities, such as monitoring, alerting, remote configuration and operations execution. It leverages on a flexible server/agent architecture. An agent allows the server to connect to a managed resource. The server gets monitoring data by agents, stores it in a database and provides a friendly use interface for data analysis and visualizations. Furthermore, server allows users to trigger operations for the remote management. Agents can be extended by means of plug-ins to add new functionalities. Let us now go through details in relation to the functionalities offered by the WA.

## Data Aggregation and Filtering

The logical dislocation of computational nodes within the distributed system assumed by the WA is inherited by the one of the Autonomic Manager. In fact, the WA exposes facilities to support aggregation and filtering of incoming monitoring data streams, in order to represent an organization of the components that can be monitored, based on the presence of logical groups that aggregate homogeneous resources. To do that, the WA exploits the advanced grouping functionalities provided by RHQ. Summarizing, the presence of logical groups serves a twofold purpose:

- Defining which access permission are applied to the monitored resources.
- Providing a way to view aggregate data and perform actions across all group members.

RHQ enables flexible group membership policies, which support not only the manual addition of resources to groups, but also the definition of regular expressions, called DynaGroups, that maintain group membership in a dynamic fashion. Once groups are defined, it is possible to specify access control polices directly to the groups of resources, instead of individual resources. By using DynaGroups, the system administrator can effectively create dynamic ACLs (Access Control Lists) to lessen the burden of security maintenance, especially against large number of resources. Compatible groups (those composed entirely of the same type of resource, e.g. all Linux platforms) have additional features available to them, such as: group-wise availability; min, max, and average metrics across the group; aggregate events viewer; operations against all group members, either serialized or concurrent execution policies; fine-grained changes to connection properties and resource configuration across one or more members of the group.

## Workload and Resource Demand Characterization

The WA has also the capability to characterize the workload and resource demand of transactional applications deployed on the Cloud-TM platform. To do that, the WA acquires a large amount of statistical information from the various layers of the Cloud-TM platform. In order to profile the behavior of transactional applications, the WA is able to compute complex statistics on the basis of data collected using a number of probes scattered across several sub-systems of the Cloud-TM's data grid. These data are externalized using JMX interfaces in order to permit their monitoring via the WPM system.

These statistics can be classified into high-level and low-level statistics. To the high-level statistics belong all the statistical data related to the identification of hot spot data items, and all the statistics aimed at identifying the maximum

degree of data parallelism for an application. For what concerns hot-spot identification, the main statistic provided is called "top-k" keys (where k is a parameter that is dynamically configurable). It derives form tracing the data accessed by the applications when:

- An update operation is issued.
- A read operation is issued, either remotely or locally - thus requiring or not a remote interaction with another node during transaction execution.
- A lock, causing no contention, contention, or abort of a transaction is issued.

This information is critical in a distributed environment for managing and optimizing the data placement and the concurrency management scheme.

The outcome of "top-k" statistics can be used for managing and optimizing the data placement and the concurrency management schemes within the data grid, and it is extremely valuable for the automatic and/or human-driven tuning of these performance-critical modules of the system. In order to minimize overheads, the process of top-k identification relies on a recently proposed algorithm coming from the world of data stream analysis. The algorithm has been presented in (Metwally, Agrawal, & Abbadi, 2006) (and implemented by the stream-lib open-source project (Clearspring Technologies, 2012). It offers several advantages in terms of limited (constant) memory space and great performance.

In addition, for what concerns the identification of maximum degree of data parallelism exposed by the applications, the WA computes an innovative metric, which is called Application Contention Factor (Didona, Romano, Peluso, & Quaglia, 2011).

The low-level statistics provide a detailed characterization of the performance and costs of the main subsystems involved in the processing of transactions along its life-cycle. These include both statistics (mean, and percentiles) on metrics typically used in SLAs (for instance, transaction execution time) and statistics useful for modeling purposes, such as the latency experienced by transactions along their various execution stages, the frequency of different types (write vs. read) of transactions and of various contention-related events (e.g. successful vs. failed lock acquisition). Among these, two types of statistics are particularly noteworthy: the probability distribution of lock inter-arrival time and the percentiles of transaction execution times.

## Workload and Resource Demand Prediction

The WA offers functionalities for post-processing collected statistics in order to have an estimation of the future workload in terms of user behavior trends and resource demand. In order to be as general and powerful as possible, rather than embedding WA specific prediction models, it relies on the well-known R statistical engine (R-project, 2012). Using R, a client of the WA is able to process in whatever manner the statistics exposed by the WA and re-inject the results again to the WA. This is made possible by exploiting the recently introduced REST APIs of RHQ, which allow exporting the statistical data gathered from the monitored platform as time-series encoded in a standard format, which of course could be parsed by R. Examples of these post-processing range from simple moving average to more complex 5% and 95% quartiles. This approach that permits to retrieve, process and then store again the results within the WA. As a final remark, the flexibility of this approach allows to use engines to post-process data that are not necessarily the mentioned R, but could be analytical models (Sanzo, Ciciani, Quaglia, Palmieri, & Romano, 2012) or machine learning tools (Couceiro, Romano, & Rodrigues, 2011; Couceiro, Romano, & Rodrigues, 2010).

## QoS Monitoring and Alert Notification

The WA provides an advanced QoS monitoring and alert notification engine, leveraging on the functionalities offered by RHQ (JBoss/Red Hat, 2012a). The latter engine is designed to provide proactive notifications about events happening throughout the monitored platform. These events can be resources becoming unavailable, specific values for metrics being collected, resource configuration being changed, operations being executed, or even specific conditions found by parsing log events. Each stream of data within the WA passes through the alerts processing engine. Here, the data can be transformed, filtered, or even correlated with data from other parts of the system. Users have full control over what they want to be notified about, and the engine keeps a full audit trail of the conditions that have triggered alerts to fire. The alerts subsystem provides a wealth of different options for being notified proactively about potential issues in the system. As a result, it supports a breadth of different configuration options that allow for deriving very specific and customized semantics.

## Adaptation Manager

The diagram in Figure 4 provides an architectural overview of the Adaptation Manager. This module is in charge of defining the global self-optimization strategy of the Cloud-TM platform and of orchestrating the platform's reconfiguration process by coordinating the tuning of the ecosystem of components forming the Data Platform, and the provisioning resources from IaaS Cloud providers. The optimization of the Cloud-TM platform is managed by the Optimization Manager component, which takes as input the following data flows:

- The QoS/Cost constraints specified by the users via the QoS API.

*Figure 4. Adaptation manager organization*

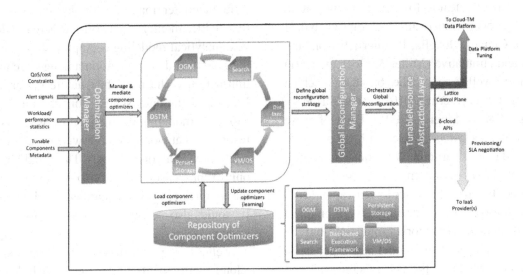

- Alert signals, performance/cost statistics and workload characterization information generated by the workload analyzer.
- The meta-data of the various tunable components of the Cloud-TM platform.

The key role of the Optimization Manager is to manage the life cycle (instantiate, interface and trigger the activation) and mediate the outputs of the set of component optimizers that will be developed throughout the project. The Cloud-TM Data Platform is in fact constituted by a complex ecosystem of components, each one associated with specific key performance indicators, utility functions and tunable parameters. Further, due to the layered architecture of the Data Platform, and to non-trivial interdependencies that exist among its constituting components, it is natural to expect that the configuration strategy of a given component, say "Comp", may strongly affect not only the efficiency of that same component, but also of the efficiency components that interact (directly or indirectly) with Comp.

Classic monolithic optimization approaches, which try to optimize the system as a whole by modeling the dynamics of all of its components using a single, unified approach, are extremely complex to use in a large and heterogeneous system such as the Cloud-TM platform. In order to master complexity, the Cloud-TM platform uses a "divide-et-impera" approach, which subdivides the global optimization task into a set of simpler local optimization sub-problems, focused on determining the optimal configuration policy for small subsystems of the Data Platform. The optimization process proceeds then in an iterative fashion, propagating the effects of the tuning of each component (such as shifts of the workload characteristics for other components, or alteration of the demands of shared system resources) along a chain that captures the existing mutual interdependencies among the Data Platform's components.

The Optimization Manager is the coordinator of this concerted optimization process, triggering its activation periodically, or upon reception of alert signals generated by the Workload Analyzer's module, and mediating the outputs (i.e. reconfiguration policies) of the various local optimizers in order to identify a globally optimal reconfiguration strategy (or at least as close as possible to the global optimum).

An important research line that we are pursuing is to investigate how to combine optimization techniques of different nature, including analytical (Sanzo, Ciciani, Quaglia, Palmieri, & Romano, 2012) and simulative (Miller & Griffeth, 1991) models, as well as approaches based on machine learning (Couceiro et al., 2010) and control theory (Wang, Zhu, & Singhal, 2005). Each of these methodologies comes in fact with its pros and cons, and results particularly adequate to control different classes of systems.

Model-based performance forecast approaches (e.g. relying on analytical or simulative techniques) typically demand very short training time, but can only be employed if the model developer has a detailed knowledge of the system's internals and dynamics. On the other hand, model-free control methods, which treat the system to control as black-boxes and learn their dynamics using statistical techniques, are more generic and robust than model-based techniques (whose accuracy is affected by the accuracy of the employed system's model), but they are better suited to deal with low-dimensional control problems, as their learning time typically grows exponentially with the number of variables to be monitored/controlled.

Some of the results achieved along this research direction include the work in (Romano & Leonetti, 2012), where analytical modeling is used to bootstrap the knowledge base of an on-line machine learner aimed to self-tune the message packing level (Friedman & Hadad, 2006) of a Group Communication System (Guerraoui & Rodrigues, 2006). This technique combines the best of the worlds: boosting, on one hand, the learning phase of the machine learner, while enhancing, on the other hand, the accuracy of the predictions initially generated by the analytical model.

Another relevant approach is represented by TAS (Didona et al., 2011), a system for automating the elastic scaling (i.e. the resource provisioning) of the Cloud-TM's in-memory transactional data grid. In this case, a divide-et-impera approach is taken, in which machine learning is used to

forecast the response of the system in presence of different contention levels for physical resources (e.g. CPU, memory, network), whereas white-box analytical modeling is employed to forecast the effects of data contention among concurrent transactions. The black-box nature of machine learning techniques spares from the burden of explicitly modeling the interactions with system resources that would be otherwise needed using white-box, analytical models. This would be not only a time-consuming and error-prone task given the complexity of current hardware architectures. It would also constrain the portability of our system (to a specific infrastructural instance), as well as its practical viability in virtualized Cloud environments where users have little or no knowledge of the underlying infrastructure. On the other hand, analytical modeling allows us to address two well-known drawbacks of machine learning, namely its limited extrapolation power and lengthy training phase. By exploiting a-priori knowledge on the dynamics of data consistency mechanisms, analytical models achieves good forecasting accuracy even when operating in previously unexplored regions of the parameters' space. Further, by narrowing the scope of the problem tackled via machine learning techniques, analytical modeling allows to reduce the dimensionality of the machine learning input features' space, leading to a consequent reduction of training phase duration (Sutton & Barto, 1998).

Returning to the diagram in Figure 4, the Adaptation Manager will store the Data Platform component's optimizers within an apposite repository that will allow both the retrieval and update of optimizers logic and data (e.g. training data-sets or other statistical information gathered by observing the results of previous self-tuning cycles).

The Adaptation Manager will include two additional building blocks, the Global Reconfiguration Manager and the TunableResource Abstraction Layer. The former will be in charge of coordinating global reconfiguration actions that entail orchestrating different layers of the Data

Platform, such as provisioning new nodes from the IaaS provider to the Data Platform, and having them join the Transactional In-memory Data Grid. Note that our architecture for reconfiguration is inherently hierarchical. Acting from a privileged, centralized perspective, the Global Reconfiguration Manager will, in fact, be able to trigger reconfiguration of complex systems (such as the In-memory transactional data grid) which may, in their turn, implement non-trivial distributed protocols to complete their own reconfiguration.

The TunableResource Abstraction Layer will serve the purpose of hiding from the Global Reconfiguration Manager the heterogeneity of interacting with the various platform's components, which will encompass modules implemented using different technologies and remotely. Under the scenes, this module will encapsulate the logic to interact with the IaaS provider, in order to automate the resource provisioning process, and with the Data Platform's components, via the Control Plane of the Lattice framework. Note that, as shown in Figure 4, in order to achieve transparent interoperability with multiple IaaS Cloud providers, the AdM exploits the delta-cloud APIs (Apache Software Foundation, 2011), a recent open-source project that has recently been accepted into the Apache Software Foundation Incubator, which provides, in its turn, an abstraction layer towards multiple IaaS Cloud providers (including Amazon EC2/S3, GoGrid, OpenNebula, Rackspace Cloud Servers/Cloud Files).

## FUTURE RESEARCH DIRECTIONS

The Cloud-TM project is, at the moment of writing, entering its third and last year, and the consortium is working intensively to materialize the vision outlined in this book chapter. In this section we overview some of the most relevant research lines that are being pursued in this stage. Note that, while we expect that these research lines will yield to

tangible results that will be incorporated in the final prototype of the Cloud-TM platform. On the other hand, some of these research problems are so broad that it is unlikely that they will be fully explored by the end of the project. Conversely, we believe that the Cloud-TM project will blaze new trails that, we hope, will be pursued in future also by other researchers active in the area of Cloud computing.

## Performance Forecasting Models for Very Large Scale DSTM Systems

As mentioned previously, the TAS system (Didona et al., 2011) represents a significant leap towards the fulfillment of the objective of automating the resource provisioning process in a DSTM system. TAS, however, addresses the scenario of fully replicated DSTM, in which each node maintains a full replica of the DSTM's state. This class of data consistency mechanisms is optimized for small-medium scale platforms, e.g. composed of 10-20 nodes.

However, the cost of propagating the state updates generated by a transaction across all the nodes in the system becomes quickly prohibitive as the system scale grows. Large scale DSTM systems, spanning hundreds or thousands of nodes, rely on inherently more scalable, so called *genuine* (Peluso, Romano, & Quaglia, 2012; Peluso, Ruivo, Romano, Quaglia, & Rodrigues, 2010), replication schemes, which ensure a limited degree of replication (hence, bounding the cost of replication even in large scale systems) and avoid the reliance on any centralized component (hence, avoiding bottlenecks in the system design).

Designing solutions capable of forecasting the effects of contention on data and physical resources on the performance of very large scale DSTM platforms represents an important line of research, which is, to the best of our knowledge, still unexplored in literature.

## Self-Tuning of Data Placement

As discussed above, a key choice when deploying a DSTM is whether to adopt a full or a partial replication model. The latter is more scalable, but, on the down side, it incurs in the costs of remote reads (as not all data are available at all nodes) during transactions' execution. Thus, a key factor affecting performance of partially replicated systems is associated with how data is distributed across the nodes of the system. This is an issue that is being intensively studied in the context of the Cloud-TM project, with the aim of designing self-tuning data placement algorithms capable of exploiting application's locality to minimize the costs of remote data fetching.

In particular, we are exploring a crucial trade-off in the design space of data placement algorithms that is associated with the granularity on whose basis data placement algorithms work. On one hand, algorithms that operate with the granularity of a single data instance have maximum flexibility, and have, consequently, the maximum potentiality of maximizing data access locality. Unfortunately, they also incur in the highest book-keeping costs, as they need to explicitly keep track of the placement of potentially a very high number of data. On the other hand, algorithms operating at the granularity of the data item type (i.e. object-type in an object-oriented data platform like Cloud-TM) incur in significantly lower book-keeping overheads, hence resulting feasible also in big data scenarios. Unfortunately, however, they also have a much more limited flexibility, which may lead to suboptimal data placement solutions.

Driven by the requirements of high scalability, the solutions developed so far in the project (Garbatov & Cachopo, 2012; Garbatov & Cachopo, 2011a; Garbatov & Cachopo, 2011b; Garbatov & Cachopo, 2011c) have been based on the object-type approach. An interesting area that is being currently explored in the Cloud-TM project is the design of instance-based techniques that exploit probabilistic techniques in order to avoid main-taining exact data placement information. The idea being pursued is to exploit space-efficient encoding techniques (such as Bloom filters (Broder & Mitzenmacher, 2005) or associative neural memories (Hassoun, 1993) to achieve the flexibility of instance-based approaches, while drastically abating their book-keepings costs, in order to achieve scalability levels comparable to those of type-based systems.

## Self-Tuning of Replication Protocols

One of the key innovative ideas explored in the Cloud-TM project is to pursue optimal efficiency by adapting dynamically the algorithms to enforce data consistency depending on fluctuations of the workload and of the scale of the DSTM platform. Polycert (Couceiro et al., 2011) represented a first important step towards the achievement of this goal. However, there are still important aspects that need to be further investigated. Polycert supports the coexistence among multiple Atomic Broadcast based (Guerraoui & Rodrigues, 2006) certification protocols, relying on machine learning techniques to determine the optimal protocol to use on a per-transaction basis. On the other hand, the design space of replication protocols for transactional systems is very wide (Couceiro, Romano, & Rodrigues, 2011), and the problem of supporting efficient re-configurations among arbitrary replication protocols remains an important open problem that we are currently addressing in our most recent efforts.

Another interesting research direction in this area is related to how to automatically identify which data consistency protocols to use given the current load/scale scenario. Machine learning techniques, as used in Polycert, are attractive due to their black box nature, which makes them capable of handling a wide range of alternative options in a relatively simple way. On the other hand, precisely due to their black box nature, they have normally relatively little extrapolation power, i.e. they have a very limited ability to predict system's performance in presence of workloads not observed during the training phase. Due to their white box nature, analytical models do not suffer of the above limitation, but they are normally much more expensive to design and validate. Exploring the, possibly combined, usage of techniques relying on statistical learning and analytical models is another intriguing research area that we plan to explore in our future work.

## CONCLUSION

Cloud-TM is an ongoing European project aimed at designing and implementing an elastic, self-tuning transactional store for the cloud. Specifically, the Cloud-TM platform aims at dynamically adjusting the amount of resources acquired from the underlying IaaS provider depending on possible fluctuations of incoming workload and user SLAs. In parallel, the Cloud-TM platform will self-tune its configuration in order to ensure maximal efficiency across scenarios characterized by different platform scales and heterogeneous workloads. From a programming perspective, the API provided by the Cloud-TM platform will be based on the abstraction of transactional memory, and will spare the programmers from dealing with the inherent complexities associated with the development of large scale distributed applications.

This chapter has overviewed the general architecture of the Cloud-TM platform. In this process we have illustrated the key motivations and challenges that were accounted for during the design of the platform and presented some of the results achieved so far within the project.

## REFERENCES

Abadi, D. J. (2009). Data management in the cloud: Limitations and opportunities. *A Quarterly Bulletin of the Computer Society of the IEEE Technical Committee on Data Engineering, 32*(1), 3–12.

Aguilera, M. K., Merchant, A., Shah, M., Veitch, A., & Karamanolis, C. (2007). Sinfonia: A new paradigm for building scalable distributed systems. In *Proceedings of Twenty-First ACM SIGOPS Symposium on Operating Systems Principles* (pp. 159–174). New York, NY: ACM.

Alonso, G., Casati, F., Kuno, H., & Machiraju, V. (2004). *Web services: Concepts, architectures and applications*. Berlin, Germany: Springer.

American National Standards Institute. (1992). *ANSI SQL-92 specification, document number: ANSI X3.135-1992*. Retrieved November 30, 2012, from http://www.contrib.andrew.cmu.edu/~shadow/sql/sql1992.txt

Amir, Y., Danilov, C., & Stanton, J. (2000). A low latency, loss tolerant architecture and protocol for wide area group communication. In *Proceedings of the International Conference on Dependable Systems and Networks* (pp. 327-336). New York, NY: ACM.

Apache Software Foundation. (2011). *δ-cloud*. Retrieved November 30, 2012, from http://delta-cloud.apache.org

Bela Ban/Red Hat. (2002). *JGroups - The JGroups project*. Retrieved November 30, 2012, from www.jgroups.org

Birman, K. P. (1993). The process group approach to reliable distributed computing. *Communications of the ACM, 36*(12), 37–53. doi:10.1145/163298.163303.

Bocchino, R. L., Adve, V. S., & Chamberlain, B. L. (2008). Software transactional memory for large scale clusters. In *Proceedings of the Symposium on Principles and Practice of Parallel Programming (PPOPP)* (pp. 247–258). New York, NY: ACM.

Broder, A., & Mitzenmacher, M. (2005). Network applications of bloom filters: A survey. *Internet Mathematics, 1*(4), 485–509. doi:10.1080/15427951.2004.10129096.

Cachopo, J. (2007). *Development of rich domain models with atomic actions.* (Unpublished doctoral dissertation). Technical University of Lisbon, Lisbon, Portugal.

Cachopo, J., & Rito-Silva, A. (2006). Combining software transactional memory with a domain modeling language to simplify web application development. In *Proceedings of the 6th International Conference on Web Engineering* (pp. 297–304). New York, NY: ACM.

Carvalho, N., Cachopo, J., Rodrigues, L., & Rito-Silva, A. (2008). Versioned transactional shared memory for the fenixedu web application. In *Proceedings of the Second Workshop on Dependable Distributed Data Management* (pp. 15-18). New York, NY: ACM.

Carvalho, N., Romano, P., & Rodrigues, L. (2010). Asynchronous lease-based replication of software transactional memory. In *Proceedings of the ACM/IFIP/USENIX 11th Middleware Conference (Middleware)* (pp. 376-396). New York, NY: ACM.

Chockler, G., Keidar, I., & Vitenberg, R. (2001). Group communication specifications: A comprehensive study. *ACM Computing Surveys*, *33*(4), 427–469. doi:10.1145/503112.503113.

Clayman, S., Galis, A., & Mamatas, L. (2010). *Monitoring virtual networks with lattice.* Paper presented at Network Operations and Management Symposium Workshops. Osaka, Japan.

Clearspring Technologies. (2012). *The stream-lib library.* Retrieved November 30, 2012, from https://github.com/clearspring/stream-lib

Codd, E. F., Codd, S. B., & Salley, C. T. (1993). *Providing OLAP (on-line analytical processing) to user-analysis: An IT mandate.* E. F. Codd & Associates.

Couceiro, M., Romano, P., Carvalho, N., & Rodrigues, L. (2009). D2stm: Dependable distributed software transactional memory. In *Proceedings of the 15th Pacific Rim International Symposium on Dependable Computing* (pp. 307-313). Washington, DC: IEEE Computer Society.

Couceiro, M., Romano, P., & Rodrigues, L. (2010). A machine learning approach to performance prediction of total order broadcast protocols. In *Proceedings of the 2010 Fourth IEEE International Conference on Self-Adaptive and Self-Organizing Systems* (pp. 184-193). Washington, DC: IEEE Computer Society.

Couceiro, M., Romano, P., & Rodrigues, L. (2011). PolyCert: Polymorphic self-optimizing replication for in-memory transactional grids. In *Proceedings of the 12th ACM/IFIP/USENIX International Conference on Middleware* (pp. 309-328). Berlin, Germany: Springer-Verlag.

Couceiro, M., Romano, P., & Rodrigues, L. (2011). Towards autonomic transactional replication for cloud environments. In Petcu, D., & Poletti, J. (Eds.), *European Research Activities in Cloud Computing.* Cambridge, UK: Cambridge Scholars Publishing.

DeWitt, D., & Stonebraker, M. (2009). *Mapreduce: A major step backwards.* Retrieved November 30, 2012, from http://www.databasecolumn.com/2008/01/mapreduce-a-major-step-back.html

Di Sanzo, P., Ciciani, B., Quaglia, F., Palmieri, R., & Romano, P. (2012). On the analytical modeling of concurrency control algorithms for software transactional memories: The case of commit-time-locking. *Performance Evaluation*, *69*(5), 187–205. doi:10.1016/j.peva.2011.05.002.

Didona, D., Romano, P., Peluso, S., & Quaglia, F. (2011). Transactional auto scaler: Elastic scaling of in-memory transactional data grids. In *Proceedings of the 9th International Conference on Autonomic Computing (ICAC 2012)* (pp. 17-21). New York, NY: ACM.

Felber, P., Fetzer, C., & Riegel, T. (2008). Dynamic performance tuning of word-based software transactional memory. In *Proceedings of the 13th ACM SIGPLAN Symposium on Principles and Practice of Parallel Programming* (pp. 237–246). New York, NY: ACM.

Friedman, R., & Hadad, R. (2006). Adaptive batching for replicated servers. In *Proceedings of the 25th IEEE Symposium on Reliable Distributed Systems* (pp. 311–320). Washington, DC: IEEE Computer Society.

Garbatov, S., & Cachopo, J. (2011a). Data access pattern analysis and prediction for object-oriented applications. *INFOCOMP Journal of Computer Science*, *4*(10), 1–14.

Garbatov, S., & Cachopo, J. (2011b). Software cache eviction policy based on stochastic approach. In *Proceedings of the Sixth International Conference on Software Engineering Advances*. IEEE.

Garbatov, S., & Cachopo, J. (2011c). Optimal functionality and domain data clustering based on latent Dirichlet allocation. In *Proceedings of the Sixth International Conference on Software Engineering Advances*. XPS.

Garbatov, S., & Cachopo, J. (2012). Decreasing memory footprints for better enterprise java application performance. In *Proceedings of the 23rd International Conference on Database and Expert Systems Applications* (pp. 430-437). Berlin, Germany: Springer.

Goetz, B., Peierls, T., Bloch, J., Bowbeer, J., Holmes, D., & Lea, D. (2006). *Java concurrency in practice*. Boston, MA: Addison Wesley.

Gramoli, V., Harmanci, D., & Felber, P. (2008). Toward a theory of input acceptance for transactional memories. In *Proceedings of the 12th International Conference on Principles of Distributed Systems* (pp. 527-533). Berlin, Germany: Springer.

Gray, J., & Reuter, A. (1993). *Transaction processing: Concepts and techniques*. Oxford, UK: Elsevier Lt.

Guerraoui, R., Herlihy, M., & Pochon, B. (2005). Polymorphic contention management. In *Proceedings of the Nineteenth International Symposium on Distributed Computing* (pp. 303-323). Berlin, Germany: Springer.

Guerraoui, R., & Kapalka, M. (2008). On the correctness of transactional memory. In *Proceedings of the 13th ACM SIGPLAN Symposium on Principles and Practice of Parallel Programming* (pp. 175-184). New York, NY: ACM.

Guerraoui, R., & Kapałka, M. (2008). On the correctness of transactional memory. In *Proceedings of the 13th ACM SIGPLAN Symposium on Principles and Practice of Parallel Programming (PPoPP)*, (pp. 175-184). New York, NY: ACM.

Guerraoui, R., & Rodrigues, L. (2006). *Introduction to reliable distributed programming*. Berlin, Germany: Springer.

Guyon, I., & Elisseeff, A. (2003). An introduction to variable and feature selection. *Journal of Machine Learning Research*, *3*, 157–1182.

Hadoop Wiki. (2012). *Hadoop map/reduce data processing benchmarks*. Retrieved November 30, 2012, from http://wiki.apache.org/hadoop/DataProcessingBenchmarks

Harris, T., & Fraser, K. (2003). Language support for lightweight transactions. *ACM SIGPLAN Notices*, *38*(11), 388–402. doi:10.1145/949343.949340.

Hassoun, M. H. (1993). *Associative neural memories: Theory and implementation*. Oxford, UK: Oxford University Press.

Herlihy, M., Eliot, J., & Moss, B. (1993). Transactional memory: Architectural support for lock-free data structures. In *Proceedings of the International Symposium on Computer Architecture* (pp. 289-300). New York, NY: ACM.

Herlihy, M., Luchangco, V., Moir, M., & Scherer, W. N., III. (2003). Software transactional memory for dynamic-sized data structures. In *Proceedings of the Twenty-Second Annual Symposium on Principles of Distributed Computing* (pp. 92–101). New York, NY: ACM.

Hibernate. (2009). *Hibernate*. Retrieved November 30, 2012, from http://www.hibernate.org

iBATIS. (2009). *iBATIS*. Retrieved November 30, 2012, from http://ibatis.apache.org

Java Community Process. (2001). *Java caching API*. Retrieved November 30, 2012, from http://jcp.org/en/jsr/summary?id=107

JBoss/Red Hat. (2001). *INFINISPAN - Open source data grids*. Retrieved November 30, 2012, from http://www.jboss.org/infinispan

JBoss/Red Hat. (2010). *Infinispan eviction, batching updates and LIRS*. Retrieved November 30, 2012, from http://infinispan.blogspot.com/2010/03/infinispan-eviction-batching-updates.html

JBoss/Red Hat. (2012a). *RHQ project*. Retrieved November 30, 2012, from http://www.rhq-project.org

JBoss/Red Hat. (2012b). *Teiid*. Retrieved November 30, 2012, from http://www.jboss.org/teiid

Jeffrey, D., & Sanjay, G. (2008). MapReduce: Simplified data processing on large clusters. *Communications of the ACM, 51*(1), 107–113. doi:10.1145/1327452.1327492.

Kalyvianaki, E., Charalambous, T., & Hand, S. (2009). Self-adaptive and self-configured CPU resource provisioning for virtualized servers using Kalman filters. In *Proceedings of the 6th International Conference on Autonomic Computing* (pp. 117-126). New York, NY: ACM.

Karger, D., Lehman, V., Leighton, T., Panigrahy, R., Levine, V., & Lewin, D. (1997). Consistent hashing and random trees: Distributed caching protocols for relieving hot spots on the world wide web. In *Proceedings of the Twenty-Ninth Annual ACM Symposium on Theory of Computing* (pp. 654–663). New York, NY: ACM.

Keleher, P., Cox, A. L., & Zwaenepoel, W. (1992). Lazy release consistency for software distributed shared memory. In *Proceedings of the 19th Annual International Symposium on Computer Architecture* (pp. 13–21). New York, NY: ACM.

Kotselidis, C., Ansari, M., Jarvis, K., Lujan, M., Kirkham, C., & Watson, I. (2008). DiSTM: A software transactional memory framework for clusters. In *Proceedings of the International Conference on Parallel Processing (ICPP)* (pp. 51–58). Washington, DC: IEEE Computer Society.

Manassiev, K., Mihailescu, M., & Amza, C. (2006). Exploiting distributed version concurrency in a transactional memory cluster. In *Proceedings of the Symposium on Principles and Practice of Parallel Programming (PPOPP)* (pp. 198–208). New York, NY: ACM.

Metwally, A., Agrawal, D., & Abbadi, A. E. (2006). An integrated efficient solution for computing frequent and top-k elements in data streams. *ACM Transactions on Database Systems, 31*(3), 1095–1133. doi:10.1145/1166074.1166084.

Microsystems, S. U. N. (1999). *Java transaction API (JTA)*. Retrieved November 30, 2012, from http://www.oracle.com/technetwork/java/javaee/jta/index.html

Microsystems, S. U. N. (2002). *Java management extensions (JMX) v1.2 specification*. Retrieved November 30, 2012, from http://jcp.org/aboutJava/communityprocess/final/jsr003/index.html

Miller, J., & Griffeth, N. (1991). Performance modeling of database and simulation protocols: Design choices for query driven simulation. In *Proceedings of the 24th Annual Symposium on Simulation* (pp. 205-216). Washington, DC: IEEE Computer Society.

Miranda, H., Pinto, A., & Rodrigues, L. (2001). Appia, a flexible protocol kernel supporting multiple coordinated channels. In *Proceedings of the 21st International DST Conference on Distributed Computing Systems* (pp. 707–710). Washington, DC: IEEE Computer Society.

Moir, M. (1997). Transparent support for wait-free transactions. In *Proceedings of the 11th International Workshop on Distributed Algorithms* (pp. 305–319). Berlin, Germany: Springer.

Olston, C., Reed, B., Srivastava, U., Kumar, R., & Tomkins, A. (2008). Pig latin: A not-so-foreign language for data processing. In *Proceedings of the International Conference on the Management of Data* (pp. 1099–1110). New York, NY: ACM.

Oracle. (2012). *Introduction to the java persistence API*. Retrieved November 30, 2012, from http://docs.oracle.com/javaee/6/tutorial/doc/bnbpz.html

Pacitti, E., Coulon, C., Valduriez, P., & Özsu, M. T. (2005). Preventive replication in a database cluster. *Distributed and Parallel Databases, 18*(3), 223–251. doi:10.1007/s10619-005-4257-4.

Peluso, S., Romano, P., & Quaglia, F. (2012). SCORe: A scalable one-copy serializable partial replication protocol. In *Proceedings of ACM/IFIP/USENIX 13th International Middleware Conference*. ACM.

Peluso, S., Ruivo, P., Romano, P., Quaglia, F., & Rodrigues, L. (2010). When scalability meets consistency: Genuine multiversion update serializable partial data replication. In *Proceeding of the IEEE 32nd International Conference on Distributed Computing Systems* (pp. 455-465). Washington, DC: IEEE Computer Society.

R-Project. (2012). *The R-project*. Retrieved November 30, 2012, from http://www.r-project.org

Ramadan, H. E., Rossbach, C. J., Porter, D. E., Hofmann, O. S., Bhandari, A., & Witchel, E. (2007). MetaTM/TxLinux: Transactional memory for an operating system. In *Proceedings of the 34th Annual International Symposium on Computer Architecture* (pp. 92-103). New York, NY: ACM.

Ranger, C., Raghuraman, R., Penmetsa, A., Bradski, G., & Kozyrakis, C. (2007). Evaluating mapreduce for multi-core and multiprocessor systems. In *Proceedings of the International Symposium on High-Performance Computer Architecture* (pp. 13–24). Washington, DC: IEEE Computer Society.

Reservoir Consortium. (2012). *Reservoir, resources and services virtualization without barriers*. Retrieved November 30, 2012, from http://www.reservoir-fp7.eu/

Riegel, T., Fetzer, C., & Felber, P. (2008). Automatic data partitioning in software transactional memories. In *Proceedings of the Twentieth Annual Symposium on Parallelism in Algorithms and Architectures* (pp. 152-159). New York, NY: ACM.

Romano, P., & Leonetti, M. (2012). Poster: Self-tuning batching in total order broadcast via analytical modelling and reinforcement learning. *ACM SIGMETRICS Performance Evaluation Review, 39*(2), 77–77. doi:10.1145/2034832.2034861.

Shavit, N., & Touitou, D. (1995). Software transactional memory. In *Proceedings of the Symposium on Principles of Distributed Computing* (pp. 204-213). New York, NY: ACM.

Shpeisman, T., Adl-Tabatabai, A., Geva, R., Ni, Y., & Welc, A. (2009). Towards transactional memory semantics for C++. In *Proceedings of the 21st Symposium on Parallelism in Algorithms and Architectures* (pp. 49-58). New York, NY: ACM.

Sonmez, N., Cristal, A., Harris, T., Unsal, O. S., & Valero, M. (2009). Taking the heat off transactions: Dynamic selection of pessimistic concurrency control. In *Proceedings of the 2009 IEEE International Symposium on Parallel & Distributed Processing* (pp. 1-10). Washington, DC: IEEE Computer Society.

Sun MicroSystems. (2003). *Java 2 platform enterprise ed. specification, v. 1.4, final release ed., 2003*. Retrieved November 30, 2012, from http://www.jcp.org/en/jsr/detail?id=151

Sutton, R. S., & Barto, A. G. (1998). *Reinforcement learning: An introduction (adaptive computation and machine learning)*. Cambridge, MA: The MIT Press.

Wang, Z., Zhu, X., & Singhal, S. (2005). Utilization and slo-based control for dynamic sizing of resource partitions. In *Proceedings of the 16th IFIP/IEEE Ambient Networks international conference on Distributed Systems: Operations and Management* (pp. 133-144). Berlin, Germany: Springer.

Xu, J., Zhao, M., Fortes, J., Carpenter, R., & Yousif, M. (2007). On the use of fuzzy modeling in virtualized data center management. In *Proceedings of the International Conference on Autonomic Computing* (p. 25). Washington, DC: IEEE Computer Society.

Yu, Y., Isard, M., Fetterly, D., Budiu, M., Erlingsson, U., Gunda, P. K., & Currey, J. (2008). DryadLINQ: A system for general-purpose distributed data-parallel computing using a high-level language. In *Proceedings of the Symposium on Operating System Design and Implementation* (pp. 987-994). New York, NY: ACM.

## KEY TERMS AND DEFINITIONS

**Elastic Scaling:** Property of a system that allows its users to use and free resources as needed, while ensuring de that the scale of system is changed in real-time to meet the demands of varying workloads.

**Self-Tuning System:** A system that is able of optimizing its own internal running parameters in order to maximize or minimize the fulfillment of an objective.

**Transactional Memory:** Programming paradigm that tries to simplify concurrent programming by allowing a group of load and store instructions to execute in an atomic way.

# Chapter 14
# Storage Security and Technical Challenges of Cloud Computing

**Shantanu Pal**
*University of Calcutta, India*

## ABSTRACT

*Cloud computing has leaped ahead as one of the biggest technological advances of the present time. In cloud, users can upload or retrieve their desired data from anywhere in the world at anytime, making this the most important and primary function in cloud computing technology. While this technology reduces the geographical barriers and improves the scalability in the way we compute, keeping data in a Cloud Data Center (CDC) faces numerous challenges from unauthorized users and hackers within the system. Creating proper Service Level Agreements (SLA) and providing high-end storage security is the biggest barrier being developed for better Quality of Service (QoS) and implementation of a safer cloud computing environment for the Cloud Service Users (CSU) as well as for the Cloud Service Providers (CSP). Therefore, cloud applications need to have increased QoS and effective security measures and policies set in place to provide better services and to decline unauthorized access. The purpose of this chapter is to examine the cloud computing technology behind innovative business approaches and establishing SLA in cloud computing applications. This chapter provides a clear understanding of different cloud computing security challenges, risks, attacks, and solutions that exist in the present heterogeneous cloud computing environment. Storage security, different cloud infrastructures, the many advantages, and limitations are also discussed.*

## INTRODUCTION

Cloud computing is an Internet-based computing paradigm (Rohini, 2011), where by shared resources, software and information are provided to computers and other devices which are available to everyone as services (Lombardi & Pietro, 2010). This technology has changed the way of delivering computation in present scenarios. In all manners of

businesses from private to governmental, everyone is now relying on the cloud applications in their everyday life. In a broader sense the term Utility Computing becomes more sophisticated in terms of cloud applications. Buyya et al in the literature (Buyya, Pandey, & Vecchiola, 2009) defined cloud computing as *Cloud is a market-oriented distributed computing system consisting of a collection of inter-connected and virtualized computers that are dynamically provisioned and presented as one or more unified computing resources based*

DOI: 10.4018/978-1-4666-3934-8.ch014

*on service-level agreements established through negotiation between the service provider and consumers*. From this definition it is clear that cloud computing is a market-oriented business paradigm that is provisioned dynamically to deliver a more flexible business environment to the clients. This technology improves the scalability as well as easy to use for end users who avail themselves of this technology pay only for the particular service they require. Moreover cloud services can be expanded or reduced depending upon the user's request by adding or removing Virtualized Machines (VM) in the system.

In the cloud, users can access their requested information from a shared resource pool, known as CDC, with minimum computer knowledge and vast computer resources to acquire the data. Users don't need to know where the data is stored or how this data is being retrieved. They only need pay to the service provider for the services that they are using, based on their SLA (Schmietendorf, Dumke, & Reitz, 2004). Generally this approach is more acceptable for online business scenarios where users and service providers are both able to benefit from the services in a cloud computing environment. SLA is the contract between the vendors (typically the CSP) and the users (typically the CSU) with legal conditions and regulations applies for using the services. One of the major characteristics of SLA is the QoS being delivered to the customers (Chaves, Westphall, & Lamin, 2010) and it should cover a transparent aspect of cost, security, legal requirements for data placement, eco-efficiency and more (Lawrence, Djemame, W"aldrich, Ziegler, & Zsigri, 2010; Buyya, Ranjan, & Calheiros, 2010). Choosing the correct vendor for a business and taking care of the right agreements is also an important factor for achieving success within the business (Zhu, 2010).

Some important issues of cloud computing can be drawn as follows: (1) large scale computing resources, (2) high scalability and elasticity, (3) shared resource pooling (virtualized and physical resources), (4) dynamic resource scheduling,

(5) general purpose, (6) flexibility, etc. Cloud computing is a broader term combining several different types of service offerings. In general it can be distinguished among Software, Platform and Infrastructure as a Service (Qian, Luo, Du, & Guo, 2009; Bleikertz, 2010; Yan, Rong, & Zhao, 2009; Stanoevska-Slabeva & Wozniak, 2010), offered by the CSP. Armbrust et al defined cloud computing as (Stanoevska-Slabeva & Wozniak, 2010):

*Cloud Computing refers to both the applications delivered as services over the Internet and the hardware and systems software in the datacenters that provide those services. The services themselves have long been referred to as Software as a Service (SaaS). The datacenter hardware and software is what we will call a Cloud. When a Cloud is made available in a pay-as-you-go manner to the general public, we call it a Public Cloud; the service being sold is Utility Computing. We use the term Private Cloud to refer to internal datacenters of a business or other organization, not made available to the general public. Thus, Cloud Computing is the sum of SaaS and Utility Computing, but does not include Private Clouds. People can be users or providers of SaaS, or users or providers of Utility Computing.*

The benefits of using cloud computing technology are clear to the end users, but however, cloud computing still faces great challenges in terms of storage security and privacy protection. One of the most important concerns is to protect user's sensitive information in a CDC. These challenges are need to be carefully addressed for deploying innovative business models into the cloud platform, particularly in a secure public cloud environment (Ren, Wang, & Wang, 2012).

The remainder of this chapter is organized as follows: At first a discussion of cloud computing for an innovative business approach is presented to understand the basic architecture behind this technology. In addition this chapter will also provide a clear understanding of different cloud computing security challenges and security risks, attacks and solutions that exist in the present heterogeneous cloud computing environment. The uses of this technology in the IT (Information Technology) world as well as different cloud applications are also briefly touched upon with the different modes of cloud application. Storage security, different cloud infrastructures, advantages, limitations and establishing SLA in a cloud computing environment are also discussed.

## CLOUD COMPUTING FOR AN INNOVATIVE BUSINESS APPROACH

Mell et al. (Mell & Grance, 2009) defined cloud computing as: *Cloud computing is a model for enabling convenient, on-demand network access to a shared pool of configurable computing resources (e.g., networks, servers, storage, applications, and services) that can be rapidly provisioned and released with minimal management effort or service provider interaction.* There is no doubt that cloud computing is a rapidly growing technology in the field of our modern computation. Many companies are now improving their business applications with a cloud computing platform to deliver more flexible as well as scalable services to the end users. From defense sector to health care services cloud computing has numerous applications. The social impact of cloud computing is now increasing day by day. Different cloud providers (such as Amazon, Google, Salesforce, IBM, Microsoft, Sun Microsystems, etc.) establish new CDC for hosting numerous cloud applications in various locations around the globe to provide redundancy and ensure reliability. Cloud can be both software and infrastructure. *'The [cloud] service is accessible via a Web browser (non-proprietary) or Web services API; Zero capital expenditure is necessary to get started; you pay only for what you use as you use it'* (Stanoevska-Slabeva & Wozniak, 2010). For initial business

setup any small company can start a Web-based business applications on its computer system, can add extra VM when needed and shut them down when there is no demand. This type of utility is called Elastic Cloud Computing (EC2) (Buyya, Yeo, Venugopal, Broberg, & Brandic, 2009).

Large investments have been made by Google to improve its data centres which provide spreadsheet applications and word processing online, keeping data and software stored on the servers. A new cloud platform called Windows Azure was created in 2008 by Microsoft. Cloud computing has been actively invested in by other hardware and software companies for the electronics industry. In addition many social networks (like facebook) have begun to move in the same direction converting into social platforms for consumer based applications (Etro, 2009). Companies like Amazon, Google and Microsoft have invested huge amount of capital to deploy most of their services over a public cloud environment (Hosseini, Sommerville, & Sriram, 2010).

Although cloud computing is facing numerous challenges in terms of security and resource protection from other users and hackers in the system, this technology shows considerable promises for delivering services in a new type of platform. Starting from the grid computing to utility computing, cloud computing is now the most important paradigm over the Web. Grid computing is a distributed computing paradigm that coordinates networked resources to achieve a common computational objective (Zhang, Cheng, & Boutaba, 2010). Using grid computing anyone can share any information with the others around the globe. For an example, Alice is doing his research at a university in California and sharing his resources with John. John is also trying to share these research resources from Sydney with Bob who is sitting at his research laboratory in Tokyo. They can easily communicate with each other by using grid computing systems, but in the case of a cloud computing paradigm they can also do a business oriented application which is not supported by the grid computing technology, for instance, John wants to provide some of the software or codes for economical purposes to Bob in Tokyo. Zhang et al in the literature (Zhang, Cheng, & Boutaba, 2010) have drawn a nice description among grid, utility and cloud computing as follows:

*The development of Grid computing was originally driven by scientific applications which are usually computation-intensive. Cloud computing is similar to Grid computing in that it also employs distributed resources to achieve application-level objectives. However, cloud computing takes one step further by leveraging virtualization technologies at multiple levels (hardware and application platform) to realize resource sharing and dynamic resource provisioning. Whereas Utility Computing represents the model of providing resources on-demand and charging customers based on usage rather than a flat rate. Cloud computing can be perceived as a realization of utility computing. It adopts a utility-based pricing scheme entirely for economic reasons. With on-demand resource provisioning and utility based pricing, service providers can truly maximize resource utilization and minimize their operating costs.*

Simply, utility computing provides high flexibility for managing the resources and grid computing provides better utilization of resources at the cost of lesser flexibility for managing those resources, whereas cloud computing provides both higher flexibility as well as higher resource utilization.

## THE MANY ADVANTAGES AND LIMITATIONS TO CLOUD COMPUTING

In cloud-based applications, services are carried out on behalf of customers (Pearson, Shen, & Mowbray, 2009). This paradigm helps to reach it in an increasingly fashionable business model.

Users typically don't know about the location of the stored data they input to a CDC or they don't have the knowledge and control over the hardware or software that are residing on them. This poses some inherent challenges in terms of storage security and data privacy for the cloud computing environment. In spite of these challenges there are various advantages of cloud computing that leads it to a more acceptable technology in electronics-business (e-business) scenarios. Some of the advantages (Qian, Luo, Du, & Guo, 2009; Bleikertz, 2010; Oh, Lim, Choi, Park, Lee, & Choi, 2010; Lee & Crespi, 2010) of cloud computing can be described as follows:

- **Infrastructural Cost Reduction:** Building of a cloud based infrastructure by the cloud users is not required for deploying their business; they (users) can depend upon any third party service provider. Thus a huge amount of cost for building those hardware supports or for its production can be reduced. Users should pay for the amount of resources they used.
- **Shared Resource Pool:** There is no doubt that cloud has a huge shared resource pool for its users, at any instance (location and place independent) users can use these services with the help of the Internet. This improves the efficiency of resource management through dynamic resource scheduling, where multiple users can use the same resources at the same time.
- **Easy to Use:** Cloud computing software can be run successfully with adequate computer knowledge; this feature makes it more acceptable to an e-business.
- **Easy to Maintain:** Users can interact with the CSP using the Internet; no physical interconnection is required with the CSP for using its application and deployment. That improves the maintenance of cloud infrastructure for end users.

- **Satisfy Business Requirements:** Resizing the resource by application with cloud computing fulfills the requirements that businesses seek as their needs change in an on demand type of business.

- **Energy Efficiency:** Cloud computing architecture needs less power consumption (Lefèvre & Orgerie, 2010; AbdelSalam, Maly, Mukkamala, Zubair, & Kaminsky, 2009). The fundamental advantage is that, it uses energy saving hardware.

- **Massive Scalability:** In numerous cloud applications; cloud provides the ability to scale thousands of systems, bandwidth and storage space to deploy business applications. Thus it increases a massive scalability for the system.

- **Elasticity:** Cloud provides the ability to increase or decrease their computing resource by users needs. Anyone can use twenty computers (VMs) today for any resource and may use only one computer (VM) for an application in the next day. Users need not to be worried about the resources, the main concern should be how many resources they need and how much they have to pay for using those services ('pay as you go' service basis).

- **Pay-as-You-go Facility:** This particular feature makes cloud more acceptable in e-business as the users only pay for the resources they use. This would also depend upon storage use, computing power and bandwidth.

- **Self-Provisioning of Resources:** Having additional resources, like processing capability, software, storage network resources, cloud computing becomes more popular to the end users.

- **Carriers' Data Center (CDC) Efficiency:** A CDC model (Zheng, Sun, & Zhou, 2009) enables rapid innovation, scalability and support of core enterprise functions, resulting in significant economies of scale. A CDC reduces the need for additional hardware, software facilities, as well as automation of server, network, storage, operating systems and middleware provisioning all of which are costly and time-consuming functions.

- **Use of Simpler Devices for Applications:** Powerful computers are not a necessity when data and software are stored in the cloud. Many electronic devices can then interface, for example an online game console, a cell phone, a personal video recorder, etc.

- **Enhanced Business Collaboration:** Allowing users to share information and applications online through the use of the cloud platform, produce new ways of working together.

While the benefits of using cloud computing promises rapid growth in e-businesses, this technology still faces great challenges in terms of security, privacy, authentication of users and so on. Some of the limitations associated with the cloud computing application are discussed in the following paragraphs.

- **Reliability and Security:** Users no longer need to know where their data is being kept and how they will transfer to the service requesting authorities. At present providing reliability and storage security is the biggest obstacle towards the development of a secure cloud computing environment.

- **Privacy Protection**: Cloud computing is facing numerous challenges, in particular for data privacy and access control. There is also a risk of data theft from machines, by its employees or by the CSP itself. It may be possible for hackers or thieves at some time to take data by breaking into a service providers' machine or even by other customers of the same service if there is inadequate separation of different customers' data at the CDC or in a machine that they share in the cloud (Brock & Goscinski, 2010).

- **User Data Privacy while Transferring Data to the Other Users**: CSP should be aware of the fact that the user's data cannot be viewed or changed by other any people or users during the transmission (Xu, Huang, Huang, & Yang, 2009). Resource protection, user provisioning and authentication and authorization should be guaranteed by the CSP.
- **Dependency on the Internet and Power**: Cloud services require uninterrupted Internet connections for delivering the services; therefore an Internet connection is a must for the cloud computing environment, in the same way power (electricity) is necessary for uninterrupted Internet connections.

In spite of all these challenges cloud computing is mentioned as the fifth generation of computing after the mainframe, personal computer, client-server computing and the Web. A fact is projected about the cloud spending details. Where in 2008 the cloud IT spending was $16 billion and with a growth of 27% it will be as $42 billion in 2012. Where the total IT spending in 2008 was $383 billion and with a growth of 7% it is projected as $494 billion in 2012. The total cloud spending in 2008 was $367 billion and it is projected that, with a growth of 4% it will be $452 billion in 2012 ($=United State Dollar) (Bechtolsheim, 2008).

## SERVICE LAYERS OF CLOUD COMPUTING

Cloud computing provides services to the customers in the form of virtualized computing resources (Oh, Lim, Choi, Park, Lee, & Choi, 2010). Customers are then able to acquire different computing resources (such as software, storage, server, and network) based on their demands and requirements. The major available cloud services are known as: Software as a Service (SaaS), Platform as a Service (PaaS), and Infrastructure as a Service (IaaS) (William, Hosame, & Feng, 2010; Bleikertz, 2010).

SaaS is the most familiar layer to the end users and focuses on multiple 'pay as you go' manners of application software packages. This service being the most visible of the service types in the cloud computing allows end-users to interact with this service directly, unlike other service types which are usually hidden from the end-users.

PaaS focuses on providing software developer's environment. In PaaS a platform is available to customers for use with their applications. The entire infrastructure is provided by PaaS to run an application over the Internet. This particular platform offers a complete application stack so customers are not required to manage and maintain its own server with components for an application stack.

IaaS focuses on providing infrastructure services such as storage or computing power over the Internet. Servers, storage disks and network devices are provisioned services offered to customers. IaaS provider offers virtualized infrastructure as a service instead of selling the basic hardware infrastructure, which includes storage, networking, and computing.

## MODES OF CLOUD APPLICATIONS

Basic outlines of the four different modes of cloud applications (Marinos & Briscoe, 2009) will be discussed in this section. They are as follows: Public, Private, Hybrid and Community cloud.

- **Public Cloud:** Public cloud services are provided by a third party (offered by a CSP) to the public as a service and typically hosts multiple cloud service customers on shared resources. An example of such cloud is Amazon Web Services. Anyone in the cloud ecosystem can use this service. Security is a big issue for deploying services over this public cloud environment.

- **Private Cloud:** Private Cloud is usually defined in terms of services where resources are available to specific types of users or companies. Private cloud service is typically provided within the enterprise and operated only for a specific customer either on- or off-premise by the customer itself or a third-party operator (Bleikertz, 2010). *It is the internal data centers of a company or other organizations. A private cloud is fully owned by a single company who has total control over the applications run on the infrastructure, the place where they run, and the people or organizations using it – simply over every aspect of the infrastructure* (Stanoevska-Slabeva & Wozniak, 2010). For an example, companies could maintain their employee's salary databases with a private cloud environment allowing only a specific group of users (such as higher officials) to access this information. Private clouds offer many of the same benefits that public clouds do, with one major difference: the enterprise is in the charge of setting-up and maintaining their private cloud infrastructure and they has full control-over and responsibility for the services. But companies may require a higher amount to set up its initial internal cloud infrastructure (such as, to setup special firewalls or security protections).

- **Hybrid Cloud:** A combination of both the public and private cloud results in a Hybrid Cloud. Management becomes the responsibility of both the enterprise and the public cloud provider. (Bleikertz, 2010). For an example, a company can launch their different types of services into public cloud platform (for everyone to access) and another part of services into the private cloud

(such as employee's salary database) for official use within the company. However, this particular type of infrastructure can be difficult in managing, governing as well as creating an effective type of security solution.

- **Community Cloud:** This type of cloud provides services for a limited set of customers from a specific community (Bleikertz, 2010), these particular type of cloud is hosted on-or-off- premises and are operated by third parties or in-house staff.

## RESOURCE MANAGEMENT THROUGH DYNAMIC RESOURCE POOLING

Virtualization is the key part of a cloud ecosystem. Virtualization is the key part of the cloud computing technology, in which both the hardware and software programs are kept away from the end users. Only provides virtualized resources to the end users. A virtualized server is commonly called a VM. The core of the cloud computing is virtualization which provides the pooling of computing resources from clusters of servers. Virtual resources are also assigned or reassigned to applications on demand (Zhang, Cheng, & Boutaba, 2010). The term cloud computing invariably describes both a type of application as well as a platform. A cloud computing platform dynamically provisions, configures, reconfigures as needed (Boss, Malladi, Quan, Legregni, & Hall, 2007). IaaS clouds offer very basic resources, specifically server virtualization and data storage. PaaS clouds offer complete hardware and software configurations and SaaS clouds offer complete software systems and application interfaces.

A secure virtualization technique (Lombardi & Pietro, 2010) can increase the level of security of cloud computing system, by protecting both of the integrity of guest VM and the cloud infrastructure components. Two kinds of virtualization, namely full virtualization and para virtualization are present in case of a cloud computing paradigm (Sangroya, Kumar, Dhok, & Varma, 2010; VMware, 2007).

## STORAGE SECURITY IN CLOUD COMPUTING

Security and privacy issues are one of the major concerns at present cloud computing research. Cloud computing databases need more security to protect sensitive information from unauthorized users and hackers. Major concerns in protecting the cloud databases are (1) to protect cloud data at CDC, (2) to protect cloud data at the time of data transmission, and (3) authorization and authentication of users and service providers in a cloud computing environment.

- **Privacy of CSU's Storage Data inside the CDC:** Sensitive information is stored by the users in the cloud storage. CSP should ensure that, this information cannot be changed or viewed by any other person or user including the CSP.
- **User Data Privacy at the Time of Transmission**: CSP should be aware of the possible data losses and CSP takes necessary measures to confirm that the user's data cannot be viewed or changed by the other people or user at runtime. This would also include security of transferring private data in cloud computing center's Intranet and Internet.
- **Authentication and Authorization of CSU and CSP:** This feature allows users as well as service providers to access cloud-data securely.

Data security in a public cloud environment needs more attention than that of the private cloud environment. In a public cloud data is available to everyone in the system and there is no specific enterprise to control-over or to take responsibility like a private cloud scenario. Major security threats in a public cloud environment are the unwanted data losses (Chow, Jakobsson, Masuoka, Molina, Niu, Shi, & Song, 2010; Yu, Wang, Ren, & Lou, 2010) and the system being crashed by the non-trusted service users and hackers. In the cloud, as the users are unaware of where their data is stored on and what security measures are given for these resources, it is vital to protect the confidentiality and integrity of the cloud data in the system. Simply, these data are stored in one or more remote server(s), where users have no access to modify, change or control over the CDC's internal operational activities. For multitenancy activities multiple users can share the same physical resources simultaneously. This feature improves the utilization of resources but creates new security issues for protecting ones sensitive information from others (Ren, Wang, & Wang, 2012; Chow, Golle, Jakobsson, Shi, Staddon, Masuoka, & Molina, 2009).

Garcia et al (Garcia & Felgar, 2008) presented a trust based approach for Web security, this approach describes about the development of Web security and to preserve its privacy for the enterprises, which integrates the WS-Trust with standards policy and ontology. A Policy-based obfuscation and de-obfuscation mechanism is discussed in (Mowbray, Pearson, & Shen, 2010). This scheme described a policy-based obfuscation and de-obfuscation mechanism to protect sensitive data within the cloud service provision, with the help of a privacy manager. Where the privacy manager has full control over to this policy based mechanism. Different security concerns and their prospective solutions are discussed in numerous studies (Zissis, & Lekkas, 2012; Pal, 2013), some of these security measures and solutions for cloud computing environments are discussed in the following section (see Table 1).

*Table 1. Different security measures and solutions for cloud computing environment*

| Proposed Scheme | Solution/ Vision | Remarks |
|---|---|---|
| Trust development for CSU and CSP in a cloud computing environment (Li & Ping, 2009) | The proposed method separates the client (CSU) and server (CSP) in a heterogeneous cloud computing environment. Then according to the scheme it assigned different trust strategies for both of them (CSP and CSU) to make the system more secure and reliable. | The proposed scheme is a domain based (trust domain) security development model which introduced a novel cloud-trust approach to solve the security issues in a multilayered cloud computing environment in which customer can choose different services within its domain. The trust recommendation strategies used in this proposed model is treated as one of the cloud services. This model successfully established a large scale 'trust recommendation' in a multilayered cloud platform that achieves both identity and behavioral authentication but not integrity. |
| Establishing trust model for multi-agent recommender systems (Lorenzi, Baldo, Costa, Abel, Bazzan, & Ricci, 2010) | It is an agent based trust recommendation approach, where agents select their tasks autonomously and perform this task with the help of the collaboration with other trusted agents or any previous solution (or interaction) records maintained in their local knowledge bases. | In this approach agents become expert for any specific kinds of tasks during the trust recommendation cycle and the improved trust degree helps to prevent any unnecessary communication with the non-trusted agents. The trust degree depends on the every communication done by the agent. |
| Trusted and collaborative agent based Approach for securing cloud computing environment (Pal, Khatua, Chaki, & Sanyal, 2012) | This scheme proposed a new trusted and collaborative agent based two-tier framework approach named as 'WAY' (Who Are You?), to protect cloud resources from unauthorized access by detecting the non trusted CSU in the system. | The proposed framework can be used to provide security in network, infrastructure, as well as data storage in a heterogeneous cloud computing environment. This technique secures the cloud databases from non trusted CSU in a domain. The uniqueness of the proposed solution is that, it ensures security and privacy both at the CSP's as well as at the CSU's end. Trust value of the CSU is checked twice (with the updates trust table) before giving any information to them. If any CSU is doing malicious activity in any domain, CSP decreases the trust value (and update the trust table) for this particular user for any future communication, instead of rapidly decreasing the trust value of the whole domain in which this malicious CSU is residing on. In this approach generating or updating the trust value depends over the CSP. Thus this framework is limited to prevent malicious activities (or to detect malicious CSU) uniquely without CSP's information. |
| A comprehensive security framework for cloud computing environment (Takabi, Joshi, & Ahn, 2010) | A security framework and existing security solutions are presented in this literature. | The proposed framework consists of different modules (such as, access control module, policy integration module, service and trust management module, etc.) to handle security, policy, trust issues of a cloud computing environment. Identity management, access control, policy integration (in multiple clouds) and trust management between different clouds as well as with its users are carried out by the different modules in this security solution. Secure service composition, integration and semantic heterogeneity among policies from different clouds are also taken care. |
| A collaboration-based security management framework for cloud computing environment (Almorsy, Grundy, & Ibrahim, 2011) | This literature describes a new cloud security management framework based on aligning the FISMA (Federal Information Security Management Act) standard. This approach focuses towards a cloud security specification based on improving and mutual collaboration among different cloud consumers in the system. | The proposed framework is based on improving collaboration among cloud providers, service providers and service consumers for managing the security in a cloud computing environment. Authors' claim that proposed approach is able to tackle both the loss of trust and security control problems in the cloud. |

*continued on following page*

*Table 1. Continued*

| Proposed Scheme | Solution/ Vision | Remarks |
|---|---|---|
| Secure dynamic trust mechanism for cloud computing environment (Zhang, Xu, Liu, Zhang, & Shen, 2006) | The dynamic nature of cloud computing makes the system more vulnerable (for protecting the resources) from other users and hackers. This literature describes an implementation of secure dynamic trust mechanism for this type of vulnerable systems. The proposed approach tries to prevent security risks and attacks as well as secures data transfer from a non-trusted party in a heterogeneous cloud computing environment. | The proposed approach successfully prevents the different types of security threats and attacks including Rootkit and System Files attacks. The trustworthiness of subjects and objects are clearly reflects with the concept of reliability. |
| User's data security in a cloud computing environment (Xu, Huang, Huang, & Yang, 2009) | The proposed architecture separates contain and format from a document, before handling and storing its data into a remote cloud server. | Using encryption function, the proposed scheme optimized authorization methods for any authorized CSU to access the cloud database. This model protects the privacy of sensitive information with an efficient methodology for the users residing in a heterogeneous cloud computing environment. Using this scheme it is difficult to handle large number of documents, thus this model is restricted for any large databases. |
| Securing cloud-data in a disc in a cloud computing environment (Sedayao, Su, Ma, Jiang, & Miao, 2009) | One of the major security concerns is to protect user's sensitive information from service provider's machine, by its employees or by the service provider itself. Proposed scheme ensures data security from the 'system administrator' or service provider as well as from other users who may read the sensitive information. | This technique protects data at 'rest' (simply data stored in disc storage). This scheme is easy to develop and cheap to implement. This model can solve the confidentiality of sensitive data stored in a CDC, where the users have an exclusive control over a private key that CSP can't view or control over. This model achieves the confidentially but unable to protect the integrity of stored data. |

## ESTABLISHING SERVICE LEVEL AGREEMENTS (SLA) FOR CLOUD COMPUTING

As cloud is a rapidly growing form of technology in the field of computing, securing more powerful Quality of Services (QoS), establishing Service Level Agreements (SLA) is by far one of the most important factors between the CSP and the CSU in a heterogeneous multi-layered cloud computing environment. Due to the dynamic nature of the cloud infrastructure, to date there are no universal definitions or agreements made for the system, which can deliver a secure business level agreement between these two parties. Thus, the establishment of a SLA is an emerging field of

research while offering increased benefits to the business. Therefore, it is imperative to provide a QoS along with added security measures in a cloud computing environment. This section will focus on the necessity of a SLA for the cloud computing environment, its challenges and opportunities for delivering a safer business environment between CSP and CSU.

SLA has an important role in a Grid and Cloud computing scenario, which can be defined as: *a part of the contract between the service provider and its customers. It describes the provider's commitments and specifies penalties if those commitments are not met* (Parrilli, 2010). One of the major goals (Takabi, Joshi, & Ahn, 2010) of a SLA is to build a new layer to create a negotiation mechanism for the contract between service provider and consumer as well as monitoring of this agreement throughout the process completion. It is a difficult task however to find the correct SLA contract to put in place for the business. Ad-hoc nature of cloud also makes it more complex for determining the correct SLA for the system (Bouchenak, 2010). If someone wants to create a SLA for a business, they should think about the correct vendors for his or her services. The same for the vendors, they should care about the authentic users who are liable for maintaining the agreements made through the SLA. All this creates a major challenge for computer technologists in establishing the SLA in a cloud computing environment. A major factor in this challenge is the correct agreements used based on the cloud paradigm between the two parties in the system. These agreements offer true gains for parties, the users and the service providers, where performance, agility and scalability are concerned for delivering better services.

## Issues of Introducing SLA in a Cloud Computing Environment

The attributes offered by the cloud, facilitates the focus of businesses on their core objectives, rather than becoming heavily involved in strategic IT decisions regarding infrastructure. Whilst easing systems management, in this respect the cloud computing paradigm also presents some challenges for the system management issues. Dodda et al. (Dodda, Smith, & Moorsel, 2009) presented architecture to facilitate the management of computer resources from different CSP in a cloud-agnostic manner with the promise to realize effectively the flexibility and adaptability in a cloud platform.

The security risks and attacks within a cloud computing environment can be quite high and because of this, the establishment of a secure SLA in a cloud environment is a challenging one. Thus the security issues should be addressed properly

while making a SLA for the business (Chaves, Westphall, & Lamin, 2010; Dodda, Smith, & Moorsel, 2009).

## Establishing SLA in a Cloud Computing Environment

The motivation behind the research is to understand and discuss the open issues related to the SLA with cloud computing and the different security risks and attacks that may affect the QoS of the services (Boss, Malladi, Quan, Legregni, & Hall, 2007). Bouchenak (2010) mentioned an automated control for SLA-aware elastic clouds. It also presents the early ideas, named as SLA aware Service (SLAaaS), which is about SLA management in cloud computing environments. Two major open issues are addressed in this literature as: (1) the integration of QoS and the SLA for a better service provisioning within the heterogeneous cloud computing environment, and (2) an automated dynamic elasticity to the cloud infrastructure for a secure and more reliable SLA management through a strong cloud capacity planning. Chaves et al. in (Chaves, Westphall, & Lamin, 2010) discussed SLA perspective in security management for cloud computing. This literature introduces Sec-SLAs that explore SLA for security in cloud computing environments. Comuzzi et al. (Comuzzi, Kotsokalis, Spanoudakis, & Yahyapour, 2009) presented a SLA management framework through the view of the service provider's perspective where the perspective of the service customer is not discussed.

Another focus should be on the technical specifications linked to the service that is provided by the SLA. QoS means in general terms and more specifically, the availability and performance levels guaranteed by the provider, but Mármol et al (Mármol, & Pérez, 2010) argue that *most of the times it is not feasible or realistic to assume the existence of service level agreements (SLA) or the presence of a centralized entity or architecture (such as a PKI), supplying reliable information regarding the actual and current behavior of every service provider in the system.* The basic objective of SLA is thus to maintain the agreement between the two parities. Service providers should be aware of the QoS and the service consumers should be aware of the policies and infrastructure of these services. Overall, everyone should maintain and adhere to the legal rules and regulations properly.

## FUTURE RESEARCH DIRECTIONS

In spite of several security threats and attacks cloud computing has many advantages in cost reduction, resource sharing, time saving for new service deployment, etc. Furthermore, cloud application does not depend on geographic barriers; it can be accessed from anywhere, anytime. From the vendors point of view it is easier to reach new customers, easy for delivering and supporting applications. But problem remains the same for privacy and security issues and securing cloud services is still in its initial stages. More development in the cloud will poses more security challenges to protect its resources and in future a more reliable cloud infrastructure is needed for deploying services securely.

## CONCLUSION

Cloud computing is one of the fastest growing technologies within the present computing scenarios. The most important security concern for it is how to secure sensitive cloud-data from unauthorized users and hackers residing on the system. There are several technologies and security features invented so far to provide a secure cloud platform for deploying businesses but these are not concrete security solutions that are able to prevent data losses and unauthorized accesses in a heterogeneous cloud computing environment.

Moreover providing more powerful QoS to the end users and establishing proper SLA between the CSP and CSU are also major concerns. It is important to provide more transparency between the CSP and CSU so that users can choose the best services according to their needs and requirements while providers provide the best mechanism to protect the sensitive cloud information. The assets and its property should be indentified to maintain while ensuring a safer cloud service. Research is ongoing in this issue to establish an ideal security solution for providing better services in all the applications running in cloud computing platform.

## ACKNOWLEDGMENT

The author would like to acknowledge and thanks to all the researchers for their ideas and works which have been described in this book chapter.

## REFERENCES

AbdelSalam, H., Maly, K., Mukkamala, R., Zubair, M., & Kaminsky, D. (2009). Towards energy efficient change management in a cloud computing environment. In *Proceedings of the 3rd International Conference on Autonomous Infrastructure, Management and Security* (LNCS), (Vol. 5637, pp. 161-166). IFIP International Federation for Information Processing. doi:10.1007/978-3-642-02627-0_13

Almorsy, M., Grundy, J., & Ibrahim, A. (2011). Collaboration-based cloud computing security management framework. In Proceedings *4th International Conference on Cloud Computing* (pp. 364 - 371). IEEE. doi:10.1109/CLOUD.2011.9

Bechtolsheim, A. (2008). *Cloud computing.* Retrieved in 2011, from http://netseminar.stanford.edu/seminars/Cloud.pdf

Bleikertz, S. (2010). *Automated security analysis of infrastructure clouds.* Retrieved from http://nordsecmob.tkk.fi/Thesisworks/Soren%20Bleikertz.pdf

Boss, G., Malladi, P., Quan, D., Legregni, L., & Hall, H. (2007). *Cloud computing.* Retrieved from http://download.boulder.ibm.com/ibmdl/pub/software/dw/wes/hipods/Cloud_computing_wp_final_8Oct.pdf

Bouchenak, S. (2010). Automated control for SLA-aware elastic clouds. In Proceedings of FeBid 2010. ACM. doi: ACM 978-1-4503-0077-3/10/4

Brock, M., & Goscinski, A. (2010). Toward a framework for cloud security. In *Proceedings of the 10th International Conference on Algorithms and Architectures for Parallel Processing* (LNCS) (Vol. 6082, pp. 254-263). Berlin, Germany: SpringerLink. doi: 10.1007/978-3-642-13136-3_26

Buyya, R., Pandey, S., & Vecchiola, C. (2009). Cloudbus toolkit for market-oriented cloud computing. In *Proceedings of the 1st International Conference on Cloud Computing,* (LNCS), (Vol. 5931, pp. 24-44). Berlin, Germany: SpringerLink. doi: 10.1007/978-3-642-10665-1_4

Buyya, R., Ranjan, R., & Calheiros, R. (2010). InterCloud: Utility-oriented federation of cloud computing environments for scaling of application services. In *Proceedings of the 10th International Conference on Algorithms and Architectures for Parallel Processing,* (LNCS), (vol. 6081, pp. 13–31). Berlin: Springer. doi:10.1007/978-3-642-13119-6_2

Chaves, S., Westphall, C., & Lamin, F. (2010). SLA perspective in security management for cloud computing. In *Proceedings of the Sixth International Conference on Networking and Services (ICNS 2010).* IEEE Computer Society. doi: 10.1109/ICNS.2010.36

Chow, R., Golle, P., Jakobsson, M., Shi, E., Staddon, J., Masuoka, R., & Molina, J. (2009). Controlling data in the cloud: Outsourcing computation without outsourcing control. In *Proceedings of the 2009 ACM Workshop on Cloud Computing Security* (pp. 85-90). ACM. doi:10.1145/1655008.1655020

Chow, R., Jakobsson, M., Masuoka, R., Molina, J., Niu, Y., Shi, E., & Song, Z. (2010). Authentication in the clouds: A framework and its application to mobile users. In *Proceedings of the 2010 ACM Workshop on Cloud Computing Security Workshop 2010.* ACM. doi: 10.1145/1866835.1866837

Comuzzi, M., Kotsokalis, C., Spanoudakis, G., & Yahyapour, R. (2009). Establishing and monitoring SLAs in complex service based system. In *Proceedings of the International Conference on Web Services, 2009 (ICWS 2009)* (pp. 783–790). IEEE. doi:10.1109/ICWS.2009.47

Dodda, R., Smith, C., & Moorsel, A. (2009). An architecture for cross-cloud system management. In *Proceedings of IC3 2009.* Springer-Verlag. doi:10.1007/978-3-642-03547-0_53

Etro, F. (2009). *The economic impact of cloud computing on business creation, employment and output in Europe.* Retrieved from http://www.intertic.org/Policy%20Papers/CC.pdf

Garcia, D. Z. G., & Felgar de Toledo, M. B. (2008). An approach for establishing trust relationships in the Web service technology. In *Proceedings of the International Federation for Information Processing,* (Vol. 283, pp. 509–516). Boston: Springer. doi:10.1007/978-0-387-84837-2_53

Hosseini, A., Sommerville, I., & Sriram, I. (2010). *Research challenges for enterprise cloud computing.* Retrieved from http://arxiv.org/abs/1001.3257

Kamara, S., & Lauter, K. (2010). Cryptographic cloud storage. In *Proceedings of the Financial Cryptography: Workshop on Real-Life Cryptographic Protocols and Standardization*. Retrieved from http://research.microsoft.com/pubs/112576/crypto-cloud.pdf

Lawrence, A., Djemame, K., W¨aldrich, O., Ziegler, W., & Zsigri, C. (2010). Using service level agreements for optimising cloud infrastructure services. In *Proceedings of ServiceWave 2010 Workshops (LNCS)* (*Vol. 6569*, pp. 38–49). Berlin: Springer-Verlag. doi:10.1007/978-3-642-22760-8_4.

Lee, G., & Crespi, N. (2010). Shaping future service environments with the cloud and internet of things: Networking challenges and service evolution. In *Proceedings of the 4th International Symposium on Leveraging Applications of Formal Methods, Verification and Validation* (LNCS), (Vol. 6415, pp. 399-410). Berlin, Germany: SpringerLink. doi:10.1007/978-3-642-16558-0_34

Lefèvre, L., & Orgerie, A. (2010). Designing and evaluating an energy efficient cloud. *Springer Journal of Supercomputing*, *51*, 352–373. doi:10.1007/s11227-010-0414-2.

Li, W., & Ping, L. (2009). Trust model to enhance security and interoperability of cloud environment. In *Proceedings of the 1st International Conference on Cloud Computing*, (LNCS), (Vol. 5931, pp. 69-79). Berlin, Germany: SpringerLink. doi:10.1007/978-3-642-10665-1_7

Lombardi, F., & Pietro, R. (2010). *Secure virtualization for cloud computing*. Elsivier Journal of Network and Computer Application.

Lorenzi, F., Baldo, G., Costa, R., Abel, M., Bazzan, A., & Ricci, F. (2010). A trust model for multi agent recommendations. *Journal of Emerging Technologies in Web Intelligence*, *2*(4), 310–318. doi:10.4304/jetwi.2.4.310-318.

Marinos, A., & Briscoe, G. (2009). Community cloud computing. In *Proceedings of the 1st International Conference on Cloud Computing* (LNCS), (Vol. 5931, pp. 472-484). Berlin, Germany: SpringerLink. doi:10.1007/978-3-642-10665-1_43

Mármol, F., & Pérez, G. (2010). Towards pre-standardization of trust and reputation models for distributed and heterogeneous systems. *Elsivier Journal of Computer Standards & Interfaces*, *32*, 185–196. doi:10.1016/j.csi.2010.01.003.

Mell, P., & Grance, T. (2009). *The NIST definition of cloud computing*. Retrieved from http://www.nist.gov/itl/cloud/upload/cloud-def-v15.pdf

Mowbray, M., Pearson, S., & Shen, Y. (2010). Enhancing privacy in cloud computing via policy-based obfuscation. *Springer Journal of Supercomputing*. Retrieved from http://www.springerlink.com/content/7438g5n0382r6937/

Oh, T., Lim, S., Choi, Y., Park, K., Lee, H., & Choi, H. (2010). State of the art of network security perspectives in cloud computing. In *Proceedings of the First International Conference on Security-enriched Urban Computing and Smart Grid*, (Vol. 78, pp. 629-637). Berlin, Germany: SpringerLink. doi:10.1007/978-3-642-16444-6_79

Pal, S. (2013). Cloud computing: Security concerns and issues. In Bento, A., & Aggarwal, A. (Eds.), *Cloud Computing Service and Deployment Models: Layers and Management*. Hershey, PA: IGI Global.

Pal, S., Khatua, S., Chaki, N., & Sanyal, S. (2012). A new trusted and collaborative agent based approach for ensuring cloud security. *Annals of Faculty Engineering Hunedoara International Journal of Engineering*, *10*(1), 71–78.

Parrilli, D. (2010). Legal issues in grid and cloud computing. In K. StanoevskaSlabeva et al. (Eds.), Grid and Cloud Computing: A Business Perspective on Technology and Applications, (pp. 97-118). Berlin: Springer-Verlag. doi: doi:10.1007/978-3-642-051937_7.

Pearson, S., Shen, Y., & Mowbray, M. (2009). A privacy manager for cloud computing. In *Proceedings of the 1st International Conference on Cloud Computing* (LNCS), (Vol. 5931, pp. 90-106). Berlin, Germany: SpringerLink. doi:10.1007/978-3-642-10665-1_9

Qian, L., Luo, Z., Du, Y., & Guo, L. (2009). Cloud computing: An overview. In *Proceedings of the 1st International Conference on Cloud Computing* (LNCS), (Vol. 5931, pp. 626-631). Berlin, Germany: SpringerLink. doi:10.1007/978-3-642-10665-1_63

Ren, K., Wang, C., & Wang, Q. (2012). Security challenges for the public cloud. *IEEE Internet Computing, 16*(1), 69–73. doi:10.1109/MIC.2012.14.

Rohini, T. (2011). Comparative approach to cloud security models. In *Proceedings of the International Conference on Computing, Communication and Control*, (Vol. 125, pp. 170-177). Berlin, Germany: SpringerLink. doi:10.1007/978-3-642-18440-6_21

Sangroya, A., Kumar, S., Dhok, J., & Varma, V. (2010). Towards analyzing data security risks in cloud computing environments. In *Proceedings of the International Conference on Information Systems, Technology, and Management*, (Vol. 54, pp. 255-265). Berlin, Germany: SpringerLink. doi:10.1007/978-3-642-12035-0_25

Schmietendorf, A., Dumke, R., & Reitz, D. (2004). SLA management – Challenges in the context of web-service-based infrastructures. In *Proceedings of the IEEE International Conference on Web Services (ICWS'04)*. IEEE Computer Society. doi:10.1109/ICWS.2004.1314788

Sedayao, J., Su, S., Ma, X., Jiang, M., & Miao, K. (2009). A simple technique for securing data at rest stored in a computing cloud. In *Proceedings of the 1st International Conference on Cloud Computing* (LNCS), (Vol. 5931, pp. 553-558). Berlin, Germany: SpringerLink. doi: 10.1007/978-3-642-10665-1_51

Stanoevska-Slabeva, K., & Wozniak, T. (2010). Cloud basics – An introduction to cloud computing. In K. StanoevskaSlabeva et al. (Eds.), Grid and Cloud Computing: A Business Perspective on Technology and Applications (pp. 47-61). Berlin: Springer-Verlag. doi: doi:10.1007/978-3-642-051937_4.

Takabi, H., Joshi, J., & Ahn, G. (2010). SecureCloud: Towards a comprehensive security framework for cloud computing environments. In *Proceedings of the 34th Annual IEEE Computer Software and Applications Conference Workshops 2010*. IEEE Computer Society. doi:10.1109/COMPSACW.2010.74

William, C., Hosame, A., & Feng, S. (2010). Cloud service architecture and related standards. In Text Book of Transforming Enterprise Cloud Services, (pp. 87-132). Berlin: Springer Science+Business Media B.V. doi: doi:10.1007/978-90-481-9846-7_3.

Xu, J., Huang, R., Huang, W., & Yang, G. (2009). Secure document service for cloud computing. In *Proceedings of the 1st International Conference on Cloud Computing* (LNCS), (Vol. 5931, pp. 541-546). Berlin, Germany: SpringerLink. doi:10.1007/978-3-642-10665-1_49

Yan, L., Rong, C., & Zhao, G. (2009). Strengthen cloud computing security with federal identity management using hierarchical identity-based cryptography. In *Proceedings of the 1st International Conference on Cloud Computing* (LNCS), (Vol. 5931, pp. 167-177). Berlin, Germany: SpringerLink. doi:10.1007/978-3-642-10665-1_15

Yu, S., Wang, C., Ren, K., & Lou, W. (2010). Achieving secure, scalable, and fine-grained data access control in cloud computing. In *Proceeding INFOCOM'10 the 29th Conference on Information Communications*. ACM.

Zhang, Q., Cheng, L., & Boutaba, R. (2010). Cloud computing: State-of-the-art and research challenges. *Journal of Internet Services and Application, 1*, 7–18. doi:10.1007/s13174-010-0007-6.

Zhang, X., Xu, F., Liu, Y., Zhang, X., & Shen, C. (2006). Trust extended dynamic security model and its application in network. In *Proceedings of the Second International Conference on Mobile Ad-Hoc and Sensor Networks* (LNCS), (Vol. 4325, pp. 404-415). Berlin, Germany: SpringerLink. doi:10.1007/11943952_34

Zheng, J., Sun, Y., & Zhou, W. (2009). Cloud computing based Internet data center. In *Proceedings of the 1st International Conference on Cloud Computing* (LNCS), (Vol. 5931, pp. 700-704). Berlin, Germany: SpringerLink. doi:10.1007/978-3-642-10665-1_75

Zhu, J. (2010). Cloud computing technologies and applications. In B. Furht & A. Escalante (Eds.), Handbook of Cloud Computing, (pp. 21-45). Berlin: Springer Science+Business Media, LLC. doi: doi:10.1007/978-1-4419-6524-0_2.

Zissis, D., & Lekkas, D. (2012). Addressing cloud computing security issues. *Future Generation Computer Systems, 28*, 583–592. doi:10.1016/j.future.2010.12.006.

## KEY TERMS AND DEFINITIONS

**Cloud Computing:** Cloud computing is a rapidly growing technology allowing users to upload or retrieve their desired data from anywhere in the world with the help of the Internet at anytime in a 'pay as you go' basis. Thus making this key element an important and primary function for cloud computing. This technology reduces the geographical barriers and improves the scalability in the way we compute.

**Cloud Data Center (CDC):** In a cloud computing environment, most of the data and software that users and providers have access to, reside in one or more remote server(s), these are typically known as Cloud Data Center or CDC.

**Cloud Service Provider (CSP):** CSP provides the required services or information to the users in the system. The infrastructure and platforms are managed by the CSP in which the different cloud computing applications run.

**Cloud Service User (CSU):** CSU uses the desired services from the CSP in the system. Users typically access desired cloud applications with the help of the Internet anytime and anywhere in the world when required.

**Electronic Business (E-Business):** E-business is the system by which individuals or groups, through the use of the Internet, can buy or sell goods and services online without actual physical interaction with one another.

**Service Level Agreements (SLA):** SLA is the agreement between two parties in the system. Providing quality service and a secure environment within the system is the primary goal of the provider, while the consumer agrees to abide by all the rules and regulations set down by the provider creating a binding SLA.

**Virtualization in Cloud Computing:** Virtualization is the key part of the cloud computing technology, in which both the hardware and software programs are kept away from the end users. Only provides virtualized resources to the end users.

# Chapter 15
# Flashing in the Cloud:
## Shedding Some Light on NAND Flash Memory Storage Systems

**Jalil Boukhobza**
*University of Western Brittany, France*

## ABSTRACT

*Data and storage systems are one of the most important issues to tackle when dealing with cloud computing. Performance, in terms of data transfer and energy cost, predictability, and scalability are the main challenges researchers are faced with, and new techniques for storing, managing, and accessing huge amounts of data are required to make cloud computing technology feasible. With the emergence of flash memories in mass storage systems and the advantages it can provide in terms of speed and power efficiency as compared to traditional disks, one must rethink the storage system architectures accordingly. Indeed, the integration of flash memories is considered as a key technology to leverage the performance of data-centric computing. The purpose of this chapter is to introduce flash memory storage systems by focusing on their specific architectures and algorithms, and finally their integration into servers and data centers.*

## INTRODUCTION

The amount of data of different forms generated today is growing exponentially. In fact, it is growing faster than Moore's law. For instance, online data indexed by Google increased by more than a 56 factor from 2002 to 2009 (5 to 280 Exabyte) (Ranganathan, 2011). This trend is not limited to Web data, enterprise data volume is also growing very fast, it observed a cumulative growth rate of 173%. (Ranganathan, 2011; Winter, 2008).

In a recent study (Farmer, 2010), EMC forecasted that the amount of digital information

created annually will grow by a factor of 44 from 2009 to 2020. It also predicts that, by 2020, more than $1/3^{rd}$ of all digital information created annually will live or pass through the cloud, which underlines the need for huge additional storage capacity.

In fact, applications are becoming more and more data intensive: transaction processing, emails, search engines, TV, social networking, video and photo sharing, etc. Those data centric applications can operate on data in many ways such as: capturing, analyzing, processing, classifying, archiving, (Ranganathan, 2011) and so putting more and more stress on I/O storage systems performances. This tendency is also confirmed

DOI: 10.4018/978-1-4666-3934-8.ch015

for scientific computing in which phenomena understanding passes through large scale data analysis (Gray, 2006a).

In 2006, data centers in the US consumed more than 1.5% of the energy generated that year, and the percentage is estimated to increase by 18% per year (Zhang, Chang & Boutaba, 2010). Moreover, the storage system represents 20 to 40% of total energy consumption in typical data centers (Carter & Rajamani, 2010). Consequently, in addition to performance and capacity considerations, energy efficiency becomes one of the most critical metric to consider in order to address the increasing cost of operating a data center (Roberts, Kgil & Muldge, 2009b).

To partly reduce energy costs, big companies such as Microsoft, Google and Yahoo have built new data centers near to large and cost efficient power sources (Vasudevan et al., 2010). In fact, Data centers are more and more driven by the management of their limited energy budget (Carter & Rajamani, 2010).

Given that only 5% of the world's data is digitalized (Lyman, & Varian, 2003; Ranganathan, 2011), the growth in capacity, performance and energy need will continue for many years.

The confluence of these trends pushes to rethink traditional architectures and memory hierarchies and makes a large room for challenging research in the area of storage systems.

Among the "*10 obstacles and opportunities for cloud computing*" discussed in (Armbrust et al., 2010), three of them are directly related to data and storage systems: 1) data transfer bottleneck, 2) performance unpredictability due to disk I/O performance, and 3) storage scalability.

The traditional approach for building high performance and capacity storage systems consists in using arrays of disk drives and distributing data across the disks to provide parallel I/O along with error detection/correction to provide fault tolerance. Because of performance and energy limitations of this approach, while considering the huge amounts of data still to be stored and managed, and in addition to technological limits of disks (heat dissipation limits the increasing of the disk RPM to enhance performance), integrating non volatile memories, especially flash memories which are the most popular and mature candidate, can be part of the answer.

In fact, the advances in adoption of flash memories are considered as "*the most important technology changes pertinent to data centric computing*" (Ranganathan, 2011).

Flash memory displays high density, consumes low idle power and provides faster access time than hard disk drives (HDD) especially for random reads. But to be efficiently integrated in a given storage system, one must necessarily take into consideration its own peculiarities: read/write performance asymmetry, limited lifetime

Flash memory can be integrated onto storage servers in three ways (Roberts, Kgil & Muldge, 2009a): 1) as an extension of the memory system, 2) as a storage accelerator where flash is managed as a cache storing frequently accessed code and data and so reducing the number of accesses to HDD, or 3) as an alternative storage device where flash Solid State Drives (SSDs) are used as a replacement to (some) HDDs.

Because of cost considerations (approximately one order of magnitude more expensive than HDDs), flash based storage system will not replace disks systems in the mean term (Gurumurthi, 2009).

From the preceding elements, we can claim that flash memories will occupy more and more space in future cloud storage systems. So to take full advantage of their integration, one must understand its intricacies and operations, this is the main objective of the chapter.

The chapter is organized as follows: in the first section, we describe the structure and algorithms of flash memories by introducing the Flash Translation Layer (FTL) and its functionalities and we present a survey of the most recent FTL schemes. In the second section, we detail different cache mechanisms designed to ease the work of FTLs and to boost performance and increase flash memory lifetime.

In the last section of the chapter, we revisit the main contributions and issues on the integration of flash memories into servers and data centers.

## FLASH MEMORY BASICS

### Background

Semiconductor chips based non volatile memories (NVM) are becoming more than widely used and not only in the embedded system area. The market of NVM is to have an average annual growth of 69% up to 2015 according to MarketResearch.com (MarketReseach, 2012). This is not only due to the extensive usage of flash memories, but also to the emergence of new NVM technologies such as Ferroelectric RAM (FeRAM), Phase Change RAM (PCRAM), Magneto-resistive RAM (MRAM), etc. Even though some firms are beginning to move toward MRAM volume production, the most mature and commonly used NVM for data storage is still NAND flash memory.

Flash memories are based on floating gate transistors and are mainly of two types (other types exist such as divided bitline NOR, AND type, and other specific embedded technologies): 1) NOR and 2) NAND flash memories. They are named after the logic gates used as the basic structure for their implementation. NOR flash memories are more reliable (no need of error correction code), support bytes random access and have a lower density and a higher cost as compared to NAND flash memories. NOR flash memories are more suitable for storing code (Brewer & Gill, 2008). NAND flash memories are, by contrast, block addressed, but offer a higher storage density at a lower cost, and provide good performance for large read/write operations. Those properties make them more suitable for storing data (Brewer & Gill, 2008).

In this chapter, we are only concerned with NAND flash memories.

NAND flash memories can be classified into three categories: 1) Single Level Cell (SLC), 2) Multi Level Cell (MLC) and 3) Triple Level Cell (TLC). In SLC flash memories, only one bit can be stored in one cell, while in MLC, two bits can be stored, and 3 bits for TLC. From a bit density and cost per bit point of view, TLC is better than MLC that outperforms SLC. From a performance and reliability point of views, SLC performs better than MLC that surpasses TLC. While TLC is more used for low end media players, mobile GPS, and more generally non critical data applications that do not require frequent updates, MLC and SLC are used for more data intensive appliances such as SSDs, mobile phones, USB sticks and memory cards, etc.

Flash memory is structured as follows: it is composed of one or more chips; each chip is divided into multiple planes. A plane is composed of a fixed number of blocks, each of them encloses a fixed number of pages that is multiple of 32, typically 64. Current versions of flash memory have between 128 KB and 1024 KB blocks (with pages of 2-8KB). A page actually consists of user data space and a small metadata area also called Out-Of-Band (OOB) area that can contain information on Error Correction Code (ECC), page state, etc. (Winter, 2008).

Three operations can be performed on flash memories: read, write and erase. Read and write operations are achieved on pages, whilst erase operations are performed on blocks. Pages in a given block must be written sequentially (see Figure 1).

### Flash Memory Characteristics

As compared to traditional magnetic storage devices, NAND flash memories present a set of specific I/O characteristics, some can be considered as advantages and others as constraints:

- **Random reads**: Mechanical disks perform poorly on random read workloads due to mechanical latencies. Flash memories are

*Figure 1. Example of a flash memory structure assuming (unrealistic) blocks of four pages and planes of 64 blocks*

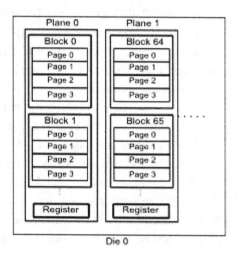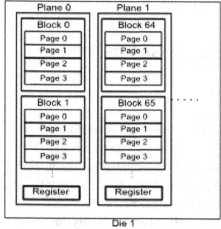

entirely electronic based components with no moving parts. Read access latency does no more depend on the physical location of data and so random reads are to perform as good as sequential ones. This makes flash memories more efficient and predictable for read operations as compared to traditional hard disk drives.

- **I/O performance asymmetry**: Another specificity of flash memories is that, unlike HDDs, reads are much faster that writes. This is due to electrical properties of the basic flash memory cell; it takes more time to program the cell to reach a stable state than simply to read it.

- **Sequential writes in a block**: In order to avoid write errors (due to electrical properties), writes must be performed sequentially within one block. Error correction codes (ECC) are implemented in hardware to cope with such errors.

- **Low power consumption**: Even though power consumption of flash based storage systems depends on its internal architecture and applied workload (Park, Kim, Urgaonkar, Lee & Seo, 2011), it remains more energy efficient than magnetic disks.

- **I/O interface**: One feature that makes easier the integration of flash memory based solid state drives (SSD) as a replacement for HDDs is the use of similar I/O interface. This characteristic can be considered as an advantage from a user point of view because no modifications have to be achieved on the operating system side. However, this may give the illusion that one must deal with flash memories the same way as with HDD which is far from being true. Note that for embedded systems, the I/O interface used for flash memories is different from past technologies.

- **Shock resistance**: This characteristic is another consequence of the absence of mechanical parts.

- **Write/Erase granularity asymmetry (C1)**: Writes are performed on pages while erase operations are realized on blocks.

- **Erase-before-write limitation (C2)**: This is one of the most important constraints on flash memories. One cannot directly overwrite data. A costly erase operation must be achieved before the data can be modified. Moreover, as mentioned earlier, erase operations are only performed on blocks.

This makes the data modification operation very costly if no specific mechanism is implemented to overcome it.

- **Limited number of Erase/Write cycles (C3)**: The average number of write/erase (W/E) cycles is approximately $10^5$ for SLC, $10^4$ for MLC, and 5000 for TLC (Bonnet & Bouganim, 2011). After the maximum number of erase cycles is reached, a given memory cell can no more retain data. Some spare storage cells exist on the chip to cope with such a wearing out.

## Flash Memory Support

In order to cope with the specific flash memory constraints noted C1, C2, and C3 in the preceding section, some mechanisms are implemented either in software or in hardware upstream of the flash memory array.

As one can see in Figure 2, those mechanisms can be either implemented in the flash memory controller through a hardware layer called the Flash Translation Layer (FTL), or through a software layer implemented by the hosting operating system that is a specific Flash File System (FFS).

In this chapter, we focus on FTL based flash memory rather than FFS based ones. The latter being dedicated to embedded system based storage such as set top boxes, mobile phones, etc.

The main FTL functionalities are the following:

- **Logical to physical block mapping**: Because of the erase-before-write (C2) limitation and unlike HDDs, data updates should be performed out-of-place meaning that the FTL must find out some free pages to write the new data. A mapping mechanism is then necessary to keep track of the physical location of the data (logical addresses). As will be described later, the mapping granularity can be as large as one block or as small as a page.

- **Garbage collection or cleaning policies**: Data updates infer basically two operations: 1) a copy to another page/block in addition to 2) the invalidation of the previous version. Over the time, invalid data tend to accumulate due to multiple modifications. So, in order to recover some clean blocks for future writes, a garbage collector

*Figure 2. Flash memory subsystems*

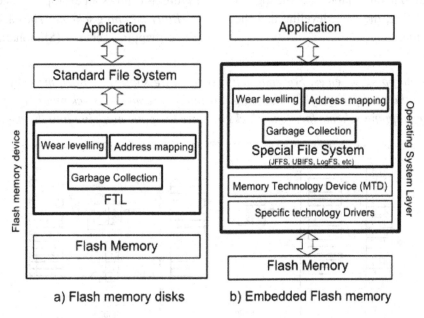

a) Flash memory disks     b) Embedded Flash memory

scans the flash memory for invalid space to recycle (erase-before-write constraint C2).

- **Wear leveling**: Due to data locality (temporal and/or spatial) observed in most workloads, writes can be concentrated in a given subset of memory blocks, and if we take into consideration the limited number of W/E cycle constraint (C3), we can easily deduce that some blocks may tend to wear out much faster than the others. In order to prevent this problem, wear leveling policies are implemented in the FTL to spread as evenly as possible the write/erase operations over the whole flash media. In addition to wear levelers, if some blocks can no more be used, because worn out prematurely, spare blocks exist to replace them.

In addition to the aforementioned mechanisms, FTL also manages the power off recovery and bad blocks management which is out of the scope of this chapter.

# FTL ALGORITHMS AND STRUCTURES

The three main functionalities of the FTL layer that are considered in this chapter are: the logical to physical mapping, the wear leveling and the garbage collection.

In this section we explore basic algorithms and structure of state-of-the-art FTLs.

## Basic Mapping Schemes

The mapping process consists in translating addresses coming from the host, and more specifically the file system layer, into physical addresses. This mapping is performed with the help of a specific table managed by the FTL. Basic mapping schemes are related to the granularity with which mapping information is managed. We can mainly classify them into page, block and hybrid mapping schemes (Chung et al., 2009).

*Page mapping scheme:* In page mapping scheme (Ban, 1995), each logical page is mapped to a given physical page independently from the other pages of the same block. This scheme is very flexible and presents very good performance. The main constraint of page mapping is the mapping table size as it grows according to the number of pages, it hardly fits into the FTL embedded RAM. If there are B blocks of P pages each, the mapping table would contain P*B entries, with each entry enclosing at least the physical address and the page state. For instance, for a 32GB flash memory of 2KB pages, if each mapping table entry consists in 8 bytes, 128MB are required which is unrealistic. Figure 3-a shows an example of such a scheme.

*Block mapping scheme:* The basic idea behind block mapping scheme (Shinohara, 1999) is to

*Figure 3. Basic mapping schemes. For simplicity reasons, we suppose a flash memory of 3 blocks of 4 pages each. In the example of hybrid mapping, the main scheme is a block mapping that can use an additional page mapping scheme for some blocks or store the page mapping into the metadata area.*

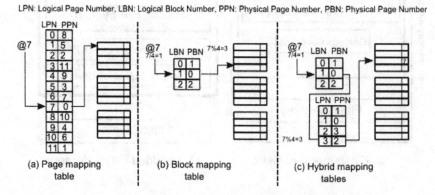

LPN: Logical Page Number, LBN: Logical Block Number, PPN: Physical Page Number, PBN: Physical Page Number

(a) Page mapping table

(b) Block mapping table

(c) Hybrid mapping tables

consider the granularity of a block rather than a page. The logical page address is composed of the logical block number and a page offset that is not modified by the mapping process. The mapping table, in this case, would contain B entries as compared to the P*B entries of the previous mapping scheme. For the same example and for blocks of 64 pages, 2MB are required for the table (additionally, we need less bytes per table entry). Even though block mapping is more feasible in terms of mapping table size, it presents an important disadvantage. When overwriting the same data in a given page, the whole block containing the page should be copied and remapped to a new free block by copying the valid and updated data. This operation happens because in a given block, offsets (page number) are always preserved. An example of such a mapping is shown in Figure 3-b.

*Hybrid mapping schemes:* Many hybrid schemes have been proposed to overcome the shortcomings of page and block mapping schemes. Hybrid schemes use both block and page mapping. Many of them use a global block map and maintain a page mapping for some given blocks. Only the block mapping table and a limited page mapping table are maintained in the SRAM. An example of such a mapping is shown in Figure 3-c.

## More Complex Mapping Schemes

In order to design a good FTL mapping scheme, one have to consider the two main drawbacks of page and block mapping: the SRAM usage for storing the (page) mapping table and the cost of additional block copies when remapping blocks.

In order to use less SRAM to store the mapping table, many FTLs are based on a global block mapping and store only some pages mapping table entries for some blocks in SRAM. Other FTLs use page mapping scheme but store part of the table on the flash media itself.

To minimize the cost of copying a whole block for each data modification, many FTLs try to absorb frequent data modification by preventing systematic block copy. This is achieved by providing additional blocks or pages, called log pages and log blocks, to use in case of a data update. Log pages can be located on the same block or in another one. This extra flash memory volume is hidden to the applicative level. For instance, when a page is modified, it is copied to the log page without performing a block copy and erase operation, and the first page version is then invalidated.

In this section, we briefly describe state-of-the-art FTLs based on these solutions.

*Mitsubishi (Shinohara, 1999):* It is a block mapping FTL that uses log pages located within the block itself. One physical block is therefore composed of general pages (data area) and log pages (spare area) called *space sectors*. Whenever a given page is updated, the FTL searches for the first free available page in the space sector area. Once found, the concerned page number (logical address) is written to the metadata area of the log page. When there are no more free pages available in the space area, and a new update operation occurs, the valid pages are copied to a new free block and the original block is erased after updating the mapping table. Mitsubishi FTL reduces the global number of copy and erase operations of classical block mapping scheme, and the price to pay is relative to the number of log pages per block. For instance, if a block is composed of 64 pages, adding two pages into the space sectors increases the percentage of spare space by 3.1%.

*M-Systems (Ban, 1999):* M-Systems FTL uses block mapping with log pages allocated in separate blocks. Each logical block is mapped to two physical blocks. When a page update happens, data are copied to the replacement block without inducing a block copy and erase operation. There exists two different algorithms named ANAND and FMAX. In ANAND, when an update of a page takes place, data are written in the replacement block by respecting the page offset. This means that a second modification of the same page would provoke a block merge operation, which means that the valid data of both the original and replacement blocks are copied to a free one. FMAX optimizes ANAND algorithm by allowing to place modified pages anywhere in the replacement block. This is made possible by storing the offsets into the metadata area of each written page. The merge operation happens consequently when the replacement block does not contain any free pages. AFTL (Wu & Kuo, 2006), for Adaptive Two-level management for FTL is a hybrid FTL that tries to optimize FMAX by dedicating a page mapping table for replacement blocks. The table is stored in SRAM and accelerates the search for the modified data.

*RNFTL (Wang, Liu, Wang, Qin & Guan, 2010):* Reuse-aware NAND FTL is a block mapping scheme that tries to reduce the number of merge operations when dealing with log blocks. Authors relied on statistics they performed on the occupation of the merged blocks. They observed that only 46% of the original blocks are full of data when merged. Their contribution consists in using the available free space of those data blocks as log pages for other blocks to reduce the number of merge operations. The merge operation in RNFTL happens only if the number of valid pages is above a fixed threshold.

*CNFTL (Hsieh, Tsai, Kuo & Lee, 2008):* Configurable NAND FTL allows having more flexibility for trading the memory usage. CNFTL resembles M-Systems FTL, but it provides a tunable mapping table by managing tables by regions (of blocks) rather than managing the whole flash memory. In addition, CNFTL addressing schemes allows a high flexibility allowing a one-to-many log page mechanism.

*BAST (Kim, Kim, Noh, Min & Cho, 2002):* Block Associative Sector Translation FTL is very similar to FMAX M-Systems FTL, but it limits the number of blocks used as log blocks. Since BAST maintains less space for the log-blocks, it can manage it more efficiently by the use of page level mapping table. BAST, however, allocates only one block from the log block pool to a given logical block. From a log block point of view, this means that we cannot have a mix of pages coming from different data blocks. A merge operation occurs whenever a new block (or a modified page) is updated while all the log blocks are allocated, or whenever a data update occurs while the log block is full of valid pages. Therefore valid data from log and data blocks are merged and copied to a free block.

*FAST (Lee et al., 2007):* The main problem with BAST is the level of associatively that is fixed to a block. That means that one data block cannot use more than one log-block at a time. This may provoke many merge operations with nearly free log-blocks. FAST, a Fully Associative Sector Translation FTL tries to make a better usage of log-blocks. Log-blocks are divided into two regions, one is dedicated for sequentially written log blocks and that behaves just like BAST, and another region, dedicated for random data, which contain a pool of log blocks in which all the log pages are used in a fully associative way, which maximizes the occupation of log blocks. The random region is managed with a page mapping table which makes FAST a hybrid mapping FTL.

*LAST (Lee, Shin, Kim & Kim, 2008):* Locality Aware Sector Translation (LAST) tries to cope with the costly merge operations of FAST that are due to the presence of many pages from different blocks into the random region log blocks. This is achieved by adding sequential locality detection based on the request size. The authors state that the bigger the request size, the better its chance to be sequentially accessed in the next requests. Big data requests (above a fixed threshold) are hence redirected toward the sequential region. LAST also partitions the random region into hot and cold regions according to temporal locality to cope with the high cost of merge operations. By doing so, LAST generates less merge operations.

*EAST (Kwon & Chung, 2008):* Even though some improvements have been noted on BAST with the help of FAST, according to Kwon (2008), there are still blocks that are merged with a bad occupancy rate. Their second observation is that merge operations on the random log region is very expensive since many pages come from different blocks (same observations as LAST). Efficient and Advanced Space management Technique (EAST) proposed two solutions for the aforementioned drawbacks. To avoid wasting space, EAST does not isolate sequentially and randomly accessed data into two different pools but uses in-place and out-of-place techniques to copy data to log blocks. EAST writes data into log blocks without modifying the offset (in-place) in a first pace, and if an additional data modification happens for the same page, it uses the rest of the log-block free pages as independent log-pages (with different offset) as in FMAX. To cope with the second drawback, EAST associates each log block with one data block but can associate a given number of log blocks to the same data block. This associativity depends on the erase and read time in addition to the number of pages per block.

*KAST (Cho, Shin & Eom, 2009):* The objective of K-Associative sector translation FTL is to limit the maximum time of merge operations by limiting the log block associatively to cope with real time predictability constraint. One of the drawbacks of FAST, as noted in LAST, is the log block associatively in the random region making the merge operation expensive. KAST allows having more than one sequential log block that can be changed to random log block if no subsequent sequential pattern is detected.

*FASTer (Lim, Lee & Moon, 2010):* It is an optimized version of FAST for OLTP workloads. It uses a second chance mechanism to better manage temporal locality. This mechanism consists in delaying the merge operation between log and data blocks and so giving a second chance for valid data of victim log blocks to stay in the log area to avoid frequent merge operations. FASTer also uses an isolation area for cold pages and progressively merge them in order to minimize the variance of response times.

*HFTL (Lee, Hyun & Lee, 2009):* Hybrid FTL also tries to cope with the lack of temporal locality consideration in FAST FTL. It does so by sepa-

rating hot and cold data and adaptively maps hot data using page mapping scheme and cold ones with a log-block mapping scheme, namely FAST.

*STAFF (Chung & Park, 2007):* State Transition Applied Fast FTL is a hybrid mapping FTL based on block mapping. It uses a state transition scheme that gives a specific state for each physical block. A block can be in 1) a free (F) state if it has been erased, 2) in a modified (M) in-place state if some pages are written with the same offset as the logical address, 3) in a complete in-place (S) state, which is a special case of the M state where all the pages have been written, 4) in the modified out-of-place (N) state in which one or many pages are written with a different offset than the logical one, or in 5) an obsolete (O) state if no valid data are present in the block

The following transitions are possible:

1.  **From F to M:** When a first write to a given page is issued.
2.  **From M to S:** When the whole pages writes are performed sequentially.
3.  **From M to N:** When some pages are modified while there is still some free pages in the concerned block, in that case modified data are written in the same block but to different offsets and a page mapping table is maintained for the block.
4.  **From S to O:** When the entire block has been written sequentially and a new write operation occurs, the data are copied to a free block that changes to the S state, and the previous block is marked with a O state.
5.  **From N to O:** When all the pages of the block in the N state have been written (with some data in out-of-place manner) and another write occurs.
6.  **From O to F:** The erase operation when a free block is needed. As all the blocks in the N state are mapped using a page mapping table hosted in SRAM.

The main issue with STAFF is the unpredictability of the SRAM usage. The number of N blocks (maintained with a page table) depends highly on the workload.

*SAST (Park, et al., 2008):* Set Associative Sector Translation FTL proposed by Park et al. (2008) manages a global set of blocks mapping table with a specific log block pool. A page mapping table is maintained for log blocks. The log page mapping table also separates hot and cold data, where the temperature is related to the number of accesses, in order to reduce the price of merge operations. An adaptive version of SAST (Koo & Shin, 2009) exists that allows to adapt the associatively according to the workload characteristics.

*Superblock FTL (Jung, Kang, Jo, Kim & Lee, 2010):* Is a hybrid mapping system similar to SAST with the difference that the page mapping table of Superblock FTL is stored into the flash memory metadata area and not into the SRAM.

*DFTL (Gupta, Kim & Urgaonkar, 2009):* Demand based FTL is a purely page mapped FTL that caches part of the mapping table, consisting of frequently accessed addresses, into the SRAM. The rest of the mapping table is stored in the flash memory itself, which can represent an important volume. CDFTL (Qin, Wang, Liu & Shaom, 2010) proposes a two level caching mechanism to enhance DFTL to exploit both temporal (1st level cache) and spatial locality (2nd level cache) of workloads. The spatial locality was not taken into account in DFTL.

*CFTL (Park, Debnath, & Du, 2009):* Convertible FTL tries to solve the shortcomings of DFTL that are the bad performance for read operations due to address translation latencies and the fact that it does not take into account spatial locality. CFTL provides an adaptive FTL in terms of block and page mapping. CFTL adapts according to the workload with the idea that read intensive workloads performs well with block mapping while write intensive workloads prefer page mapping for data modification reasons. CFTL also uses a caching strategy for both block and page mapping tables and exploits both temporal and spatial locality for cache management of the mapping table.

*S-FTL (Jiang, Zhang, Yuan, Hu & Chen, 2011):* Spatial locality aware FTL is another page mapping FTL based on caching part of the mapping table. S-FTL reduces the sizes of the mapping table to put into the cache by exploiting the sequentiality of the workload. In S-FTL, if the workload is sequential, there is no need to load in the cache every page containing the mapping information of the accessed data, sequential addresses are inferred by calculating the corresponding offset.

*WAFTL (Wei et al., 2011):* The Workload Adaptive FTL dynamically stores data according to their access pattern into either a page mapped blocks (PMB) or a block mapping blocks (BMB) just like CFTL. PMB stores random data and partial updates while BMB stores sequential data and mapping tables. WAFTL also uses a part of the flash memory to buffer sequential writes before sending them to BMB or PMB. WAFTL maintains only a part of the page mapping table into SRAM.

Table 1 summarizes the different FTL characteristics.

## Wear Leveling Algorithms

As described earlier, each flash memory cell can support a limited number of W/E cycles. Beyond this limit, the cell becomes unusable. The objective of wear leveling techniques is to keep the whole flash memory volume usable as long as possible. To do so, the system has to ensure an even wear of memory cells.

In this chapter, we use the same differentiation between wear leveling and garbage collection as Kwon et al. (2011). Wear leveling is concerned by block level management while garbage collection is concerned by page level management as it is explained in the following.

Wear leveling algorithms are based on the number of erase operations performed on a given block. If this number is smaller than the average of all the flash memory blocks, the block is said to be

*Table 1. This table summarizes the characteristics of state-of-the-art FTLs. We distinguish between hybrid mapping (page and block map at the same level) and block mapping for the primary mapping scheme column. "In-place" and "out-of-place" refer to associativity of pages in the log blocks while "one to one" and "many to many" refers to how data blocks are mapped to log blocks.*

| | Primary mapping scheme | Mapping scheme properties | Characteristics |
|---|---|---|---|
| **Mitsubishi** | Block | Log pages in each data block / out-of-place | Log pages mapping stored in metadata area |
| **M-Systems ANAND** | Block | 1 to 1 Log blocks / in-place | Same offset in log and data blocks |
| **M-Systems FMAX** | Block | 1 to 1 Log blocks / out-of-place | Log pages mapping stored in metadata area |
| **AFTL** | Block | 1 to 1 Log blocks / out-of-place | Log pages mapping table stored in SRAM |
| **RNFTL** | Block | Log blocks then log pages / in and out-of-place | Fill log blocks with pages from other data blocks to optimize merge operations |
| **CNFTL** | Block | One-to-many / Log page / out-of-place | Optimize SRAM mapping table usage by partitioning the flash memory. |
| **BAST** | Block | One-to-one / Log-block / in-place | Page mapped pool of log blocks |
| **FAST** | Block | Many-to-many / log-blocks / in and out-of-place | In-place for the sequential log block and out-of-place for the random region that is managed with page mapping table. |
| **LAST** | Block | Many-to-many / log-blocks / in or out-of-place | Additional spatial locality detection according to request size. Random log region partitioning according to hot / cold data (temporal locality) |
| **EAST** | Block | Many-to-many / log-blocks / in and out-of-place | Writing in-place and fill the rest of the log block in out-of-place. Limited associatively. No more rand. and seq. region. |
| **KAST** | Block | Many-to-many / log-blocks / in and out-of-place | More than one sequential blocks in the seq. region. Limited (K) associatively to limit the merge operation time. |
| **FASTer** | Block | Many-to-many / log-blocks / in and out-of-place | FAST+ second chance algorithm in log blocks for temporal locality. |
| **HTFL** | Hybrid | Page map + block map (with log block – FAST) | Detecting hot data: mapped by page, and cold data: mapped by blocks with log blocks |
| **STAFF** | Hybrid | State transition / state stored in metadata/ page map for N state and block map for the rest | Sequential updates managed with block mapping while random ones managed with page mapping |
| **SAST** | Block | Block set / log-blocks and log-pages / Many-to-many / in and out-of-place | Page mapping for log blocks (block set). Cold / hot data separation for log-page mapping. Limited associatively. A-SAST: adapt associatively to workload |
| **Superblock FTL** | Block | Block set / log-blocks and log-pages / Many-to-many / in and out-of-place | Page mapping for log pages (block set) stored in metadata area. Temporal and spatial locality detection. |
| **DFTL** | Page | Reserved flash area for the page table | Caching part of the page mapping table using spatial locality. |
| **CDFTL** | Page | Reserved flash area for the page table | 2 level cache: 1st level for spatial locality and 2nd level for temporal locality. |

*continued on following page*

*Table 1. Continued*

| | Primary mapping scheme | Mapping scheme properties | Characteristics |
|---|---|---|---|
| **CFTL** | Hybrid | Reserved flash area for the page and block table / Adaptive FTL | Block map for read intensive / page map for write intensive workloads. Caching of parts the mapping tables: spatial and temporal locality. |
| **SFTL** | Page | Reserved flash area for the page table | Reduces the use of mapping table by using offsets for sequential accesses. |
| **WAFTL** | Hybrid | Reserved flash area for the page and block table / Adaptive FTL | Block mapping for sequential data and page mapping for random data. Buffer on flash to detect sequentiality |

cold. Conversely, if it is higher than the average, it is said to be hot. Wear leveling algorithms try to maintain the gap between hot and cold blocks as small as possible. This can be achieved by swapping data from hot blocks (more exactly data that made that block hot) and cold blocks. This operation is costly and cannot be performed many times. In fact, one has to compromise between wear leveling and performance.

We can group wear leveling algorithms into two categories: those based on the erase number count, and those based on write counts.

*Erase count based wear levelers:* In these algorithms the erase count is maintained for each block and stored whether in the mapping table or in the block metadata. The wear leveler is launched whenever a given disparity is observed between blocks erase count. It is easier to monitor such algorithms when the count is stored in SRAM, otherwise partial read/write operations have to be performed in the block metadata area, and the number of partial (metadata) writes in flash memory pages is generally limited.

One of the wear leveling techniques based on erase count was described in (Assar, Namazie & Estakhri, 1995) and called dual pool. It refers to two additional tables used with the standard block mapping table: hot-block and cold-block table. The hot-block table contains a given number of overused empty blocks sorted according to the number of erase count in descending order,

while the cold-block table contains underused free blocks sorted in the ascending order. In dual pool algorithm, each time a free block is required, it is taken from the cold block table and the hot blocks stay unused. Periodically, the system recalculates the average erase count number and the difference between each block's erase count and the calculated average. It then compares the difference with a given threshold and according to the result, it puts the respective block into the hot or cold table. The smaller the threshold, the better the wear leveling and the more it impacts performance because of the generated data movements. Some wear levelers do only take into account the erased (free) blocks in the wear leveling process while others consider the entire space. More specifically, if one block contains rarely modified data (called static or cold data), some wear levelers (Assar et al., 1995; Chang, Qawami & Sabet-Sharghi, 2006) copy that data into hot / dynamic regions.

*Write count based wear levelers:* They are algorithms that maintain a count of write operations performed on blocks or set of blocks. In (Achiwa, Yamamoto & Yamagata, 1999), a write count is preserved in the SRAM, in addition to block erase count, and is updated each time the write is performed on the block. Blocks with a given erase count are grouped together. The objective of the wear leveler is to store highly written data to the least frequently erased blocks and to store rarely written data into the most frequently erased blocks.

In (Chang, 2007), the system does the same as in (Assar et al., 1995) but by maintaining, this time, the number of write accesses rather than the erasures. It manages two tables, one for the highly written blocks and a second for the less written ones. The mechanism swaps data between highly and lowly accessed regions, however in (Chang, 2007) the two tables have flexible sizes that depend upon the workloads.

Another wear leveling category described in (Kwon, Ranjitkar, Ko & Chung, 2011) consists in considering groups of blocks as cold/hot rather than blocks. This is more an optimization, in our point of view, than a category by itself. Managing groups instead of blocks reduces very much the SRAM usage necessary to control the wear leveling (Lofgren, Norman, Thelin & Gupta, 2005; Conley, 2005).

## Garbage Collection Algorithms

Garbage collection is the process used in FTL to recycle free space from previously invalidated pages in different blocks. The term of cleaning policy or algorithm can also be used (Kwon et al., 2011).

In (Chiang & Chang; 1999) a garbage collector should answer given number of questions: 1) when the garbage collector should be launched, 2) which blocks should be concerned by the garbage collection operation and how many of them should be chosen, 3) How should valid data be written out in the new blocks. We omitted the last task that is "where to write the new data" because we think that this is the job of the wear leveler. The garbage collection can also be coupled with the wear leveler to operate synchronously like in the JFFS file system (Woodhouse, 2001).

A good garbage collector should minimize the cleaning costs while maximizing the recycled space without being very intrusive. This cost in-cludes the number of erase operations and valid data copies.

Garbage collectors are generally automatically launched when the number of free blocks passes under a predefined threshold and optionally triggered during I/O timeouts.

One of the main metrics taken into account when choosing a dirty block to recycle, is the ratio of dirty pages in the given block or group of blocks. To do so, garbage collectors consider the state of each page, which can be very resource consuming. Some garbage collectors maintain the page state table in SRAM while others just use the metadata area of each page.

Basic garbage collectors copy valid pages from the dirty blocks into newly allocated blocks and erase the previous ones.

Yet again, the hot/cold data separation is very important to perform garbage collection, and this partly answers the question about how data should be written to new blocks. In order to perform a good garbage collection, one has to separate cold and hot data to different blocks. Indeed, if cold and hot data coexist in a given block, there is a higher chance that garbage collector will be called due to hot data updates. This will induce a costly copy of cold data. Conversely, if the block contains only hot data, there is a higher probability that only an erase operation is needed (no data copy) since all the pages are hot (updated).

Many contributions were based upon this hot/cold data separation (Chiang, Cheng & Wu, 2008; Chang & Kuo, 2002; Syu & Chen, 2005; Hsieh, Kuo & Chang, 2006; Cho et al., 2009). For instance, Dynamic dAta Clustering (DAC) (Chiang et al., 2008) partitions the flash memory into many regions according to the update frequencies. The two levels LRU (Chang & Kuo, 2002) uses two lists: one containing hot block address list managed in LRU fashion and another one containing candidate (to be hot if accessed once again) block addresses.

Having an efficient hot/cold separation helps in selecting the dirty block/group to clean up. The main objective of the selection policy is to free the higher amount of blocks at the lower cost, which implies selecting the block/group containing the less valid data and less usable space. The greedy policy simply selects the block with the higher number of invalid pages. This policy can be very efficient if the workload is accessing the flash memory blocks uniformly.

The number of dirty pages contained in the block/group, is however always taken in consideration when calculating the cost benefit of cleaning some blocks. In (Kawaguchi, Nishioka & Motoda, 1995), the utilization of the block "u" is taken into consideration in addition to the elapsed time since the most recent modification (age in the equation): age * (1-u)/2*u. The terms "2u" and "1-u" respectively represent the cost for copying valid data (read and write) and the free space reclaimed. The block(s) with the highest score is/are chosen to be cleaned. In Cost Age Times (CAT) policy (Chiang, Chang, 1999), hot blocks are given more time to accumulate invalid data, the equation that calculates the score is: Cleaning_cost * (1/age) * Number_of_cleaning, where the cleaning cost is u/(1-u) and the number of cleanings is the number of erase operations.

Every garbage collection policy has its own advantages and drawbacks and can be very closely related to the wear leveling mechanism and the underlying mapping scheme.

In addition to FTL algorithms, some buffering mechanisms can contribute in optimizing the performance of flash based storage systems. The next section reviews some flash specific caching systems.

## CACHE ALGORITHMS FOR OPTIMIZING FLASH BASED SYSTEMS

In order to optimize the performance of write operations, many implementations of cache buf-

fers placed on top of the FTL have been proposed. Those buffers allow mainly two optimizations:

1. Absorbing some page/block writes at the cache level and thus avoiding reporting them to the flash media.
2. Trying to reveal sequentiality by buffering write operations and reorganizing them before sending them to the flash media.

In this section, some state-of-the-art caching mechanisms are reviewed.

*CFLRU (Clean First LRU) (Park, Jung, Kang, Kim & Lee, 2006):* This algorithm takes into account the read/write asymmetry cost in the page replacement policy of caches for flash systems. It uses an LRU list divided into two regions: the working region containing recently used pages, and the clean-first region containing pages that are candidate for eviction. CFLRU evicts first clean pages that do not generate any flash write operations, if not possible it cleans a dirty page in LRU manner. This algorithm can be interesting if one needs both a read and a write cache and if they have to cohabit in the same pool.

*FAB (Flash Aware Buffer policy) (Jo, Kang, Park, Kim & Lee, 2006):* Keeps a given number of pages in the buffer. FAB is managed in an LRU order, a group of pages is moved to the beginning of the list whenever one page of the group is accessed. For selecting the victim pages, FAB takes into account the biggest group of pages that belongs to the same block. When many blocks can be chosen as victim, recency is taken into consideration.

*CLC (Cold and Largest Cluster) (Kang, Park, Jung, Shim & Cha, 2009):* System implements two pools of clusters of pages in the cache, a size-independent and a size-dependant pool. A cluster (named *group* in FAB) is a set of pages belonging to the same block. The size independent pool receives write operations and is managed in LRU, when there is no more space in the size independent pool, the least recently used cluster is moved to the size dependent pool where it is stored according to the number of pages it contains. When a victim is to be selected for flushing, the biggest cluster of the size dependent pool is evicted.

*BPLRU (Block Padding Least Recently Used) (Kim & Ahn, 2008):* Is a write buffer that uses three main techniques: 1) block level LRU management scheme, 2) page padding: before flushing a victim block, it reads clean pages from the flash memory to fill blocks in the cache, and 3) LRU compensation: moving sequentially written blocks to the tail of the LRU.

*BPAC (Block-Page Adaptive Cache) (Wu, Eckart & He, 2010):* Partitions the cache into two parts: an LRU page list used to store data with high temporal locality, and a list of blocks divided into two data clusters organized by recency and size.

*LB-Clock (Debnath, Subramanya, Du & Lilja, 2009):* Large Block Clock uses clock block replacement algorithms. The block to evict is the one for which the reference bit is 0 and that contains the largest number of pages. This algorithm uses both recency and block space utilization metrics.

*PUD-LRU (Hu, Jiang, Tian & Xu, 2010):* Predicted average Update Distance LRU is a dual pool buffer that mixes frequency and recency to decide which block to evict depending on the predicted update distance frequency.

All the described caching systems are to be used above an FTL to optimize its performance. Some give better performance on specific FTLs.

*C-lash (Cache for flash) (Boukhobza, Olivier, & Rubini, 2011; Boukhobza & Olivier, 2011):* Is different from the previous cache systems as it does not suppose the existence of an underlying wear leveler and garbage collector. C-lash tries to explore what would be the performance if we use flash memories just like disks with only a cache (specific to flash architectures) upon the flash array. It uses a dual pool cache composed from a page space that maintains accessed pages and a block space managed in LRU and that receives biggest cluster of pages (belonging to the same block) from the page space. Flushing is performed

following an LRU algorithm on the block space. C-lash shows better performances for a set of workloads as compared to some efficient FTLs, but it does not well manage very small intensive random writes.

Most of the proposed buffer systems use page and block granularities and are based upon recency, frequency. They highly increase the performance of the FTL systems. In our opinion, one way to make those buffering techniques more efficient is to move toward a more collaborative cache/ FTL schemes.

## INTEGRATION INTO DATA SERVERS

After having described the intricacies of flash memories, we try in this section, to depict how flash memories can be integrated into larger storage architectures, and how they can leverage performance and energy efficiency in data intensive application in the Cloud.

In order to apprehend the integration of flash memories into storage system architectures, one must understand their performance behavior and how does it compare to traditional magnetic drives. The objective of the next section is to position flash memory according to traditional drives from a performance and energy points of view.

### Performance and Energy Considerations of Flash Memories

We observed from 2006 up to now nearly an exponential growth of published work on flash memories. There is a real enthusiasm of researchers for this technology as they see it as candidate to upgrade storage systems.

During the last couple of years, a large number of studies on performance measurements, modeling and analysis have been achieved on flash based systems. We try to briefly summarize their main results in this section.

*Flash disks outperform hard disk drives* in most cases:

- Sequential read and write performance in flash memories are at least as good as in HDD and generally better.
- Random read performance in flash memories is far better than in HDDs.
- Performance of random writes is very dependent on the internal architecture of the flash disk. Some flash disks perform better than HDD while others give very bad performances. However strided write patterns do perform better in flash disks, this is probably due to efficient caching mechanisms and/or efficient FTLs.
- Flash disks are generally always outperforming disks from the energy consumption point of view (more than 5 times better in some specific cases) but here again it highly depends on the nature of the workload and the flash disk internals (Park et al., 2011).

*Flash disk performance is heterogeneous:* Even though flash disks are outperforming HDDs, they show big disparities in both performance and energy consumption according to the used technology (SLC, MLC, or TLC), the internal structure, and workload. In (Grupp et al., 2009), performance and energy measurements on different flash disks show big disparities. From the performance point of view, latency and bandwidth have been measured and it was observed that: 1) performance fluctuations between SSDs from different constructors and between different technologies can be significant, 2) a wide performance asymmetry between read and write performances. From the energy point of view, the same conclusions were drawn, for instance the average read power of a single operation can vary from 7,4 mW (SLC) to 31.1 mW (MLC) (Grupp et al., 2009). Another important metric is the provisioning space left for the work of the FTL. The more free space we have, the better is the performance of the FTL (in general), and this is a very new situation as this parameter did have no impact on disk design (if one do not consider the fragmentation problem). So FTL designers try to save some free space to insure a minimal performance limit while keeping the usable data space percentage above a certain bound.

As stated in (Bonnet & Bouganim, 2011), what database system designers should have to efficiently use flash memory based storage systems, is a clear distinction between well and bad performing I/O patterns. Unfortunately, up to now, even though we can have a clear position for some patterns, it is still ambiguous for others. The I/O behavior is not predictable enough for DBMS designers and depends on the SSD internal structure.

*Flash memory design space is large:* The main reason behind flash memory disk different behaviors is the very large design space the constructors have to deal with. In addition to the use of different FTLs (mapping, wear leveling and garbage collectors), (Cagdas & Jacob, 2009) performance can be tuned by varying the degree of concurrency of accesses by partitioning flash memory in different topologies. This performance variation is also relevant for the energy consumption metric (Park et al., 2011). In (Agrawal et al., 2008), the authors also emphasize on the different design tradeoffs for SSDs like the diverse parallel schemes (ganging interleaving, etc.) and interconnect density. Authors also cite the product market category that drives the design of flash memories: 1) consumer portable storage like music players, 2) laptop disk replacement, and 3) enterprise/database accelerators. According to the category, awaited performance can grow by two orders of magnitude.

As a conclusion, flash memories are outperforming disks for many workloads except very random writes, but they does not present to the applicative layer a homogeneous enough model to lie upon for precisely optimizing performance. Despite this drawback (in addition to cost), they represent a serious alternative for many applications and an indispensable solution for energy constrained systems. This technology is maturing very rapidly and we have no doubt on the fact that the raised problems will be addressed very soon.

## Architecting Flash Memories in Data Servers

Gray (2006b) rightly stated that flash memories are to disks what disks were to tapes. However, tapes have not yet disappeared and so one has not to bury disks prematurely. Flash memories are still very expensive and not mature enough (even if it grows in maturity very fast) because there is not enough feedback and hindsight on the current implementations in enterprise systems. It is too early to draw precise conclusions on the reliability and lifetime of flash memories.

The integration of flash memories onto data center servers can follow three main models according to Roberts (2009), to which we added a last category that can encompass two main possibilities as discussed later:

- Flash memory as an extension of system memory.
- Flash memory as a storage accelerator.

- Flash memory as an alternative storage device.
- Flash memory as a complementary storage device.

We will give, in this section, an overview of each type of integration by giving some design and implementation examples (see Figure 4).

*Extension of the system memory:* As flash memory presents performances that are in between DRAM and disks, it can be integrated with both. Flash memory can be combined to the system memory principally for power saving reasons. Another reason can also be the difficulty to integrate more DRAM for electrical and interfacing constraints. To do so, operating systems must be aware of this new memory hierarchy organization. The operating system kernel should be modified to take into account flash memory peculiarities. Data placement issues must be managed in addition to all flash memory issues treated earlier in this chapter.

FlashCache (Roberts et al., 2009a) is a good example of such tiered system where the DRAM size is reduced and flash memory added and used as a file cache buffer of the Linux kernel. Extending the DRAM with flash memory allows to achieve three main optimizations according to the authors:

*Figure 4. Flash memory integration models*

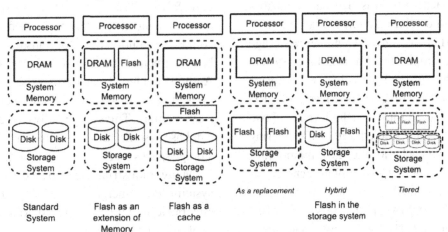

1) reducing the system power consumption as flash memory consumes less than DRAM especially the idle power, 2) reducing the overall main memory cost as flash memory is cheaper than DRAM, and 3) insuring a quicker startup as there is no need to warm up the flash memory thanks to its nonvolatile property. Obviously, this does not go without an increase in the memory hierarchy complexity. This study has also been extended to PCRAM caches (Roberts et al., 2009a).

Another work concerning this type of integration is (Kang, Lee & Moon, 2012), in which the authors presented FaCE (Flash as a Cache Extension) for a recoverable database. FaCE uses flavors of LRU and FIFO algorithms on DRAM and flash and takes advantage of non-volatility of flash to support database recovery, it was shown to give very good performance for an OLTP (OnLine Transaction Processing) benchmark (TPC-C).

*Storage accelerator (flash as a cache):* The flash memory here is used as a cache for the underlying storage system thereby reducing accesses to HDDs gaining performance and power. The flash storage management, in this case, is achieved by the user application, device driver stack and the firmware (for instance FlashPCI Express). The flash storage in that case should be shared between the different applications (and kernel) that make use of it.

This model allows a short term integration of flash memories into traditional memory hierarchy.

This approach has been used in many contributions linked to database systems. The 3LA (Ou & Härder, 2011), or 3 *Layer Architecture* storage system, is an example of such a cache based system where a flash memory layer is inserted between the DRAM and the disk layers. Flavors of LRU algorithms are used for the cache levels and two cache structures are studied: either considering the DRAM as a cache for the flash memory, or considering both of them as a global cache avoiding to have the same data on both.

In (Creasey, 2005) was proposed one of the first attempts to integrate flash memory technology as complementary cache (in addition to DRAM) of a HDD in order to optimize I/O performance and energy consumption in laptops.

*Alternative storage device:* In this model, the flash disk is supposed to replace HDDs. This would improve latency, throughput and the power consumption cost. Those advantages are compensated by the main brake to flash memory expansion that is the higher cost per GByte. This is the main reason why flash memory is presently more seen as a mean to enhance traditional HDDs rather than a way to replace them at short term (Leventhal, 2008). Flash disks can be used in this case to architect the same storage platforms such as NAS (Network Attached Storage) or SAN (Storage Area Networks). For all the reasons stated throughout this paper, additional (and sometimes highly complex) reliability and performance mechanisms are added at the level of the flash controller.

One example of exclusively based storage system architecture is Gordon (Caulfield, Grupp & Swanson, 2009), a flash memory based cluster architecture for massively parallel data centric applications. Gordon framework combines three technologies: peta-scale data-centric parallel programming, low power processors, and flash memory.

Many studies in database systems have been realized to evaluate the benefit of flash memories for database applications. In, (Lee, Moon, Park, Kim, & Kim, 2008), some exhaustive performance measurement have been performed in order to compare execution times of transaction log, rollback segments, and some other table operations. Authors concluded that for some database applications, it is worth to replace traditional storage by flash memory. This is especially relevant because database systems are configured to have separate storage spaces for the above-mentioned elements.

Many industrial flash-based only storage systems have emerged in the last years, one may cite: Fusio-io, Intel, Kaminario, RamSan (TMS), Violin, Virident, etc.

*Complementary storage device:* In this model, we may distinguish two possibilities for flash memory to complement traditional storage systems:

1.  To build tiered storage architecture consisting of flash disks at the storage system front end for performance and traditional disks as a back end for capacity (Gurumurthi, 2009).
2.  To have hybrid storage systems with flash disks and traditional disks at the same level and depending on the application requirements and characteristics data can be placed into flash or magnetic drives.

Using flash memory in a multi-tiered architecture consists in adding an array of flash disks tier as a cache for a tier of HDDs. The difference with the integration of flash memory as storage accelerator is that in a tiered architecture, rather than having some flash memory in each storage device (or dedicated to it), it is centralized in an upstream level. When dealing with the integration of flash storage in tiered architectures, some important points are to consider among which we find: the dimensioning of the storage systems (e.g. how much SSDs, HDDs?), the energy proportionality issue, and data migration from one tier to another.

In (Narayanan, Thereska, Donnelly, Elnikety & Rowstron, 2009), tradeoffs and dimensioning of tiered storage systems with SSD tier as a cache to disk tier were described. The study has been performed on a set of real workloads and takes into account the point of view of an administrator that needs to upgrade or define the storage architecture according to workload requirements. Even though the conclusions of the paper are quite pessimistic about the relevance of the use of SSDs because of price considerations, we think that one must reconsider the problem by taking into account the evolution of costs (and performance) that is in favor of flash memories.

Another important issue to consider out is energy proportionality (Gurumurthi, 2009) which also plays in favor of flash memories. This property has been used in (Felter, Hylick & Carter, 2011) to design a power and reliability-aware hybrid storage systems. Indeed, disk based storage systems are not energy proportional as they consume almost the same energy amount in idle (spinning) state as in active state. The authors showed the benefit of relying on the synergy of both flash-caching and disk spin down in order to increase the global energy proportionality of the storage system. This is realized by considering many disk power states and by having an explicit management of disk reliability through a token bucket algorithm.

When dealing with tiered storage systems, data migration between SSD and HDD tier in time is a very important issue to investigate because of changing data access patterns over time. In (Zhang, Chiu & Liu, 2010), an adaptive data migration mechanism between storage tiers in the cloud is proposed, especially to take full advantage of, and capitalize on the expensive flash memory based (SSD) limited tier. The solution is based upon the dynamic use of I/O profile to guide the migration of hot data toward SSD tier in order to capitalize on the expensive SSD tier. The authors use a look-ahead migration scheme that takes into account many parameters to determine the optimal look-ahead factor. Examples of such parameters include: the heat information of data, the migration deadline, the tradeoff between the gain in migrating the selected workload to higher level SSD tier and the degradation from the ongoing workload, etc.

In hybrid storage systems, SSD storage is at the same level as traditional HDDs, data can be exclusively stored in one or the other storage system. When conceiving such a system, designers must implement some allocation techniques (how to decide where to put data) and migration algorithms. This is done according to the storage system characteristics discussed above on performance and energy, in addition to access patterns.

Lightning (Kaushik, Campbell, Nahrstedt & Cherkasova, 2010) is an example of hybrid storage for cloud systems based on a multi zone approach. The cloud storage servers are logically dynamically partitioned into hot and cold zones. Each zone having its own characteristics: performance, cost, data layout and power behavior. Flash storage is used in this architecture in the first zone, the one that contains a subset of the hottest data, more exactly for read intensive data. The other zones contain HDDs with different characteristics, and the last zone (4th one) is used for backup allowing long sleep (idle state) periods though consuming less energy. In order to perform high energy-conservation, lightning uses data-classification policies, application hints, and file system derived insights to place files in specific zones that are managed differently from the energy point of view.

In (Wu & Narasimha Reddy, 2009) was presented another data migration mechanism for hybrid flash/disk storage systems. The presented work transparently and automatically manages the migration of data through the storage system according to their access patterns. In this approach, the system dynamically keeps track of the access behavior (throughout counters) to measure read and write accesses. In order to have a transparent and generic approach, the system manages the devices' characteristics with the help of continuous and dynamic I/O performance measurements for both read and write operations. This study focused on pure I/O performance and did not take into account energy consumption.

Some contributions on putting flash and magnetic storage at the same level for database applications also exist. Authors of (Koltsidas & Viglas, 2008) tried to answer the two main issues:

1.  Adapting to the changing workload by migrating data from one storage media to another.
2.  Data placement of newly written pages with the help of three different algorithms (conservative, optimistic, and hybrid algorithm). Read intensive data are placed in flash disk

while write intensive data are placed in magnetic disks which resembles to some previously discussed contributions.

More generally, in the database area, flash memory is being largely discussed because it presents many interesting research issues (Athanassoulis, Ailamaki, Chen, Gibbons & Stoica, 2010). Three aspects of traditional relational database management systems were investigated: transactional logging in memory-resident OLTP systems, data layout in flash-resident OLTP systems, and finally using the flash memory as an update cache in HDD-resident data warehousing. Generally, database community showed a real enthusiasm in integrating flash memories in database systems.

## CONCLUSION AND FUTURE RESEARCH DIRECTIONS

Research on flash memories has made an extraordinary leap forward these last couple of years. Many issues have been identified and some relevant solutions proposed. But there is still a lot to do in many directions:

- Flash memory internals better mechanisms to dynamically adapt FTLs supporting different workloads, reducing the SRAM space and the provisioning space, generating less erase operations, performing better wear leveling, reducing the overhead of garbage collection, investigating real time FTLs, and all this with a minimal energy consumption of the controller. The flash disk cache design is also an important issue; caches must absorb part of the erase operations, reveal sequentiality between interleaved requests. Another direction is the implementation of efficient tools for design exploration of flash memories (number of chips, busses, caches, etc.) according to the applicative level.

- From the architectural point of view, many directions are to be explored depending on the chosen model of integration. High level exploration tools for a better dimensioning can help administrators to decide of the better configuration of their storage systems. When using flash as a cache for hard disk drives, one have to take into account specific constraints of flash memories to design efficient caching algorithms (read and write, eviction policies, perfecting algorithms, etc.) according to the supported workloads. When using the flash memory in storage system level, one should find the better architecture for its specific applications: hierarchical (tiered or zoned architectures), or non hierarchical. Whatever solution should take into account the data placement problem, and the migration of data according to the changes of the workload and state of the storage system. Changing configuration by adapting to newly added storage elements is also a key point to consider out for evolving storage systems. Integration of heterogeneous storage systems is a key element in the future of storage system architectures.

The metrics to consider out are the same as those of traditional storage systems to which one can add: the reliability, as harder constraints apply to flash memories, and energy consumption and proportionality. Because of the exponential growth of data the energy argument becomes the cornerstone of an efficient storage system design. Predictability is also another important metric to focus on as database management system designers need clear rules to lie upon for optimizing their systems.

Flash memories will occupy more and more space in future cloud storage systems and their integration is considered as a key to leverage the performance of data centric computing. A better understanding of its structures and algorithms is essential to make the most out of it.

We proposed in this chapter an overview of flash memory systems throughout 1) the description of its internal structure and specificities, and 2) a discussion about its integration into storage systems. The first part of the chapter is necessary to understand the performance issues and integration possibilities.

Flash memory is currently the most mature NVM technology and studies achieved to optimize its usage will probably help in making other NVM technologies emerge quickly even though some of the constraints are different. PCRAM, FeRAM, MRAM are all new candidates that open up new opportunities to explore and challenges to tackle in this data centric era.

## REFERENCES

Achiwa, K., Yamamoto, A., & Yamagata, O. (1999). *Memory systems using a flash memory and method for controlling the memory system.* United States Patent, No 5,930,193. Washington, DC: US Patent Office.

Agrawal, N., Prabhakaran, V., Wobber, T., Davis, J. D., Manasse, M., & Panigrahy, R. (2008). Design tradeoffs for SSD performance. In *Proceedings of the USENIX Annual Technical Conference (ATC)*. USENIX.

Armbrust, M., Fox, A., Griffith, R., Joseph, A. D., Katz, R., & Konwinski, A. et al. (2010). A view of cloud computing. *Communications of the ACM, 53*(4), 50–58. doi:10.1145/1721654.1721672.

Assar, M., Namazie, S., & Estakhri, P. (1995). *Flash memory mass storage architecture incorporation wear leveling technique.* United States Patent, No 5,479,638. Washington, DC: US Patent Office.

Athanassoulis, M., Ailamaki, A., Chen, S., Gibbons, P., & Stoica, R. (2010). Flash in a DBMS: Where and How? *A Quarterly Bulletin of the Computer Society of the IEEE Technical Committee on Data Engineering, 33*(4), 28–34.

Ban, A. (1995). *Flash file system*. United States Patent, No 5,404,485. Washington, DC: US Patent Office.

Ban, A. (1999). *Flash file system optimized for page-mode flash technologies*. United States Patent, No 5,937,425. Washington, DC: US Patent Office.

Bonnet, P., & Bouganim, L. (2011). Flash device support for database management. In *Proceedings of the 5th Biennial Conference on Innovative Data Systems Research (CIDR)*. CIDR.

Boukhobza, J., & Olivier, P. (2011). An efficient hierarchical dual cache system for NAND flash memories. *International Journal of Digital Information and Wireless Communications, 1*(1), 175–194.

Boukhobza, J., Olivier, P., & Rubini, S. (2011). A cache management strategy to replace wear leveling techniques for embedded flash memory. In *Proceedings of the 2011 International Symposium on Performance Evaluation of Computer & Telecommunication Systems (SPECTS)*. SPECTS.

Brewer, J. E., & Gill, M. (Eds.). (2008). *Nonvolatile memory technologies with emphasis on flash*. IEEE Press.

Cagdas, D., & Jacob, B. (2009). The performance of PC solid-state disks (SSDs) as a function of bandwidth. In *Proceedings of the International Symposium of Computer Architecture (ISCA)*. IEEE.

Carter, J., & Rajamani, K. (2010). Designing energy efficient servers and data centers. *Computer, 43*(7), 76–78. doi:10.1109/MC.2010.198.

Caulfield, A. M., Grupp, L. M., & Swanson, S. (2009). Gordon: Using flash memory to build fast, power-efficient clusters for data-intensive applications. In *Proceeding of the 14th International Conference on Architectural Support for Programming Languages and Operating Systems (ASPLOS)*. ASPOLOS.

Chang, L. (2007). On efficient wear leveling for large-scale flash-memory storage systems. In *Proceedings of the 2007 ACM Symposium on Applied Computing (SAC)*. ACM.

Chang, L. P., & Kuo, T. W. (2002). An adaptive striping architecture for flash memory storage systems of embedded systems. In *Proceedings of the 8th IEEE Real-Time and Embedded Technology and Applications Symposium (RTAS)*. IEEE.

Chang, R. C., Qawami, B., & Sabet-Sharghi, F. (2006). *Method and apparatus for managing an erase count block*. United States Patent, No 7,103,732. Washington, DC: US Patent Office.

Chiang, M., & Chang, R. C. (1999). Cleaning policies in mobile computers using flash memories. *Journal of Systems and Software, 48*(3), 213–231. doi:10.1016/S0164-1212(99)00059-X.

Chiang, M., Cheng, C., & Wu, C. (2008). A new FTL-based flash memory management scheme with fast cleaning mechanism. In *Proceedings of the International Conference on Embedded Software and Systems (ICESS)*. ICESS.

Cho, H., Shin, D., & Eom, Y. I. (2009). KAST: K-associative sector translation for NAND flash memory in real-time systems. In Proceedings of Design, Automation, and Test in Europe (DATE), (pp. 507-512). DATE.

Chung, T., Park, D., Park, S., Lee, D., Lee, S., & Song, H. (2009). A survey of flash translation layer. *Journal of Systems Architecture, 55*, 332–343. doi:10.1016/j.sysarc.2009.03.005.

Chung, T. S., & Park, H. S. (2007). STAFF: A flash driver algorithm minimizing block erasures. *Journal of Systems Architecture, 53*(12), 889–901. doi:10.1016/j.sysarc.2007.02.005.

Conley, K. M. (2005). *Zone boundary adjustment for defects in non-volatile memories*. United States Patent, No 6,901,498. Washington, DC: US Patent Office.

Creasey, J. (2005). Hybrid hard drives with non-volatile flash and longhorn. In *Proceedings of Windows Hardware Engineering Conference (WinHEC)*. WinHEC.

Debnath, B., Subramanya, S., Du, D., & Lilja, D. J. (2009). Large block CLOCK (LB-CLOCK): A write caching algorithm for solid state disks. In *Proceedings of the 17ᵗʰ IEEE International Symposium on Modeling, Analysis & Simulation of Computer and Telecommunication Systems (MASCOTS)*. IEEE.

Farmer, D. (2010). *Study projects nearly 45-fold annual data growth by 2020*. Retrieved August, 2012, from http://www.emc.com/about/news/press/2010/20100504-01.htm

Felter, W., Hylick, A., & Carter, J. (2011). Reliability-aware energy management for hybrid storage systems. In *Proceedings of the IEEE 27th Symposium on Mass Storage Systems and Technologies (MSST)*. IEEE.

Gray, J. (2006a). *E-science: The next decade will be exciting*. Retrieved August, 2012, from http://research.microsoft.com/en-us/um/people/gray/talksETH_E_Science.ppt

Gray, J. (2006b). *Tape is dead, disk is tape, flash is disk, RAM locality is king*. Redmond, WA: Storage Guru Gong Show.

Grupp, L. M., Caulfield, A. M., Coburn, J., Swanson, S., Yaakobi, E., Siegel, P. H., & Wolf, J. K. (2009). Characterizing flash memory: Anomalies, observations, and applications. In *Proceedings of the 42ⁿᵈ Annual IEEE/ACM International Symposium on Microarchitecture (MICRO)*. IEEE/ACM.

Gupta, A., Kim, Y., & Urgaonkar, B. (2009). DFTL: A flash translation layer employing demand-based selective caching of page-level address mappings. In *Proceedings of the 14th International Conference on Architectural Support for Programming Languages and Operating Systems (ASPLOS)*. ASPLOS.

Gurumurthi, S. (2009). Architecting storage for the cloud computing area. *IEEE Micro, 29*(6), 68–71. doi:10.1109/MM.2009.92.

Hsieh, J., Kuo, T., & Chang, L. (2006). Efficient identification of hot data for flash memory storage systems. *ACM Transactions on Storage, 2*(1), 22–40. doi:10.1145/1138041.1138043.

Hsieh, J., Tsai, Y., Kuo, T., & Lee, T. (2008). Configurable flash-memory management: Performance versus overheads. *IEEE Transactions on Computers, 57*(11), 1571–1583. doi:10.1109/TC.2008.61.

Hu, J., Jiang, H., Tian, L., & Xu, L. (2010). PUD-LRU: An erase-efficient write buffer management algorithm for flash memory SSD. In *Proceedings of the 2010 IEEE International Symposium on of Modeling, Analysis & Simulation of Computer and Telecommunication Systems (MASCOTS)*. IEEE.

Jiang, S., Zhang, L., Yuan, X., Hu, H., & Chen, Y. (2011). SFTL: An efficient address translation for flash memory by exploiting spatial locality. In *Proceedings of 2011 IEEE 27th Symposium on Mass Storage Systems and Technologies (MSST)*. IEEE.

Jo, H., Kang, J., Park, S., Kim, J., & Lee, J. (2006). FAB: A flash-aware buffer management policy for portable media players. *IEEE Transactions on Consumer Electronics, 52*(2), 485–493. doi:10.1109/TCE.2006.1649669.

Jung, D., Kang, J. U., Jo, H., Kim, J. S., & Lee, J. (2010). Superblock FTL: A superblock-based flash translation layer with a hybrid address translation scheme. *ACM Transactions on Embedded Computing Systems, 9*(4), 1–41. doi:10.1145/1721695.1721706.

Kang, S., Park, S., Jung, H., Shim, H., & Cha, J. (2009). Performance trade-offs in using NVRAM write buffer for flash memory-based storage devices. *IEEE Transactions on Computers, 58*(6), 744–758. doi:10.1109/TC.2008.224.

Kang, W., Lee, S., & Moon, B. (2012). Flash-based extended cache for higher throughput and faster recovery. *Proceedings of the VLDB Endowment, 5*(11), 1615–1626.

Kaushik, R., Campbell, R., Nahrstedt, K., & Cherkasova, L. (2010). Lightning: Self-adaptive, energy-efficient, storage-efficient, tiered, automated policy-driven green cloud storage system. In *Proceedings of the 19th ACM International Symposium on High Performance Distributed Computing (HPDC)*. ACM.

Kawaguchi, A., Nishioka, S., & Motoda, H. (1995). A flash memory based file system. In *Proceedings of the USENIX 1995 Annual Technical Conference (ATC)*. USENIX.

Kim, H., & Ahn, S. (2008). BPLRU: A buffer management scheme for improving random writes in flash storage. In *Proceedings of the 6th USENIX Conference on File and Storage Technologies (FAST)*. FAST.

Kim, J., Kim, J. M., Noh, S. H., Min, S. L., & Cho, Y. (2002). A space-efficient flash translation layer for compact flash systems. *IEEE Transactions on Consumer Electronics, 48*(2), 366–375. doi:10.1109/TCE.2002.1010143.

Koltsidas, I., & Viglas, S. D. (2008). Flashing up the storage layer. *Proceedings of the VLDB Endowment, 1*(1), 512–525.

Koo, D., & Shin, D. (2009). Adaptive log block mapping scheme for log buffer-based FTL (flash translation layer). In *Proceedings of the International Workshop on Software Support for Portable Storage (IWSSPS)*. IWSSPS.

Kwon, S. J., & Chung, T. (2008). An efficient and advanced space-management technique for flash memory using reallocation blocks. *IEEE Transactions on Consumer Electronics, 54*(2), 631–638. doi:10.1109/TCE.2008.4560140.

Kwon, S. J., Ranjitkar, A., Ko, Y., & Chung, T. (2011). FTL algorithms for NAND-type flash memories. *Design Automation for Embedded Systems, 15*(3-4), 191–224. doi:10.1007/s10617-011-9071-9.

Lee, H., Yun, H., & Lee, D. (2009). HFTL: Hybrid flash translation layer based on hot data identification for flash memory. *IEEE Transactions on Consumer Electronics, 55*(4), 2005–2011. doi:10.1109/TCE.2009.5373762.

Lee, S., Moon, B., Park, C., Kim, J., & Kim, S. (2008). A case for flash memory SSD in enterprise database applications. In *Proceedings of the 2008 ACM SIGMOD International Conference on Management of Data*. ACM.

Lee, S., Park, D., Chung, T., Lee, D., Park, S., & Song, H. (2007). A log buffer based flash translation layer using fully associative sector translation. *ACM Transactions on Embedded Computing Systems, 6*(3), 1–27. doi:10.1145/1275986.1275990.

Lee, S., Shin, D., Kim, Y., & Kim, J. (2008). LAST: Locality aware sector translation for NAND flash memory based storage systems. *ACM SIGOPS Operating Systems Review, 42*(6), 36–42. doi:10.1145/1453775.1453783.

Leventhal, A. (2008). Flash storage memory. *Communications of the ACM, 51*(7), 47–51. doi:10.1145/1364782.1364796.

Lim, S., Lee, S., & Moon, B. (2010). FASTer FTL for entreprise-class flash memory SSDs. In *Proceedings of the 2010 International Workshop on Storage Network Architecture and Parallel I/Os (SNAPI)*. SNAPI.

Lofgren, K. M. J., Norman, R. D., Thelin, G. B., & Gupta, A. (2005). *Wear leveling techniques for flash EEPROM systems*. United States Patent, No 6,850,443. Washington, DC: US Patent Office.

Lyman, P., & Varian, H. R. (2003). *How much information?* Retrieved August, 2012, http://www2.sims.berkeley.edu/research/projects/how-much-info-2003

Market Research. (n.d.). *Advanced solid state non-volatile memory market to grow 69% annually through 2015.* Retrieved August, 2012, from http://www.marketresearch.com/corporate/aboutus/press.asp?view=3&article=2223

Narayanan, D., Thereska, E., Donnelly, A., Elnikety, S., & Rowstron, A. (2009). Migrating server storage to SSDs: Analysis of tradeoffs. In *Proceedings of the ACM European Conference on Computer Systems (EuroSys).* ACM.

Ou, Y., & Härder, T. (2011). Trading memory for performance and energy. In *Proceedings of the 16th International Conference on Database Systems for Advanced Applications (DASFAA).* DASFAA.

Park, C., Cheon, W., Kang, J., Roh, K., Cho, W., & Kim, J. (2008). A reconfigurable FTL (flash translation layer) architecture for NAND flash based architectures. *ACM Transactions on Embedded Computing Systems, 7*(4), 1–23. doi:10.1145/1376804.1376806.

Park, D., Debnath, B., & Du, D. (2009). *CFTL: A convertible flash translation layer with consideration of data access patterns* (Technical Report 09-023). Minneapolis, MN: University of Minnesota.

Park, S., Jung, D., Kang, J., Kim, J., & Lee, J. (2006). CFLRU: A replacement algorithm for flash memory. In *Proceedings of the 2006 International Conference on Compilers, Architecture and Synthesis for Embedded Systems (CASES).* CASES.

Park, S., Kim, Y., Urgaonkar, B., Lee, J., & Seo, E. (2011). A comprehensive study on energy efficiency of flash memory storages. *Journal of Systems Architecture, 57*(4), 354–365. doi:10.1016/j.sysarc.2011.01.005.

Qin, Z., Wang, Y., Liu, D., & Shao, Z. (2010). Demand-based block-level address mapping in large-scale NAND flash storage systems. In *Proceedings of the 2010 IEEE/ACM/IFIP International Conference on Hardware/Software Codesign and System Synthesis (CODES+ISSS).* IEEE/ACM/IFIP.

Ranganathan, P. (2011). From microprocessors to nanostores: Rethinking data-centric systems. *Computer, 44*(1), 39–48. doi:10.1109/MC.2011.18.

Roberts, D., Kgil, T., & Mudge, T. (2009a). Integrating NAND flash devices onto servers. *Communications of the ACM, 52*(4), 98–106. doi:10.1145/1498765.1498791.

Roberts, D., Kgil, T., & Mudge, T. (2009b). Using non-volatile memory to save energy in servers. In *Proceedings of the Design, Automation and Test in Europe conference (DATE).* DATE.

Shinohara, T. (1999). *Flash memory card with block memory address arrangement.* United States Patent, No 5,905,993. Washington, DC: US Patent Office.

Syu, S., & Chen, J. (2005). An active space recycling mechanism for flash storage systems in real-time application environments. In *Proceedings the 11th IEEE International Conference on Embedded and Real-Time Computing Systems and Applications (RTCSA),* (pp. 53-59). IEEE.

Vasudevan, V., Andersen, D., Kaminsky, M., Tan, L., Franklin, J., & Moraru, I. (2010). Energy-efficient cluster computing with FAWN: Workloads and implications. In *Proceedings of the 1st International Conference on Energy-Efficient Computing and Networking (e-Energy '10).* E-Energy.

Wang, Y., Liu, D., Wang, M., Qin, Z., Shao, Z., & Guan, Y. (2010). RNFTL: A reuse-aware NAND flash translation layer for flash memory. In *Proceedings of the ACM SIGPLAN/SIGBED 2010 Conference on Languages, Compilers, and Tools for Embedded Systems (LCTES).* ACM.

Wei, Q., Gong, B., Pathak, S., Veeravalli, B., Zeng, L., & Okada, K. (2011). WAFTL: A workload adaptive flash translation layer with data partition. In *Proceedings of 2011 IEEE 27th Symposium on Mass Storage Systems and Technologies (MSST)*. IEEE.

Winter, R. (2008). *Why are data warehouses growing so fast?* Retrieved August, 2012, from http://www.b-eye-network.com/view7188

Woodhouse, D. (2001). JFFS: The journaling flash file system. In *Proceedings of Ottawa Linux Symposium*. Linux.

Wu, C., & Kuo, T. (2006). An adaptive two-level management for the flash translation layer in embedded systems. In *Proceedings of the 2006 IEEE/ ACM International Conference on Computer-Aided Design*. IEEE/ACM.

Wu, G., Eckart, B., & He, X. (2010). BPAC: An adaptive write buffer management scheme for flash-based solid state drives. In *Proceedings of 2010 IEEE 26th Symposium on Mass Storage Systems and Technologies (MSST)*. IEEE.

Wu, X., & Narasimha Reddy, A. L. (2009). Managing storage space in a flash and disk hybrid storage system. In *Proceedings of the 2009 IEEE International Symposium on Modeling, Analysis & Simulation of Computer and Telecommunication Systems (MASCOTS)*. IEEE.

Zhang, G., Chiu, L., & Liu, L. (2010). Adaptive data migration in multi-tiered storage based cloud environment. In *Proceedings of the 3rd IEEE International Conference on Cloud Computing (CLOUD)*. IEEE.

Zhang, Q., Cheng, L., & Boutaba, R. (2010). Cloud computing: State-of-the-art and research challenges. *Journal of Internet Services and Applications*, 1(1), 7–18. doi:10.1007/s13174-010-0007-6.

## KEY TERMS AND DEFINITIONS

**Flash File System (FFS):** A file system designed to store files on a flash memory media. In addition to standard file system services, FFS includes mechanisms to achieve the three flash-specific tasks that are: logical-to-physical address mapping, wear leveling, and garbage collection.

**Flash Translation Layer (FTL):** A hardware/software layer that performs flash memory management. Typical functionalities offered by FTLs are: logical-to-physical address mapping, wear leveling, and garbage collection. Other functionalities might be covered by the FTL: error correcting codes, power off recovery and bad blocks management (those three are not covered in this chapter).

**Garbage Collection:** Is the process used in FTLs and FFS to recycle free space from previously invalidated pages in different blocks of the flash memory.

**Logical-to-Physical Address Mapping:** The used mechanism that keeps track of the physical location of the data in the memory. This mechanism is used as modify in-place is not allowed in flash memories due to performance and lifetime considerations.

**Non-Volatile Memory (NVM):** Memory that does retain data even when power is turned off. Some examples of such memories include Ferroelectric RAM (FeRAM), Phase Change RAM (PCRAM), Magneto-resistive RAM (MRAM), and flash memory.

**Solid-State Drive (SSD):** A storage subsystem device based on integrated circuit components that stores data on a solid-state (actually flash) memory.

**Wear Leveling:** A process that allows to prolong the flash memory lifetime by balancing the erase operations over all the flash memory blocks. Without wear leveling, some blocks would tend to wear out much more quickly than the others due to temporal and spatial locality of I/O workloads.

# Chapter 16
# XtreemFS:
## A File System for the Cloud

**Jan Stender**
*Zuse Institute Berlin, Germany*

**Michael Berlin**
*Zuse Institute Berlin, Germany*

**Alexander Reinefeld**
*Zuse Institute Berlin, Germany*

## ABSTRACT

*Cloud computing poses new challenges to data storage. While cloud providers use shared distributed hardware, which is inherently unreliable and insecure, cloud users expect their data to be safely and securely stored, available at any time, and accessible in the same way as their locally stored data. In this chapter, the authors present XtreemFS, a file system for the cloud. XtreemFS reconciles the need of cloud providers for cheap scale-out storage solutions with that of cloud users for a reliable, secure, and easy data access. The main contributions of the chapter are: a description of the internal architecture of XtreemFS, which presents an approach to build large-scale distributed POSIX-compliant file systems on top of cheap, off-the-shelf hardware; a description of the XtreemFS security infrastructure, which guarantees an isolation of individual users despite shared and insecure storage and network resources; a comprehensive overview of replication mechanisms in XtreemFS, which guarantee consistency, availability, and durability of data in the face of component failures; an overview of the snapshot infrastructure of XtreemFS, which allows to capture and freeze momentary states of the file system in a scalable and fault-tolerant fashion. The authors also compare XtreemFS with existing solutions and argue for its practicability and potential in the cloud storage market.*

## INTRODUCTION

Cloud computing is emerging as a pioneering paradigm for service hosting and on-demand computing. By providing computation and storage as a utility without requiring an up-front commit-ment by users, clouds offer a flexible alternative to traditional solutions that are built upon dedicated hardware (Armbrust et al., 2009).

Especially with respect to data storage, cloud computing presents various new challenges. From a user's point of view, a storage cloud is expected to behave like a reliable and exclusively owned storage resource with unlimited capacity. Stor-

DOI: 10.4018/978-1-4666-3934-8.ch016

age clouds convey this impression by addressing issues like *elasticity, isolation, availability,* and *robustness*:

- **Elasticity:** Providers of cloud computing systems aim to lead users to believe that unlimited amounts of resources are available on demand. Accordingly, they must be able to dynamically adjust the scale of the underlying hardware installation, subject to the demand of their users. In the context of cloud computing, such on-demand scalability is referred to as *elasticity*.

An elastic storage cloud must be able to extend or shrink the capacity by means of adding or removing resources. In doing so, new resources must be able to become seamlessly integrated into an existing storage installation. As a consequence, cloud storage systems require a distributed system architecture that comprises a network of loosely coupled, independent storage components.

- **Isolation:** To handle accesses from many users in a cost-efficient manner, users of a cloud share the same pool of physical resources. Accordingly, a storage cloud implements a many-to-many relationship between users and storage devices, regardless of any trust relationships between users. Storage devices may further reside in an untrusted environment, where data is exposed to the threat of unauthorized access, which may affect privacy and integrity. To take potential security concerns of cloud users into account, storage clouds have to meet high standards in terms of security and data isolation. This involves a comprehensive security infrastructure with support for a secure authentication and authorization of users as well as the encryption of stored data.
- **Availability and Robustness:** To encourage users to submit their data to a storage cloud, the cloud provider has to guarantee that all data is safely stored and available at any time. Data access must be impervious to network partitionings and downtimes as well as permanent failures of system components, which may occur as a consequence of misconfiguration, power cuts, hardware failures or disasters. Such outages have to be handled internally by the storage system and hidden from users to the best possible extent. Robustness especially matters in connection with elasticity, as failures on the underlying hardware layer have proven to be the norm rather than the exception on large-scale storage installations (Ghemawat, Gobioff, & Leung, 2003).

The advent of cloud computing as a new paradigm for utility computing and the resulting new challenges have leveraged a variety of novel cloud storage systems (e.g., Amazon S3[1], Windows Azure[2] or Google Cloud Storage[3]). Most of them offer a proprietary, typically HTTP-based interface with vendor-specific semantics, which are incompatible with those of traditional file systems (e.g. POSIX), thereby requiring users to adapt their application to the underlying cloud storage infrastructure. This can be a tedious and time-consuming task for cloud users, not only because it involves a learning effort to get acquainted to new data management schemes and APIs, but also because adapting existing applications to a specific data management framework involves a potentially large additional programming and maintenance effort.

As a solution, we present XtreemFS (Hupfeld et al., 2008), a distributed, secure, highly available and fault-tolerant cloud file system. XtreemFS comes with a range of useful features for the cloud. It can be accessed by any application that uses a traditional file system to store data, as it offers a common file system interface with POSIX semantics. XtreemFS is inherently elastic because of its object-based architecture (Factor, Meth,

Naor, Rodeh, & Satran, 2005, Mesnier, Ganger, & Riedel, 2003); data is stored on a resizable pool of independent, intelligent object storage devices, which can be scaled out in order to increase the total data capacity and throughput. In terms of security, it provides for encrypted connections, authentication and authorization of users through SSL, X.509 certificates and POSIX ACLs. It guarantees high availability and fault tolerance by means of replication, with strong replica consistency and automatic fail-over when individual replicas are unavailable. Moreover, snapshots make it possible to create consistent on-line backups and to revert to prior states in the event of data loss or inadvertent changes at application level.

The remainder of the chapter is structured as follows. Section 2 gives an overview of related work in the area of cloud storage and distributed file systems. Section 3 describes the general architecture and components of XtreemFS, including the mechanisms to enable secure data access in untrusted environments. Section 4 provides a comprehensive and detailed summary of replication techniques employed in XtreemFS and how they are used to ensure consistency, durability and high availability of data. Section [REMOVED REF FIELD]5 presents the XtreemFS snapshot infrastructure, with a particular focus on version management and the approach to capture a consistent image of a distributed data volume. Section 6 discusses future research directions based on user and developer feedback and Section 7 concludes the chapter with a summary of results.

## BACKGROUND

The storage and administration of large data volumes is a fundamental issue of today's cloud providers and data center operators. Over the last decade, a multitude of distributed and parallel storage systems have been developed for different environments and purposes. Systems with practical relevance can be roughly categorized into:

- **Cloud Storage Systems:** Which offer users high availability, durability and secure access to data on a shared, remotely hosted data management infrastructure;
- **Parallel File Systems:** Which are designed for a high throughput and low-latency access to data in a trusted, local cluster environment.

## Cloud Storage Systems

The landscape of cloud storage systems is diverse and covers a multitude of different technologies and approaches, such as databases, file storage, as well as backup and archiving services. We will consider cloud storage services and cloud file systems in the following, as they can be best compared with XtreemFS.

## Cloud Storage Services

Cloud storage services offer storage and access to data "as a service", typically through an HTTP-based interface. Rather than supporting a full file system directory tree, data is organized into a flat hierarchy of objects, which reside in containers. Objects can be modified by means of *put* and *get* primitives, typically with relaxed consistency guarantees.

Various such cloud storage systems have gained access to the cloud computing market. One of the most prominent and widely used examples is Amazon's Simple Storage Service (S3). To protect objects from unauthorized access, S3 encrypts data on the server before being stored. Access to objects can be restrained to certain users by means of access control lists, which are attached to each object. All objects are replicated for high availability and durability by means of cross-site replication.

Similar solutions have been presented by various other vendors. Notable examples are Microsoft's Azure Storage Service and Google's Cloud Storage. Such commercial cloud storage services provide for a high availability and durability of data by means of replication, but they typically have limitations in terms of consistency, especially if replicas reside on different WAN-connected sites. For instance, Amazon S3 only ensures eventual consistency of such replicas. If data encryption is supported, encryption keys are typically stored on the servers, which constitutes a potential security gap if encryption servers are compromised.

## Cloud File Systems

A drawback of cloud storage services are their heterogeneous, vendor-specific interfaces and consistency guarantees. Cloud applications have to be aware of these and need to be specifically tailored to the respective storage service. Some systems, such as DropBox[4], Ubuntu One[5], ZumoDrive[6] and SpiderOak[7], tackle the problem by making cloud storage resources available through a file system interface. As such services have been designed for data sharing and backup rather than data processing in the cloud, however, they do not offer complete POSIX semantics, especially if individual files are updated concurrently.

The idea of providing cloud storage in a highly available, durable, secure and POSIX-compliant way has also been seized by HekaFS[8]. HekaFS runs on top of GlusterFS[9] and provides various features, such as data and traffic encryption, high availability, durability, as well as POSIX compliance. GFarm (Kobayashi, Mikami, Kimura, & Tatebe, 2011) aggregates local storage resources of compute nodes in a cloud and makes them accessible through a POSIX interface. Files and metadata are replicated. To maximize performance, it ensures that data is placed on local compute nodes. However, GFarm is not suitable

for being used in an untrusted environment, as user authentication depends upon a shared secret between clients and servers.

## Parallel File Systems

Parallel file systems provide access to scalable storage through a POSIX file system interface. Well-known examples are Lustre (Braam, 2004), PVFS (Carns, III, Ross, & Thakur, 2000), GPFS (Schmuck & Haskin, 2002), Panasas Active Scale (Tang et al., 2004) and Ceph (Weil, Brandt, Miller, Long, & Maltzahn, 2006). Although some of these resemble XtreemFS with respect to their architectures, their fields of application are different. Purpose of these file systems is to provide high-throughput, low-latency access to large data volumes, which is typically required by high performance computing applications running on a local cluster. Accordingly, issues like security and data durability are not of prime importance and typically only handled in a preliminary manner.

## XTREEMFS ARCHITECTURE

XtreemFS implements the concept of object-based storage (Factor et al., 2005, Mesnier et al., 2003), which has emerged as a flexible and scalable alternative to architectures of parallel file systems like NAS and SAN. As the name suggests, it relies on the abstraction of an *object* as a means of storing, accessing and transferring data. An object is a container that encapsulates a range of bytes associated with a file. Unlike blocks managed by a block storage device, objects are flexibly sized units that are independent of the underlying storage device. The interface through which objects are accessed and modified resembles that of a file system rather than a block device, as objects are attached to device-independent identifiers and can be read and written at byte granularity.

Object-based storage architectures combine the best features of NAS and SAN (Mesnier et al., 2003): As with NAS, files are managed by intelligent storage devices with capabilities that go beyond simple read and write access to disk blocks. Data is read and written over the network through a high-level interface in a secure and platform independent manner. As with SAN, clients communicate with storage devices directly rather than through a head node, thus providing similar scalability and performance characteristics. Consequently, object storage systems overcome the limitations of NAS in terms of scalability and performance and those of SAN in terms of security — both are important features for an elastic and secure cloud file system.

## Components

Figure 1 illustrates the modular client-server architecture of XtreemFS. Clients and servers are connected via an IP-based network, such as the Internet, with no specific requirements in terms of security, fault tolerance and performance. Servers can be run on arbitrary commodity hardware with the ability to perform computations, to persistently store data, and to communicate with remote clients and servers.

The separation of the compute-intensive management of metadata from the I/O-intensive

*Figure 1. XtreemFS architecture*

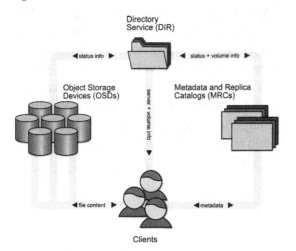

management of file content is a design principle found in many object-based file systems (Braam, 2004, Tang et al., 2004, Weil et al., 2006). XtreemFS resorts to different types of servers for these tasks, which typically run on different physical machines. To maximize scalability, metadata and storage servers are loosely coupled; they have independent life cycles and do not directly communicate with each other.

## OSD

*Object Storage Devices (OSDs):* Manage file content in the form of objects and provide an interface to access and modify individual objects of a file. Each OSD resorts to a local file system to store its objects persistently. This guarantees POSIX semantics with local reads and writes and makes it possible to benefit from operating system features like the page cache to enhance performance.

Aside from providing the basic functionality for accessing and modifying file content, OSDs implement various advanced features, such as replication, versioning, scrubbing and checksumming of file content. By adding new OSDs, the storage capacity and I/O throughput of an XtreemFS installation can be increased at runtime.

## MRC

*The Metadata and Replica Catalogs (MRCs):* Manage all metadata of an XtreemFS installation. Metadata is a collective term for all types of data that need to be managed by a file system except for file content. Pivotal pieces of metadata are the hierarchy of directories (required by POSIX) as well as attributes of individual files and directories such as file names, file sizes, access timestamps, access rights, ownership information and references to OSDs with file content replicas.

Metadata is grouped into volumes. Each volume has its own directory tree and specific set of policies (e.g., for access control and the assignment of OSDs to files). Since POSIX requires access rights to be evaluated on each component of the path when accessing a file or directory, and because requests to the MRC should be answered with a single communication round-trip in order to minimize latency, there is no partitioning scheme for metadata at sub-volume granularity. To mitigate potential drawbacks in terms of scalability, it is recommended to manually implement a partitioning scheme at volume granularity, e.g., by assigning each user her own volume and distributing volumes across multiple MRCs.

MRCs are internally built on BabuDB (Stender, Kolbeck, Högqvist, & Hupfeld, 2010), a non-relational database optimized for the storage of file system metadata. BabuDB maintains metadata in the form of key-value pairs. The directory hierarchy of each volume is thus mapped onto a flat key-value scheme, which supports the retrieval of a metadata record with a single lookup in $O(log(n))$ time if the database contains $n$ records. BabuDB provides a number of useful features such as fast point-in-time snapshots of databases for file system snapshots, transparent replication for durability and crash resilience of metadata, atomic updates of multiple key-value pairs for atomic file system operations such as rename, and append-only disk writes for a fast creation of new files and directories.

## DIR

*The Directory service (DIR):* Implements a registry for all services and file system volumes. It maintains configuration and runtime information about individual servers.

MRCs and OSDs initially register at the DIR and report status information in regular intervals. By retrieving such information, clients are able to locate the MRC responsible for a mounted volume, and MRCs can determine the set of OSDs for new files. The DIR also uses BabuDB to store all data and thus also capitalizes on features like replication and atomic updates.

## Client

*The Client:* Acts as the access point to the file system. It provides a common file system interface, which allows users to access mounted XtreemFS volumes in the same way as locally mounted file systems. Internally, it receives file system-related calls from the operating system, which it translates into interactions with MRCs and OSDs.

Access to a file on a POSIX file system requires multiple file system calls. First, the file is opened by means of its path name, which generates a file handle. The file handle can then be used to repeatedly read or write the file until it is closed. As illustrated in Figure 2, the client issues an open call with the respective path name to the MRC when receiving an open call from the local operating system. If successful, the MRC responds with a set of all replicas, each of which contains an individual distribution pattern for the objects and a list of OSDs for the pattern. Supported distribution patterns are "single OSD" and RAID 0. Subsequent read or write calls on the file handle are then translated into object-related calls on the respective OSDs of a replica.

Client modules are available for Linux, MacOS or Windows. We decided in favor of a user-space module based on FUSE[10] (Linux, MacOS) and Dokan[11] (Windows) rather than a respective kernel module to facilitate code development and maintenance. At its core, a cross-platform library libxtreemfs implements all client-server interactions as well as advanced functionality like caching and replica fail-over. Accordingly, XtreemFS bindings for FUSE and Dokan are implemented as thin layers on top of libxtreemfs.

## Figure 2. File access with XtreemFS

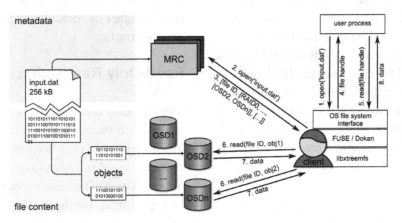

## Security

Security is of paramount importance for storage systems, as it protects the privacy of individual users and keeps data safe from unauthorized manipulation in the face of shared resources and inherently insecure environments. Relevant aspects of the security architecture include the authentication of users, the authorization of accesses and the encryption of messages and data.

## Authentication

XtreemFS clients and servers are not required to run in a trusted environment. Clients running on any machine may access any XtreemFS installation that is reachable over the network. Consequently, servers cannot assume that clients are inherently trustworthy, nor can clients assume that servers are trustworthy.

To solve the problem, XtreemFS supports SSL connections between all clients and servers. When establishing a new server connection, e.g., in the course of mounting a volume or initially writing a file, clients and servers exchange X.509 certificates to ensure a mutual authentication. The distinguished name of a client certificate reflects the identity of the user on behalf of whom subsequent operations are executed. User and group IDs are thus unforgeable and allow for a secure authentication of individual users.

## Authorization

A complementary issue is the assignment and evaluation of access rights. XtreemFS offers a common POSIX authorization model with different access flags for the owning user, the owning group and all other users. An optional extension are POSIX access control lists (ACLs), which allow the definition of access rights at the granularity of individual users and groups.

File system calls with path names are directed to the MRC, where they can be authorized locally, as the MRC stores all relevant metadata to perform access control. For calls with file handles, POSIX does not stipulate a renewed verification of access rights, as it can be assumed to have happened with the precedent path name call. However, OSDs need to be able to verify that a file was opened on a trusted MRC in order to inhibit unauthorized access to file content.

XtreemFS solves the problem by means of specific security tokens, so-called capabilities (Gobioff, 1999), which are issued by the MRC when files are opened, deleted, replaced or truncated. In essence, a capability is a datagram that contains the desired access mode, information about the accessing client's identity (e.g., its IP address), and an expiry timestamp indicating when the capability becomes invalid. To protect capabilities against forgery, a cryptographic hash value is appended, which covers the capability's attributes and a secret passphrase shared between all trusted servers. Before processing a request from a client, each OSD verifies that the capability (1) has a valid hash value, (2) has not yet expired, (3) was received from the correct client, and (4) grants sufficient authorization for the requested operation. This allows OSDs to authorize users asynchronously without having to communicate with MRCs and without MRCs having to maintain internal state for each open file.

## Encryption

As a consequence of using SSL connections between clients and servers, the network traffic is encrypted and thus protected from unauthorized access and manipulation on the network layer. To ensure that data is also protected on the storage devices, we envision an end-to-end encryption scheme on the client side. Such a scheme causes data and metadata to be encrypted before being written and decrypted after having been read. Thereby, the user data remains secure even when storage servers should become compromised.

Such an end-to-end encryption scheme has not yet been implemented in XtreemFS. Since XtreemFS is POSIX-compliant, however, it is possible to use file system encryption tools like EncFS[12] which can be stacked on top of any existing file system to encrypt file names and file content.

## REPLICATION

XtreemFS supports two kinds of file replication. The first one, read-only replication, allows to asynchronously replicate immutable files with a focus on the fast and efficient distribution of data at the cost of a write-once semantics. It is ideally suited for building content distribution networks or for distributing virtual machine images that are accessed by a multitude of nodes in parallel. The second replication mechanism, read/write replication, synchronously replicates every file operation

and guarantees availability and durability at the cost of higher operation latencies and additional network traffic.

## Read-Only Replication

The read-only replication is limited to write-once files, which means that they cannot be changed anymore after having been initially written and closed. Since this limitation obviates the need for a coordination of updates, the implementation can be kept simple. We therefore laid our main focus on a fast and efficient distribution of data.

## Approach

To replicate a file, the user first has to mark it as read-only at the MRC. Having done this, he can add new replicas to the replica set of the file at the MRC. XtreemFS allows to automate these steps by configuring a volume as read-only replicated and setting a default replication factor i.e., the number of replicas per file. Read-only flags and replicas will then be automatically added to newly created files when they are closed after having been written.

The actual replication of data happens between the OSDs in the replica set. It is triggered asynchronously with respect to adding replicas i.e., the client does not block when adding a replica or closing a file. Thus, the read-only replication does not affect the write performance of the client.

Data is transferred at object granularity. Object transfers are receiver-initiated in a similar way as data transfers via BitTorrent (Cohen, 2003). Instead of pushing objects to a replica, OSDs fetch missing objects from the remaining replicas.

## Full and Partial Replicas

The read-only replication supports two replica types: full replicas and partial replicas. When adding a full replica to a file, the client leads the OSD to immediately fetch all objects. To ensure redundancy as quickly as possible, this is done on a rarest-first basis: objects with the lowest redundancy across all replicas are transferred first.

With partial replicas, object transfers are exclusively triggered on demand. Figure 3 illustrates the principle. When a client attempts to read a replica on an OSD that does not have the requested object, the OSD blocks the read request and retrieves the object from the remaining replicas. Once the object has been successfully transferred, the OSD stores it locally and sends the requested data to the client.

Consequently, partial replicas only consume disk space for objects that were actually read by clients. This is ideal for accelerating access to large files that are only partially read, such as virtual machine images that are started on hundreds of nodes in parallel. In order to mask the additional transfer time of the on-demand replication in case of sequentially read files, partial replicas automatically pre-fetch subsequent objects when a client attempts to access a missing object.

## Read-Write Replication

The read-write replication in XtreemFS provides transparent replication of files without the read-only restriction. It maintains POSIX semantics and tolerates failures of replicas.

*Figure 3. Reading an object from a partial replica which automatically fetches the missing object*

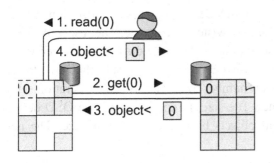

## Background

POSIX dictates the level of consistency the replication has to provide. In particular, the POSIX specification requires that after a successful write, any subsequent read returns the previously written data (IEEE Std 1003.1-2008, 2008). Consequently, the file system has to enforce a total order on all operations on a file. To ensure a total order in the face of multiple replicas, XtreemFS implements a primary/backup scheme at file granularity. Operations have to be executed on the OSD that takes the primary role for the file, which in turn propagates modifying operations to the backup OSDs. Hence, the primary acts as sequencer, which serializes all operations on the file.

XtreemFS uses leases to allow a fail-over of the primary. A lease grants an OSD the primary role for a file for a defined period of time. When a lease has expired, one of the former backup OSDs can become the new primary. Therefore the duration of a lease represents the maximum time for which the system may become unavailable if the primary fails.

The replication makes progress as long as a majority of replicas respond. The underlying assumption for this is the quorum intersection property (Thomas, 1979, Agrawal & Abbadi, 1990), which states that the intersection of two quorums is never empty. As long as operations are executed on a majority of replicas, the failure of a minority of replicas is tolerated.

## Approach

The processing of a replicated file operation on the OSD can be separated in the following three phases, which are sequentially executed.

1.  **Lease Acquisition:** When a client accesses a file replica on an OSD $o$, $o$ tries to acquire the lease for the file and thus to become primary. If another OSD $o'$ already holds the lease, $o$ redirects the client to $o'$.

2. **Replica Reset:** Once *o* has acquired the lease and became primary, it has to ensure that its local version of the file is up to date in order to support local reads. It may have missed updates in the past, as operations have to be executed only on a majority of replicas. Therefore *o* has to detect its outdated objects and fetch their up-to-date counterparts.

3. **Data Dissemination:** When *o* is up to date, it can answer read requests locally and execute write operations on the majority of replicas. If an object is modified through a write request, the primary sends the updated object to the backup OSDs. Once a majority of OSDs have written and acknowledged the update, the primary responds to the client that the object was successfully written.

The processing of subsequent file operations can be performed without executing the lease acquisition and replica reset phases again, since *o* maintains an open state for the file. The open state remains active and the lease is automatically renewed in the background until the file is closed.

In the following we give a more detailed description of the lease acquisition and replica reset phases. Thereby we assume that the set of replicas of a file is fixed and must not be changed. The section 4.2.5 describes how replica sets can be changed in XtreemFS.

## Decentral Lease Coordination with Flease

We designed and implemented Flease (Kolbeck, Högqvist, Stender, & Hupfeld, 2011), a scalable and fault-tolerant algorithm for the coordination of leases in distributed systems. Flease resorts to a variant of Lamport's Paxos algorithm (Lamport, 1998) to ensure consensus on a lease across multiple distributed nodes. A detailed description of Flease and a proof of its correctness can be found in (Kolbeck et al., 2011).

Flease handles leases in a decentralized fashion without a dedicated lock service. In XtreemFS, it coordinates the lease for a file among the OSDs that hold replicas of the file, thus allowing for scalability with the number of OSDs and files. Flease is fault-tolerant since it requires only a majority of replicas to respond in order to make progress. It supports crash-recovery without requiring stable writes by exploiting the fact that leases expire and become invalid after their expiration.

The approach of using Paxos to issue leases in a fault-tolerant fashion has been implemented in distributed lock services like Google's Chubby (Burrows, 2006) or Microsoft's Centrifuge (Adya, Dunagan, & Wolman, 2010). However, Paxos without modifications requires two writes to stable storage per lease acquisition in order to support the crash-recovery of processes. Consequently, a Paxos implementation in the OSD would be limited by the performance of the disks and, even worse, it would affect the performance of I/O operations on the OSD.

## Replica Reset

The replica reset phase ensures that an OSD becoming primary for a file has the file's latest version. Updates may have been missed, as update operations must only be executed on a majority of replicas.

To obtain the latest file version, the primary reconstructs the total order of update operations that were previously applied to the file. The total order is preserved through file version numbers, which are incremented with each update operation and stored persistently.

POSIX defines two update operations for file content: write and truncate. The respective write operation on the OSD creates a new version of the affected object and attaches the new file version number to it. The truncate operation sets a new file size. In consequence, the OSD deletes all objects beyond the new file size. The new file version number and file size are stored in a truncate log for the file.

The new primary starts the replica reset phase by requesting a list of version numbers attached to all objects and the truncate log from each OSD in the replica set. Once a majority has responded, it determines the current file version by means of all received version lists. In doing so, it generates a version list that represents the file's current version from the union of all known lists. If the union contains multiple versions for an object, only the highest file version number is kept. Additionally, all received truncate logs are applied to the resulting list by removing version numbers of objects that were deleted due to a truncate operation.

The primary uses the version number list to determine the set of object versions it has missed. If a local object has the same file version number as in the list, it is up to date and does not have to be synchronized. Any object versions in the list with larger version numbers are fetched from the respective OSDs.

The replica reset phase only ensures that the primary has the most up-to-date file version. To also allow backup replicas to catch up on missing updates, the primary sends information on the latest file version to the backup OSDs in the background on a best-effort basis.

*Master Epochs:* In the face of primary fail-overs, the total order of update operations may not be preserved in case of incomplete writes. If a file version number was not successfully written on a majority of replicas e.g., due to a crashed primary, it is possible that a new primary reassigns the same file version number to a new object version. This may cause replicas to become inconsistent, as the replica reset protocol rests on the assumption that objects with the same file version number are identical. To maintain the total order in the face of primary fail-overs, a master epoch is attached to each assigned file version, which is only incremented when a new primary is elected.

To prevent conflicting assignments of master epochs, it is necessary to ensure that a master epoch is known by a majority of OSDs in the file's replica set. Coordinating master epochs as part of the replica reset phase would require an additional message round, which would increase latency. To save this message round, we developed $Flease_m$, an enhanced version of the Flease algorithm that finds out the latest master epoch, increments it and stores the new value on a majority in the course of negotiating a lease. Unlike Flease, $Flease_m$ has to use stable storage to persistently store the master epoch, which, however, is only required in case of a primary fail-over.

## Replica Set Changes

Replica set changes are necessary when replicas have to be added or removed e.g., in order to replace a defective machine. Changes from a current replica set $R$ to a new replica set $R'$ must be carefully coordinated to ensure that the quorum intersection property is never violated.

*Background:* Newly added replicas initially have an empty state and therefore must not form a majority in $R'$. Consequently, only up to

$$x = |R' \setminus R| < \left\lceil \frac{|R'| + 1}{2} \right\rceil$$

replicas can be added. In $R'$ the majority of replicas must have the latest file version i.e.

$$q_{R'} = \left\lceil \frac{|R'| + 1}{2} \right\rceil$$

replicas. This is guaranteed by successfully executing the replica reset on at least $q_{R'}$ replicas before the actual replica set change. Since only replicas in $R$ can be used therefore, $x$ is constrained by $q_{R'} \leq |R'|$. Additionally, if $q_{R'}$ exceeds the number of available replicas, the value $x$ has to be further decremented.

Removed replicas have to be informed that they are no longer part of $R'$. Otherwise they could form a majority with respect to $R$ and return outdated values. Consequently, removed replicas are invalidated before the replica set will be changed.

*Replica Sets Versioning:* The XtreemFS architecture defines that the file's replica set is stored at the MRC and passed to clients as part of the open response. Clients send their copy of the replica set with every file operation to the OSD. To support the detection of the latest replica set, replica sets are augmented by a version number. Additionally, all respective OSDs of the file's replicas persistently store the latest known version number and the information if the current replica set was invalidated. If a client sends an OSD a replica set with a higher version number, the OSD can update its local value. If the version number is lower or the replica is invalidated, the OSD rejects the request and the client has to fetch the latest replica set from the MRC.

*Replica Sets Change Protocol:* The actual change of the replica set is driven by the MRC. Once the prerequisite is fulfilled that $q_{R'}$ replicas have the latest file version, the replica set can be changed. The required sequence of commands resembles a two-phase commit and involves locking the replica set first, applying the changes and unlocking the replica set.

The old replica set $R$ is effectively locked by the MRC which persistently stores both $R$ and $R'$ and thereby marks the replica set change as in progress. Subsequently, the replicas in $R$ are invalidated. After a majority of the respective OSDs acknowledged the invalidation, the MRC can change the replica set to $R'$. In the last step all replicas in $R'$ are informed about the new version number and reverse the invalidation.

## Replication of Metadata

Aside from replicating file content, XtreemFS also replicates metadata. Multiple instances of the DIR or MRC can be configured to act as a replicated service, which means that any of them can be accessed by a client, and consistency is guaranteed through a replication protocol that runs between the instances.

The internal replication protocol resembles the one for the read-write replication, in that it is also based upon a primary/backup scheme with automatic fail-over through Flease. Unlike OSDs, which implement a replication scheme for individual files, however, the DIR and all MRCs are replicated at database level. Flease negotiates a primary instance among all BabuDB instances that run inside the services. The primary BabuDB instance propagates all updates in the form of database log entries to the backup instances. The total ordering of updates and the synchrony of the primary after the replica reset phase are ensured through the sequence numbers of the log entries.

## Replica Placement and Selection

XtreemFS supports the automatic placement and selection of replicas. Replica placement can be useful to control the assignment of OSDs to new replicas. For instance, it may be necessary to create replicas across different data centers to guarantee durability in the event of local disasters, close to their consumers to guarantee short network routes and low accesses latencies, or exclusively on OSDs in certain geographical regions for legal reasons. Similarly, replica selection allows to find the most suitable replicas among all available ones, e.g., to allow clients to retrieve their data as quickly as possible.

XtreemFS offers different policies to control the placement and selection of replicas. When replicas are automatically added to a file (e.g., because of a default on-close replication policy), the respective replica placement policy determines the OSDs for the new replicas. It selects the most suitable OSDs, based on the set of all available OSDs and information on the client's location, such as the client's IP address. A replica selection policy determines the order in which the replica set of a file is sent to clients that access the file, so as to lead the client to access those replicas first that are preferred according to the policy.

Different replica placement and selection policies exist, which implement the selection of OSDs and replicas based on OSD identifiers and domain names, static data center maps that define distances between domains and IP address ranges, as well as dynamically measured and estimated network latencies, which are provided by an implementation of the Vivaldi algorithm (Dabek, Cox, Kaashoek, & Morris, 2004). Besides these default policies, users can implement custom policies.

## SNAPSHOTS

XtreemFS supports snapshots to allow users to revert to prior versions of their data in the event of data loss or corruption caused by themselves or their applications. Snapshots also allow to create consistent on-line backups of the file system.

Traditional approaches for snapshots in file systems capture all files and directories in their momentary states by deferring concurrent changes. For XtreemFS, which distributes file content and metadata across a large number of servers, this is not an option. Taking a snapshot could lead to extended periods of unavailability because of failures or slow network connections; frequent snapshots could even keep the system from making progress at all. As a solution, XtreemFS resorts to a snapshot algorithm (Stender, Högqvist, & Kolbeck, 2010) that does not defer any changes, scales with the number of servers and tolerates arbitrary server failures and network partitionings.

### Approach

The snapshot algorithm keeps versions of all changed data by implementing a versioning scheme across all servers. OSDs record new ver-

sions of their files, either on every write or when a file is closed after writing. MRCs record versions of entire volumes when receiving snapshot requests from a client.

The relationship between versions and snapshots is established through timestamps. A timestamp is attached to each version, which originates from the responsible server's local clock. Server clocks are (loosely) synchronized to ensure that timestamps from different servers can be compared in a meaningful manner. This is done by running a clock synchronization protocol on each server, which involves regular communication with the DIR, an external NTP server, or a local GPS device.

### File Content Versioning

To record versions of files, OSDs implement a *copy-on-write* scheme at object granularity. We chose copy-on-write because it is easy to implement and fits well together with the internally used principle of storing objects as files on the OSD's local file system. An OSD records a new object version by creating a copy of the file with the previous version and applying the write to the copy. The resulting object version file is tagged with a timestamp.

New file versions are created when writing or closing a file, depending on the file's versioning policy. To create a file version, the OSD records the current time and file size in a persistent *file version log*. The log is necessary to ensure correctness in the presence of truncate operations and sparse files, and to ensure that an "on-close" versioning policy causes consistent versions to be captured.

### Metadata Snapshots

The MRC uses BabuDB (Stender, Kolbeck, et al., 2010) to store the metadata of its volumes. BabuDB is a fast key-value store. It uses log-structured merge trees (O'Neil, Cheng, Gawlick, & O'Neil, 1996) in a similar way as Google's Bigtable (Chang et al., 2006). This allows BabuDB to take snapshots of all metadata of a whole XtreemFS volume within a very short, constant period of time. Figure 4 illustrates the building blocks of BabuDB:

- A log which persistently records metadata changes to prevent data loss in case of shutdowns and failures.
- A persistent on-disk index for each volume and snapshot, which contains an efficiently searchable representation of all metadata.
- A stack of in-memory search trees for each volume, each reflecting a snapshot together with all other in-memory trees beneath and the on-disk index.

Updates are recorded in the log and also in the top in-memory tree, the *active tree*. To create a snapshot, it is sufficient to create a new active tree by adding an empty in-memory tree on top of the stack. This converts the formerly active tree into an immutable in-memory representation of a snapshot. To reduce the memory footprint, a snapshot tree can be merged in the background with

*Figure 4. Internal architecture of BabuDB*

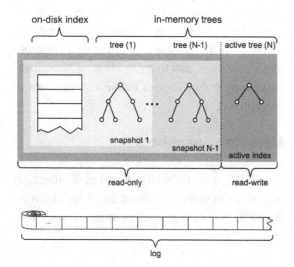

all subjacent in-memory trees and the volume's on-disk index. This results in a new on-disk index, which contains all metadata of the snapshot. The in-memory tree as well as obsolete parts of the log can then be discarded.

## Snapshot Access

XtreemFS users and administrators can take snapshots of entire volumes or individual subdirectories by means of a snapshot tool. To record a snapshot, the tool invokes a snapshot operation on the MRC, which records a volume or subtree snapshot at database level. The MRC assigns a timestamp to the snapshot, as well as a descriptive name if requested.

## Retrieving Object Versions

A snapshot can be accessed by mounting it, similar as a volume. Opening a file on the snapshot leads the MRC to attach the snapshot timestamp $t_s$ to the capability. To read an object of the file, the OSD has to retrieve the correct object version. To perform this task in an efficient manner, it maintains a memory-resident object version table for each open file. The object version table is sorted by its keys and effectively maps combined keys of object identifier and object version timestamp to the respective object versions. It is allocated and populated when the file is first accessed after having been opened and discarded when the file is closed.

The retrieval of object versions is illustrated in Figure 5. To find an object version attached to a specific snapshot, the OSD first seeks the respective file version timestamp $t_f$ in a memory-resident representation of the file version log. $t_f$ is largest timestamp that is smaller than or equal to $t_s$. In a second step, it performs a lookup in the object version table for the respective object version with the largest timestamp $t_o$ that is smaller than or equal to $t_f$. After having retrieved the object version, it is still is necessary to make sure that

*Figure 5. Illustration of a version retrieval of object #2 for a snapshot timestamp 2011-12-27 08:01:02*

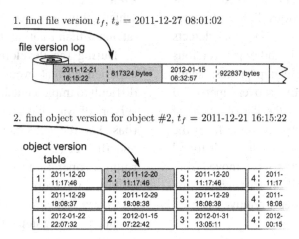

it actually belongs to the file version. This may not be the case if the file has been truncated since the object was created. Thus, it is necessary to compare $t_o$ to all file version timestamps $t'_f$ in the file version log with $t_o \leq t'_f \leq t_f$ and make sure that the file size attached to the respective file version log entry is large enough to cover the requested object identifier.

## Ensuring Consistency

A snapshot represents the latest versions of all files that were recorded up to the time when the metadata snapshot was recorded, as seen from the MRC's local clock. Given that a snapshot is recorded at time $t$ and the clock drift between any two servers never exceeds $\varepsilon$, a snapshot reflects all changes to files that were made up to $t - \varepsilon$ and no changes that were made later than $t + \varepsilon$. For any changes made within an $\varepsilon$ time frame around $t$, it is unspecified whether it is included or not.

The approach allows to efficiently capture a snapshot within a bounded time frame of $\varepsilon$, without any communication between servers. However, snapshots may be inconsistent if message latencies are smaller than $\varepsilon$. An application that changes a file and takes a snapshot right after having received the acknowledgment for the change expects the change to be included in the snapshot. If both performing the change and

requesting the snapshot happen within an $\varepsilon$ time frame, however, this is not guaranteed.

To solve the problem, each server piggybacks its current local time to any message sent in response to a local change. A client receiving a timestamped response message attaches the timestamp to any subsequent update requested on a server. When receiving a timestamped message, a server delays its execution until its local clock has advanced to some time later than the received timestamp. In practice, such artificial delays are unlikely and typically very short, as message transfer times are usually greater than $\varepsilon$, and clock synchronization protocols like NTP are capable of restraining $\varepsilon$ to milliseconds even on wide area networks (Mills, 1991).

## Version Cleanup

Since OSDs record new versions of their files and objects after files are closed (or with every write if desired), file and object versions can accumulate to large numbers. However, not all of these versions are effectively bound to a snapshot. If a file is updated multiple times before taking a snapshot on the MRC, only the latest of the resulting versions will be accessed. All other versions are superseded by the latest version and can thus be removed. The same issue may arise if metadata snapshots are deleted.

XtreemFS provides a cleanup tool to dispose of obsolete file and object versions. The tool triggers a cleanup process on a given OSD, which detects and removes superseded file and object versions in the background. The cleanup process scans each of its files. To be able to discover superseded versions, it initially fetches the list of snapshot timestamps for the respective volume from the MRC. If a superseded version of the file is found by means of the timestamp list, it is removed from the file version log, and all object versions that are exclusively assigned to it are removed as well.

## FUTURE DIRECTIONS AND LESSONS LEARNED

Based on the feedback of our users, we identified some functional extensions which could be incorporated into XtreemFS in the future. For instance, some users would prefer to sacrifice consistency of replicas for reduced latency of operations or offline access to a locally available replica. Another issue of the Read/Write file replication is that it requires at least three replicas and accordingly twice as much additional storage capacity to provide fault tolerance. Regarding the snapshot functionality, some users would like to revert to any previous file version, even if no snapshot was explicitly created.

In the future, we plan to look into possible solutions to these issues, such as disconnected operations, erasure codes, as well as continuous data protection mechanisms. However, some solutions e.g., giving up strong consistency, would break full POSIX compliance, which is one of the cornerstones of XtreemFS. Besides that, we will also investigate techniques to provide quality-of-service, autonomous replica management, hierarchical storage management, deduplication-aware data placement, and secure and fast end-to-end encryption. We expect that future solutions will be influenced by the emergence of commonly available flash-based storage mediums like SSDs which allow to persistently store data at lower latencies than rotating hard disks.

During the development of XtreemFS, we experienced that event-driven architectures are difficult to implement and debug. The XtreemFS server software has an event-driven architecture (based on the ideas presented in "Welsh, Culler, and Brewer (2001)"), which requires that long running operations (e.g., the communication with other servers) must not block and have to provide a callback function that triggers subsequent processing steps. This hinders the developer from writing source code that is easy to read and maintain, and makes it particularly difficult to debug complex distributed algorithms such as those for the replication in XtreemFS. Therefore, we do not recommend to choose this architecture for the implementation of distributed algorithms with a large state space.

## CONCLUSION

XtreemFS was designed with the goal to fill the gap between the fast parallel file systems used in clusters and high-performance computers (e.g., Lustre, PVFS, Panasas, Ceph) and the storage systems used in global data centers (e.g., Amazon S3, Google Cloud Storage). Both are tailored towards their specific usage scenarios: The former provide fast parallel data access to tightly connected, POSIX-compliant storage, while the latter support simple HTTP interfaces for storing large amounts of data without a hierarchical file system.

To a certain extent, XtreemFS serves both parties: It allows to run legacy applications in the Cloud without the need to adapt their file interface. This is possible, because XtreemFS supports the complete POSIX semantics and API. It provides elasticity, isolation, availability, and robustness in distributed environments with unreliable hardware components.

XtreemFS is an open-source project with an active user community. Source code, binaries and further information are available at http://www. xtreemfs.org. The project has reached a mature state and is used in several cloud computing projects, mostly as a backend for content delivery systems.

## ACKNOWLEDGMENT

The XtreemFS project would not have been possible without the contribution of many individuals who contributed to its design and implementation. We thank especially Felix Hupfeld and Björn Kolbeck, who headed the development of XtreemFS in the EU projects XtreemOS and Contrail, respectively. Financial support came from the EU projects XtreemOS (2006-2010) and Contrail (2010-2013) and also from the German BMBF project MoSGrid (2009-2012).

## REFERENCES

Adya, A., Dunagan, J., & Wolman, A. (2010). Centrifuge: Integrated lease management and partitioning for cloud services. In *Proceedings of the 7th USENIX Symposium on Networked Systems Design and Implementation*. USENIX.

Agrawal, D., & Abbadi, A. E. (1990). The tree quorum protocol: An efficient approach for managing replicated data. In *Proceedings of the 16th International Conference on Very Large Data Bases* (pp. 243–254). San Francisco, CA: Morgan Kaufmann Publishers Inc.

Armbrust, M., Fox, A., Griffith, R., Joseph, A. D., Katz, R. H., & Konwinski, A. etc. (2009). Above the clouds: A Berkeley view of cloud computing (Tech. Rep.). Berkeley, CA: EECS Department, University of California.

Braam, P. J. (2004). *The Lustre storage architecture*. Academic Press.

Burrows, M. (2006). Chubby distributed lock service. In *Proceedings of the Symposium on Operating System Design and Implementation, OSDI'06*. Seattle, WA: OSDI.

Carns, P. H., III, Ross, R. B., & Thakur, R. (2000). PVFS: A parallel file system for Linux clusters. In *Proceedings of the 4th Annual Linux Showcase and Conference* (pp. 317–327). USENIX Association.

Chang, F., Dean, J., Ghemawat, S., Hsieh, W. C., Wallach, D. A., Burrows, M., et al. (2006). Bigtable: A distributed storage system for structured data. In *OSDI '06: Proceedings of the 7th Symposium on Operating Systems Design and Implementation* (pp. 205–218). OSDI.

Cohen, B. (2003). Incentives build robustness in bittorrent. In *Proceedings of the Workshop on Economics of Peer-to-Peer Systems* (Vol. 6, pp. 68–72). IEEE.

Dabek, F., Cox, R., Kaashoek, F., & Morris, R. (2004). Vivaldi: A decentralized network coordinate system. In *Proceedings of the 2004 Conference on Applications, Technologies, Architectures, and Protocols for Computer Communications* (pp. 15–26). New York, NY: ACM.

Factor, M., Meth, K., Naor, D., Rodeh, O., & Satran, J. (2005). Object storage: The future building block for storage systems. In *Proceedings of the 2nd International IEEE Symposium on Mass Storage Systems and Technologies* (pp. 119–123). IEEE.

Ghemawat, S., Gobioff, H., & Leung, S. T. (2003). The Google file system. In *Proceedings of the Nineteenth ACM Symposium on Operating Systems Principles* (pp. 29–43). ACM.

Gobioff, H. B. (1999). *Security for a high performance commodity storage subsystem.* (Unpublished doctoral dissertation). Carnegie Mellon University, Pittsburgh, PA.

Hupfeld, F., Cortes, T., Kolbeck, B., Stender, J., Focht, E., & Hess, M. et al. (2008). The XtreemFS architecture – A case for object-based file systems in grids. *Concurrent Computing: Practical Experiments, 20,* 2049–2060. doi:10.1002/cpe.1304.

Kobayashi, K., Mikami, S., Kimura, H., & Tatebe, O. (2011). The gfarm file system on compute clouds. In *Proceedings of the 2011 IEEE International Symposium on Parallel and Distributed Processing Workshops and PhD Forum* (pp. 1034–1041). Washington, DC: IEEE Computer Society.

Kolbeck, B., Högqvist, M., Stender, J., & Hupfeld, F. (2011). Flease - Lease coordination without a lock server. In *Proceedings of the 25th IEEE International Symposium on Parallel and Distributed Processing (IPDPS 2011)* (pp. 978-988). IEEE.

Lamport, L. (1998). The part-time parliament. *ACM Transactions on Computer Systems, 16*(2), 133–169. doi:10.1145/279227.279229.

Mesnier, M., Ganger, G., & Riedel, E. (2003). Object-based storage. *IEEE Communications Magazine, 8,* 84–90. doi:10.1109/MCOM.2003.1222722.

Mills, D. L. (1991). Internet time synchronization: The network time protocol. *IEEE Transactions on Communications, 39*(10), 1482–1493. doi:10.1109/26.103043.

O'Neil, P., Cheng, E., Gawlick, D., & O'Neil, E. (1996). The log-structured merge-tree (LSM-tree). *Acta Informatica, 33*(4), 351–385. doi:10.1007/s002360050048.

Schmuck, F., & Haskin, R. (2002). GPFS: A shared-disk file system for large computing clusters. In *Proceedings of the 1st USENIX Conference on File and Storage Technologies* (pp. 231–244). USENIX.

Std, I.E.E.E. 1003.1-2008. (2008). *POSIX.1-2008, the open group base specifications issue 7.* Retrieved from http://pubs.opengroup.org/onlinepubs/9699919799/

Stender, J., Högqvist, M., & Kolbeck, B. (2010). Loosely time-synchronized snapshots in object-based file systems. In *Proceedings of the 29th IEEE International Performance, Computing, and Communications Conference* (pp. 188–197). IEEE Computer Society.

Stender, J., Kolbeck, B., Högqvist, M., & Hupfeld, F. (2010). BabuDB: Fast and efficient file system metadata storage. In *Proceedings of the 2010 International Workshop on Storage Network Architecture and Parallel I/OS* (pp. 51–58). Washington, DC: IEEE Computer Society.

Tang, H., Gulbeden, A., Zhou, J., Strathearn, W., Yang, T., & Chu, L. (2004). The Panasas ActiveScale storage cluster - Delivering scalable high bandwidth storage. In *Proceedings of the ACM/IEEE SC2004 Conference (SC'04)* (p. 53). ACM/IEEE.

Thomas, R. H. (1979). A majority consensus approach to concurrency control for multiple copy databases. *ACM Transactions on Database Systems, 4*(2), 180–209. doi:10.1145/320071.320076.

Weil, S. A., Brandt, S. A., Miller, E. L., Long, D. D. E., & Maltzahn, C. (2006). Ceph: A scalable, high-performance distributed file system. In *Proceedings of the 7th Symposium on Operating Systems Design and Implementation (OSDI)* (pp. 307–320). OSDI.

Welsh, M., Culler, D., & Brewer, E. (2001). Seda: An architecture for well-conditioned, scalable internet services. *SIGOPS Operating Systems Review*, *35*(5), 230–243. doi:10.1145/502059.502057.

## KEY TERMS AND DEFINITIONS

**Cloud File System:** A cloud file system provides access to distributed data resources in the cloud through a common file system interface.

**Copy-on-Write:** Copy-on-write is a version management mechanism that protects data from being overwritten by creating a copy prior to applying the write.

**Distributed Lease Negotiation Protocol:** A distributed lease negotiation protocol is a protocol for determining a lease in a network of distributed processes. A lease grants a client exclusive access to a resource for a given time period.

**Loosely Synchronized Clocks:** Loosely synchronized clocks are used in distributed systems to provide the illusion of a global time e.g., by applying a clock synchronization protocol.

**Object-Based File System:** An object-based file system stores the data on an elastic pool of independent, intelligent object storage devices, which can be scaled out in order to increase the total data capacity and throughput.

**Paxos:** Paxos is a protocol for determining consensus in a network of unreliable distributed processes.

**POSIX File System:** A POSIX file system is compliant with the POSIX standard for the file system interface and semantics, which means that it offers the same interface and semantics as a common local file system.

**Snapshot:** A snapshot represents the state of a system in a particular point in time.

**Strong Replica Consistency:** Strong replica consistency requires that all replicas see all write operations in the same order, and all write operations appear in the order given by the program code (program order).

## ENDNOTES

[1] http://aws.amazon.com/s3
[2] http://www.windowsazure.com
[3] http://www.google.com/enterprise/cloud/storage
[4] http://www.dropbox.com
[5] http://one.ubuntu.com
[6] http://www.zumodrive.com
[7] http://spideroak.com
[8] http://hekafs.org/
[9] http://www.gluster.org
[10] http://fuse.sourceforge.net/
[11] http://dokan-dev.net/en/
[12] http://www.arg0.net/encfs

# Compilation of References

Abadi, D. J. (2009). Data management in the cloud: Limitations and opportunities. *A Quarterly Bulletin of the Computer Society of the IEEE Technical Committee on Data Engineering, 32*(1), 3–12.

AbdelSalam, H., Maly, K., Mukkamala, R., Zubair, M., & Kaminsky, D. (2009). Towards energy efficient change management in a cloud computing environment. In *Proceedings of the 3rd International Conference on Autonomous Infrastructure, Management and Security* (LNCS), (Vol. 5637, pp. 161-166). IFIP International Federation for Information Processing. doi:10.1007/978-3-642-02627-0_13

Abu-libdeh, H., Princehouse, L., & Weatherspoon, H. (n.d.). *Racs: A case for cloud storage diversity*. Academic Press.

Achiwa, K., Yamamoto, A., & Yamagata, O. (1999). *Memory systems using a flash memory and method for controlling the memory system*. United States Patent, No 5, 930,193. Washington, DC: US Patent Office.

Adya, A., Dunagan, J., & Wolman, A. (2010). Centrifuge: Integrated lease management and partitioning for cloud services. In *Proceedings of the 7th USENIX Symposium on Networked Systems Design and Implementation*. USENIX.

Agarwal, S., Dunagan, J., Jain, N., Saroiu, S., Wolman, A., & Bhogan, H. (2010). Volley: Automated data placement for geo-distributed cloud services. In *Proceedings of the 7th Usenix Conference on Networked Systems Design and Implementation* (p. 2). Berkeley, CA: USENIX Association. Retrieved from http://portal.acm.org/citation.cfm ?id=1855711.1855713

Agrawal, D., & Abbadi, A. E. (1990). The tree quorum protocol: An efficient approach for managing replicated data. In *Proceedings of the 16th International Conference on Very Large Data Bases* (pp. 243–254). San Francisco, CA: Morgan Kaufmann Publishers Inc.

Agrawal, N., Prabhakaran, V., Wobber, T., Davis, J. D., Manasse, M., & Panigrahy, R. (2008). Design tradeoffs for SSD performance. In *Proceedings of the USENIX Annual Technical Conference (ATC)*. USENIX.

Aguilera, M. K., Merchant, A., Shah, M., Veitch, A., & Karamanolis, C. (2007). Sinfonia: A new paradigm for building scalable distributed systems. In *Proceedings of Twenty-First ACM SIGOPS Symposium on Operating Systems Principles* (pp. 159–174). New York, NY: ACM.

Alhamad, M., Dillon, T., & Chang, E. (2010b). SLA-based trust model for cloud computing. In Proceedings of Network-Based Information Systems (NBiS). NBiS. doi: doi:10.1109/NBiS.2010.67.

Alhamad, M., Dillon, T., & Chang, E. (2010a). Conceptual SLA framework for cloud computing. In *Proceedings of Digital Ecosystems and Technologies (DEST)*. IEEE. doi:10.1109/DEST.2010.5610586.

Almorsy, M., Grundy, J., & Ibrahim, A. (2011). Collaboration-based cloud computing security management framework. In Proceedings *4th International Conference on Cloud Computing* (pp. 364 - 371). IEEE. doi:10.1109/CLOUD.2011.9

Alonso, G., Casati, F., Kuno, H., & Machiraju, V. (2004). *Web services: Concepts, architectures and applications*. Berlin, Germany: Springer.

Amazon S3 SLA. (2009). *Amazon S3 service level agreement*. Retrieved from http://aws.amazon.com/s3-sla/

Amazon S3. (2009). *Amazon simple storage service.* Retrieved from http://aws.amazon.com/s3/

*Amazon simpledb* . (n.d.). Retrieved from http://aws.amazon.com/ simpledb/

American National Standards Institute. (1992). *ANSI SQL-92 specification, document number: ANSI X3.135-1992.* Retrieved November 30, 2012, from http://www.contrib.andrew.cmu.edu/~shadow/sql/sql1992.txt

Amir, Y., Danilov, C., & Stanton, J. (2000). A low latency, loss tolerant architecture and protocol for wide area group communication. In *Proceedings of the International Conference on Dependable Systems and Networks* (pp. 327-336). New York, NY: ACM.

Anderson, C. (2006). *The long tail: Why the future of business is selling less of more.* New York: Hyperion.

Andrieux, A., Czajkowski, K., Dan, A., Keahey, K., Ludwig, H., & Nakata, T. ... Xu, M. (2005). *Web services agreement specification (WSAgreement).* Retrieved from http://www.ggf.org/Public_Comment_Docs/Documents/Oct-2005/WS-AgreementSpecificationDraft050920.pdf

*Apache DeltaCloud.* (n.d.). Retrieved from http://delta-cloud.apache.org/

*Apache Hbase Reference Guide* . (n.d.). Retrieved from http://hbase.apache.org/book.html

Apache Software Foundation. (2011). *δ-cloud.* Retrieved November 30, 2012, from http://deltacloud.apache.org

*ApacheLibCloud.* (n.d.). Retrieved from http://libcloud.apache.org/

*Argus Authorization Service.* (n.d.). Retrieved from https://twiki.cern.ch/twiki/bin/view/EGEE/AuthorizationFramework

Armbrust, M., Fox, A., Griffith, R., Joseph, A. D., Katz, R. H., & Konwinski, A. etc. (2009). Above the clouds: A Berkeley view of cloud computing (Tech. Rep.). Berkeley, CA: EECS Department, University of California.

Armbrust, M., Fox, A., Griffith, R., Joseph, A. D., Katz, R., & Konwinski, A. et al. (2010). A view of cloud computing. *Communications of the ACM, 53*(4), 50–58. doi:10.1145/1721654.1721672.

Aronovich, L., Asher, R., Bachmat, E., Bitner, H., Hirsch, M., & Klein, S. T. (2009). The design of a similarity based deduplication system. In *Proceedings of Systor 2009: The Israeli Experimental Systems Conference* (pp. 6:1–6:14). New York, NY: ACM. Retrieved from http://doi.acm.org/10.1145/1534530.1534539

Assar, M., Namazie, S., & Estakhri, P. (1995). *Flash memory mass storage architecture incorporation wear leveling technique.* United States Patent, No 5,479,638. Washington, DC: US Patent Office.

Athanassoulis, M., Ailamaki, A., Chen, S., Gibbons, P., & Stoica, R. (2010). Flash in a DBMS: Where and How? *A Quarterly Bulletin of the Computer Society of the IEEE Technical Committee on Data Engineering, 33*(4), 28–34.

*Atmos Online Programmer's Guide.* (2010). Retrieved from https://community.emc.com/docs/DOC-3481

*AWS Identity and Access Management (IAM).* (n.d.). Retrieved from http://aws.amazon.com/iam/

Ban, A. (1995). *Flash file system.* United States Patent, No 5,404,485. Washington, DC: US Patent Office.

Ban, A. (1999). *Flash file system optimized for page-mode flash technologies.* United States Patent, No 5,937,425. Washington, DC: US Patent Office.

Banerjee, A. (2011). *Addressing big data telcom requirements for real-time analytics.* Retrieved August from http://www.sybase.com/files/White_Papers/Sybase-Big-Data-WP-3-9-11.pdf

Bechtolsheim, A. (2008). *Cloud computing.* Retrieved in 2011, from http://netseminar.stanford.edu/seminars/Cloud.pdf

Bela Ban/Red Hat. (2002). *JGroups - The JGroups project.* Retrieved November 30, 2012, from www.jgroups.org

Belaramani, N., Dahlin, M., Gao, L., Nayate, A., Venkataramani, A., Yalagandula, P., & Zheng, J. (2006). PRACTI replication. In *Proceedings of the USENIX Symposium on Networked Systems Design and Implementation (NSDI).* USENIX.

Belaramani, N., Dahlin, M., Nayate, A., & Zheng, J. (2008). *PADRE: A policy architecture for building data replication systems.*

Bhagwat, D., Eshghi, K., Long, D. D. E., & Lillibridge, M. (2009). Extreme binning: Scalable, parallel deduplication for chunk-based file backup. In *Proceedings of Mascots* (pp. 1–9). Mascots. doi:10.1109/MASCOT.2009.5366623.

Birman, K. P. (1993). The process group approach to reliable distributed computing. *Communications of the ACM, 36*(12), 37–53. doi:10.1145/163298.163303.

Bleikertz, S. (2010). *Automated security analysis of infrastructure clouds*. Retrieved from http://nordsecmob.tkk.fi/Thesisworks/Soren%20Bleikertz.pdf

Blumer, A., & Ligon, W. B. (1994). *The parallel virtual file system*. Paper presented at the 1994 PVM Users Group Meeting. New York, NY.

Bocchino, R. L., Adve, V. S., & Chamberlain, B. L. (2008). Software transactional memory for large scale clusters. In *Proceedings of the Symposium on Principles and Practice of Parallel Programming (PPOPP)* (pp. 247–258). New York, NY: ACM.

Boniface, M., Phillips, S. C., Sanchez-Macian, A., & Surridge, M. (2007). Dynamic service provisioning using GRIA SLAs. In *Proceedings of the 5th International Workshops on Service-Oriented Computing, ICSOC'07.* ICSOC.

Bonnet, P., & Bouganim, L. (2011). Flash device support for database management. In *Proceedings of the 5th Biennial Conference on Innovative Data Systems Research (CIDR)*. CIDR.

Boss, G., Malladi, P., Quan, D., Legregni, L., & Hall, H. (2007). *Cloud computing*. Retrieved from http://download.boulder.ibm.com/ibmdl/pub/software/dw/wes/hipods/Cloud_computing_wp_final_8Oct.pdf

Bouchenak, S. (2010). Automated control for SLA-aware elastic clouds. In Proceedings of FeBid 2010. ACM. doi: ACM 978-1-4503-0077-3/10/4

Boukhobza, J., Olivier, P., & Rubini, S. (2011). A cache management strategy to replace wear leveling techniques for embedded flash memory. In *Proceedings of the 2011 International Symposium on Performance Evaluation of Computer & Telecommunication Systems (SPECTS)*. SPECTS.

Boukhobza, J., & Olivier, P. (2011). An efficient hierarchical dual cache system for NAND flash memories. *International Journal of Digital Information and Wireless Communications, 1*(1), 175–194.

Braam, P. J. (2004). *The Lustre storage architecture.* Academic Press.

Bradshaw, D. (2012). *Cloud in Europe: Uptake, benefits, barriers, and market estimates.* Academic Press.

Brandic, I., Emeakaroha, V. C., Maurer, M., Dustdar, S., Acs, S., Kertesz, A., & Kecskemeti, G. (2010). LAYSI: A layered approach for SLA-violation propagation in self-manageable cloud infrastructures. In *Proceedings of Computer Software and Applications Conference Workshops (COMPSACW)*. IEEE.

Brewer, J. E., & Gill, M. (Eds.). (2008). *Nonvolatile memory technologies with emphasis on flash.* IEEE Press.

Brinkmann, A., & Effert, S. (2008). Redundant data placement strategies for cluster storage environments. In *Proceedings of the 12th International Conference on Principles of Distributed Systems* (pp. 551–554). Berlin: Springer-Verlag. Retrieved from http://dx.doi.org/10.1007/978-3-540-92221-6 38

Brock, M., & Goscinski, A. (2010). Toward a framework for cloud security. In *Proceedings of the 10th International Conference on Algorithms and Architectures for Parallel Processing* (LNCS) (Vol. 6082, pp. 254-263). Berlin, Germany: SpringerLink. doi: 10.1007/978-3-642-13136-3_26

Broder, A., & Mitzenmacher, M. (2005). Network applications of bloom filters: A survey. *Internet Mathematics, 1*(4), 485–509. doi:10.1080/15427951.2004.10129096.

Burrows, M. (2006). Chubby distributed lock service. In *Proceedings of the Symposium on Operating System Design and Implementation, OSDI'06.* Seattle, WA: OSDI.

Burrows, M. (2006). The chubby lock service for loosely-coupled distributed systems. In *Proceedings of the 7th Symposium on Operating Systems Design and Implementation* (pp. 335–350). Berkeley, CA: USENIX Association. Retrieved from http://portal.acm.org/citation.cfm?id=1298455.1298487

Buyya, R., Pandey, S., & Vecchiola, C. (2009). Cloudbus toolkit for market-oriented cloud computing. In *Proceedings of the 1st International Conference on Cloud Computing*, (LNCS), (Vol. 5931, pp. 24-44). Berlin, Germany: SpringerLink. doi: 10.1007/978-3-642-10665-1_4

Buyya, R., Ranjan, R., & Calheiros, R. (2010). InterCloud: Utility-oriented federation of cloud computing environments for scaling of application services. In *Proceedings of the 10th International Conference on Algorithms and Architectures for Parallel Processing*, (LNCS), (vol. 6081, pp. 13–31). Berlin: Springer. doi:10.1007/978-3-642-13119-6_2

Cachopo, J. (2007). *Development of rich domain models with atomic actions*. (Unpublished doctoral dissertation). Technical University of Lisbon, Lisbon, Portugal.

Cachopo, J., & Rito-Silva, A. (2006). Combining software transactional memory with a domain modeling language to simplify web application development. In *Proceedings of the 6th International Conference on Web Engineering* (pp. 297–304). New York, NY: ACM.

Cagdas, D., & Jacob, B. (2009). The performance of PC solid-state disks (SSDs) as a function of bandwidth. In *Proceedings of the International Symposium of Computer Architecture (ISCA)*. IEEE.

Cardosa, M., Korupolu, M. R., & Singh, A. (2009). Shares and utilities based power consolidation in virtualized server environments. In *Proceedings of the 11th IFIP/IEEE International Conference on Symposium on Integrated Network Management* (pp. 327–334). Piscataway, NJ: IEEE Press. Retrieved from http://portal.acm.org/citation.cfm?id=1688933.1688986

Carns, P. H., III, Ross, R. B., & Thakur, R. (2000). PVFS: A parallel file system for Linux clusters. In *Proceedings of the 4th Annual Linux Showcase and Conference* (pp. 317–327). USENIX Association.

Carter, J., & Rajamani, K. (2010). Designing energy efficient servers and data centers. *Computer, 43*(7), 76–78. doi:10.1109/MC.2010.198.

Carvalho, N., Cachopo, J., Rodrigues, L., & Rito-Silva, A. (2008). Versioned transactional shared memory for the fenixedu web application. In *Proceedings of the Second Workshop on Dependable Distributed Data Management* (pp. 15-18). New York, NY: ACM.

Carvalho, N., Romano, P., & Rodrigues, L. (2010). Asynchronous lease-based replication of software transactional memory. In *Proceedings of the ACM/IFIP/USENIX 11th Middleware Conference (Middleware)* (pp. 376-396). New York, NY: ACM.

Castro-Leon, E. et al. (2012). *Global IT manageability policies across service boundaries in a cloud environment*. Intel Technology Journal. doi:10.1109/SRII.2012.48.

Caulfield, A. M., Grupp, L. M., & Swanson, S. (2009). Gordon: Using flash memory to build fast, power-efficient clusters for data-intensive applications. In *Proceeding of the 14th International Conference on Architectural Support for Programming Languages and Operating Systems (ASPLOS)*. ASPOLOS.

Chang, F., Dean, J., Ghemawat, S., Hsieh, W. C., Wallach, D. A., Burrows, M., et al. (2006). Bigtable: A distributed storage system for structured data. In *Proceedings of the 7th USENIX Symposium on Operating Systems Design and Implementation* (vol. 7, p. 15). Berkeley, CA: USENIX Association. Retrieved from http://portal.acm.org/citation.cfm?id=1267308.1267323

Chang, L. (2007). On efficient wear leveling for large-scale flash-memory storage systems. In *Proceedings of the 2007 ACM Symposium on Applied Computing (SAC)*. ACM.

Chang, L. P., & Kuo, T. W. (2002). An adaptive striping architecture for flash memory storage systems of embedded systems. In *Proceedings of the 8th IEEE Real-Time and Embedded Technology and Applications Symposium (RTAS)*. IEEE.

Chang, R. C., Qawami, B., & Sabet-Sharghi, F. (2006). *Method and apparatus for managing an erase count block*. United States Patent, No 7,103,732. Washington, DC: US Patent Office.

Chang, V., Wills, G., & De Roure, D. (2010). A review of cloud business models and sustainability.[IEEE.]. *Proceedings of IEEE CLOUD, 2010*, 43–50.

Chaves, S., Westphall, C., & Lamin, F. (2010). SLA perspective in security management for cloud computing. In *Proceedings of the Sixth International Conference on Networking and Services (ICNS 2010)*. IEEE Computer Society. doi: 10.1109/ICNS.2010.36

Chiang, M., Cheng, C., & Wu, C. (2008). A new FTL-based flash memory management scheme with fast cleaning mechanism. In *Proceedings of the International Conference on Embedded Software and Systems (ICESS)*. ICESS.

Chiang, M., & Chang, R. C. (1999). Cleaning policies in mobile computers using flash memories. *Journal of Systems and Software, 48*(3), 213–231. doi:10.1016/S0164-1212(99)00059-X.

Cho, H., Shin, D., & Eom, Y. I. (2009). KAST: K-associative sector translation for NAND flash memory in real-time systems. In Proceedings of Design, Automation, and Test in Europe (DATE), (pp. 507-512). DATE.

Chockler, G., Keidar, I., & Vitenberg, R. (2001). Group communication specifications: A comprehensive study. *ACM Computing Surveys, 33*(4), 427–469. doi:10.1145/503112.503113.

Chou, T. (2009). *Seven clear business models*. New York: Active Book Press.

Chow, R., Golle, P., Jakobsson, M., Shi, E., Staddon, J., Masuoka, R., & Molina, J. (2009). Controlling data in the cloud: Outsourcing computation without outsourcing control. In *Proceedings of the 2009 ACM Workshop on Cloud Computing Security* (pp. 85-90). ACM. doi:10.1145/1655008.1655020

Chow, R., Jakobsson, M., Masuoka, R., Molina, J., Niu, Y., Shi, E., & Song, Z. (2010). Authentication in the clouds: A framework and its application to mobile users. In *Proceedings of the 2010 ACM Workshop on Cloud Computing Security Workshop 2010*. ACM. doi: 10.1145/1866835.1866837

Chung, T. S., & Park, H. S. (2007). STAFF: A flash driver algorithm minimizing block erasures. *Journal of Systems Architecture, 53*(12), 889–901. doi:10.1016/j.sysarc.2007.02.005.

Chung, T., Park, D., Park, S., Lee, D., Lee, S., & Song, H. (2009). A survey of flash translation layer. *Journal of Systems Architecture, 55*, 332–343. doi:10.1016/j.sysarc.2009.03.005.

Cisco. (2012). *Cisco visual networking index: Global mobile data traffic forecast update, 2011-2016*. Retrieved from http://www.cisco.com/en/US/solutions/collateral/ns341/ns525/ns537/ns705/ns827/white_paper_c11-520862.pdf

Clayman, S., Galis, A., & Mamatas, L. (2010). *Monitoring virtual networks with lattice*. Paper presented at Network Operations and Management Symposium Workshops. Osaka, Japan.

Clearspring Technologies. (2012). *The stream-lib library*. Retrieved November 30, 2012, from https://github.com/clearspring/stream-lib

Close, T. (2009). *ACLS don't*. Retrieved from http://www.hpl.hp.com/techreports/2009/HPL-2009-20.pdf

Cloudswitch. (2011, May). *CloudSwitch entrreprise*. Retrieved from http://www.cloudswitch.com/page/enterprise-cloud -computing-product-overview Dell boomi

Codd, E. F., Codd, S. B., & Salley, C. T. (1993). *Providing OLAP (on-line analytical processing) to user-analysis: An IT mandate*. E. F. Codd & Associates.

Cohen, B. (2003). Incentives build robustness in bittorrent. In *Proceedings of the Workshop on Economics of Peer-to-Peer Systems* (Vol. 6, pp. 68–72). IEEE.

Comuzzi, M., Kotsokalis, C., Spanoudakis, G., & Yahyapour, R. (2009). Establishing and monitoring SLAs in complex service based system. In *Proceedings of the International Conference on Web Services, 2009 (ICWS 2009)* (pp. 783–790). IEEE. doi:10.1109/ICWS.2009.47

Conley, K. M. (2005). *Zone boundary adjustment for defects in non-volatile memories*. United States Patent, No 6,901,498. Washington, DC: US Patent Office.

Cooper, B. F., Ramakrishnan, R., Srivastava, U., Silberstein, A., Bohannon, P., Jacobsen, H.-A., et al. (2008). Pnuts: Yahoo!'s hosted data serving platform. *Proceedings of VLDB Endowment, 1*(2), 1277–1288. Retrieved from http://dx.doi.org/10.1145/1454159.1454167

Cossu, R., Pacini, F., Goncalves, P., & Fusco, L. (2010). Data and computing intensive applications in GENESI-DR. In *Proceedings of EGU General Assembly Conference* (p. 14169). EGU.

Couceiro, M., Romano, P., & Rodrigues, L. (2010). A machine learning approach to performance prediction of total order broadcast protocols. In *Proceedings of the 2010 Fourth IEEE International Conference on Self-Adaptive and Self-Organizing Systems* (pp. 184-193). Washington, DC: IEEE Computer Society.

Couceiro, M., Romano, P., & Rodrigues, L. (2011). PolyCert: Polymorphic self-optimizing replication for in-memory transactional grids. In *Proceedings of the 12th ACM/IFIP/USENIX International Conference on Middleware* (pp. 309-328). Berlin, Germany: Springer-Verlag.

Couceiro, M., Romano, P., Carvalho, N., & Rodrigues, L. (2009). D2stm: Dependable distributed software transactional memory. In *Proceedings of the 15th Pacific Rim International Symposium on Dependable Computing* (pp. 307-313). Washington, DC: IEEE Computer Society.

Couceiro, M., Romano, P., & Rodrigues, L. (2011). Towards autonomic transactional replication for cloud environments. In Petcu, D., & Poletti, J. (Eds.), *European Research Activities in Cloud Computing*. Cambridge, UK: Cambridge Scholars Publishing.

Creasey, J. (2005). Hybrid hard drives with non-volatile flash and longhorn. In *Proceedings of Windows Hardware Engineering Conference (WinHEC)*. WinHEC.

*Cross-Enterprise Security and Privacy Authorization - XSPA- Profile of XACMLv2.0 for Healthcare Version 1.0.* (n.d.). Retrieved from http://www.oasis-open.org/committees/document.php?document id=34164&wg abbrev=xacml

Crunchbase. (2011). *Crunchbase.* Retrieved from http://www.crunchbase.com/company/signiant

Dabek, F., Cox, R., Kaashoek, F., & Morris, R. (2004). Vivaldi: A decentralized network coordinate system. In *Proceedings of the 2004 Conference on Applications, Technologies, Architectures, and Protocols for Computer Communications* (pp. 15–26). New York, NY: ACM.

Dan, A., Franck, R., Keller, A., King, R., & Ludwig, H. (2002). *Web service level agreement (WSLA) language specification.* Academic Press.

Das, S., Agrawal, D., & El Abbadi, A. (2010). G-store: A scalable data store for transactional multi key access in the cloud. In *Proceedings of the 1st ACM Symposium on Cloud Computing* (pp. 163–174). New York, NY: ACM. Retrieved from http://doi.acm.org/10.1145/1807128.1807157

*Data Deduplication.* (n.d.). Retrieved from http://searchstorage.techtarget.com/definition/data-deduplication

Debnath, B., Subramanya, S., Du, D., & Lilja, D. J. (2009). Large block CLOCK (LB-CLOCK): A write caching algorithm for solid state disks. In *Proceedings of the 17th IEEE International Symposium on Modeling, Analysis & Simulation of Computer and Telecommunication Systems (MASCOTS)*. IEEE.

DeCandia, G., Hastorun, D., Jampani, M., Kakulapati, G., Lakshman, A., Pilchin, A., et al. (2007). Dynamo: Amazon's highly available key-value store. *SIGOPS Operating Systems Review, 41*, 205–220. Retrieved from http://doi.acm.org/10.1145/1323293.1294281

Delaet & Joosen. (2009). Managing your content with cimple-a content-centric storage interface. In *Proceedings of Local Computer Networks, 2009*. IEEE.

*Dell Press Releases.* (n.d.). Retrieved from http://content.dell.com/us/en/corp/d/press-releases/2011-10-25-dell-boomi-fall11-v5

DeWitt, D., & Stonebraker, M. (2009). *Mapreduce: A major step backwards.* Retrieved November 30, 2012, from http://www.databasecolumn.com/2008/01/mapreduce-a-major-step-back.html

DeWitt, D. J., & Gray, J. (1990). Parallel database systems: the future of database processing or a passing fad? *SIGMOD Record, 19*, 104–112. Retrieved from http://doi.acm.org/10.1145/122058.122071 doi:10.1145/122058.122071.

Di Martino, B., Petcu, D., Cossu, R., Goncalves, P., Gulyas, L., & Loichate, M. (2011). Building a mosaic of Clouds. *Lecture Notes in Computer Science, 6586*, 529–536. doi:10.1007/978-3-642-21878-1_70.

Di Sanzo, P., Ciciani, B., Quaglia, F., Palmieri, R., & Romano, P. (2012). On the analytical modeling of concurrency control algorithms for software transactional memories: The case of commit-time-locking. *Performance Evaluation, 69*(5), 187–205. doi:10.1016/j.peva.2011.05.002.

Didona, D., Romano, P., Peluso, S., & Quaglia, F. (2011). Transactional auto scaler: Elastic scaling of in-memory transactional data grids. In *Proceedings of the 9th International Conference on Autonomic Computing (ICAC 2012)* (pp. 17-21). New York, NY: ACM.

*Distributed Databases Survey* . (n.d.). Retrieved from http://wiki.toadforcloud.com/index.php/Surveydistributeddatabases#Overview

DocumentCloud. (2011). *DocumentCloud*. Retrieved from http://www.documentcloud.org/featured

DocumentCloud. (2012). *DocumentCloud*. Retrieved from http://blog.documentcloud.org/blog/2011/06/new-home-at-ire/

Dodda, R., Smith, C., & Moorsel, A. (2009). An architecture for cross-cloud system management. In *Proceedings of IC3 2009*. Springer-Verlag. doi:10.1007/978-3-642-03547-0_53

Dong, W., Douglis, F., Li, K., Patterson, H., Reddy, S., & Shilane, P. (2011). Tradeoffs in scalable data routing for deduplication clusters. In *Proceedings of the 9th USENIX Conference on File and Storage Technologies* (p. 2). Berkeley, CA: USENIX Association. Retrieved from http://portal.acm.org/citation.cfm?id=1960475.1960477

*Dropbox* . (n.d.). Retrieved from https://www.dropbox.com/

EBU. (2002). *EBU*. Retrieved from http://www.ebu.ch/CMSimages/en/DSG_final_report_E_tcm6-5090.pdf

Eigler, F. C. (2006). Problem solving with Systemtap. In *Proceedings of the Linux Symposium*. Ottawa, Canada: Linux.

Elmroth, E., & Larsson, L. (2009). Interfaces for placement, migration, and monitoring of virtual machines in federated clouds. In *Proceedings of the 2009 Eighth International Conference on Grid and Cooperative Computing* (pp. 253–260). Washington, DC: IEEE Computer Society. Retrieved from http://dx.doi.org/10.1109/GCC.2009.36

Elmroth, E., & Tordsson, J. (2005). An interoperable, standards-based grid resource broker and job submission service. In *Proceedings of the First International Conference on E-Science and Grid Computing* (pp. 212–220). Washington, DC: IEEE Computer Society. Retrieved from http://13portal.acm.org/citation.cfm?id=1107836.1107876

*Emc Avamar*. (n.d.). Retrieved from http://www.emc.com/collateral/software/data-sheet/h2568-emc-avamar-ds.pdf

EMC Corporation Community Network. (2012). *Atmos programmer's guide 1.4.1*. Retrieved April 2012, from https://community.emc.com/docs/DOC-10508

EMC Corporation Website. (2012). *Atmos - cloud storage, big data - EMC*. Retrieved April 2012, from https://http://www.emc.com/storage/atmos/atmos.htm

EMC Corporation White Papers. (2012). *Emc atmos cloud optimized storage for web services*. Retrieved April 2012, from http://www.emc.com/collateral/software/white-papers/h7067-atmos-cloud-optimized-storage-wp.pdf

Emeakaroha, V. C., Brandic, I., Maurer, M., & Dustdar, S. (2010). Low level metrics to high level SLAs - LoM2HiS framework: Bridging the gap between monitored metrics and SLA parameters in cloud environments. In Proceedings of High Performance Computing and Simulation (HPCS). HPCS.

Emeakaroha, V. C., Netto, M. A. S., Calheiros, R. N., Brandic, I., Buyya, R., & De Rose, C. A. F. (2011). Towards autonomic detection of SLA violations in cloud infrastructures. *Future Generation Computer Systems*. doi: doi:10.1016/j.future.2011.08.018.

ENISA. (2009). *Cloud computing - Benefits, risks and recommendations for information security*. ENISA.

Etro, F. (2009). *The economic impact of cloud computing on business creation, employment and output in Europe*. Retrieved from http://www.intertic.org/Policy%20Papers/CC.pdf

Factor, M., Meth, K., Naor, D., Rodeh, O., & Satran, J. (2005). Object storage: The future building block for storage systems. In *Proceedings of the 2nd International IEEE Symposium on Mass Storage Systems and Technologies* (pp. 119–123). IEEE.

Farmer, D. (2010). *Study projects nearly 45-fold annual data growth by 2020*. Retrieved August, 2012, from http://www.emc.com/about/news/press/2010/20100504-01.htm

Felber, P., Fetzer, C., & Riegel, T. (2008). Dynamic performance tuning of word-based software transactional memory. In *Proceedings of the 13th ACM SIGPLAN Symposium on Principles and Practice of Parallel Programming* (pp. 237–246). New York, NY: ACM.

Felter, W., Hylick, A., & Carter, J. (2011). Reliability-aware energy management for hybrid storage systems. In *Proceedings of the IEEE 27th Symposium on Mass Storage Systems and Technologies (MSST)*. IEEE.

*Filesystem in Userspace*. (n.d.). Retrieved from http://fuse.sourceforge.net/

*Fit4green*. (n.d.). Retrieved from http://www.fit4green.eu/

*Force.com*. (n.d.). Retrieved from http://www.force.com/

Ford, D., Labelle, F., Popovici, F. I., Stokely, M., Truong, V.-A., Barroso, L., et al. (2010). Availability in globally distributed storage systems. In *Proceedings of the 9th USENIX Conference on Operating Systems Design and Implementation* (pp. 1–7). Berkeley, CA: USENIX Association. Retrieved from http://portal.acm.org/citation.cfm?id=1924943.1924948

Foundation, K. (2012). *Knight foundation*. Retrieved from http://knightfoundation.org/about/

Friedman, R., & Hadad, R. (2006). Adaptive batching for replicated servers. In *Proceedings of the 25th IEEE Symposium on Reliable Distributed Systems* (pp. 311–320). Washington, DC: IEEE Computer Society.

Fusco, L., Cossu, R., & Retscher, C. (2008). Open grid services for Envisat and earth observation applications. In Plaza, A., & Chang, C. (Eds.), *High Performance Computing in Remote Sensing* (pp. 237–280). London: Chapman & Hall.

Ganesan, P., Bawa, M., & Garcia-Molina, H. (2004). Online balancing of range-partitioned data with applications to peer-to-peer systems. In *Proceedings of the Thirtieth International Conference on Very Large Data Bases* (vol. 30, pp. 444–455). VLDB Endowment. Retrieved from http://portal.acm.org/citation.cfm?id=1316689.1316729

Garbatov, S., & Cachopo, J. (2011b). Software cache eviction policy based on stochastic approach. In *Proceedings of the Sixth International Conference on Software Engineering Advances*. IEEE.

Garbatov, S., & Cachopo, J. (2011c). Optimal functionality and domain data clustering based on latent Dirichlet allocation. In *Proceedings of the Sixth International Conference on Software Engineering Advances*. XPS.

Garbatov, S., & Cachopo, J. (2012). Decreasing memory footprints for better enterprise java application performance. In *Proceedings of the 23rd International Conference on Database and Expert Systems Applications* (pp. 430-437). Berlin, Germany: Springer.

Garbatov, S., & Cachopo, J. (2011a). Data access pattern analysis and prediction for object-oriented applications. *INFOCOMP Journal of Computer Science, 4*(10), 1–14.

Garcia, D. Z. G., & Felgar de Toledo, M. B. (2008). An approach for establishing trust relationships in the Web service technology. In *Proceedings of the International Federation for Information Processing*, (Vol. 283, pp. 509–516). Boston: Springer. doi:10.1007/978-0-387-84837-2_53

Garcia-Molina & Salem. (1992). Main memory database systems: An overview. *IEEE Transactions on Knowledge and Data Engineering, 4*(6), 509–516. doi:10.1109/69.180602.

Ghemawat, S., Gobioff, H., & Leung, S. T. (2003). The Google file system. In *Proceedings of the Nineteenth ACM Symposium on Operating Systems Principles* (pp. 29–43). ACM.

Ghys, F., Mampaey, M., Smouts, M., & Vaaraniemi, A. (2003). *3G multimedia network services, accounting, and user profiles*. Boston: Artech House.

*GIS*. (2012). Retrieved from http://www.3gis.net/default.asp?lang=eng

Gilbert, S., & Lynch, N. (2002). Brewer's conjecture and the feasibility of consistent, available, partition-tolerant web services. *SIGACT News, 33*, 51–59. Retrieved from http://doi.acm.org/10.1145/564585.564601

*Glusterfs Wiki*. (n.d.). Retrieved from http://en.wikipedia.org/wiki/ GlusterFS

*GlusterFS*. (n.d.). Retrieved from http://www.gluster.org/

GNU. (2001). *The GNU C library reference manual*. Retrieved from http://www.gnu.org/software/libc/manual/htmlnode/Name-Service-Switch.html

Gobioff, H. B. (1999). *Security for a high performance commodity storage subsystem*. (Unpublished doctoral dissertation). Carnegie Mellon University, Pittsburgh, PA.

Goetz, B., Peierls, T., Bloch, J., Bowbeer, J., Holmes, D., & Lea, D. (2006). *Java concurrency in practice*. Boston, MA: Addison Wesley.

*GoGrid*. (n.d.). Retrieved from http://www.gogrid.com/

Golpayegani, N., & Halem, M. (2009). Cloud computing for satellite data processing on high end compute clusters. In *Proceedings of the IEEE International Conference on Cloud Computing* (pp. 88-92). IEEE.

*Google App. Engine*. (n.d.). Retrieved from https://developers.google.com/appengine/

*Google Cloud Storage*. (n.d.). Retrieved from http://www.google.com/enterprise/cloud/ storage/

Gramoli, V., Harmanci, D., & Felber, P. (2008). Toward a theory of input acceptance for transactional memories. In *Proceedings of the 12th International Conference on Principles of Distributed Systems* (pp. 527-533). Berlin, Germany: Springer.

Gray, J. (1995). Queues are databases. In *Proceedings 7th High Performance Transaction Processing Workshop*. Asilomar, CA: Prentice Hall.

Gray, J. (2006a). *E-science: The next decade will be exciting*. Retrieved August, 2012, from http://research.microsoft.com/en-us/um/people/gray/talksETH_E_Science.ppt

Gray, J. (2006b). *Tape is dead, disk is tape, flash is disk, RAM locality is king*. Redmond, WA: Storage Guru Gong Show.

Gray, J., & Reuter, A. (1993). *Transaction processing: Concepts and techniques*. Oxford, UK: Elsevier Lt.

*Green Data Centers* . (n.d.). Retrieved from http://www.green-datacenters.eu/

*Green Grid* . (n.d.). Retrieved from http://www.thegreengrid.org/

Green, J. (2012, July 31). *OTT VoIP to cost telcos $479 billion to 2020*. Retrieved from http://ovum.com/2012/07/31/ott-voip-to-cost-telcos-479-billion-to-2020/

Grupp, L. M., Caulfield, A. M., Coburn, J., Swanson, S., Yaakobi, E., Siegel, P. H., & Wolf, J. K. (2009). Characterizing flash memory: Anomalies, observations, and applications. In *Proceedings of the 42nd Annual IEEE/ACM International Symposium on Microarchitecture (MICRO)*. IEEE/ACM.

Guardian. (2012, June 30). *Guardian*. Retrieved from www.guardian.co.uk

Guerraoui, R., & Kapalka, M. (2008). On the correctness of transactional memory. In *Proceedings of the 13th ACM SIGPLAN Symposium on Principles and Practice of Parallel Programming* (pp. 175-184). New York, NY: ACM.

Guerraoui, R., Herlihy, M., & Pochon, B. (2005). Polymorphic contention management. In *Proceedings of the Nineteenth International Symposium on Distributed Computing* (pp. 303-323). Berlin, Germany: Springer.

Guerraoui, R., & Rodrigues, L. (2006). *Introduction to reliable distributed programming*. Berlin, Germany: Springer.

Gulati, A., Ahmad, I., & Waldspurger, C. A. (2009). Parda: Proportional allocation of resources for distributed storage access. In *Proceedings of the 7th Conference on File and Storage Technologies* (pp. 85–98). Berkeley, CA: USENIX Association. Retrieved from http://portal.acm.org/citation.cfm?id=1525908.1525915

Gulati, A., Kumar, C., Ahmad, I., & Kumar, K. (2010). Basil: Automated io load balancing across storage devices. In *Proceedings of the 8th USENIX Conference on File and Storage Technologies* (p. 13). Berkeley, CA: USENIX Association. Retrieved from http://portal.acm.org/citation.cfm?id=1855511.1855524

Gupta, A., Kim, Y., & Urgaonkar, B. (2009). DFTL: A flash translation layer employing demand-based selective caching of page-level address mappings. In *Proceedings of the 14th International Conference on Architectural Support for Programming Languages and Operating Systems (ASPLOS)*. ASPLOS.

Gurumurthi, S. (2009). Architecting storage for the cloud computing area. *IEEE Micro, 29*(6), 68–71. doi:10.1109/MM.2009.92.

Guyon, I., & Elisseeff, A. (2003). An introduction to variable and feature selection. *Journal of Machine Learning Research, 3*, 157–1182.

Hadoop Wiki. (2012). *Hadoop map/reduce data processing benchmarks*. Retrieved November 30, 2012, from http://wiki.apache.org/hadoop/DataProcessingBenchmarks

Harnik, D., Naor, D., & Segall, I. (2009). Low power mode in cloud storage systems. In *Proceedings of the 2009 IEEE International Symposium on Parallel & Distributed Processing* (pp. 1–8). Washington, DC: IEEE Computer Society. Retrieved from http://portal.acm.org/citation.cfm?id=1586640.1587438

Harnik, D., Pinkas, B., & Shulman-Peleg, A. (2010). Side channels in cloud services: Deduplication in cloud storage. *IEEE Security and Privacy, 8*, 40–47. Retrieved from http://doi.ieeecomputersociety.org/10.1109/MSP.2010.18

Harris, T., & Fraser, K. (2003). Language support for lightweight transactions. *ACM SIGPLAN Notices, 38*(11), 388–402. doi:10.1145/949343.949340.

Hassoun, M. H. (1993). *Associative neural memories: Theory and implementation*. Oxford, UK: Oxford University Press.

HBase Apache Hadoop Project. (2012a). *Apache HBase reference guide*. Retrieved April, 2012, from http://hbase.apache.org/book.html

HDFS Apache Hadoop Project. (2012b). *Hdfs architecture guide*. Retrieved April 2012, from http://hadoop.apache.org/common/docs/r1.0.2/hdfs_design.html

HDFS Apache Hadoop Project. (2012c). *Hadoop 1.0.2 java api*. Retrieved April 2012, from http://hadoop.apache.org/ common/docs/current/api/

*Hdfs, Apache Hadoop Project* . (n.d.). Retrieved from http://hadoop.apache.org/hdfs/

Herlihy, M., Eliot, J., & Moss, B. (1993). Transactional memory: Architectural support for lock-free data structures. In *Proceedings of the International Symposium on Computer Architecture* (pp. 289-300). New York, NY: ACM.

Herlihy, M., Luchangco, V., Moir, M., & Scherer, W. N., III. (2003). Software transactional memory for dynamic-sized data structures. In *Proceedings of the Twenty-Second Annual Symposium on Principles of Distributed Computing* (pp. 92–101). New York, NY: ACM.

Hibernate. (2009). *Hibernate*. Retrieved November 30, 2012, from http://www.hibernate.org

Hosseini, A., Sommerville, I., & Sriram, I. (2010). *Research challenges for enterprise cloud computing*. Retrieved from http://arxiv.org/abs/1001.3257

Hsieh, J., Kuo, T., & Chang, L. (2006). Efficient identification of hot data for flash memory storage systems. *ACM Transactions on Storage, 2*(1), 22–40. doi:10.1145/1138041.1138043.

Hsieh, J., Tsai, Y., Kuo, T., & Lee, T. (2008). Configurable flash-memory management: Performance versus overheads. *IEEE Transactions on Computers, 57*(11), 1571–1583. doi:10.1109/TC.2008.61.

Hu, J., Jiang, H., Tian, L., & Xu, L. (2010). PUD-LRU: An erase-efficient write buffer management algorithm for flash memory SSD. In *Proceedings of the 2010 IEEE International Symposium on of Modeling, Analysis & Simulation of Computer and Telecommunication Systems (MASCOTS)*. IEEE.

Hui, L. (2009). Challenges in SLA translation. *SLASOI, FP7216556, 1-6. Sla translation 27 30 Violation 28 29.*

Hupfeld, F., Cortes, T., Kolbeck, B., Stender, J., Focht, E., & Hess, M. et al. (2008). The XtreemFS architecture – A case for object-based file systems in grids. *Concurrent Computing: Practical Experiments, 20*, 2049–2060. doi:10.1002/cpe.1304.

*Hypertable Inc* . (n.d.). Retrieved from http://hypertable.com/

iBATIS. (2009). *iBATIS*. Retrieved November 30, 2012, from http://ibatis.apache.org

*IBM Cast Iron*. (n.d.). Retrieved from http://www-01.ibm.com/software/integration/cast-iron-cloud-integration/#

*IBM General Parallel File System* . (n.d.). Retrieved from http://www-03.ibm.com/systems/software/gpfs/

IBM. (2012). *Many eyes*. Retrieved from http://www-958.ibm.com/software/data/cognos/manyeyes/page/About.html

Ioannidis, J., Ioannidis, S., Keromytis, A. D., & Prevelakis, V. (2003). Fileteller: Paying and getting paid for file storage. In *Proceedings of the 6th International Conference on Financial Cryptography* (pp. 282–299). Berlin: Springer-Verlag. Retrieved from http://portal.acm.org/citation.cfm?id=1765278.1765298

*Isilon Onefs Operating System* . (n.d.). Retrieved from http://www.ndm.net/isilonstore/isilon/isilon-onefs-operating-system

Java Community Process. (2001). *Java caching API*. Retrieved November 30, 2012, from http://jcp.org/en/jsr/summary?id=107

JBoss/Red Hat. (2001). *INFINISPAN - Open source data grids*. Retrieved November 30, 2012, from http://www.jboss.org/infinispan

JBoss/Red Hat. (2010). *Infinispan eviction, batching updates and LIRS*. Retrieved November 30, 2012, from http://infinispan.blogspot.com/2010/03/infinispan-eviction-batching-updates.html

JBoss/Red Hat. (2012a). *RHQ project*. Retrieved November 30, 2012, from http://www.rhq-project.org

JBoss/Red Hat. (2012b). *Teiid*. Retrieved November 30, 2012, from http://www.jboss.org/teiid

*Jclouds*. (n.d.). Retrieved from http://code.google.com/p/jclouds/

Jeffery, K. et al. (2010). *The future of cloud computing: Opportunities for European cloud computing beyond 2010*. Academic Press.

Jeffrey, D., & Sanjay, G. (2008). MapReduce: Simplified data processing on large clusters. *Communications of the ACM*, *51*(1), 107–113. doi:10.1145/1327452.1327492.

Jiang, S., Zhang, L., Yuan, X., Hu, H., & Chen, Y. (2011). SFTL: An efficient address translation for flash memory by exploiting spatial locality. In *Proceedings of 2011 IEEE 27th Symposium on Mass Storage Systems and Technologies (MSST)*. IEEE.

Jo, H., Kang, J., Park, S., Kim, J., & Lee, J. (2006). FAB: A flash-aware buffer management policy for portable media players. *IEEE Transactions on Consumer Electronics*, *52*(2), 485–493. doi:10.1109/TCE.2006.1649669.

*JSON Web Token*. (n.d.). Retrieved from http://self-issued.info/docs/draft-jones-json-Web-token.html

Jung, D., Kang, J. U., Jo, H., Kim, J. S., & Lee, J. (2010). Superblock FTL: A superblock-based flash translation layer with a hybrid address translation scheme. *ACM Transactions on Embedded Computing Systems*, *9*(4), 1–41. doi:10.1145/1721695.1721706.

Kalyvianaki, E., Charalambous, T., & Hand, S. (2009). Self-adaptive and self-configured CPU resource provisioning for virtualized servers using Kalman filters. In *Proceedings of the 6th International Conference on Autonomic Computing* (pp. 117-126). New York, NY: ACM.

Kamara, S., & Lauter, K. (2010). Cryptographic cloud storage. In *Proceedings of the Financial Cryptography: Workshop on Real-Life Cryptographic Protocols and Standardization*. Retrieved from http://research.microsoft.com/pubs/112576/crypto-cloud.pdf

Kang, S., Park, S., Jung, H., Shim, H., & Cha, J. (2009). Performance trade-offs in using NVRAM write buffer for flash memory-based storage devices. *IEEE Transactions on Computers*, *58*(6), 744–758. doi:10.1109/TC.2008.224.

Kang, W., Lee, S., & Moon, B. (2012). Flash-based extended cache for higher throughput and faster recovery. *Proceedings of the VLDB Endowment*, *5*(11), 1615–1626.

Karger, D., Lehman, V., Leighton, T., Panigrahy, R., Levine, V., & Lewin, D. (1997). Consistent hashing and random trees: Distributed caching protocols for relieving hot spots on the world wide web. In *Proceedings of the Twenty-Ninth Annual ACM Symposium on Theory of Computing* (pp. 654–663). New York, NY: ACM.

Karp, A. H. (n.d.). *From ABAC to ZBAC: The evolution of access control models*. Retrieved from http://www.hpl.hp.com/ techreports/2009/HPL-2009-30.pdf

Kaushik, R. T., Cherkasova, L., Campbell, R., & Nahrstedt, K. (2010). Lightning: Self-adaptive, energy-conserving, multi-zoned, commodity green cloud storage system. In *Proceedings of the 19th ACM International Symposium on High Performance Distributed Computing* (pp. 332–335). New York, NY: ACM. Retrieved from http://doi.acm.org/10.1145/1851476.1851523

Kawaguchi, A., Nishioka, S., & Motoda, H. (1995). A flash memory based file system. In *Proceedings of the USENIX 1995 Annual Technical Conference (ATC)*. USENIX.

Keleher, P., Cox, A. L., & Zwaenepoel, W. (1992). Lazy release consistency for software distributed shared memory. In *Proceedings of the 19th Annual International Symposium on Computer Architecture* (pp. 13–21). New York, NY: ACM.

Keller, A., & Ludwig, H. (2003). The WSLA framework: Specifying and monitoring service level agreements for web services. *Journal of Network and Systems Management*, 11.

Kernel. (2005). *Linux-pam*. Retrieved from http://www.kernel.org/pub/linux/libs/pam

Kim, H., & Ahn, S. (2008). BPLRU: A buffer management scheme for improving random writes in flash storage. In *Proceedings of the 6th USENIX Conference on File and Storage Technologies (FAST)*. FAST.

Kim, J., Kim, J. M., Noh, S. H., Min, S. L., & Cho, Y. (2002). A space-efficient flash translation layer for compact flash systems. *IEEE Transactions on Consumer Electronics, 48*(2), 366–375. doi:10.1109/TCE.2002.1010143.

Kobayashi, K., Mikami, S., Kimura, H., & Tatebe, O. (2011). The gfarm file system on compute clouds. In *Proceedings of the 2011 IEEE International Symposium on Parallel and Distributed Processing Workshops and PhD Forum* (pp. 1034–1041). Washington, DC: IEEE Computer Society.

Kolbeck, B., Högqvist, M., Stender, J., & Hupfeld, F. (2011). Flease - Lease coordination without a lock server. In *Proceedings of the 25th IEEE International Symposium on Parallel and Distributed Processing (IPDPS 2011)* (pp. 978-988). IEEE.

Kolodner, E. K., Tal, S., Kyriazis, D., Naor, D., Allalouf, M., & Bonello, L. … Wolfsthal, Y. (2011). A cloud environment for data-intensive storage services. In *Proceedings of Cloud Computing Technology and Science (CloudCom)*. IEEE.

Kolodner, H., Naor, D., Tal, S., Koutsoutos, S., Mavrogeorgi, N., & Gogouvitis, S. … Salant, E. (2011). Data-intensive storage services on clouds: Limitations, challenges and enablers. In *Proceedings of eChallenges e-2011 Conference*. eChallenges.

Koltsidas, I., & Viglas, S. D. (2008). Flashing up the storage layer. *Proceedings of the VLDB Endowment, 1*(1), 512–525.

Koo, D., & Shin, D. (2009). Adaptive log block mapping scheme for log buffer-based FTL (flash translation layer). In *Proceedings of the International Workshop on Software Support for Portable Storage (IWSSPS)*. IWSSPS.

Koponen, C., & Chun, E. K. Shenker, & Stoica. (2007). A data-oriented (and beyond) network architecture. In *Proceedings of the 2007 Conference on Applications, Technologies, Architectures, and Protocols for Computer Communications, SIGCOMM '07*, (pp. 181–192). New York, NY: ACM Press.

Kotselidis, C., Ansari, M., Jarvis, K., Lujan, M., Kirkham, C., & Watson, I. (2008). DiSTM: A software transactional memory framework for clusters. In *Proceedings of the International Conference on Parallel Processing (ICPP)* (pp. 51–58). Washington, DC: IEEE Computer Society.

Kwon, S. J., & Chung, T. (2008). An efficient and advanced space-management technique for flash memory using reallocation blocks. *IEEE Transactions on Consumer Electronics, 54*(2), 631–638. doi:10.1109/TCE.2008.4560140.

Kwon, S. J., Ranjitkar, A., Ko, Y., & Chung, T. (2011). FTL algorithms for NAND-type flash memories. *Design Automation for Embedded Systems, 15*(3-4), 191–224. doi:10.1007/s10617-011-9071-9.

Lakshman, A., & Malik, P. (2009). Cassandra: Structured storage system on a p2p network. In *Proceedings of the 28th ACM Symposium on Principles of Distributed Computing* (p. 5). New York, NY: ACM. Retrieved from http://0-doi.acm.org.millennium.lib.cyut.edu.tw/10.1145/1582716.1582722

Lamanna, D. D., Skene, J., & Emmerich, W. (2003). SLAng: A language for defining service level agreements. In *Proceedings of the Ninth IEEE Workshop on Future Trends of Distributed Computing Systems (FTDCS'03)*. IEEE.

Lamport, L. (1998). The part-time parliament. *ACM Transactions on Computer Systems*, *16*(2), 133–169. doi:10.1145/279227.279229.

Lawrence, A., Djemame, K., W¨aldrich, O., Ziegler, W., & Zsigri, C. (2010). Using service level agreements for optimising cloud infrastructure services. In *Proceedings of ServiceWave 2010 Workshops (LNCS)* (Vol. 6569, pp. 38–49). Berlin: Springer-Verlag. doi:10.1007/978-3-642-22760-8_4.

Lawson, J. (2009). *The cloud: OSS model 3.0*. Paper presented at the O'Reilly Conference. San Jose, CA. Retrieved from http://en.oreilly.com/oscon2009/public/schedule/detail/10369

Le, K., Bianchini, R., Martonosi, M., & Nguyen, T. D. (n.d.). *Cost-and energy-aware load distribution across data centers*.

Lee, G., & Crespi, N. (2010). Shaping future service environments with the cloud and internet of things: Networking challenges and service evolution. In *Proceedings of the 4th International Symposium on Leveraging Applications of Formal Methods, Verification and Validation* (LNCS), (Vol. 6415, pp. 399-410). Berlin, Germany: SpringerLink. doi:10.1007/978-3-642-16558-0_34

Lee, S., Moon, B., Park, C., Kim, J., & Kim, S. (2008). A case for flash memory SSD in enterprise database applications. In *Proceedings of the 2008 ACM SIGMOD International Conference on Management of Data*. ACM.

Lee, H., Yun, H., & Lee, D. (2009). HFTL: Hybrid flash translation layer based on hot data identification for flash memory. *IEEE Transactions on Consumer Electronics*, *55*(4), 2005–2011. doi:10.1109/TCE.2009.5373762.

Lee, S., Park, D., Chung, T., Lee, D., Park, S., & Song, H. (2007). A log buffer based flash translation layer using fully associative sector translation. *ACM Transactions on Embedded Computing Systems*, *6*(3), 1–27. doi:10.1145/1275986.1275990.

Lee, S., Shin, D., Kim, Y., & Kim, J. (2008). LAST: Locality aware sector translation for NAND flash memory based storage systems. *ACM SIGOPS Operating Systems Review*, *42*(6), 36–42. doi:10.1145/1453775.1453783.

Lefèvre, L., & Orgerie, A. (2010). Designing and evaluating an energy efficient cloud. *Springer Journal of Supercomputing*, *51*, 352–373. doi:10.1007/s11227-010-0414-2.

Leigh, D., & Davies, N. (2010). *Guardian data blog*. Retrieved from http://www.guardian.co.uk/world/2010/jul/25/afghanistan-war-logs-military-leaks

Leung, A. W., Miller, E. L., & Jones, S. (2007). Scalable security for petascale parallel file systems. In *Proceedings of the 2007 ACM/IEEE Conference on Supercomputing* (pp. 16:1–16:12). New York, NY: ACM. Retrieved from http://doi.acm.org/10.1145/1362622.1362644

Leventhal, A. (2008). Flash storage memory. *Communications of the ACM*, *51*(7), 47–51. doi:10.1145/1364782.1364796.

Levine, A., Prevelakis, V., Ioannidis, J., Ioannidis, S., & Keromytis, A. D. (2003). Webdava: An administrator-free approach to web file-sharing. In *Proceedings of the Twelfth International Workshop on Enabling Technologies: Infrastructure for Collaborative Enterprises*. Washington, DC: IEEE Computer Society. Retrieved from http://portal.acm.org/citation.cfm?id=938984.939757

Li, J., Agarwal, D., Humphrey, M., van Ingen, C., Jackson, K., & Ryu, Y. (2010). eScience in the cloud: A MODIS satellite data reprojection and reduction pipeline in the Windows Azure platform. In *Proceedings of the 2010 IEEE International Symposium on Parallel & Distributed Processing* (pp. 1-10). IEEE.

Li, W., & Ping, L. (2009). Trust model to enhance security and interoperability of cloud environment. In *Proceedings of the 1st International Conference on Cloud Computing*, (LNCS), (Vol. 5931, pp. 69-79). Berlin, Germany: SpringerLink. doi:10.1007/978-3-642-10665-1_7

Lillibridge, M., Eshghi, K., Bhagwat, D., Deolalikar, V., Trezise, G., & Camble, P. (2009). Sparse indexing: Large scale, inline deduplication using sampling and locality. In *Proceedings of the 7th Conference on File and Storage Technologies* (pp. 111–123). Berkeley, CA: USENIX Association. Retrieved from http://portal.acm.org/citation.cfm?id=1525908.1525917

Lim, S., Lee, S., & Moon, B. (2010). FASTer FTL for entreprise-class flash memory SSDs. In *Proceedings of the 2010 International Workshop on Storage Network Architecture and Parallel I/Os (SNAPI)*. SNAPI.

Liu, F. (2011). NIST cloud computing reference architecture. *Special Publication 500-292*.

Lofgren, K. M. J., Norman, R. D., Thelin, G. B., & Gupta, A. (2005). *Wear leveling techniques for flash EEPROM systems*. United States Patent, No 6,850,443. Washington, DC: US Patent Office.

Lombardi, F., & Pietro, R. (2010). *Secure virtualization for cloud computing*. Elsevier Journal of Network and Computer Application.

Lorenzi, F., Baldo, G., Costa, R., Abel, M., Bazzan, A., & Ricci, F. (2010). A trust model for multi agent recommendations. *Journal of Emerging Technologies in Web Intelligence*, 2(4), 310–318. doi:10.4304/jetwi.2.4.310-318.

Luhn, A., & Jaekel, M. (2009). *Cloud computing – Business models, value creation dynamics and advantages for customers*. Retrieved from https://www.it-solutions.siemens.com/b2b/it/en/global/Documents/Publications/CloudComputing_Whitepaper_PDF_e.pdf

*Lustre* . (n.d.). Retrieved from http://www.lustre.org

Lyman, P., & Varian, H. R. (2003). *How much information?* Retrieved August, 2012, http://www2.sims.berkeley.edu/research/projects/how-much-info-2003

MacCormick, J., Murphy, N., Ramasubramanian, V., Wieder, U., Yang, J., & Zhou, L. (2009). Kinesis: A new approach to replica placement in distributed storage systems. *Transitional Storage, 4*, 11:1–11:28. Retrieved from http://doi.acm.org/10.1145/1480439.1480440

Manassiev, K., Mihailescu, M., & Amza, C. (2006). Exploiting distributed version concurrency in a transactional memory cluster. In *Proceedings of the Symposium on Principles and Practice of Parallel Programming (PPOPP)* (pp. 198–208). New York, NY: ACM.

Manocha, I. (2011). *IDG connect*. Retrieved from http://www.idgconnect.com/blog-abstract/263/ian-manocha-uk-on-road-open-data

Marinos, A., & Briscoe, G. (2009). Community cloud computing. In *Proceedings of the 1st International Conference on Cloud Computing* (LNCS), (Vol. 5931, pp. 472-484). Berlin, Germany: SpringerLink. doi:10.1007/978-3-642-10665-1_43

Markatchev, N., Curry, R., Kiddle, C., Mirtchovski, A., Simmonds, R., & Tan, T. (2009). A cloud-based interactive application service. In *Proceedings of the Fifth IEEE International Conference on e-Science* (pp. 102-109). IEEE. mOSAIC Consortium. (2011a). *D3.1: Cloud usage patterns*. Retrieved from www.mosaic-cloud.eu

Market Research. (n.d.). *Advanced solid state non-volatile memory market to grow 69% annually through 2015*. Retrieved August, 2012, from http://www.marketresearch.com/corporate/aboutus/press.asp?view=3&article=2223

Mármol, F., & Pérez, G. (2010). Towards pre-standardization of trust and reputation models for distributed and heterogeneous systems. *Elsivier Journal of Computer Standards & Interfaces, 32*, 185–196. doi:10.1016/j.csi.2010.01.003.

Maurer, M., Brandic, I., Emeakaroha, V. C., & Dustdar, S. (2010). Towards knowledge management in self-adaptable clouds. In *Proceedings of the 4th International Workshop of Software Engineering for Adaptive Service-Oriented Systems, SEASS'10*. SEASS.

Mell, P., & Grance, T. (2009). *The NIST definition of cloud computing*. Retrieved from http://www.nist.gov/itl/cloud/upload/cloud-def-v15.pdf

*Memopal – Online Backup* . (n.d.). Retrieved from http://memopal.com/ en/

Mense, M., & Scheideler, C. (2008). Spread: An adaptive scheme for redundant and fair storage in dynamic heterogeneous storage systems. In *Proceedings of the Nineteenth Annual ACM-SIAM Symposium on Discrete Algorithms* (pp. 1135–1144). Philadelphia, PA: Society for Industrial and Applied Mathematics. Retrieved from http://portal.acm.org/citation.cfm?id=1347082.1347206

Mesnier, M., Ganger, G., & Riedel, E. (2003). Object-based storage. *IEEE Communications Magazine, 8*, 84–90. doi:10.1109/MCOM.2003.1222722.

Messmer, E. (2009). *Are security issues delaying adoption of cloud computing*. Retrieved from http://www.networkworld.com/news/2009/042709-burning-securitycloud-computing.html

Metwally, A., Agrawal, D., & Abbadi, A. E. (2006). An integrated efficient solution for computing frequent and top-k elements in data streams. *ACM Transactions on Database Systems, 31*(3), 1095–1133. doi:10.1145/1166074.1166084.

Microsoft Corporation. (2009). *Windows Azure pricing and service agreement*. Retrieved from http://www.microsoft.com/windowsazure/pricing/

Microsystems, S. U. N. (1999). *Java transaction API (JTA)*. Retrieved November 30, 2012, from http://www.oracle.com/technetwork/java/javaee/jta/index.html

Microsystems, S. U. N. (2002). *Java management extensions (JMX) v1.2 specification*. Retrieved November 30, 2012, from http://jcp.org/aboutJava/communityprocess/final/jsr003/index.html

Miller, J., & Griffeth, N. (1991). Performance modeling of database and simulation protocols: Design choices for query driven simulation. In *Proceedings of the 24th Annual Symposium on Simulation* (pp. 205-216). Washington, DC: IEEE Computer Society.

Mills, D. L. (1991). Internet time synchronization: The network time protocol. *IEEE Transactions on Communications, 39*(10), 1482–1493. doi:10.1109/26.103043.

Miltchev, S., Prevelakis, V., Ioannidis, S., Ioannidis, J., Keromytis, A. D., & Smith, J. M. (2003). Secure and flexible global file sharing. In *Proceedings of the USENIX 2003 Annual Technical Conference (Freenix Track)* (pp. 165–178). USENIX.

Miltchev, S., Smith, J. M., Prevelakis, V., Keromytis, A., & Ioannidis, S. (2008). Decentralized access control in distributed file systems. *ACM Computer Survey, 40*, 10:1–10:30. Retrieved from http://doi.acm.org/10.1145/1380584.1380588

Miranda, H., Pinto, A., & Rodrigues, L. (2001). Appia, a flexible protocol kernel supporting multiple coordinated channels. In *Proceedings of the 21st International DST Conference on Distributed Computing Systems* (pp. 707–710). Washington, DC: IEEE Computer Society.

Mitchel, R. L. (2009). *Cloud storage triggers security worries*. Retrieved from http://www.computerworld.com/s/article/340438

Moir, M. (1997). Transparent support for wait-free transactions. In *Proceedings of the 11th International Workshop on Distributed Algorithms* (pp. 305–319). Berlin, Germany: Springer.

mOSAIC Consortium. (2011b). *D3.2 platform use cases*. Retrieved from www.mosaic-cloud.eu

Mowbray, M., Pearson, S., & Shen, Y. (2010). Enhancing privacy in cloud computing via policy-based obfuscation. *Springer Journal of Supercomputing*. Retrieved from http://www.springerlink.com/content/7438g5n0382r6937/

*Mozy*. (n.d.). Retrieved from http://mozy.com

Narayanan, D., Thereska, E., Donnelly, A., Elnikety, S., & Rowstron, A. (2009). Migrating server storage to SSDs: Analysis of tradeoffs. In *Proceedings of the ACM European Conference on Computer Systems (EuroSys)*. ACM.

Nelson, T. (1988). *Literary machines*. New York: Mindful Press.

Nesse, P. E. (2011). Exploiting cloud computing - A proposed methodology of generating new business. In *Proceedings of ICIN 2011*. ICIN.

*Network-Attached Storage*. (n.d.). Retrieved from http://en.wikipedia.org/wiki/Network-attached_storage

*Nirvanix Service Level Agreement*. (n.d.). Retrieved from http://www.nirvanix.com/sla.aspx

NIST. (2012). *Security and privacy controls for federal information systems and organizations.* Retrieved from http://securecloudreview.com/2011/10/cloud-security-transfers-some-responsibility-but-not-accountability/

Niu, Z., Jiang, H., Zhou, K., Yang, T., & Yan, W. (2009). Identification and authentication in large-scale storage systems. In *Proceedings of the 2009 IEEE International Conference on Networking, Architecture, and Storage* (pp. 421–427). Washington, DC: IEEE Computer Society. Retrieved from http://dx.doi.org/10.1109/NAS.2009.72

*Nosql Databases .* (n.d.). Retrieved from http://en.wikipedia.org/wiki/NoSQL

O'Neil, P., Cheng, E., Gawlick, D., & O'Neil, E. (1996). The log-structured merge-tree (LSM-tree). *Acta Informatica, 33*(4), 351–385. doi:10.1007/s002360050048.

*OAUTH 2.0.* (n.d.). Retrieved from http://oauth.net/2/

Objectivity.com. (2012a). *Data replication in objectivity/db.* Retrieved April 2012, from http://www.objectivity.com/pdf/documents/DataReplication.pdf

Objectivity.com. (2012b). *The objectivity/db technical overview.* Retrieved April 2012, from http://http://www.objectivity.com/pages/downloads/whitepaper/pdf/oodb_techOverview.pdf

*Oco Analytic Applications for SAP BusinessObjects On-Demand.* (n.d.). Retrieved from http://ecohub.sap.com/catalog/#!solution:bisolutions

Oh, T., Lim, S., Choi, Y., Park, K., Lee, H., & Choi, H. (2010). State of the art of network security perspectives in cloud computing. In *Proceedings of the First International Conference on Security-enriched Urban Computing and Smart Grid,* (Vol. 78, pp. 629-637). Berlin, Germany: SpringerLink. doi:10.1007/978-3-642-16444-6_79

Oldham, N., Verma, K., Sheth, A., & Hakimpour, F. (2006). Semantic WS-agreement partner selection. In *Proceedings of the 15th International Conference on World Wide Web (WWW '06).* ACM.

Olston, C., Reed, B., Srivastava, U., Kumar, R., & Tomkins, A. (2008). Pig latin: A not-so-foreign language for data processing. In *Proceedings of the International Conference on the Management of Data* (pp. 1099–1110). New York, NY: ACM.

*Online Analytical Processing.* (n.d.). Retrieved from http://en.wikipedia.org/wiki/Online_analytical_processing

*Online Transaction Processing.* (n.d.). Retrieved from http://en.wikipedia.org/wiki/Online_transaction_processing

*OpenID.* (n.d.). Retrieved from www.openid.net

Oracle. (2012). *Introduction to the java persistence API.* Retrieved November 30, 2012, from http://docs.oracle.com/javaee/6/tutorial/doc/bnbpz.html

Ou, Y., & Härder, T. (2011). Trading memory for performance and energy. In *Proceedings of the 16th International Conference on Database Systems for Advanced Applications (DASFAA).* DASFAA.

Owen, T. (2012, April 18). *Data security and the small/medium enterprise (SME).* Retrieved August 2012, from http://www.allenport.com/blog/2012/04/18/data-security-and-the-smallmedium-enterprise-sme-part-2/

Pacitti, E., Coulon, C., Valduriez, P., & Özsu, M. T. (2005). Preventive replication in a database cluster. *Distributed and Parallel Databases, 18*(3), 223–251. doi:10.1007/s10619-005-4257-4.

Pal, S. (2013). Cloud computing: Security concerns and issues. In Bento, A., & Aggarwal, A. (Eds.), *Cloud Computing Service and Deployment Models: Layers and Management.* Hershey, PA: IGI Global.

Pal, S., Khatua, S., Chaki, N., & Sanyal, S. (2012). A new trusted and collaborative agent based approach for ensuring cloud security. *Annals of Faculty Engineering Hunedoara International Journal of Engineering, 10*(1), 71–78.

Panica, S., Neagul, M., Craciun, C., & Petcu, D. (2011). Serving legacy distributed applications by a self-configuring cloud processing platform. In *Proceedings of the 6th IEEE International Conference on Intelligent Data Acquisition and Advanced Computing Systems: Technology and Applications* (pp. 139-145). IEEE.

*Parallel Virtual File System (PVFS) Wiki .* (n.d.). Retrieved from http://en.wikipedia.org/wiki/ParallelVirtualFileSystem

Park, D., Debnath, B., & Du, D. (2009). *CFTL: A convertible flash translation layer with consideration of data access patterns* (Technical Report 09-023). Minneapolis, MN: University of Minnesota.

Park, S., Jung, D., Kang, J., Kim, J., & Lee, J. (2006). CFLRU: A replacement algorithm for flash memory. In *Proceedings of the 2006 International Conference on Compilers, Architecture and Synthesis for Embedded Systems (CASES)*. CASES.

Park, C., Cheon, W., Kang, J., Roh, K., Cho, W., & Kim, J. (2008). A reconfigurable FTL (flash translation layer) architecture for NAND flash based architectures. *ACM Transactions on Embedded Computing Systems*, 7(4), 1–23. doi:10.1145/1376804.1376806.

Park, S., Kim, Y., Urgaonkar, B., Lee, J., & Seo, E. (2011). A comprehensive study on energy efficiency of flash memory storages. *Journal of Systems Architecture*, 57(4), 354–365. doi:10.1016/j.sysarc.2011.01.005.

Parrilli, D. (2010). Legal issues in grid and cloud computing. In K. StanoevskaSlabeva et al. (Eds.), Grid and Cloud Computing: A Business Perspective on Technology and Applications, (pp. 97-118). Berlin: Springer-Verlag. doi:doi:10.1007/978-3-642-051937_7.

Pearson, S., Shen, Y., & Mowbray, M. (2009). A privacy manager for cloud computing. In *Proceedings of the 1st International Conference on Cloud Computing (LNCS)*, (Vol. 5931, pp. 90-106). Berlin, Germany: SpringerLink. doi:10.1007/978-3-642-10665-1_9

Peluso, S., Romano, P., & Quaglia, F. (2012). SCORe: A scalable one-copy serializable partial replication protocol. In *Proceedings of ACM/IFIP/USENIX 13th International Middleware Conference*. ACM.

Peluso, S., Ruivo, P., Romano, P., Quaglia, F., & Rodrigues, L. (2010). When scalability meets consistency: Genuine multiversion update serializable partial data replication. In *Proceeding of the IEEE 32nd International Conference on Distributed Computing Systems* (pp. 455-465). Washington, DC: IEEE Computer Society.

Petcu, D., Panica, S., & Neagul, M. (2011). From grid computing towards sky computing: Case study for earth observation. In *Proceedings of the Cracow Grid Workshop 2010* (pp. 11-20). Cracow.

Popa, R. A., Lorch, J., Molnar, D., Wang, H. J., & Zhuang, L. (2011). Enabling security in cloud storage SLAS with cloudproof. In *Proceedings of the 2011 USENIX Conference on USENIX Annual Technical* Conference *(USENIXATC'11)*. USENIX Association.

Pritchett, D. (2008). Base: An acid alternative. *Queue*, 6(3), 48–55. doi:10.1145/1394127.1394128.

Qian, L., Luo, Z., Du, Y., & Guo, L. (2009). Cloud computing: An overview. In *Proceedings of the 1st International Conference on Cloud Computing (LNCS)*, (Vol. 5931, pp. 626-631). Berlin, Germany: SpringerLink. doi:10.1007/978-3-642-10665-1_63

Qin, Z., Wang, Y., Liu, D., & Shao, Z. (2010). Demand-based block-level address mapping in large-scale NAND flash storage systems. In *Proceedings of the 2010 IEEE/ACM/IFIP International Conference on Hardware/Software Codesign and System Synthesis (CODES+ISSS)*. IEEE/ACM/IFIP.

*Rackspace Cloud Files*. (n.d.). Retrieved from http://www.rackspace.com/cloud/cloud_hosting_products/files/

*Rackspace*. (n.d.). Retrieved from http://www.rackspace.com/

Ramadan, H. E., Rossbach, C. J., Porter, D. E., Hofmann, O. S., Bhandari, A., & Witchel, E. (2007). MetaTM/TxLinux: Transactional memory for an operating system. In *Proceedings of the 34th Annual International Symposium on Computer Architecture* (pp. 92-103). New York, NY: ACM.

Ranganathan, P. (2011). From microprocessors to nanostores: Rethinking data-centric systems. *Computer*, 44(1), 39–48. doi:10.1109/MC.2011.18.

Ranger, C., Raghuraman, R., Penmetsa, A., Bradski, G., & Kozyrakis, C. (2007). Evaluating mapreduce for multi-core and multiprocessor systems. In *Proceedings of the International Symposium on High-Performance Computer Architecture* (pp. 13–24). Washington, DC: IEEE Computer Society.

Raybum, D. (2011, June 27). *Telcos and carriers forming new federated CDN group called OCX*. Retrieved August 31, 2012, from http://blog.streamingmedia.com/the_business_of_online_vi/2011/06/telco-and-carriers-forming-new-federated-cdn-group-called-ocx-operator-carrier-exchange.html

*Redundant Array of Independent Disks*. (n.d.). Retrieved from http://en.wikipedia.org/wiki/Redundant_array_of_independent_disks

Ren, K., Wang, C., & Wang, Q. (2012). Security challenges for the public cloud. *IEEE Internet Computing*, *16*(1), 69–73. doi:10.1109/MIC.2012.14.

Reservoir Consortium. (2012). *Reservoir, resources and services virtualization without barriers*. Retrieved November 30, 2012, from http://www.reservoir-fp7.eu/

Ried, S. (2011). *Cloud broker - A new business model paradigm*. Forrester Research Report.

Riegel, T., Fetzer, C., & Felber, P. (2008). Automatic data partitioning in software transactional memories. In *Proceedings of the Twentieth Annual Symposium on Parallelism in Algorithms and Architectures* (pp. 152-159). New York, NY: ACM.

*RightScale Multi Cloud Platform*. (n.d.). Retrieved from http://www.rightscale.com/products/multicloud-platform.php

Roberts, D., Kgil, T., & Mudge, T. (2009b). Using non-volatile memory to save energy in servers. In *Proceedings of the Design, Automation and Test in Europe conference (DATE)*. DATE.

Roberts, D., Kgil, T., & Mudge, T. (2009a). Integrating NAND flash devices onto servers. *Communications of the ACM*, *52*(4), 98–106. doi:10.1145/1498765.1498791.

Rochwerger, B., Breitgand, D., Epstein, A., Hadas, D., Loy, I., Nagin, K., et al. (2011). Reservoir - When one cloud is not enough. *Computer*, *44*, 44–51. Retrieved from http://dx.doi.org/10.1109/MC.2011.64 doi: http://dx.doi.org/10.1109/MC.2011.64

Rochwerger, B., Breitgand, D., Levy, E., Galis, A., Nagin, K., Llorente, I. M., et al. (2009). The reservoir model and architecture for open federated cloud computing. *IBM Journal of Reservoir Development*, *53*, 535–545. Retrieved from http://portal.acm.org/citation.cfm?id=1850659.1850663

Rogers, S. (2010). *Guardian data blog*. Retrieved from http://www.guardian.co.uk/news/datablog/2010/nov/19/government-spending-data

Rogers, S. (2012). *Guardian data blog*. Retrieved from http://www.guardian.co.uk/news/datablog/2012/jun/28/open-data-white-paper

Rogers, T. (2012). *About journalism*. Retrieved from http://journalism.about.com/od/reporting/a/newsworthy.htm

Rohini, T. (2011). Comparative approach to cloud security models. In *Proceedings of the International Conference on Computing, Communication and Control*, (Vol. 125, pp. 170-177). Berlin, Germany: SpringerLink. doi:10.1007/978-3-642-18440-6_21

Romano, P., & Leonetti, M. (2012). Poster: Selftuning batching in total order broadcast via analytical modelling and reinforcement learning. *ACM SIGMETRICS Performance Evaluation Review*, *39*(2), 77–77. doi:10.1145/2034832.2034861.

R-Project. (2012). *The R-project*. Retrieved November 30, 2012, from http://www.r-project.org

*SAML SimpleSign*. (n.d.). Retrieved from http://www.oasis-open.org/committees/download.php/28046/sstc-saml-binding-simplesign-cs-01.pdf

Sangroya, A., Kumar, S., Dhok, J., & Varma, V. (2010). Towards analyzing data security risks in cloud computing environments. In *Proceedings of the International Conference on Information Systems, Technology, and Management*, (Vol. 54, pp. 255-265). Berlin, Germany: SpringerLink. doi:10.1007/978-3-642-12035-0_25

*SAP BusinessObjects BI OnDemand*. (n.d.). Retrieved from http://www.biondemand.com/businessintelligence

Schmietendorf, A., Dumke, R., & Reitz, D. (2004). SLA management – Challenges in the context of web-service-based infrastructures. In *Proceedings of the IEEE International Conference on Web Services (ICWS'04)*. IEEE Computer Society. doi:10.1109/ICWS.2004.1314788

Schmuck, F., & Haskin, R. (2002). GPFS: A shared-disk file system for large computing clusters. In *Proceedings of the 1st USENIX Conference on File and Storage Technologies*. Berkeley, CA: USENIX Association. Retrieved from http://portal.acm.org/citation.cfm?id=1083323.1083349

Schubert, L., & Jeffery, K. (2012). *Advances in cloud – Research in future cloud computing*. Academic Press.

Sedayao, J., Su, S., Ma, X., Jiang, M., & Miao, K. (2009). A simple technique for securing data at rest stored in a computing cloud. In *Proceedings of the 1st International Conference on Cloud Computing* (LNCS), (Vol. 5931, pp. 553-558). Berlin, Germany: SpringerLink. doi: 10.1007/978-3-642-10665-1_51

Seidel, J., Wäldrich, O., Ziegler, W., & Yahyapour, R. (2007). Using SLA for resource management and scheduling-a survey. *Network*, 8, 335–347. Retrieved from http://www.coregrid.net/mambo/images/stories/TechnicalReports/tr-0096.pdf.

Shavit, N., & Touitou, D. (1995). Software transactional memory. In *Proceedings of the Symposium on Principles of Distributed Computing* (pp. 204-213). New York, NY: ACM.

Sheth, A. P., & Larson, J. A. (1990). Federated database systems for managing distributed, heterogeneous, and autonomous databases. *ACM Computing Surveys*, 22, 183–236. doi:10.1145/96602.96604.

*Shibboleth*. (n.d.). Retrieved from http://www.shibboleth.net/

Shinohara, T. (1999). *Flash memory card with block memory address arrangement*. United States Patent, No 5,905,993. Washington, DC: US Patent Office.

Shpeisman, T., Adl-Tabatabai, A., Geva, R., Ni, Y., & Welc, A. (2009). Towards transactional memory semantics for C++. In *Proceedings of the 21st Symposium on Parallelism in Algorithms and Architectures* (pp. 49-58). New York, NY: ACM.

Signiant. (2012). *Signiant*. Retrieved from http://www.signiant.com/company/company-profile/

Silk, D. (2010). *CDMI and cloud federation*. Paper presented at the SNIA Storage Developer Conference. New York, NY.

Simon, H., & Wuebker, G. (1999). Bundling – A powerful method to better exploit profit potential. In Fuerderer, R., Herrmann, A., & Wuebker, G. (Eds.), *Optimal Bundling: Marketing Strategies for Improving Economic Performance* (pp. 7–28). Berlin: Springer Verlag. doi:10.1007/978-3-662-09119-7_2.

*Simple Cloud Identity Management*. (n.d.). Retrieved from https://sites.google.com/site/clouddir/draft1

*SMEStorage*. (n.d.). Retrieved from http://www.smestorage.com/

*SNIA*. (1997). Retrieved from http://www.snia.org/cdmi

SNIA. (2010). *Managing private and hybrid clouds for data storage*. Retrieved from www.snia.org/forums/csi/Private-HybridCloudWhitePaper.pdf

SNIA. (n.d.). *Cloud data management interface (CDMI)*. Retrieved from http://snia.org/cdmi

*Software as a Service (SaaS)*. (n.d.). Retrieved from http://www.gartner.com/it-glossary/software-as-a-service-saas/

Sonmez, N., Cristal, A., Harris, T., Unsal, O. S., & Valero, M. (2009). Taking the heat off transactions: Dynamic selection of pessimistic concurrency control. In *Proceedings of the 2009 IEEE International Symposium on Parallel & Distributed Processing* (pp. 1-10). Washington, DC: IEEE Computer Society.

Stanoevska-Slabeva, K., & Wozniak, T. (2010). Cloud basics – An introduction to cloud computing. In K. StanoevskaSlabeva et al. (Eds.), Grid and Cloud Computing: A Business Perspective on Technology and Applications (pp. 47-61). Berlin: Springer-Verlag. doi: doi:10.1007/978-3-642-051937_4.

Std, I. E. E. E. 1003.1-2008. (2008). *POSIX.1-2008, the open group base specifications issue 7*. Retrieved from http://pubs.opengroup.org/onlinepubs/9699919799/

Stender, J., Högqvist, M., & Kolbeck, B. (2010). Loosely time-synchronized snapshots in object-based file systems. In *Proceedings of the 29th IEEE International Performance, Computing, and Communications Conference* (pp. 188–197). IEEE Computer Society.

Stender, J., Kolbeck, B., Högqvist, M., & Hupfeld, F. (2010). BabuDB: Fast and efficient file system metadata storage. In *Proceedings of the 2010 International Workshop on Storage Network Architecture and Parallel I/OS* (pp. 51–58). Washington, DC: IEEE Computer Society.

Stonebraker, M., Madden, S., Abadi, D. J., Harizopoulos, S., Hachem, N., & Helland, P. (2007). The end of an architectural era: It's time for a complete rewrite. In *Proceedings of the 33rd International Conference on Very Large Data Bases* (pp. 1150–1160). VLDB Endowment. Retrieved from http://portal.acm.org/citation.cfm?id=1325851.1325981

*Storage Area Network*. (n.d.). Retrieved from http://en.wikipedia.org/wiki/Storage_area_network

*Strace*. (n.d.). Retrieved from http://linux.die.net/man/1/strace

Sun MicroSystems. (2003). *Java 2 platform enterprise ed. specification, v. 1.4, final release ed., 2003*. Retrieved November 30, 2012, from http://www.jcp.org/en/jsr/detail?id=151

Sutton, R. S., & Barto, A. G. (1998). *Reinforcement learning: An introduction (adaptive computation and machine learning)*. Cambridge, MA: The MIT Press.

*Symantec Netbackup*. (n.d.). Retrieved from http://www.symantec.com/ netbackup

Symantec. (2011). *State of cloud survey*. Retrieved August 2012, from http://www.symantec.com/content/en/us/about/media/pdfs/symc-state-of-cloud-report-global.pdf

Syu, S., & Chen, J. (2005). An active space recycling mechanism for flash storage systems in real-time application environments. In *Proceedings the 11th IEEE International Conference on Embedded and Real-Time Computing Systems and Applications (RTCSA),* (pp. 53-59). IEEE.

Takabi, H., Joshi, J., & Ahn, G. (2010). SecureCloud: Towards a comprehensive security framework for cloud computing environments. In *Proceedings of the 34th Annual IEEE Computer Software and Applications Conference Workshops 2010*. IEEE Computer Society. doi:10.1109/COMPSACW.2010.74

Tang, H., Gulbeden, A., Zhou, J., Strathearn, W., Yang, T., & Chu, L. (2004). The Panasas ActiveScale storage cluster - Delivering scalable high bandwidth storage. In *Proceedings of the ACM/IEEE SC2004 Conference (SC'04)* (p. 53). ACM/IEEE.

Telco 2.0 Research. (2012). *The value of smart pipes to mobile network operators*. Retrieved August 2012, from http://www.telco2research.com/articles/WP_the-value-of-smart-pipes_Summary

Telco 2.0. (2012). *Euro telcos: Fiddling while the platform burns?* Retrieved August 31, 2012, from http://www.telco2research.com/articles/EB_euro-telcos-fiddling-while-platform-burns_Summary

Telenor Group. (2012). *Strategy*. Retrieved from http://telenor.com/about-us/our-strategy/

Telenor. (2011, June 14). *Telenor and Telia join forces to create Denmark's best network*. Retrieved August 2012, from http://telenor.com/news-and-media/press-releases/2011/telenor-and-telia-join-forces-to-create-denmarks-best-network/

The Hindu. (2012, July 24). *Uninor to scale down in four circles*. Retrieved August 2012, from http://www.thehindu.com/business/companies/article3679206.ece

*The Apache Cassandra Project*. (n.d.). Retrieved from http://cassandra.apache.org/

Thomas, R. H. (1979). A majority consensus approach to concurrency control for multiple copy databases. *ACM Transactions on Database Systems, 4*(2), 180–209. doi:10.1145/320071.320076.

*Tivoli Storage Manager*. (n.d.). Retrieved from http://www-01.ibm.com/software/tivoli/products/storage-mgr/

Tordssona, J., Monterob, R. S., Moreno-Vozmedianob, R., & Llorente, I. M. (n.d.). *Optimized placement of a computational cluster across multiple clouds*. Academic Press.

Torry Harris. (n.d.). *Cloud computing services - A comparison*. Retrieved from http://www.thbs.com/pdfs/Comparison of Cloud computing services.pdf

Tosic, V., Pagurek, B., & Patel, K. (2003). WSOL - A language for the formal specification of classes of service for web services. In Zhang, L.-J. (Ed.), *ICWS* (pp. 375–381). CSREA Press.

*Trusted Computer System Evaluation Criteria*. (1985). Retrieved from http://csrc.nist.gov/publications/history/dod85.pdf

Vasudevan, V., Andersen, D., Kaminsky, M., Tan, L., Franklin, J., & Moraru, I. (2010). Energy-efficient cluster computing with FAWN: Workloads and implications. In *Proceedings of the 1st International Conference on Energy-Efficient Computing and Networking (e-Energy '10)*. E-Energy.

Versant Developer Center. (2012a). *How to evaluate an object database*. Retrieved April 2012, from http://developer.versant.com/developer/resources/objectdatabase/whitepapers/WP_Evaluate2002.pdf

Versant Developer Center. (2012b). *Versant object database fundamentals manual*. Retrieved April 2012, from http://developer.versant.com/developer/resources/objectdatabase/documentation/VODFundamentals.pdf

Versant Developer Center. (2012c). *Versant object database*. Retrieved April 2012, from http://developer.versant.com/developer/resources/objectdatabase/overview

Videonet. (2010, September 23). *Broadband ready to become a serious TV platform*. Retrieved August 31, 2012, from http://www.v-net.tv/Broadband-ready-to-become-a-serious-TV-platform/

*VISION Cloud*. (2010). Retrieved from http://www.visioncloud.eu/

Vogels, W. (2009). Eventually consistent. *Communications of the ACM*, 40–44. doi:10.1145/1435417.1435432.

*Voldemort Distributed Database*. (n.d.). Retrieved from http://project-voldemort.com/voldemort/

Voulodimos, A., Gogouvitis, S., Mavrogeorgi, N., Talyansky, R., Kyriazis, D., & Koutsoutos, S. ... Varvarigou, T. (2011). A unified management model for data intensive storage clouds. In *Proceedings of the IEEE First International Symposium on Network Cloud Computing and Applications*. Toulouse, France: IEEE.

Wäldrich, O. (n.d.). *WS-agreement for JAVA (WSAG4J)*. Retrieved 2012, from http://packcs-e0.scai.fraunhofer.de/wsag4j/

Wang, Y., Liu, D., Wang, M., Qin, Z., Shao, Z., & Guan, Y. (2010). RNFTL: A reuse-aware NAND flash translation layer for flash memory. In *Proceedings of the ACM SIGPLAN/SIGBED 2010 Conference on Languages, Compilers, and Tools for Embedded Systems (LCTES)*. ACM.

Wang, Z., Zhu, X., & Singhal, S. (2005). Utilization and slo-based control for dynamic sizing of resource partitions. In *Proceedings of the 16th IFIP/IEEE Ambient Networks international conference on Distributed Systems: Operations and Management* (pp. 133-144). Berlin, Germany: Springer.

Wang, Y., Wang, S., & Zhou, D. (2009). Retrieving and indexing spatial data in the cloud computing environment. *Lecture Notes in Computer Science*, *5931*, 322–331. doi:10.1007/978-3-642-10665-1_29.

Wei, Q., Gong, B., Pathak, S., Veeravalli, B., Zeng, L., & Okada, K. (2011). WAFTL: A workload adaptive flash translation layer with data partition. In *Proceedings of 2011 IEEE 27th Symposium on Mass Storage Systems and Technologies (MSST)*. IEEE.

Weil, S. A., Brandt, S. A., Miller, E. L., & Maltzahn, C. (2006). Crush: Controlled, scalable, decentralized placement of replicated data. In *Proceedings of the 2006 ACM/IEEE Conference on Supercomputing*. New York, NY: ACM. Retrieved from http://doi.acm.org/10.1145/1188455.1188582

Weil, S. A., Brandt, S. A., Miller, E. L., Long, D. D. E., & Maltzahn, C. (2006). Ceph: A scalable, high-performance distributed file system. In *Proceedings of the 7th Symposium on Operating Systems Design and Implementation (OSDI)* (pp. 307–320). OSDI.

Welsh, M., Culler, D., & Brewer, E. (2001). Seda: An architecture for well-conditioned, scalable internet services. *SIGOPS Operating Systems Review, 35*(5), 230–243. doi:10.1145/502059.502057.

*What is DFS ?* (n.d.). Retrieved from http://technet.microsoft.com/en-us/library/cc779627.aspx

William, C., Hosame, A., & Feng, S. (2010). Cloud service architecture and related standards. In Text Book of Transforming Enterprise Cloud Services, (pp. 87-132). Berlin: Springer Science+Business Media B.V. doi: doi:10.1007/978-90-481-9846-7_3.

Wilson, T. (2009). *Security is chief obstacle to cloud computing adoption, study says.* Retrieved from http://www.darkreading.com/securityservices/security/perimeter/showArticle.jhtml?articleID=221901195

*Windows Azure – Data Management .* (n.d.). Retrieved from http://www.windowsazure.com/en-us/home/features/data -management/

*Windows Azure Storage Services API Reference.* (2010). Retrieved from http://msdn.microsoft.com/en-us/library/dd179355.aspx

*Windows Azure.* (n.d.). Retrieved from http://www.windowsazure.com/en-us/

Winter, R. (2008). *Why are data warehouses growing so fast?* Retrieved August, 2012, from http://www.b-eye-network.com/view7188

Woodhouse, D. (2001). JFFS: The journaling flash file system. In *Proceedings of Ottawa Linux Symposium.* Linux.

*WSLA Documents.* (n.d.). Retrieved from http://researchWeb.watson.ibm.com/wsla/documents.html

*WSLA.* (n.d.). Retrieved from http://www.research.ibm.com/wsla/

Wu, C., & Kuo, T. (2006). An adaptive two-level management for the flash translation layer in embedded systems. In *Proceedings of the 2006 IEEE/ACM International Conference on Computer-Aided Design.* IEEE/ACM.

Wu, G., Eckart, B., & He, X. (2010). BPAC: An adaptive write buffer management scheme for flash-based solid state drives. In *Proceedings of 2010 IEEE 26th Symposium on Mass Storage Systems and Technologies (MSST).* IEEE.

Wu, X., & Narasimha Reddy, A. L. (2009). Managing storage space in a flash and disk hybrid storage system. In *Proceedings of the 2009 IEEE International Symposium on Modeling, Analysis & Simulation of Computer and Telecommunication Systems (MASCOTS).* IEEE.

*XtreemFS .* (n.d.). Retrieved from http://www.xtreemfs.org/

Xu, J., Huang, R., Huang, W., & Yang, G. (2009). Secure document service for cloud computing. In *Proceedings of the 1st International Conference on Cloud Computing* (LNCS), (Vol. 5931, pp. 541-546). Berlin, Germany: SpringerLink. doi:10.1007/978-3-642-10665-1_49

Xu, J., Zhao, M., Fortes, J., Carpenter, R., & Yousif, M. (2007). On the use of fuzzy modeling in virtualized data center management. In *Proceedings of the International Conference on Autonomic Computing* (p. 25). Washington, DC: IEEE Computer Society.

Xu, L., & Jennings, B. (2009). A framework for automated creation and deployment of consolidated charging schemes for service compositions. In *Proceedings of the 7th European Conference on Web Services* (pp. 49-57). IEEE.

Yan, L., Rong, C., & Zhao, G. (2009). Strengthen cloud computing security with federal identity management using hierarchical identity-based cryptography. In *Proceedings of the 1st International Conference on Cloud Computing* (LNCS), (Vol. 5931, pp. 167-177). Berlin, Germany: SpringerLink. doi:10.1007/978-3-642-10665-1_15

Yu, S., Wang, C., Ren, K., & Lou, W. (2010). Achieving secure, scalable, and fine-grained data access control in cloud computing. In *Proceeding INFOCOM'10 the 29th Conference on Information Communications.* ACM.

Yu, Y., Isard, M., Fetterly, D., Budiu, M., Erlingsson, U., Gunda, P. K., & Currey, J. (2008). DryadLINQ: A system for general-purpose distributed data-parallel computing using a high-level language. In *Proceedings of the Symposium on Operating System Design and Implementation* (pp. 987-994). New York, NY: ACM.

Zhang, G., Chiu, L., & Liu, L. (2010). Adaptive data migration in multi-tiered storage based cloud environment. In *Proceedings of the 3rd IEEE International Conference on Cloud Computing (CLOUD).* IEEE.

Zhang, X., Xu, F., Liu, Y., Zhang, X., & Shen, C. (2006). Trust extended dynamic security model and its application in network. In *Proceedings of the Second International Conference on Mobile Ad-Hoc and Sensor Networks* (LNCS), (Vol. 4325, pp. 404-415). Berlin, Germany: SpringerLink. doi:10.1007/11943952_34

Zhang, Q., Cheng, L., & Boutaba, R. (2010). Cloud computing: State-of-the-art and research challenges. *Journal of Internet Services and Application, 1*, 7–18. doi:10.1007/s13174-010-0007-6.

Zheng, J., Sun, Y., & Zhou, W. (2009). Cloud computing based Internet data center. In *Proceedings of the 1st International Conference on Cloud Computing* (LNCS), (Vol. 5931, pp. 700-704). Berlin, Germany: SpringerLink. doi:10.1007/978-3-642-10665-1_75

Zhu, B., Li, K., & Patterson, H. (2008). Avoiding the disk bottleneck in the data domain deduplication file system. In *Proceedings of the 6th USENIX Conference on File and Storage Technologies* (pp. 18:1–18:14). Berkeley, CA: USENIX Association. Retrieved from http://portal.acm.org/citation.cfm?id=1364813.1364831

Zhu, J. (2010). Cloud computing technologies and applications. In B. Furht & A. Escalante (Eds.), Handbook of Cloud Computing, (pp. 21-45). Berlin: Springer Science+Business Media, LLC. doi: doi:10.1007/978-1-4419-6524-0_2.

Zissis, D., & Lekkas, D. (2012). Addressing cloud computing security issues. *Future Generation Computer Systems, 28*, 583–592. doi:10.1016/j.future.2010.12.006.

# About the Contributors

**Dimosthenis Kyriazis** received the diploma from the Dept. of Electrical and Computer Engineering of the National Technical University of Athens, Athens, Greece in 2001, the MS degree in Techno-Economic Systems (MBA) co-organized by the Electrical and Computer Engineering Dept - NTUA, Economic Sciences Dept - National Kapodistrian University of Athens, Industrial Management Dept - University of Piraeus and his Ph.D. from the Electrical and Computer Engineering Department of the National Technical University of Athens in 2007. He is currently a Research Engineer in the Telecommunication Laboratory of the Institute of Communication and Computer Systems (ICCS). Before joining the ICCS he has worked in the private sector as Telecom Software Engineer. He has participated in numerous EU / National funded projects (such as IRMOS, 4CaaSt, ARTIST, VISION Cloud, NextGRID, Akogrimo, BEinGRID, HPC-Europa, GRIA, Memphis, CHALLENGERS, HellasGRID, etc.). His research interests include Grid computing, scheduling, Quality of Service provision and workflow management in heterogeneous systems and service oriented architectures.

**Athanasios Voulodimos** was born in Athens, Greece, in 1984. He received his Dipl.-Ing. degree from the School of Electrical and Computer Engineering of the National Technical University of Athens (NTUA) in 2007, ranking among the top 2% of his class. In 2010, he acquired an MSc in "Techno-economic Systems" after completing a two-year Master's program co-organized by the National Technical University of Athens and the University of Piraeus. In 2011, he received his PhD from the School of Electrical and Computer Engineering of NTUA in the area of computer vision and machine learning focusing on behavior recognition from video. He has been and is currently involved in National and European research projects, such as SCOVIS, My-e-Director 2012, and VISION Cloud. He is currently leading the Construction Activity of the EU EXPERIMEDIA IP project. He has published more than 35 papers in international conferences, workshops, and journals. His main research interests include computer vision, machine learning, as well as ubiquitous and cloud computing.

**Spyridon V. Gogouvitis** was born in Athens, Greece in 1982. He received the Dipl. -Ing. from the School of Electrical and Computer Engineering of the National Technical University of Athens (NTUA) in 2006. He is currently pursuing his Ph.D. while working as a Researcher in the Telecommunication Laboratory of the Institute of Communication and Computer Systems (ICCS). In the past he has been actively involved in several EU and National funded projects such as the Interactive Realtime Multimedia Applications on Service Oriented Infrastructures (IRMOS) project. He has also worked as a developer for the Hellenic Army Information Systems Support Centre and as a consultant for the General Secretariat for Information Systems of the Hellenic Ministry of Economy and Finance. Currently he is NTUA's team leader in the VISION Cloud EU Project. His research interests include Grid and Cloud Computing, Workflow Management, as well as Mobile and Ubiquitous Computing.

**Theodora A. Varvarigou** received the B. Tech degree from the National Technical University of Athens, Athens, Greece in 1988, the MS degrees in Electrical Engineering (1989) and in Computer Science (1991) from Stanford University, Stanford, California in 1989, and the Ph.D. degree from Stanford University as well in 1991. She worked at AT&T Bell Labs, Holmdel, New Jersey between 1991 and 1995. Between 1995 and 1997, she worked as an Assistant Professor at the Technical University of Crete, Chania, Greece. Since 1997, she was elected as an Assistant Professor while since 2007 she is a Professor at the National Technical University of Athens, and Director of the Postgraduate Course "Engineering Economics Systems." Prof. Varvarigou has great experience in the area of semantic Web technologies, scheduling over distributed platforms, embedded systems, and grid computing. In this area, she has published more than 170 papers in leading journals and conferences. She has participated and coordinated several EU funded projects such as IRMOS, SCOVIS, POLYMNIA, Akogrimo, NextGRID, BEinGRID, Memphis, MKBEEM, MARIDES, CHALLENGERS, FIDIS, and others.

* * *

**Miriam Allalouf** received her B.Sc. and M.Sc. degrees in computer science from the Hebrew University in Jerusalem, Israel and her PhD degree at the Tel-Aviv University School of Electrical Engineering. She is currently a staff member in the Jerusalem College of Engineering (JCE), Israel. Before that, she worked as a research staff member at IBM Research - Haifa, Israel. At IBM she participated and led research activities in the storage fields such as power management, intrusion detection and storage cloud in the frame of the EU VISION project. Formerly, Miriam has worked in development, design, and management positions in the Hi-Tech industry, mainly related to networking and database. Her research interests include data communication subjects such as QoS routing, cloud and big data related area and storage research. Miriam contributed to this book during her tenure at IBM.

**Kanchanna Ramasamy Balray** has a Bachelor of Computer science Engineering degree from the University of Madras, India followed by an International Masters in IT from Scuola Superiore Sant Anna, Pisa, Italy. She successfully completed the Masters with a thesis in the Netx project with Engineering group and eventually joined the R&D laboratory of Engineering group in October 2009. Her research interests are Infrastructure resource management solutions, Cloud infrastructure Interoperability standards, Benchmarking of cloud applications, Identity and Access management, Federated Identity Management, SOA Security and Single-sign-solutions for Portals. Currently, she is working in the ARTIST EU-funded project in designing and developing a benchmarking and testing platform.

**João Barreto** is an Assistant Professor at the Computer and Information Systems Department at the Technical University of Lisbon (Instituto Superior Técnico - IST/UTL), Portugal. He received his Ph.D. degree in Computer Science in 2009, from IST/UTL, the same university where he completed his M.Sc. (2004) and Bs.E.E. (2002). He is a researcher at INESC-ID since 2001, as a member of the Distributed Systems Group. His research interests are distributed systems and operating systems, in particular: transactional memory, optimistic replication in mobile, pervasive and ubiquitous environments, and distributed data deduplication. He has participated in a number of international projects and is author or co-author of over 20 peer-reviewed scientific communications. He is a member of ACM and IEEE.

**Michael Berlin** is a PhD candidate and research assistant at the department for parallel and distributed systems at Zuse Institute Berlin. In 2011, he graduated in Computer Science from Humboldt University of Berlin, Germany and received his Diplom. After his studies, he worked jointly at Zuse Institute Berlin and started to work on the distributed file system XtreemFS. Since 2012, he leads the research and development team of XtreemFS at the institute. His research interests are in distributed systems and data-management in the cloud.

**Lucia Bonelli** gratuated in Computer Science at the University of Rome "La Sapienza" in 1998. Her IT career started at Engineering Ingegneria Informatica R&D laboratory as Information Security software engineer. In 2000 she joined Schumberger Worldwide, where she worked both as project manager and technical consultant in the area of SIM Card applications. Then she moved to Schumberger Security Consultants team where she was appointed as technical responsible of the "PKI and IAM framework" (including card management system, PKI, SSO, secure access) in a 5-years project for a Public Administration Institution. In October 2009 she joined again the R&D lab of Engineering Ingegneria Informatica, where she's currently team leader in technical activities related to security and compliance in cloud infrastructures in European Research Projects including VISION Cloud.

**Roberto Borgotallo** graduated in Telecommunication Engineering at *Politecnico di Torino* in 1999. Since 2001, he has been working for RAI - Radiotelevisione Italiana at the R&D department in Turin. Since the beginning, he was involved in several internal projects gravitating around indexing and access of the multimedia material of the company. He subsequently worked in a RAI team for the realisation of systems related to automatic metadata extraction from the content and for the high quality digitisation of legacy media carriers with a special focus on quality control. He participated to several national and EU funded projects gravitating around high quality digitisation, digital content preservation, and automatic metadata extraction.

**Jalil Boukhobza** received his electrical engineering degree (with honors) from I.N.E.L.E.C (Institut Nationale d'Electricité et d'électronique), Boumerdès, Algeria in 1999, and M.S and PhD degrees in computer science from the University of Versailles, France, respectively in 2000 and 2004. He was a research fellow at the PRiSM laboratory (University of Versailles, France) from 2004 to 2006. Jalil Boukhobza is currently Associate Professor at the University of Western Brittany (université de Brest), Brest, France, since 2006, and member of the Lab-STICC laboratory in the CACS team (Communication, Architecture, and Circuits). His main research interests include flash-based storage system design, performance evaluation and energy optimization, and embedded operating systems design and optimization.

**Fabrice Brito** is the co-founder of Terradue Srl a private company focusing its activities on the use of Web Services, Grid, Cloud, and peer-to-peer technologies to support distributed spatial data management and high performance computing applications in collaborative digital environments and exploits and strengthens best practices in distributed data discovery, processing and archiving, putting the emphasis on the delivery of robust operational systems while adhering to a concrete roadmap to build the next generation of data processing and storage systems.

**Ghislain Chevalier** has been working for Orange since October 1983. After being an Operating System and Data Base Administrator, he managed a team in charge of validating the exploitability of Orange service platforms (TV, VoIP,...). After moving to Orange R&D, he was in charge of the functional qualification process of the Orange Storage Enabler and its associated services. After being in charge of the integration of a Proof of Concept on Content Distribution in a P2P Storage Cloud, he became in charge of the technical architecture of an Innovative Orange distributed cloud storage solution called Clostera. Ghislain also participated in the definition of the Orange Business Service STorage as a Service solution. He evaluated cloud storage solutions like Scality, Mezeo, Openstack Swift, Hitachi Content Platform, and cloud gateways like Ctera. In Vision Cloud storage Project, Ghislain participates in the specification of the FT use case and contributes his expertise in cloud storage systems and service architecture.

**Roberto Cossu**, working in ESA since 2005, has been working in several projects dealing with different aspects of Earth Observation applications and related innovation technologies, like Grid, Cloud, Open GIS, emerging Web-based and e-collaboration technologies with the overall aim of providing the users with an easy access to heterogeneous Earth Observation data and related processing services for their exploitation. He currently acts as Project Director of GENESI-DEC and technical Director of GEOWOW.

**Michel Dao** is a project leader and expert at Orange Labs in Paris. He worked in different areas throughout his career from graphical interactivity, object modeling and programming, queuing systems, etc. He is the author of numerous publications and has been part of several international conferences program committees. Currently, he is involved in the effort by Orange to provide rich and efficient cloud computing based services. He is in charge of Orange's contributions to VISION Cloud project and leads telecommunication use casework package for this project as well as the experimentation and validation work package for 4CaaSt project.

**Claudio Di Giulio**, working in ESA since 2011, has been working in projects dealing with different aspects of innovation technologies, like Grid, Cloud, Open GIS, emerging Web-based and e-collaboration technologies. Before experience has been in Physics and Astroparticles Physics computing and related processing services.

**Sebastian Dippl** works as Software Architect for Siemens AG's central research unit Corporate Technology in the area of systems integration with a primary focus on distributed systems and cloud computing technologies. In the past, he was responsible for a variety of development projects ranging from P2P VOIP systems, harbour automation and e-mobility solutions. Currently he is active as a technology consultant for the Siemens business units and is actively involved in research projects. Sebastian holds a university diploma in computer engineering from the University of Würzburg.

**Pierangelo Di Sanzo** has a Master Degree and a Ph.D. in Computer Engineering by the Sapienza University of Rome, where he was a research associate and a lecturer of computer engineering courses in the area of parallel and concurrent programming, database systems, and performance analysis of computer systems. Currently he is a researcher at the Consorzio Interuniversitario Nazionale per l'Informatica (CINI), where he is involved in a European Union funded project on transactional memory systems in cloud computing platforms. His research interests are mainly focused on distributed and transactional systems, including performance modeling and optimization, concurrency control schemes, adaptivity, and self-tuning.

**Francisco Javier Martínez Elicegui** holds a Degree in Computer Science from Technical University of Madrid (UPM), Master in Expert Systems from University of Salamanca and currently preparing a PhD on Auditory Computation & Psychoacoustics. Computer system engineer with an extensive experience in several industrial sectors, such as manufacturing, banking, space engineering, public administration, and more than 20 years in the telecommunication sector. Since joining Telefonica I+D he has got expertise in a variety of areas, being the most relevant ones: Graphical Interfaces, remote supervision of telecommunication nets, Data Warehouse and Business Intelligence, Service Oriented Architectures, Financial Services, Semantic Technologies, and Cloud Computing at present.

**Emilio Javier García Escobar** received his Master degree in Telecommunication Engineering in 2001 from Technical University of Madrid (UPM). During the period 2001-2004, he worked for Agora Systems, where he was involved both in coordination and development tasks in several IST projects (MIND, 6POWER, DAIDALOS) in the fields of IP mobility, 3G+ networks and multimedia services. In 2005, he joined the Telematics Department of UPM, being involved in FP7 projects (ECOSPACE, C@R, GLOBAL) in the field of collaborative working environments, and working towards his PhD, also as a member of W3C HTML WG. From March 2011 he has been working for Telefónica I+D in the Cloud Computing area as a researcher in European projects 4CaaSt, VISION, and participating in new proposals, as well as a patent request. He holds multiple publications in international congresses.

**Luisa Giudicianni** is graduated in Mathematics at University of Naples "Federico II" in 1999. She has been working for Engineering group since May 2000. She is a solution developer for Web applications in their functional, development and presentation aspects. She also worked on European Research project in the field of Cloud Computing, where she contributed both to the specification of security compliance requirements and to the design and implementation of a tool supporting security audit and assessment in a distributed and virtualized infrastructure.

**Danny Harnik** is a research staff member at IBM Research - Haifa, Israel. Danny received his M.Sc. and PhD degrees in computer science from the Weizmann institute of Science and his B.Sc in mathematics and computer science from Tel Aviv University. Before joining IBM, he also held a post-doc position in the Technion and UCLA/IPAM and was employed at M-Systems, Flash Disk Pioneers. During his academic tenures Danny's work focused in the fields of cryptography and complexity. His current research interests include storage systems, data reduction techniques, cryptography, and security.

**Uwe Hohenstein** received a diploma degree in computer engineering and a Dr. degree in Informatics, both from TU Braunschweig in Germany. Since 1990, he is a senior research scientist in the Corporate Technology division within Siemens AG. His responsibility is to coach the efficient and effective use of various database technologies in modern software architectures. Uwe was involved in several large-scale projects in the field of automation and telecommunication, using several database technologies such as relational, object-oriented, XML, and NoSQL databases. He accumulated about 25 years of research experience in the area of database benchmarking, data migration, federated database systems, and cloud computing, thereby co-authoring more than 50 publications. His current research interests are in the area of Cloud computing with a special emphasis on Cloud storage solutions.

**Angelo Immediata** is graduated in Electronic Engineering from the University of Salerno. He's solution architect with ten-years of SOA experience developed in many IT markets related projects, Workflow Managment systems and Big data systems. He got several certifications such JBoss for advanced J2EE developer and PMPO. He was involved in European Research Projects PASSIVE and VISION Cloud, where he worked both on the architecture design and the implementation of a tool based on SIEM approach to support Security Audit and Assessment in the Cloud.

**Peter Izsak** is a research intern at SAP Research, CEC, Ra'anana (Israel). Researching in the area of Computer Systems and Cloud infrastructures while also participating in SAP's contribution to FP7 VISION Cloud project as a developer. Peter received a BS.c in Computer Science from Technion - Israel Institute of Technology, and currently perusing a MS.c. degree in Information Systems in the Technion as well.

**Michael C. Jaeger**, at Siemens Corporate Technology, works in different roles: as research scientist, project manager, software architect, trainer and consultant for distributed systems, storage technology, server applications and their development with an emphasis on open source software. Michael has more than 10 years of experience in professional research and development work and has participated in 5 EU-funded research projects so far. Michael received a diploma degree in computer engineering and a Dr.-Ing. degree in Informatics, both from TU Berlin in Germany.

**Mirko Lorenz** is a hands-on journalist with software development skills. For the last 15 years, he worked on technologies for newsrooms. Recently he launched Datawrapper, a free open source tool for Journalists to easily create charts. He is a co-author of the Data-Journalism Handbook. Before joining Deutsche Welle in 2008 Mirko worked for a variety of large media companies in Germany and the US.

**Achim Luhn** received a doctoral degree in Physics from the Technical University in Munich. He joined the Siemens central research labs in 1986 and moved through various positions and business units in Siemens since. He has long-time industry experience as lead solution architect in designing large IT systems, mainly for the public sector, and strategic innovation management in the IT services industry. In the latter role he analyzed the disruptive potential of Cloud Computing for classical IT services business and supported the resulting corporate-wide action plan. As part of the Siemens Cloud Computing Initiative he was helping the Siemens business units to leverage cloud computing for their products and solutions in the Energy, Industry and Healthcare sectors. His current affiliation is with the European Institute of Innovation and Technology ICT Labs.

**Antonio Luzzi** is graduated in Electronic Engineering from the University of Salerno. He's solution architect with ten-years of SOA experience developed in many IT markets related projects, such as IP Multimedia System for Telecommunication, Business Process Management system for a Supply Chain Management company, and SCADA system in the Automation Domain. He's got several certifications such as SunSCJP1.6, Oracle Web Component Developer and JBoss for advanced J2EE developer. He was involved in some European Research Project in the area of Cloud Computing including VISION Cloud, where he worked both on the architecture design and the implementation of a tool based on SIEM approach to support Security Audit and Assessment in the Cloud.

**Alberto Messina** began his collaboration as a research engineer with RAI in 1996, when he completed his MS Thesis about objective quality evaluation of MPEG2 video coding. After starting his career as a designer of RAI's Multimedia Catalogue, he has been involved in several internal and international research projects in digital archiving, automated documentation, and automated production. His current interests are from file formats and metadata standards to content analysis and information extraction algorithms. R&D coordinator since 2005, his current competence area is Automated Information Extraction & Management/Information and Knowledge Engineering, where he is author of more than 70 technical and scientific publications. He has extensive collaborations with national and international research institutions, in common research projects and students' tutorship. He has a PhD in the area of Computer Science. He is active member of several EBU Technical projects, former chairman of EC-M/SCAIE project on automatic metadata extraction and of the Expert Community on Metadata, now leads the Strategic Programme on Media Information Management. He worked in the EC PrestoSpace project and currently in PrestoPRIME, TOSCA-MP, and VISION Cloud. He has served in the Programme Committee of several international conferences including AI*IA 2007, Web Intelligence 2009 and 2010, SDM Workshop on Multimedia Data Mining 2009, SAC 2009 e 2010 (IAR track), Machine Learning and Applications 2009 (ICMLA 2009), Semantic and Media Technologies 2009, MMM 2012. He is General Co-Chair of the International Workshop on Automated Information Extraction in Media Production workshop. He's ACM Professional member since 2005 and nominated Contract Professor at Politecnico di Torino from 2012. He actively participates in International Standardisation bodies, mainly in EBU and MPEG, where he contributed to MPEG-7 Audiovisual Description Profile.

**Maurizio Montagnuolo** received his Laurea degree in Telecommunications Engineering from the Polytechnic of Turin in 2004, after developing his thesis at the RAI Research Centre. In 2008 he received his Ph.D. in "Business and Management" at the University of Turin, in collaboration with RAI. His initial contributions to computer science were in the area of artificial intelligence, specifically in the semantic classification of audiovisual content. He participated to several national and EU funded projects in automatic content analysis, indexing and search. His current research interests are mostly addressed in the context of Web data mining and multimedia data mining. He is also co-*author of several scientific* works published on Journals or in International Conferences in these subject areas.

**Shantanu Pal** received his M.Tech in Information Technology from the University of Calcutta, India. Prior to that, he did his B.Tech in Information Technology from the West Bengal University of Technology, India. He was visiting researcher at the Ca' Foscari University of Venezia, Venice, Italy in 2010. His current research interest is in the broad area of distributed computing, computer communications, cloud computing, networking security. Shantanu has also served in the committees of some international conferences. He is the reviewer of the IJCSIS journal and the *IEEE Potentials* magazine. He was the coordinator of the 'IEEE All India Young Engineers' Humanitarian Challenge' for 2010 and 2011. He is also a board member of the 'Membership Growth and Sustainability Committee (MGSC)' of the IEEE Computer Society Chapter India Council.

**Roberto Palmieri** obtained the Ph.D. in Computer Engineering in 2012 by "Sapienza" University of Rome. He is member of the High Performance and Dependable Computing Systems group (HPDCS). His research interests are focused on differentiated aspects of computing and service oriented applications and platforms, spanning from theory to modeling, design, and implementation. In such contexts, he worked on the definition and implementation of frameworks and protocols for dependability in transactional systems, with special attention to systems based on Software Transactional Memories. He is also interested to the definition and validation of accurate performance models for components or sub-systems forming the core of transactional systems (DBMS or STM). His main research topics are Distributed Computing,Transactional Systems,Software Transactional Systems, Dependability, Modeling, and Performance Evaluation.

**Dana Petcu** is Professor at West University of Timisoara and Executive Director of Research Institute e-Austria Timisoara, Romania.Her main research activities are related to Cloud, Grids, Cluster and Super-computing. She leads or and has lead several national and European projects, currently FP7 HOST and Romanian AMICAS, concerning high-performance computing, respectively Cloud computing, as project coordinator, and FP7 mOSAIC and MODAClouds, concerning Cloud computing, as scientific coordinator, respectively collaboration coordinator.She is involved also in policy forums like EC FP7 ICTC, Cloud expert group, e-Infrastructure Policy Forum, or e-Infrastructure Reflection Group.

**Linda Rath-Wiggins,** is a PhD candidate at the University of Bonn in Germany and holds an M.Sc. degree in Communication Science. The focus of her work revolves around technical and organizational processes of journalism with regards to social media and data journalism. Her areas of expertise include the relevance of cloud computing and social media as part of journalists' daily workflows. For Deutsche Welle's Akademie, Linda has conducted several journalism workshops around the world.

**Alexander Reinefeld** is the Head of the Computer Science Department at Zuse Institute Berlin and a Professor at the Humboldt University of Berlin. He received his PhD and Diploma from the University of Hamburg in 1987 and 1982, respectively. He has been awarded a PhD scholarship by the German Academic Exchange Service and a Sir Izaak Walton Killam Post Doctoral Fellowship from the University of Alberta. Reinefeld has served as an Assistant Professor at the University of Hamburg and as the Managing Director at the Paderborn Center for Parallel Computing. He co-founded the North German Supercomputing Alliance HLRN, the European Grid Forum, the Open Grid Forum, and the German e-Science initiative D-Grid. His research interest is on scalable and fault-tolerant distributed algorithms, distributed data management, and high-performance computer architecture.

**Paolo Romano** has a Master degree (2002) summa cum laude in Computer Engineering by the Rome University "Tor Vergata." He obtained the PhD in Computer and Systems Engineering (2006) by the Rome University "La Sapienza." From 2002 to 2008, he was a lecturer at the Rome University "La Sapienza." Since 2008, he is a senior researcher at INESC-ID, Lisbon, Portugal, and since 2011, he is assistant professor in the Computer Engineering department of Instituto Superior Tecnico of Lisbon. He is currently coordinator of the FP7 STREP project Cloud-TM and Chair of the Euro-TM COST ACTION. His research interests include dependability of parallel and distributed systems, autonomic systems, performability modelling and evaluation, cloud and high performance computing. In these areas, he has published more than 70 papers and serves regularly as Program Committee member and reviewer for prestigious international conferences and journals (e.g. IEEE TKDE, IEEE TPDS, ACM TOPLAS, OPODIS).

**Wilfried Runde** holds a degree as an Information Specialist from the University of Applied Sciences in Cologne and obtained his training as a journalist at the Cologne City Magazine. He has worked as an Information specialist, researcher and TV-journalist for German broadcaster WDR and its ARD Broadcasting Network studios in Brussels, New York and Washington. After joining Deutsche Welle (DW) in 2001, Runde led a number of R&D and media projects as a project manager and editor. As off September 2010 he is Head of the Innovation Projects unit. Wilfried Runde has extensive experience in various broadcasting-related domains - both on the journalistic as well as on the technical side.

**Aidan Shribma** is a Senior Researcher at SAP Research, CEC, Ra'anana (Israel) leading SAP's contribution to FP7 VISION Cloud. Prior to that Aidan lead a software team in SAP R&D, and worked as a software developer at Checkpoint and Jungo. Aidan received a BS.c. in Computer Science from Technion - Israel Institute of Technology, and has an MBA from Tel-Aviv University Israel.

**Alexandra Shulman-Peleg** is a research staff member at IBM Haifa Research Lab, Israel. She holds a Ph.D. and M.Sc. in computer science as well as B.Sc. in mathematics and computer science from Tel Aviv University, Israel. Her academic research focused on developing algorithms in the fields of computational biology and structural bioinformatics. Prior to joining IBM, she had a position of a software development team leader at RAD Data Telecommunications LTD, designing embedded systems. Her current interests include cloud architectures as well as their security and access control aspects.

**Fredrik Solsvik** received his MSc degree in communication technology in 2005 from the Norwegian University of Science and Technology (NTNU), Norway. Since graduating, he has been working as a research scientist at Telenor ASA in Trondheim, focusing on the research and development of open services platforms by involvement in projects related to open interfaces in telecommunication networks, open service innovation, and machine-to-machine communication. He has experience in research and development for European and local projects in fields such as context/rich presence, cloud computing and Web services. Currently, his main activity in Telenor ASA is leading the Telenor research contribution to the VISION Cloud project telecommunication use case.

**Jan Stender** is managing director and co-founder of Xtreem Storage Systems, a spin-off company for distributed storage solutions. After having studied computer science and received his Diploma in 2005, he has been working at the department for parallel and distributed systems at Zuse Institute Berlin, where he received his PhD in 2013. He has many years of experience with large-scale distributed data management and is one of the core developers of XtreemFS, a scalable and distributed file system for cloud environments. He is particularly interested in the management of metadata and snapshots as well as the consistent replication of data.

**Paola Sunna** graduated in Electronic Engineering from Turin Polytechnic University in 1997 and took her MBA in 2005. Since 1997, she has been with the RAI Research and Technical Innovation Centre in Turin, involved in studies to define the performances of video coding systems for broadcast and broadband scenarios. In the past, she chaired the activities of the EBU (European Broadcasting Union) groups B-VIM (Video in Multimedia) and WMT (Web Media Technologies). Her current activities are in the field of end-to-end delivery of OTT (over-the-top) multimedia interactive services at user's home, Web technologies evolution, 2D/3D TV encoding issues, connected TV, and second screen companion TV applications.

**Sivan Tal** worked for 13 years at IBM in various positions including R&D team leader in the area of cloud storage; security strategy leader (modular servers and storage); various research projects in the storage area; and research staff member at the storage subsystems R&D, in development of IBM storage system products. Since August 2011, he works for Infinidat - an Israeli storage startup company, as a developer and development manager. He is now VD R&D at Infinidat. Sivan holds B.A. in Computer Sciences (cum laude) from the Technion. Sivan contributed to this book during his tenure at IBM.

**Lei Xu** is a researcher at Dublin City University, school of computing. Prior to this, he was a post-doctoral research fellow with the Cloud and Grid Computing Group, Department of Computing Science, Umea University, Sweden. His research interests include: monitoring, billing and pricing; resource allocation and workload balance; Virtual Machine (VM) placement and live migration; elastic resource management; policy-based workflow management. He holds a Ph.D. from Telecommunications Software & Systems Group, Waterford Institute of Technology, Ireland, and a M.Sc. from University of Durham, United Kingdom.

# Index